Pearson
BTEC National
Information Technology

Student Book

Jenny Phillips

Alan Jarvis

Mark Fishpool

Richard McGill

Tim Cook

David Atkinson-Beaumont

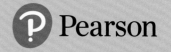

Published by Pearson Education Limited, 80 Strand, London, WC2R 0RL.

www.pearsonschoolsandfecolleges.co.uk

Copies of official specifications for all Edexcel qualifications may be found on the website: www.edexcel.com

Text © David Atkinson-Beaumont, Tim Cook, Mark Fishpool, Alan Jarvis, Richard McGill and Jenny Phillips, 2016
Edited by Julie Bond
Designed by Andy Magee
Typeset by Tech-Set Ltd, Gateshead
Original illustrations © Pearson Education Ltd, 2016
Illustrated by Tech-Set Ltd, Gateshead
Cover design by Vince Haig
Picture research by Susie Prescott

The rights of David Atkinson-Beaumont, Tim Cook, Mark Fishpool, Alan Jarvis, Richard McGill and Jenny Phillips to be identified as authors of this work have been asserted by them in accordance with the Copyright, Designs and Patents Act 1988.

First published 2016

19 18 17
10 9 8 7 6 5 4

British Library Cataloguing in Publication Data
A catalogue record for this book is available from the British Library

ISBN 978 1 292 14041 4

Acknowledgements
We would like to give a special thanks to Ian Bruce for his invaluable help, expertise and advice in the development this content.

The authors and publisher would like to thank the following individuals and organisations for their approval and permission to reproduce their photographs:

(Key: b-bottom; c-centre; l-left; r-right; t-top)

123RF.com: 79tr; **Alamy Images:** Artur Marciniec 39tl, Glyn Allan 7l, Ian Dagnell 385cr, Joe Belanger 37tl, Kurt Miller 422bl, Robert Kneschke 179; **Apple, Inc:** 18tl; **Courtesy of Logitech G:** 429bl; **Courtesy of Unity Technologies:** 431cl; **Fotolia.com:** alvarez 423t, Andrey Popov 409bl, Hugo Félix 332tl, Jacob Lund 446cr, kavzov 333, michaeljung 171tr, Oleksiy Mark 1, Svyatoslav Lypynskyy 275tr, vege 85, 379, Volker Witt 331tr; **Getty Images:** alvarez 465tr, Colin Anderson 419, 437bc, ODD ANDERSEN / AFP 13bl; **JTAG Technologies:** 231br; **Microsoft Limited:** 18bl; **Science Photo Library Ltd:** JIM REED 277; **Shutterstock.com:** Andrey_Popov 347cr (bottomL), arek_malang 218tl, charnsitr 426cr, Darrin Henry 347cr (topR), Eldad Carin 395t, Ilike 347cr (bottomR), iurii 437bl, Kzenon 219, michaeljung 377tr, Oleksiy Mark 15br, Olga Zelenskaya 347cr (CentreL), paul prescott 418tl, pkchai 466tl, racorn 217tr, 417tr, Roger Jegg Fotodesign-jegg.de 378tl, sheff 347cr (topL), wavebreakmedia 426cl, ZouZou 276tl

Cover images: *Front:* **Shutterstock.com:** Juanjo Tugores

All other images © Pearson Education

The authors and publisher would like to thank the following individuals and organisations for their approval and permission to reproduce their materials:

p.70-71: adapted from https://www.gov.uk/government/case-studies/risk-management-of-the-enterprise-it-for-cesg-digital, © Crown copyright. Contains public sector information licensed under the Open Government Licence (OGL) v3.0. http://www.nationalarchives.gov.uk/doc/open-government-licence/version/3/; **p.187, Fig 3.1:** Google, © 2016 Google Inc. All rights reserved. Google and the Google Logo are registered trademarks of Google Inc.; **p.191, Fig 3.2:** Twitter, Inc., Twitter, Tweet and Twitter Bird Logo are trademarks of Twitter, Inc. or its affiliates; **p.199, 200 and 201:** Google, © 2016 Google Inc. All rights reserved. Google and the Google Logo are registered trademarks of Google Inc.; **p.210-212:** Screenshots from Hootsuite, with permission of Hootsuite, DIY Photography, Facebook, Inc., Tumblr, Inc. and Twitter, Inc. Twitter, Tweet and Twitter Bird Logo are trademarks of Twitter, Inc. or its affiliates. Facebook is a trademark of Facebook, Inc. The LinkedIn logo and the IN logo are registered trademarks or trademarks of LinkedIn Corporation and its affiliates. Google and the Google Logo are registered trademarks of Google Inc.; Screenshots on pages 360-71 from Notepad++, licensed under GNU GPL v.3; **p.231, Fig 4.9:** webstyleguide.com, Copyright © 2009 Lynch and Horton, all rights reserved; **p.312, Table 5.5:** from Microsoft Corporation, Used with permission from Microsoft product screenshot(s) reprinted with permission from Microsoft Corporation; **p.349, Fig 6.6 and Fig 6.7:** Pearson Education UK website; **p.356, Fig 6.11:** Pearson Education UK website; **p.358, Fig 6.12:** Boston College; **p.360-371:** all screenshots used with permission from Notepad++, licensed under GNU GPL v.3; **p.384, Fig 7.1:** gammaplay.com, © 2016 Google; **p.385 Fig 7.2:** Apple Inc, screenshot reprinted with permission from Apple Inc.; **p.387, Fig 7.6; p.389, Fig 7.8;** with permission from android.com; **p.393, Fig 7.13:** with permission from audacityteam.org, Copyright © 2016 Audacity Team; **p.394, Fig 7.14; p.397, Fig 7.18; p.398, Fig 7.19 and Fig 7.20** all with permission from android.com; **p.408, Fig 7.33, p.409, Fig 7.34, Fig 7.35, Fig 7.36; p.410, Fig 7.38 and Fig 7.39** all with permission from android.com, Android is a trademark of Google Inc. The Android robot is reproduced or modified from work created and shared by Google and used according to terms described in the Creative Commons 3.0 Attribution License; **p.424, Fig 8.3:** Concept art by Ewon Harding; **p.431, Fig 8.8:** with permission from unity3d.com, Copyright © 2016 Unity Technologies; **p.432, Fig 8.9 and Fig 8.10:** with permission from Unreal® Engine; **p.435, Fig 8.12:** with permission from Limbo © Playdead; **p.446, Table 8.3:** adapted from http://www.pegi.info/en/index/id/33/, for more information visit www.pegi.info; **p.448, Fig 8.18:** with permission from Autodesk, Inc., Autodesk screenshots reprinted courtesy of Autodesk, Inc.; **p.450, Fig 8.19; p.452, Fig 8.20; p.453 Fig 8.21 and Fig 8.22; p.455, Fig 8.23 and Fig 8.24; p.456, Fig 8.25; p.457, Fig 8.26; p.460, Fig 8.26:** all with permission from Unreal® Engine.

Microsoft product screenshot(s) reprinted with permission from Microsoft Corporation.

Every effort has been made to trace copyright holders and we apologise for any omissions. We would be pleased to insert the appropriate acknowledgement in any subsequent editions.

Websites
Pearson Education Limited is not responsible for the content of any external internet sites. It is essential for tutors to preview each website before using it in class so as to ensure that the URL is still accurate, relevant and appropriate. We suggest that tutors bookmark useful websites and consider enabling students to access them through the school/college intranet.

A note from the publisher
In order to ensure that this resource offers high-quality support for the associated Pearson qualification, it has been through a review process by the awarding body. This process confirms that this resource fully covers the teaching and learning content of the specification or part of a specification at which it is aimed. It also confirms that it demonstrates an appropriate balance between the development of subject skills, knowledge and understanding, in addition to preparation for assessment.

Endorsement does not cover any guidance on assessment activities or processes (e.g. practice questions or advice on how to answer assessment questions), included in the resource nor does it prescribe any particular approach to the teaching or delivery of a related course.

While the publishers have made every attempt to ensure that advice on the qualification and its assessment is accurate, the official specification and associated assessment guidance materials are the only authoritative source of information and should always be referred to for definitive guidance.

Pearson examiners have not contributed to any sections in this resource relevant to examination papers for which they have responsibility.

Examiners will not use endorsed resources as a source of material for any assessment set by Pearson.

Endorsement of a resource does not mean that the resource is required to achieve this Pearson qualification, nor does it mean that it is the only suitable material available to support the qualification, and any resource lists produced by the awarding body shall include this and other appropriate resources.

Contents

Introduction   iv

1   **Information Technology Systems**   JENNY PHILLIPS   1

2   **Creating Systems to Manage Information**   ALAN JARVIS   85

3   **Using Social Media in Business**   ALAN JARVIS   179

4   **Programming**   MARK FISHPOOL   219

5   **Data Modelling**   RICHARD McGILL   277

6   **Website Development**   TIM COOK   333

7   **Mobile Apps Development**   MARK FISHPOOL   379

8   **Computer Games Development**   DAVID ATKINSON-BEAUMONT   419

Glossary   467

Index   473

How to use this book

Welcome to your BTEC National Information Technology course!

The BTEC National in Information Technology qualification is a vocational qualification that will help prepare you for a huge range of careers. You may be thinking of pursuing a career either as a programmer, software or web developer or as a project manager with a focus on an organisation's IT infrastructure.. A BTEC National in Information Technology will expose you to a wide range of IT topics that will enhance your options for employment or for further study in higher education.

You will develop a common core of IT knowledge and study areas such as the relationship between hardware and software that form an IT system, managing and processing data to support business and using IT to communicate and share information, including through social media. You will also study computational thinking skills, the principles of designing and developing computer programs, websites and mobile apps.

You may be considering joining the information technology industry as a software developer. This job requires you to have an understanding of how IT systems inter-relate to ensure the design and implementation of solutions are efficient. You will also need to know the principles of computational thinking and programming to develop your ability to analyse a problem and produce efficient and effective solutions. Software developers can work in a wide variety of areas within the information technology sector including PC software application development, website development, mobile apps development or they may be able to get a job in the competitive computer games industry. The computer games industry has been growing year on year and has become a multi-billion pound industry. With the prevalence of computing devices, games consoles and mobile devices, this growth shows no sign of slowing.

You may instead want to work in the expanding social media industry, either managing a business' social media campaign as a social media specialist or working for a social media site company as a content or web developer. Social media websites provide many opportunities for businesses to interact with people to promote their business, to provide customer service and to encourage sales of products and services. Alternatively, you may want to help businesses make informed decisions about IT systems or through the application of data modelling to make informed business decisions. Data modelling provides the computational ability to, consider alternative processes or solutions, compare consequences and suggest potential courses of action. These skills would be very useful to employers and would help you progress to an information technology or business-related higher education course .

How your BTEC is structured

Your BTEC National is divided into **mandatory units** (the ones you must do) and **optional units** (the ones you can choose to do). The number of units you need to do and the units you can cover will depend on the type of qualification you are doing.

The number of mandatory and optional units will vary depending on the type of BTEC National you are doing. This books supports all the mandatory units and the optional units to allow you to complete the:

- Certificate
- Extended Certificate
- Foundation Diploma.

Your learning experience

You may not realise it but you are always learning. Your educational and life experiences are constantly shaping you, your ideas, your thinking, and how you view and engage with the world around you.

You are the person most responsible for your own learning experience so it is really important you understand what you are learning, why you are learning it and why it is important both to your course and your personal development.

Your learning can be seen as a journey which moves through four phases.

Phase 1	Phase 2	Phase 3	Phase 4
You are introduced to a topic or concept; you start to develop an awareness of what learning is required.	You explore the topic or concept through different methods (e.g. research, questioning, analysis, deep thinking, critical evaluation) and form your own understanding.	You apply your knowledge and skills to a task designed to test your understanding.	You reflect on your learning, evaluate your efforts, identify gaps in your knowledge and look for ways to improve.

During each phase, you will use different learning strategies. As you go through your course, these strategies will combine to help you secure the core knowledge and skills you need.

This student book has been written using similar learning principles, strategies and tools. It has been designed to support your learning journey, to give you control over your own learning and to equip you with the knowledge, understanding and tools to be successful in your future studies or career.

Features of this book

In this student book there are lots of different features. They are there to help you learn about the topics in your course in different ways and understand it from multiple perspectives. Together these features:

▶ explain what your learning is about

▶ help you to build your knowledge

▶ help you understand how to succeed in your assessment

▶ help you to reflect on and evaluate your learning

▶ help you to link your learning to the workplace.

In addition, each individual feature has a specific purpose, designed to support important learning strategies. For example, some features will:

▶ get you to question assumptions around what you are learning

▶ make you think beyond what you are reading about

▶ help you make connections across your learning and across units

▶ draw comparisons between your own learning and real-world workplace environments

▶ help you to develop some of the important skills you will need for the workplace, including team work, effective communication and problem solving.

Features that explain what your learning is about

Getting to know your unit

This section introduces the unit and explains how you will be assessed. It gives an overview of what will be covered and will help you to understand *why* you are doing the things you are asked to do in this unit.

Getting started

This appears at the start of every unit and is designed to get you thinking about the unit and what it involves. This feature will also help you to identify what you may already know about some of the topics in the unit and acts as a starting point for understanding the skills and knowledge you will need to develop to complete the unit.

Features that help you to build your knowledge

Research

This asks you to research a topic in greater depth. Using these features will help to expand your understanding of a topic as well as developing your research and investigation skills. All of these will be invaluable for your future progression, both professionally and academically.

Worked example

Our worked examples show the process you need to follow to solve a problem, such as a maths or science equation or the process for writing a letter or memo. This will also help you to develop your understanding and your numeracy and literacy skills.

Theory into practice

In this feature you are asked to consider the workplace or industry implications of a topic or concept from the unit. This will help you to understand the close links between what you are learning in the classroom and the affects it will have on a future career in your chosen sector.

Discussion

Discussion features encourage you to talk to other students about a topic in greater detail, working together to increase your understanding of the topic and to understand other people's perspectives on an issue. This will also help to build your team working skills, which will be invaluable in your future professional and academic career.

Safety tip

This provides advice around health and safety when working on the unit. It will help build your knowledge about best practice in the workplace, as well as make sure that you stay safe.

Key terms

Concise and simple definitions are provided for key words, phrases and concepts, allowing you to have, at a glance, a clear understanding of the key ideas in each unit.

Link

This shows any links between units or within the same unit, helping you to identify where the knowledge you have learned elsewhere will help you to achieve the requirements of the unit. Remember, although your BTEC National is made up of several units, there are common themes that are explored from different perspectives across the whole of your course.

Step by step:

This practical feature gives step-by-step descriptions of particular processes or tasks in the unit, including a photo or artwork for each step. This will help you to understand the key stages in the process and help you to carry out the process yourself.

Further reading and resources

This contains a list of other resources – such as books, journals, articles or websites that you can use to expand your knowledge of the unit content. This is a good opportunity for you to take responsibility for your own learning, as well as preparing you for research tasks you may need to do academically or professionally.

Features connected to your assessment

Your course is made up of a series of mandatory and optional units. There are two different types of mandatory unit:
- externally assessed
- internally assessed.

The features that support you in preparing for assessment are below. But first, what is the difference between these two different types of units?

Externally assessed units

These units give you the opportunity to present what you have learned in the unit in a different way. They can be challenging, but will really give you the opportunity to demonstrate your knowledge and understanding, or your skills in a direct way. For these units you will complete a task, set directly by Pearson, in controlled conditions. This could take the form of an exam or it could be another type of task. You may have the opportunity in advance to research and prepare notes around a topic, which can be used when completing the assessment.

Internally assessed units

Most of your units will be internally assessed. This involves you completing a series of assignments, set and marked by your tutor. The assignments you complete could allow you to demonstrate your learning in a number of different ways, from a written report to a presentation to a video recording and observation statements of you completing a practical task. Whatever the method, you will need to make sure you have clear evidence of what you have achieved and how you did it.

Assessment practice

These features give you the opportunity to practise some of the skills you will need when you are assessed on your unit. They do not fully reflect the actual assessment tasks, but will help you get ready for doing them.

Plan – Do – Review

You'll also find handy advice on how to plan, complete and evaluate your work after you have completed it. This is designed to get you thinking about the best way to complete your work and to build your skills and experience before doing the actual assessment. These prompt questions are designed to get you started with thinking about how the way you work, as well as understand why you do things.

Getting ready for assessment

For internally assessed units, this is a case study from a BTEC National student, talking about how they planned and carried out their assignment work and what they would do differently if they were to do it again. It will give you advice on preparing for the kind of work you will need to for your internal assessments, including 'Think about it' points for you to consider for your own development.

Getting ready for assessment

This section will help you to prepare for external assessment. It gives practical advice on preparing for and sitting exams or a set task. It provides a series of sample answers for the types of questions you will need to answer in your external assessments, including guidance on the good points of these answers and how these answers could be improved.

Features to help you reflect on and evaluate your learning

⏸ PAUSE POINT
Pause points appear after a section of each unit and give you the opportunity to review and reflect upon your own learning. The ability to reflect on your own performance is a key skill you'll need to develop and use throughout your life, and will be essential whatever your future plans are.

Hint
Extend
These also give you suggestions to help cement your knowledge and indicate other areas you can look at to expand it..

Reflect
This allows you to reflect on how the knowledge you have gained in this unit may impact your behaviour in a workplace situation. This will help not only to place the topic in a professional context, but also help you to review your own conduct and develop your employability skills.

Features which link your learning with the workplace

Case study
Case studies are used throughout the book to allow you to apply the learning and knowledge from the unit to a scenario from the workplace or the industry. Case studies include questions to help you consider the wider context of a topic. This is an opportunity to see how the unit's content is reflected in the real world, and help you to build familiarity with issues you may find in a real-world workplace.

THINK ▶FUTURE

This is a special case study where someone working in the industry talks about the job role they do and the skills they need. This comes with a *Focusing your skills* section, which gives suggestions for how you can begin to develop the employability skills and experiences that are needed to be successful in a career in your chosen sector. This is an excellent opportunity to help you identify what you could do, inside and outside of your BTEC National studies, to build up your employability skills.

About the authors

David Atkinson-Beaumont

David has worked in Games and Computing education for over ten years following a career as a programmer and IT Consultant. He currently manages Truro and Penwith College's Vocational Arts and Community department based in Penzance, looking after courses from Level 1 to Level 6 and has worked for Pearson as a course writer, textbook contributor and external verifier.

Tim Cook

Tim is a Team Leader for QCF and NQF BTEC Computing qualifications, and has worked for Pearson in a variety of consultancy roles for over eight years. He has contributed to writing several computing specifications, including the new NQF 2016 BTEC Level 3 Computing qualification. Alongside his work for Pearson, he teaches BTEC computing qualifications at Boston College. He has done this for over fifteen years, and has delivered computing based units from Level 1 up to HND.

Mark Fishpool

Mark has 26 years of working within further and higher education. He was Head of Computing and IT at Gloucestershire College, managing its successful Centre of Vocational Excellence and trailblazing programmes in Interactive Games Design and Forensic Computing at Level 3. He has taught at most academic levels (including pre-16 and post-16), developed and lead written BTEC IT programmes at level 2 and 3 and has led the development of a new nationally recognised Technical qualification in Cyber Security. Currently he is taking a break from academia by pursuing a career in commercial web development after contributing software for an award winning EDF project.

Alan Jarvis

Alan started his career working in the IT industry and then spent 20 years working as a lecturer in Further Education. Alan has contributed to a number of text books and recently has been working with Pearson on qualification development, preparing teaching support materials and training centres in preparation for new versions of the BTEC qualifications.

Richard McGill

Richard is currently a level 3 BTEC course team leader at SGS Filton College with over 25 years experience in delivering and leading BTEC IT and Computing qualifications at this centre. Previously he was a Senior Analyst at Lloyds Bank. He has worked for more than two decades for Edexcel and Pearson with current roles including Senior SV Team Leader, OSCA writer and Lead Examiner. In his spare time, Richard rides a motorcycle and plays bass guitar with a large band in Bristol.

Jenny Phillips

Jenny is an educational consultant advising colleges, training providers, employers and schools on high quality education and training. Jenny fulfilled her ambition to train as a lecturer, whilst working in industry 20 years ago, running her own business and that of others. Jenny's consultancy work involves national and internal travel and varied tasks. She has written many books and articles, multi-media resources and educational film scripts. Her specialist subjects are computing, IT and all aspects of business, having gained 40 related qualifications including several undergraduate and postgraduate degrees in education, research, business and computer science. She is currently working on her doctoral thesis.

Information Technology Systems 1

Getting to know your unit

Information technology (IT) systems are involved in almost everything we do in society and have a significant role in our way of life. IT systems have benefited our society in many ways such as communication, finance, medicine and farming. Having a good understanding of how to effectively select and use appropriate IT systems for both personal and business use will put you in a strong position when considering higher education or getting a job in the IT industry.

You will be learning about hardware and software and how they come together and interact with each other to form an IT system. You will also be learning about the relationship between users and systems and the decisions that businesses and individuals need to make. You will be exploring issues related to using IT systems and their impact on us as individuals and also how they affect business practices.

In this unit, you will draw on your learning from across your programme to complete assessment tasks set by your teacher.

This unit will give you a fundamental and synoptic understanding of all areas of IT, which will support progression to an IT-related higher education course.

How you will be assessed

This unit is externally assessed by means of a written examination, which will last for two hours. You will be assessed on your understanding of computer systems and the implications of their use in personal and professional situations.

Grade descriptors

To achieve a grade, you will be expected to demonstrate the following attributes across the essential content of the unit. The maximum number of marks for this unit is 90.

To pass this unit:

▸ you will be able to apply knowledge and understanding of key information technology concepts to a range of familiar vocational contexts

▸ you will apply knowledge and understanding of IT systems to deconstruct problems in common situations and apply standard IT conventions to produce solutions with supporting reasoning

▸ you will be able to identify the impact of effective and ineffective uses of IT systems and recommend ways in which IT can be developed and/or improved

▸ you will explore and make judgements on the impact of the use of IT on individuals and organisations.

To achieve a distinction:

▶ you will be able to analyse complex information, data and situations, in vocational contexts, in order to draw conclusions and make valid observations

▶ you will be able to synthesise your knowledge and understanding of IT systems to deconstruct complex problems, drawing on various sources of information to develop effective solutions

▶ you will evaluate the effectiveness of IT systems and make justified recommendations for further developments and future actions

▶ you will make valid, justified judgements on the impact of IT on individuals, organisations and wider society.

Assessment outcomes

AO1 Demonstrate knowledge and understanding of information technology terms, standards, concepts and processes.

Command words: identify, give, state, name, complete, draw.

Marks: ranges from 1 to 6 marks.

AO2 Apply knowledge and understanding of information technology terms, standards, concepts and processes.

Command words: complete, draw, describe, explain, calculate, produce, demonstrate.

Marks: ranges from 1 to 10 marks.

AO3 Select and use information technologies and procedures to explore likely outcomes and find solutions to problems in context.

Command words: explain, calculate, produce, develop, demonstrate.

Marks: ranges from 1 to 6 marks.

AO4 Analyse and evaluate information, technologies and procedures in order to recommend and justify solutions to IT problems.

Command words: discuss, demonstrate, analyse, produce, write.

Marks: ranges from 6 to 12 marks.

AO5 Make connections between the application of technologies, procedures, outcomes and solutions to resolve IT problems.

Command words: write, produce, evaluate.

Marks: ranges from 6 to 12 marks.

Information technology impacts on our lives on a daily basis. We rely on computers to perform even basic tasks such as telling the time.
List any devices that you use. Add those that you are aware of but have never used. Update the list as you learn about other types of technology.

A Digital devices in IT systems

This section introduces you to the concepts and implications of the use of the devices that form IT systems and the relationships between them. You are already familiar with a variety of IT systems and have probably come to rely on them in your everyday life. It must be hard to imagine that you are part of possibly the first generation to grow up with IT systems from birth.

Here are some of the digital devices, their functions and uses, some of which you may not have used before or maybe not even heard about.

Digital devices, their functions and use

Although IT devices are becoming more sophisticated at a rapid pace, businesses have been reliant on multiple digital technologies to manage their practices for quite a long time. Many of us are unaware that computers are relied upon for the functioning of familiar everyday items, such as:

- ovens
- washing machines
- tractors
- motor cycles
- medical equipment
- lighting.

- watches
- cars
- hearing aids
- aircraft
- heating systems

You are going to consider in more detail those more sophisticated digital devices that we rely on to form IT systems in our personal lives and those affecting businesses. You will look at the features and uses of digital devices in IT systems to meet the needs of individuals and organisations

Digital devices that form part or all of IT systems

There are a number of digital devices that go to make up standard IT systems for both personal and business use.

Multifunctional devices

Multifunctional devices (**MFDs**) are also known as **AIOs**. MFDs perform several different purposes. They include printers which not only print, but also scan, photocopy, fax and email.

> ### Key terms
>
> **AIO** – an all-in-one (AIO) device is one which is multifunctional. They are also known as MFDs.
>
> **MFD** – a multifunctional device, such as a smartphone, a camera which connects to the internet or a printer which also scans and photocopies. They are also known as AIOs.
>
> **Standalone computer** – a computer not reliant on any other computers or digital devices to function; therefore it can be used independently.

Personal computers

Personal computers (PCs) are those which are general purpose and available in a range of sizes, levels of power and capacity, and which are affordable to many for personal use. They operate as **standalone computers** and are very often lightweight and portable. (Personal computers includes laptops and netbooks as well as static tower PCs.)

PCs first came onto the market in the late 1970s when 'micro-computers' were launched to the market. Until that time, computers were large pieces of equipment, often filling entire rooms dedicated solely for computer systems.

PCs combine multiple digital functions, as well being able to store large amounts of data produced in spreadsheets and word-processed documents. They also provide storage and manipulation for images, music and videos. It is standard for PCs to have:

- access to the internet
- sound and other media software
- integrated microphones and webcams for communicating visually as well verbally.

PCs execute software, such as the widely used Microsoft® Office® suite, so that it can be employed by the user, and can connect to other digital devices, making it possible to share files across all of your personal devices (for example smartphone, tablet or camera).

Mainframe computers

There are still some circumstances in which computers fill large amounts of space. These are known as mainframe computers and they are used for processing enormous amounts of data, which even the most powerful of standalone computers are unable to do.

Large mainframe computers are used by very large organisations, such as Amazon, eBay, IBM and some major airlines. Some government agencies also rely on mainframe computers where large amounts of data are processed. Mainframe computers are not the same as servers. Servers are powerful computers that provide network services such as network applications, storage and other resources for users on the same and other computers.

Research

Search online for businesses that use large mainframe computers. Make a list and try to identify what they use them for.

Mobile devices

Mobile device is a term given to any digital device which can be carried around easily and which is usually WiFi enabled. They typically weigh less than a bag of sugar and can fit into a pocket or bag comfortably. Examples of manufacturers of mobile devices include:

- Motorola
- Apple
- LG
- Huawei
- Microsoft
- Samsung.

Mobile devices such as these have become a must-have personal item, enabling us to keep in touch while on the move. Since the introduction of smartphones for general sale from IBM in 1994, we have had a world full of information at our fingertips. With the introduction of smartphones came touchscreens and the ability to access email and the internet on our phones. As you can imagine, flagship models displaying the latest technology are quite expensive.

Early smartphones were ahead of their time as we did not have the wireless infrastructure that we have today. You might liken this to the invention of the telephone by Alexander Graham Bell; he had a phone but who could he call? When smartphones were first invented the internet was a much smaller place and far fewer people had the internet at home or owned smartphones.

Servers

Servers provide services for other computers on the network. The network could comprise a series of cables which connect the server to other computers, perhaps in a small office, or could provide virtual connections via the internet. Your place of study will probably operate in the same way. All the computers are networked together using network infrastructure. A server then manages the logical access to the resources.

Servers are used not only to store data files centrally so that several people can access them, but also to store software centrally to relieve storage space on individual PCs. As all the data is stored centrally, it can be backed up from one location. Servers also allow shared access to devices such as printers and scanners. They authenticate users and perform account management for users.

You may have heard of, or use the cloud. The cloud is a term used to mean servers that are geographically separate from the user. These servers often offer some sort of storage service.

Link

We shall look at some options for cloud servers in the section Online systems.

Entertainment systems

Entertainment systems are multifunctional, comprising sound and vision. They manage music and video files, which contain large amounts of data and can quickly reduce the available capacity of a PC or mobile device. Entertainment systems can be operated from a central server, known as a digital media server. Central servers for home use have recently become much more readily affordable and simple to use.

Entertainment systems often combine the facility to record, and many provide facilities for editing and mixing digital (music or video) files. Many connect to the internet and interact with other peripheral devices. The most familiar of these systems, which are considerably variable in size and price include:

- MP3 and MP4 players
- home video theatre
- in-car entertainment systems
- Apple TV
- NOW TV
- music centres
- DAB radios
- Amazon Fire TV
- Google Chromecast
- Roku.

Link

For more about peripheral devices see Peripheral devices and media.

Smart TVs can be defined as entertainment systems, in addition to PCs, tablets and many other digital devices. The digital world now makes it possible to have devices and systems which provide a wide range of entertainment options, which not so long ago would have required multiple devices.

Larger entertainment systems include those you might have seen at concerts, the theatre or in clubs or bars.

Digital cameras

Digital cameras capture two different types of images.

▶ Still – images that do not move (photos). They occupy much less storage space than moving images.

▶ Video – moving images which comprise a series of frames to make a film. Videos include sound and can be edited to include subtitles. It is also possible to capture single frames from a video as a still image.

Digital cameras encode digital images by breaking a picture into tiny squares called pixels and store the images onto a memory card. The resolution of the image captured is a count of how many pixels are used to make up the image. A high resolution image may contain several million pixels (1 million pixels = 1 megapixel). A modern digital camera is between 10 and 20 megapixels. Several digital devices have camera functions, for example smartphones and tablets, and can store photos on the hard drive or an SD card.

SLR cameras are becoming increasingly popular again with the development of digital SLRs. Digital SLRs (DSLRs) are especially popular for specialist photography, because of the high quality of the images produced, depending on the quality of the camera lens.

Special-effect lenses and interchangeable lenses can be bought for DSLR cameras, for example:

▶ wide angle

▶ fish-eye

▶ macro (for close-up photos)

▶ multi-faceted (for star-burst effects)

▶ zoom (for long distance photos).

Navigation systems

Navigation systems are those which use **GPS** or GPS working alongside Global Navigation Satellite System (GLONASS) to navigate to locations. In addition, they can provide information about:

▶ traffic congestion

▶ road works

▶ accidents

▶ weather

▶ points of interest.

Navigation systems can be standalone, such as TomTom or Garmin products. These products are portable and can be ftted into vehicles to enable the driver to navigate. Many vehicles now come with factory-fitted GPS, either as standard or as an extra. Some motorbikes also come fitted with navigation systems.

You may have a navigation system integrated in your smartphone which enables you to find your way around while driving, cycling or walking.

Data capture and collection systems

Data capture and collection systems, also known as electronic data capture (EDC), are those which take information and collect it to perform a specific task. Examples are:

▶ credit and debit card readers for payment transactions

▶ iris and fingerprint recognition systems for biometric entry and authentication systems

▶ medical scanning machines such as magnetic resonance imaging (MRI), dual-energy X-ray absorptiometry (DEXA) and computed tomography (CT) scanners

▶ radio-frequency identification (RFID) used in stock control, race timing systems

▶ personal digital assistants (PDAs) with integrated barcode scanners for stock control

▶ automatic number plate recognition (ANPR) cameras for crime prevention and enforcement

▶ barcode readers for fast data entry such as at checkouts and for courier services.

▶ A data capture system

Data capture and collection systems are reported to be used frequently in clinical trials to gather data for analysis.

Link

For more about iris and fingerprint recognition systems, see http://findbiometrics.com/solutions/iris-scanners-recognition/.

For more about data capture and collection systems used in clinical trials, visit http://www.bioclinica.com/ and http://journal.frontiersin.org/researchtopic/363/electronic-data-capture-representation-and-applications-in-neuroimaging.

Communication devices and systems

With such a diverse mix of systems and devices in information systems today, communication is essential. Communication devices and systems allow digital devices to communicate with each other, whether in the same room or on the other side of the world. The growing demands of digital devices to interact with each other and the cloud has resulted in the resilient global communications we see today. Some of the devices and systems used for communication are.

▶ Satellites – these operate without cables by using satellite dishes as a two-way method of transmitting data (This is an option for remote areas where broadband is not available.)

▶ WiFi (IEEE 802.11 wireless) – connects devices without wires using high frequency radio waves.

▶ FTTC (fibre to the cabinet) – fibre-optic **broadband** offers speedier broadband connections than copper cabling alone. With FTTC, the customer's local cabinet has fibre and the last section of the connection to the premises is traditional copper.

▶ FTTP (fibre to the premises) – fibre-optic broadband offers even speedier broadband connections than FTTC.

▶ 4G/LTE – these are high-speed mobile data networks offering connectivity while on the move at speeds up to 50Mbps.

▶ Bluetooth – this is often used for personal area networks (PANs) to connect peripherals such as headsets, mice, keyboards and bar code scanners to PCs and mobile devices.

Link

Bluetooth is another method for transferring information between devices and is discussed in more detail later in the unit.

Key terms

Broadband – a high-speed transmission technique, whereby a wide band of frequencies are used to transmit messages. It commonly refers to internet access via a range of networks including DSL, WiFi, 3G and 4G. Today, broadband is a very familiar term in the UK and all of our digital devices, such as smartphones, games consoles and internet-enabled TVs, use broadband to connect to the internet and share data all the time.

The function and use of digital devices

We would probably feel lost without the digital technology we now take for granted. Although technology is a global phenomenon, it is still not available or accessible to everyone. Some of the areas of life that have benefited from digital devices are discussed below. We will look at the function of digital devices for these different areas of modern life.

Education and training

Education and training traditionally were nearly always done face to face in a classroom. The emergence of digital devices has both expanded the reach of the classroom and also brought about different ways of educating and training people.

If you attend a school or college, then it is likely that your teachers have used interactive white boards (IWBs) for front-of-class teaching. These IWBs connect to a PC as the input device and enable access to a wide range of features. If work displayed on the IWB is stored on a network, then it can be changed, drawn over, manipulated and saved to a central server.

You may have experienced using e-learning resources yourself. For example, perhaps your tutor has uploaded e-learning resources to a shared virtual learning environment (VLE) for you to study at a convenient time or so that you can complete an assignment independently.

Training is available as computer based training (CBT) on almost any subject one can imagine, from flower arranging to games programming. Enthusiasts use the power of YouTube and Instructables to record instructional videos on even the most niche of hobbies.

Large academic organisations have created massive online open courses or MOOCs to offer courses to unlimited numbers of people, and these are often self paced and certificated. Journals and research papers are available to a much wider audience now as almost everything that has ever been written has been digitised and stored somewhere or other.

The benefits of digital devices combined with the communications technologies today bring about unprecedented opportunities for collaboration, for example using services such as Google Docs and video conferencing and surveying tools.

Education and training can now happen remotely, anywhere in the world, without the tutor and students ever meeting. Virtual classrooms can be used in which the tutor communicates with students via web conferencing technology. The tutor and students can share access to class materials and a forum for class discussions.

Personal

Over the last few decades, the personal use of digital devices has transformed how people in society live. We are now able to communicate more easily, at the touch of a button or by means of our smartphones. Our personal digital devices are highly integrated into our lives and we can carry out many everyday tasks in moments, directly from our smartphones or tablets.

They allow us to communicate with friends and family anywhere in the world through phone calls, instant messages, email, voice-over-the-internet protocols (VoIPa) such as Skype, and through social media applications. They allow us to create, edit and watch visual media in the form of photos and videos, and this is not confined to specialist

devices (such as DSLRs) but is available to all on even the most basic smartphones. We can also read e-books using e-readers and tablets.

Digital devices also enable us to manage our lives through banking apps which allow us to make transactions remotely, and through the use of diary and alarm clock applications. It is now even possible to pay for small purchases by holding a contactless card or enabled mobile phone close to a terminal. Our digital devices let us access the vast information sources of the internet, wherever we happen to be so, for example, you can find an appealing restaurant nearby having never visited that place before that day. Your smartphone might even decide to tell you there is a great restaurant nearby using location aware services and targeted advertising. With the right software applications, we can operate our homes (the heating, lighting and entertainment system) without getting out of our chairs, or even if we are overseas with the growth of the interconnected home and the 'Internet of Things'.

The use of the humble smartphone to manage our daily lives also has its drawbacks. Natives of the digital age are often lost when their device fails or is forgotten, or the battery runs flat. Society today is so reliant and engrossed in technology that sometimes the real world takes a back seat. Living our lives online and being so connected brings with it brings some pretty big risks too. Security is a huge concern – it is all too easy to 'steal' someone's identity or gain access to control their home if simple precautions are not taken.

Social

Our social lives revolve around our digital devices and the world of social media that we can access on them. Many of us check our social media newsfeeds regularly throughout the day and well into the evening. We always want to know what new thing has been posted or tweeted by our friends, family and celebrities. We also use social media to make arrangements to meet up with friends and family and much of our social life with them is even conducted virtually through social media.

Some would say that our use of social media has become disruptive, destructive and occupies too much of our time. Before digital technology, we probably visited friends and family more often. Now it is often the case that, even when you visit people, you might spend time looking at social media rather than talking to each other.

Link

For more on social media, see Unit 3: *Using Social Media in Business.*

As mentioned above, digital devices have given us access to vast amounts of information at the touch of a button. However, we are also bombarded by vast amounts of data that we do not request, such as spam email and unsolicited advertising on social media.

Research

The unwanted data that we are bombarded with was claimed in 2011 to be the equivalent of around 174 newspapers per day. Explore the amount of internet traffic there is nowadays; read the article on The Zettabyte Era on at www.cisco.com.

We are now so reliant on technology, which is often promoted as a time saver, that we seem to have less time than before. Keeping up to date with social media, emails and texts is very time consuming. It seems that we cannot go anywhere without some form of digital device, and need to be 'connected' all of the time. While our lives appear to have been enhanced by the digital revolution, it is worth considering what life might be like without it.

Reflect

What would your life be like without the digital devices you use everyday? How would you arrange to meet up with friends? How would you do research for a college project? How would you put together an assignment for college? (Putting aside the fact that you would probably be studying something other than IT.)

Retail

Retail operations have been made much simpler by digital devices. Consider how supermarkets use electronic scanners to read barcodes on merchandise rather than relying on a sales assistant to manually key the price into the till. Until relatively recently, shop assistants were required to perform mental arithmetic to add up the customer's purchases and work out the change required, but this is all done by digital cash registers now, and these usually have touch screens.

Supermarkets are employing new technology at a fantastic rate. RFID is being introduced to automatically track stock from factory to store. The technology exists to read every product in your shopping trolley simultaneously as you pass it through a special reader, eliminating the prospects of mistakes or theft. Large supermarkets have self-checkouts and scan-as-you-shop systems, where the traditional role of a checkout operator is eliminated.

Contactless, Apple Pay and android pay are all RFID. Security systems can now track and identify people automatically by their facial features.

As you learnt earlier, electronic funds transfer at point of sale (EFTPOS) systems are used for transactions with credit and debit cards. We rarely require cash, and when we do we mostly use another machine, an automated teller machine (ATM), to withdraw money. These are often situated near or inside retail outlets.

Retailers, such as supermarkets, garages and clothing stores, that encourage us to sign up for loyalty cards, gather data on our preferences. They use that information to send us enticements to buy again and to promote products that might suit our lifestyle and preferences.

The barcodes on purchases update shop stock records, and automated systems ensure that stock is systematically ordered from the supplier without the need for human intervention.

Organisational use

Organisations use digital devices to support an extensive range of functions. For example, they use digital devices to carry out administrative functions such as:

▶ accounts

▶ sales

▶ stocktaking

▶ procurement (acquiring goods to sell).

Organisations also use digital devices to carry out a number of specialist functions in the following areas.

▶ Design – The design industry (textiles, architecture and furniture) will use computer-aided design (CAD) software to create their technical drawings.

▶ Manufacturing and construction – The manufacturing and construction industries use **CNC** machines for milling, turning, moulding and cutting materials with precision.

Key terms

CNC – computer numerically controlled (CNC) machines are automated using software programs to carry out precision production of parts used in manufacturing and construction.

Link

To learn more about CNC machining, see http://machcnc.co.uk/.

Business have benefited significantly by using technology to speed up operations and the internet has enabled easy communication and access to information. Organisations can easily maintain links with suppliers, customers and their workforce, regardless of their location.

The internal and external dissemination of information is rapidly improved with technology. Central records are now stored on a server, which can be accessed remotely at any time, providing up-to-the-minute information. Geographical differences, time zones and cultures are no longer the barrier they used to be because all information is digital. Before the availability of digital technology, information was almost entirely kept in paper format and it would take considerably longer to perform transactions.

Discussion

In small groups, share your experiences of any part-time work you might do or your experiences as a customer.

What IT systems are involved in performing work tasks and transactions? Which replace older manual methods? Can you identify any businesses still relying on manual methods that are more usually carried out using technology today?

Discuss the advantages and disadvantages of the digital and manual methods.

Creative

The creative industries, one of the fastest growing sectors over recent years, have also benefited significantly from the use of technology. Consider the humble photograph and the time delay that used to exist between capturing an image on film and then getting it processed and the cost of the wastage created by taking numerous frames. Instead, we take digital images which do not cost anything to capture and we can easily delete those we are not happy with, freeing up memory on our digital cameras/ smartphones.

Link

Technology has now also provided us with 3D imaging, which opens up many more opportunities to be creative. For more on 3D imaging, see http://www.wisegeek.com/what-is-3d-imaging.htm.

The media, music and film industries can now replicate sounds digitally and even edit them on the move. Computer generated imagery (CGI) and 3D computer graphics have revolutionised media productions and contributed to the rapid global growth of software developers, particularly in computer gaming. It is highly unlikely any computer games you enjoy now are 2D and you will probably have watched 3D films in the cinema or on a home TV.

Link

For more on the use of digital devices in the creative industries, see *Unit 8: Computer Games Development*.

Peripheral devices and media

This section is about the features and uses of peripheral devices and media in IT systems to meet the needs of individuals and organisations.

Peripheral devices used with other digital devices to form part of an IT system

A peripheral device is **hardware** that is auxiliary (supplementary) to the computer. If you can touch it, then it is hardware (and is therefore not **software**, although it may contain software).

There are different types of peripheral devices:

▸ input devices

▸ output devices

▸ storage devices – these store information externally from the computer and provide extra memory

▸ communication devices, for example, WiFi, Bluetooth, radio and serial ports.

Key terms

Hardware – computer equipment that you can physically touch. It includes computers and other digital devices themselves and also peripheral devices such as the keyboard, monitor and mouse.

Software – applications or programs which are installed onto a digital device. They enable us to carry out certain functions such as word processing or creating spreadsheets, using media, accessing websites or playing computer games.

Input devices

Input devices are those which interact with or send information to the computer. They may pass data to the computer but do not store data. The following are all examples of input devices which can be connected via a cable or wirelessly to a digital device.

▸ Keyboard – This can be connected to a computer, laptop, tablet or smart TV. Using the keys, users transmit instructions or input data into the digital device.

- Mouse – This is a pointing device that allows users to make selections on a computer screen.
- Webcam – This is a video camera which transmits moving images through an internet connection. Webcams make it possible to see friends and family on the other side of the world.
- Microphone – This is used in conjunction with a webcam. A microphone allows us to transmit sounds across the internet or to give commands to the computer using our voices.
- Joystick – This is similar to a computer mouse. A joystick allows users to make selections or navigate through computer generated environments in a computer game.

The following are types of connection commonly used by input devices.

- USB – A Universal Serial Bus (USB) is a form of connection used for many peripheral devices. USB flash drives are data storage devices. A WiFi dongle, which is a USB peripheral, can also transmit a WiFi connection so can be attached to a digital device such as an internet-enabled TV to connect it to the internet.
- Bluetooth adaptors and wireless dongles – These contain radio communication hardware and will have some degree of firmware on them. They connect to other devices with similar connectivity which may allow a connection to the internet. A Bluetooth dongle is commonly used to add Bluetooth capability to connect to a device such as a mouse or headset.

Bluetooth adaptors transmit data over short distances and rely on software to connect to another device, whereas a wireless dongle contains firmware and connects to a USB port.

Output devices

Output devices provide information to the user from the computer. They perform a function using data or software stored in a computer. The following are all examples of output devices which can be connected via a cable or wirelessly to a digital device.

- Printers – Conventional printers are used to reproduce text and images according to instructions which they receive from any digital device. The printer receives data from the digital device which it replicates on paper. Three-dimensional printers are used to produce objects using materials such as plastic and even chocolate from instructions that they receive from any digital device.
- Monitors – A monitor is a visual display of whatever software and/or data is being accessed on the digital device at any given time. They are crucial to human interaction with computers, because otherwise we would not know what was stored on the digital device

or be able to access the internet through it. Monitors show us how we are interacting with the digital device via a keyboard, mouse or joystick.

- Projectors – These are similar to monitors as they are visual displays of whatever is being accessed on a digital device. Projectors are used to project the digital display onto a white or silver screen. They are mostly used to project films in cinemas (commercial and home) and for presentations in front of large groups of people where there are too many people to gather around a small computer monitor.
- Speakers – A sound card converts digital signals into analogue signals which are then converted into audible sound by the speakers. They are used to listen to music or videos and enable users to hear people in other locations during web conferences.

Some devices are both input and output devices. Joysticks are generally input devices but you can get ones that have haptic feedback, which is an output. Haptic feedback is a tactile sensation that users feel in their hands in response to something happening in the software they are using. The most common use of haptic feedback is in computer games, as this enables users to feel sensations corresponding to things happening in the game, for example, crashing into another car in a racing game.

Storage devices

Storage devices are peripheral devices that are used for storing data for the following reasons:

- to save space on your computer's hard drive
- to transfer files physically rather than over the internet
- to share files with another person or another digital device physically (if a network connection is not available)
- to back up data in order to protect against damage or loss.

The following are examples of storage devices.

- External hard drives – These are used to back up data or to store large amounts of data. Digital devices such as laptops and tablets have limited storage space, so by storing data on an external hard drive you can increase your storage capacity.
- USB flash drives – These can store smaller amounts of data which you wish to keep a copy of, or they can be used for temporary storage when moving data from one digital device to another.
- SD (secure digital) cards – SD cards provide high-capacity memory storage in a small space. They are most commonly used in small digital devices, particularly for storing still images.

- Optical disks – DVDs (digital versatile disks) are a form of optical disk technology similar to CD-ROMs. They are most commonly used to store movies. Blu-ray is an advancement on the DVD technology that uses different wavelengths and materials to realise a massive increase in storage capability.

> **Link**
>
> For more about the cloud, see Online systems.

Storage devices are often used as both input and output devices (they are known as I/O devices), which means that you can copy or transfer the data from the device as well as onto it. Some storage devices will not allow you to reuse them, so that you cannot change the data that is stored on them. These devices are read only.

Manual and automatic data processing

You may have heard the saying that what comes out of a computer is only as good as what goes in. Loosely speaking this is true. However, computers can read through optical character recognition, and can write through output of data. Also some of what comes out of the computer could be 'created' by the computer. Output is generated by the software, which was written by a person.

> **Tip**
>
> In your assessment, ensure that what you put into the computer is what you want to get out. Make sure that you always proofread your work or ask someone to help you do this, as a fresh pair of eyes often spots things you will not. You will also need to be exact when writing programming code, so make sure to check everything you write..

A computer has no decision making capability unless it is programmed in. A computer will only do exactly what it is told to do. Take, for example, a simple calculator which is a basic form of computer. It is very easy to assume that the answer a calculator gives must always be right. However, if the calculation or the figures which were put into it were wrong, then the answer will also be wrong. (The calculator will calculate correctly the figures put into it, but it will not know if these were the wrong figures.)

Despite the limitations, we would struggle to imagine life today without computers and their capacity to process enormous amounts of data rapidly.

Now consider examples of different types of data processing, both manual and automatic, that are performed by businesses.

Manual

The following are examples of some possible manual processes:

- keying in mail and telephone orders
- entering customer details from paper forms
- processing sales (checkout operators at a supermarket)
- marking exam scripts
- entering or collecting survey responses.

Automatic

Automatic data processing is data collection or processing carried out by a computer, sometimes with very little human input. The following are examples of uses of automatic data processing:

- smart meters (measuring electricity and gas)
- seismometer (used for predicting and measuring earthquakes)
- satellites (such as the Hubble telescope, observatories such as Mauna Kea and in the search for extraterrestrial intelligence (SETI))
- processing of ATM transactions
- race timing systems (RFID)
- bitcoin mining.

Accessibility devices

Accessibility devices are those which provide alternative input and output options for using digital technology when standard methods are not an option, for example because of a physical disability. They are also referred to as adaptive technologies. The following are examples of accessibility devices.

- Voice or speech recognition software – This software allows users to give instructions to digital devices or to input data using their voices (rather than fingers). It is particularly useful for anyone with a visual impairment or physical impairment to their hands. Examples of this kind of software are Express Scribe Free, Speakonia and Dragon. Many digital devices now have a 'personal assistant' which is controlled by your voice, such as Siri on Apple iPhones and Cortana on Microsoft products.
- Screen readers – This software will read aloud the words or content of the computer screen. This is particularly useful for people with visual impairments. The screen reader will read the words on the screen and also read out **alt text** for images and other media. Examples of this kind of software are JAWS, Supernova, Thunder, Window-Eyes and ReadHear, among many others.

▶ Touch screens – As well as touch screens being an interactive and useful way for anyone to input data into a mobile digital device, they can be of particular benefit for anyone who is unable to use a keyboard easily.

▶ Keyboards with big keys – Keyboards with big keys are useful for visually impaired people or for those who find it physically difficult to use standard keyboards.

▶ Ergonomic keyboard and mouse – Ergonomically-shaped keyboards and computer mice can benefit people who suffer with repetitive strain injuries when using a standard keyboard and mouse for long periods.

▶ Screen magnifiers – Screen magnifiers benefit those with visual impairments as they make it easier for them to read what is on the computer screen.

▶ Screen overlays – These are helpful for those with visual impairment or conditions such as dyslexia as they make the text easier to read by changing features of the screen, for example the background colour. This is an example of an in-built accessibility option in Microsoft Windows.

▶ Eye motion sensors, head motion trackers, sip-and-puff systems or light operated mouse and keyboard – These accessibility devices/adaptive technologies make certain tasks possible for people with significantly limited physical movement or paralysis. The choice of these devices will be dependent on the specific disabilities of each individual.

▶ Adaptive technology in action

▶ Keyless cars – This technology can be convenient for anyone but is also particularly useful for anyone with dexterity difficulties.

As you will learn towards the end of this unit, legislation exists to prevent people and businesses from putting barriers in the way of anyone accessing technology.

Characteristics and implications of storage media used to form part of an IT system

Earlier, we started to consider the use of servers to store data. They are often used as central locations for software applications which are accessed by multiple users via networked computers, rather than installing the software on individual computers. Servers are most commonly used by businesses and organisations, such as schools and colleges, because they allow large numbers of people to share data, software and resources easily.

▶ Storage devices including USB flash drives, DVDs, CD-ROMs and external hard drives are most commonly used by individuals. Many businesses prevent the use of personal or transportable storage devices as they pose a risk to the business of computer viruses being spread across devices and of sensitive data being lost if it is only stored on one standalone storage device.

▶ Businesses usually have formal procedures in place for storing media centrally over a network so that other employees can gain access to information which needs to be shared. Certain protocols will also exist about the structure of that stored data so that it can be located easily by anyone using the network and for routine backups.

- ▶ Businesses use servers to store data on fixed disks. They usually also use a system called RAID (redundant array of independent disks) to spread data across a number of different physical disks. This has the advantages of both increased speed and redundancy if configured in the correct way. If a file needs to be accessed, it may be spread across 10 disks, which means that each physical disk only needs to read a tenth of the file, and this can happen simultaneously cutting down read times by a factor of 10. If one disk fails, the data can be reconstructed using the data from the remaining good disks.

Computer software in an IT system

This section is about the concepts and implications of the use of, and relationships between, hardware and software that form large- and small-scale IT systems. You will also consider the impact of IT systems on individuals and organisations.

Types of operating system

An operating system is the **platform** which enables software installed on a digital device to work. It includes the necessary functions which act as an **interface** between the hardware and the software. You will probably know about some of the operating systems that exist, such as those developed by Microsoft (Windows), Apple (iOS), Android and ChromeOS. These systems operate with graphical user interfaces (**GUIs**). You may also have heard of DOS (disk operating system), which was the first, most commonly installed operating system on PCs.

Real-time operating system

A real-time operating system (RTOS) is a system which processes data in current (real) time, for example, RTLinux and Windows CE.

Single-user single task

Single-user single task operating systems can only run one user application at any one time (such as on a basic mobile phone), unlike a smartphone, which runs several software applications at the same time.

Single-user multi-tasking

Single-user multi-tasking operating systems deal with multiple applications running at the same time, which is what smartphones use. For example, when you are using spreadsheets, word processing, surfing the internet and listening to the radio on your PC at the same time, you are demonstrating that the operating system you are using is single-user multi-tasking.

Multi-user

A multi-user operating system, for example Unix, enables several users to operate the same, or different, software applications at the same time, for example through a server. Cloud servers enable multiple users to contribute to the same document, such as a spreadsheet, at the same time.

The role of the operating system

You have started to learn how operating systems manage many different functions. Operating systems also have functions to manage, in addition to running applications, and you will explore five of these here.

Networking

A networking operating system (NOS) controls access to resources and devices on a network. Networking operations include tasks such as managing remote printing, user management and backing up files.

Link

For more information about NOS services, including the programming language used for early operating systems on different platforms visit

http://computernetworkingnotes.com/comptia-n-plus-study-guide/network-operating-systems.html.

Security

Operating systems that manage security run ongoing checks for attacks to the system and its software. They gather data, which is analysed and collated to form huge amounts of intelligence about the health of the IT system. Manufacturers of software collate this data to help with combating cyberattacks. They also use it to develop new software or to adapt existing software to make it more secure against attacks.

Discussion

How do you know whether your data and IT system is protected?

Discuss this in a small group. Consider what you can do to protect your data and IT system from cyber attacks.

Memory management

Operating systems require memory to run, and the larger the IT system, the greater the memory needed to run all its functions. This is the reason why multi-user operating systems run from a server (or collection of servers), because otherwise the computers would fail to operate efficiently. For an operating system to work, there has to be sufficient memory for its application workload, to enable it to work out how best to use the memory it has for conducting each task.

Link

For more about the types of memory that digital devices use, see Memory and storage in *Unit 8: Computer Games Development*.

Multi-tasking

The modern operating systems of today continually multi-task. Think of your classroom PC – it is constantly scanning for viruses, maybe allowing you to research on the internet while also editing your assignment work on a document and playing a selection of music, all at the same time. The operating system provides you with information about your system, such as how much storage remains or how much battery life is left in addition to the management of your running applications. However, a PC can in fact only do one thing at a time! So how does it multi-task?

Multi-tasking is managed by the operating system by allowing each process access to a tiny amount of processor time in turn. This happens so fast that it appears that it is doing it all at once. The downside to all of this is that there is only so much processing power and memory to go around, so things can begin to slow down when using lots of applications at once.

Device drivers

The operating system manages your peripheral devices by using a **driver** to link the digital device with peripherals such as printers.

Key term

Driver – a routine program used to operate peripheral devices such as monitors and keyboards.

Factors affecting the choice and use of user interfaces

User interfaces (UIs) provide a communication link between a computer's operating system and the user, whether the device is operated by using GUIs or by writing a sequence of programming code to perform each action. You will now consider the factors which affect the choice of UI, depending on the intended use.

Graphical

The majority of PC users are probably very familiar with using graphical user interfaces (GUIs), as Microsoft has a significant market share in supplying software and operating systems for personal and public use. As previously mentioned, GUIs allow users to operate a computer through the selection of graphical icons. Therefore GUIs enable users to operate their devices effectively without needing programming knowledge and with limited computing skills. However, because of this, GUIs require significantly more memory and power to operate than other UI methods.

▶ Examples of GUIs

Apple describes GUI functions as 'WIMP computing' (windows, icons, menus and pointer) and could be said to have revolutionised the way in which we use computers and digital devices. WIMP computing has made computer usage accessible to many billions of people of almost any age group by being an intuitive, easy-to-use UI, whereby users can perform multiple actions with little or no prior knowledge or training.

Command line

The command line is the starting point shown on a computer screen where programming code is typed, informing the operating system what to do next. Essentially, the computer is operated via the inputting of text, specifically commands. A command line UI provides more flexibility than a preprogrammed GUI, but requires the user to have knowledge of the OS specific commands to use it. The advantage of a command line UI is that it can be used to operate lower specification computers.

Menu based

Menu based UIs provide alternative methods to perform functions, through a menu, and require less memory than GUIs. They may provide additional options to those of a GUI but require user knowledge about which menu provides each function. Users who are less familiar with the software, or who are risk averse, are more likely to prefer GUIs to menu based UIs as a way to navigate and operate their devices.

Adapted

Factors that influence the choice of UI include the ability to adapt it, for example the options routinely provided by Microsoft for adapting the colour, font size and positioning of GUIs on the desktop. The ability to adapt a UI is an important factor for users, particularly if they have specialist needs such as a visual impairment.

> **Link**
>
> You will learn more about accessibility guidelines and current legislation in the section entitled Legal, moral and ethical issues.

Factors affecting the choice of operating system

You have already starting learning about some of the features of operating systems. These features will help you make a choice about which operating system is likely to be most suitable to meet your needs.

Most people will want to have access to a single-user multi-tasking operating system so that they can carry out more than one function at the same time, because such digital devices are more powerful and useful. PCs used by individuals and businesses will be single-user multi-tasking. Some businesses may also have access to a multi-user operating system for collaborative working, which will be accessed via a server or the cloud.

If you are planning to become a **software developer**, **data engineer** or an IT technician who problem solves network and security issues, you will need to interact directly with the operating system by using operating system tools and sometimes the command line. There are often quite accessible graphical interfaces in a modern server operating system. Microsoft Windows can almost be exclusively managed by a graphical interface as can modern implementations of Linux. A networking device such as a Cisco Router, however, is programmed solely by the command line through a terminal window.

However, if you (or a future customer of yours) interact with the digital device for the purposes of administration or leisure pursuits, then the operating system used will need to be configured for efficiency and usability. For a relatively new digital user or for someone who has little interest in anything more than basic functions which are simple to use, save time, enhance daily living or simply for entertainment, then a WIMP style GUI operating system is likely to be the appropriate choice.

Many individuals will also have one or more mobile digital devices such as a smartphone or tablet. Some of these may be single-user single task, but the majority these days will be multi-tasking.

RTOSs will be used by specific digital devices which require real-time data processing, such as GPS devices to enable people to navigate through traffic.

> **Key terms**
>
> **Software developer** – someone who contributes to producing computer programs (software applications) or computer games.
>
> **Data engineer** – someone who designs and produces database programs known as information systems.

Factors affecting use and performance of an operating system

The amount of data you want your digital device to process at any one time will affect the performance of the operating system. A device running multiple applications and performing numerous operations, especially simultaneously, will use considerable amounts of memory and processing power (for example, a device streaming music and videos while also editing a presentation). In contrast, on a device used entirely for administrative purposes, producing spreadsheets and word processing documents will use significantly less memory and processing power. In both examples, the operating system is single-user multi-tasking, but the smaller amount of memory required and the fewer applications running simultaneously, the faster and more effectively an operating system can perform.

The amount of data analysis performed will increase the memory usage. A PhD student performing complex mathematical analysis on copious amounts of data for a major research project will require considerably better operating system performance than a book-keeper of a small business who has relatively small amounts of new data at any one time.

Utility software

Utility software is system software that runs alongside the operating system to distinguish between applications and to carry out routine tasks to maintain and optimise the system operation.

The purpose, features and uses of utility software

The purpose of utility software is to undertake routine tasks. The following are all examples of features and uses of routine tasks carried out by utility software:

▶ security checks
▶ identifying and removing viruses
▶ cleaning up files
▶ software updates
▶ backing up data
▶ issuing warnings or alerts that updates or backups are required
▶ managing peripheral devices (such as cameras, printers and webcams).

Another use of utility software is to gather data to clean up the system and speed up performance by searching for junk data and purging it (removing it) to free up storage space. Utility software varies in the amount of memory it takes up according to its features.

Factors affecting the choice and performance of utility software

Factors affecting the choice of utility software depend on what the user expects to get out of their device in terms of performance. If the device is mainly for browsing the internet or talking to friends using VOIP, it may not require utility software such as a printer driver. Users will choose utility software based on their needs. Most digital devices

come with integrated software update processes but it will be up to users whether they choose to add security and virus protection or to set up backup utility software.

Factors which can affect the performance of utility software include the amount of memory available on the digital device for utility software, as mentioned above. Other factors include:

▶ bandwidth
▶ conflicts with other utility software (such as multiple antivirus applications running on one device)
▶ memory failures.

Application software

Application software enables users to interact with their digital devices to perform many different functions. They are constructed using computing programming code. It is highly likely that you use several applications every day, such as Microsoft Word and Excel, as well as internet browsers or apps on mobile devices. Other examples of software applications include specialist business software used to manage stock control or accounting functions. If you are studying computer programming, you may become familiar with programming software such as Windows Visual Basic, Python and Java.

The purpose, features and uses of application software

Since the development of application software, business processes have been greatly enhanced. Software applications enable businesses to cut costs, increase production and control quality through the use of automated digital processes and greater data processing power. There are also a number of businesses that benefit from the introduction of IT systems using application software that may not immediately occur to you. These include following examples.

▶ **Farming** – Software applications are used to manage harvesting, sorting, cleaning and packing produce.
▶ **Textiles** – Software applications are involved in the design and manufacturing processes used to produce textiles.

Factors affecting the choice, use and performance of application software

One of the many reasons why Microsoft products have been so popular worldwide is their versatility and usability (ease of use). Businesses needing general office applications mostly favour those with which the majority of people are familiar (and most people are familiar with Microsoft's Office suite), and those with interoperability. When employing administrative staff, it is easiest to only require previously learnt skills, such as how to use Microsoft Office applications.

Apple products are most likely to be favoured by businesses in creative industries, such as advertising and graphic design, because the software that Apple initially designed had floating point processing power and excellent graphics capability that was more suitable for creative processes. Since then, they have built on that reputation. Some users simply prefer the design of Apple software although Microsoft Office operates on PCs and offers a version for Apple Macs. A great deal of industry-standard graphic, video and music production software is specifically designed for Apple Macs and takes full advantage of their unique capabilties.

▶ Home screens on different computers

Open source and proprietary operating systems and software

Behind all operating systems and software there is programming code, known as the source code. You may have come across this if you have looked at the source code of a web page in **HTML**. There are two types of source code that are generally created – open source and proprietary.

Key term

HTML – stands for hypertext markup language and is used to create web pages.

Link

For more on HTML see *Unit 6: Website Development*.

Open source

Open source code is a collaborative effort where more than one programmer contributes to the programming of the source code. It relies on peer review for testing its uses and functionality, and to fix any problems. Its main distinguishing feature is that the source code is open for use by anyone. Individuals can copy open source operating system and software code and, if they have the knowledge required, they can adapt it to their needs. Another distinguishing feature of open source software is that it is free.

Link

For more about open source, go to www.webopedia.com and search What is Open Source Software?

One of the implications of using open source software is that it can be copied and modified by individuals with a malicious intent, by expert programmers who do not share the same philosophy or responsibility to its integrity as the originators or simply by inexperienced programmers. However, this risk can be mitigated by individuals by checking the source of the open source code you download. On the positive side, open source programming provides opportunities for individuals to be creative and share their knowledge and expertise globally and freely. It gives access to sophisticated software to people who would not be able to afford the proprietary software. Developers of open source software do it 'for the love of good software', and bug fixes and feature developments are usually rapid.

Proprietary

Proprietary source code for operating systems and software, unlike open source, is privately owned. Examples of proprietary operating systems and applications are those produced by Sage, Microsoft, Apple and Pegasus. Proprietary operating system and software code will also have been produced by more than one programmer but as employees of a particular private company. Proprietary operating systems, software specifications and code are kept secret within a company to avoid copies being made and to stop modifications being made by anyone other than the company's designated programmers. Proprietary operating systems and software need to be purchased by individuals and businesses, but they are only able to use the operating systems and software, not change the source code.

One of the main implications of using proprietary software is that it can be costly. Another is that it restricts development to particular employed or contracted programmers. However, because the developers have control over the code, they are able to gather data on problems which occur and can use this information to correct programming issues. They are able to create code 'patches' that can then be delivered to registered users of the software. (Updates are also possible with open source software: developers develop the code and users upgrade.)

The impact and features of user interfaces in computer software

User interfaces (UIs) are the front-facing link between humans and computers. The command line is the point at which the user enters command text sequences, to instruct the computer to perform a task. In the early days of PCs, the only way to operate the computer was to input a lengthy command, known as a string, at the initial prompt which showed on the screen when the computer was turned on, as shown in the picture below.

UIs have been revolutionised by the use of graphics (GUIs) so users do not need to input command line code. GUIs provide prompts and directions so that even the most novice user can operate a digital device with little or no training.

Possibly the most important and influential impact of GUIs in computer software is their universal accessibility, which enables billions of users to interact with technology by:

▶ increasing levels of technological skills even without formal training

▶ providing creative and effective ways for users who are disabled or who have specific sensory impairments to interact with computers.

The features of common file types and formats

The data within a digital device are divided up into different file types, for different types of data. File types help the computer determine which software should be associated with the file (that is, which software will be used to access the file) and how or where it should be stored. File types are automatically assigned to routine files. There are many different types and formats used for creating files and these are identified by a suffix following a filename and a dot. For example, you may be aware that Microsoft Word files are identified as '.docx' in the current version, whereas the Word template file type is '.dotx'.

Other examples of file types include the following which are used for different kinds of data.

▶ Image file types include:
  - .bmp (BITMAP)
  - .tif (TIFF)
  - .jpg (JPEG)
  - .gif (GIF)
  - .raw (RAW).
▶ Video file types include:
  - .mov (MOV)
  - .avi (AVI)
  - .mp4 (MPEG4).
▶ Application software files are saved using different file types, the most familiar being Microsoft Office's Word (.docx), Excel (.xlsx) and Access (.mdb).

Use and selection of file types and formats

There are a number of implications on IT systems, individuals and organisations depending on the use and selection of file types and formats.

The method used for storing a file will vary according to the type of data it contains, the software used to access it and the type of file produced. Therefore decisions can be made about how you save a file in a different format depending on which will save memory, increase performance or, for example, retain the clarity of an image.

The implications of using and selecting some file types are discussed below.

BITMAP

BITMAP file types are associated with Microsoft Windows, although they are compatible with many other brands of software. A bitmap is a lossless image file format that does not lose quality or resolution. The downside is that it results in large files.

JPEG

JPEG files can be opened by most software applications and take up less memory than many other file types because the file is compressed when it is saved, losing some data and therefore quality in the process. Therefore JPEGs are particularly useful for attaching to emails, but the image quality might not be high enough for some purposes.

TIFF

TIFF files retain the quality of the image when saving, but TIFF files are not compatible with some software applications and so will not open and cannot be used in these applications. Therefore it is not the most versatile file type.

RAW

RAW files are uncompressed and the raw camera data. RAW file types can be used for images which require editing but require the relevant sophisticated software to open and manipulate them. The RAW file types are mostly used by cameras, specifically DSLRs, and each manufacturer has its own proprietory RAW file type.

PNG and GIF

PNG stands for portable network graphics. PNGs are file types which support lossless data compression. GIF stands for graphics interchange format and is a lossless format used for both still and animated images. There are patented restrictions on using GIF files, whereas the PNG file types do not carry the same restrictions and so are more commonly used. PNG file types can also be used as an alternative to TIFF file types.

> **Link**
>
> You will learn about lossless data compression later in this unit in Types of compression.

As with GIF and JPEG file types, PNGs were created for use on websites, each file type offering different levels of resolution. GIF file types do not support sophisticated animation such as those used, for example, in **Flash** files and often in logos. One of the benefits of using PNG file types, which were initially designed to replace the GIF format, is that software developers and web designers are not restricted by patenting laws as they might be when reading and writing other file types, such as GIF.

> **Link**
>
> To learn more about image file types, visit the Windows website, windows.microsoft.com.

> **Key term**
>
> **Flash** – authoring software used to create and play animated images.

MP3 and MP4

The MP3 file type only stores audio files, unlike the MP4, which holds both audio and video data of fairly high quality. MP4 files with video are significantly larger than MP3 files. However, MP3 and MP4 are not protected file types, which has led to piracy.

> **Link**
>
> To learn more about the difference between MP3 and MP4 files, visit www.differencebetween.com

DOC or RTF

Word processing documents can take the form of a document, such as Microsoft Word's DOC file type, or can be saved as a rich text file (RTF). Saving long and complex documents as an RTF is a useful tactic because they take up much less storage space than DOC files and is especially useful if the files are to be shared with users who have newer versions of software or different software makes. However, you cannot preserve a heavily formatted document in RTF. So if you wish to preserve formatting or tables and graphics, you will need to use the software file type.

ⓘ PAUSE POINT   Think about what has influenced you in your choice of software and devices for your own personal use. What choices would you make now, based on what you have learnt in this unit so far?

> **Hint**   Identify the devices and software you use and make a list. Analyse and evaluate the advantages and disadvantages of each item on your list. Then consider which devices and software you might choose now.

> **Extend**   Create a list of the software and devices used at your place of study. You might want to choose a specific department to focus on. Identify the advantages and disadvantages of each in relation to the purposes they are used for and make suggestions for improvements. Compare with a peer and explain the reasons for your evaluations and recommendations.

Compatibility

Files of different types will not necessarily open in different software and may be incompatible. For example, you will not be able to open a spreadsheet in a word processing application and you may not be able to open a file saved in a later version of the software in an earlier version.

Emerging technologies

New technologies are emerging at a rapid pace. Consider that your personal smartphone will contain more computer processing capacity and software than the Apollo 11 rocket that landed on the moon in 1969.

> **Link**
>
> In fact, the computing power of the Apollo 11 rocket was less than that of basic calculators used in the early 1980s. For more about moon technology, visit www.itpro.co.uk and read the 'Man on the Moon: Technology then and now' article.

The concepts and implications of how emerging technologies affect the performance of IT systems

The extent to which technology can be developed appears boundless. However, some might argue that we have tried to run before we can walk by creating a world reliant on using technology before the world is fully equipped to be able to access technology or understand how to maximise even a small percentage of its capabilities.

The requirements of producing emerging technologies impact on the performance of IT systems because they put demands on our current systems, which in turn places demands on our environment and day-to-day living. In recent years, the launch of streaming media from a wide range of organisations has put enormous strain on already saturated infrastructure. The network providers have to

plan ahead and expand the capacity of their networks to cope with the exponential growth in demand and use. The use of VOIP has again increased traffic but, in this case, a quality of service issue arises as calls cannot be delayed and must be given high priority when travelling through the hands of unknown couriers or organisations. Considerations include:

▸ technology is always expected to be on

▸ the exponential growth of data collection (big data) and the necessary processing and analysis of data

▸ the raw materials needed to manufacture IT equipment

▸ the environment needed to run electronic devices

▸ the infrastructure required for implementing and maintaining telecommunications and networks

▸ the cost of emerging technologies

▸ pressure on individuals to become **early adopters**.

> **Key term**
>
> **Early adopter** – an individual who feels compelled to obtain the latest products and technology as soon as they become available. For example, robotic vacuum cleaners, smart TVs and watches.

You will now explore the implications of emerging technologies on IT systems that are used by individuals and organisations.

Implications of emerging technologies on the personal use of IT systems

Ever since the 'birth' of the **worldwide web** by Tim Berners-Lee in 1989, and especially since the introduction and rise in popularity of smartphones and tablets, we have had access to more information on a daily basis than people from previous generations did in their entire lifetimes.

Link

For more about the inventor of the world wide web, Tim Berners-Lee, visit www.w3.org.

Link

It is reported that 'almost one-third of the world's 6.8 billion people use the internet regularly'. To find out more about the invention of the internet, visit www.history.com.

While the **internet** as a communication medium is a wonderful invention and the emergence of the worldwide web making use of this has changed the way we run our businesses and everyday lives, it has impacted on the way we communicate with family and friends (through email and social media and less in person) and how we conduct our daily lives. We are now easily drawn into making snap decisions about purchases or enticed by promises of rapid wealth through social media advertising.

Key term

Worldwide web – also referred to as the Web, is a method of accessing information over the internet.

Internet – the networking infrastructure which enables communication and access to information between internet-enabled digital devices with potentially infinite range.

Link

Read more about the internet and the worldwide web at www.computerhistory.org and computer.howstuffworks.com. (Try searching for 'what is the difference between the internet and the worldwide web?')

Most of us can probably name an instance when IT systems have stopped working but, because we have learnt to rely on them, we overlook how we can manage without them. Examples of everyday tasks where we are now reliant on IT systems whereas, previously, we managed without include making a purchase, performing banking transactions, talking to friends and family, washing our clothes or keeping our homes warm.

Yet the benefits of emerging technologies for our personal usage on a daily basis are many, including:

▸ keeping in touch with friends and family by text, phone, email, VOIP and social media

▸ instant access to world news, TV programmes, films and music

▸ multiple functions contained in one single device

▸ the ability to take and store thousands of images using high-quality cameras which can be integrated into mobile devices.

Research

LG has recently (February 2016) launched a new smartphone, the first of its kind, which is modular in that plug-in modules can be purchased to add more functions to the device.

Research this technology and whether any other manufacturers have since developed similar devices.

Implications of emerging technologies on the use of IT systems in organisations

As referred to earlier, technology has massively impacted on the way businesses are managed. For example, it enables businesses to source supplies globally and to market products and services internationally. However, it is easy for businesses to become burdened with the high costs of supplying and maintaining technology, finding ways to accommodate expensive equipment and also to train staff to use these IT systems.

Nevertheless, there are also many advantages of investing in emerging technologies for businesses, especially for undertaking tasks that would have been high risk for humans to undertake. Examples include mining, extended space travel, carrying out delicate medical operations, or the use of unmanned devices to work in Fukushima or Chernobyl.

PAUSE POINT   What examples can you find of where farming has benefited from the use of technology?

Hint   Try searching the internet for the British apple farmer who uses digital imagery to sort 130 million apples.

Extend   Compare two examples of where technology is being used in farming. Identify the advantages and disadvantages of relying on technology, analyse the impact on the farmer and employees and evaluate how farming methods have changed since the introduction of technology.

Research

Learn more about emerging technologies from BBC's Click programme.

Choosing IT systems

With so much choice and so many options, choosing IT systems can be complicated. .

The features of an IT system can affect its performance and/or the performance of a larger IT system, such as an IT system running two pieces of software which are incompatible with each other. One such example is the IT network used by the NHS. Currently, the software used by GP doctors' surgeries for keeping patient medical records around the country does not interact with and is not compatible with that used by hospitals to gather and store patient data.

Factors affecting the choice of digital technology

There are many factors that determine our choice of digital technology and these are discussed below.

User experience

When choosing an IT system, the experience it gives to the user is of particular importance, whether it is being used for personal or business use. User experience is the experience a user has of using a device or piece of software, and whether they have a good user experience depends on whether the device or piece of software meets their needs.

For example, an elderly person wanting to purchase their first mobile phone primarily for emergencies is likely to want a simple-to-use phone which makes and receive calls, has large keys and a clear screen with few, if any, other features. In contrast, an individual looking to upgrade their smartphone will base their decisions on previous experience and may be looking for additional or enhanced features such as extended WiFi range, screen resolution and memory capacity. Other factors, such as cost, will also be a consideration for users and, while many sign up for monthly payment contracts, an elderly person, as mentioned above, may be wise to buy their phone on a pay-as-you-go contract.

There are a number of aspects of user experience that will affect choices of digital technology.

▶ Ease of use – Devices or systems which are easy to use, or are more likely to save time are going to be preferred by most people, whether for personal or business use. Too many systems are overly complex and so only a minor portion of those IT systems are actually used.

Link

Other examples of complex systems are mobile virtualisation tools. To find out more, go to http://www.computerweekly.com/news/2240149820/Mobile-virtualisation-tools-unpopular-despite-IT-consumerisation.

▶ Performance – According to whether the technology is to be used for pleasure, business or academic research, the level of desirable performance will vary. The variety of functions a device can perform is also a factor. For example, an elderly person may want a mobile phone for emergencies only so will not need particularly good performance and will choose based on a single criterion. However, a business may make the choice based on high levels of performance if it requires its employees to be contactable while on the move. Employees may also need to be able to access a central server for customer records, to analyse financial data and produce complex reports. Therefore businesses make choices based on many criteria.

▶ Availability – People demand a service or an app that is there when they want it. Always on means always available. It is no good having a retail website that shuts when the shop does – one of the big advantages of e-commerce is that it extends your market. A retailer that was only open 9 to 5 in one town before a web presence would now be open 24/7 worldwide!

▶ Accessibility – Accessibility or adaptability of technology may dictate digital technology choices, especially if the user requires specialist devices such as speech recognition software, digital personal assistants or perhaps automated wheelchairs.

User needs

Users will have different needs which inform the criteria they use to make digital technology choices. For example, your place of study requires IT systems which may need to accommodate the needs of staff to use Microsoft Office software, communicate by email and store files on a central server. IT students will use computers for their studies, to learn about new software, to apply programming skills and to study networking techniques (access to a variety of digital technology is required for this).

Specifications

According to user needs, the system **specifications** will vary. Software designers may require different types of systems according to the tasks they are undertaking. For example, for programming they might use fairly basic systems, but they will probably want significant processing power and **RAM** for compiling programs or testing games.

Compatibility

Compatibility means whether two or more things that need to connect and interact with one another do so properly. If they do not connect (physically in terms of cables or connectors) or interact with one another (do not work together) then they are incompatible. Decisions about choosing IT systems will be based on the needs of the whole organisation. Just as you might choose the same make for several devices out of personal preference and because you know they will work together, businesses are concerned about compatibility and whether the IT systems they choose will interact with each other.

Connectivity

An individual, and usually an organisation, may choose a system based on its ability to connect to either a network and/or the internet reliably. Some individuals may only require their system for internet use, while an organisation may employ sales staff or engineers who spend most of their time on the road. These remote staff are likely to require VLAN access and mobile data. They will also need stable connectivity via, for example **Bluetooth** and **WiFi**, to communicate with customers and the organisation.

Cost

The cost of an IT system is very much a factor when making a choice. Businesses will allocate a budget for their IT systems. This budget is likely to include maintenance and upgrades. The cost varies according to the specifications and manufactured quality of the IT system. Cost is obviously an important factor for individuals too, and their budgets are likely to be much smaller than that of organisations. Quite often, manufacturers market their headline cost but businesses and consumers need to consider much more than this. Take a printer as an example – the cost of consumables varies a great deal between different manufacturers. Businesses will normally calculate the total cost of ownership (TCO) using standard formulae for the range of devices and not just look at the initial purchase cost.

Efficiency

How **efficient** an IT system needs to be depends on an individual's or organisation's users' needs. If a business is operating with low specification IT systems which underperform, it will take employees longer to complete tasks and this will cost the business money.

Implementation

Choosing a system can depend on the speed of its implementation. For example, an individual and organisation are likely to choose to use a system that runs the same software as they currently use for everyday tasks to avoid unnecessary time lost for training. The IT system will be chosen for performance, but also perhaps for space saving, mobility and weight, to make it easier to implement without having to find new locations for the system or to move around special equipment. However, if specialist software is developed, such as that being implemented in the NHS (http://systems.hscic.gov.uk/scr), it may require new IT systems to implement the change.

The urgency for implementing IT systems will influence choices.

▶ Timescales – The preferred IT system may not be readily available or the lead time for implementation may be too disruptive for the organisation or individual. Perhaps you decide that your personal computer is underperforming and you want to upgrade to one with greater performance but cannot get the same make as it is out of stock. In order to avoid a break in your studies, you may choose an alternative make or model because it is available straight away.

▶ Testing – It is hard and possibly irresponsible to choose an IT system without having tested it first. Depending on what it is needed for, you might want to test it for compatibility and stability. A keyboard user, rather than a mouse user, will probably want to try out the keyboard for touch, size and positioning of keys. Someone purchasing a GPS will want to test it for ease of use and readability in different weather conditions.

▶ Migration to new system(s) – Transferring data, software and files to a new IT system can be stressful as well as time consuming. The process of migration needs to be straightforward and reliable. Some suppliers include data migration as a service when purchasing a new IT system, perhaps transferring contacts, favourites and apps to another mobile phone for you. Even migrating to a new operating system can cause disruption and, when making choices about new systems, the OS for an individual or business can appear to be imposed on you whether or not you wish to migrate.

If at first you don't succeed

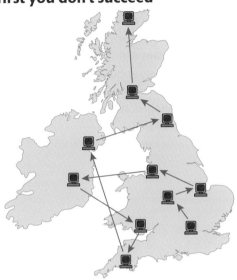

▶ **Figure 1.1:** How systems can be linked geographically

The NHS is striving for efficient, improved IT systems which subsequently save billions of pounds. Due to the potential of digital technology and its functionality, the NHS intends to go paperless by 2018 by implementing a system which maximises electronic communication, such as:

- text messaging
- electronic prescriptions
- paperless referrals
- shared patient records across the country and with other social care agencies.

The NHS has experienced many problems with its IT systems over the years, reportedly costing nearly £10 bn. Some of the problems encountered with the systems include:

- old systems which are incompatible with replacements
- migrating patient records
- lack of integration with records held by other support services

- inability to share information across regions
- escalating costs for implementing and maintaining systems
- budget overspending due to compensation for cancellation of projects.

Due to the inefficiency of the current IT systems, there still remains a reliance upon:

- administrators to send out appointment letters to patients following doctors' requests
- patients having to explain conditions and medical history to doctors rather than patient records being readily available
- patients being relied upon to inform their GP of hospital visits and outcomes.

All of these slow down productivity, efficiency and, most importantly, patient care.

There are early signs that technology is being used more readily and automatically in the NHS. For example, images from X-rays and scanners are stored digitally, digital cameras are occasionally used to measure progress made during treatment and some doctors' surgeries routinely welcome emails from patients for repeat prescriptions. At some surgeries, booking appointments can also be arranged online while the telephone is also a means of triaging patients who may not require a face-to-face or doctor's appointment.

Check your knowledge

1 State why it is important for the NHS to change its IT systems.

2 Identify at least five reasons why previous NHS IT systems have been unsuccessful.

3 Name examples of where the NHS has already made improvements to its processes.

4 Give at least three examples of where standards could be improved by choosing the right IT systems.

⏸ **PAUSE POINT**   How can digital technology improve current NHS processes?

　　　　　Hint   Read more about the NHS intentions by visiting
- Jeremy Hunt challenges NHS to go paperless by 2018', www.gov.uk
- The care.data programme – collecting information for the health of the nation', www.nhs.uk.

　　　　Extend   How would you describe the concept of the intended NHS system? Tip: Try drawing your concept of the intended system.

Productivity

Businesses very often make a decision to upgrade, change or implement new IT systems to increase **productivity**. Productivity in industry is a measurement based on the quantity of work carried out or products made in a given time period. For example, a Japanese farm near Kyoto (Kameoka farm) runs entirely without farmers, using robots to carry out all of the work. Productivity increased from an average of 30,000 heads of lettuce harvested a year to 10 million a year.

> **Link**
>
> For more about the Kameoka farm, visit http://spread.co.jp/en/factory/.

Security

IT system security is of constant concern. Frequent news reports feature examples of major breaches in security due to hacking into personal and business records. While we have become fairly savvy about the need for security software or using passwords to access IT systems and files, we remain less vigilant with mobile devices. Organisations will make their choices about IT systems according to the security precautions in place, especially where sensitive information is managed, such as police, health and financial records.

B Transmitting data

Computers process and transmit data either internally through the operating system or externally between digital devices. In this section, you are going to learn more about the concepts, process and implications of transferring data within and between IT systems.

Connectivity

Connectivity is the ability to process digital data by connecting the operating system with applications and systems and with each other.

Wireless and wired methods of connecting devices and transmitting data within and between IT systems

There are a number of different methods to connect devices and transmit data between systems wirelessly or using wired cables. Nowadays, we expect our portable devices to connect to the internet via WiFi automatically. When on the move, we rely on our digital devices to detect wireless signals and prompt us if we need to connect manually by simply choosing the network available and inputting a security code, if needed.

However, connecting devices by wired cables was the only option when computers were first being adopted by businesses. Computers, printers, scanners and web cams were all joined together by cables. It was usual to see cables resting on desks and along the floor to join digital devices together or to a server.

Within IT systems there is the need to connect peripherals and devices to perform input or output functions such as printers, keyboards, mice, webcams, speakers and monitors. There are a range of both wired and wireless technologies that enable this.

▶ USB – This is the most prevalent wired connection in today's IT landscape. It is a bidirectional bus which means it can both transmit and receive data and a single port can provide connectivity for up to 127 individual devices. One big advantage of USB is that it can also provide power to peripherals.

▶ Bluetooth – This is a wireless method often used to connect mice and keyboards as well as audio devices such as headphones. Its range is approximately 100 metres.

▶ VGA, HDMI, DisplayPort – These are video interconnects that permit connection of some form of visual display, such as an LCD monitor, projector or TV. HDMI also facilitates the transmission of digital sound and is becoming the standard in this respect.

▶ Parallel – This is older technology used to connect printers over very short distances.

▶ Serial – This is slow technology used for communication devices such as modems. It is also used to connect accessibility devices and to create console systems for commercial internet routers.

There are many available methods of communication between IT systems. Technologies such as WiFi and

Bluetooth allow wire-free connection to a network, which might be a corporate network or be through your phone using 'tethering' and the 3G or 4G mobile data network. In businesses, wired connections are the most common form as they offer enhanced speed and reliability compared with wireless networks and, in some cases, they offer increased security.

We take for granted the functions that our digital devices perform to enable them to connect automatically and **sync** with other devices for access and so that data can be shared between them. For example, although we might own multiple digital devices, we can sync our data into one storage place so that we can access files, images and contacts whether we use our phone, tablet or even a smart TV. Usually, cloud storage is used to achieve this syncing of data.

Key term

Sync – is short for 'synchronise' or 'synchronisation' which means to match up and pull together, for example, to make sure that multiple devices have the same copy of the relevant files in many places.

When video recorders and TVs first became available to the public at more affordable prices, in the late 1980s, remote controls were also connected by a cable.

Link

For more about early television remotes, go to www.earlytelevision.org.

Remote controls using radio transmitted signals were first used by the military to control weapons in each of the world wars. Now all of our everyday remote controls for smart TVs and FreeView, Sky or Virgin boxes use infrared signals.

When the internet was originally available to the public, wired cables were used to connect computers and telephone lines to enable access the internet. The dial-up process was tedious, noisy and unreliable. Considerably less data was able to be downloaded then than can be today due to the limitations of the **bandwidth**. The introduction of broadband enabled quicker internet access with a faster response time and it gave people the ability to download large quantities of data fairly rapidly.

Key term

Bandwidth – the available amount of data transmission capability.

Theory into practice

Interview your relatives, neighbours and anyone living in a different area of the country from your home. Ask them about their experiences with technology and how they managed without in the past. Compare their responses and analyse the information according to, for example, their location, age group, gender. What similarities and differences are there and what evaluations can you draw from your findings?

We now have access to many different internet-enabled digital devices which we can operate wherever we are, assuming we have an internet connection. There are many different products available which enable us to operate our homes, even if we are on the other side of the world. We can turn the heating on and off, arrange for lighting to come on automatically or change the settings using our digital devices. If we are at home watching the TV, we can use any internet-enabled device to change the TV programme using an app and use smart TVs to access the internet.

How the features of connection types can meet the needs of individuals and organisations

Even though broadband is widely available and even taken for granted by many, there are many areas, even in this country, where broadband is either not available, has limited bandwidth or is not wanted or cannot be afforded by householders. For example, the information gathered by the Government in its last census of 2012 reported that 80 per cent of households have internet access. This meant that one-fifth of all households did not, at that time, have internet access. It would be hard to imagine life without internet access, particularly in the UK.

Link

For more about the census information on internet access visit the Office for National Statistics http://www.ons.gov.uk/ons/.

Theory into practice

Imagine what your life would be like without internet access. Try living without any form of internet access for a whole day. Find alternative ways of living without it. Keep a diary of what you did and the alternative methods you used. Share with a peer.

Wired systems using cabling are still used to network computers together for shared access to servers, especially by businesses. In some cases, the connection to the internet is now shared with telephone lines through which broadband is received. In other cases, it might be cable broadband. Alternatively, people can use mobile broadband as their only means of connecting to the internet.

Businesses transmit data to speed up their productivity and efficiency using a mixture of wireless and **hardwired** or cabled systems. For example, vehicle manufacturers such as Mercedes Benz monitor the performance history of their vehicles which they gather remotely, directly from the vehicle. The vehicle also gathers data on its performance which is analysed by the processor in the vehicle and provides updates to the driver. The collection and analysis of this data enables more rapid and accurate diagnosis of problems. The manufacturer is able to automatically schedule servicing or replacement of parts before they become worn out.

Since the introduction of **fibre-optic** cabling and **4G** connectivity, systems for accessing the internet and streaming videos have become more reliable, quicker and effective than before.

Fibre-optic wiring increases the broadband speed, enabling users to utilise multiple digital devices in their homes and offices without experiencing the latency, unreliability or slow download speeds experienced when using traditional broadband connections. Since reports suggest that households own at least three different internet-enabled devices, on average, the demands on instant and reliable connectivity are increasing.

The development of 4G has enabled us to use multiple applications on mobile devices and to have a swifter connection to the internet than previously experienced. As yet, neither 4G nor fibre-optic connections are available to everyone because they are dependent on where you are located in the country and each connection type comes at an increased cost.

> **Link**
>
> Another type of 4G technology is referred to as 4G LTE which stands for 'long term evolution'. To find out more, visit www.pcadvidsor.co.uk.

> **Key term**
>
> **Fibre optics** – a collection of very fine **strands of** silica glass which use light to transmit data at high speeds.
>
> **4G** – stands for 4th generation and is intended to replace 3G for accessing the internet at much higher speeds via mobile.
>
> **Hardwired** – a permanent connection between components of an IT system with dedicated wired cabling. Modern buildings are often purpose built with the cables integrated into the fabric of the building and internet connections are provided for direct connection of non-mobile digital devices such as PCs, servers and machinery.

The implications of selecting and using different connection types

Recent advancements in technology may have made some internal cabling redundant (that is, internet cabling within houses and offices). However, in those areas of the country with limited bandwidth, the ability to access the internet via wires is still useful. Also, cables provide greater stability when using smart TVs and surround-sound systems, and can be hardwired directly into the device.

It was not until the late 2000s that some homes and offices were being built with cables embedded into the building infrastructure, so many businesses still show signs of trailing wires between IT systems. Increased health and safety requirements have raised awareness of the potential hazard from trailing cables.

There is a greater demand from businesses to have reliable remote connectivity for employees to communicate remotely between offices and across the world. Increasingly, more employees work remotely and interact with customers and suppliers around the globe at any time of day.

Such considerations are important when making choices about selecting different methods to connect digital devices.

The type of usage is also an important consideration when selecting the method of connection. In a warehouse, where staff are constantly on the move picking stock or collecting orders, then the use of WiFi with handheld computers would be an excellent fit. Likewise, using tablets to access live patient records at the bedside is better suited to a wireless technology, although security in this situation is a key concern, given the sensitive personal data that is being accessed. A business in the creative industry that produces advertisements and which is often editing high resolution video and imagery would benefit from cabled fibre to the desktop, so as to offer maximum speed of data transfer.

However, most businesses are content with copper to the desktop as a middle ground of reliability and speed.

The impact of connection types on the performance of an IT system

Choosing a suitable connection type will impact on the performance of an IT system. This could mean the compatibility of the cables and their connectors to transfer data between digital devices or the ability of the software applications to interact effectively. For example, a business relying on the stability and speed of multiple systems to transfer large amounts of data, such as banks, government offices and the health services, will want the fastest broadband connection available, which is currently fibre optic. In the case of the Stock Exchange, reports have suggested that via changes to its connection types between companies with which it trades, the potential benefit to traders could be to the tune of £12bn a year. The ability for finance houses to get data across the Atlantic milliseconds before their competitors has the opportunity to significantly affect the profitability of trade.

In some industries, the reasons for choosing a more expensive connection type are not as obvious. There can be very high levels of electromagnetic interference as a result of some processes which would cause problems with traditional copper cabling; in these cases the added expense of fibre to the desktop is a necessity to prevent data loss and network degradation.

> **Research**
>
> Read more about how customers benefit from the changes to connectivity undertaken by the Stock Exchange, which increased customer access from 2Mb to 10Gb, at www.lseg.com.

> **Link**
>
> There are potentially negative impacts of connection types on the performance of an IT system. For one such example, read 'Six reasons why the NHS National Programme for IT failed' at www.computerweekly.com.

The DVLA's newly implemented IT system enables vehicle tax evasion to be reported to the police directly, whereas previously the two systems were unconnected. As a result, this has significantly reduced offending to less than one per cent. Previously, manual systems also relied on licensing requests to be serviced manually and paper tax discs were issued for cars. The intention for the DVLA to become completely digital has resulted in paper tax discs being abolished and has cut costs considerably in the administration processes. The DVLA forecast an 85 per cent take up in 2016–17, although this relies even more on individuals and businesses using online systems.

> **Link**
>
> To find out more about the DVLA's newly implemented IT system, read the 'DVLA Business Plan 2015-16' at www.gov.uk.

Networks

You have already started to consider what networking means and how or where it is used. You are now going to learn more about the concepts and implications for individuals and organisations of connecting devices together to form a network.

The features, use and purpose of different networks

This section discusses the different types of network and their features, use and purpose.

▶ Personal Area Network (PAN) – A wirelessly connected network between an individual's digital devices such as their smartphone, laptop, printer and car. This kind of network is used by individuals to sync their data across their devices for personal or business use.

▶ Local Area Network (LAN) – A local network which provides a connection between digital devices within a small area or building. The organisation 'owns' the communication links (cabling, infrastructure etc.) employed to support the network. It might be used to network two computers and their internet connection within an office.

▶ Wide Area Network (WAN) – A WAN uses telecommunications over a wider area than a LAN, with the potential to connect digital devices around the globe. The Internet is a collection of WANs. This global potential enables businesses to connect with each other across wider geographical areas such as the IT system now being used by the DVLA and police force in the UK. The advantage of a WAN over a cloud system for users is that it will be self-contained and can be made more secure, which is why organisations such as the police force use it. To connect using a WAN, the user usually pays a subscription to the telecommunications provider. WANs originally only transmitted voice but can now also carry data. The link uses telecommunications infrastructure that is not owned by the organisation.

- Virtual Private Network (VPN) – This type of network provides a contingency for business expansion with little disruption to computing services. It works by using the internet to securely connect remote digital devices together. So it is useful for businesses whose employees work remotely around the country or at different sites internationally. VPN is a relatively recent development, replacing the need for dedicated communication links such as **ISDN** for home or remote workers. Instead, these workers can now use a public network such as the internet to 'pipe' a private (and secure) connection to their own LAN.

Theory into practice

Identify at least one example of where each network type is used in different businesses, other than the examples given. What reasons can you give why these businesses would connect using the means they do rather than alternative methods?

Share with a peer and explain your rationale to each other.

What have you learnt from this activity? If you agreed entirely with each other, share with another peer or in a small group.

Factors affecting the choice of network

As with choosing an IT system, there are several factors which will influence the choice of network type. Some of these factors are discussed here.

User experience

- Ease of use – This is how easy is the network to use. Users are likely to choose networks that are easy for them to use or gain access to. For example, if certain types of network are hardwired in their building they are more likely to adopt them. Smartphone users are also more likely to keep to the same mobile phone network provider because of familiarity with their service. Users do not like overcomplicated processes. A device that connects automatically to a data service is preferable to a complicated configuration process that requires complex passwords or keys to be entered.
- Performance – Level of performance will be more important to some users than others, depending on the purpose of the digital device. As in the examples above,

a video editing studio would require far more from their connection method than a corner shop. For example, if a user often has to use an internet connection to download significant amounts of data, then the user might choose a 4G or fibre optics for broadband connection, whereas an occasional data user would be satisfied with a (cheaper) 3G service.

- Availability – There are limitations to the availability of some network services, such as fibre-optic services and even standard broadband or WiFi. These depend on the locations of transmitters, especially in rural locations, and will affect the possible choices of network that a user can make.

- Accessibility – This determines whether a user can access data across a network, perhaps from a server or another device or perhaps access information from an **intranet** or **extranet**. You may be familiar with using the intranet at your place of study, possibly for information and resources uploaded by your teacher and for uploading your assignments for feedback. Accessibility can also mean how suitable a network is for particular users with specialist needs or a disability.

Key terms

Intranet – a local network website where access is restricted to internal users, such as within an organisation.

Extranet – an intranet system which can be accessed by authorised external users to retain data security.

Reflect

How would you make a choice of network for personal use? Make a list of reasons and rank these in the order you believe are most important to you, with the most important being number 1.

How would you make a choice of network for your school or college using the same process?

Discuss your evaluations with those of a peer.

User needs

The needs of the user vary with what they need an IT network for, whether they are an individual setting up a network for personal use or a business. Individuals use technology for different purposes. You are likely to use your digital devices in different ways and for different reasons to those of your family members. A family may need to share a network so will need one that will meet the needs of everyone in the family.

A business will have similar considerations about network usage which will depend on the size of the business, number of employees and where they are distributed. If they have several office sites, they will want to transmit data and share files over the network, perhaps globally.

Specifications

Depending on the needs of the user or users, the specifications of the required network will also vary. Although office software is a fairly standard requirement, the versions installed will vary according to need. The performance of digital devices will also vary according to need: that is, the expected speed of connection, capacity and operating power required to undertake complex tasks will vary depending on the kind of business in question. For example, the specifications will be more demanding in a graphic design or music/film industry office than in one which is solely administrative.

Connectivity

An individual user might want to sync their digital devices together to share contact lists, files and photos and, according to usage, might want a more powerful broadband connection such as fibre optic. However someone else who just wants to use a tablet for browsing the internet or sending emails on occasions may prefer to pay a lower price for standard broadband.

As many businesses will need to connect to other offices across the country or globally for sales or suppliers, they will need to ensure that their access for the internet is very stable. Therefore they will need to choose a stable network and connection type. Businesses will also need to decide upon the size of servers, their type and the performance power of digital devices to be used in the network, depending on their business needs.

Cost

Cost is another factor in the choice of network – the higher the specification, the greater the cost. Some businesses and individuals prefer to make up their own specification for an IT system, whereby each component part is costed according to its function and performance, for example different types of **CPU**. It is possible, in this way, to get the same specification IT system for less money. However, it requires more technical knowledge and practical experience to set up.

> **Key term**
>
> **CPU** – central processing unit which acts as the computer's brain to process instructions.

Efficiency

The busier our lives become, the greater the demands we put on the technology we use. We demand maximum efficiency. Just as we are no longer satisfied with dialling into the internet once we have tried broadband, the same will be the case for those who use fibre-optic connections because they are more efficient: that is, they can download more data in the same time period.

Compatibility

Our choice of telecommunications network will depend on its compatibility to communicate between a variety of digital devices that we own. Any exchange of data will need to be in a format which each device understands. If a network is to be used to support workers who are constantly mobile, such as for quality control workers on a production line, then a fibre network is unsuitable. Some form of wireless technology would suit them better as they do not have a 'fixed base'. Likewise, WiFi is likely to be unsuitable for a data analyst working with large data sets due to the necessity for the data to be error free and available instantly.

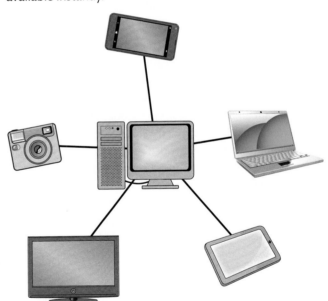

▶ **Figure 1.2:** Compatibility between devices is important

Implementation

The decisions we make about the types and makes of device we buy and the telecommunications network providers we choose will be influenced by the ease and simplicity to implement them (set them up).

▶ Timescales – For a business time is money and the purpose of the installation will often dictate the timescale. A network installation in temporary buildings to accommodate seasonal demand needs to be installed quickly. For this purpose, wireless can be set up and running in minutes. However, for a permanent office, a more resilient structured cabling solution would be more suitable, but would take many days to install properly. Similarly, for external communications, temporary circuits in copper can be installed much more quickly than a permanent fibre-to-the-premises installation.

▶ Testing – A business needs to be able to rely on its network infrastructure as it is often the core holding every other system together. A properly planned installation will take into account this element of testing and a business might specify that the installation is categorised and certified to meet international standards as a way of ensuring reliability. A business IT system will also need to be tested and this may take a long time depending on the demands for the system. For example, testing needs to be carried out between digital devices for connectivity, especially if overseas. An individual will need to test their IT system, even on a very small scale such as using the internet or testing the time taken to upload and download data. If the download speed is too slow, they may choose to implement a different network.

▶ Downtime – This is a period of time when the digital devices or networks are out action, such as when the internet is unavailable, perhaps due to engineering works. Businesses and individuals want to avoid downtime as much as possible so a network that has significant amounts of downtime would not be chosen or would quickly be replaced. When considering the implementation of a network, the downtime that might occur when upgrading infrastructure needs to be planned in advance so that the business does not lose money. It might be planned for night times when demand is low, or might be carried out in phases so that parts of the network are unaffected while others are upgraded.

Productivity

Productivity means the speed at which instructions and data are processed, together with the quality of the outcome, for example the less downtime, the greater the productivity. The telecommunications network we choose is influenced by its performance and reliability, because we are likely to choose one that is more productive.

Security

Communicating over networks increases the risk to the security of that data. Simple precautions can be taken in the first instance, such as not sharing passwords and **encrypting** important or sensitive information. Businesses, as well as individuals, are likely to choose a network that provides them with an appropriate level of security for their needs.

> **Key term**
>
> **Encrypting** – converting data into a code to avoid it easily being accessed by unauthorised users. Specialist software is used to encrypt data.

> **Tip**
>
> Treat your password like a bank card PIN number – do not share it with anyone.

However, there are many examples of breaches in data security, for example in February 2015, the personal details of TalkTalk customers were put at risk of identity theft.

Your place of study will have an IT security policy and, depending on the restrictions imposed on the intranet, you may not be able to access the intranet when off-site or when using other digital devices.

How the features of a network and its component parts affect the performance of an IT system

A network is often made up of a variety of different components working together. The demands of the network make the choice of components critical, for example an enterprise network in a large company is unlikely to use products sold for the home market. A business needs their network to be resilient, and often auditable with redundant hardware to minimise the risks of failure, whereas a home user does not need the same level of resilience or auditing. For example, the failure of a core switch in a call centre employing thousands of people will result in those employees being unable to work, and customers unable to contact the company. The failure of your network switch at home is often just merely inconvenient. An enterprise firewall will log attacks and allow intervention and traceability. However, these features are not needed for home use.

Issues relating to transmission of data

You have probably experienced issues with transmitting data on occasions. Perhaps the network connection has failed temporarily or a file will not attach to an email. Sometimes the files will not attach because the **email host** you are using has an internal problem, rather than it being an issue with the file size.

Key terms

Email host – an internet provider that offers an email service to its users.

This section is about how the features and processes of data transmission affect the use and performance of IT systems.

Reflect

What are your experiences and to what can you attribute the reasons why your connection failed? Is there anything you could do to prevent the situation happening again?

Protocols used to govern and control data transmission for common tasks

In IT systems, protocols are essential to allow systems to communicate. A protocol is like a language, that is, it is a set of rules governing how the communication takes place. The use of international standards and protocols allows devices of different manufacturers and operating systems to work with each other seamlessly. The protocol will dictate how the transmission is initiated, how data is encoded and how it is terminated. Just as when speaking to someone you begin a conversation with 'Hello', follow with sentences using your chosen language and end with 'Goodbye', data transmission follows a set pattern. We will look at some common tasks and the specific protocols that are used.

Email

When sending an email, you do not need to know what type of device your recipient is using – it is enough to know their email address. Email, by its very nature, connects people and devices across the world and it is likely that an email will pass through devices of many

different manufacturers and operating systems before being delivered. The common protocols used by email are:

▶ post office protocol (POP3) – this is used to retrieve mail from a server by a mail client such as Mozilla's Thunderbird or Microsoft's Outlook

▶ simple mail transfer protocol (SMTP) – this is used to transmit mail to a server either from a mail client or another server

▶ internet message access protocol (IMAP) – this is used to access mail on a remote server by a mail client (the main difference between POP3 and IMAP is that IMAP does not remove mail from the server but merely acts as a method of accessing the mail)

▶ exchange – this is a proprietary protocol used by Microsoft with their Microsoft Exchange Server and Outlook; it works in a similar way to IMAP.

Voice and video calls over the internet

A common and popular way to communicate is to talk over the internet. There are a numbe of voice-over-the-internet applications such as Skype, FaceTime and Google Hangouts. They are especially popular because the basic functions are free to use. There are numerous providers offering paid-for voice-over-the-internet services which may vary in the service they provide and any charges they make. However, the connections can be unstable or unreliable and applications are not always compatible between devices, such as FaceTime which only communicates between Apple devices.

VOIP allows businesses and individuals to make financial savings by routing traditional telephone calls over the IP network (the internet) instead of using traditional phone lines. VOIP-enabled devices can often call VOIP addresses as well as traditional phone numbers. The use of standard protocols such as RTP and SIP (session initiation protocol) allow VOIP services from many different providers to work together seamlessly.

Web pages

Information about almost anything is now accessible through web pages, and it is estimated that there are over one billion websites online in 2016. It is the ease of access combined with the interactivity and immersive aspect of web pages that have made them so widespread. Web pages began life called 'hypertext pages' because text had links to other pages (hyperlinks). The protocol used to transfer these pages therefore became http (hypertext transfer protocol). The http protocol describes how a web browser requests pages from a server using a GET command such as *GET /index.html HTTP/1.0*. The server responds with a response code (you have probably seen the dreaded 404 response meaning File Not Found). The more normal response is 200, which means OK. A special version of http exists called https which is a secure version used for applications such as banking and the transfer of sensitive data. HTTPS makes use of SSL (secure sockets layer) or TLS (transport layer security) to encrypt the data transfer using public key cryptography.

Secure payment systems

The world of e-commerce as we know it is made possible by consumer confidence in safe and secure payment. Secure payment relies on much more than just the secure data transmission provided by https. The process of payment also needs to be secure and safe from phishing attempts and social engineering. Possibly the most well-known secure payment system is PayPal which uses the internet to undertake financial transactions in real time. Users need to register with PayPal and provide details of their bank and/or credit cards. When making payments they then need only log on through PayPal rather than giving out their sensitive payment data to other organisations. PayPal has built in protections and is incredibly popular for consumer-to-consumer transactions such as online auctions.

> **Link**
>
> For more about PayPal, visit https://www.paypal.com/uk/.

However, PayPal has experienced problems, for example reports during 2015 say that the site was down at one point for two hours and therefore unusable. This can occur when servers are down or because of with problems connecting to other networks.

> **Link**
>
> For more about the problems that PayPal, like many other websites, have experienced, visit https://downtoday.co.uk/paypal/.

Fraudsters often target users randomly by emailing them with claims that they need to share personal data in order to resolve account issues. Examples of where this occurs not only relate to PayPal but also include banks, building societies and HMRC. With regards to HMRC, the spam emails often claim to be tax overpayments which will be paid directly into personal bank accounts once you have shared your bank account details by return of email.

Businesses such as banks also provide secure payment systems, for example paying by credit or debit cards using a PIN number and making payments using their purpose-built banking apps. However, these are also open to abuse because credit and debit card details and PINs can be stolen. Banks providing online systems use techniques such as only requesting characters from your passcode rather than the full code or by using a 'challenge response' system using dongles such as the one available from HSBC.

> **Tip**
>
> You should never reply directly to emails from your bank or other organisations such as HMRC which request you to email them your personal or financial account details. They are almost certainly fraudulent. You can check the authenticity of any communication with the company via their websites (do not use telephone numbers provided in the potentially fraudulent email).
>
> The British police also provide a dedicated website for reporting scam emails: visit www.actionfraud.police.uk

Security issues and considerations when transmitting data over different connection types and networks

As we become even more security conscious, those who specialise in hacking into IT systems strive to find alternative ways to break through security systems. Examples include the cyber attack suffered by Serco in 2012 on US federal retirement plans.

> **Link**
>
> For more about the cyber attack on Serco in 2012, visit www.securityweek.com.

Businesses routinely transfer sensitive data across their data networks and security of this data must always be considered carefully. It might be that simple encryption is employed or more sophisticated security depending on the perceived risk of the data being transferred. For an internal corporate network, security must start at the physical level, as protection of the physical network prevents simple eavesdropping attacks. For example, it would be prudent to ensure that any network ports in public areas are not enabled. Similarly, links between sites need to be adequately secured. A fibre link could be employed, as fibre is inherently secure because it cannot be 'tapped' in the same way that a copper cable can. Once data leaves a corporate network, then security is out of the business's control; because of this it is essential to consider how to protect this data when travelling over a public network such as by email. Email is sent as plain text and readable by any servers along the way. There are some secured networks, such as the GSI or government secured intranet (email addresses ending in .gsi.gov.uk) used by government departments, within which you can be assured of security.

Encryption and digital certificates allow security for data sent across public networks if this is essential. Tools such as PGP (pretty good privacy) allow easy access to encryption tools.

Factors affecting bandwidth and latency

Bandwidth is a measure of the data carrying capacity of a network connection. This may be your external broadband connection or even an internal corporate network. The speed is measured in bits per second (bps) and is often quoted in megabits per second (Mbps). A connection speed of 10 Mbps means that a connection can theoretically carry 10 Megabits of data each second. The performance of a connection is also sometimes expressed by quoting the **ping** time, which is calculated as the time taken to reach a destination and return (measured in milliseconds). A lower ping time is best; high ping times mean increased latency on your network. Your bandwidth will impact on the speed at which data is transmitted and other actions such as downloading or streaming of videos actions can be performed. Reasons for variation in bandwidth include:

▸ time of day (there are different loads at different times of day - for example, first thing in the morning, many people will be logging on to check emails)

▸ distance to your nearest telecommunications exchange

▸ volume of data being transmitted overloading the network

▸ hardwiring is usually faster than wireless.

These factors can result in increased **latency** of the system or connection.

The implications of bandwidth and latency on the use and performance of an IT system

If a business relies on international communications, it might be decided to transmit a large amount of data at a particular time because there will be a greater bandwidth available due to the daily peaks and troughs of international data links. A system with high latency can cost businesses enormous sums of money and loss of business. For example, an aircraft relying on stable and reliable connections with air traffic control could face a major disaster if the IT system was subject to increased latency as critical systems like this rely on real-time control.

Types of compression

Data can be compressed so that it takes up less space, and uses less bandwidth, when being transmitted across a network. There are two types of compression:

Lossy – Lossy means removing data, that is, data is lost in order to compress the file (make it smaller). As data is lost from the file this may result in loss of information. For example, if an audio file loses too much data, then it will not sound good. Image files saved in the file type JPEG will be lossy (they will contain less data and therefore be of a lower quality than the original RAW image file). The compression algorithm works to remove data that would be less noticeable. For example, in an MP3, it removes sounds that would be virtually inaudible due to the presence of other overpowering sounds – this is why some audiophiles often say that MP3s do not have the same feel.

Key terms

Ping – a test of end-to-end connectivity, which times the return of an ICMP packet between two hosts.

Latency – the 'delay' experienced, for example, when playing online games. High latency results in you seeing the movements you made to a character a longer period of time after you made them..

Link

Technological failure is often blamed for air disasters, whether it is the cause or not. To find out more about technical failures involved in air disasters, go to www.tibco.com.

▶ Lossless – Lossless is the opposite to lossy. It reduces the size of the data file by filtering out unnecessary data by reducing the number of **bits**, rather than by losing relevant data. In essence, it is squeezed rather than cut down. Lossless compression includes, for example, the compression of a file or files into a zip file.

> **Key term**
>
> **Bit** – short for binary digit. Bit is the smallest component of data represented as a zero (0) or a one (1).

The applications and implications of data compression

Lossy compression is used, for example, in cameras and DVDs, and overwrites any previous formatting. Therefore it can reduce audio or visual clarity of the file. Applications for lossy compression include:

▶ MP3

▶ WMA (Windows Media Audio)

▶ JPEG

▶ AAC (advanced audio **codec**) which is a newer addition popularised by Apple and considered superior to MP3.

> **Key term**
>
> **Codec** – a device or program that compresses data for faster transmission.

> **Link**
>
> Google developed WebP for Android combining both lossy and lossless compression. For more information, visit www.developers.google.com.

Applications for lossless compression include:

▶ Windows Media Lossless

▶ FreeMp (free audio player).

Programs such as Microsoft Office include the option to compress a file as a zip file or to save as a different file type. Unlike lossy compression, lossless data can be retrieved and saved in other formats without loss of quality, as uncompression recreates a new file as it was.

The use and implications of codecs when using and transmitting audio and video in digital format

Codecs encode and decode data. Sometimes this results in the compression of data but sometimes it is just digitally encoded. Transmitting or storing encoded files is significantly quicker and takes up far less space than pre-codec. For example, smartphones have the capacity to store numerous videos, music, other audio and data files and images.

Audio and visual codecs are revolutionary in the way that digital audio is compressed while retaining, and even improving, quality by removing unnecessary sounds or silences.

Compatibility is the main implication – you need to be certain that the intended recipient is able to decode the data in order to be able to view the video/listen to the audio. Another problem may be if there are bugs in the codec program itself.

The sky's the limit

▶ The world's largest and most powerful observatory

In the remotest group of islands in any ocean, the big island of Hawaii is home to the world's largest and most powerful observatory. Situated about 2,000 miles from mainland USA, the observatory and its 13 telescopes are located on the volcano of Mauna Kea which measures, at its peak, 32,000 feet from the ocean floor. The telescopes are used by researchers to study the universe.

The reason for choosing the highest volcanic peak in the world for situating these observatories is due to the purity of the air and cloud conditions. This enables greater access to gather astronomical data for processing, some of which is undertaken by its headquarters in Hilo, the capital of Hawaii. However, due to location, the observatories are exposed to extreme weather conditions including strong winds, rapidly changing temperatures and snow.

These telescopes rely on digital technology to receive, transmit and analyse data that is collected as light and other waves. Surprisingly, scientists and astronomers rarely look directly through these telescopes as the information gathered by computers is invisible to the naked eye. The telescopes can be used to track satellites as well as identify stars and give scientists information about their speed, size, age and distance. Telescopes do not usually store data, but act as an interface, transmitting data to computers.

Satellites rely on technology when they transmit data from distances further away from Earth than can be observed by telescopes on Earth. The software between all devices must be compatible or translatable for computers and scientists to interpret the results.

Probably the world's most famous telescope is the Hubble, which has been orbiting Earth since 1990. It is the 'length of a school bus and weighs as much as two adult elephants, (www.nasa.gov/) and takes its energy from the Sun. When it was first launched, it had problems with a mirror which affected the clarity of images. This problem was fixed but, due to its age and technological advancements, the Hubble is going to be replaced. The Hubble transmits about 140 gigabits of data per week (**http://hubblesite.org/**) but there are problems with gathering data because this is distorted by the Earth's atmosphere. Latest technologies will enable increased data transmission and overcome the problems with distortion for more accurate and frequent data gathering.

Check your knowledge

1 State what type of connectivity enables the transmission of data between telescopes and observatories.

2 Interpret the connectivity between a telescope, observatory and astronomers.

3 Give at least four factors which could affect transmission at Mauna Kea.

4 Describe the reasons for replacing for the Hubble telescope.

Ⅱ **PAUSE POINT**   What have you learnt about networks and transmitting data from this case study?

Hint   Identify and list the different factors that affect networks and transmission of data. You can add to your list as you continue to gain new knowledge.

Extend   What similarities and differences can you identify when comparing networks for data transmission at Mauna Kea with your own personal use?

Tip

Explore websites about Mauna Kea and the Hubble telescope to expand your understanding.

You meet a fellow student in the refectory and get chatting about the courses each of you are studying. Kamelia has just started a foundation degree course in zoology and hopes to specialise later in the study of amphibians. She is pleased to make a new friend as she is homesick and has little time for socialising. Kamelia shows an interest in your studies and asks if you would help her to make a decision about the technology she should use and how to get the most out of it, while spending very little. With Kamelia's help, you produce a list of criteria identifying her needs:

- method for networking laptop, phone and camera
- connectivity enabling WiFi access while in Malaysia, on field trips, and in the UK
- maximising storage space, especially images
- securing data against loss and attacks
- options for finding research material, storing, processing and printing findings
- ways to meet like-minded people.

Kamelia also tells you that she might be able to use part of a grant she has been given to purchase some software or technology, providing it adds value to what she already has. She also tells you she is colour blind and that English is not her first language. She wants to know if there is anything available now, or possibly being developed, to help her.

She will be learning more about photographing wildlife and possibly underwater photography, but wants to make sure that the images retain their clarity. She also tells you that she will be studying when back in Malaysia as well as on the move and wants to be sure that she has sufficient bandwidth to send large files to her tutors for assessment.

As Kamelia admits to having a fairly basic understanding of computing concepts, she has asked if you would be able to:

- identify options
- explain clearly what they are
- demonstrate how networking concepts work by drawing a diagram
- produce a short checklist as a troubleshooting guide of simple things that are likely to go wrong and what to do about them.

Plan
- What is the task?
- What are the success criteria for this task?
- Are there any areas I think I may struggle with in this task?
- What resources am I going to need?

Do
- I have planned my time appropriately to do my research and complete the task.
- I can identify when I have gone wrong and make amendments to improve the outcome.
- I set milestones and evaluate my progress and success at those intervals.
- I provide a glossary of common technical terms.

Review
- I can assess what went well and what I need to improve.
- I can explain why I went wrong or struggled in some areas more than others.
- I can identify what I have achieved by undertaking this task.
- I know what I need to learn next.

C Operating online

Many of us rely on the internet for work (communication, marketing and selling products or services) or in our personal lives (to communicate with friends and family through video calling and social media, to stream music and videos, and to browse and shop online). During downtime of our IT systems, our activities are interrupted and this is not just frustrating but costs businesses money due to loss of productivity. In this section, you will learn about the implications for individuals and organisations of using online IT systems.

Online systems

First, you will learn about some of the features, impacts and implications of the use of online IT systems to store data and perform tasks.

The personal and professional uses and applications of cloud storage

Cloud storage operates like a virtual server, providing the user with connectivity (through any form of connection:

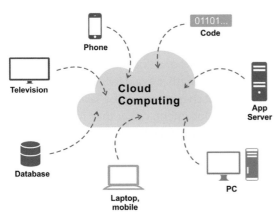

▶ **Figure 1.3:** Cloud storage allows you to store and access files across different platforms.

commonly an internet connection) to the cloud storage system selected, such as those provided by Microsoft, Google and Apple. Cloud storage provides a massive amount of space by using numerous servers all linked together. You may have experienced problems attaching a file to an email which exceeds your quota and so, instead, used cloud storage applications such as Dropbox or Google Docs. These applications allow you to store files on a cloud storage profile to which you can give others access. This enables you to transfer large files to them.

Cloud storage is not an infinite resource and nor is it totally free. Some smartphone manufacturers have offers linked with cloud services, for example Android handsets are linked with Google Drive and Windows phones have additional space on OneDrive. Providers of cloud storage entice you to use them without making an initial payment, allocating you a limited and fairly small space. Then when you get close to exceeding the limit, you are sent alerts to increase the storage capacity for an additional fee, which is often an annual subscription payment.

Personal

If you have a smartphone, it is possible that you back up your data to the cloud, either by choice or automatically. Doing so provides a virtual backup for your contact lists, emails, calendar, music, and image files. You might also choose to back up up your data files from other digital devices, such as a PC, to the cloud rather than have a separate hard drive. This means that you can access your files anywhere, providing you have access to the internet.

Cloud storage can be especially useful for sharing photos of special occasions, which is made simple by uploading and sharing the link for the photos with those you choose to have access to view the images. Both the person uploading the photos and those receiving an invitation to view them are taken through each stage of the process in simple terms, making no assumptions about their technical knowledge

or expertise. Images can be viewed on internet-enabled devices such as phones, tablets and smart TVs.

Professional

Many businesses also use cloud storage for backup, enabling their employees to access files remotely and at any time. Cloud storage is especially useful for employees who travel on business and rely on numerous digital devices to carry out their business functions.

The British Government reported in early autumn 2015 that millions of commuters now use free WiFi on public transport in the UK. This means that commuters with cloud storage can sit on public transport and carry out work while on the move.

> **Reflect**
>
> Do you use cloud storage? If so, what do you use it for and how?

> **Theory into practice**
>
> Explain to someone who is less familiar with using the cloud (perhaps a family member or friend) how to use it, its advantages and possible disadvantages.
>
> Reflect on how clear your explanation was. How could you improve on your articulation of a technical instruction to a less technical individual?

The personal and professional uses and applications of cloud computing

Cloud computing provides access to software, resources and information via a virtual server, as with cloud storage. It is often referred to as being 'available on demand' although, of course, cloud computing also relies on having a suitable network connection, often to the internet. As there are increasingly more WiFi hotspots available and more and more people have access to 4G devices, they are able to access files, chat to friends and browse the internet while on the move.

> **Link**
>
> One example of a cloud computing company is The Cloud. You can find out more about The Cloud by visiting https://www.thecloud.net/.

Personal

Cloud computing saves people money and space on their own digital devices because they do not have to physically purchase and download software which then needs to be stored on their device. Instead, they pay a subscription to use whatever software and resources they wish, depending on the specification of their contracts. They need not bother themselves with downloads, upgrades of software, backing up their data and purchasing individual security software as this is all taken care of by the provider of their cloud computing service. You might imagine cloud computing as having a technical team on hand day and night looking after your system.

There are also lots of free cloud computing applications that only perform limited functions, but, used in combination, they can provide people with similar capabilities to paid-for cloud computing services. However, the users need to manage their applications a little more and ensure that they have adequate security on their devices. Examples of uses of the cloud include Google Docs and Office 365.

Professional

Although a cost is involved in cloud computing services, businesses may view the cost as significantly less than the cost of purchasing individual software and licences for each of their employees. Businesses also save time because preparing computers with the necessary software and making them ready to operate takes longer than if staff are given access to an online cloud computing service account. This approach to mass purchasing (in this case, of a cloud computing service) results in significant savings due to economies of scale, rather like the savings that can be made when purchasing in bulk through a cash and carry outlet.

Many businesses run their applications using cloud computing, rather than installing them onto a server or individual computers on their premises. One of the benefits to accessing applications through the cloud is that demand on processing power and storage is never exceeded, whereas, on a local server, these often would be exceeded.

The use of cloud services such as Microsoft's Azure or Amazon Web Services allows businesses to dynamically scale the available server capability to meet the demand. Retailers experience huge peaks of demand on events such as the Black Friday sales and the use of this scaleable power ensures they do not lose out on sales when their own servers cannot cope with demand. They only pay for the power they actually use so need not plan for or anticipate this demand.

Employees who use applications through a cloud computing service are able to collaborate on documents in a way that is not possible using traditional software that needs to be downloaded onto individual PCs. This is one of the biggest advantages of the cloud. Members of a team can concurrently (at the same time) type into and update documents that they are working on together, so improving productivity and avoiding the need to have multiple versions of a document which then need to be pulled back together again (which might result in discrepancies). All changes would be saved and tracked using one single document, rather than multiple versions which relied on an individual to coordinate. The team members do not need to be in the same office to work on cloud-based documents but can make changes and contribute to content or structure while working remotely and in real time.

Working in this way does come with the risk that you expose the document to errors as there is no control over what changes are being made and you cannot easily undo large changes (as others may have made changes since you made yours). Therefore consideration should be given before setting up documents as to what their purpose is and whether it is best to use cloud computing or whether to use the traditional method of one individual creating a document which is then uploaded and commented on by others (using cloud storage but not cloud computing). For example, if you are producing a textbook, it would be best to use the traditional method so that version control is maintained. However, if a team of work colleagues are updating a log sheet indicating whether they are in the office that week or working from home, which is useful for everyone to be able to see in real time, this document could be created and managed via cloud computing.

The impact and implications on individuals of using cloud storage and computing

Cloud storage and computing provides flexible access to data and applications, although it can come at a price. As an individual, you may have limited cloud storage included in your telecommunications contract and can pay extra for increasing the storage limit on your mobile digital devices. For personal users that own many connected devices, the ability to use the cloud to keep all devices in sync is invaluable. Each user need only maintain a single calendar and have it available on their home and work PCs as well as on their smartphone. However, applications such as Google's Gmail and Docs are free and provide ample cloud storage and computing features for most personal use.

Using the cloud is not without its concerns, especially regarding security or downtime. Without access to the internet you will not be able to access your data, so to ensure constant access you need to pay for a reliable connection. You should use appropriate safeguards to store financial or sensitive information on the cloud, even if it is encrypted.

The impact and implications on organisations of using cloud storage and computing

There are obvious benefits to businesses of using the cloud storage and computing which include the following:

▶ provides unlimited storage facilities

▶ reduces costs

▶ reduces the need for specialist in-house IT support

▶ enables employers to focus on core business objectives rather than technology

▶ provides flexibility in terms of meeting the needs of the workforce: for example they are able to hold virtual meetings over Skype or make contact with customers using chat rooms, emails and by sharing files easily, as well as collaborating on files.

Managers need to compare the cost of using the cloud with the cost of purchasing and maintaining their own servers. They should also consider the benefits of knowing that the responsibility and expertise needed to maintain and develop the cloud does not sit with them but with the cloud computing service. A new start-up is probably unable to afford the intial expense of powerful servers and processing so can use a cloud service to host their new platform without the worry that it will not cope. AWS (Amazon Web Services) offer a range of plans where users are billed according to the actual bandwidth and processing power used. This allows the company to meet the demand without paying for something that may never be used if an idea does not take off. If a new business idea does take off, then the service will dynamically scale up to cope with the new traffic and demand.

However, as with individual use, concerns continue about potential loss of data and breaches in security. Businesses will have policies on what they perceive to be acceptable practice, such as:

▶ using business cloud computing/storage for professional use only

▶ contingency plans for periods of downtime

▶ what information is not to be stored on the cloud, such as financial and government documents.

▶ Some businesses may choose to store sensitive data files using the cloud if they believe that the security risk is greater if they were stored locally on their premises.

▶ During any system maintenance or upgrading, the cloud provides a less disruptive option for businesses. Any downtime will impact on a business's ability to carry out its functions and any employees who are working remotely may also be affected during these periods, as they will not be able to access files stored on the cloud.

Systems that enable and support remote working

There are two important types of IT system that enable and support employees' ability to work remotely. These are virtual private networks and remote desktop technologies.

Virtual private networks (VPNs)

VPNs enable users to be part of a local area network (LAN) while they are physically located remotely. A 'virtual' tunnel is created across the public network (the internet). VPNs do not use the cloud, as the servers they connect to are physical. Instead, they provide access remotely through an internet connection.

There are many providers of VPNs offering secure, unlimited bandwidth, a few of which are listed here:

▶ ExpressVPN

▶ IPVanish

▶ VyprVPN

▶ CentreStack.

VPN systems enable users to become part of a remote network that tunnels over a public network.

> **Link**
>
> To find out how to set up a VPN to access your office files remotely, visit www.sumac.com.

VPNs only work if the individual's device is recognised as operating online. If your device defaults to working offline when using it remotely, then until the settings are configured to recognise your online status, you will only view the files made available to view offline.

VPNs do not enable the same type of collaboration that cloud computing does. However, they do make it possible for employees to access all the files that they can access in the office, at home or while on the move.

Remote desktop technologies

Remote desktop technologies enable any authorised individual to access your system remotely. You may have experienced this if you have had problems when using a device, for example a smartphone. The support technician helping you may have asked for access to your phone to check for any faults or misunderstandings in how to operate the device. By accessing your device remotely, they are better able to deal with the problem quickly and satisfactorily. They might also provide remote training on how to resolve the problem or how to use the device.

Microsoft systems have the built-in Remote Desktop that allows technicians full control, with permission. There are also utilities such as TeamViewer, VNC (virtual network computing) and Chrome Remote Desktop that all allow remote access for free.

Computer repair services and software issues are also commonly dealt with remotely for both personal devices and business PCs. This way of working means that no time is wasted by physically having to take a device in for repair and perhaps sending it away to the manufacturer (which might be for several weeks, as was often the case in the past).

Theory into practice

Ask your tutor if they can demonstrate or ask a technician to demonstrate remote desktop technology to you. You can try out some of the free utilities at home, but make sure that you only give your details to a trusted friend. Alternatively, try asking your mobile phone or other digital device manufacturer if they can assist you with trying out a feature remotely. Of course, check whether there is a charge for this service first.

Tip

If you are a Barclays Bank customer you could try their Digital Eagles IT support programme which uses remote desktop technology to support customers in how to use IT applications.

Theory into practice

If you are unsuccessful with experiencing remote desktop technology through the ways suggested above, try this activity with a peer. Agree upon a small IT problem to resolve, such as the exact procedure for logging on, accessing a file in the user area or connecting to the internet via WiFi. Sit back to back with one of you describing the step-by-step instructions (the navigator role) and the other carrying out those instructions exactly as described (the pilot role). The pilot is not allowed to ask any questions or seek guidance.

Take turns by swapping roles. Reflect on the experiences and discuss what went well, and what could be improved upon. Evaluate the advantages and disadvantages of using remote desktop technology compared to the pilot and navigator technique. Discuss what you have learnt through this experience.

Factors affecting the use and selection of online systems

You started to learn about some of the issue involved when using online systems in the previous sections. In this section, we will look a bit more closely at factors affecting the use and selection of online systems.

Security

Breaches in security can occur when transferring data over an online network as well while stored on a particular online account. Internet websites which do not include 'https:' at the beginning of their **URL** are less secure and should be used with caution. The 's' in 'https:' stands for 'secure'. If you examine the URL of websites, you will see that web addresses which include 'https:' at the beginning display a padlock symbol to show that the site is secure.

The use of a VPN by remote employees puts them 'inside the corporate LAN' so that they have the protection of a company firewall and filtering despite being remotely located. VPN connections are by their nature encrypted and secured, and a number of different protocols are available that offer different degrees of security. Online systems and tools such as VPNs are essential for a business to maintain the integrity and security of their data and ultimately the confidence of their customers.

Key term

URL – stands for uniform resource locator and is the term given to the address of a website.

Tip

Most cloud computing and storage services, including free ones, are likely to be secure websites, but it is worth checking this before you sign up and certainly before you store personal files on such a service. You should also make sure that you understand the privacy policy when you store files on cloud services.

Cost

Although there is a cost involved in using online systems, and this can escalate as you become dependent on the cloud, there are also pay-as-you-go options and short-term contracts, as well as free applications for individual use. Small businesses are attracted by the pay-as-you-go options and often evaluate the benefits of cloud computing as greatly outweighing the costs involved, including the amount they can save on resources alone.

In addition to the costs advertised for servers and cloud applications, there are all the connected costs associated with operating 'in the cloud'. A business will need reliable and fast connectivity to support their employees, there are the fees to register your identity on the internet and a domain name such as mybusiness.com. Having mobile workers 'always on' while being mobile brings with it the demand for data plans with sufficient allowance for the expected use; this is often hard to forecast.

Ease of use

Access and availability online systems of almost wherever you are means that both individuals and businesses can function without having to carry around numerous devices or files of paper, which could be lost or damaged.

If a system or service is not easy to use, then users will not use it. Therefore, if you want users, then you must ensure that your system is easy and intuitive no matter what device someone uses to access your service. Web applications are expected to be 'responsive', that is, to adapt the format of their user interface to the device used to access them. This might mean resizing icons and headers for smaller screens or changing the layout from a table to columns to be more appropriate for mobile users.

Features

Making a decision about which online system to choose will depend on the features it offers. Primarily, the security measures in place should be paramount, but also the type and quality of technical support available should be considered, along with the storage capacity. Any additional benefits offered should also be considered, such as low start-up costs, metered services or the ability to scale up and down the level of service you receive.

Connectivity

To access the cloud, you will require internet access and therefore your choice of internet service provider will depend on stability and, of course, availability. Technology is advancing continually and the Government aims for the entire British population to have broadband access by the end of its current administration.

Access to the internet is available through many different technologies, each presenting different qualities that are

more suited to different markets. Table 1.1 lists some of the commonly available broadband connections available and the relative speeds.

> **Link**
>
> For more about the Government's broadband access aims visit https://www.gov.uk/government/policies/broadband-investment.

Online communities

It is highly likely that you belong to at least one online community. In this section, you will explore the features of online communities and the implications of their widespread use for organisations and individuals.

Ways of communicating and interacting with online communities

A wide range of digital devices, such as smartphones, gaming consoles and tablets, enable access to online communities.

Social media

Probably the most well-known worldwide social media website is Facebook and the second is Twitter. Despite concerns by many, and frequent media reports about the disadvantages, both of these websites are used by government departments, other public sector agencies, and most private sector organisations, enabling people to network around the worldwide. Other popular social media websites include LinkedIn and Google+. Customers are resorting more and more directly to social media to contact companies due the public 'naming and shaming' that can take place.

> **Link**
>
> For more about social media see *Unit 3: Using Social Media in Business*.

▶ **Table 1.1:** Available broadband connections and their relative speeds

Connection	Speed	Technology
ADSL	Up to 20Mbps.	Copper telephone cabling.
FTTC	Up to 80Mbps.	Fibre to the local cabinet and copper cabling for the final connection.
FTTP	Up to 330Mbps.	Fibre direct to the premises.
Satellite broadband	1Gbps down. 10Mbps up.	Linked to geostationary satellites. Sometimes uses slower copper lines for the upstream connection.
Mobile broadband	Up to 50Mbps.	Using 3G or 4G technology.

Blog, microblog, vlog

Blogs are like online journals, although they are normally for public viewing, and are contributed to and read by millions. There are blogs relating to numerous topics including gossip, hobbies, interests and news articles. Computing and software manufacturers have blogs that provide information on use, research and development, and for responding to customer queries. (Social media is also used by businesses in this way.)

Microblogs are shorter posts than blog posts and therefore take up less storage space, but the primary reason for the popularity of services such as Twitter is the shorter time it takes to follow a microblog due to the nature of the 'snippets' of information posted.

A vlog is a video form of a blog. One such vlogging website is vlog.it, although YouTube also has a partner program for vloggers which also allows users to make money from their vlogs.

Theory into practice

You may never have produced a blog, vlog or even a microblog before. Work with a peer to create one. You may have a blog app already installed on your smartphone, such as Apple Podcasts, PocketVideo or Vlog Camera. Other examples of downloadable software include Google+, Ghost and Pamela for Skype, which is free.

Wiki

A wiki is a website or database which is contributed to by a community of users who work together to add content about a particular topic. Wikis can be added to or edited by anyone, meaning the information cannot be assumed as reliable, current or accurate. The most famous wiki of all is Wikipedia which encourages quality control from contributors by providing authentic sources.

Chatrooms

It is likely you have used a chatroom, perhaps as an alternative to a video call on Skype or WhatsApp. Chatrooms enable virtual meetings or social networks to take place, regardless of where individuals or groups are located. Google Hangouts is an example of a virtual meeting environment. Netmums Coffee House is another example that is used, primarily, by mothers to talk about issues relating to bringing up children. Chatrooms, however, are sometimes unfriendly places and there are inherent risks involved in using them.

Instant messaging

There are few individuals in this country who have not used instant messaging. Instant messaging can be over the internet using an instant messaging app such as Facebook Messenger, Skype, WhatsApp, etc. Texting has become a way of life in the way we communicate, whether it is for pleasure or business. For example, some GP surgeries and hospitals use texting to remind patients about appointments. Instant messaging over the internet is usually free, unlike texting which normally costs a few pence. These instant messaging apps allow users to communicate quickly and privately with their friends and family and to also send images and other files. Instant messaging (IM) apps are beginning to take over from short message service (SMS) messaging, due to their immediacy and chat-like presentation.

Podcasts

You may not have produced a podcast yet but it is a very effective means for communicating audio information as an alternative to, or in addition to, text. News articles often provide a podcast alternative which enables access to someone with a visual impairment. Podcasts can be downloaded onto digital devices, such as your smartphone, so that you can listen to it at a more convenient time. Podcast websites include PodOmatic and Podbean. Some podcast websites, such as ipadio, translate the audio file into text which can be printed.

Forums

An online forum is where individuals are invited to participate in a discussion, usually focusing on a topic in which they share a vested interest. Each forum member can contribute by posting their comments and opinions which can be read later. Although interacting online using a forum or other methods, such as messaging and emailing, involves a transaction between each party, none are actually in real time, as is the case with a chatroom. Unlike a chatroom, the posted interactions to a forum can be difficult to order resulting in losing track of the flow of conversations.

You are likely to have been invited to join a virtual student forum at your place of study so that you can share ideas or ask questions of your peers. A forum can be localised to restrict access to users; therefore your school or college might have a forum as part of their intranet or extranet, perhaps using Moodle. Other forum websites include Yuku and Social Forum.

> **Link**
>
> For more about Moodle, visit https://moodle.org.

> **Theory into practice**
>
> With a peer or in a small group, identify an example of each type of online community and make notes about the purpose, impact and execution in each case.
>
> Compare each one by analysing and evaluating their advantages and disadvantages for both individual and business use.

The implications for individuals of using and accessing online communities

Using and accessing online communities should be undertaken responsibly and can bring significant benefit to users. You will now explore some of the implications.

User experience

▶ Ease of use – Most online communities are easy to use and are user-friendly. Users are more likely to stick with communities that are easy to use and which enable them to form online friendships easily. Although needing to do anything more than 'one click' is considered a nuisance, it can provide reflecting time before you post something that goes global and cannot be undone.

▶ Performance – Performance of online communities depends on the internet connection, the server load and its capability. It also depends on how simple and flexible it is to implement and use.

▶ Availability – Availability of an online community can be restricted (for example, closed user groups such as selected alumni of a college) or extended to widen the community. Users of online communities do not solely engage in social networking but use them for making contact with lost friends or relatives, attracting new business or for getting advice.

▶ Accessibility – For those individuals who are immobile or at least unable to travel far, online communities provide companionship, information and news updates. Adaptive or assistive technologies enable access to online communities for people who are not able to use a standard keyboard and mouse or keys on smartphones. Alternatives include speech recognition software, electronic pointing devices and sip-and-puff systems.

> **Link**
>
> For more on assistive technologies, visit Microsoft's Accessibility website www.microsoft.com.

Meeting needs

Online communities enable users to extend their social networks, often with a shared interest or to keep in touch from remote locations. However, there are implications of meeting all of those needs, including the inability for:

▶ every individual to have access to technology or connectivity

▶ those with extreme difficulties or disabilities to fully interact with websites

▶ accurate interpretation by speech recognition software of languages and colloquialisms (although research is being undertaken, for example by Microsoft).

Cost

Implementing an online community comes at a cost. Although individuals might have free access to social networking websites, revenue is obtained from businesses that promote their products and services on the website. Otherwise, the online communities could not afford to run the service to users for free. However, this advertising puts temptation in your way and may tempt you to purchase something you cannot afford or do not need. Some users experience a psychological need to feel connected to the community. This results in such users 'needing' better connectivity and spending more and more money on better connections, for example 4G.

Privacy

The openness of the internet and the proliferation of scammers mean that it is potentially a very dangerous place. Identity theft and fraud are commonplace and so being careful with your data and the sites you visit is essential. However, there are some reputable websites, such as Skype and Google, which endeavour to provide a more private and secure service.

Security

You can never be absolutely certain that your online communications are secure. You should remain vigilant and be aware of what is posted. Even if *you* are conscientious, there will be others who are less so and unscrupulous individuals who want exploit those who are careless or vulnerable. You also need to consider the consequences of posting inappropriate content online. Potential employees often now look up an individual's online community accounts to see what kind of person they are, and if they do not like what they see, they are not likely to hire you.

The implications for organisations of using and accessing online communities

The internet has opened up boundless opportunities for businesses to communicate. Online communities enable them to source suppliers, market and sell products or services, and to expand their operations on a much wider scale than ever before.

Employee and customer experience

Both employees and customers are able to benefit from a very different experience today than even ten years ago and this is largely down to the use of online communities in business.

▶ Ease of use – This puts a massive amount of pressure on organisations. They need to ensure that their online presence is as user-friendly and 'modern' as their competitors' and this is a never ending battle. Customers can buy clothes, food or search for properties without leaving their homes. Employees are able to work remotely or at flexible times to meet the needs of customers who could be located anywhere around the globe. Online community systems are mostly simple to use for both customers and employees, regardless of any other IT skills they might have.

▶ Performance – If the internet is down, it can interrupt an interaction at a crucial stage, leaving employees or customers unsure of what to do next. For example, an employee may be drafting an email which requires some refining before sending to a customer, which could have inadvertently been sent during interruptions in performance.

▶ Availability – Many businesses expect employees to be available outside normal working hours to manage online communities. With customers and individuals being geographically dispersed, online communities enable contact across time zones and consumers expect now that businesses respond quickly day and night so they need to be available through different devices, regardless of location or time. Businesses might, therefore, have to set up shift working patterns for their employees. A business can appear to be available and operating 24/7 without the cost of opening a store. Businesses may employ cheaper offshore labour to handle the quieter overnight periods since responding to emails and social media is anonymous and so location is immaterial.

▶ Accessibility – As an employee, accessibility to online communities provides opportunities for keeping in touch with colleagues and customers outside normal hours. Although this might seem unreasonable, if you are responsible for an entire sales transaction and a bonus awaits you as a result (such as for an estate agent or stockbroker), you would be very happy to see it through. Businesses that only operate online restrict their services to those customers with access and IT skills. Employers can provide adaptive or assistive technologies for any staff with disabilities in order to facilitate their ability to work and give them equal opportunities.

Customer needs

As life appears to be busier than ever, customers require more flexibility to source and purchase products which can be sent to their home and be easily returned, if necessary. Customers have become much more discerning and therefore businesses are exposed to greater competition, particularly as online businesses are more far-reaching than local shops. Businesses strive to retain their market share by seeking creative ways to make their business a priority website for customers. Customers are able to undertake research and easily make comparisons between products and services.

Customers now have a huge advantage in the increased availability of the market place with stores being available 24/7 and access to global markets is instant and troublefree over the internet. If you have a customer care department, then there is an expectation that you will be available online and that you will respond and be able to deal with queries instantly at any time of the day or night.

Theory into practice

With a peer or in a small group, devise a questionnaire to survey family and friends about their experiences and preferences when using or accessing online communities, and then analyse and evaluate the results.

Seek out some employers willing to be surveyed to compare the results with the outcomes from individuals (friends and family).

Cost

Although operating online may be cost effective in many ways and expands the range of businesses promoting their products and services, the problem is that competition drives down costs. There is so much choice and availability that businesses have to try to find ways of keeping costs down and productivity up.

Having a social media presence is not without cost for a business. As well as the need to pay staff to respond and update the presence there is the additional cost of boosting the business's prominence in an online community. Facebook provides tools for businesses to promote posts (adverts) and boost their status for a fee. The tools that social media sites provide are incredibly powerful and allow, for example, a business to specifically target teenagers aged 16–19 in a particular geographical area who have shown they have a liking for outdoor activities. The selection of the demographics is very granular so, while not a cheap option for advertising, the chances of suitable returns are high as you are specifically targeting only the audience you require.

Implementation

An online community takes time to implement and delays can occur at each stage of the set-up.

▸ Timescales – Planning stages can take considerably longer than expected to convert an idea into a series of structured actions, text and images which will successfully link to the data that sits behind the web pages of an online community.

▸ Testing – During implementation, the online community will be tested. This will be carried out at numerous stages and will involve many different users.

Replacement or integration with current systems

If the online community is replacing one that currently exists, then users will be familiar with the current system and may be reluctant to engage with any change. During the replacement or integration with an existing community there may be a period of downtime and this inactivity can lose users to other communities. If the implementation is a total integration with an existing system, then the period of inactivity or problems encountered by users may be greater than replacement. Reasons for this may include:

▸ links between the two systems which may have been overlooked need to be changed

▸ it confuses users more than starting afresh

▸ it does not sufficiently address or develop the community to expand on its features.

Productivity

A new online community should provide greater productivity by, for example:

▸ offering more features such as accessibility

▸ being easier for users to interact with

▸ meeting user needs, such as links to similar businesses, economic performance, recruitment and training opportunities

▸ offering greater security

▸ offering greater activity by increasing popularity among users.

However, additional features might attract greater risk to the security of information. For example, competitors could gain a greater insight into company practices by having access to its employees in chatrooms.

Working practices

▸ Organisations suffer from loss of employee productivity by users engaging in social networking during working hours, despite policies against such use for personal interest. Some people have lost their jobs over their inappropriate use of social media at work, because they have overlooked the fact that posts, such as those on Twitter, are visible to everyone including their boss.

Reflect

Have you ever used social media when you should have been participating in something else, perhaps in a lesson? How did you catch up with what you missed? If you relied on a friend to fill in the gaps, consider the time taken to do so, which was unproductive. Were you caught by your teacher? What were the consequences in terms of punishment but also in the time you needed to carry out the work you should have completed?

Security

Security is always going to remain a risk no matter how sophisticated an IT system is. Reputable online communities have security policies regarding their use for the safety of their users. However, unless businesses ensure that their staff are fully aware of and understand the policy (which should be monitored for user compliance), breaches of security can occur very easily and without intention.

> **Link**
>
> You can find a template social media security policy at www.biba.org.uk.

Reported trends in breaches of data security in 2013 stated that two-thirds of instances were as a result of human error and system glitches, with hacking being responsible for the remaining third.

> **Link**
>
> For more about trends in breaches of data security, visit www.symantec.com.

Case study

Gaming is not always fair play

In April 2011, Sony's PlayStation network was interrupted following a major breach in security. Users of Sony's PlayStation and Music on Demand Service learnt that the personal information of possibly as many as 77 million user accounts had been infiltrated (hacked). The data at risk included:

- user accounts
- passwords
- potentially 10 million credit card details
- names, postal and email addresses and birth dates.

The attack was identified as originating from an application server on Sony's network, originally disguised as a purchase and therefore not spotted by their internal security systems. Sony suffered a blow to its reputation and the risk of losing customers. Users were left without access to their systems until services resumed with security reassurances. Sony incurred more costs by offering extended subscriptions and limited free downloads to its customers by way of an apology.

In late 2014, Sony's customers experienced another security breach which led to employees filing lawsuits against the company for its inability to protect their personal data. Although there were only 47,000 records reportedly involved, the attack was aimed at hurting people by infiltrating their personal data for identity theft rather than their financial data.

Breaches of security can go undetected for long periods of time and it is not until threats are made to users or there are obvious signs of malfunction that the attack is revealed. The sources of attacks are difficult to identify with some being instigated by the organisation itself. One reported way was 'by infiltrating trusted business partners and stealing legitimate credentials for accessing the victims' networks. Once inside, they moved from machine to machine until they reached the subnets containing point-of-sale machines, which they infected with scrapers to steal card numbers and expiration dates'.

Check your knowledge

1 Identify at least three different types of online community which are vulnerable to security breaches of personal data.

2 Explain what was unusual about the second security breach compared with the first example given.

3 Describe the implications for organisations, customers and employees when security breaches occur.

4 Produce a list of ways in which security breaches can occur.

 PAUSE POINT   How often have you put your personal data at risk?

> **Hint**   Produce a list of online communities and networks that you belong to and complete it by adding ways in which you could reduce your risks.
>
> **Extend**   Describe or draw a procedure for using online communities safely and responsibly.

Assessment practice 1.2   A01 A02 A03

In the heart of rural England, Mollie developed her love of baking, and especially making preserves, into a small cottage industry making and selling jams and chutneys to the local community. As demand for delicious, tasty bottled preserves made from locally grown produce grew, she found herself expanding her business and attending county fairs and specialist markets.

Mollie runs her business from home, using her large kitchen and range cooker to produce the preserves, the triple garage for storage and distribution and the adjacent purpose-built shed for packaging orders. She has managed her business until now with little IT presence apart from a professionally developed website and, more recently, a smartphone. Business has continued to boom as orders have flooded in through the website and Mollie has taken on extra help to assist with boxing up orders and taking them to the post office for despatch.

However, as the business expands she finds that most of her day is taken up with cooking, she spends weekends at fairs, markets and sourcing local produce and every evening is spent on business administration.This includes:

- responding to website enquiries
- placing orders with suppliers for packaging, jars and bottles
- writing packaging labels
- stocktaking
- updating customer records
- paying bills, issuing invoices and chasing outstanding payments.

Plan
- What is the task? What am I being asked to do?
- How confident do I feel in my own abilities to complete this task? Are there any areas I think I may struggle with?

Do
- I know what it is I'm doing and what I want to achieve.
- I can identify where I've gone wrong and adjust my thinking/ approach to get myself back on course.

Review
- I can explain what the task was and how I approached it.
- I can explain how I would approach the hard elements differently next time (i.e. what I would do differently).

Mollie has a laptop and printer and uses word processing to produce invoices. However, she keeps her account and stock records in a book and all her customer details on an index card system. She knows that there are probably more efficient methods, but has not got the time to do her research into suitable options, nor will her business support any extra hired help. Mollie is keen to introduce more automation to the business and is seeking your advice and guidance on what options are open to her. She is willing to invest in a new system or additional equipment to work with her existing IT equipment, which is fairly new. Naturally, Mollie wants to ensure that whatever choices she makes are cost effective and will enable her to spend more time growing the business and less time on administration. She has set aside a budget of £5,000, but is hoping to spend less than that. Your task is to:

- identify the opportunities for automation which will enable Mollie's business to run more efficiently
- produce a list of recommendations
- explain the advantages and disadvantages of the options you provide
- describe the benefits to Mollie's business operations of the options
- calculate the potential costs associated with the options suggested.

As Mollie is an entrepreneur and always looking for ways to grow the business, she will respond to innovative ideas which are presented creatively. She has asked if you would also present your ideas as drawings to demonstrate how they might work in the context of her business.

⏸ PAUSE POINT   How do you ensure that you remain objective and advise Mollie on what is best in her situation and not be seduced by the budget?

Hint   Explore how other small business owners use IT systems to run their operations. Search local directories for contacts – maybe you have a friend or relative who runs a small business or knows someone who does.

Extend   What recommendations would you make to Mollie for developing a strategy for the use of IT in an expanding business over the next two years?

D Protecting data and information

You have started to learn about the implications of using IT networks and online communities, and in this section you will learn more about the issues and implications of storing and transmitting information in digital form.

Threats to data, information and systems

In this section, you will explore the implications of accidental and malicious threats to the security and integrity of data held in, and used by, IT systems.

The characteristics of threats to data

There are a number of characteristic types of threats to data that you will look at in this section. First, consider these extremely common ways in which you, or any individual, may put business and personal data at risk. Anyone can put data at risk by:

▶ using obvious passwords such as your favourite pet, place or date of birth

▶ disclosing passwords with other users

▶ leaving devices open to other users, such as not locking a PC when going to the toilet or not locking a mobile phone

▶ using the same login details for multiple website accounts

▶ posting information globally without thinking first as to whether it is sensible to do so

▶ using personal devices for business operations.

Reflect

We are all guilty of some of these ways of putting data at risk. Consider which ones apply to you. Think about ways in which you could avoid putting data at risk in these ways in the future.

Viruses and other malware

You may have experienced a virus on your PC or smartphone. When normal performance is interrupted, suspicions about a virus or other **malware** are raised.

Key term

Malware – short for malicious software, is software created to steal data by gaining access to an IT system without the user's consent.

A virus is a form of malware. It is software designed to harm your IT system, not just access it for unlawful purposes. Viruses can be passed from one device to another, most commonly by devices such as USB sticks, through downloading software or via files from the internet. A virus can corrupt files and compromise the data.

Link

Find out more about threats to data security at http://ict4u.net.

Early signs that you may have malware in your IT system include annoying behaviour such as applications crashing frequently or the cursor behaving strangely.

Ransomware is a form of virus that attempts to hold companies to ransom by encrypting their data and then demanding a large sum of money to release the data. Even law enforcement can fall for these attacks. For example, in 2015 a number of US police departments suffered attacks and, despite security experts working to assist, they ended up paying the ransom demand to regain access to their systems. In February 2016, Lincolnshire council suffered an attack in which they were unable to access 300 of their machines.

Hackers

Hacker is the term used for anyone who attempts to access an IT system without permission of the owner/user. Hackers are not just groups or individuals who infiltrate secret data or perform identity theft – there is a more ethical side of hacking. Ethical hackers are employed by businesses to test out their defences and try to gain unauthorised access to systems with a view to then repairing the vulnerability to prevent real hackers gaining access intending to do harm.

Phishing

To phish is to attempt to fraudulently gain information by unlawfully making claims via phone or email that the user should share personal data or financial details. Examples of frequent phishing attacks are those pretending to be from banks, including HSBC and Santander, and also from PayPal and MSN.

Research

Explore services that enable you to restrict nuisance calls and unsolicited emails or postal mail.

Accidental damage

It is very easy to accidentally lose data or at least think that you have. While applications such as Microsoft Office applications issue reminders to users to save files before closing, if the whole system crashes or there is a power cut before a file is saved, it could result in a loss of data (and waste of hard work and effort). Sometimes we think that we have lost a file when we have filed it incorrectly or saved it under an irrelevant name. Although software alerts us to think before deleting a file, if we are hurried or distracted, it is easy to overlook this. It is also easy to save over a file without thinking, which will permanently overwrite the previous file.

> **Tip**
>
> It is important to regularly save your work as well as ensuring that autosave functions are set up in applications that have that feature.

The impact of threats to data, information and systems on individuals

Users experience stress and time being wasted to varying degrees when threats to data occur. Some of these, such as phishing threats, can cause unnecessary anguish, especially to those users who are unaware of the source of these malicious emails and unwittingly share sensitive data.

If your personal device develops a virus, it will prevent or compromise the performance you expect from that device. The system might need to be taken to an expert to fix, leaving you without alternative means to work, potentially exposing your data to even greater risk. You may need to replace your device with a new one if it is deemed irreparable or too costly to repair.

Nowadays, photos are usually stored in digital image files rather than photo ablums. The impact of this data becoming corrupted is often immeasurable to an individual: a lifetime of irreplaceable memories can be wiped out by a simple disk failure. Backup solutions are becoming just as important for individuals as they are to businesses as our lives transition to the digital world.

> **Research**
>
> Explore the options available for insuring your devices against security threats. Compare these with strategies that you can deploy for protecting your devices and data to avoid potentially unnecessary and costly insurance.

> **Link**
>
> For guidance on suitable strategies to protect against data threats, visit:
>
> www.computerweekly.com
>
> www.computerworld.com
>
> www.cisco.com.

The impact of threats to data, information and systems on organisations

When threats occur in organisations, it can impact on all users and the productivity of the business. Just as in the example of Sony's 2014 experience, businesses can face claims for damages from employees or customers and it also can also result in loss of business. Even the smallest breach of data, regardless of its sensitivity, can be incredibly damaging to a business. Public confidence in any system is on a fragile balance and, once this is upset, it can take a great deal of time and money to restore confidence.

If your site is 'down', even just for maintenance, the public perception is that you are unreliable as a business, irrespective of whether or not this is actually the case!

> **Research**
>
> What other examples can you find of businesses exposed to data threats which impacted on the company's reputation? Share your findings with a peer or in a small group.

Protecting data

Having explored some of the threats and implications, you will now learn about some of the features, uses and implications of systems and procedures that are used to protect the data of individuals and organisations.

Processes and implications of techniques for protecting data and systems

Organisations have, or should have, processes in place for protecting data and systems. However, unless these are comprehensive, kept up to date and the policies are followed by all users at all times, the threats to data remain. Some simple processes and techniques for protecting data and systems include the following.

File permissions

Access to files can be restricted through the use of password protection or by setting the file as a read-only file, which prevents inadvertent editing, when sharing with colleagues who do not need to edit it.

Reflect

What reasons can you suggest for needing to create read-only files? How might you restrict access to a file?

Access levels

Giving users access to only those systems or applications that they need to fulfil their roles, and restricting the level of access they have, protects data because fewer people are able to put it at risk. For example, limiting permission to filter and query in a database, or making it so that permission is required to add records, will limit the number of people who can change or delete data accidentally.

Link

For more about database access levels see *Unit 2: Creating Systems to Manage Information.*

Backup and recovery procedures

Everyone should back up their data files regularly, regardless of the degree of usage. Most organisations will have a formal procedure which routinely backs up data on a very frequent basis. They may undertake incremental backups which only back up those files which have been amended since the previous backup. A full backup might be undertaken monthly, depending on the size of the organisation and the amount of data produced. Backups do not just back up files but also the contents of servers, systems and processes.

Systems often have automatic recovery procedures, such as the ability to undelete a file or recover a file following a premature software or system closure. Organisations should have a formal recovery plan which enables the system to return to a predetermined point from which operation can continue if the system fails. Larger organisations have full disaster recovery plans in place to minimise any disruption as a result of things such as a natural disaster or criminal attack. These plans can sometimes even involve the maintaining of warm backup sites that mirror the primary base of operations. Alternatively, they can have off-site backups and a contract with a disaster recovery company who will get the backups running on a mobile server farm within hours.

Link

Explore some examples of recovery procedures and backup plans. Search for the following articles on the internet:

'Developing Backup and Restore Procedures', https://technet.microsoft.com

'Recover system procedure', www.ibm.com

'HP System Recovery Procedures'.

Passwords

Passwords should be kept secret, regardless of whom you may trust. Think of your passwords like your bank account details or PIN number, which you would not share. Weak passwords can be easily identified and are often repeated by users for different websites and purposes. Strong passwords should have between 12 and 14 characters, and use upper and lower case letters, numerals and symbols.

Link

See The characteristics of threats of data, for more on how not to use passwords.

Physical access control

Leaving your computer or device unattended and unlocked exposes your data to others, whether you are present or not. Locking, shutting down or removing the device protects your data from immediate access by a passer-by. Not logging out properly or fully from your system or an online account leaves your data exposed to potential risk. Organisations have restricted physical access to data centres and cabling for their computer systems.

Digital certificates

Digital certificates are unique codes which are assigned to you by a business to verify your identity when performing a transaction, such as a money transfer or requesting a bank statement. It is sometimes called a public key certificate and works in a similar way to a passport. Digital certificates are also issued by certificate authorities to facilitate SSL (https).

Protocols

Protocols are the agreement between devices regarding how a communication might take place. There are a range of protocols that are concerned with security. Secure data transfer relies on some form of encryption – for websites this is SSL or TLS which uses public key cryptography.

There are also human operating protocols, such as policies for using equipment or creating passwords, but the difficulty is in remembering numerous ones for different systems, devices and actions. Common password rules include using a mix of letters, numbers and symbols in upper and lower case. Additional passwords are used by websites such as those performing financial transactions. It is not unusual for some users to store their passwords on their computer in a file or diary. Another option is to use a password vault, e.g. LastPass or 1Password.

Reflect

How secure are your user areas? What strategies do you use to remember your login details or various passwords? How could you improve the security of your data?

The features, characteristics and implications of using antivirus software to protect data

There are numerous organisations developing antivirus software in an attempt to keep our data and systems secure, including:

▶ Kaspersky

▶ McAfee

▶ AVG

▶ Symantec (Norton).

Antivirus software is designed to search out and stop attempts to corrupt your IT system or files using viruses or any malware. Different antivirus software approach this in different ways, but common features include:

▶ real-time scanning to check files as they are saved or opened

▶ deep or full scans used periodically to check an entire storage device

▶ heuristic analysis to look for 'virus-like' activity as well as known viruses

▶ virus definition databases.

However, the more you expose your system to a wider network, the greater risk to your system. For example, your IT system and data are more exposed when you use cloud computing, but many people do use it because of the benefits.

Antivirus software manufacturers provide similar, yet different, types of protection, including seeking out updates to antivirus software via the cloud. Antivirus software needs to be working continually to check for threats and should be installed before commencing any computing operations. However, the constant scanning and checking for threats required by antivirus software increases the load on a system, including the CPU, memory and disk activity.

Theory into practice

Compare different types of antivirus software in terms of their features and what they cost. Compare those that you can download for free with those for which you pay a subscription. Evaluate which are most suitable to meet personal and business needs.

Research

With a peer or in a small group, share your experiences of antivirus software. Explore the advantages and disadvantages of at least six different types of antivirus software according to their features, prices, versatility and impact on other software and processes.

The features, characteristics and implications of using firewalls to protect data

Firewalls

A firewall performs a different function to antivirus software. It monitors the network traffic and decides whether or not to let the traffic in or out. It can protect the IT system from unauthorised access and can be both hardware and software. Hardware firewalls are usually part of the **router** whereas software firewalls are applications. Software firewalls, the likely choice for individuals, must be stored locally on the device, not on a network. They can be manipulated by users who may reduce the restrictions on traffic, or be turned on and off to speed up performance or allow access to prohibited websites. Like any software, updates should be installed whenever they become available.

Firewalls can use a variety of methods to protect a network, from the basic port blocking where the firewall simply refuses incoming access to the network to the more advanced stateful packet inspection (SPI) where the firewall uses active connection data to look at where packets are from and to to decide whether the incoming data is legitimate and connected to an active connection. Firewall configuration is a skilled task that can easily have a major performance impact on a network if not done correctly.

Key term

Router – an electronic device that enables data to be transmitted between networks.

Reflect

What immediate actions will you take to protect your data from risk of loss or damage?

The features, applications and implications of encryption methods used to protect data

Stored data

Methods for encrypting data which you intend to store include using specialist software which can:

▶ create hashes, which are fixed-length signatures for the text

▶ use a key to crypt and decrypt messages (known as private key cryptography); therefore anyone with the key can access the contents of the message

▶ using a public key to allow one-way encryption of data which is decrypted using a matching secret private key.

> **Link**
>
> For more about data encryption methods visit http://datashieldcorp.com.

The implications of using encryption methods include:

▶ if the code or key is forgotten, then the data may never be decrypted

▶ the way in which the key is shared with those entitled to access the data can result in other risks to security.

Data during transmission

Data is often assumed to be secure when it is not. For example, an email is sent in plain text between servers and can be read by anyone along the way. The encryption of data in transit is essential when communicating information which may be confidential or sensitive. As you have already seen, web pages make excellent use of encryption when using https (SSL or TLS). It might also be desirable to encrypt all network traffic to ensure security. Pretty good privacy (PGP) can be used to encrypt the contents of emails which are then sent in plain text, but would be unreadable to any unauthorised access without the appropriate decryption key.

> **Discussion**
>
> In your group, discuss the following. Who watches the watchers? Should governments have access to private keys and therefore the means to decrypt secret data?

> **Reflect**
>
> Have you ever used any form of encryption method? What did you use and how did it work? Try using other methods. What have you learnt from the experience that would help you when advising others?

If a break occurs during the transmission of encrypted data, the data may continue being decrypted and expose itself to threats. For example, when performing a bank transaction, data is encrypted and decrypted to protect the holder of the account. If that holder takes a break or becomes distracted, the data is accessible to others during this period. It is advisable therefore to avoid disruptions and breaks in such sessions and, especially, to avoid using public access devices for such transactions.

The role of current legislation in protecting data and IT systems from attack and misuse

Chief Information Security Officer of Honeycomb Connect Banking Information Technology said in a webcast to his members in 2006, 'Other than everyone who works for us and everyone who doesn't work for us, we have no one to fear.' That is, everyone could be a potential threat, intentionally or unintentionally. Legislation is necessary to provide legal remedies for breaches; it acts as a deterrent and it sets clear acceptable limits that describe what unauthorised access actually is (see Table 1.2 for information about current legislation)

> **Link**
>
> For more about Honeycomb Connect visit www.honeycombconnect.com.

Therefore, legislation such as the Computer Misuse Act of 1990, which legislates against computer crime, is necessary to protect data and IT systems from attack by:

▶ hackers

▶ fraud and theft

▶ copyright infringement

▶ abuse, for example:

- cyber bullying
- trolling (deliberately trying to cause arguments or offence)
- child pornography
- harassment.

> **Link**
>
> For more about legislation, such as the Computer Misuse Act of 1990, see Legal, moral and ethical issues.

▶ **Table 1.2:** Current legislation protecting IT systems

Legislation	What does it protect?	What are the consequences for breaching?
Data Protection Act 1998	The storage and processing of personal data. The right to accurate storage and proportional use.	Fines of up to £500,000.
Computer Misuse Act 1990	Protects IT systems against: • unauthorised access • unauthorised access with intent to commit crime • unauthorised modification of material.	• Two years in prison. • Five years in prison. • Ten years in prison.
Freedom of Information Act 2000	Places a legal obligation on public bodies to release information in response to requests from the public.	• No penalties.

Reflect

Do you know, or think you know, of anyone who has been a victim of some form of cyber bullying? What would you do or did you do?

Discuss with a peer what steps you should take if you were concerned about cyber bullying that is happening to yourself or someone you know.

Research

Try searching for case studies about cyber bullying, such as the 2014 Channel 4 drama Cyber Bully, starring Maisie Williams, or government guidance at www.gov.uk.

The impact on individuals and organisations of legislation designed to protect data and IT systems

Government legislation exists to protect data. This is known as the Data Protection Act of 1998. As with all legislation, it is frequently monitored and reviewed for its relevancy and to accommodate changes which impact on its promises.

Link

For more about the Data Protection Act of 1998, visit http://www.legislation.gov.uk/ and http://ico.org.uk/.

The Data Protection Act requires that personal data is not shared without the permission of the individual it relates to and also provides individuals with permission to ask for information held about them by organisations. There are eight principles with which all records must comply:

▶ fairly and lawfully processed

▶ processed for limited purposes

▶ adequate, relevant and not excessive

▶ accurate and up to date

▶ not kept for longer than is necessary

▶ processed in line with your rights

▶ secure

▶ not transferred to other countries without adequate protection.

The act entitles everyone to read their own medical records and the records held about you by your place of study. There are certain exceptions to this, and a charge may be levied. The people responsible for inputting the data must be aware of any consequences arising from sharing that data.

Information about registered companies is also accessible to anyone under the Companies Act of 2006. Therefore businesses and individuals can seek trading information about other businesses, providing they are registered with Companies House.

Public bodies have been heavily affected by the introduction of the Freedom of Information Act which means that they are required by law to release information to the public if asked for it. The intention of this Act was to provide much greater transparency to government bodies. It revealed some surprising data which has led to legislative change, for example the MPs' expenses issues of recent times.

Link

For more about legislation designed to protect data and IT systems, see Legal, moral and ethical issues .

The purpose, role and impact, on individuals and organisations, of codes of practice for the protection of data produced by the Information Commissioner's Office (UK) and professional bodies

The Information Commissioner's Office (ICO) is the UK's independent body intended to 'uphold information rights in the public interest, promoting openness by public bodies and data privacy for individuals'.

For individuals, the ICO provides assistance in accessing your data, stopping nuisance telephone calls and raising concerns about organisations. As well as performing a monitoring and reporting role, it provides individuals with the opportunity to update their records, for example information contained within the electoral register.

Professional bodies enforce the legislation relating to their sector of expertise by prescribing a code of conduct or practice. Examples of such professional bodies include:

Link

For more about the Information Commissioner's Office (ICO), visit https://ico.org.uk/.

▶ Association of Chartered Certified Accountants

▶ Law Society

▶ British Medical Association (BMA).

For organisations, the ICO also provides guidance and interpretation of legislation such as data protection. It provides a filter for legislation which must be complied with according to the business sector. For example, small businesses can learn about data protection and use the training leaflets provided to train their employees. Those in marketing roles can find guidance about what affects the way they operate, and there are rules about maintaining customer databases or environmental regulations.

Organisations may be required to register as a data controller with the ICO if they process personal information. For example, if your local leisure centre sends you a text to remind you of an appointment, it should also be registered with the ICO under the Privacy and Electronic Communications guidance.

Professional bodies, such as the Crown Prosecution Service, become involved when reported breaches lead to prosecution.

Some of the other professional bodies include:

Link

For more about the professional code of practice laid down by the BMA, visit www.gmc-uk.org.

▶ General Teaching Council

▶ General Medical Council

▶ Care Quality Commission.

Each of these professional bodies also prescribes a code of practice which must be followed, such as that laid down by the BMA and the Hippocratic Oath for those in the medical profession.

Assessment practice 1.3

A03 A04

A small business owner, Serena, has asked for your advice about protecting the data on her system. She runs an engineering business that produces steel products to customer specifications, some of which are uniquely designed sculptures. She is concerned about her customer records, especially the unique designs and their copyright. She has heard that there is legislation about protecting such information but does not know what it entails or how to implement it.

The business currently operates on a single computer used by the administrator/receptionist but, as the business grows, she wants to be prepared for taking on at least two new members of staff, one for technical drawing and another for managing all customer information and accounting procedures. Serena is interested in what systems and software she should budget for and how to secure the data. She has arranged for additional funding from the bank and has £15,000 set aside for the next stage, although knows that she may have to spend more in the future. She has asked you to:

- discuss the options available to her that best suit the short-term business plan

- demonstrate how they will provide her with peace of mind and fulfil any legislative requirements

- calculate software and hardware costs

- analyse at least two different options for suitability

- write an evaluation of your findings and make recommendations for her to consider.

Plan

- I shall prioritise the tasks and prepare a checklist of things to do.
- I shall identify a range of resources to help me.
- I will keep a detailed list of all my sources which anyone can locate.
- I will allow for some buffer time as a contingency.

Do

- I have structured my schedule to ensure that I cover all the criteria.
- I am double checking my calculations and finding alternative costings.
- I am putting the customer needs first beyond my own preferences.
- I am providing alternatives for the technical language and terminology .

Review

- I am pleased with the outcome and I do not think I could improve it at this stage.
- I know what I need to learn to expand my current knowledge.
- I can recognise what progress I have made from undertaking this activity.

 **PAUSE POINT**   How could you have presented the outcomes differently if the customer was from a different sector or had more technical knowledge?

Hint   Try putting yourself in the position of a business owner and viewing the outcomes through 'different eyes'.

Extend   Find yourself a local business mentor who can give you constructive feedback about your suggestions.

Theory into practice

What strategies for safe online working have you learnt that you could recommend to your workplace or where you study?

Impact of IT systems

In this section, you will be learning about the uses, issues and implications of IT systems and their impact on individuals and organisations.

Online services

Firstly, we shall explore how the features of online services are used to meet the needs of individuals and organisations. Since the year 2000, global internet usage has increased from 360 million to more than three and a quarter billion, an increase exceeding 800 per cent. The largest usage is in Asia, with more than 1.5 billion users, while the greatest proportion of a population using the internet is the USA, with almost three-quarters of the population using online services.

The internet provides services for almost everything we want, from ordering takeaway meals to finding our long lost relatives and ancestors. However, the more we expose ourselves and our personal data by using online services, the greater the risk of fraud.

Link

For more about online services, see *Unit 3: Using Social Media for Business*.

The features and implications of using online services

In this section, you will look at the features and implications of using online services to support a selection of key industry sectors and aspects of everyday life.

Retail

We can purchase almost anything we want over the internet. While this means that we can shop at a time and place to suit us and we have an immeasurable amount of choice, it also means that we have access to products or services which are not regulated by government standards, such as unlicensed medication and pirated products. We are also exposed to the risk of any payment being taken without goods being provided or receiving unregulated products.

Financial services

Financial services include advice and services for mortgages, investments, banking, debt and loans. The UK's financial services are regulated by the FCA (Financial Conduct Authority) and PRA (Prudential Regulation Authority) but, because we have global access online, not all of the services you use can be confirmed as being authentic or reliable. We also have relative newcomers to the financial marketplace with incredibly popular providers such as PayPal now becoming a dominant force on the internet.

Link

For more about the FCA, visit www.fca.org.uk.

Education and training

You may have searched for courses, career guidance and training providers prior to enrolling at your place of study. The way in which we are taught and study has also been influenced by online services. We are now able to research online and use this method more than using reference books (although these are still useful) and we can learn from digital activities and virtual teachers. Academic institutions across the world are getting involved with launching MOOCs, as discussed earlier in this chapter, which can access new audiences and bring education to the masses. Unfortunately, there are also many examples of where unscrupulous training organisations and rogue universities issue certificates which are unregulated.

Link

For more about the threat of rogue certificate authorities, visit www.jurinnov.com.

Tip

Expand your research by using Google Scholar to access research journals and articles.

News and information

It is suggested that we are bombarded online with more information every day than the equivalent of the content of almost 200 newspapers. Due to the ease of availability of online services and the range of technology enabling us to access those services, we churn out enormous amounts of data daily, far exceeding the amount we produced just 20 years ago. Although we have the opportunity to be better informed, we are also able to produce more meaningless information, which can cause disruption to work patterns and periods of concentration. News is now being broadcast in real time thanks to the global nature of technology and communication networks. For example, when the 9/11 attacks occurred in 2001, almost immediately footage was being broadcast around the world with hundreds of camera angles. News gets 'out there' so quickly that it is harder now for authorities to delay news to help investigations. Photographs of incidents such as the Shoreham Air disaster in 2015 hit the internet almost instantly, which meant that authorities really had a race against time to inform families of any victims before they found out through the media.

Entertainment and leisure

You may have subscribed to films directly from your television or by using an app on your mobile device. We can watch our favourite TV programmes whenever we want rather than missing them or having to record them using other devices. Having the ability to do so can also dominate our lives because this can occupy more waking hours than when TV was only available for a restricted number of hours a day. Another implication of this is that programmes unsuitable for children and vulnerable adults are now available without a time constraint (known as the watershed). However, it is also possible to put safety locks on devices so that a password is required to access certain channels or to turn on the TV. The bringing into the home of services such as online casinos also brings with it problems. No longer do people who wish to gamble have to go out and visit the casino – they can play (and potentially lose thousands of pounds) without ever leaving their armchair; so the impact of increased access to leisure services online is not entirely positive.

Productivity

The services available to employees can result in happier, more productive employees; using tools such as remote working, flexible working and collaborative cloud workspaces allows employees to access and use their productivity at any time and wherever they may be. However, this could be seen as intrusive into one's personal life as employees may be expected to check and respond to work communications outside of work time.

On the other hand, the generation of large amounts of data and information online can severely interrupt our work patterns. That is, we can become easily distracted by text messaging, emails and social media rather than focusing on our work and other priorities.

Some organisations confiscate mobile devices and monitor staff internet usage, especially emails and social media. Many businesses have policies which have led to employees being disciplined or sacked due to the loss of productivity resulting from their inappropriate use of the internet.

Link

The suggested cost to businesses of staff using online services at work is in the billions of pounds. For more on this story, visit www.hubpages.com.

Theory into practice

What is the policy regarding using the internet for staff and for students at the place where you study?. Would you make any improvements to it and, if so, how would you go about trying to influence the management into making those changes?

Booking systems

Receiving paper tickets as evidence for travel will soon be a thing of the past on all means of public transport. Online services provide us with the ability to search out competitive fares, book travel in advance or at the last minute and receive an e-ticket as proof of purchase. There is always a security risk when relying on online services as personal data is collected during transactions. In theory, if someone were to hack this data they might be able to find out your address and would know that you will be away from your residence for a holiday and so could commit burglary.

The method of opting out of further contact from online services is often made difficult to locate on websites and sometimes requests made by websites to use your data for marketing purposes can result in continuing contact, which is a considerable nuisance.

Reflect

What is your experience with nuisance online marketing? What have you done about it?

The uses, impact and implications of different online services

In this section, you will look at the uses, impact and implications for individuals and organisations of different online services.

Transactional data

Transactional data includes the information that is recorded every time a transaction is made, whether it is a personal or business-related financial transaction. Businesses collect data from transactions which can be used to inform them of your preferences, for example websites you have searched, including those you have not used in a while. Therefore businesses generate masses of data that can be analysed. They monitor browsing patterns through websites and buying patterns using tools such as loyalty cards and they can adjust their promotions to meet the market demands. The prevalence of online systems brings with it the inherent logging and audit trail that benefits all, as it is an indisputable record of what went on.

Targeted marketing

One of the ways in which businesses use transactional data is to target their marketing at likely customers, such as sending them offers to purchase similar products or engage in similar leisure interests. They will offer enticements, such as vouchers towards your next online shop with them.

Less scrupulous business practices include examples of companies that collect on behalf of charities targeting individuals with requests for contributions, especially around Christmas time. These begging and phishing emails and phone calls have a considerable negative impact on vulnerable adults, especially the elderly who feel pressured into making contributions or signing up to new services without fully understanding what they are agreeing to.

Another argument is that the quality of advertising is increased. It is more relevant to what you need and becomes almost helpful rather than an annoyance. With this in mind it is essential that companies are competitive as they really do need to compete in a global marketplace.

> **Reflect**
>
> Have you been influenced by targeted marketing or do you know someone who has? What examples can you identify that have led to a positive outcome for the business and what advice would you give to someone to avoid being easily led?
>
> With a peer or in a small group, explore positive forms of targeted marketing that businesses could deploy.

Collaborative working

Online services enable individuals to work together regardless of where they are located. This provides individuals with opportunities to work in extended groups and on larger projects, while businesses can build teams based on individual strengths from a wider group of individuals. This can save businesses time and money.

Collaborative working online also means that two or more individuals can have remote access at the same time to central files which are shared for reading, editing and contributing to, using cloud computing. Levels of authorisation and restrictions need to be in place to avoid

any risk to the integrity of the data. Collaborative working relies on internet access and is also at risk from hackers, as is any online activity.

Impact on organisations

Technology has developed so rapidly that it is hard even for those who have been in business for 20 years to recall the impact it has made on the way we operate commercially. When electronic word processors began to arrive in offices in the mid- to late 1980s, before PCs were widely available, these were seen as revolutionary in the way they could store short phrases and enable limited word processing before printing onto paper. These machines quickly replaced the old typewriters and the need for bottles of correction fluid.

By the mid-1990s, desktop computers (PCs) were a familiar sight in offices although the internet was still rarely available. Businesses were becoming automated with the use of office software suites and accounting software. Individuals and businesses alike were able to produce their own professional-looking documents and notices using desktop publishing software. Retailers moved from manual or basic electric cash registers to using digital tills by the end of the twentieth century, although self-service checkouts were not introduced in the UK until 2010, by Tesco.

In the mid-1990s when mobile phones were first being used by businesses, they were generally car phones with a handset which could be removed for safety. Mobile phones as we know them today were not available and were not only heavy and cumbersome pieces of equipment but also extremely expensive to buy and operate. Mobile phone service providers were distinguishable by the phone number issued by the network and the signal was often unreliable.

Fast-forwarding ahead to the current day, the developments in technology have been described as beyond imagination and are even said to be running our lives rather than the other way round. It is probably impossible to spend a day in the modern world without using or observing someone using technology. Developments are such that organisations expect us to manage our lives using technology. Examples include:

▶ online shopping, including buying food, for which we no longer need to step outside our homes

▶ social media websites for support with using unfamiliar items that we may have purchased

▶ borrowing money, which previously would require an interview with a bank manager for a large purchase

- organising travel and accommodation
- medical consultations over the telephone
- internet dating and matching services.

The features and implications of IT systems used by organisations for various processes

As the internet has become a feature of almost every business operation, the impact has possibly been most obviously felt through internet shopping. It seems hard to believe that online shopping has only been around for only a couple of decades. It has multiplied in its popularity year on year with shoppers spending twice as much in 2013 as ten years ago. Online sales were already exceeding £50 billion by 2012. Reports suggested that, by 2016, one-fifth of all high street stores would close due to lack of demand, but this has not proved to be true.

Reports also suggest that the reasons for the growth in online shopping is not only access to the internet, mobile devices and familiarity with using technology, but is particularly due to confidence in making purchases online and less concern over the security and safety of our financial details.

Research

Learn about the ways in which technology is used by organisations such as the Samaritans (at www.samaritans.org), how governments are using social media for sharing information (https://govtrequests.facebook.com/) and why chat lines can benefit business (www.inc.com).

Reflect

How much do you and your family rely on internet shopping? How would you manage without it and how would this impact on the way you manage your life?

A major benefit to businesses from IT systems, and networking in particular, is the opportunity to source suppliers and materials and promote their businesses across a wider area. This is known as e-commerce.

Business operations have been automated and are now more reliable, although this does not necessarily replace the need to understand the basic principles of manual processes, such as accounting and stocktaking. You will now explore some of the automated processes relied upon in business today.

Stock control

Controlling stock has become more efficient and effective since the introduction of online systems whereby bar codes automatically populate databases and show stock levels. Stocktaking is simplified and levels can be monitored digitally so that retailers are less likely to run out of supplies. In the case of large businesses such as supermarkets, their stock levels are monitored centrally and supplies are ordered from central sources. Sometimes, RFID is used to automatically track stock from factory through distribution to the consumer. This allows a business to instantly inform a consumer about the status of their order.

While this type of stock control system may reduce staff numbers formerly required for placing orders, it also results in staff not knowing what stock is likely to be received until it arrives.

Data logging

A data logger is a digital device which measures, monitors and records information in real time such as a CCTV camera, weather station or carbon monoxide sensor. As these become more sophisticated, and as many rely on wireless connection rather than standalone systems which interface with computers, reports can be interrupted if the wireless connection is broken. Therefore alternative means such as a battery backup are required for continuity, for example in burglar alarms. They allow for more responsive ordering, for example a filling station might use data loggers that report the amount of fuel in the fuel tanks automatically and order replacement fuel when a preset level is reached, so removing the possibility for this to be overlooked by staff.

Data analysis

The data gathered in a data logger is analysed to monitor performance, for example those used in motor racing and horse racing. Analysis can provide information about vehicle performance or photo finishes, although such systems are also open to abuse through the manipulation of data. Your PC or smartphone also logs performance data and analysis can provide information of activity. This information can also be hacked into remotely if security measures are not in place.

A good example of data analysis is that of a supermarket that uses loyalty schemes to track shopping habits which can then be analysed extensively. The term 'big data' has arisen as the handling and 'mining' of these vast data stores. For example, a retail business might use this data to forecast when consumers begin purchasing their holiday essentials – this way they can more accurately order the stock to be available at the time when people want to purchase these goods.

General office tasks

General office tasks include administrative operations such as communicating by letter or email, producing invoices, which can be automatically generated from transactions, and producing company accounts using specialist accounting software. General office tasks are performed by a wider range of employees than in former times where dedicated personnel, such as secretaries, were employed to carry out administrative tasks. This is because the systems used to carry out administrative tasks are easier to use and the general population has more IT skills. Difficulties arise where individuals become overloaded by administration, which impacts on the time they have to perform their craft or trade, such as doctors, nurses and teachers. Administration can get forgotten about. Smaller businesses, in particular, can lose money by forgetting to issue invoices or by not following up on quotations and orders.

Research

With a peer or in a small group, identify a small local business and explore their operations to identify how and where they use IT systems. What implications are they likely to face and how do IT systems benefit their daily practices?

Tip

Why not visit a local employer who is willing to show you how they use IT in their daily practice? Perhaps a local charity shop will assist you or the office of your local MP or a nearby school.

Creative tasks

Technology enables a plethora of options for being creative. Even untrained individuals can create film shows from static images by adding transitions, subtitles and sound using software which is often free. Designers, such as those in car manufacture, or architects can produce drawings using software such as **CAD** to create 3D imagery and combine **QR codes** to produce virtual rooms which enable clients to better visualise concepts in their own settings.

The sophistication of 3D and 4D software enables the production of professional-looking drawings which could

mislead individuals who may overlook the credentials of the company and their ability to actually implement the construction to the specifications of the drawings, because they are being seduced by the quality of the graphics.

Key terms

CAD – computer-aided design software which is used for detailed technical drawings. It is used to help design cars and buildings.

QR codes – quick response codes which provide direct links to, for example, websites or make a payment, using a QR code reader app such as Red Laser.

Link

Search on the internet for more information about 3D and 4D software.

Advertising

Technology has revolutionised advertising by providing access to techniques previously used by the trade, such as software that provides easy-to-use templates and through the use of social media and the internet, for example:

▶ pop-up adverts when surfing the internet

▶ adverts embedded in social media interactions.

Organisations now have the ability to pinpoint the target audience for any advertising.

Theory into practice

What positive and negative methods of advertising can you describe? Share these with a peer and explain what makes them positive or negative, in your opinion.

The benefits to businesses are that they can advertise more widely and avoid using specialist and costly advertising companies by generating adverts in-house or relying on their websites.

The implications of making advertising simpler and easier for many include other activities such as:

▶ phishing – an illegal practice and form of social engineering

▶ **viral** marketing and advertising – where the quirkiness of an advert promotes sharing by the public, which eliminates distribution and display costs.

Manufacturing

Technology has significantly benefited the manufacturing industry. For example, data from digital drawings can be transferred to automated machines to create precision-produced components such as:

▸ car parts

▸ components for buildings

▸ medical prosthetics.

The implications are that employee numbers are reduced as they are replaced by automated machines. Machines are mostly reliable, accurate and increase productivity by working around the clock and they can produce in larger quantities.

Security

CCTV and burglar alarms are common means of security, and most people use antivirus software to protect their digital devices. Systems such as aircraft flight recorders are far more complex and vital for logging data to establish any breaches in security, especially in extreme cases such as air crashes.

As we become more security conscious, there is a feeling of being constantly under surveillance, for example when shopping. The technology exists to tag more expensive items and the store's CCTV automatically can keep a customer under surveillance while carrying such an item. The introduction of convergent networks means that additional CCTV cameras can be added quickly and easily to the existing network cabling.

The impact and implications for organisations of using IT systems

In this section, you will look at the impact and implications for organisations of using IT systems in terms of the following aspects.

User experience

The way in which businesses operate has changed since the implementation of IT systems, in every sector. Employees spend long periods of time using computers, inputting and generating data and probably less time communicating verbally, for example to resolve problems and plan projects.

▸ Ease of use – Systems continue to become more intuitive and easy to use.

▸ Performance – Using technology can be seen to save time, enabling employees to tackle greater workloads and undertake a wider range of tasks.

▸ Availability – Online systems are readily available, which can have a positive impact on employee performance because they can be more productive. On the other hand, they may be distracted by the easy access they have to social media.

▸ Accessibility – Not everyone has easy access to IT systems, especially those with specialist needs such as physical disabilities or learning difficulties.

Employee and customer needs

Employees and customers both benefit from businesses that use IT systems. For example, IT systems allow for the immediate allocation of a product or service to a customer, such as seating on a train or aircraft. However, technology can result in loss of personal interaction, through automated services such as customer helplines. Due to data logging and businesses wanting to generate greater productivity, procedures can be set up to monitor time devoted per customer, such as in fast food outlets.

Cost

Businesses benefit from reduction in employee costs by reducing the number of workers required to perform tasks which can now be managed by fewer individuals or machines. However, there is an increase to certain costs, such as those relating to technology for:

▸ maintenance

▸ upgrades

▸ replacement systems

▸ training and retraining staff.

Implementation

Before technology and the reliance upon IT systems, businesses employed staff who could carry out their duties almost immediately, depending on their skills and knowledge. For example, secretaries and administrators who knew the procedures for their roles and shop assistants who could deal with customer transactions. However, technology can interrupt businesses practices, especially where bespoke systems are implemented, such as specialist **CRM**, **MIS** and **SAP** systems or those for stock control or accounting. These interruptions may be due to the following factors.

▸ Timescales – Delays in decision making, availability of budget and delivery or installation of new systems.

▸ Testing – Time to test the new system under different circumstances and conditions.

▶ Downtime – The period when the old system is being replaced with the new one can result in no system being available at all (such as the transition experienced by the NHS with loss of or limited access to patient records). Downtime can impact on productivity while staff are being retrained or getting used to a new system, or simply due to employees displaying some resistance to becoming familiar with the changes.

> **Key terms**
>
> **CRM** – customer relationship management system.
>
> **MIS** – management information system.
>
> **SAP** – systems, applications and products is a data processing system.

Replacement or integration with current systems

There are risks associated with replacing systems or integrating changes to existing systems. Both of these methods will interfere with working schedules and contingencies should be considered to mitigate loss of business or revenue. In some businesses, such as those which operate 24 hours every day, finding suitable solutions might involve a decision made upon the time of day, or day of the week, when business is at its slowest and therefore loss to services is the least disruptive. For example, software changes were made to reflect the fare increases across London's public transport system at the start of 2016 on the Bank Holiday. The impact resulted in systems not recognising prepaid travel cards and passengers enjoyed free travel, albeit for a short period of time. Although this occurrence may well have been unexpected, the loss in revenue could still be significant but not as bad as if it were done in rush hour at a busy time of year.

Productivity

Automated services provided by IT systems are recognised as being beneficial to productivity. For example, automation in the manufacturing industry greatly increases the quantity of products which can be produced and reduces rejects due to the accuracy of preprogrammable machines, such as those using computer-aided manufacturing (**CAM**). However, as you have been exploring, the introduction of or changes to IT systems can also interrupt productivity. Introducing multiple computer processes into industry can also impact negatively on productivity, for example if employees are required to operate a series of machines sequentially and lose concentration or become distracted from their routine.

> **Key term**
>
> **CAM** – computer-aided manufacturing is done by machines that use software to operate tools and machinery for manufacturing, so providing greater precision and accuracy.

Working practices

Normal productivity can be disrupted by even the threat of new systems being implemented and certainly during the period of implementation. Staff can be exposed to changes to their routine and the way they work and even the terminology that is familiar to them. Any changes to working practices, even if they will bring out greater productivity in the long run, may have a negative impact in the short term. The expectation, even if not verbalised, of staff needing to be 'switched on' 24/7 can be stressful. With home working, there are no longer the clear home/work boundaries.

Staff training needs (initial and ongoing)

Any new system usually requires some training to use and the cost and time implications to businesses can be considerable. The difficulty also lies in the skilfulness of those providing the training and the timing of that training. For example, training that is all up-front, that is at the start or before using a new system, is less effective than phased training which enables users to ask questions and pose scenarios to resolve queries they have encountered personally when starting to use a new system, rather than those that might be encountered.

User support

IT systems and those providing networking solutions usually offer user support, such as Microsoft's and Apple's online and telephone support services. However, specialist systems require specialist, dedicated support for that system and, where systems are bespoke, they are more restricted in the type of support available to respond to individual queries and may incur additional costs.

Security

Ensuring that sufficient and adequate security measures are in place while implementing an IT system, before it becomes operational, can have an impact not only on the lead time for users but also on the costs involved, both during set-up and for ongoing maintenance. Whatever measures are implemented, they need to be constantly monitored for their effectiveness. This may require dedicated staff time to check data-logging records and analyse risk levels.

Using and manipulating data

Having explored some of the benefits and implications of IT systems used by organisations, you will now learn more about the uses, processes and implications for individuals and organisations of accessing and using data and information in digital form.

Sources of data

Source data is often referred to as raw data, which means that it is unrefined and that something has to be done with the data in order for it to become information. There are two types of data sources: primary and secondary.

Primary

Primary data is data that the organisation has collected or produced itself.

Primary data might, for example, be a list of customers' details. This primary data can be input into a CRM in order for a mailshot containing a promotional leaflet to be generated, by merging their names and addresses, or to produce labels for envelopes.

Secondary

Secondary data is data that is 'bought in' or collected by someone else.

Secondary data includes data which is second-hand, as it has already been through some sort of data-handling process. This includes:

▶ research articles
▶ government reports
▶ journalist accounts
▶ reference materials.

> **Reflect**
>
> What are the main methods you use for getting information? Which do you use least and why?

> **Theory into practice**
>
> Revisit one of your recent assignments or activities from this unit. Explore a wider range of sources of data, which should include, at least, all the examples of secondary data given above and one additional source. Analyse the data and evaluate its usefulness. Consider the impact that your latest findings would have on the outcomes you produced for the assignment or activity. If they differ, why do they and what are the implications? If they do not differ, why not?
>
> What have you learnt by undertaking this activity? What will you do differently in the future?

Judging and ensuring the reliability of data

You cannot assume that everything you hear or read is reliable. One such example is when police investigations dismiss witness accounts which are purely hearsay and where there is no solid evidence to verify the information provided. An internet wiki is another example of where information can be dubious. You have probably noticed that Wikipedia invites individuals to provide reference sources to validate the data as reliable.

> **Link**
>
> For more about factors affecting the quality of information see *Unit 5: Data Modelling.*
>
> For more on reliability of data see Methods of ensuring data accuracy.

Data generates an audit trail just as you do when you produce your assignments. You will be expected to reference your sources to validate their reliability. You are guilty of plagiarism if you claim that any of the work is yours when it has been directly taken from other sources. Plagiarism is a serious offence.

> **Reflect**
>
> How would you feel if you discovered that someone had copied your work or repeated something you had suggested and claimed that it was their idea?

The characteristics and implications of methods of collecting data and opinions

Data can be gathered in many forms and, potentially, even without a person's knowledge or consent. This section focuses on different methods of gathering data and opinions.

Survey

Qualitative data is data that is based on categories, such as colour of hair or make of car. Quantitative data is data that is based on numerical measurements, such as height. Surveys include instances where individuals are asked their opinions, perhaps about their experience with a hair product or a leisure event. Market researchers may approach people in busy shopping streets or centres, but now more surveys are conducted over the phone or online. Online surveys save businesses time and money. Online surveys encourage users of websites to give feedback and opinions on products or services they have used. Often this feedback can be used to rate those products or services. Once such example is Trip Advisor, where customer reviews and ratings form the advice that users are given about hotels and restaurants, for example.

Attempts are made by companies using online surveys to ensure the reliability of the data. Otherwise, a business may find themselves blacklisted by users. Surveys such as these have limited usefulness because it is difficult to measure and compare individual opinions as each person's experience is personal and biased.

Questionnaire

You may have completed questionnaires at your place of study, perhaps to provide information about your personal experience as a student and as a measure of your satisfaction with the quality of the teaching or facilities. Questionnaires tend to be more structured than surveys and, although they are still open to an individual's opinions, the data gathered can be more useful as it can be made quantifiable. For example, specific questions can be asked and users can rank their answers from 1 to 5.

Regardless of method for gathering data, assurances should be given about the purpose for gathering the data and also about the use of any personal data which could identify the individual.

> **Tip**
>
> Producing questions which generate the responses you need to answer a specific research question is quite difficult. Keep the questions simple and, if you are seeking opinions, avoid closed or leading questions which rely on yes/no answers. If you ask open questions (how, why...) consider how you are going to analyse the responses as this will help you word the questions appropriately.

Focus groups

Using focus groups is a useful method of gathering information from groups of individuals with a similar interest which, although they are often held on a face-to-face basis, only require each question to be asked once to each group. However, the information gathered can be less reliable where responses are skewed by the solidarity of a group or reticence to provide detail and be identified as the source of an opinion.

Interview

Interviewers can gather information or provide information or both. An interview is a very powerful method of data collection as it is interactive and allows the interviewer to probe for clarity and gain a really clear understanding of the views canvassed. The difficult part of this method is getting respondents to agree to be interviewed as it can be seen to be really quite intrusive. A systems analyst or developer can use interviews to excellent effect to gain an insight into a user's working life and therefore produce a system more ideally suited to their needs. An interviewer must be well prepared and knowledgeable of the intended outcome, as they may be called upon to provide information during the interview.

Reasons for ensuring data accuracy

Inputting accurate data is crucial to business operations. Unfortunately, we all make mistakes and cannot eradicate human error which is why it is so important to ensure that procedures include checking data entry and that systems are designed to undertake validity checks. You will learn more about what that means and how to do this later in this section.

With technology advancements and the reliance on having vast amounts of information just a click away, we are becoming more intolerant when we do not get the information we expect. This could be because we have typed in the wrong questions, or that the information received is inaccurate. You may have noticed, in the disclaimers on the Wikipedia website, concerns about the validity of the data and requests for site users to provide sources and verify its accuracy.

> **Reflect**
>
> Identify an occasion when your information was inaccurate or not found, perhaps when you contacted a business about the guarantee on an item or to seek support using software or a device you recently purchased. Ask yourself what might have happened if the information was not located. If you were the employee searching for the information, what questions would you ask or what strategies would you try to locate the information?
>
> Discuss your example and conclusions with a peer.

> **Theory into practice**
>
> With a peer, explore the implications of your medical records going missing or if they were inaccurate so that you were mistaken for another patient. What methods could be used to ensure that this did not happen?

There are many reasons why data may be inaccurate. For example:

▶ careless data entry (spelling mistakes, inaccuracy)
▶ misheard or misread data
▶ duplications
▶ inadequate **data cleansing**
▶ omissions (gaps in data should always be avoided).

> **Key term**
>
> **Data cleansing** – ongoing checking of data for accuracy, currency and completeness.

It is likely that you have wrongly dialled or stored a telephone number by missing out a digit or putting them in the wrong order. In business, it is vital that data is input accurately and that it is checked frequently. For example, if addresses of Amazon customers became jumbled or were entered inaccurately, then orders would not be received by the people who purchased them.

If a business orders the wrong stock or amount, they could lose custom or find that they have a large amount of stock which they cannot sell and for which they have paid in advance. Inaccurate data is useless data.

> **Theory into practice**
>
> With a peer, produce a questionnaire which can be used to gather data on eating preferences of young adults. Select how you will gather your data and analyse the results. Compare with secondary sources and evaluate the outcome.
>
> Share your experiences with your peers and identify what went well and why, and what you would change if you were to undertake this study again.

Methods of ensuring data accuracy

There are two methods for ensuring the accuracy of data: verification and validation.

Verification

Verification means checking the data with its original source to find inaccuracies. Another method is to enter the data twice and check against both versions.

Validation

To validate data requires a preprogrammed instruction, perhaps a macro or set of parameters, designed to check that the data makes sense and appears reasonable. For example, if the parameters cover a range between 50–80 and the entry is 95, then this will be identified as an error.

If the parameters expect specific data types, such as your postcode, then any inaccuracy will be recognised. This restriction is known as an **input mask**. Parameters can also be set to refuse blank fields so that omissions are not allowed, for example in a National Insurance number, which is unique to every individual.

The process of validation does not check for inaccuracies just as a spellchecker in Microsoft Word cannot proofread. In other words, the program will check whether a word might be misspelt but is not able to identify a wrong telephone number or a missing word. Each of these entries might be recognised as valid entries by the spellchecker, although they may be inaccurate.

> **Link**
>
> For more about Validation and verification of data, see *Unit 5: Data Modelling*.

> **Key term**
>
> **Input mask** – a database instruction which restricts or controls the type, format or amount of data entered.

Methods of extracting and sorting data

Digital **databases** enable the extraction and sorting of data with ease. Actually, any file containing a collection of data which can be manipulated in some way to provide an answer, such as using a spreadsheet to sort information numerically and alphabetically in either direction, can be referred to as a database. For example a list of numerical values can be sorted from low to high and *vice versa*, or words can be alphabetically sorted A–Z or Z–A.

Data can be extracted very quickly and simply using a filter. All data entries containing an exact match are filtered. This works with simple **queries** using a single criterion at a time.

To extract more complex data, constructs using more than one criterion require a more complex query and, for this reason, a dedicated database software program is more likely to be used as it will include the facility to construct queries using multiple criteria. A query can be created in a digital database using another query, which may be referred to as a nested query, rather than recreating a query which repeats the criteria already included in an existing query but requires a refined result.

For example, an existing query might interrogate a database to find all those customers who made a purchase in August 2016 and a new query might be designed using this query and then refining it by asking for all those customers in Birmingham who purchased during that period. Queries can be saved, so those you are likely to need again do not have to be recreated.

Link

For more about databases and queries, read *Unit 2: Creating Systems to Manage Information*.

Key terms

Database – a collection of data which can be in digital or paper form, such as a telephone directory.

Query – a way of interrogating data by applying a set of criteria.

Numerical and data modelling

The processes of numerical and data modelling are used in software engineering.

Numerical modelling

Numerical modelling is the process of producing a mathematical model to perform predetermined actions such as calculations in a spreadsheet. An individual might design a numerical model to calculate their personal finances and manage their budget. A business will use numerical modelling to forecast sales, manage their cash flow and perform projections for future business growth.

Financiers will use numerical modelling for making assumptions about potential growth in stocks and shares or movements in interest rates. Numerical models use formulae and equations and the results can also be used to **amortise** payments over periods of time.

Key term

Amortise – gradually write off the initial cost of an asset over a period of time, because regular payments are made.

Data modelling

Data modelling means to create a conceptual image (a model) of the meaning of the data in order to help consider alternatives. Modelling the data in different ways enables you to evaluate the usefulness of the model and how to justify decisions. Databases are set up to make use of a particular set of data and are modelled in a particular way so as to find out specific information. For example, your place of study needs to keep records of every student, which includes:

▶ personal details

▶ course studied

▶ progress

▶ study support.

The planning of a database is almost more important than the final product. A procedure is required for ongoing maintenance to ensure that the database provides the required information and initial testing should be carried out before any data is input into the database in case changes need to be made to the data model.

Databases can be planned out on paper and each of the features required needs to be defined to ensure that parameters are in place so that the data, when entered and manipulated, are retained. Each line of entry is called a record and each of the records will be broken down into fields, for example:

▶ title

▶ first name

▶ last name

▶ house name/number.

Each field will need to be identified as a particular datatype, for example:

▶ text

▶ number (integers, currency, decimal).

Each field needs to have its parameters set, for example:

▶ format (capitals, lower case, numbers and/or letters)

▶ length (number of characters).

One of the most important features of a database is to ensure that data is stored efficiently and robustly; the most effective databases minimise repeated and redundant data. Queries are used to perform database searches to provide the data required at any particular time.

The planning stage involves refining the database model so that data is stored in separate compartments (tables) which all have something in common so that they can relate to each other. Unlike a spreadsheet or word-processed table, which are usually single tables (flat files) and can become unwieldy, an effective database relies on relationships with other tables in the same or from other databases.

Link

For more about databases, queries and relationships, read *Unit 2: Creating Systems to Manage Information*.

For more about data modelling, read *Unit 5: Data Modelling*.

Presenting data and results

The tables containing the raw primary data are known as the backend of the database. These tables are usually protected and inaccessible to those inputting data to avoid deletions and threats to data integrity. Routine actions are performed at the frontend, known as the dashboard.

Well-planned databases include a variety of methods and means of presenting the data and the results from the interrogation of data, through data modelling. These include:

▶ Reports – Combining text, images and numbers. Calculations can be performed by a database and presented in different formats in a report.

▶ Forms – Raw data can be merged into a predefined form, such as a registration form, perhaps to be completed or signed by the person registering at a leisure centre.

▶ Graphical representation – Numerical data can be presented as a graph and integrated into a report.

Once the database has been set up properly and considerable thought has been given to anticipating what will be required from the raw data (that is, whether it has been modelled correctly), these actions can be performed very simply and easily.

Link

For more on user interfaces (dashboards) and presenting data, see *Unit 5: Data Modelling*.

The characteristics and implications of user interfaces for data collection and processing systems

You are likely to be familiar with systems that are designed to contain or gather and process data. You may have designed a database or possibly used one which was designed for a business, such as a customer database or for stock control.

As databases become increasingly sophisticated, we are largely unaware of the philosophy involved in designing such a system. If you use a spreadsheet to manage your personal finances, this could also be viewed as a sort of database and you will have thought about how you will structure it, that is, the headings for the columns and rows. You may use a filter or sort the data and possibly you will include some formulae to perform calculations. You may have created a database using software such as Microsoft Access and begun to become familiar with the complexities of how to structure the database to ensure that it meets its intended purpose.

When you store the contact details of your friends and family in your phone, this information is contained in a database. As mobile phones have become more sophisticated, your input into gathering and storing this information becomes minimal. For example, recent smartphones can seek out content from messages and emails and then prompt you with a suggestion that new data should be added to existing records or that a new record be created.

Therefore, if you are designing a database system for storing a list of your contacts or for manipulating data for a research project, there are many aspects to consider long before structuring or implementing the system. You will explore some of these aspects now.

Ease of use

The intention of every database is to input, manipulate and extract data with ease. Basic requirements to ensure ease of use are things such as titling fields to avoid ambiguity or misinterpretation, for example using the term first name rather than Christian name, and last name rather than surname.

Accessibility

The dashboard is the user interface which provides users with guidance on how to use the database. For example, an icon might say 'data entry' which, when pressed, will open the window to where new records can be entered.

Depending on the design of the dashboard, databases can be made accessible to the majority of users. Points to consider include:

▶ language and terminology

▶ colour

▶ size of dashboard, text and icons

▶ layout

▶ position (where the dashboard sits in relation to the monitor used)

▶ number of clicks to perform each action.

Link

For more about accessibility, see Accessibility of devices.

Error reduction

User interfaces should be designed to reduce or prevent errors when entering data. If an input mask or other parameter has been implemented, a warning message should appear informing the user about why the data are being refused. Any attempt to delete or alter a record should be preceded by a warning.

Intuitiveness

A well-designed database should be intuitive to use and not require intensive training for daily use. The more sophisticated or bespoke databases often require considerable training over longer periods of time. Making the layout of an on-screen form match that of a physical form aids intuitiveness, as the system is immediately familiar.

Functionality

As database users and those requiring reports generated from the raw data expand their needs and review its capabilities, the database can be refined or expanded to become even more functional. For example, as a business increases its range of products or services, the database might need to be expanded or generate new reports. A business will input employee records and may expand the database to automatically generate salary adjustments based on appraisal outcomes.

This ongoing maintenance relies on the initial structure of the database being sufficiently well thought through during the design process as any changes can affect the integrity of the data.

Performance, usability and cost

User interfaces enable greater performance and usability by reducing the complexities and potential fear attached to using a database, particularly for users less familiar with technology. However, database software can be expensive, especially if designed specifically for a business using a bespoke system. Databases also demand greater storage capacity and performance from IT systems.

Compatibility

Using a database from a software suite, such as Microsoft Office, provides advantages in that the format of the data is compatible to other programs in the suite and is often recognised by other software packages. For example, the ability to export data using a **CSV** file type.

> **Key term**
>
> **CSV** – comma-separated values is a file type which stores records in a line and presents data in plain text as individual fields, where each field is separated by a comma.

Case study

IT enterprise risk management for CESG Digital

CESG is the information security arm of GCHQ, and the National Technical Authority for Information Assurance within the UK. This means that they are the definitive voice on the technical aspects of information security in Government. CESG works in partnership with industry and academia, the Centre for Protection of National Infrastructure (CPNI), MI5 and the Secret Intelligence Service (MI6). The team working on risk management needed a solution to create and share documents. The team put together a small enterprise IT service and the choices they made formed part of a series of blog posts. They initially set some overarching principles, which were, in summary:

- manage risk responsibly
- take decisions based on evidence, react promptly to events, and seek expert advice when needed

- be sensible when making technological decisions that result in risk
- record significant decisions.

The team do not have a separate risk management process, but that they make sensible decisions throughout their project, based fundamentally on security. Basic initial principles included identifying:

- the needs of the users
- the information they expected to secure
- rules for how different types of data would be handled
- which decisions and risks could be taken in-team and those that needed escalating.

For each technological decision, they followed this process.

- They assessed each set of options or approaches against user needs.

- For each option that met user needs, they assessed how well it fitted with decisions made previously and how it measured up against the security factors that were most important for this particular decision.

- They made decisions based on assessments, with a preference for the most usable service that was acceptable against other criteria.

- They escalated the decision if they did not feel empowered to make it locally.

- They recorded the decisions made and tracked any risks which were not fully mitigated.

- They made sure that the right people were in their team, and ensured that those people were trusted by accountable people (outside of the team) to make decisions which they would support.

- All decisions would consider a range of viable options, with decisions made on the basis of evidence and professional judgement.

- Important decisions would be discussed in the team, with two or more people being responsible for more challenging decisions.

- Risks would not be taken if the team did not feel empowered, informed or qualified to take them.

- Help would be sought when required from independent experts in specific areas.

- The team agreed to follow this approach.

They used the Cloud Security Principles, the End User Device Security Principles, or asked some of their security experts what the most important security considerations were for any given decision, and assessed the viable options against them. They also:

- recognised that security needs to be adequate for the purpose

- demonstrated why they made the decisions

- accepted that there will always be uncertainty

- ensured that the business understood the risks it was taking

- were careful to speak in plain English in all internal workings and external outputs

- acknowledged that everyone is part of the delivery team

- recognised that decisions are interconnected.

Because this is a new approach for CESG, they are missing some supporting tools to help track decisions and resulting risks effectively. They used documents to do this, but would like to use a web tool to help with this in the future and some tools to help produce summaries and understand quickly how much cumulative risk they are exposed to.

Check your knowledge

1 Why did CESG need a secure system?

2 How did they go about starting the project?

3 Name at least five factors that CESG believe are important when embarking on projects.

4 What plans do CESG have for improving their procedure further?

Discussion

Discuss this case study with your peers and identify further improvements for your information security procedures.

PAUSE POINT   What risks can you identify from CESG operations in the case study above and what procedures would you put in place?

Hint   Read through the Cloud Security Principles and CESG blogs at www.cesg.gov.uk and www.gov.uk.

Extend   Draw a diagram which demonstrates how you have developed a procedure for protecting your data and information.

F Issues

The final section of this unit explores further the concepts, impacts and implications of issues resulting from the use of IT systems.

Moral and ethical issues

What we use IT systems for and how we use or access them can raise **moral** and **ethical** issues. In this section, you will learn more about the implications for individuals, organisations and wider society of the moral and ethical factors of using information technology.

> ### Key terms
>
> **Moral** – principles about what is right and wrong behaviour.
>
> **Ethical** – relating to the knowledge of moral principles: that is, how we behave.

> ### Reflect
>
> What are your principles and values? How do they compare with those of your peers? What influences your views of what is right and wrong?

The moral and ethical factors of the use of information technology

Our views about morality and ethics will differ depending on our cultural backgrounds. An example of morally and ethically poor practice relates to the ease with which pay-day loans can be activated online or over the phone, enticing vulnerable adults to sign up to high interest rate loans that they cannot afford to pay back.

Privacy

It is not unusual for someone to experience onlookers when reading or writing messages or emails, or for someone to be listening in to phone calls. Some users are quite happy to share their devices but, morally, it is usually considered impolite to engage in others' conversations, whether verbally or digitally, without being invited.

It is not uncommon, however, for conversations to take place over mobile phones in public places without any consideration to others around, even if the content is somewhat sensitive or private in a business context. Likewise the use of multimedia in public places where others are subject to interference and noises, particularly in places designated as quiet areas, such as some train carriages, libraries or waiting rooms.

Personal details are often unwittingly shared with others in public areas by people working in professional situations. Examples include hotel receptionists repeating customer addresses and phone numbers during check-in and doctors' receptionists sharing patients' phone numbers and dates of birth to verify their identity.

As soon as you begin placing personal details online there will be concerns about privacy. Who is storing your data, where is it stored physically, who has access and how is it protected? While there is legislation to protect your personal data, as discussed earlier in this chapter, it is useless if the holder of the data is not in the same jurisdiction as you. Wherever you choose to store your personal data, it is always worth taking note of the privacy policies listed on websites as to what you are agreeing to, that is, what can they do with your data?

> ### Theory into practice
>
> Keep a log for a day as you go about your daily activities, making notes about your regular habits when using any digital device. Note also how others behave and log the circumstances and location of each event.
>
> Assess the impact of these actions and what the risks are regarding the potential invasion of privacy or inadvertent sharing of private data.
>
> What changes will you make to how you will respect others' privacy in the future and what can you do to mitigate the risk of others inadvertently sharing your data?
>
> Carry out this activity again in two or three weeks' time. Have you changed your behaviour? What else have you discovered from this activity?

Environmental

Factors of morality and ethics affect the environment. One well-known example is the disposal of IT equipment such as hardware and printer cartridges, which may be carcinogenic. The use of technology also impacts on the environment by draining natural resources and adding to our carbon footprint.

Despite this, the environment has benefited indirectly from technology because users can gain a better understanding of ways to improve and maintain the environment and those within it by sharing information globally. For example, charities can promote their messages and seek funding from numerous sources. However, morally this method of promotion can also be considered as invasive, especially when TV appeals are shown at mealtimes when they are likely to gain the attention of millions of viewers. Sharing images of those considered less fortunate than ourselves, especially where actors are used to portray misfortune, can be considered immoral.

Research

With a peer, identify at least five examples of risks to the environment due to immoral or unethical practice.

Search for case studies of major organisations. You could start by searching government websites.

Unequal access to information technology

Another ethical and moral consideration is the inequality regarding access to IT. Although much is being done to improve the access to IT systems for all people, through adapted devices or assistive technology, there is still a large percentage of the world's population without any access to IT systems at all.

In 2015, it was estimated that almost half of the population of the world had no access to the internet but that does not indicate how many actually are without any technology. Google and Facebook have initiatives to bring internet access to developing nations. In the more privileged countries, such as the UK and USA, a child without the latest technology can feel stigmatised and disadvantaged when compared with their peers.

Online behaviour and netiquette

There are differing opinions about how to behave online. You may have devised your own rules as peers and decided what is acceptable and what is not, such as the way you write messages, and you might start and sign off with terms of endearment that you would not use when communicating with your employer or teacher.

Generally, you should follow some basic rules of **netiquette** regardless of cultural background:

▶ never use abusive language

▶ do not harass others with demands or personal questions

▶ if a third party is asked to join a discussion, give them access to the string of previous messages in a discussion

▶ get permission before sending other people's content to a third party

▶ do not share personal information (yours or other people's) insecurely or unnecessarily.

Key term

Netiquette – a word derived by combining internet (net) with correct behaviour (etiquette); it is especially related to online discussions and forums but also emails.

Tip

Read the online behaviour and netiquette protocols relating to the online communities you are using.

Theory into practice

Check if your place of study has a netiquette policy. Review the current policy and make recommendations for changes to reflect latest developments relating to moral and ethical behaviour.

Globalisation

As the world is interconnected by the use of IT, the moral and ethical issues appear greater. For example, advertisers need to consider the impact of their promotional material on multi-cultural groups and economic situations.

Research

'The gap between rich and poor is still very large…40% of the world's population live on less than $2 per day'. For more about the ethical dilemmas of globalisation visit www.ethicalfocus.org.

What examples can you identify of inequality due to globalisation? How would you judge whether this inequality is immoral and unethical? Discuss with a peer.

Freedom of speech and censorship

There appears to be conflict between the ability to exercise freedom of speech and the suppression of speech through censorship. Morally and ethically, freedom of speech should follow protocols such as those explored earlier: that is, netiquette.

Acceptable use

Many businesses implement acceptable use (of IT) policies (AUP) which state protocols for what are deemed morally and ethically acceptable, including:

▸ constraints (websites, activities, time)

▸ devices (types and their use, including whether personal devices can be used for business activities and vice versa)

▸ security (complying with legislation, keeping data secure).

> **Link**
>
> For more about AUPs, visit http://whatis.techtarget.com.

The purpose and role of codes of practice produced by professional bodies for the use of IT systems

In the section Protecting data and information, you began to learn about codes of practice for the protection of data and you will now explore further the purpose and role of codes such as those produced by the:

▸ Information Commissioner's Office (ICO)

> **Link**
>
> For more about the Information Commissioner's Office (ICO), visit https://ico.org.uk/.

▸ Care Quality Commission

> **Link**
>
> For more about the Care Quality Commission, visit http://www.cqc.org.uk/.

▸ Chartered Institute of Library and Information Professionals.

> **Link**
>
> For more about the Chartered Institute of Library and Information Professionals, visit http://www.cilip.org.uk/.

The purpose of codes such as these is to protect users and customers and to provide assurance regarding data protection and also clear guidance about their values. Values are based around moral and ethical considerations.

The impact of codes of practice on individuals and organisations

Codes of practice are also self-regulated, which means that any individual can report a breach as a cause for concern for investigation to the organisation itself, rather than to an independent body. Each of the promises identified in the code of practice will also be formally monitored and regulated. Therefore anyone in breach of any aspect of the code of practice will be dealt with in accordance to the organisation's policies and legislation.

The benefits of having a code of practice are consistency of use of an IT system and that it provides a set of common ground rules to avoid misunderstandings or misinterpretations. Individuals are responsible for making themselves aware of the requirements of such codes.

Legal issues

There are many examples of where individuals' personal data have been violated, such as hacking into bank accounts or stealing personal identities. We shall now explore some of the legal issues relating to the use of IT systems and the implications for individuals, organisations and wider society.

The role of current legislation (and subsequent additions and amendments) in protecting users and their data from attack and misuse

We all have opinions about legal, moral and ethical issues, particularly if it affects someone close to us. However, as you may have been discovering, we do not all share the same views, nor can we do much about what we consider to be an injustice without the support of greater forces, such as that provided by government legislation and enforcement.

As technology and its uses continue to evolve and expand, legislation is reviewed for its currency and updated to combat risk. Ensuring legislation is fit for purpose in accordance with current expectations and behaviours is really complicated, as laws must work together in harmony and not contradict other laws. Hence working parties devote considerable time and effort to producing legislation based on many sources of data which are gathered, analysed and evaluated.

Businesses and individuals are responsible for ensuring that they are aware of current legislation and any changes. You will note from the following examples that amendments, additions and convergences exist to address the changes.

Link

Full legislation and amendments can be found at http://www.legislation.gov.uk/.

Computer Misuse Act 1990

The Computer Misuse Act 1990 is a generic set of rules prohibiting unauthorised access to data and unlawful treatment of data where access is permitted. The act links to other legislation by identifying the scope of the legislation and the territory covered by the act. Changes are currently being made to keep up with technological developments over the last 25 years. The Computer Misuse Act lists three basic offences. These are:

▶ unauthorised access to a computer system – punishable by up to 2 years in prison and a hefty fine

▶ unauthorised access with intent to commit a criminal act – punishable by up to 5 years in prison and a hefty fine

▶ unauthorised access and modification of a computer system – punishable by up to 10 years in prison and a hefty fine.

The act covers all offences, ranging from minor intrusions into a company database by an employee to an incident that may impact on national security.

Police and Justice Act 2006 (Computer Misuse)

The Police and Justice Act 2006 (Computer Misuse) expands on the impact of breaching the Computer Misuse Act through amendments which include:

▶ penalty by imprisonment and/or fine

▶ length of imprisonment

▶ making explicit the constituents of unauthorised acts, such as making, supplying or obtaining offensive material.

Copyright Designs and Patents Act 1988

The Copyright Designs and Patents Act 1988, also referred to as the CDPA or CDP Act, sets out the rules for copyright and artistic licence relating to all multimedia, specifically:

▶ broadcasting

▶ films and recordings

▶ ownership

▶ databases, computer design and backup copies

▶ rental and loans (differentiating between permissions for public and personal use)

▶ accessibility (typefaces, printing).

The Copyright (Computer Programs) Regulations 1992

The Copyright (Computer Programs) Regulations 1992 expand upon the CDPA in terms of:

▶ jurisdiction (Northern Ireland is included)

▶ literary work (preparatory design material for a computer program is included)

▶ restrictions to issuing copies of, adapting or converting computer programs

▶ permission to back up copies of programs when for lawful use.

The Health and Safety (Display Screen Equipment) Regulations 1992

The Health and Safety (Display Screen Equipment) Regulations 1992 sets out rules for using 'any device or equipment that has an alphanumeric or graphic display screen' because of the implications to health, in particular **RSI**. The Regulations advise taking regular breaks and engaging in other activities to reduce the risk of RSI. Businesses are required to consider the moral and ethical issues of employees expected to spend extended lengths of time in front of computer screens.

Link

For more about the Health and Safety (Display Screen Equipment) Regulations, visit http://www.hse.gov.uk/.

Key term

RSI – repetitive strain injury.

Data Protection Act 1998

Copying someone else's data without their permission or acknowledgement is against the law and both morally and ethically inappropriate. The Data Protection Act 1998 extends beyond the obvious restrictions in sharing data and also includes rules about disclosing and the use of data.

For example, a business must disclose the use of telephone or CCTV recordings. The law requires businesses to notify the ICO as to why they are using CCTV. It would not be morally or ethically acceptable for a business to use CCTV for observing staff working.

Link

For more about data protection in regards to the use of CCTV, visit www.gov.uk.

Guidelines and current legislation (and subsequent additions and amendments) designed to ensure the accessibility of IT systems

Legislation is there to protect everyone and ignorance is not excusable in the eyes of the law. Businesses often monitor compliance by appointing someone to remain up to date with changes to legislation and to implement procedures for employees to follow.

Disability Discrimination Acts 1995 and 2005

The Disability Discrimination Acts 1995 and 2005 (DDA) legislate against unlawful discrimination of those with disabilities and with specialist needs such as learning difficulties. (These acts have now been repealed and replaced by the Equality Act 2010 (except in Northern Ireland).) Discrimination can occur when those intended to be protected by the law do not have the same rights or access as those without these characteristics.

A business cannot discriminate when recruiting or employing staff by the way they advertise or the duties to be undertaken. Neither can they discriminate against customers gaining access to services or products. For example, a recruitment advert which is inaccessible to those with visual impairment or a job requiring use of IT without provision made for adaptive or assistive technology would be in breach of the law.

Equality Act 2010

The Equality Act of 2010 has replaced the DDA to promote equality regardless of characteristics. For example, it legislates against unlawful behaviour such as that described in the previous section and makes explicit the characteristics of vulnerable groups, known as those with protected characteristics.

> **Link**
>
> For more about the Equality Act 2010, visit www.equalityhumanrights.com.

British Standards Institute (BSI) codes of practice

The BSI includes the code of practice known as whistleblowing. The whistleblowing code permits the right of individuals and employees to 'blow the whistle' on those in breach of legislation.

> **Link**
>
> For more about the BSI ,visit http://www.bsigroup.com/en-GB/, and for more about whistleblowing, visit http://www.pcaw.org.uk/bsi/.

Perhaps you feel that a fellow student is being discriminated against by being excluded from accessing some specialist software needed for their course, which is available to everyone else; then you might report it to the appropriate person.

Open Accessibility Framework (OAF)

The purpose of the OAF is to 'conduct research...to enable the development of embeddable assistive technologies for the desktop and for mobile devices'. The six framework steps are:

1 define accessible
2 stock elements
3 development/authoring tools
4 platform support
5 the app itself
6 assistive technology.

> **Link**
>
> For more about the Open Accessibility Framework, visit http://www.oaeg.org/.

Web Content Accessibility Guidelines (WCAG) 1.0 and 2.0 and World Wide Web Consortium (W3C®)

In 1994, Tim Berners-Lee founded the W3C to initiate universal accessibility codes of practice for accessibility of the internet. The WCAG defines guidance for creating web content which avoids discrimination, by providing three basic tips on:

▶ user interface and visual design

▶ writing and presenting content

▶ markup and coding.

> **Link**
>
> For more on the WCAG, visit http://www.w3.org/.

As the use of the internet continues to grow and develop, W3C® continues to strive to eradicate inaccessibility, for example, by, defining terminology, user needs, providing guidelines and resources for use and designing for inclusion, such as mobile accessibility and content.

> **Link**
>
> For more about mobile accessibility, visit www.w3.org.

The moral and ethical factors in the use of IT systems

This section covers the moral and ethical factors involved in the use of IT systems.

Health and safety

Health and safety is all around us and there exist many risks when using digital devices. If we look at the traditional office workstation, users should ensure that they take frequent breaks from using screens, keyboards and other peripherals, and they should be provided with fully adjustable seating to prevent RSI and back problems. Employees are entitled to DSE (display screen equipment) risk assessments to consider their specific needs if they regularly use IT equipment. Trailing cables, glare, eye strain, electrical concerns and work–life balance all present their own health and safety risks.

Outside the workplace, less obvious factors include using digital devices which could cause a fire, such as:

▶ using a digital device at a petrol station

▶ using digital device as a torch to locate a gas leak in a dark space.

In addition, digital devices should not be used when crossing a road or when driving or controlling machinery. The frequent use of smartphones may cause RSI due to constantly performing fine motor movements to interact with a touch screen.

Theory into practice

Ask your tutor for your centre's DSE risk assessment and carry out a risk assessment of your workstation in class. What could you do to mitigate any risks you identified?

Copyright

Copyright laws and plagiarism rules are the same whether content is copied from a paper book or digital material and whether it is text, image, sound or any other media which you have not created. It is all too easy in the digital age to accidentally breach copyright legislation. Simply using an image from Google Images, for example, in a website could result in a lawsuit for unauthorised use of images. If you are using images found on the internet, it is essential that you obtain permission to use them. There are many sources that are licensed under the Creative Commons licence which allow easy reuse with a clear conscience and free of the risk of potential legal action.

Computer misuse

Using a computer other than your own should be within the realms of the regulations laid down by the owner, whether a friend or a business. Conducting personal activities using a business computer or other device without permission, whether in work time or over a break, can be viewed as immoral and unethical. This is because the data on that computer or in the network it is attached to is put at a greater security risk through your personal use of it. Using a company mobile for personal communication and other use is also not moral or ethical unless agreed to by the company.

Protection of data

It is your responsibility to protect your data and also to protect the data belonging to others. Simple precautions such as locking access or not copying or removing data from its original source should be followed. Using the internet through public access puts data at risk of exploitation. Ensure that you are not looking over someone's shoulder when they use an ATM or a PIN number for a transaction, and make sure that you are not overlooked when you are doing the same.

Privacy

It is neither moral nor ethical to listen to others' telephone calls or to read another's emails without permission. Equally, it is not appropriate to randomly capture images or record videos without the permission of those in the image or recording, or to post the content onto the internet.

Accessibility

Creating or accommodating a situation which discriminates someone from using IT systems is neither moral nor ethical. Therefore accessibility and inaccessibility are important considerations whether programming, producing a blog, typing an email or leaving a message.

Further reading and resources

Websites

Useful websites for further information relating to Unit 1:

- http://www.cisco.com/
- http://computer.howstuffworks.com/
- http://www.dummies.com/
- https://books.google.co.uk/
- http://www.howtogeek.com/
- http://www.ibm.com/
- https://technet.microsoft.com

Assessment practice 1.4

The Canadian Health Commission (CHC) is looking to improve the data collection system across the health care system in Canada by introducing a standardised approach. The problem they have identified is trying to overcome the challenges faced when trying to collect data on patients' race, ethnicity, language and communication needs.

The organisation is striving to create a comprehensive system that combines data collected from multiple agencies, which include:

- hospitals
- community health centres
- physician practices
- health plans
- government or federal agencies.

The organisation recognises that each agency faces opportunities and challenges in how to collect the data sensitively and consistently.

To identify the next steps towards improving data collection they have recognised that, in some instances, the opportunities and challenges are unique to each type of organisation while, in others, they are common to all, including how to:

- ask existing and potential patients questions about race, ethnicity, and language and communication needs
- train staff to elicit this information in a respectful and efficient manner
- address the discomfort of registration/admission staff about requesting this information.

You have been asked to:

1 write a report which might help them solve the problem of how staff could elicit sensitive information consistently, perhaps by producing a checklist or questionnaire

2 include an evaluation of UK codes of practice

3 analyse and synthesise codes of practice from UK and W3C®

4 provide recommendations for CHC justified by your findings.

Plan

- What do I need to find out?
- What is my timeframe?
- What will the structure of the report look like?
- How can I demonstrate that this meets the required standard for distinction?

Do

- I know how to locate where my weaker areas are and how to improve.
- I understand what is being asked of me.
- I can check that all the criteria are met.
- I can make improvements to my analytical and evaluating skills.

Review

- I can describe how to improve further.
- I can recognise my strengths.
- I can explain how I tackled each part of this activity.
- I can explain how this knowledge and experience will be useful to me elsewhere.

Ⅱ PAUSE POINT   What ethical and moral factors feature in this assessment activity and on whom do they have an impact?

Hint   Try exploring other case studies or talking to a mentor or business colleague.

Extend   How would you develop an outline for logging the data electronically?

THINK ▶FUTURE

Tom Churchill,
BTEC National
Student

It wasn't until I was part way through my BTEC National that I started to realise 'I can do this!' I joined the course mainly because I didn't know what else to do and I like computers. I don't mind admitting I was worried I wouldn't make the grade but I enjoyed studying.

So after getting some careers advice from my tutor and student services I found a Uni course I fancied and applied. It meant filling in a UCAS form and I wasn't very confident but I had help to write about what I am good at and why I wanted to go into higher education. I can't wait to go on to do a degree as I shall be the first person in my family to go to Uni. I have done some research about possible jobs in the future and it seems they're crying out for software developers.

It wasn't until I talked to my parents about my plans and they asked me to explain what software developers do that I realised I needed to be more focused. When I looked through the courses again I realised I needed to be specific in what I wanted and identify what my strengths were. I also realised then that I wanted to make a success of the course and not struggle with something that might not interest me. I especially enjoyed learning about design philosophy and knew that my creative skills would be useful when designing software.

I explained to my parents that I would be preparing for a job where I would work in a team on projects which might also involve me researching clients' needs to inform the design. This got me thinking about the research I had done on this course and how much I had developed from when I first started. I must admit I didn't think very hard about the information I found and now I know about ways to check it is accurate before relying on it. However, I have a lot more to learn.

My parents are proud of my achievements so far and especially pleased that I have a mission to follow! Most of all, I am proud of myself and can't wait to continue my journey. I'm not saying it's going to be easy though!

Focusing your skills

Skills health check and preparing to apply to higher education

It is important to promote the skills you have gained as they can be used in the future in lots of different situations. Here are some ideas for you.

1. Make a list of the skills you have and how they will help you in higher education.

2. Divide your list into four skills sections: employment, creative, study, social.

3. Rate each one to identify what you are really good at and what you need to improve on.

4. Ask someone who knows your skills well to check your list in case you have missed anything.

5. Research the variety of higher education courses on offer and read through the syllabus of those you find most interesting.

6. Arrange to visit some universities that offer courses that interest you to assess which suits you and where you might fit in best. Perhaps start by visiting https://www.ucas.com.

   - You should also consider preparing for any visits and possible interviews by producing:
     - an updated CV
     - examples of where you have applied your skills as a student or employee
     - a list of sensible and interesting questions
     - a bibliography of your sources used for research and your application.

Getting ready for assessment

This section has been written to help you to do your best when you take the external examination. Read through it carefully and ask your tutor if there is anything you are not sure about.

About the test

The set task should be carried out under supervised conditions.

▶ You must not bring anything into the supervised environment or take anything out without your tutor's knowledge and approval. You will need to use a black ink or ball-point pen. Make sure you bring one with you and it might be sensible to have a spare as well.

▶ You should make sure that you back up your work regularly. You should save your work to your folder using the naming instructions that will be indicated in each activity.

▶ Do not forget anything else you might need, such as glasses for reading the assessment paper.

Preparing for the test

This unit is assessed under supervised conditions and the number of marks for the unit is 90. Pearson sets and marks the task.

The marks for each question will be shown in grey boxes next to each question. Use this as a guide as to how much time to spend on each question.

Additional information and stimulus material needed to answer the questions can be found in the additional information booklet.

The external assessment will last for 2 hours. You will be assessed on your understanding of IT systems and the implications of their use in personal and professional situations.

The assessments for this unit are available in January and May/June each year.

Make sure that you arrive in good time for the assessment. Check that you have everything you need for the test ahead of time. Plan out your time to ensure that you leave yourself enough time to complete all of the questions and to check through your work at the end. Try to answer every question. Proofread and correct any mistakes before handing in your work. Ensure that you have checked all sides of the assessment paper before starting.

Listen to, and read carefully, any instructions you are given. Lots of marks are often lost through not reading instructions properly and misunderstanding what you are being asked to do.

Key terms typically used in assessment

There are some key terms that may appear in your assessment. Understanding what these words mean will help you understand what you are being asked to do.

The following table shows you the command words that will be used consistently in your assessments to ensure that you are rewarded for demonstrating the necessary skills.

Please note: the list below will not necessarily be used in every paper/session and is provided for guidance only. Only a single command word will be used per item in your test.

Key term	Definition
Analyse	Learners examine in detail a scenario or problem to discover its meaning or essential features. Learners will break down the problem into its parts and show how they interrelate. There is no requirement for any conclusion.
Assess	Learners give careful consideration to all the factors or events that apply and identify which are the most important or relevant. They make a judgement on the importance of something.
Calculate	Learners apply some form of mathematical or computational process.
Complete	Learners complete a diagram or process. This can apply to problems/solutions of varying complexity.
Demonstrate	Learners illustrate and explain how an identified computer system or process functions. This may take the form of an extended writing response, a diagram or a combination of the two.
Describe	Learners provide an account of something, or highlight a number of key features of a given topic. May also be used in relation to the stages of a process.
Develop	Learners provide a solution to a problem, typically using an existing system or structure that must be improved or refined.
Discuss	Learners investigate a problem or scenario showing reasoning or argument.
Draw	Learners represent understanding through the use of a diagram or flowchart.
Explain	Learners denote a series of linked points needed and/or justify or expand on an identified point required.
Evaluate	Learners review and synthesise information to provide a supported judgement about the topic or problem. Typically, a conclusion will be required.
Identify	Learners assess factual information, typically when making use of given stimuli. This requires a single word or short sentence answer.
Produce	Learners provide a solution that applies established constructs to a given computing problem.
State, name, give	Learners assess factual information. This requires a single word or short sentence answer.
Write	Learners produce a solution, or mechanism used as part of a solution to a given computing problem.

A few more guidelines

▶ Always make a plan for your answer before you start writing. Sketch this out so that you can refer to it throughout – remember to include an introduction and a conclusion and think about the key points you want to mention in your answer. On this plan, think about setting yourself some timeframes so that you make sure that you have time to cover everything you want to and, importantly, have time to write the conclusion!

▶ Try and keep your answer as focused on your key points as possible. If you find your answer drifting away from that main point, refer back to your plan.

▶ Make sure that you understand everything being asked of you in the activity instructions. It might help you to underline or highlight the key terms in the instructions so that you can be sure your answer is clear and focused on exactly what you have been asked to do.

Sample answers

For some of the questions you will be given some background information on which the questions are based.

Look at the sample questions which follow and our tips on how to answer these well.

Worked example

Exam text

Sarah works as administrator of a small advertising company. Since starting her job she has been keeping a list of all the places where they have advertised and the responses generated from the adverts.

The owner of the business wants to know which adverts have been the most successful in terms of responses and whether the cost of each advert is viable.

Sarah has been keeping all the records and advertising costs on a spreadsheet but she thinks she needs to use a database program before the list becomes too big to manage. She has found someone who could produce an integrated system which will interact with all her administrative duties which include invoicing, credit control and producing reports for her boss. Her boss has agreed that Sarah meet with the developer to explain what the business requires and how the system would be used.

Answering extended answer questions:

1. Sarah wants to reorganise her administrative duties using an integrated system. Explain **two** implications for the business when designing an IT system.

For a question using the word 'implication' you must do more than just describe what needs doing. You will need to justify the reasons why they have to be done this way and what the advantages and disadvantages might be.

Exam sample answer

An IT system requires considerable planning to meet employer and user needs. Sarah will need to explain to the developer what the system will be used for and who will be using it so that the data are secure and that access is easy for her employer and other authorised users can operate the system should she leave the business.

Sarah will need to discuss with the developer the working practices of the business and what the impact might be when the new system is being implemented. Sarah's boss is concerned about lost data and whether there will be more expense while everyone is being trained.

Sarah will need to check if the system will run automatic backups and the protocols that need to be followed to make sure that the accounts are safe. Sarah will also need to check how the system will verify and validate the data as it is input to ensure that it is accurate. Sarah currently verifies data manually by checking against the invoices for costs of adverts, but current methods for validating data have been time consuming and unreliable.

2. Sarah's boss has said he will need to provide monthly reports to his accountant on a routine basis. The problem is that the accountant will ask for different information depending on what he needs at the time. Some requests are VAT related while others might be relating to outstanding payments.

The accountant lives 300 miles away and sometimes travels abroad and has asked for reports to be sent by email to him so that he can check the records at any time.

a) Describe two options for enabling the accountant to access the information required.

b) Explain the advantages and disadvantages of each option and what Sarah could offer as a solution.

> For a question asking you to explain advantages and disadvantages, you will need to demonstrate that you understand complex situations and can justify your reasons and provide recommendations for a solution that could be acceptable.

Exam sample answer

If the accountant contacted Sarah to produce reports whenever he needed them, this would provide the accountant with bespoke reports as required. However, the disadvantages include the impact on Sarah's workload and the time delay in getting the information back to the accountant, especially at times when Sarah is not at work. The main consideration is the risk to the security of the data if sent via email as either an attachment or in the email itself. The data could be at risk of hackers or be sent to the wrong person in error.

The accountant could also access the area of the local system containing the financial data needed via a VPN across the internet. Another alternative is that the system may also be stored in the cloud allowing collaborative access and ensuring that the data would be current and is backed up automatically using cloud storage.

The access would be password protected and, if the system has limited permissions, the data would be more secure by restricting the use by the accountant, so that the information required can be accessed but changes could not be made.

The advantages of the accountant having access to the system remotely include being able to obtain the information immediately when needed, anywhere and at any time of the day or night and not making Sarah responsible. This information might be required urgently by HMRC or to chase a long-standing debt.

Disadvantages to using cloud computing and VPN are that if the accountant is working remotely in an area with unstable internet or limited bandwidth then the information might not be easily available. The accountant might not be able to respond to urgent and important requests due to downtime. The employer might also have to pay the accountant for the time spent trying to access the data although productivity is interrupted.

You might be asked to present your answer as a diagram to provide a thorough model of data sharing and connection types to respond to a scenario. In this case, you will need to ensure that your diagram is clearly annotated so that examiners can assess how well you understand and explain your answer.

Creating systems to manage information 2

Getting to know your unit

Information technology is all about managing and manipulating information. Database software applications are very widely used to support many business processes and internet facilities. Google™, Facebook™ and YouTube™ are all based around a database, as are many other applications.

In this unit, you will explore the purpose and structure of relational databases. You will look at the structure of data. You will look at how you can design and then implement an effective database system solution. Note that, though the screenshots in this unit show a particular database, the information in this unit can be applied to whichever database you are using.

How you will be assessed

This unit is externally assessed by a practical task which will be completed under supervised conditions for 10 hours in a 1 week period which can be arranged over a number of sessions. You will be assessed on your ability to design, create, test and evaluate a relational database system to manage information.

Grade descriptors

To achieve a grade, a learner is expected to demonstrate these attributes across the essential content of the unit. The maximum number of marks for this unit is 66.

To pass the unit

▸ You will be able to use your knowledge and understanding of database design and development terminology, standards, concepts and processes.
▸ You can apply problem-solving skills to design and develop a solution in context.
▸ You can demonstrate your understanding of how to use standard database. constructs to develop a functioning solution that evidences testing and evaluation.

To achieve a distinction

▸ You can evaluate a given problem and develop a detailed and complex solution to meet all requirements of the brief.
▸ You can apply an in-depth understanding of database constructs, using test results to produce an optimised solution.
▸ You are able to evaluate the quality, performance and usability of your database with supporting justification.

Assessment outcomes

AO1 Demonstrate knowledge of database development terminology, standards, concepts and processes

AO2 Apply knowledge and understanding of database development terminology, standards, concepts and processes to create a software product to meet a client brief

AO3 Analyse information about database problems and data from test results to optimise the performance of a database solution

AO4 Evaluate evidence to make informed judgements about the success of a database's design and performance

AO5 Be able to develop a database solution to meet a client brief with appropriate justification

Getting started

Data is all around us, your social media newsfeed, mobile phone call list, the weather forecast, your college or school timetable. Data becomes information when it is useful to us and we can use it in a meaningful way. Think of all the sources of data that you have accessed recently. Were they useful to you? Could they have been presented in a different way to make them more useful? What would be the implications if the data you accessed had been inaccurate? In this unit, you will develop an understanding of database technology which is central to how so much of the internet-centric world around us operates. This understanding will be essential to you as you work towards a career in Information Technology.

A The purpose and structure of relational database management systems

Databases are used to provide a wide range of applications, from e-commerce and customer billing through to games and social media. In this section, you will look at the purpose and structure of relational database management systems.

Relational database management systems

First, we will cover the types of relational database management systems (RDBMS).

Types of RDBMS and their characteristics

There are a number of different types of RDMBS, which can be broadly categorised in the following way:

▶ Desktop systems – These are designed for personal use. The best known of these is Microsoft® Access®, which we will use throughout this unit. Microsoft® Access® is part of the Microsoft® Office® suite and is focused on single-user or small-departmental applications. Access® includes an end user interface and features such as 'Wizards' to simplify the creation of databases for end users. Access® only runs on computers with the Windows® operating system.

▶ Client–server database systems – These are designed for distributed multi-user databases with the database files stored on a server computer. Databases in this category are developer tools and they need a lot more developing before they include the end user interface features found in Access®. This category of RDBMS can be further divided into the following.

- Open source database systems – The best known and most widely used **open source** database system is MySQL™. MySQL™ runs on a wide range of operating

systems including Windows®, Linux™ and Apple® OSX, and is a popular choice for web applications.

- Proprietary database systems – The most widely used **proprietary** database systems are Microsoft®'s SQL Server®, Oracle® Database and IBM®'s DB2®.

Research

MySQL® and Oracle® Database are the two most widely used database software applications. What are the differences and similarities between them?

Relational data structures

To understand the relational model, it is a good idea to start by thinking of simple real-life data examples. For example, if you drew up a list of Christmas presents to buy your family, it might look something like the list in Figure 2.1.

▶ **Figure 2.1:** Christmas present list

If you wanted to, you could create a budget for your Christmas spending by putting this data into a spreadsheet and adding up the cost of the items. This is often called a flat file database as it contains a single list of data (in database terminology, this is a table). Please read the worked example, which will explain how two tables of data are used to create a relational database, before going on to learn more about relational database terminology.

In *relational database* terminology, a table of data is known as a *relation*. Every relation has columns which represent the different data that is stored in the relation. In the customer details table in our example, this would be items like customer number, first name, surname, house number and postcode. Each of these items is called an *attribute*. Each attribute has a range of allowable values, which is known as a *domain*. An example of the attributes and domains for the customer details table are shown in Table 2.1.

▶ **Table 2.1:** Attributes and domains in the customer details table

Attribute	Domain name	Domain definition
Customer number	CUST_NO	Numeric, 6 digits
Customer first name	F_Name	Character, size 25
Customer surname	S_Name	Character, size 25
Address line 1	Addr_1	Character, size 25
Address line 2	Addr_2	Character, size 25
Town	Town	Character, size 25
Postcode	Postcode	Character, size 8

Worked example: Ordering from an online store

Imagine that you ordered all of your Christmas presents (see Figure 2.1) from an online store. Due to the fact that you might place several orders with the same online store, they would keep at least two tables of data. One table would hold the information about you, the customer, and the other table would hold information about the orders that you have placed.

In theory this data could all be held in one table, but then every time you placed an order you would need to include all of your details (such as name and address) again. This would mean duplicating a lot of data; therefore, it is a much better solution to have two tables.

However, there needs to be a way to link (relate) the two tables (those holding your customer details and other holding your orders) together because the online store needs to know which customer has placed each order. We could use the customer's name to relate the two tables but, as there might be several people with the same name, a better idea is to use a unique identifier for each customer, such as a customer number. Therefore, every order that a particular customer places is identified by including the customer number, from the *Customer* table, in the orders placed by that customer in the *Orders* table. The two tables are said to be related by the customer number.

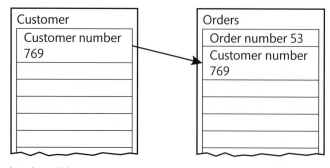

▶ **Figure 2.2:** The Customer and Orders tables

The number of attributes that a relation contains is known as its *degree*. The degree of the customer details relation is 7 (because there are seven attributes listed in the table). The domain definition describes the type and size of the data to be stored in that attribute; this is often called the *datatype*.

> **Key term**
>
> **Datatype** – Datatypes are used in both programming and in database development as the definition of the type of data that is to be stored (in the case of database) in a field. The most commonly used datatypes are text and number, but there are variations on these and other datatypes too.

> **Research**
>
> What datatypes does Microsoft Access® support? What kind of data can they store? How might you use the different datatypes?

The rows within a relation represent complete sets of attributes, sometimes called records but, in relational database terminology, they are called *tuples*. The uniqueness of the attributes within a relation is called the *cardinality* of the relation. In Table 2.1, the Town attribute is likely to have the same value in many records (e.g. London or Manchester) as there are a limited number of towns within the UK, whereas the Cust_no attribute is different for each record so its cardinality is equal to the number of records in the customer table. Access® and other database software applications sometimes use different terminology to the standard relational database terminology. Table 2.2 compares the standard relational database terminology with that used by Access®.

▸ **Table 2.2:** Comparison between standard relational database terminology and that used by Access®

Standard relational database terminology	Access® terminology for commonly used terms that differs from the standard
Relation	Table
Attribute	Field
Tuple	Record

In this book, to avoid confusion, we will use the terminology used in Access®, because it is likely that you will use this database software application to complete this unit.

Step by step: Creating tables

8 Steps

1 When using Access®, all the tables within a single database are stored in the same database file. When you start Access®, it displays the screen shown. From this screen, to create a new database file to which tables can be added, click the Blank desktop database icon.

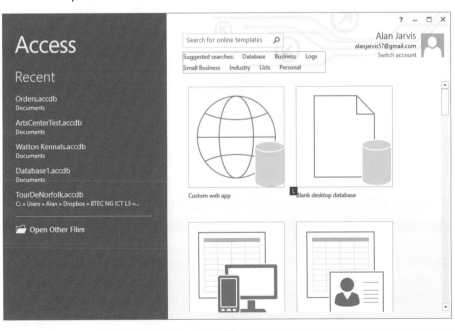

2 You will then be asked for a filename and a location for the database file. Once you have done this, you will see this screen.

3 Access® creates a table for you and you can complete the fields in this Datasheet View. To get more control over how the table is structured, it is best to swap to Design View, so click the View icon on the far left of the toolbar and choose Design View from the drop-down menu. Access® will now ask you to save the table. Type a meaningful table name (e.g. Customers) and click OK. You will now see this display.

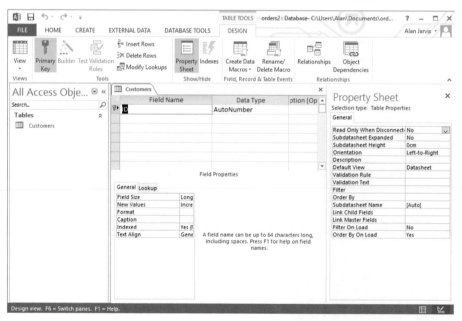

4 Access® creates a field, that it calls 'ID' for you, which it sets as the primary key. It has a datatype of AutoNumber, which means that Access® will automatically give each record in the table a unique consecutive number, starting from 1. This can be a good idea for a primary key field, as we will see later, but 'ID' is not a good name. Something more meaningful like 'Customer_Number' would be a better choice.

5 The next field to be added is 'F_Name' in the second row of the field name list. Access® automatically adds the datatype of 'Short Text', which allows up to 255 characters (which should be more than enough characters). The display should now look like this.

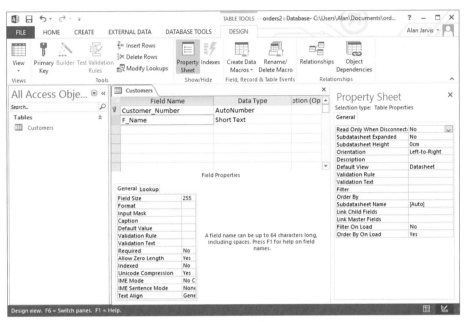

6 Under the field name grid you can see the properties for whichever field you have selected in the grid. Here, for example, you could adjust the field size, if required, to the 255 characters listed in the example in step 5. All the other fields from that example are text so they can be added in the same way as the F_Name field. However, suppose that you also wanted to add the customer's date of birth. This time, where Access® adds the default datatype of Short Text, you need to click in the box and choose Date/Time from the drop-down menu, as shown here.

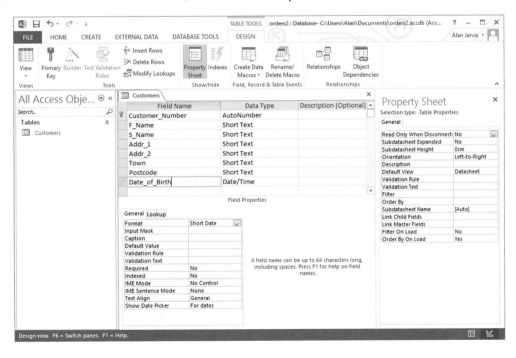

7 In the properties for this field, you can see that there is no size property, but there is a format property. Clicking in the Date/Time box will drop down a list of different date and time formats. In this case, the 'Short date' format (e.g. 20/12/2015) is fine. You can add as many fields as you like. Once they are all added, you can swap to Datasheet View and try entering some data. Click on the View icon in the toolbar and choose Datasheet View (Access® will require you to save the table design first).

▼

8 Once in Datasheet View, you cannot type in the Customer_Number field as it is an AutoNumber field, meaning that Access® completes it for you. You can type in all the other fields but, because the 'Date_of_Birth' field is formatted as a date, you must enter a valid date, otherwise you will get an error message.

Tip

It is very important that you check that your table design is correct, particularly with regard to datatypes, before you add large numbers of records. Correcting design mistakes later, when the table is full of data, can be complex and time consuming.

Relational algebra

The theoretical basis behind relational databases and query languages such as **SQL** is known as relational algebra. The practical applications of relational algebra are database queries (or relational algebra operations) that allow us to extract useful information from the tables within a database.

Key term

SQL – stands for structured query language and is a special purpose programming language used for managing data in relational databases. SQL is a standard language (developed by ISO, the International Organisation for Standardisation) used by all the main database programs.

There are a number of different relational algebra operations that we can apply to tables. Some simple examples are given below. Each operation is represented by a special *symbol*.

Select

The *select* operation involves selecting a subset of records from a table that match certain criteria. It is written as

$$\sigma \text{ condition}^{(\text{relation})}$$

The 'condition' is a Boolean expression in which rows are selected if true. For example, suppose you had a table

(relation) which contains books, and one of the fields is the subject, then the following expression will display all the books with a subject of "computing"

$$\sigma \text{ Subject = "computing"}^{(\text{books})}$$

Join

The *join* operation, as the name suggests, involves joining two tables together. There are several versions of the join operation, the simplest of which is the *natural join*. The symbol for natural join is ⋈. To carry out a natural join, the two tables must have at least one common field. For example, imagine a college database with a table of all the courses, as shown in Table 2.3 (just a few fields are shown for simplicity).

▶ **Table 2.3:** Table of all the Courses offered by a college

Course ID	Course name	Department
001	BTEC IT L3	Computing
002	HNC Child care	Health and social care
003	A level Business	Business studies
004	A Level Computing	Computing

The second table holds details of the college departments and who is the head of each department, as shown in Table 2.4 (again just a few fields are shown for simplicity).

▶ **Table 2.4:** Table of all the Departments at a college and the names of the heads of departments

Department	Head of department
Computing	Wendy Smith
Health and social care	Alan Jones
Business studies	Mohammed Ahmed

Therefore the join operation *Courses* ⋈ *Departments* would produce the following, see Table 2.5.

Table 2.5: Table produced by join operation Courses ⋈ Departments

Course ID	Course name	Department	Head of department
001	BTEC IT L3	Computing	Wendy Smith
002	HNC Child care	Health and social care	Alan Jones
003	A level Business	Business studies	Mohammed Ahmed
004	A Level Computing	Computing	Wendy Smith

Union

The *union* operation requires the two tables to have the same fields, and it involves taking all the records that are in one table or in the other table (or in both) and putting them together. Duplicate records are eliminated. The symbol for union is ∪. For example, imagine two separate tables containing customer details (see Tables 2.7 and 2.8).

Table 2.6: Customer_table1

Name	Address	Postcode	Telephone number
J Smith	10 High Street	NR6 2ZZ	01883 12345
A Jones	22 Station Road	IP95 1QQ	01999 22222
B Williams	105 London Road	N65 6XX	01888 33333
G Anderson	4 North Lane	E88 4VV	02946 11133

Table 2.7: Customer_table2

Name	Address	Postcode	Telephone number
A Jones	22 Station Road	IP95 1QQ	01999 22222
S Evans	165 Main Avenue	AB69 4KK	0345 998877
G Anderson	4 North Lane	E88 4VV	02946 11133
T Thomas	52 Harbour Lane	SW8 9ZQ	01998 88888

Therefore the *union* operation *Customer_table1* ∪ *Customer_table2* would produce the following (see Table 2.8).

Table 2.8: Table produced by union operation Customer_table1 ∪ Customer_table2

Name	Address	Postcode	Telephone number
J Smith	10 High Street	NR6 2ZZ	01883 12345
A Jones	22 Station Road	IP95 1QQ	01999 22222
B Williams	105 London Road	N65 6XX	01888 33333
G Anderson	4 North Lane	E88 4VV	02946 11133
S Evans	165 Main Avenue	AB69 4KK	0345 998877
T Thomas	52 Harbour Lane	SW8 9ZQ	01998 88888

Intersect

The *intersect* operation is similar to the union operation but only those records that appear in both the tables are selected (the records where the two tables intersect or overlap). The symbol for intersect is ?. For example, using the same two customer details tables from the union operation section, the intersect operation *Customer_table1* ? *Customer_table2* would produce the following (see Table 2.9).

Table 2.9: Table produced by intersect operation Customer_table1 ? Customer_table2

Name	Address	Postcode	Telephone number
A Jones	22 Station Road	IP95 1QQ	01999 22222
G Anderson	4 North Lane	E88 4VV	02946 11133

Database relations

We have already mentioned how, in a relational database, tables can be related to each other. These relationships between tables model real-world relationships and are called entity relationships.

Entity relationships

Entities (table) are real-world things like customers, books, courses, authors and teachers. Entities often have relationships with each other which are called entity relationships. So for example, customers order goods, books are written by authors and courses are taught by teachers.

There are three types of entity relationships, the most common of which is one-to-many.

One-to-many entity relationships

Look back at the Worked example: Ordering from an online store. The example we used was of a customer who ordered goods from an online store and the store recorded the order, but kept the data about the customer in a separate table to the data about the order.

The tables in that example were linked using the customer number. This means that the customer details only need to be recorded once, no matter how many orders the customer places. Therefore one customer record can be related to as many different order records as the customer places. However, in the Orders table, each record is related to one and only one customer, since the same order cannot be placed by two different customers. This is called a *one-to-many relationship* (between one customer and many orders). To help conceptualise databases designs, it is common to draw a diagrammatic representation of the relations and the relationships between them using an *entity-relationship diagram (ERD)*. The relationship between the Customer and the Orders tables (Figure 2.2) would be drawn as follows (see Figure 2.3).

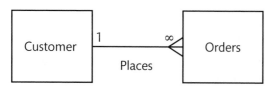

▶ **Figure 2.3:** An ERD showing the relationship between the Customer and Orders tables

Note that the connecting line which shows the relationship has a '1' at the customer end and a ∞ at the order end. This shows that the Orders table can have many records related to one record on the Customer table.

Although the one-to-many entity relationship is the most common, there two other types of entity relationships which can exist.

One-to-one entity relationships

In a one-to-one entity relationship, one record in the first table is related to one and only one record in the other table. An example of this might be an employee database. Some employees might have a company car or van. Data about company cars is likely to be kept on a separate table (the Company car table) from general employee data (the Employee table), because it is not data about the employee directly and not every employee will have a company car or van (only those who need to travel to complete their work). However, no employee can have more than one company car, so the relationship between the Employee table and the Company car table is a one-to-one relationship. Every record on the Company car table is related to one and only one record on the Employee table. Similarly, one and only one record on the Employee table is related to one and only one record in the Company car table. When drawn in an ERD diagram, the relationship looks as shown in Figure 2.4.

▶ **Figure 2.4:** An ERD diagram showing the one-to-one entity relationship between the Employee and Company car tables

Many-to-many entity relationships

The final type of relationship is the many-to-many entity relationship where one record in the first table can be related to many records in the second table, and *vice versa*. So, unlike with a one-to-many relationship, one record in the second table can also be related to many records in the first table. Imagine a database of college students and the subjects that they study. In the Student table, each student record will be related to many subjects (listed in the Subject table) that each student studies. However, in the Subject table, each subject record would be related to the many different students that take that subject (listed in the Student table).

Many-to-many relationships cannot be represented directly in a relational database and have to be broken down into three tables with a link or mapping table linking the two main tables. The example of the Student and Subject tables can be used to explain how this works. As already mentioned, linked tables require a unique identifier for each record so, in this example, the unique identifier for the Student table is likely to be a student number, while for the Subject table it is likely to be a subject code. To make the mapping table (which can be called Student-subjects) the unique identifier attribute is taken from each table and used to create a link between students and subjects. Where a single student is, for example, taking four subjects, four records are created in the Student-subjects table, all with the same student number but with each record containing a different subject code for the four subjects they are studying. See Figure 2.5 for an ERD diagram for the many-to-many relationship between students and subjects.

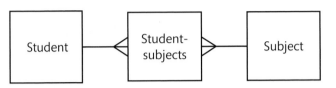

▶ **Figure 2.5:** An ERD diagram showing the relationship between the Student and Subjects tables using a mapping table called Student-subjects

In addition, the Student-subjects mapping table has a one-to-many relationship with the Student table (one student can be related to many mapping table records) and, likewise, the Subject table has a one-to-many relationship with the Student-subjects table, so one subject record is related to many records on the Student-subjects table.

Generic and semantic

Relationships can be modelled in a *generic* way (that is, generalised and non-specific) when you first attempt to understand the design of a complex system. Then, as your understanding develops, you can create a *semantic* (that is logical) model of the relationship between specific data items. The topic of designing database relations is covered in more detail under section B, when conceptual and logical data models are explained.

Link

For more on designing database relations see Relational database design.

Relational keys

We have already mentioned the need for unique identifiers, such as a customer number or subject code, in the tables of a relational database. These unique identifiers are known as keys. Keys not only uniquely identify records within a database, but they can also be used to speed up searching for records because the database keeps an index

of keys so that it can find key values without searching through the whole database.

Primary key

The unique identifier for a table is known as the **primary key**. Each table should have a primary key and, within the table, each key value must be unique.

Candidate keys

When designing a database table you may have a choice of fields which may make a suitable primary key. For example, a company may have a database of its employees. Possible primary keys that they could use might be the employees' national insurance (NI) numbers or unique employee numbers. These different possible primary keys are known as the **candidate keys**. During the database design process, the decision must be made as to which of the candidate keys is to be chosen as the primary key, as there can only be one primary key per table in a database.

Foreign keys

As already explained, when creating a relationship between two tables, the primary key value of one table is inserted into the table that it is linked to. So, using the example discussed earlier of the online ordering system, orders are related to the customer that ordered them by taking the customer number (the primary key) from the Customer table and putting it into the orders saved on the Orders table, which shows the orders that the particular customer has placed. This value (customer number) could not be the primary key value on the Orders table because a customer can place many orders, so it would not be unique in the Orders table. Instead, the Orders table would most likely have a primary key of order number. However, the customer number in the Orders table is known as a **foreign key** because it is a key in another table.

Key term

Primary key – a field which can uniquely identify one and only one record in a table.

Candidate key – a field or combination of fields which could provide a unique identifier for a table. Typically in a table there may be several candidate keys which could be chosen as the primary key for the table.

Foreign key – the primary key from a record in a table at the 'one' end of a one-to-many entity relationship, which is used as a field in records in the table at the 'many' end, to provide the link between the records.

Composite keys

In some situations it may be necessary to combine several attributes to create a unique key for a table. This is known as the **composite key** (also called a super key). For example, imagine a database of books in a library. The book title alone would not necessarily uniquely identify a book, as two books could have the same title. However, the book title combined with the author's name might be a better choice. But suppose there were several editions of the book. In this case, the book title and author name would not be unique, but including the edition number in the composite key as well would create a unique value (a super key). There might, of course, be several copies of the book in the library, in which case the copy number would also need to be included in the super key.

Integrity constraints

The integrity of the data in a database is important. For example, in the online ordering system, what would happen if there was a record in the Orders table with no related record on the Customer table, perhaps due to an invalid customer number? This would be a 'lost' order with no customer to deliver it to. The issues of entity and referential integrity are covered in detail later in this unit.

Manipulating data structures and data in relational databases

Having data organised into related tables is all very well but, for the database to be useful, there must be a way to find and extract data from the database. There also need to be methods for giving users access to the database, and for securing and recovering the database.

We have already used the tools that Access® provides to create tables. Once a table has been created, data can be entered into the table using the Datasheet View. You can also modify data in the table in Datasheet View. You can return to the Design View of the table at any time and modify its structure, although care should be taken in making changes to fields which already contain data. For example, if you change the datatype of a field from text to a numeric datatype, then data already in the field will not match the new datatype. You can also delete records in Datasheet View.

Typically, in a database containing a large number of records, you would want to be able to find a specific record (or group of records) within a table which match certain requirements. This can be done using the standard database query language known as SQL, which can be used on almost any relational database, not just Microsoft® Access®.

SQL

Structured query language (SQL) is the standard language used to create queries and extract data from a relational database. SQL is used to define, modify and remove data structures and data, including allowing you to insert new records into a database, delete records and update records.

Retrieval of data for queries and reports

SQL can be used to retrieve data for queries and reports using the SQL command select query.

Step by step: SQL Select query   4 Steps

1 To demonstrate how to use SQL commands to retrieve data, we will use a simple single table Access®
database that might be used by an animal charity to keep records for rescue dogs awaiting adoption. The single
table (called Rescue_Dogs) is shown here.

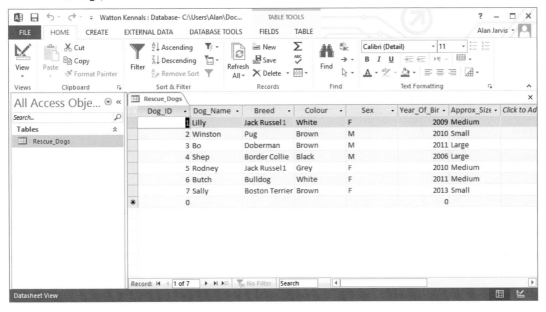

2 To create a query in Access®, click on Create in the menu bar, then chose Query Design in the toolbar. Access®
will ask you which table you want to add to the query: there is only one, Rescue_Dogs, so click Add, and then
Close to close the Show Table dialog box.

The default view that Access® provides for creating queries is the Design View, which provides a visual drag and
drop interface for creating queries. However, you want to use SQL View, so click on the View icon (far left of the
toolbar) and choose SQL View from the drop-down list. You will then see the display shown here.

3 One of the simplest things you can do with the SQL Select statement is just display certain fields. Suppose you just wanted to display the dog name and breed. The SQL statement for that is:

SELECT dog_name, breed FROM Rescue_Dogs

You can see this in SQL View here.

4 Now click the View icon again and select Datasheet View. You should see something like this.

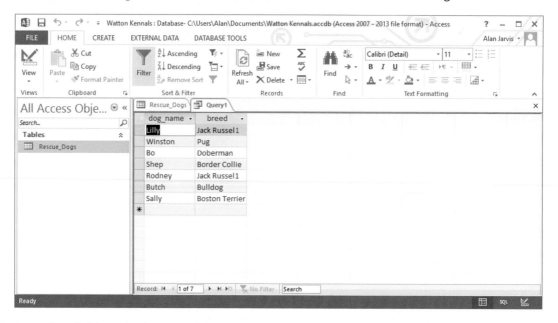

Using SQL to select fields to display is useful, but what is even more useful is the ability to select records from the database which match certain criteria. This can be done using the SQL SELECT...WHERE clause.

Step by step: SQL Select...where

1 Suppose, for example, you were only interested in medium size dogs. This kind of selection uses the SELECT... WHERE clause. To display all the fields you use the * symbol, so the command would be:

SELECT * FROM Rescue_Dogs WHERE approx_size = 'Medium'

This is shown here.

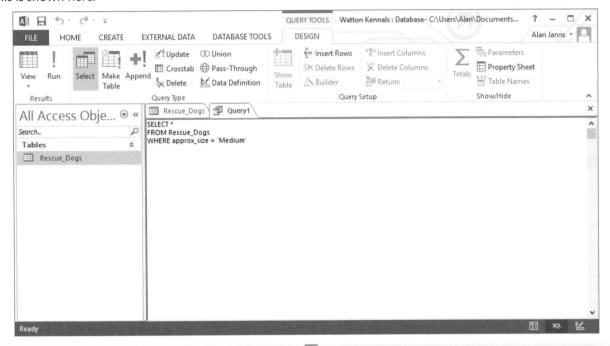

2 If you swap from the Query View to the Datasheet View, you can see the result of the SQL command, with just medium dogs listed, as shown here.

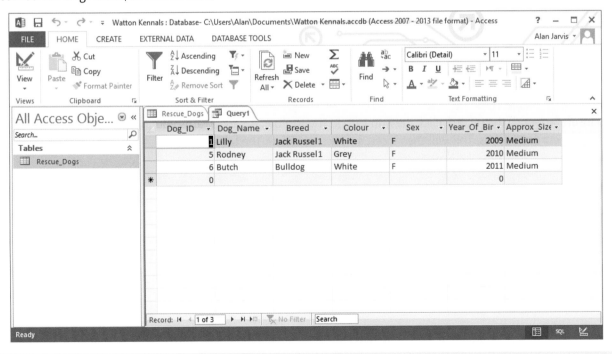

Inserting

You can also use SQL to insert new records. This is done using the SQL command INSERT INTO.

Step by step: SQL Insert into

2 Steps

1 Change the type of query to an Append Query by clicking the Append icon in the toolbar. Access® will ask you where you want to append the records to, so select the only table: Rescue_Dogs. The correct command to insert a single record is as follows:

> INSERT INTO Rescue_Dogs (Dog_ID, Dog_Name, Breed, Colour, Sex, Year_Of_Birth, Approx_Size)
>
> VALUES (8, 'Patch', 'Alsatian', 'Black', 'M', 2013, 'Large')

(Note that the text fields are enclosed in quotes but the numeric fields are not.)
The command is shown typed into SQL View here.

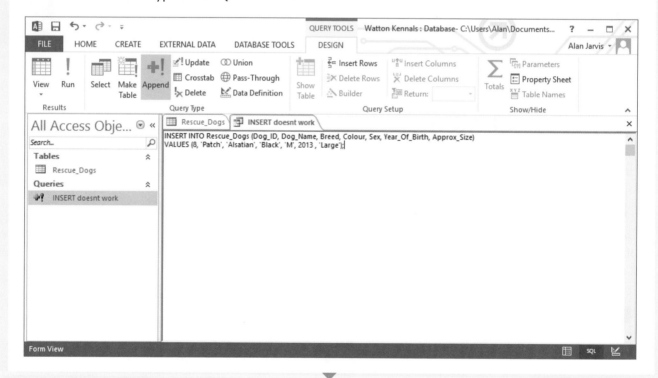

2 To insert (append) the record, click the Run icon in the toolbar. Access® warns you that you are about to append a record. Click Yes. This will then insert a new record into the table.

Updating

The final SQL command that you will need is the Update command. As the name suggests, this allows you to update existing records.

Step by step: SQL Update　　　　　　　　　　　　　　　　　　3 Steps

1 To create the command, first use the Create menu to make a new Query Design. Add the Rescue_Dogs table, as before, then click the Update icon in the toolbar to make it an update query. Now swap to SQL View. Suppose it was discovered that a mistake had been made and the Border Collie breed of dogs should have been classified as 'Medium' size rather than 'Large'. The SQL command to update the data accordingly is:

    UPDATE Rescue_Dogs SET Approx_Size='Medium'

    WHERE Breed='Border Collie'

This can be seen here.

2 Click the Run icon and Access® warns you that you are about to update a record. Click Yes and the update is completed.

3 You can also delete a record using SQL. The command is used in a similar way to the select command, so the command would delete all the medium sized dogs from the table. Care should be taken when using delete. There is no 'undo' option.

    DELETE FROM Rescue_Dogs WHERE approx_size = 'Medium'

Using SQL like this seems very longwinded compared with using the drag-and-drop query design interface. However, you would not normally use SQL like this – it would be built into a database procedure which runs automatically without user intervention.

The output from SQL statements or queries can be displayed in the table format shown here, but more commonly reports or forms are used to format and display the output.

> **Link**
>
> There is a lot more you can do with SQL. You can find a full SQL course with examples at www.w3schools.com.

Administration of users and database security

Where a database is used by multiple people, that is, a multi-user database, it is important that there are procedures in place to control what actions different users can carry out on the database. This is because not all users need to be able to edit and they may only want to view the database. It can also be safer to not allow editing access to all users so that human error is less likely to occur. It is unlikely that all users would be allowed full access to every part of the database.

Controlling which actions can be carried out by different users is typically done by creating users and then granting them permissions, such as the ability to insert, update and delete records. The primary method of maintaining database security is by maintaining the system of database permissions, as described above, by ensuring that users have strong passwords and that they only have the permissions required to do their jobs and no more.

In addition, the following security procedures can help to secure a database.

▶ Hardening of the underlying system by the application of standard security procedures: ensuring the system has up-to-date software, virus protection, and through the use of firewalls.
▶ Database auditing and monitoring can be used with sensitive data. Logs are kept of the changes to the database and are reviewed regularly. Database monitoring systems can automatically look for unusual activity on the database in an attempt to identify things such as credit card fraud or an attack by a hacker.

Integrity and recovery

Ensuring the integrity of a database is a very important consideration and there are two main aspects to it: design integrity and physical integrity.

> **Link**
>
> The topic of design integrity is covered in the section on Database anomalies.

The design of a database needs to ensure that there are no inconsistencies in the structure of the tables (entities) and the ways in which they are related: this is entity integrity. The process of normalisation, as described in the next section, is used to check the entity integrity of the database.

Physical integrity

There must be mechanisms in place to ensure that data stored on disk is protected from corruption: this is physical integrity.

Multi-user server-based database systems are usually implemented on high availability hardware. These include RAID disk systems, which use multiple disks to provide protection from single disk hardware failures, and other duplicated hardware. They provide a good degree of protection from hardware failure. However, the system can still be vulnerable to software failure. If the database system crashes part way through a **database transaction,** this can lead to inconsistencies and a mechanism to recover the database is required. Depending on the application, certain types of transaction must be completed, either in their entirety or not at all.

> **Key term**
>
> **Database transaction** – A complete set of actions required to complete some task in a database. Transactions related to database systems, such as withdrawing money from an ATM machine or booking an airline ticket, are made up of several steps such as authentication of the user, selecting the required item and paying for a purchase.

Many database transactions consist of data being added or updated on several tables. For example, when booking an airline ticket, there are several parts to the transaction, such as reserving the seat and paying for the ticket. In order to ensure the integrity of the transactions, database systems keep a log of changes to the database which have been completed and commit points where transactions have been successfully completed. Should the system crash, the log is used to identify any transactions which have not reached the commit point (that is, they have not been successfully completed). Those changes which are part of an incomplete transaction are then undone or rolled back, to the previous commit point. This ensures that the database is recovered to a consistent state.

(II)   PAUSE POINT   What kinds of database need strong security? From time to time, commercial databases are attacked and you may read in the news about the problems they have encountered. Have you heard of any recent attacks? How was data stolen and what were the consequences?

Hint   SQL injection is a software vulnerability which can be used by hackers to gain access to data held on databases associated with web applications. SQL injection has been used in a number of recent high profile attacks in which large quantities of data have been stolen.

Extend   What is SQL injection and how does it work?

How can you protect against it?

Normalisation

When considering a real-life situation that you want to model using a relational database, it can sometimes be difficult to see how to divide up the data into different related tables in the most efficient way. The process of normalisation has been developed to help database designers create designs that avoid data redundancy (duplicated data), which, in turn, minimises storage requirements and helps to avoid the problems that occur with duplicated data. For example, if a customer's postcode is held on a database in two different tables, then should the customer move house and change their postcode, it may not be updated in more than one table, which may cause anomalies.

The process of normalisation is an important part of the database design process. The outcome of the process of normalisation will be a **verified** database design which identifies the main structure of the database, including:

▶ the tables that the database will be split into

▶ the indexes used, including the primary and foreign keys and any composite keys required for the tables

▶ the structure of the individual tables from which the data dictionary can be created.

> **Key term**
>
> **Verification** – Verification is the process of checking that something is correct. Normalisation is the process used to verify the database design.

Following on from the normalisation process, database designers need to consider the issue of referential integrity and how the updating and deletion of records on related tables is dealt with.

The stages of normalisation

Normalisation is a three-stage process which begins with raw data, such as you might extract from a paper-based system that the database you are designing will replace.

Summary of the stages of normalisation

1 The process starts off with raw data, which is referred to as un-normalised (UNF).

2 The first stage takes raw data and modifies its structure to the meet the requirements of 1st normal form (1NF).

3 The second stage further modifies the 1NF structure to meet the requirements of 2nd normal form (2NF).

4 The third stage takes the 2NF data structure and modifies it to meet the requirements of 3rd normal form (3NF).

To demonstrate the process we will return to the example of the online ordering system. Figure 2.6 gives an idea of the sort of paper-based order form the database will emulate.

This is our un-normalised data (UNF). Note that the order number and the customer details appear just once but the product details repeat for each item ordered.

Universal Products Ltd

Order No 1

Customer: Bert Smith
　　　　　　10 High Street
　　　　　　Norwich

Ordered Items

Product ID	Product description	Price	Quantity	Total
P33	Camera	£35.00	1	£35.00
P09	Book	£8.00	3	£24.00
P21	Headphones	£22.00	2	£44.00
			Total	£103.00

▶ **Figure 2.6:** Paper-based order form

Stage 1: 1st Normal form

The first stage of normalisation involves modifying the data to meet the requirements of 1st normal form (1NF) by doing the following.

▶ Remove any calculated fields (such as total order value).

▶ Make sure that each data item is **atomic**. The customer name is not atomic since it can be split into 'First name' and 'Surname'. The same is true of the customer address but, for simplicity, we will ignore this attribute.

▶ Remove repeating groups so that there is a data item for every record for each attribute. So for example, in the paper-based order form, the order number and customer number occur just once but we must include them in each record on our new 1NF table.

▶ Finally, we must select a primary key (which needs to be unique). There is no one value which is unique but we can create a composite key using the Order Number and the Product ID.

The completed 1NF table is shown here (Table 2.10). More orders have been added to make the process clearer. The key fields are indicated by underlining the attribute name.

<aside>
Key term

Atomic – in this context, atomic means broken down into individual parts. For example, in terms of its suitability for a database field a person's name is not atomic because it can be broken down into title, first name, middle names and surname.
</aside>

▶ **Table 2.10:** Completed 1NF table (underlined attributes are the key fields)

Order no.	Product ID	Customer no.	Customer FName	Customer SName	Description	Price	Quantity
1	P33	C10	Bert	Smith	Camera	£35	1
1	P09	C10	Bert	Smith	Book	£8	3
1	P21	C10	Bert	Smith	Headphones	£22	2
2	P09	C5	Wendy	Jones	Book	£8	1
2	P15	C5	Wendy	Jones	Trainers	£40	1
3	P21	C12	Alice	Williams	Headphones	£22	1
3	P19	C12	Alice	Williams	Pen	£6	2

Stage 2: 2nd Normal form

The second stage of normalisation is to modify the data to meet the requirements of 2nd normal form (2NF). If a table has a primary key based on a single attribute, then nothing needs to be done at the 2NF stage. However, our table does have a composite key. In this case, we need to move any data that is only **dependent on** one part of the composite key attributes to a separate table.

The data that are only dependent on one part of the composite key attributes are the Description and Price, as these only depend on the Product ID and should not be in the OrderNumber table. If you know the Product ID, then you can find the Description and Price, but knowing the order number alone will not uniquely identify the product (as several items may be on the order). The completed 2NF tables now look like this (Tables 2.11–12).

> **Key term**
>
> **Dependent on** – one field depends on another if you can only find out the unique value of the second field if you know the value of the first one. For example, if you know the Product ID, then you can find the description and the price.

▶ **Table 2.11:** Completed 2NF – Product table

Product ID	Description	Price
P33	Camera	£35
P09	Book	£8
P21	Headphones	£22
P15	Trainers	£40
P19	Pen	£6

▶ **Table 2.12:** Completed 2NF – Main table

Order no.	Customer no.	Customer FName	Customer SName	Product ID	Quantity
1	C10	Bert	Smith	P33	1
1	C10	Bert	Smith	P09	3
1	C10	Bert	Smith	P21	2
2	C5	Wendy	Jones	P09	1
2	C5	Wendy	Jones	P15	1
3	C12	Alice	Williams	P21	1
3	C12	Alice	Williams	P19	2

Note that the duplicates are removed from the Product table but the Product ID is left in the main table as a foreign key.

Stage 3: 3rd Normal form

The third and final stage in normalisation is to modify the data to meet the requirements of 3rd normal form (3NF). The requirement of 3NF is that none of the non-primary key attributes should depend on any other attributes. If they do, then they need to be moved to another table, leaving a copy of the primary key field for the new table in the original table as a foreign key.

In the main table, Customer no. will allow you to find a unique customer name (First and Surname) and, since these are not key attributes, they need to be moved to another table (the Customer table) with a copy of the key for that new table (customer number) left in the main table as a foreign key. The 3NF tables are shown here (Tables 2.13–15).

▶ **Table 2.13:** 3NF – Product table

Product ID	Description	Price
P33	Camera	£35
P09	Book	£8
P21	Headphones	£22
P15	Trainers	£40
P19	Pen	£6

▶ **Table 2.14:** 3NF – Main table

Order no.	Customer no.	Product ID	Quantity
1	C10	P33	1
1	C10	P09	3
1	C10	P21	2
2	C5	P09	1
2	C5	P15	1
3	C12	P21	1
3	C12	P19	2

▶ **Table 2.15:** 3NF – Customer table

Customer no.	Customer FName	Customer SName
C10	Bert	Smith
C5	Wendy	Jones
C12	Alice	Williams

However, the data shown in Tables 2.13–15 are not fully normalised yet because in the main table there is dependence between Order number and Customer number. Since an order is only placed by one customer, if you know the order number, you can find the customer number. Order number and customer number therefore need to go in their own table (the Orders table) as shown here in the completed 3NF tables (Tables 2.16–19).

▶ **Table 2.16:** Completed 3NF – Product table

Product ID	Description	Price
P33	Camera	£35
P09	Book	£8
P21	Headphones	£22
P15	Trainers	£40
P19	Pen	£6

▶ **Table 2.17:** Completed 3NF – Customer table

Customer no.	Customer FName	Customer SName
C10	Bert	Smith
C5	Wendy	Jones
C12	Alice	Williams

▶ **Table 2.18:** Completed 3NF – Orders table

Order no.	Customer no.
1	C10
2	C5
3	C12

▶ **Table 2.19:** Completed 3NF – Order products table

Order no.	Product ID	Quantity
1	P33	1
1	P09	3
1	P21	2
2	P09	1
2	P15	1
3	P21	1
3	P19	2

Note that the remaining table is named the Order products table since it identifies which products are on each order.

Database anomalies

The process of normalisation is designed to help reduce the possibility of anomalies occurring as the database is used. To see how anomalies might occur in a database which has not been fully normalised we shall look at an expanded version of the table we used to demonstrate how data at 1NF looked in the section Stage 1 of The stages of normalisation (see Table 2.20).

Research

Although for this qualification you only need to understand the process of normalisation up to 3rd Normal form (3NF), there are higher levels of normalisation. Find out what these are and why they might be needed.

▶ **Table 2.20:** Expanded version of Completed 1NF table

Order no.	Product ID	Customer no.	Customer FName	Customer SName	Address	Description	Price	Quantity
1	P33	C10	Bert	Smith	10 High St	Camera	£35	1
1	P09	C10	Bert	Smith	10 High St	Book	£8	3
1	P21	C10	Bert	Smith	10 High St	Headphones	£22	2
2	P09	C5	Wendy	Jones	3 Station Rd	Book	£8	1
2	P15	C5	Wendy	Jones	3 Station Rd	Trainers	£40	1
3	P21	C12	Alice	Williams	2 London Rd	Headphones	£22	1
3	P19	C12	Alice	Williams	2 London Rd	Pen	£6	2

The following type of anomalies can occur with this kind of 1NF database table:

▶ insert

▶ delete

▶ update.

Link

See the original table of data at 1NF in the section Stage 1 of The stages of normalisation Table 2.10

Insert anomalies

To insert a new order into the database, the customer's name has to been entered even if that customer has previously placed an order. This gives rise to the possibility of errors or inconsistencies.

Another possible source of anomalies is the fact that an existing customer might need to enter their address every time they place an order. Compare this with the 3NF version of the database (Table 2.17). In this, the customer details (only Customer Fname and Sname are shown, but address details would be in the same table) are recorded once only per customer in the Customer table. Only the Customer no. attribute needs to be recorded in the Orders table.

Another issue would be registering of new customers. In the 1NF version of the database, a new customer could only be registered if they placed an order as the Product ID is part of the composite key. Therefore, it is not possible to create a record with a null value in the Product ID attribute (that is, it is impossible to create a customer account without placing a record).

Delete anomalies

If a customer places an order and then later cancels it, it needs to be deleted. However, if that customer does not have any other orders, then all their details will be lost since without an order you cannot have any customer details (you cannot have a customer record). This is avoided in the 3NF version of the database as customer details are held in a separate table.

Update anomalies

If a customer changes their address, for example, then all the records containing orders for that customer may need to be searched to change the address on those orders too. Again, this is avoided in the 3NF version of the database, as customer details are held in a separate table.

Another issue which makes the 1NF version of the database unworkable is that of products and their details. In this version, only products which have been ordered can exist on the database. The only way to add a new product is if someone orders it. This clearly would not be acceptable in practice.

As you can see from the normalisation example we have completed, the process helps you to decide on the indexing, including the primary, foreign and composite keys required for each table. The completed table diagrams can be used as the basis for the data dictionary, which will include full details of the tables, attributes, data types and validation required for the whole database.

Referential integrity and cascading update/delete

One issue that can occur with a relational database is how to deal with linked records when deleting or updating a record at the 'one' end of a one-to-many relationship. Consider the Customer and Orders relationship. One customer can place many orders and the link is made by placing the Customer table primary key attribute as a foreign key in the Order table.

But what happens if a customer closes his account with the company? If we delete the customer record alone, that will leave orders on the Order table with no corresponding customer. These might be considered 'lost' orders and might cause problems with an application which expects to see every order linked to a customer record. One alternative is to use cascading updates, where deleting a record on the Customer table would automatically delete related records on the Order table. Microsoft® Access® (and SQL Server) provides an option to switch this facility on, which is known as referential integrity.

> **Reflect**
>
> In reality, would you want to completely delete a customer record and their associated orders?
>
> What alternatives might there be?
>
> Are there any legal implications of retaining customer details for people who close their accounts?

Another problem may occur if you were to allow updates to the key field to which other records are related. Imagine an employee database where the key field for the Employee table was the employee's NI number. Staff annual appraisal records are linked to the employee record by inserting the primary key from the Employee table (the NI number) as a foreign key on the Appraisals table. Consider what would happen if it was discovered that a data entry error had been made in one employee's NI number and it was updated to be correct. This would mean that all of the employee's appraisal records would be 'lost' because the NI number on the parent record had changed. The referential integrity setting in Microsoft® Access® and SQL Server allows you to prevent changes to key fields which exist as foreign keys in other tables.

> **Reflect**
>
> Is the use of an employee's NI number as the primary key field a good idea?
>
> What alternative key fields could be used to avoid the problem of updates?

Step by step: Creating relationships in Access® | 6 Steps

1 You can create as many tables as you like in a single Access® database. Linking them together can be done as long as your design is correct and you have used the primary key from the 'one' end of a relationship as a foreign key in the table at the 'many' end of the relationship.

2 Assume that, as well as the Customer table that we created earlier, you have also created tables for Products, Orders and Order-Products following the design created during the normalisation process described in the Stages of normalisation.

3 To link them together, go to the Database Tools menu in Access® and click on the Relationships icon in the toolbar. The Show Table dialog box will appear, asking which tables you want to create relationships for. Click each of the tables in turn and click Add then, after you have added them all, click Close. The relationships display should now look like this.

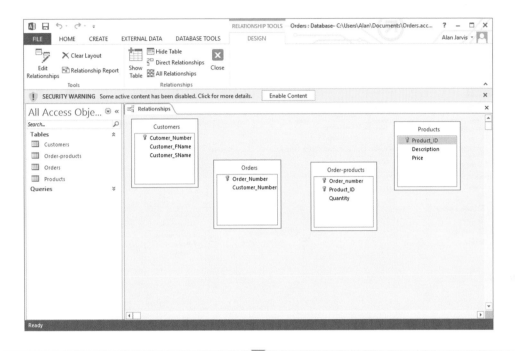

4 First, we will create the relationship between the Customer table and the Orders table. Click on the Customer_Number field in the Customer table (the primary key) and drag it over to the Customer_Number field in the Orders table (the foreign key). The dialog box shown here will appear.

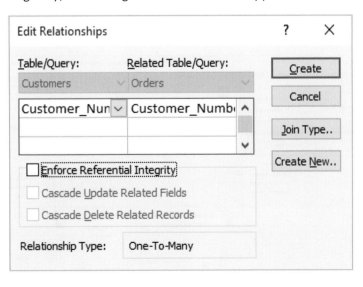

5 The appearance of the dialog box shows that Access® has identified that this is a one-to-many relationship (it knows this because the field is a primary key on the Customer table). It also gives you the option to enforce referential integrity so that it will not allow you to delete records or modify the primary key value of records on the Customer table that have related orders. You can also turn on the Cascade Update and Cascade Delete features so that if a customer is deleted from the customer table all of their orders will automatically be deleted (rather than you just getting an error message), or if you update the Customer number field on the Customer table related records on the orders will also be updated. Turn these options on and then click Create. The relationships display should now look like this.

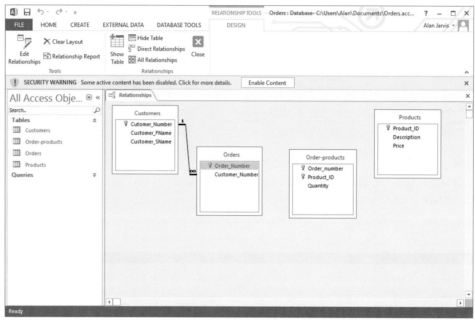

6 Now do the same with Order_Number in the Orders table (primary key) and the Order_number in the Order-products table. Finally create the relationship between the Product_ID (primary key) in the Products table and the Product_ID in the Order-products table. The relationships should now look like this.

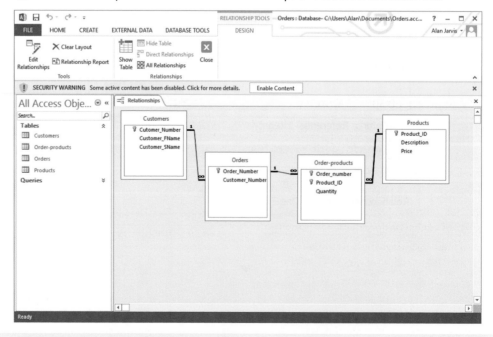

Standard methods and techniques to design relational database solutions

Now that you have looked at the theoretical structure of RDBMS, you will investigate the standard methods and techniques used to design relational database solutions. As with any software application development, the process starts with building an understanding of the user requirements and progresses through to creating more and more detailed models and designs for the system.

Relational database design

In many cases, databases can be very large and complex and a lot of design work needs to go into their creation and development. The design needs to be carefully considered, as resolving design errors during the development or implementation of the database can be difficult and costly. As well as the designs for the application, the selection of suitable hardware, software tools, techniques and processes needs to be considered. With a multi-user server database, hardware needs to be selected which has sufficient performance and capacity to support the expected transaction volumes.

Database design

The designing of a large and complex database system involves a number of phases. The first phase is a broad conceptual overview of the database design, after which more detail and complexity are added in later design phases. The design process is an iterative one, with continual refinements and improvements being made. There are often three phases to the design process.

1 Conceptual database design – This is the first phase and involves building a **conceptual model** of the information used in the database system based on the details provided in the user requirements specification. It does not take into account the physical implementation details such as the database software to be used or hardware platforms. It involves the identification of tables and their relationships, as well as the drawing of an outline ERD.

2 Logical database design – This phase takes the conceptual model and refines it further into a **logical model**. The process of logical design involves arranging data into a series of logical relationships (tables and fields) and taking into account the requirement of the relational database model and the selected RDBMS software. The logical design defines the detailed structure for the tables, relationships and fields. This design is then validated using the normalisation process.

3 Physical database design – This final phase involves deciding how the database will actually be implemented on the chosen RDBMS software and hardware. It includes calculations of the required storage space. It defines the storage structures, methods of access that will be used and security protection that will be applied.

Key term

Conceptual model – is based on generalisation and ideas (concepts) such as 'a customer places an order'.

Logical model – takes the concepts and applies rules (logic) to the concepts (including verifying them with normalisation) and adding details such as the nature of the relationship which exists between customer and order (via the primary and foreign keys).

The table below (Table 2.21) shows at which phase various aspects of the design are defined.

▶ **Table 2.21:** Phases at which design aspects of a database are defined

Design feature	Design phase		
	Conceptual	**Logical**	**Physical**
Entity names	✓		
Entity relationships	✓		
Fields		✓	
Keys (primary and foreign)		✓	
Field names			✓
Field datatypes			✓

Link

An example of conceptual and logical design models can be found in the section on Design documentation.

Relational algebra

As part of the design process, the types of relationship between tables will be defined using entity-relationship (ER) models and tested using normalisation. Most relationships are likely to be one-to-many, with the primary and foreign keys identified as part of the design process. There may also be some one-to-one relationships required. Remember that many-to-many relationships, identified in the conceptual design phase, will need to be split into separate linked tables at the logical design phase.

Link

For a reminder of the various different types of entity relationships, see Database relations.

The queries used to extract data from the database also need to be designed, using SQL and Boolean operators such as AND, OR and NOT and comparison operators such as > (greater than), < (less than), ≥ (greater than or equal to), ≤ (less than or equal to).

Link

For more on Boolean operators, see *Unit 5: Data modelling, Logical functions*, and for more on comparison operators, see *Unit 7: Mobile apps development, Operators*.

RDBMS and SQL selection

There are a range of different RDBMS software applications available, almost all of which include the SQL language. The main considerations for selecting a RDBMS are the following.

▶ What is the size of the implementation? – For small desktop databases, software application products such as Microsoft® Access® are suitable. For much larger client server-based requirements and web-based databases, software application products such as Oracle® Database, MySQL™ and Microsoft® SQL Server® are suitable.

Step by step: Using comparison and Boolean operators in SQL   6 Steps

1 These examples use the Rescue dogs table that was previously used to explain the basics of SQL (see Step by steps in the section SQL).

2 The comparison operators can only be used with numeric fields. So, for example, to find dogs born after 2010 you would enter:

    SELECT * FROM Rescue_Dogs WHERE Year_of_Birth > 2010

You can of course use the other comparison operators to get different results.

3 The Boolean operators allow you combine selection criteria. The AND operator finds records which match both the criteria you set. Suppose you wanted a small male dog. The SQL statement would be:

    SELECT * FROM Rescue_Dogs WHERE sex = 'M' AND approx_size = 'Small'

4 The OR operator selects records which match either of the criteria you set. So this statement will list all the male dogs and all the small ones (whatever sex they are):

    SELECT * FROM Rescue_Dogs WHERE sex = 'M' OR approx_size = 'Small'

5 You can also combine criteria and operators, for example this statement will find the female dogs who are either black or white:

    SELECT * FROM Rescue_Dogs WHERE sex = 'F' AND (colour = 'Black' or colour = 'White')

6 You can also use NOT in a WHERE condition. If you wanted to find all the dogs which are not the Doberman breed the command would be:

    SELECT * FROM Rescue_Dogs WHERE NOT Breed = 'Doberman'

▶ Is proprietary or open source software preferable? –
   MySQL™ is open source, while products from Oracle®
   and Microsoft® are proprietary and require a licence fee
   to be paid.

Application design

As with any software development project, the database
application 'front-end' needs to be designed, that is, the
interface that users see, as well as the structure. Many
database systems are accessed through a web-based front-
end (user interface) so this is one area where this topic
overlaps with website development.

> **Link**
>
> For more on principles that will be useful when
> designing the user interface for a database software
> application, see Unit 6: Website development, Principles
> of website design.

The user interface design will need to define the layout
of each screen, including labels (text to guide the users),
fields, controls (such as drop-down boxes and command
buttons), error messages and colour schemes. There will
also probably need to be software application designs that
define the procedures which connect the user interface to
the underlying database.

Database implementation techniques

Like any software development project there are a number
of ways in which the database and associated applications
can be designed and implemented. The approach taken
with a particular project will depend on a number of
factors including whether this is an entirely new database
application or if it is replacing some existing computer or
paper-based system.

Prototyping

The use of prototyping is one way to attempt to ensure
that the eventual product (database solution) meets
the users' requirements. Prototyping involves building a
simplified version of the system with limited functionality.
The prototype can then be demonstrated to the users to
see if it matches their requirements. Prototypes can be
further refined and added to and further demonstrations
done for the users. However, the problem with
prototyping is that it can delay the software development
process as building, demonstrating and refining the
prototypes can be time consuming. On the other hand,
by not prototyping and not getting confirmation from the
users that your design fulfils their requirements, you risk
building a database solution that does not meet the users'
requirements, therefore wasting time and money.

Data conversion

In cases where the new database system replaces an
existing system, the issue of data conversion needs to
be considered. Existing systems may contain very large
amounts of data which may need to be reformatted and
split into a different structure of tables and relationships.

Data may also need 'cleaning', that is, the removal of
inaccurate, invalid or erroneous data that, over time, has been
included amongst the valid data in the existing database.

These data conversion steps can be very time consuming if
a large volume of data is involved.

Testing

Once the design and development work is complete, the
database and its associated applications must be tested,
using the test data and plans created during the design
phase. If the system is large and developed in several parts,
it may be possible to test each part as it is completed.
However, once all the parts are complete, integration
testing of the whole system must also be done.

Quality, effectiveness and appropriateness of the solution

The quality, effectiveness and appropriateness of the
database solution design all need to be considered before
it is implemented.

Quality

The quality of the design has a direct impact on the eventual
quality of the completed database system. Although changes
can be made to the design where faults or omissions are
discovered during implementation, these can cause major
delays to the project and cost additional money.

Effectiveness and appropriateness

The effectiveness and appropriateness of the solution
is usually judged by the degree to which it meets the
user requirements, which is why understanding those
requirements is so important. The user requirements
themselves may contain a number of differing views.

For example, the people who will use the system may have
different requirements from those who are paying for the
development of the database (they are not always the
same people). These conflicts in user requirements should
be addressed by the database designer early on through
discussion with the people/organisation paying for the
development of the database. They need to consider the
needs of the users of the database, just as the designer
does, because if they do not then users either will not
purchase the database or not use it correctly.

Other factors

There are a number of other areas to be considered.

▸ Normalisation and relationships between data – The normalisation process should help to validate the design of the relationships between the data and the overall structure of the database.

▸ Correctness of data – It is very important that the data put into the database is as correct (accurate) as possible. Every opportunity should be taken to validate data. Also, the design of the user interface should, wherever possible, prevent the user from making invalid inputs. Clear error messages should be used, where appropriate, to make it clear why inputs are rejected.

▸ Data integrity – Careful consideration needs to be given as to how to maintain data integrity. This can include deciding whether or not to use the cascading update and delete features built into the database software to preserve referential integrity.

Reflect

Over the years, there have been a number of high profile database system developments which have failed for a variety of reasons. Perhaps the best known is the NHS patient records system – Google 'NHS system failure' for details. It may be that the user requirements were not well enough understood or the system was too complex.

How can you ensure, at the outset of a database development project, that it can be implemented successfully?

Design documentation

The design of a database needs to be documented so that the structure and component parts are implemented according to the design and to meet the user requirements. Also it is likely that, in the real world, the software development of the database system is designed and implemented by different people within a team.

In this section you will look, in detail, at the techniques and associated documentation that is created during the database design process.

Requirements of the brief

The first step in designing a database is to understand the client brief. This can be quite difficult as, often, the client will understand their business much better than the developer. The requirements need to be discussed with the client and a formal document, which describes the requirements in as much detail as possible, should be created and agreed on.

The requirements of the client brief are often the user requirements but they may also (or instead) be the requirements that the client has for the database, which may include constraints such as time for development and a budget.

The users of the database are known as the audience, and it is important to understand who they are and what they require from the database: that is, understand what their user requirements are. The purpose of the database means what it is for and what questions it needs to be able to answer – this should be part of the client brief.

Link

For more on the topic audience, purpose and client brief see *Unit 8: Computer games development, Audience, purpose and client requirements*.

Security and legal considerations

Many databases hold information about living individuals and, as such, come under the requirements of the Data Protection Act 1998 and The European Union (EU) Directive on Data Protection legislation.

When designing the database, the requirements in the Data Protection Act 1998 need to be considered.

This act stipulates that the data must be correct, it should be held securely and additional personal data not required for the application should not be collected

Correctness of data

Correctness of data is a major consideration for the database design and not just for the data protection requirements. Designers need to consider a number of different methods to try to ensure that the data that is recorded in the database is correct (accurate). This can include techniques such as validation of input data, as discussed earlier.

Securing data

Securing the database so that only those people who need to have access to the data can view or edit it can be done in a number of ways.

With a desktop database created with Access®, the database can be password protected and encrypted. This is particularly important if the database is stored on a laptop, which is vulnerable to theft.

Worked example: Dissford Arts Centre 1

A local arts centre has a small hall and a couple of studios which they rent out to music, drama and art groups to run workshops and performances. They have won a lottery grant to improve their facilities and build a small theatre and some music practice rooms. They want to replace the paper-based booking diary with a more sophisticated booking database.

The centre would like a prototype of the system to be developed before the complete database solution is implemented so that they can check that it meets their requirements.

The details of the requirements of the brief for the prototype database system are as follows.
- Audience – Initially, the arts centre staff will be the only users of the database, although eventually an online booking will be added.
- Purpose – The purpose of the database is to allow staff to search for and book free slots for the arts centre rooms. Initially, there will be just four rooms on the system: the large theatre hall, the small hall and two multi-purpose studios. Each room can be booked for an afternoon or an evening session.

The client's requirements are as follows.
- Users should be able to pull up a list of free slots (i.e. dates and sessions which are not already booked) for a given room within a date range.
- Users should be able to select and book a free slot.
- When booking a slot, users can select an existing client (i.e. person or organisation making the booking) or create a new client.

With a server-based database, a user access regime needs to be designed which restricts the access of users or groups of users to the database, so that they can carry out their jobs with regards to the database, but cannot do anything more to the database.

> **Link**
>
> For more on security and legal considerations, see *Unit 6: Website development, Legal and ethical considerations*.
>
> For more about the Data Protection Act 1998, see the Information Commissioner's Office website, www.ico.org.uk.

Data structure designs

The first step in designing data structures will probably be to look at any paper-based records and to take these through the process of conceptual, logical and physical modelling described earlier. The end result of the process should be a detailed ERD showing how the tables are related and a data dictionary which defines the fields required for each table. Ensuring that the data which ends up in the database is correct is very important and there are a number of ways you can help prevent incorrect data being accepted. This includes the details contained in the data dictionary about field dataatypes, lengths and validation rules.

Data dictionaries

The data dictionary for a database needs to define a number of things about each table in that database.
▶ Field names – Each field within a table needs to have a meaningful name.

> **Link**
>
> See Naming conventions for more on how to choose meaningful names for fields.

▶ Datatypes – You need to select an appropriate datatype for each field. Datatypes help to validate data as they prevent accidental errors. For example, by setting a numeric datatype for a field, you cannot accidentally enter text or, if you set a date field, you cannot enter invalid dates. Access® provides a range of text and numeric datatypes plus special ones such as date, currency and Boolean (Yes/No).

> **Tip**
>
> Note that the short text datatype defaults to a length of 255 characters, which is quite large, so you might want to make it shorter.

▶ Validation rules – You can also add a variety of rules to prevent invalid data being entered. For example, only 'M' or 'F' can be entered into a field recording a person's gender. This can use a short text datatype, of one character length. The easiest way to make sure that only the values of 'M' or 'F' are entered is use a lookup table. Lookup tables work fine where there are a defined number of options for a field but would not work where there is a range of numeric or date values. In this case, a validation rule is required. The following Step by step will show you how to use lookup tables to restrict values entered into a field. The second Step by step will show you how to set validation rules.

Lookup tables

Step by step: Lookup tables

4 Steps

1 To use a lookup table to restrict the values that can be entered into field, first go to the Design View for the table and then for the field in question. Select Lookup wizard from the drop-down list of datatypes. In this example, we will use the Rescue dogs table that we worked with previously, as shown here.

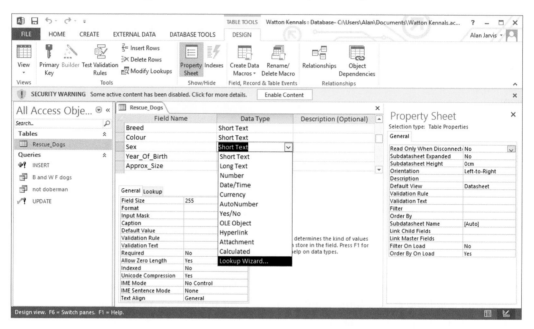

2 The Lookup wizard will then ask you if you want to look up the values in another table or query (which can be useful if there are a lot of values) or if you want to type them in yourself. As we only require 'M' or 'F', typing the values in yourself is the easiest option, so select this one and click Next. You will then see this next step of the wizard, as shown here.

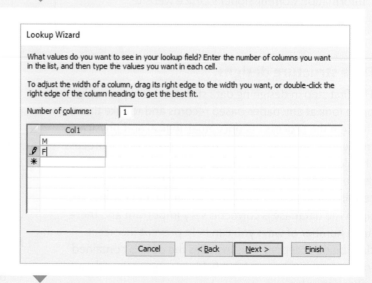

Care must be taken creating validation rules as, unless the validation text is clear, users may not understand why they cannot enter certain values in a field. Also, note that if you change the validation rules on an existing database table which contains data, all the records in the table need to be checked to ensure they do not violate the rule, which can take a long time if there are a lot of records. This is one of the reasons why it is important to get the design of the database right before you put lots of data in it.

Worked example: Dissford Arts Centre 1

Conceptual model

In order to create the design for the Dissford Arts Centre booking system database, the first step is to work on the conceptual model. From the current paper-based diary shown earlier, we can extract the following fields.

- Date (the date of the booking).
- Room name (can be Large theatre, Small hall, Studio 1 or Studio 2).
- Session (can be afternoon or evening).
- Client name.
- Client telephone number (plus other details such as address etc.).

If we put this into a single table and add some actual data, it would look something like this.

Date	Room	Session	Client name	Client tel	Client address	Client town
9/11/15	Large theatre	Afternoon				
9/11/15	Large theatre	Evening	Drama Club	012345678	10 High St	London
9/11/15	Small hall	Afternoon				
9/11/15	Small hall	Evening	J Smith	079999999	28 Station Rd	Norwich
9/11/15	Studio 1	Afternoon	Art Society	012398765	66 Main Rd	Watton
9/11/15	Studio 1	Evening	Art Society	012398765	66 Main Rd	Watton
9/11/15	Studio 2	Afternoon				
9/11/15	Studio 2	Evening	Rock band	079988888	3 London Rd	Thetford

This shows all the booking slots for one day (9 November). Note that some of the slots are free (no client details recorded).

Based on this information, it is fairly clear that there are three entities: Clients, Rooms and Booking slots. Clients 'reserve' booking slots and Rooms 'are booked'. The conceptual ERD looks like this (see Figure 2.7).

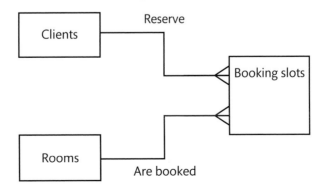

▶ **Figure 2.7:** Conceptual ERD

Logical model

From this conceptual model of the database, we can now develop the logical model.

We know that each table needs to have a primary key and that this key needs to be unique and that it is best if it takes a numerical value which does not have meaning outside the database (e.g. Client name does not make a good primary key). Therefore, our data table should now look like this (for simplicity the client address and town have been left out).

Booking slot ID	Date	Room ID	Room name	Session	Client ID	Client name	Client tel
1	9/11/15	1	Large theatre	Afternoon			
2	9/11/15	1	Large theatre	Evening	1	Drama Club	012345678
3	9/11/15	2	Small Hall	Afternoon			
4	9/11/15	2	Small Hall	Evening	2	J Smith	079999999
5	9/11/15	3	Studio1	Afternoon	3	Art Society	012398765
6	9/11/15	3	Studio1	Evening	3	Art Society	012398765
7	9/11/15	4	Studio2	Afternoon			
8	9/11/15	4	Studio2	Evening	4	Rock band	079988888

From this we can create our logical ERD (see Figure 2.8).

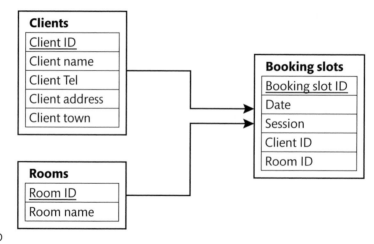

▶ **Figure 2.8:** Logical ERD

Data dictionary

We can also create the data dictionary for each table, which describes each table and their fields in much more detail.

Data dictionary: Clients table			
Field name	**Key?**	**Datatype**	**Validation**
Client_ID	Primary	Integer	Automatically created by Access
Client_name		Text, 25 characters	
Client_tel		Text, 12 characters	
Client_address		Text, 25 characters	
Client_town		Text, 25 characters	

Data dictionary: Booking slots table

Field name	Key?	Datatype	Validation
Booking_slot_ID	Primary	Integer	Automatically created by Access
Date		Short date	
Session		Text, 10 characters	Can only be afternoon or evening
Client_ID	Foreign key from Clients table	Integer	Must exist on Client table
Room_ID	Foreign key from Rooms table	Integer	Must exist on Rooms table

Data dictionary: Rooms table

Field name	Key?	Datatype	Validation
Room_ID	Primary	Integer	Automatically created by Access
Room_name		Text, 25 characters	

For the sake of simplicity, only a small number of fields have been included in these tables; in a real database there are likely to be many more fields.

Naming conventions

There are a range of conventions (rules) which can be used for naming database objects such as tables, fields, queries etc. The most important rules are the following.

▶ Do not use spaces – rather than First Name, use First_Name or FirstName. Access® allows you to use spaces, but it can cause problems if you use the database on a web server or with other database software.

▶ Do not use names that are reserved words – such as 'date'. (Access® will not allow you to do this anyway.)

Entity-relationship designs

ERDs need to be created at the conceptual design phase and refined in the logical design phase. Examples of ERDs are given in the worked example above.

Normalisation

As described earlier, the process of normalisation is used mainly as a validation technique to check if the conceptual and logical model of the database design is correct. The normalisation process needs to be documented with descriptions of the way in which each stage was completed.

Worked example: Dissford Arts Centre 3

The normalisation for this data is fairly simple. If we look at the first table under the heading 'Logical model', in the previous Worked example, then the Booking slot ID is a suitable primary key, and since it is not a compound key this data is already in 2NF.

Remember that the requirement of 3NF is that if non-key attributes depend on other attributes within the data, then they need to be moved to another table. In the data shown in this table, if we know the room ID then we can identify the room name, so these two need to be moved to a separate table.

The same is true of the Client ID – if we know this, we can uniquely identify the client name and their telephone number. Therefore the normalisation exercise produces the same result as shown in the logical ERD, validating that our design is correct.

User interface design

The user interface can usually be broadly divided into the parts of the interface used for data entry and those used to present information to the user.

Data entry

The most important aspect of designing a data entry interface is to ensure that, as far as possible, the data that is entered is correct. There are a number of ways to ensure the correctness of data.

▶ Validation – Various validation methods can be used. For example, dates can be validated to ensure that they fall within the correct ranges (so a date of 31st February is clearly recognised by the database as being incorrect). The use of a 'date picker' (miniature pop-up calendar) is one way to make date entry easy and to help reduce errors.

▶ Verification – Verification is used where the correctness of data entered is essential. It involves entering the data twice and checking that both entries are the same. It is often used for setting passwords and entering email addresses into forms.

▶ Calculated fields – Calculated fields can also be used to check numerical data. 'Check digits' are a commonly used example of a calculated field that are used by banking applications to avoid errors in the manual inputting of bank account and debit/credit card numbers. This involves the addition of one or more digits to a number which are calculated from the preceding numbers.

▶ Input masks – Input masks can be used where the data follows a pre-set format, for example NI numbers. These always consist of two upper case characters, followed by six numbers and a final single upper case character. The mask ensures that the data that is entered into the NI field must fit this pattern.

▶ Directed input – Directed input can be implemented where only a fairly small range of different values is acceptable. An example would be a value for gender, which can only be 'Male' or 'Female'. Methods of directed input include radio buttons (where there are only very few values) and drop-down lists.

Task automation

The user interface design should make the user's life easy and should automate procedures whenever possible. Fortunately, Access® provides a number of facilities that make automation of many tasks quite easy. However, details of how each task will be automated should be included in the design. Some of the areas where automation could be used include the following.

▶ Imports – Data may need to be imported into a new database from an existing one, so a design needs to be produced that maps the tables and fields across from the old to the new database. Access® provides a step-by-step import facility, which is covered in the Step by step: Importing data and using an action query to manipulate it. You can save the import steps so that you can run the automated import any time you need to.

▶ Updates – Automated updates to a table can be done using action queries. These are a special type of query which as well as selecting data based on certain criteria can also modify data. Action queries used to update data can be designed in the same way as select queries. An example of this is the Worked example: Dissford Arts Centre 2.

▶ Deletions – As with updates, action queries can also be used to automate the deletion of unwanted fields or records.

Data reports and presentation

The most important design consideration for the parts of the user interface that present data to the user (such as queries and forms) is that the data is reported/presented in a clear way with the correct fields shown in the correct order.

The use of colours, lines and boxes within the tables may also help the user to understand the data. As well as presenting information on the screen, many databases will need to produce printed reports.

Step by Step: Creating forms

1 Access® provides a simple way for you to create forms to use for data entry or displaying data. This example uses the online orders database that was discussed earlier.

2 To create a form for the Customers table, first make sure that you have the Online orders database open and the Customers table selected. Then go to the Create menu and choose the Form Wizard icon. This will take you through a step-by-step process to create a simple form. First, it will ask you which fields you want to be included in the form, as shown here.

3 In this case, you want all the fields, so click the double arrow to move them all over to the selected fields box and then click Next. Then it will ask you what layout you want. This is something you can experiment with to see what kind of results you get, but for now just leave 'Columnar' selected and click Next. Finally, it will ask you what text you want for the title of the form. The default setting of the table name (Customers) is fine. Also leave the default setting selected which will open the form and view data (rather than opening it in design view). Click the Finish button and you should see the form displayed, as shown here.

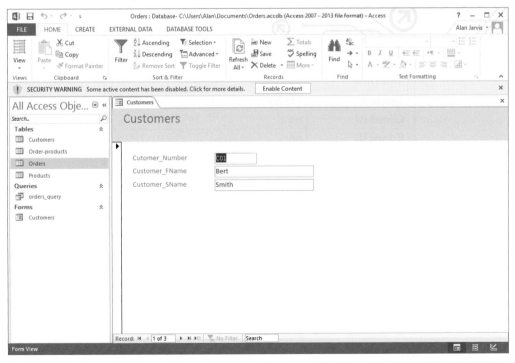

Worked example: Dissford Arts Centre 4

One of the main requirements of the prototype database system is that users can enter a date range and then see a list of all the available slots for rooms during that period, and then proceed to book one of the free slots. The user interface design for this process could look something like this.

Step 1: The user enters the date range for when they want to see the available slots, as shown in Figure 2.9.

Start Date	
End Date	

▶ **Figure 2.9:** Date range data entry design

Step 2: The user is presented with a list of available booking slots as shown in Figure 2.10.

Available slots

Booking slot ID	Slot Date	Session	Room name	
nnnnn	nn/nn/nn	Xxxxxx	xxxxxxx	Book
nnnnn	nn/nn/nn	Xxxxxx	xxxxxxx	Book
nnnnn	nn/nn/nn	Xxxxxx	xxxxxxx	
nnnnn	nn/nn/nn	Xxxxxx	xxxxxxx	

▶ **Figure 2.10:** Available booking slots design

Step 3: The user clicks a button next to the available slot they want to book and is presented with a form on which they complete the booking, as shown in Figure 2.11.

Make Booking

Booking slot ID	nnnnn
Slot Date	nn/nn/nn
Session	Xxxxxx
Client ID	nn
Room ID	nn
Room name	xxxxxxx

▶ **Figure 2.11:** Make booking design

Extracting and presenting data

One of the main benefits of using a relational database is its ability to extract and present data in many different ways.

Queries

Queries provide the main way to extract data from a database. We have looked briefly at how to use SQL to extract records from a table which match certain criteria, but there are many more powerful features you can make use of.

The visual interface that Access® provides for creating queries can be easier to use than SQL and it also provides a number of useful features. You can, of course, always look at the SQL that is created by selecting the SQL View.

The same Online orders database that was used for the normalisation exercise will be used as an example. This database has four tables: Orders, Customers, Products and Order-products. Given the way that the database is structured, the details of an individual order are not stored in one table, but spread across the tables. A query can therefore be used to bring all the information about an order together.

> **Link**
>
> See The stages of normalisation.

Step by step: Queries   6 Steps

1 To create a new query in Access®, first, go to the Create menu and choose the Query Design icon in the toolbar. Access® will then display the Show Table Dialog shown here.

2 Click on each of the tables and then click Add. Then click close and you will see the Query Design View, as shown here.

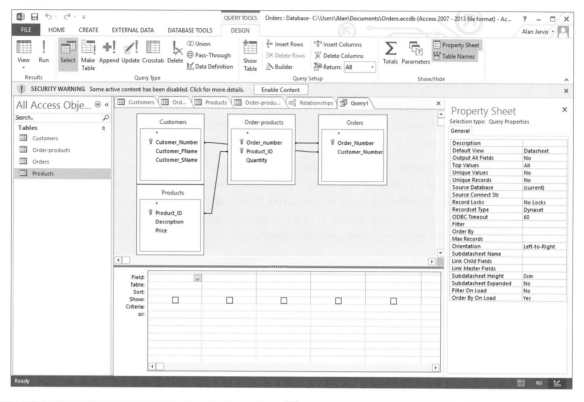

▼

3 From the Orders table (in the top part of the Design View), click and drag the field 'Order_Number' down into the first 'Field' column of the query grid in the lower part of the display, as shown here.

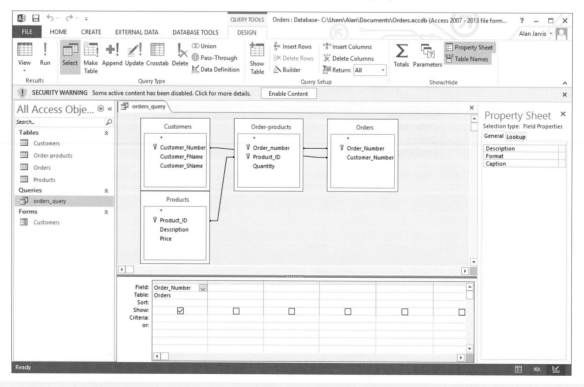

4 Next do the following:
- from the Customers table, drag the field Customer_SName into the next column of the query grid
- from the Products table, drag the Description and Price fields into the query grid
- from the Order-products table, drag Quantity.

The query grid should now look like this.

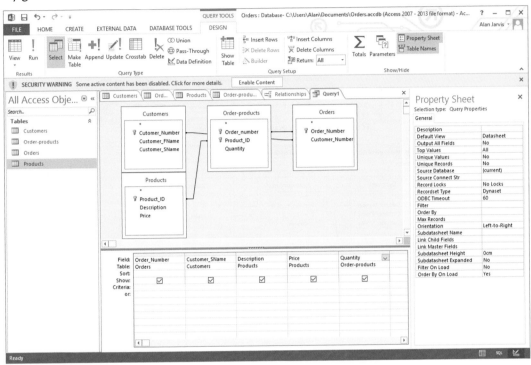

5 To run the query, click the Run icon in the toolbar and you should see the results, as shown here.

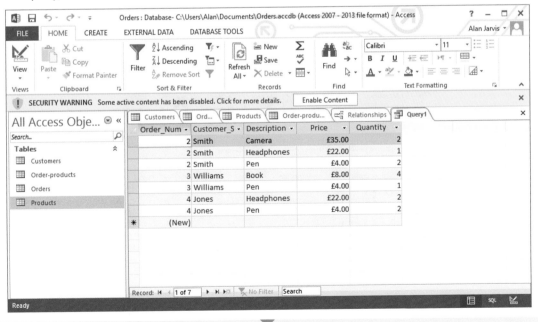

6 Save the query by right clicking in its tab and choosing Save. Give the query a meaningful name such as 'Orders_query'.

Calculated queries

You can also create calculated fields in queries. For example, in the query just created it might be useful to multiply each product price by the quantity to get the total cost of each product ordered.

Step by step: Calculated fields in queries

2 Steps

1 To do this, open the previous Step by step, 'Orders_query', and return to the Design View. In the empty right-hand column of the query grid, type the following expression:

Total: [Price]*[Quantity]

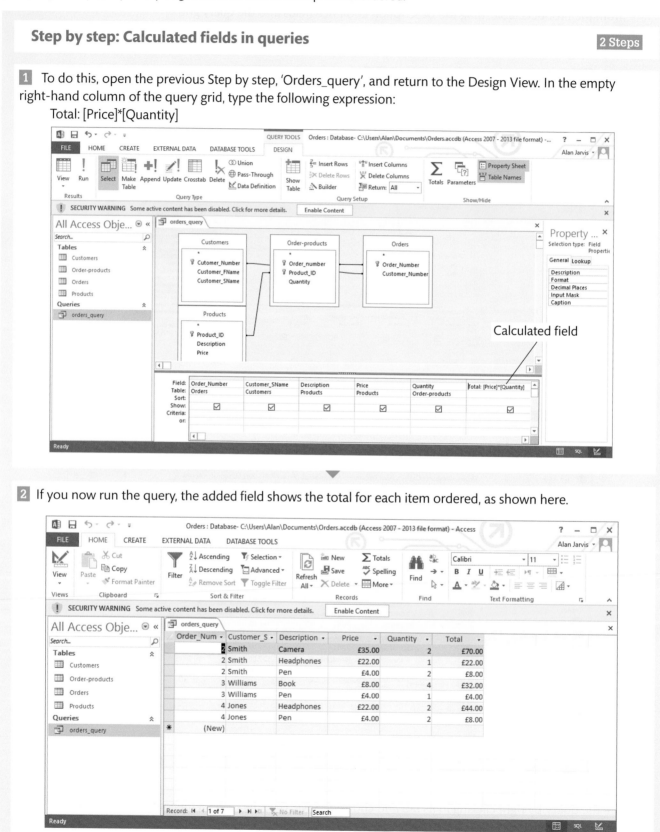

Calculated field

2 If you now run the query, the added field shows the total for each item ordered, as shown here.

Queries using multiple criteria

As well as typing the criteria that you wish to apply to a query directly into the query grid, a query can also pick up values used as selection criteria elsewhere. The simplest method is to use a pop-up dialog box to collect values for the criteria from the user.

Step by step: Queries using multiple criteria   4 Steps

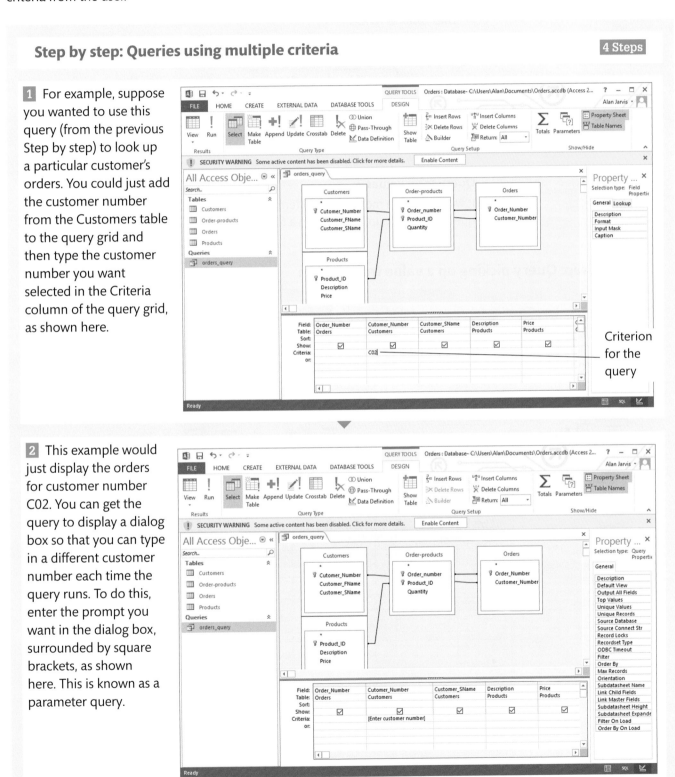

1 For example, suppose you wanted to use this query (from the previous Step by step) to look up a particular customer's orders. You could just add the customer number from the Customers table to the query grid and then type the customer number you want selected in the Criteria column of the query grid, as shown here.

Criterion for the query

2 This example would just display the orders for customer number C02. You can get the query to display a dialog box so that you can type in a different customer number each time the query runs. To do this, enter the prompt you want in the dialog box, surrounded by square brackets, as shown here. This is known as a parameter query.

3 Now when you run the query, you will see the dialog box, as shown here.

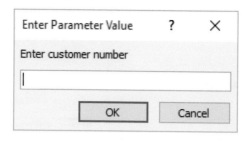

4 When you enter a valid customer number, it will display only matching records.

Query form values

It would be even more useful, in terms of creating an easy-to-use application, if the query could pick up a value from a form.

Step by step: Query picking up a value from a form

`6 Steps`

1 In the Step by step: Creating forms, we created a simple form for the Customers table. Now we are going to add a button which will open the query showing the orders that a customer has placed. To add the button, open the form that you created earlier, then click the View icon and choose Design View. This will display the form in Design view, as shown below. Drag the Form footer down a little to create some space for the button.

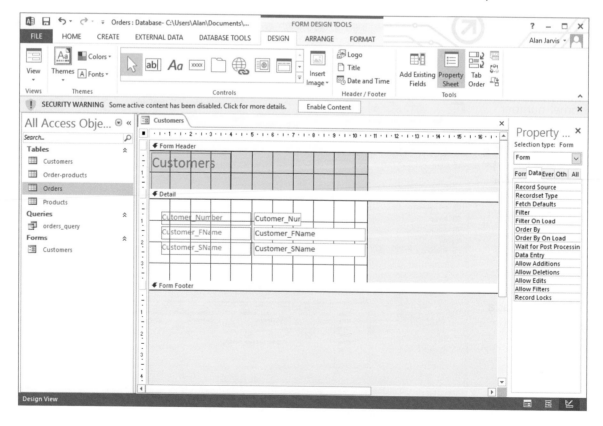

2 Now, in the Controls section of the toolbar, click the Command Button control and drag out a button on the lower part of the form. This will open the Command Button Wizard, as shown here.

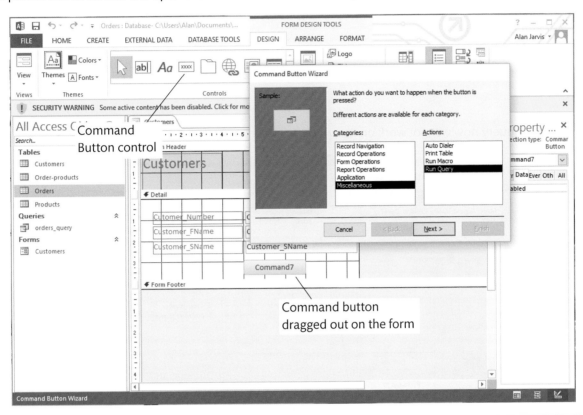

3 Choose Miscellaneous in the list on the left-hand side and then Run Query on the right-hand side. Click Next and choose the name of the query you are working on. Click Next again to select Text to appear in the box. Enter something like 'View Orders', as shown here.

4 Now you can click Finish and the button is added to the form. At the moment, the button will show the query, but will show all the orders for every customer. We want to transfer the current Customer_Number field to the query criteria. Save the form and open the query in Design View. The expression we need to add in the Criteria column is as follows:

[Forms]![Customers]![Customer_Number]

This tells the query to obtain the criteria from a form called 'Customers' and a field called 'Customer_Number', as shown here.

5 Note that the query now will not work on its own; it will only work when opened from the form.

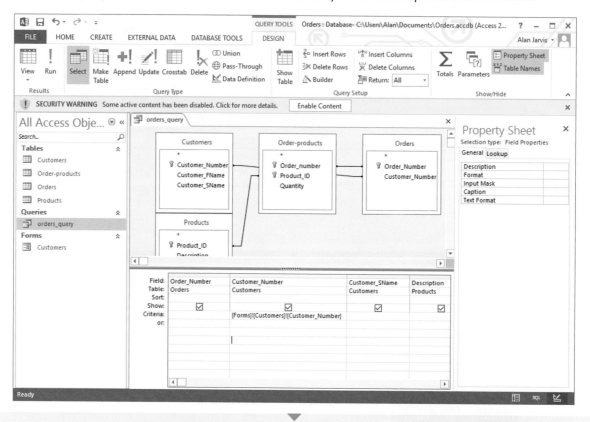

6 Save and close the query. Open the form again, use the navigation buttons at the bottom to select a particular customer, then click the button and the query will display only those orders for the current customer displayed on the form.

Worked example: Dissford Arts Centre 5

You have already completed the user interface design for the main booking process (finding an available booking slot and then making a booking in a free slot). Now you will need to use a query to find free booking slots. You can use a parameter query to select the date range of the booking slots and, by setting a criteria of only those booking slots which have no client ID in them (i.e. they have not already been booked), the query will select only available booking slots. Since Client_ID is a numeric field, it has a zero in it if no booking has been made. We can outline the design for the query like this (another possibility would be to look at the SQL for the query by selecting SQL view).

Query name:	Find_slot				
Tables:	Booking_slots	Rooms			
Query grid:					
Field	Booking_slot_ID	Date	Session	Room_name	Client_ID
Table	Booking_slots	Booking_slots	Booking_slots	Rooms	Booking_slots
Sort		In date order (ascending)			
Criteria		Between start and end dates			0
Notes					(does not need to be displayed)

Action queries

All the queries mentioned so far have just been used to select and display data, but Access® also supports action queries, which can make changes to data. Being able to make changes to data is useful, for example if you needed to update every record in a large database.

There are various types of action query:

▸ an update query can update every record in a table that matches some criteria

▸ a delete query can delete records which match certain criteria

▸ an append query can append (add) records from one table to another

▸ a make table query can create a new table based on records from an existing table.

Action queries can be useful if you need to create a set of related tables from a raw set of data held in a single file.

Step by step: Importing data and using an action query to manipulate it   13 Steps

1 It is likely that, in the assessment for this unit, you will be given a file of raw data which you need to import and split into tables, following the design you create for the database. Look at how this can be done with the 1NF version of the data that was used in the normalisation example earlier (see The stages of normalisation).

Here is a reminder of what the data looks like.

Order no	Product ID	Customer no	Customer FName	Customer SName	Description	Price	Quantity
1	P33	C10	Bert	Smith	Camera	£35	1
1	P09	C10	Bert	Smith	Book	£8	3
1	P21	C10	Bert	Smith	Headphones	£22	2
2	P09	C5	Wendy	Jones	Book	£8	1
2	P15	C5	Wendy	Jones	Trainers	£40	1
3	P21	C12	Alice	Williams	Headphones	£22	1
3	P19	C12	Alice	Williams	Pen	£6	2

2 You can import various types of file into Access® including text files and Microsoft® Excel® spreadsheet files. First, open a database file (or create a new one) into which you want to import the data. Then, from the External Data menu, click on the icon for the type of file you want to import, which is Excel in this example. First, you will see the dialog box, as shown here.

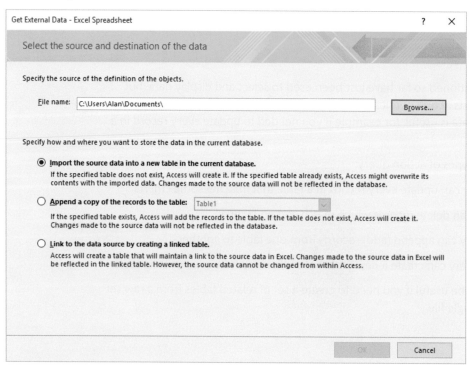

3 Browse to find the Excel® file you want to import and then click OK. Next you will see a preview of the data from the chosen file and you can select which worksheet within the Excel® file it is in, as shown here.

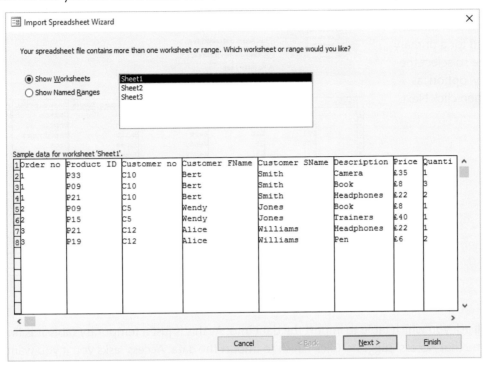

4 The next screen will ask you to confirm that the first row contains the column (field) headings, which it does in this example, so just click Next. Then you have the opportunity to adjust the field names and datatypes of each field by clicking in the field and adjusting the setting at the top, as shown here. When you are happy with the names and datatypes click Next.

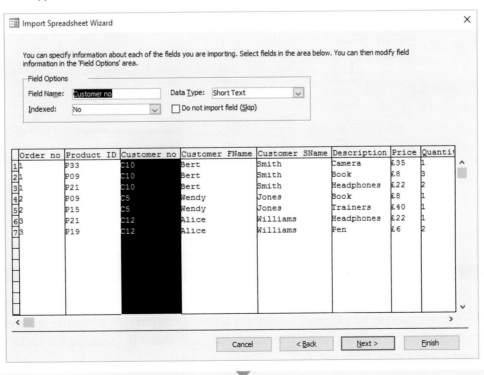

5 Access® will then offer to add a primary key field to the data. Since this data will be split up into different tables, there is no need for a primary key at this stage so select the 'no primary key' option, as shown here. Then click Next.

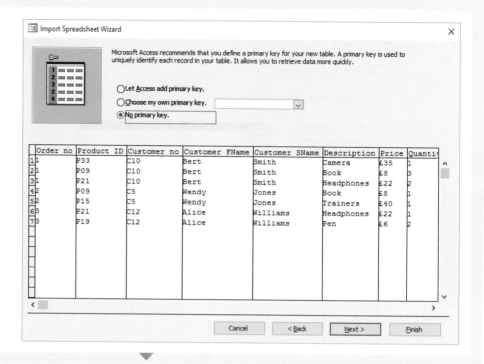

6 Finally, it will ask you which table to import the data into. As this is just a temporary table it is fine to go with the default name that Access® suggests. Click Finish to import the data. Access® asks you if you want to save the import steps, but there is no need to do this; just click Close. All the data should now be imported to a single table, as shown here.

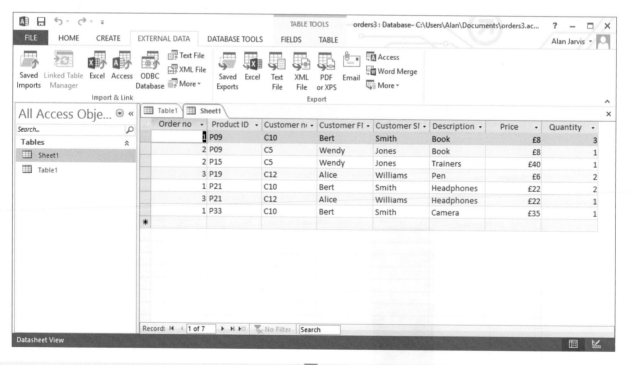

7 Now that the data is imported into Access®, we can use action queries to split it into the required tables. It is a good idea to start off with a standard select query and make sure that it has selected the correct records before you convert it into a make table query.

8 To create the Products table, first go to the Create menu and click the Query Design icon, and then add the table created from the imported data. For the Products table, the only fields we need are Product ID, Description and Price. Drag these into the query grid, as shown here.

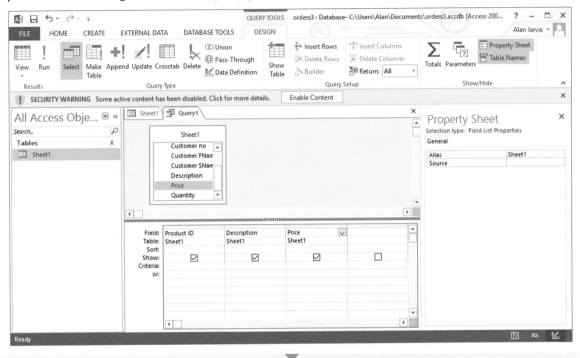

9 If you run this query, you will see that some products appear multiple times (because they have been ordered on different orders). You need to create the product table so that each product only occurs once in the query results. To show only unique values, you need to click in the light blue background in the top part of the query screen, which will display the query properties in the right side panel. The fourth property in the list is called Unique Values and, by default, it is set to No. Change this to Yes, as shown here.

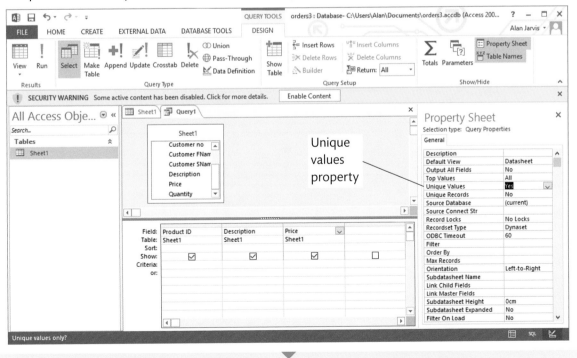

10 Now when you run the query you will only get each product displayed once, as shown here.

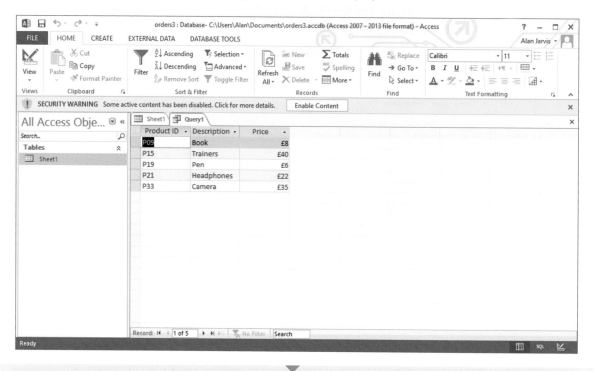

11 This query can now be converted into a make table query and used to create the products table. To do this, click the Make Table icon in the Design toolbar. Access® will then ask you the name of the table that you want to create. In this case it is Products, as shown here.

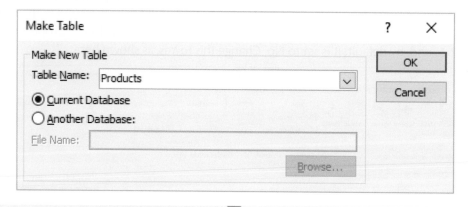

12 Before you can run the query in Make Table mode, you will need to click the Enable Content button below the toolbar and save the query. Open the query again and a warning message will appear telling you that the query will modify data, as shown here.

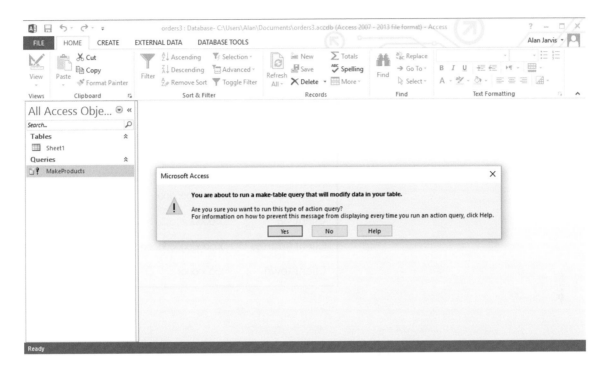

13 Click Yes. Another message will appear telling you that you are about to paste five rows (records) into a table. Click Yes again. Then your new Products table will be created. Only run the query once. You will also need to go into the Design View for the new Products table and make the Product ID the primary key for the new table. The other tables for the database can be created in the same way.

Wild cards

Queries can also use so called 'wild cards' for their criteria. A wild card is a special character which can be substituted for any other character(s). In Access® queries, there are several wild card characters as follows.

▶ To substitute any number of characters use '*': so North* will find North West, North London and Northend.

▶ To substitute a single character use '?': so B?ll will find Bill, Ball.

To substitute a single digit use '#': so 1#2 will find 123, 103.

Reports

Reports are produced to show the outcomes of queries and can be printed to present the data to users.

As the final part of the process of finding and then booking an available room at the arts centre, a printed confirmation sheet needs to be produced to be sent to the client as a reminder of their booking. This is done using an Access® report. The design for the report is shown here.

Booking Report	
Booking slot ID	nnnn
Session	
Slot Date	nn/nn/nn
Room name	n
Client name	xxxxxxxxxxxx
Client Tel	xxxxxx
Client address	xxxxxxxxxxxxxxxxxx
Client town	xxxxxxxx

Test plans

Testing that a completed database meets the user requirements and works correctly is an important step. To do this you will need to create a test plan which shows each individual test that you will carry out and the expected outcome of each test. Your test plan should be created at the design stage and then used to test the database once it has been developed.

Correctness of data

It is important to ensure that all the data input into a database is correct. You must ensure that the data validation that has been defined in the data dictionary works correctly and that only data that meets the requirements for each table/field is accepted, and that data which does not meet the requirements is rejected with a suitable error message.

When creating the test data to be included in the test plan for each table, there are three main types of test data to be created:

▶ Normal – This is data which can be considered the ordinary/typical (normal) type of data you would expect to be input to the field and that should be accepted.

▶ Erroneous – This is data that is incorrect for this field (e.g. a text value in a number field) and should be rejected with a suitable error message.

▶ Extreme – This is data which is at the limit of what should be accepted. This might be in terms of the maximum and minimum acceptable values in a numeric field, or a value with the maximum number of characters for a text field. Extreme values (for test data) should include those on the limit of what is acceptable (and so should be accepted) and just over the limit (and so should be rejected).

For example, here is the data dictionary for the Rescue dogs table.

▶ **Table 2.22:** Data dictionary for the Rescue dogs table

Field name	Key?	Datatype	Validation
Dog_ID	Primary	Integer	Automatically created by Access
Dog_name		Text, 15 characters	
Breed		Text, 15 characters	
Colour		Text, 15 characters	
Sex		Text, 1 character	M or F only
Year_of_birth		Integer	Must be less than current year and no more than 20 years in the past
Approx_size		Text, 6 characters	Small, medium or large only

Here is an example of suitable test data for each of the fields which have validation applied (assuming that the current year is 2016).

▶ **Table 2.23:** Suitable test data for each of the fields of the Rescue dogs table

Field	Test data type	Data item	Expected outcome	Actual outcome (completed when the database is tested)	Action required?
Sex	Normal	M	Accepted		
Sex	Normal	F	Accepted		
Sex	Erroneous	X	Rejected		
Year_of_birth	Normal	2010	Accepted		
Year_of_birth	Erroneous	Text	Rejected		
Year_of_birth	Extreme	2016	Accepted		
Year_of_birth	Extreme	2017	Rejected		
Year_of_birth	Extreme	1996	Accepted		
Year_of_birth	Extreme	1995	Rejected		
Approx_size	Normal	Small	Accepted		
Approx_size	Normal	Medium	Accepted		
Approx_size	Normal	Large	Accepted		
Approx_size	Erroneous	Big	Rejected		

This gives examples of the different types of test data that could be used. However, where a field has a limited number of acceptable entries (such as the Sex and Approx_size fields) the best method of ensuring that only valid data is entered is by using the Lookup wizard, as described earlier.

Functionality

The user interface needs to be tested to ensure that all of its features, including forms and reports, work correctly. This is called testing the user interface's functionality.

Testing the functionality of a user interface is rather more complex than testing the data. You need to create a series of scenarios which mimic the way that users will use the completed database system. (You need to include, in these scenarios, data which is normal, extreme and erroneous, where appropriate.)

Consider the database design created earlier for the process of searching for available booking slots and then making a booking in the Worked example: Dissford Arts Centre. Booking scenarios for this process would need to have some existing data in the database, including clients and available and booked booking slots.

> **Link**
>
> For more on using the Lookup wizard see Lookup tables.

When booking a room, the data that is entered into the database system is the date range of available slots to search for (start and end dates) and the client ID. So test data which is normal (for example, a client ID who does exist) and erroneous (for example, a client ID who does not exist) needs to be created.

An example of the test data that could be used is shown below. Note that the date ranges will depend upon the example data which has been loaded into the database.

▶ **Table 2.24:** Test data for Worked example: Dissford Arts Centre booking database

Field	Test data type	Data item	Expected outcome	Actual outcome (completed when the database is tested)	Action required?
Date range	Normal	1/11/15 to 10/11/15	Accepted, produces list of free slots		
Date range	Erroneous	20/12/15 to text	Error message		
Date range	Erroneous	Date in the past to date in the past	Error message		
Client ID	Normal	2 (valid client ID)	Accepted, client ID saved in the booking slot table for the date selected		
Client ID	Erroneous	999 (invalid client ID)	Rejected with error message		

Usability and accessibility

The user interface can also be tested for usability and accessibility.

▶ Usability – Usability testing is rather more subjective than functionality testing and tests need to be conducted by real users who then give their opinion about how easy the interface is to use and any suggestion for improvements. This cannot really be done at the design stage. Usability tests need to be conducted using either a prototype of the user interface or the completed version.

▶ Accessibility – The accessibility of the user interface needs to be tested against existing guidelines for making computer interfaces accessible, such as the Royal National Institute of Blind People (RNIB) guidelines for web accessibility. These guidelines will give consideration to things such as font size and colour and the use of white space.

> **Link**
>
> The RNIB guidelines for web accessibility can be found at http://www.rnib.org.

PAUSE POINT

How much testing is enough? Do you think it would be ok to just check that the basic things work and then give the database to the users for them to find any faults for you to fix?

Hint   What might the consequences of this approach be?

Extend   Testing is a big subject with many different aspects to it. Research different types of testing and consider how they might be applied to a database system.

Creating a relational database structure

Once the design of a database is complete, you can start work on developing the relational database solution.

Producing a database solution

In this section, you will learn about selecting and configuring appropriate RDBMS and SQL tools to produce a database solution to meet the client's requirements.

Creating data tables, relationships and validation rules

Using the data dictionary developed during the design stage, the database tables can now be created. This can either be done by defining the fields, datatypes and validation rules in the Access® table Design View or, if the tables will use imported data, this can either be done at the import stage or using action queries to split up a single imported file. Once the tables have all been created, you can then create the relationships between them.

> **Link**
>
> **Creating data tables**
>
> Details of how to create tables in Access® is covered in the Step by step: Creating tables.
>
> **Creating links and relationships between data tables**
>
> Details of how to create relationships in Access® is covered in the Step by step: Creating relationships in Access®.
>
> **Applying data validation rules**
>
> Details of how to create lookup tables and validations rules is in the Step by step: Lookup tables and validation rules.

Worked example: Dissford Arts Centre 7

Tables can be created for this booking database using the data dictionary and ERD created earlier. The Design View of the Client table is shown in Figure 2.12 on the following page.

An AutoNumber datatype is used for the Client_ID so that each client will have a unique number automatically created by Access®.

(Note also that the Client_tel is a text field, as a telephone number is not a number in the mathematical sense (e.g. you never need to add phone numbers together!) and using a numeric data type will prevent you from adding leading zeros, which most phone numbers require.)

Remember that when you use a foreign key in another table, such as the Client_ID in the Booking_Slots table, you must use a datatype that matches the primary key in the linked table. In this example, as the Client_ID is an AutoNumber field, so you must use the data type of Number, long integer.

Once the tables are created, you can create the relationships between them using the Relationships window, as described earlier. The relations set up between the tables for the arts centre booking system are shown in Figure 2.13 on the following page.

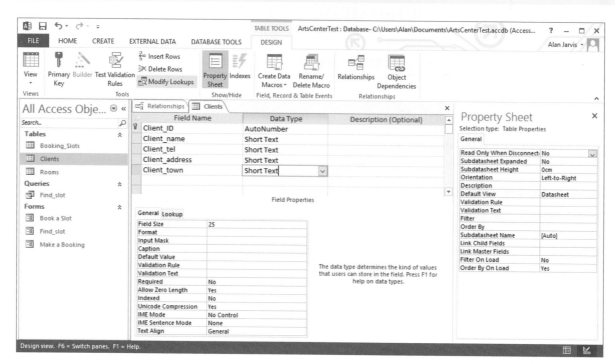

▶ **Figure 2.12:** The Client table design

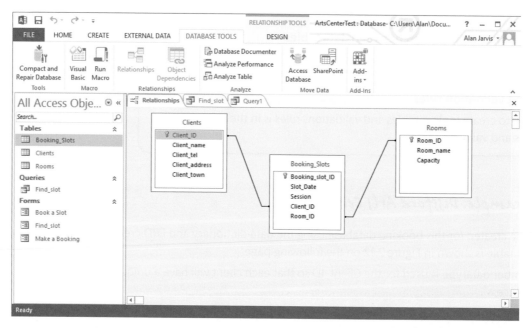

▶ **Figure 2.13:** The relationships for the arts centre database system

At this stage, you should enter a small amount of test data into the tables, just to ensure that they work as expected and to provide something for you to test queries and forms and to report with. It is unwise to enter large amounts of data until you are sure that the database works as expected. If the data has already been provided for the table, now is the time to import it and, if necessary, divide it up into the required tables using action queries, as described earlier.

Worked example: Dissford Arts Centre 8

An important concept in a booking database of any type (for hotel rooms or airline tickets, for example) is that of available booking slots. With the Online orders database, when no orders are placed, then there are no records on the Order table, but with the bookings database the concept is a bit different and you need to populate the Booking_Slots table with unbooked slots to allow users to search for and book available slots.

Typically, this would be done for three- or possibly six-month periods in advance, and in a real database system they would probably be generated automatically. An easy way to create booking slots for the arts centre system is to use a spreadsheet as it is easier to copy and paste data in a spreadsheet and the autofill feature will create dates for you.

You will need to create an afternoon and evening session booking slot for every room on every date. This creates quite a lot of records (8 per day), as shown in Figure 2.14.

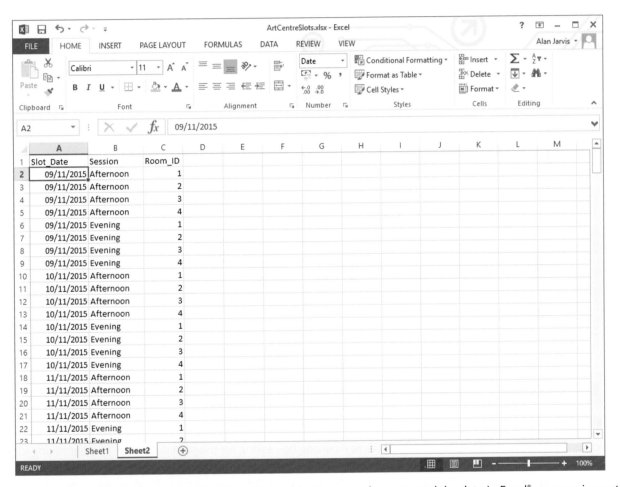

Figure 2.14: Spreadsheet data for the Booking_Slots table. Once you have created the data in Excel®, you can import it into the Booking_Slots table in Access®.

Generating outputs

The next step in developing the database is to create queries. In many cases, forms and reports rely on queries to provide their data, so you can start developing the queries before the forms and reports. However in some cases, such as where a query takes its criteria from a form, you may need to develop them together.

User generated queries

Database users can, of course, generate their own queries to answer *ad hoc* questions about the data, but many queries will run automatically in the background, triggered by the forms and reports that use their data.

Worked example: Dissford Arts Centre 9

You have already created a design for a query that will find available booking slots. Now you can start to implement that design. First, you will create the basic query to find available slots, later you will integrate it with two forms to provide a facility to find and then book an available slot.

The data shown in the table in Worked example: Dissford Arts Centre 2 has been added to the tables that provide both booked and available slots, to allow us to test the query. Figure 2.15 shows the query design for this.

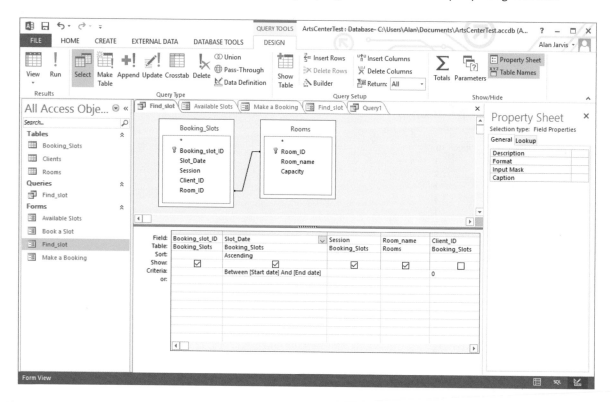

▶ **Figure 2.15:** Query design

The criteria added for the Slot_Date field will display a dialog box asking for the start date, then another asking for the end date of the search range. Slots will appear in ascending order (earliest first). With the criteria for the client_ID set to zero, only those booking slots with no client ID (i.e. available slots which are not booked) will appear. Because the 'Show' option is not selected, this will not appear in the query results. Figure 2.16 shows the typical output from this query with a date range set to between 9/11/15 and 10/11/15.

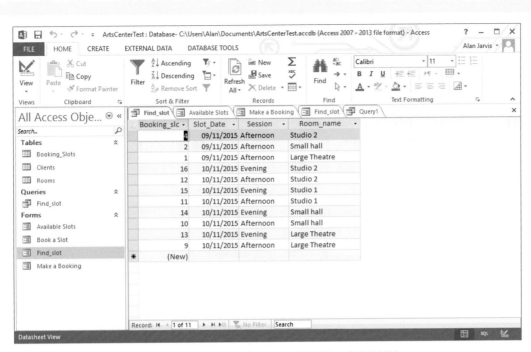

▶ **Figure 2.16:** Typical query output with a date range set to between 9/11/15 and 10/11/15

The query that you have just created will not be directly visible to the user. Instead, it will work while being automatically hidden behind the form that the user will see. The next step is therefore to create that form.

Worked example: Dissford Arts Centre 10

Creating a form that will list all the available slots that the query has found is quite straightforward if we use the Form Wizard icon (found in the Create toolbar). Start from the Design View of the query that you have just developed; the form will automatically be based on it. Select all the fields from the query, as shown in Figure 2.17.

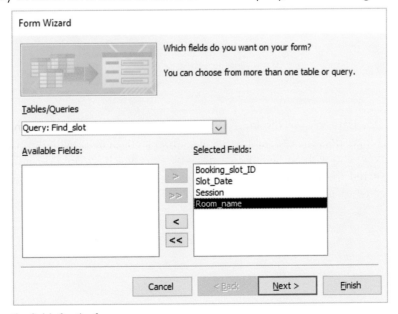

▶ **Figure 2.17:** Selecting the fields for the form

Creating systems to manage information

Then click Next and choose a Tabular layout so that it displays many records on a single form. Click Next. Choose a title for the form such as 'Available Slots' and then click Finish. Because the form is based on the query, it will now run the query and ask for start and end dates. Enter these and you should see the data from the query displayed in the newly created form, as shown in Figure 2.18.

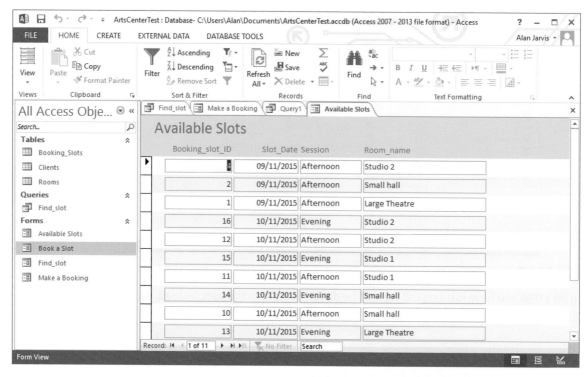

▶ **Figure 2.18:** The completed form

Now the first stage in the process is complete. The user can enter dates and see a list of available booking slots. The next stage is to allow the user to select a particular booking slot and make a booking for that slot.

Worked example: Dissford Arts Centre 11

First, a simple query is required to select the record in the Booking_Slot table that has been chosen (i.e. the one the client wants to book). This query is very similar to the Find_slot query just created (in Worked example: Dissford Arts Centre 10) but it needs to pick up the Booking_slot_ID that the user has selected from the form that has just been created. The criterion required to pick out that record is shown in the query design for the new query, in Figure 2.19.

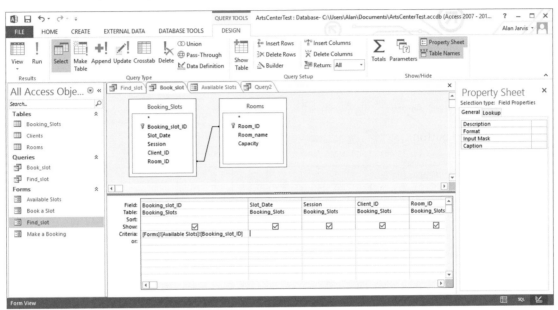

▶ **Figure 2.19:** Criterion for the Booking_slot_ID

This query is now saved. In this example, it has been give the name Book_slot.

You now can create a form which will display the data from the Book_slot query. Open the query in Design View and then, from the Create menu, choose the Query Wizard. Make sure it is using the Book_slot query and select all the fields (see Figure 2.20). Click Next.

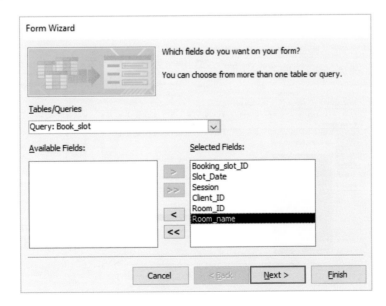

▶ **Figure 2.20:** Selecting the fields

This time, use a Columnar layout (as only one record will be displayed in the forms – the one the user has chosen to book) and give the form a title such as Make_Booking.

If you complete the Form Wizard and the new form attempts to open, you will get an error message because the query that provides the data for the form is looking for a value for the Booking_slot_ID from the Available Slots form. The new Make_Booking form does not work on its own – it only works in conjunction with the Available Slots form. Therefore, you need to modify the Available Slots form to link the two forms together. Click Cancel on the error message and close the form.

Now return to the Available Slots form and open it in Design View, as shown in Figure 2.21. You are going to add a command button which will open the Make_Booking form.

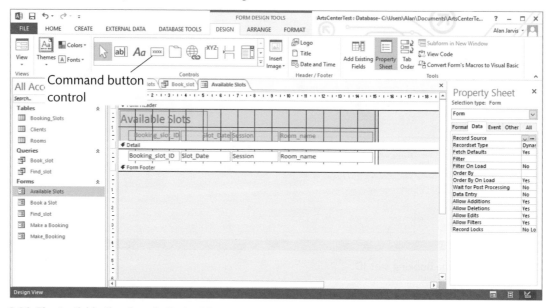

▶ **Figure 2.21:** The Available Slots form in Design View

Make sure that you have Design View selected in the menu bar, and, in the Controls section of the toolbar, you need to click on the Button control and then drag out a button on the form design to the right of the Room_name field. This will open the Command Button Wizard, as shown in Figure 2.22.

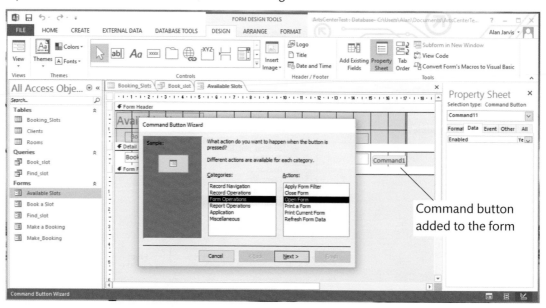

▶ **Figure 2.22:** The Command Button Wizard

From the Categories section choose Form Operations, and then, in the Actions section, choose Open Form. Click Next. Now choose the Make_Booking form as the form to be opened, click Next and in the next step leave the option set to 'Open the form and show all the records'. Click Next again. In the next step (see Figure 2.23), set the text for the button to 'Book' and then click Next.

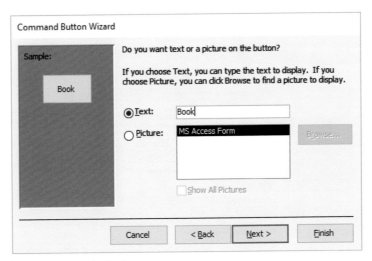

▶ **Figure 2.23:** Setting the text to appear on the button

This will take you to the final step of the wizard where you can just click Finish. The form should now contain a button labelled 'Book' as shown in Figure 2.24.

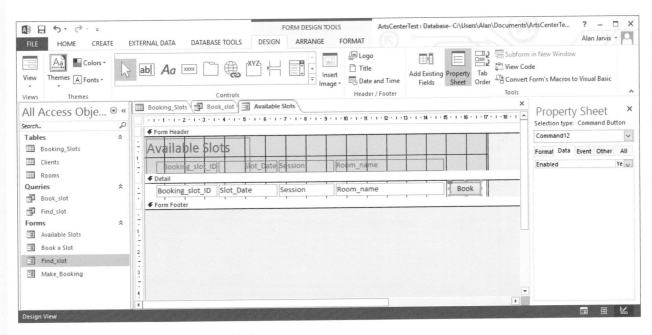

▶ **Figure 2.24:** Form design with a button added

Save and close the form.

Now it is time to test the whole process of searching for an available booking slot, selecting the one to book and booking it. Open the Available Slots form and enter a valid date range. The form should open, showing all the available booking slots, with a 'Book' button next to each one (see Figure 2.25).

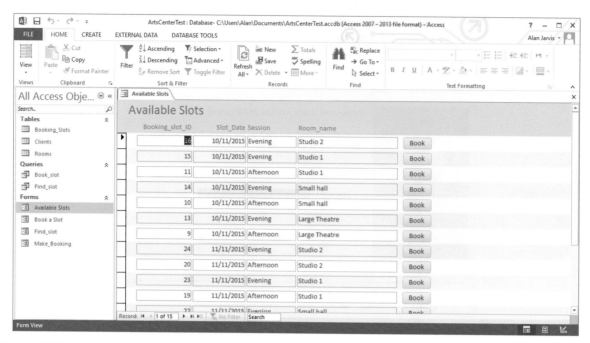

▶ **Figure 2.25:** Slots available for booking

Select one slot and click the Book button. The Make_Booking form should now appear with the booking slot you chose in the previous form shown (see Figure 2.26).

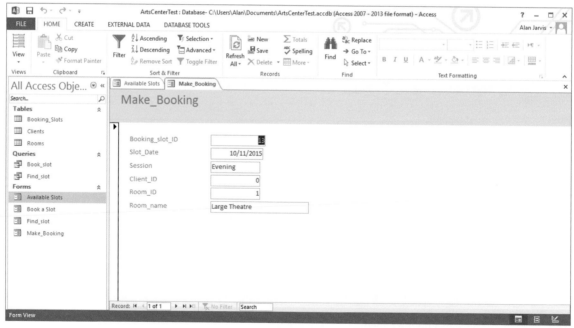

▶ **Figure 2.26:** The Make_Booking form

The Make_Booking form in Worked example: Dissford Arts Centre 11 works because it displays only the Booking_Slots record that the user clicks in the Available Slots form and a booking can be made by entering a Client_ID value in that field on the form.

However it is not fit for purpose for a number of reasons.

▸ The user can type in all the fields of the form and change their values. The room ID and name, date, session and the Booking slot_ID must not be changed as they are related to this particular booking and changing them might create duplicate booking slots. The only field the user should be able to change is the Client_ID. This must be changed to allocate the booking slot to a client.

▸ As stated above, the booking is made by changing the Client_ID from zero to a valid Client_ID. But how does the user know what Client_ID relates to a particular client? They can type any number in the Client_ID field, including invalid ones.

To resolve these issues, you need to lock all the fields on the form so that the user cannot type in them, only view them, and provide a drop-down list of valid client IDs that the user can select from.

Worked example: Dissford Arts Centre 12

To select the Client_ID, we will provide the user with a drop-down list of valid Client_IDs and names from which they can select the correct one. This will prevent any invalid data from being entered.

(Note that it does require that the client exists on the database before a booking can be made for that client.)

View the Make_Booking form in Design View. Select the Client_ID field and label and delete them (right click on them and choose Delete). Now drop down the list of controls under the Design menu and choose the Combo Box control (see Figure 2.27).

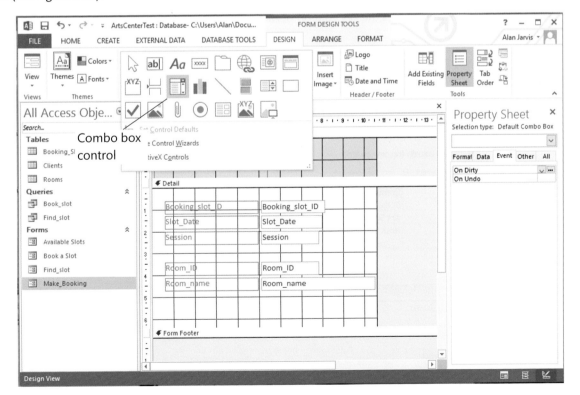

▸ **Figure 2.27:** The Combo Box control

Then drag out a combo box in the space left by the Client_ID field. The Combo Box Wizard will then start. In the first step of the wizard, leave the option 'I want the Combo Box to get the values from another table or query' selected and click Next. Then choose the table called Clients as the source of values for the combo box, and click Next. Select the Client_ID and the Client_name as the fields to be displayed (see Figure 2.28).

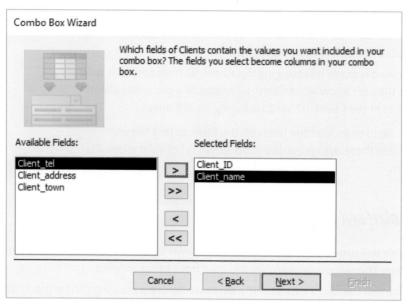

▶ **Figure 2.28:** Fields to be displayed in the Combo Box

Click Next to take you to the step where you can choose a sort order. This is not really needed here, so just click Next. Then uncheck the box which hides the key column because you need to use this field (see Figure 2.29).

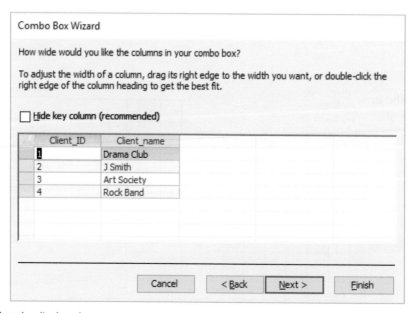

▶ **Figure 2.29:** Fields to be displayed

You will now be asked which field you want to store in the database. Make sure that Client_ID is selected and click Next. This field needs to be stored in the Client_ID field in the Booking Slots table, so select this, as shown in Figure 2.30.

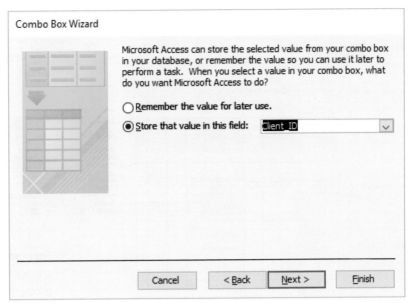

▶ **Figure 2.30:** Storing the Client_ID

Click Next. Give the Combo Box a suitable title, such as Client ID, and click Finish. The form should now look like Figure 2.31.

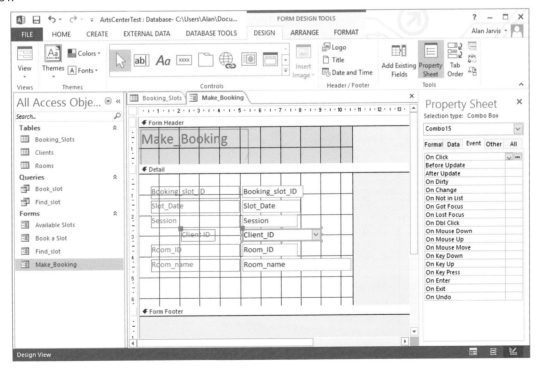

▶ **Figure 2.31:** Form with Combo Box added

Finally, we need to lock all the other fields to prevent the user changing them. Click on each of the fields in turn (except the Combo Box you just created) and, on the right-hand side of the display in the Property Sheet, select the Data tab and set the Enabled property to 'No' and the Locked property to 'Yes', as shown in Figure 2.32.

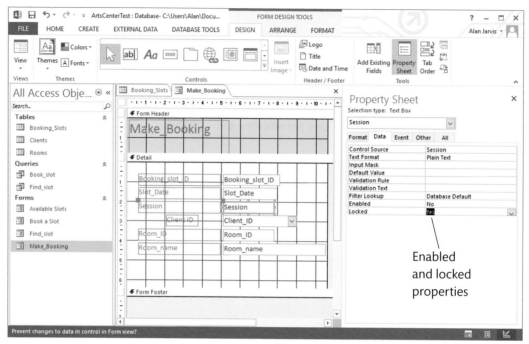

▶ **Figure 2.32:** Setting the Enabled and Locked properties

One final change needs to be made to the form. The user needs an easy way, once they have selected the correct client, to be able to save the change that they have made. Therefore we will add a Save command button to provide this. Use the Command Button Wizard, as before, to add a button at the bottom of the form. Choose the Category 'Record Operations' and Action 'Save Record'. Add some text such as 'Save Booking' to the button.

Save the form and return to Form View to see the finished form. It should look something like Figure 2.33.

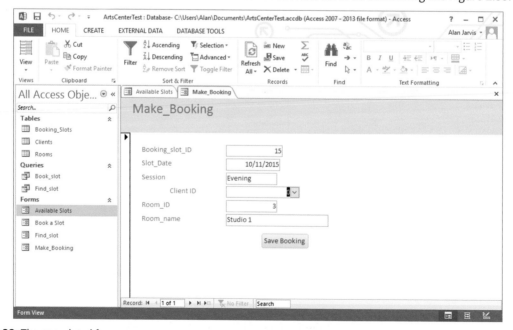

▶ **Figure 2.33:** The completed form

Reports

Creating printed reports in Access® is quite easy to do because there is a step-by-step wizard provided to create report layouts. Reports can be based on either tables or queries.

Worked example: Dissford Arts Centre 13

This example creates a report in the form of a booking receipt for the Dissford Arts Centre. The first task is to create a simple query that will provide the data for the report. This needs to select a specific booking slot and then bring together the data about the client who made that booking. First, create a query in Design View, as shown in Figure 2.34.

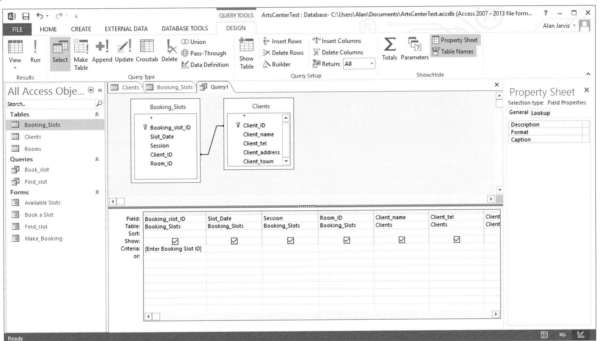

▶ **Figure 2.34:** The Query Design

Note that this query is a parameter query, which will ask the user for the booking ID.

You can check that this query works, save it (in this example it has been called Booking_report) and then move on to create the report based on it. To do this, go to the Create menu and select the Report Wizard icon. Make sure that you have the Booking_report query selected and then choose all the fields in the query, as shown in Figure 2.35.

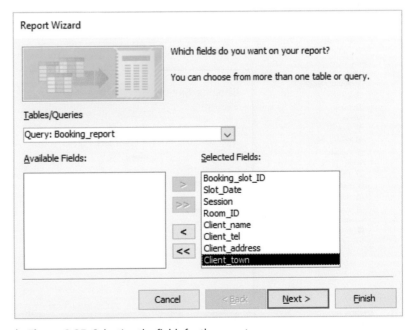

▶ **Figure 2.35:** Selecting the fields for the report

Click Next and then leave the question about how you want to view your data set to 'by Booking slots'. Click Next again. You do not need to add any groups or levels so leave this option set as it is and click Next. You also do not need to sort the records in any order, so just click Next. On the next step of the wizard, choose Columnar layout, as shown in Figure 2.36.

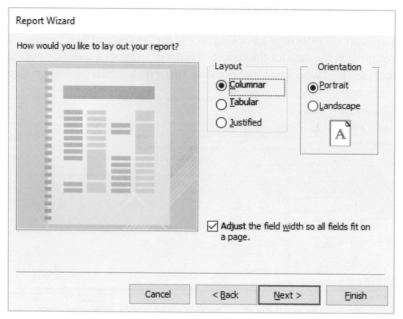

▶ **Figure 2.36:** Selecting a layout for your report

Click Next again and leave the title as suggested. Then click Finish. Because the report is based on the parameter query we created earlier, you will be asked for a Booking slot ID. Enter an ID number that has been booked and you should see the completed report, as shown in Figure 2.37.

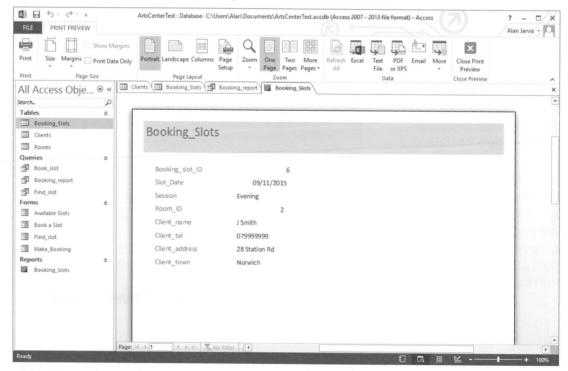

▶ **Figure 2.37:** The completed report

> **Tip**
>
> The Report Wizard does not always set out your report in the neatest way. You can edit your report in the Report Design View and move the fields around to improve the layout.

User interface

The user interface will primarily consist of forms, and we have already looked at some examples of how to create forms and link them to tables and queries.

Two useful additional features that you can add to forms are navigation buttons and subforms.

Navigation

Navigation buttons simply provide easy-to-use buttons to navigate through the records of the table or query that a form is based on. You can add these in the Design View of a form.

Worked example: Dissford Arts Centre 14

Suppose you created a form for the Clients table of the Dissford Arts Centre database example using the wizard, as previously described. To add navigation buttons, choose the Design View for the form. Drag the form footer down a little to create some space and then, in the toolbar, click the Button icon in the Controls group and drag out a button into the space you just created. This will open the Command Button Wizard, as shown in Figure 2.38.

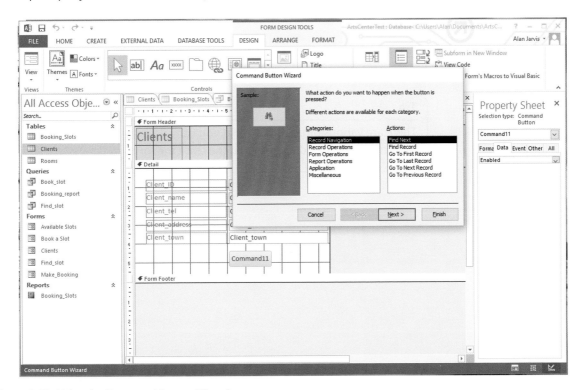

▶ **Figure 2.38:** Using the Command Button Wizard

Leave the Categories list set to Record Navigation and in the Actions list choose Go to Next Record. Then click Next. Then you can choose the text or picture you want to appear on the button. Make your choice and click Finish. The Command Button will now appear on the form and, if you return to Form View, you can see and use the button you added, as shown in Figure 2.39.

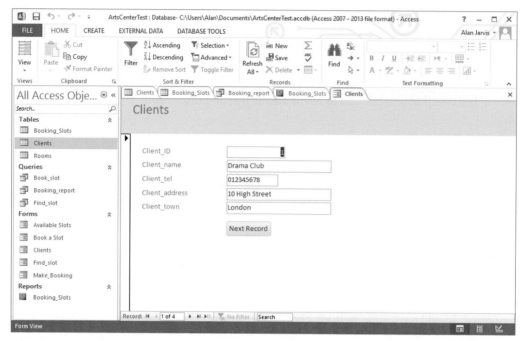

▶ **Figure 2.39:** The complete navigation button

You can, of course, add more record navigation buttons, for example to go to the previous record.

> **Tip**
>
> There are various other buttons that you can add to forms with the Command Button Wizard, including ones that the close the form.

Subforms

Subforms are useful because they allow you to display related records from another table within the same form.

Worked example: Dissford Arts Centre 15

Using the client form to which you have just added the navigation button, you can also add a subform which will display the bookings that each client has made. Open the form in Design View again, and drag the footer bar down further to create more space under the button that you just added. Click the expand button on the right side of the Controls icon and then choose the Subform/Subreport icon (see Figure 2.40).

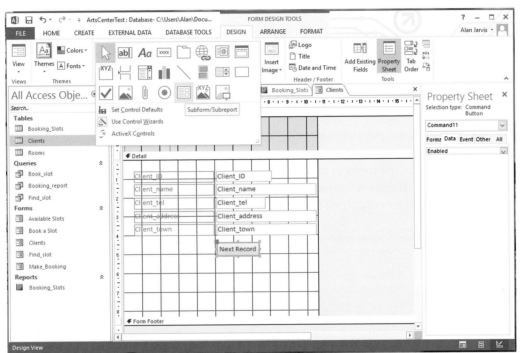

▶ **Figure 2.40:** The Subform/Subreport icon

Drag out a large box under the Next Record button that you have created and the SubForm Wizard will start. In the first step, leave the 'Use existing Table or Queries' button selected and click Next. Then select the Booking_Slots table and choose all the fields (see Figure 2.41).

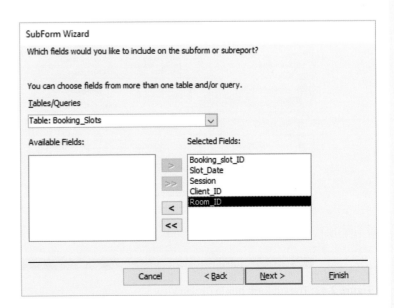

▶ **Figure 2.41:** Choosing the table and fields

In the next step, Access® should have identified the link between the two tables (as they are related) (see Figure 2.42).

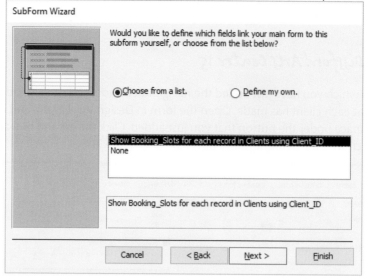

▶ **Figure 2.42:** The link fields between the two tables

Click Finish. You should now see the subform box in your Design View (see Figure 2.43). You might need to drag the form footer down further to make room for the subform. Because the subform will be displayed in Datasheet View, it is best to make the box for it wider rather than longer.

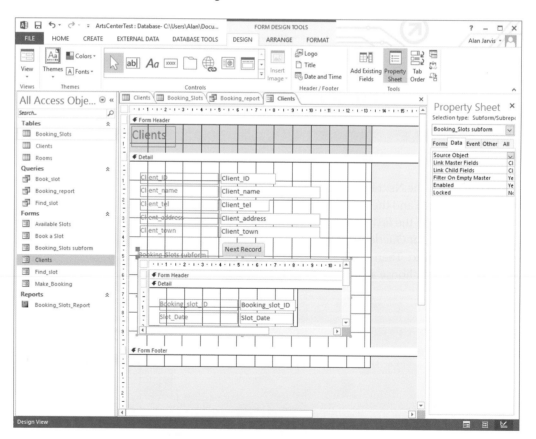

▶ **Figure 2.43:** The subform box in Design View

Now change back to Form View and you should see the related booking displayed in the subform for whichever client you are viewing in the main form (see Figure 2.44).

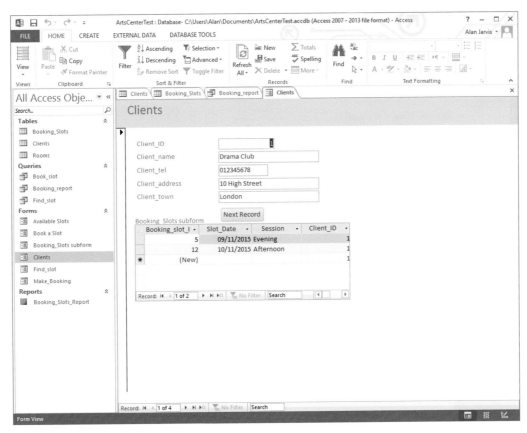

▶ **Figure 2.44:** The main and subforms in Form View

Populating the database

You will need to enter or import some test data, as shown in the worked examples, in order to check the functionality of the queries, reports and forms you create. You may also need to import data, as described in the Step by step: Importing data and using an action query to manipulate it.

Link

See the Step by step: Importing data and using an action query to manipulate it.

Tip

The formatting and layout of main and subforms is quite complex and requires some practice.

Applying security levels

You can apply security measures to your database to control access to the data. There are two main ways to make your database secure: password protection and user access levels.

Passwords

You can keep an Access® database secure by password protecting it.

Step by step: Password protecting an Access® database

3 Steps

1 Before you can protect a database with a password you must first open it in exclusive mode. To do this, go to the File menu, then choose Open (do not use the Recent Files option). Select the location of your database (e.g. the Documents folder) and, when the Open dialog box opens, click the down arrow on the Open button and choose Open Exclusive, as shown here.

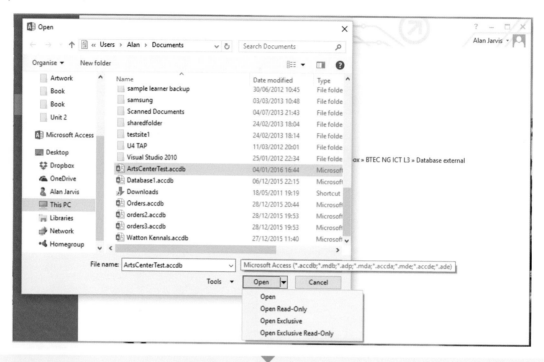

2 Once the database has opened, choose the File menu again, and click the Encrypt with Password button, as shown here.

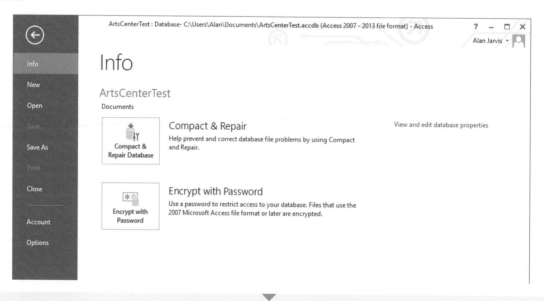

3 You will then be asked to enter and verify a password for the database. The database is now password protected and encrypted. DO NOT lose the password otherwise the database will be inaccessible.

User access levels

Access® database up to version 2003 allowed user-level access control. It was removed from later versions of Access (2007 and 2010, for example) as it was considered too complex.

You can still apply user-level access control using more recent versions of Microsoft® Access®, but only if you first save the database as an Access 2002–2003 version (a .mdb file).

> **Link**
>
> For more on database security, please go to www.databases.about.com

---

Step by step: Applying user access levels   `4 Steps`

1 To save your database as an Access 2002–2003 version (a .mdb file), so that you can apply user access level, go to the File menu, choose Save As and then select the Database file type to be Access 2002-2003 Database (.mdb).

▼

2 Once you have done this, you will need to add the User-Level Security Wizard to the Ribbon. Go to the File menu, then choose Options (bottom of the list on the left). Once the Access Options dialog box appears, choose Customize Ribbon from the menu on the left. Click Database Tools on the right and click the New Group button, as shown here.

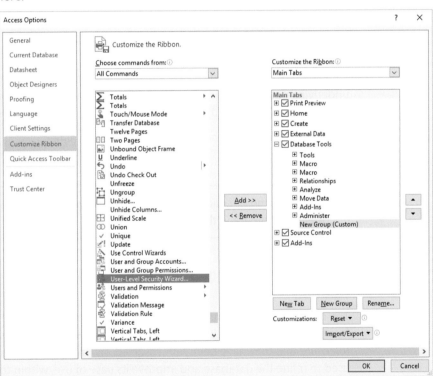

▼

3 Then, from the drop-down box entitled Choose commands from (top centre left of the dialog) choose All commands. From the list underneath, scroll down and find User-Level Security Wizard (the list is alphabetical). Now click the Add button in the centre of the dialog to add the command into the new group that you previously created. Then click OK. You should now see the User-Level Security Wizard in the Ribbon under the Database Tools menu.

▼

4 The User-Level Security Wizard takes you, step by step, through allowing you to control which users and groups of users have access to all the different database objects (such as tables, queries, forms) and what kind of access they have (such as read or modify).

Testing and refining the database solution

Once the main work of implementing the relational database solution has been completed, work can start on testing the database. It is important to test and refine a database, as you need to ensure that the end result matches the design and that it fulfils the user requirements.

Recording appropriate test documentation

The functionality of the database will be tested using the test plans created during the design phase.

> **Link**
>
> Example test plans are shown in the section Test plans.

Each test is carried out and the actual outcome of the test recorded next to the expected outcome in the test plan. In instances where the expected and actual outcomes differ, further investigation (including correction of any errors) is required and should be documented in the test plan.

Different types of testing

Functionality testing should cover the main features of the user interface and the underlying database structure, including referential integrity issues. Testing of the usability, accessibility and security of the database should also be completed.

This testing will require the use of appropriate test data.

> **Link**
>
> For more on the selection and use of appropriate test data see the section Correctness of data in the Test plans section.

Using testing outcomes to improve and refine the database solution

The database functionality testing should help to ensure that the database system is free from errors and works as expected. Any errors should be resolved and re-tested to ensure that they have been fully resolved. Usability and accessibility testing can be used to refine the database and improve its ease of use, within the constraints of time and the client's budget.

Ⓘ PAUSE POINT   The Access® database software has so many features that it can be difficult to remember how to use them all or to find the correct feature to do what you need. Were there things you wanted to do with the database but could not find or features that you did not know how to use?

Hint   There are lots of resources available online to learn more. See Further reading and resources.

Extend   Think of additional features that would be needed to make the Dissford Arts Centre database system fully functioninal. Try to implement some of them to develop your skills at using Access®.

Assessment practice 2.1   A01 A02 A03

A local charity runs a dogs' home where they look after abandoned dogs and try to find them a new home. They have asked you to create a database of the dogs they have in the home which will allow them to search for a dog which meets the requirements of people looking to re-home one of their dogs. The facilities they need are as follows.

- Each dog's ID number, Name, Breed, Colour, Sex, Year_of_birth, Approx_size (can be large, medium or small), Weight (in kg), Date of last vaccination and Comments (text field for a short description of the dog's history and temperament).
- The charity requires there to be a form on which to enter each dog's details.
- They require a query to allow them to search for dogs meeting a client's requirements. They should be able to input the Colour, Sex and Approx_size and see a list of matching dogs. The results of the query should be presented in a report.
- They also need to record details of the families with which dogs have been re-homed. They need to have the details of the family (name, address, telephone number etc.) and the dog that has been re-homed with them.
- They require a form-based user interface to allow them to link a dog with the family that has re-homed the dog.

You need to:
- produce a design for these requirements including:
  - an ERD showing the relationships between entities
  - documentation describing the normalisation process for this data
  - a data dictionary for the required tables
  - user interface designs
  - designs for the queries and reports
  - test plans to test your solution.
- implement your design and using the test plans created at the design stage, test the system works as expected.
- resolve any issues and optimise your solution as a result of your testing of the database to improve the functionality and usability of the system.

Plan
- What is the task?
- What are the success criteria for this task?
- Are there any areas I think I may struggle with in this task?
- What resources am I going to need?

Do
- I have planned my time appropriately to do my research and complete the task.
- I can identify when I have gone wrong and make amendments to improve the outcome.
- I can set milestones and evaluate my progress and success at those intervals.
- I can provide a glossary of common technical terms.

Review
- I can assess what went well and what I need to do to improve.
- I can explain why I went wrong or struggled in some areas more than others.
- I can identify what I have achieved by undertaking this task.
- I know what I need to learn next.

D   Evaluating a database development project

Evaluation is an important part of any project because, by evaluating how the project went, you can learn from your experiences and do better next time. You will evaluate the database design, the database created, the testing processes used and the overall success of the relational database solution.

> **Tip**
>
> One method that can really help you to evaluate the process of designing and creating a database is to keep notes as you go through the process. Note down things that you had problems with and how you resolved them, and also tasks that were completed with no problems. Then, when you come to the end of the process of designing, developing and testing the database, you can refer back to these notes as a reminder of how things went and the issues you had to deal with. This will make writing an evaluation much more straightforward.

Database design evaluation

The design of a database, as with any software development project, is a critical part of the process. No matter how good the creation and implementation of the database system is, if the design is flawed, then the end result is unlikely to meet the requirements.

Hopefully, the majority of design errors will be spotted during the implementation stage and the design will be corrected. Errors which only become evident once the system is implemented are often much harder to resolve. This is especially the case where large volumes of data are involved, as changes to tables or relationships will take a long time to complete if there is a lot of data already in the tables.

There are a number of things you might consider when evaluating the design of a database against the given requirements while completing or after completion of the development process.

▶ Use and application of an ERD – How easy was it to understand the conceptual stage of the database design? Was it clear which tables would be needed and how they were to be related? Were you able to draw up the conceptual ERD easily? Was it clear what type of relationship existed (one-to-one, one-to-many, many-to-many) between the entities?

▶ Normalisation – Did your conceptual design translate easily into the logical design? Were you able to verify the logical design of the table relationships with the normalisation process?

▶ Data dictionary – Did the data dictionary accurately and correctly list the fields, datatypes, field sizes and validation required?

▶ Functionality requirements and identification of any omissions – How well did the design meet the user functionality requirements? To a certain extent, this depends on how well the user requirements are defined. There might have been some areas that were omitted from the requirements, for example. How did you deal with this? You need to consider the stated purpose of the database and how the user wanted to be able to access the data. There might be stated requirements, such as that the database should be easy to use, in which case you will need to consider if your user interface designs were clear and intuitive. Were any of the requirements omitted from the database design? Some of the answers to these questions may not become evident until you have created and tested the database and its user interface.

▶ Design strengths and weaknesses and potential further improvements – What are the strengths and weaknesses of your design? This may also only become clear when you have implemented and tested the whole system. Weaknesses in the design are going to include those parts of the design that you had to change when it came to implementation or testing. You might also want to consider whether your design was detailed enough or if there were parts of it that did not meet the requirements or omitted any of them. What further improvements could you carry out to your database to ensure that it does meet the requirements?

Evaluation of database testing

Testing is vital to ensure the correctness and robustness of your database before it gets released it to users. You will need to evaluate the application of test data to ensure that the database solution meets requirements.

The testing of the database should reveal any errors, which should then be corrected. If the testing does not reveal any errors then it is likely that the testing has not been rigorous enough.

When evaluating database testing, there are a number of areas you should consider.

▶ Test data – Was your selection of test data appropriate, did you have a full range of normal, erroneous and extreme test data? Could your selection of test data have been more rigorous and extensive?

▶ Recording of actual results and test records – Were the results of testing fully documented? You should have created detailed test plans at the design stage. Once the database had been developed, these plans should have been used to test the database and you should have entered the actual outcomes against the expected outcomes for each test.

> **Tip**
>
> Where appropriate, you should take screenshots of the actual outcomes of your tests for inclusion with your analysis and evaluation of the database.

▶ Analysis and commenting on results – Did you make use of the actual test outcomes? Have you commented on the results and analysed them? Were there different issues that you needed to investigate? Have you done this and resolved any issues? You should also keep detailed records of the changes you have made to resolve the issues and commented on what your tests revealed.

▶ Iterative processes – Once all the issues have been resolved, the whole database should be tested again, and results of the new set of tests documented. The reason for this is that the changes made to correct the issues identified in the first round of tests may have inadvertently introduced other problems. This iterative process helps to improve the quality (accuracy, readability and robustness) of the final product.

▶ Identifying and recording which tests were successfully met and which test data issues were not resolved – Which tests were met successfully? Were there any issues that your testing identified that you were not able to resolve? What were the reasons for not being able to resolve the issues? Constraints on time or money perhaps?

Evaluation of the database

The acid test for any software development project is whether or not it meets the requirements of the users. Every software product will have its strengths and weaknesses and, when evaluating the final database product, there are a number of things that should be considered in terms of its strengths and weaknesses.

Is it fit for purpose?

The purpose of the database should have been defined at the outset by those who commissioned the database, based on who will use the product (i.e. the client and user requirements). You can consider how well it achieves that purpose.

Given that in the assessment for this unit you will have limited time, there may well be facilities that will be needed to enable the database to achieve its purpose which you do not have time to implement. You may only be asked to complete certain facilities, so there may be things that, if the database were to be used in real life, you would need to add to make it a complete application.

Consider the Dissford Arts Centre booking system that we have been using as an example (see Worked examples throughout this unit). Although we completed the part of the system that allows staff to search for available slots and make a booking, there are a number of other facilities

that would be required by a real-life database, such as the ability to modify an existing booking.

Is it easy to use?

This can be difficult for you, as the creator of the database, to judge. Remember that the users of the database will probably not be IT professionals, so things that are obvious to you may be less so for them. You might find it helpful to show your user interface designs to your peers and, if possible, to others who are not IT specialists to get their opinions on how intuitive and usable the interface is. Of course you cannot do this in the final assessment for this unit, but it might help you get some ideas about what users might find difficult to understand about interfaces, and then you can apply what you have learnt in your assessment.

Are some aspects of the system constrained by the software used?

As mentioned at the start of this unit, Microsoft® Access® is designed for use as a desktop database and it lacks many of the features required to support true multi-user environments. With a database, this is particularly limiting as data, by its nature, is best when shared with others. Access® is also not really suitable for creating databases which are accessed via the internet. Therefore, you should consider what other database software options are available to you.

How easy is it to maintain the database?

Would it be easy for someone else to update, correct and add to your database? The ease of maintenance of an Access® database will depend upon how detailed and accurate your design documentation is. This documentation should allow someone else to understand how your database has been designed and created.

Does the database meet its given requirements?

To a certain extent, this will depend on how detailed those requirements were in the first place. In many ways this question is a combination of all the questions above. Evaluation of the database against its requirements essentially requires you to ask the following question: Does the database do what it was required to do and how well does it do it?

Write a justification and an evaluation of the database development project that you undertook for the dogs' home in Assessment practice 2.1.

Your justification and evaluation should consider the following questions.
- How well does the system that you developed meet the user requirements, as outlined in the scenario?
- How effective have you been in creating a high quality database solution which performs appropriately and is easy to use?
- What were the changes that you needed to make to the system during the implementation and testing phases?
- What improvements would you like to make, given more time?

Plan
- What is the task and how will my success be judged?
- What might I find difficult with this task?
- How does an evaluation and a justification differ from an explanation?
- What resources will I need?

Do
- I have collected together my notes and the work I completed for assessment practice 2.1.
- I have set task milestones and checked my progress against these.
- I have drafted out answers to the questions listed in the task.
- I have checked that what I have written provides a justification of the actions that I took in assessment practice 2.1.
- I have checked that I have evaluated the work that I completed for assessment practice 2.1.

Review
- I can assess which parts of the work went well and which parts I found difficult.
- I understand places where I might have gone wrong.
- I know what I have learnt by completing this task.
- I know what my next steps will be.

Further reading and resources

Training manuals

There are lots of free training materials on the internet including:
- Support.office.com – The official Microsoft® Office® website. It contains training material for various versions of Access®.
- docs.oracle.com/en/database/ – Oracle database documentation. It includes information on database concepts.
- http://www.lynda.com/Access-training-tutorials/140-0.html – Access® tutorials on Lynda.com.

Books

Connolly, T. and Begg, C. (2014) *Database Systems: A Practical Approach to Design, Implementation, and Management* (Pearson) ISBN 9781292061184
This is a comprehensive book on database theory. It is a standard university text and quite technical.

Alexander, M. and Kusleik, R. (2013) *Access 2013 Bible* (John Wiley) ISBN 9781118490358
This gives comprehensive and detailed examples of how to use all the features of Access, including advanced level ones.

Fuller, L.U. and Cook, K. (2013) *Access 2013 for Dummies* (John Wiley) ISBN 9781118516386
This is an easy-to-follow book in the Dummies' easy-to-read style.

THINK ▶FUTURE

Hesmita Patel,

BTEC National
Student

I wanted to do this course

because I know that so many jobs require IT skills. I found it quite hard going, as there is a lot of technical content. I had thought that databases were pretty straightforward so it was quite a surprise that they can get quite complex. However, I did enjoy the challenge and, after a while, I began to enjoy using database software. I find it very interesting to see all the things you can do with it and I'm sure these skills will come in very handy in the business world.

I'm a bit apprehensive about the assessment, as there are lots of skills and techniques I need to be able to use for both making the design and creating the database, so I need to make sure that I am fully prepared for it.

In the future, I would like to learn more about web and server-based database systems as I think this is a really key skill for someone interested in using databases professionally.

Focusing your skills

Development plan

It is important to work out which skills you need to develop in the future. Here are some ideas to help you create a development plan.

1 Make a development plan listing the skills you currently have and those you want to develop. For the skills you need to develop, you should investigate ways of developing them and include this information in your plan.

2 Take every opportunity to develop your skills. There are lots of free resources available on the internet and lots of widely used web development tools, including database software, which is available free of charge.

3 Practise your skills by either setting up databases for your own use or look for work experience opportunities where you can practise these skills.

Getting ready for assessment

This section has been written to help you to do your best when you take the external examination. Read through it carefully and ask your tutor if there is anything you are not sure about.

About the test

The set task should be carried out under supervised conditions.

▸ Electronic templates for use in task activities will be provided, ahead of your assessment, for centres to download for you. These will be supplied to you at the start of your assessment.

▸ Work should be completed on a computer. Make sure that you have a power lead if you are using a laptop.

▸ Internet access is not permitted.

▸ During any break, materials must be kept securely by your tutor.

▸ You must not bring anything into the supervised environment or take anything out without your tutor's knowledge and approval.

▸ You should make sure that you back up your work regularly. You should save your work to your folder using the naming instructions that will be indicated in each activity.

▸ Remember to bring anything else you might need, such as glasses for working onscreen and refreshments.

▸ Turn off your mobile phone to avoid distractions!

Preparing for the test

This unit is assessed under supervised conditions. The number of marks for the unit is 66. Pearson sets and marks the task.

The external assessment will last for 10 hours in a 1 week period, and can be arranged over a number of sessions. You will be assessed on your ability to design, create, test and evaluate a relational database system to manage information.

Make sure that you arrive in good time for each test session and check that you have everything you need for the test beforehand. Make a schedule for the task to ensure that you leave yourself enough time at the end to check through your work.

Listen to, and read carefully, any instructions that you are given. Marks are often lost through not reading instructions properly and misunderstanding what you are being asked to do. Ensure that you have checked all sides of the assessment task before starting.

Proofread and correct any mistakes before handing in your work.

Key terms typically used in assessment

There are some key terms that may appear in your assessment. Understanding what these words mean will help you understand what you are being asked to do.

▶ The following table shows you the key terms that will be used consistently in your assessments to ensure that you are rewarded for demonstrating the necessary skills.

▶ Please note: the list below will not necessarily be used in every paper/session and is provided for guidance only. Only a single command word will be used per item in your test.

Key terms	Definition
Annotated screen shot	Image copy of a computer screen (obtained by pressing the print screen key then pasting into a document) with added annotations explaining what the image shows.
Database structure	The structure is composed of fields (a single piece of data, e.g. a name or date of birth), records (a complete set of fields, e.g. an employee's personnel record) and tables (a collection of records, e.g. all employees' personnel records).
Data dictionary	A centralized repository of information about data, such as meaning, relationships to other data, origin, usage, tables, fields and format.
Entity-relationship diagram (ERD)	A diagrammatical representation of database tables and their relationships to other data, origin, usage, tables, fields and format.
Evaluate	A review and synthesis of each stage of database design, (i.e. development, processes and outcomes) to provide a supported judgement about the quality. Typically, a conclusion will be required.
Normalisation	The process of organising raw data into separate related tables to minimise data redundancy.
Query	An SQL select statement which extracts data from a table or tables which match defined criteria.
Report	A database report presents information from a database. Information should be displayed simply and efficiently. Printed reports from the database should allow the viewing of information quickly and easily.
Test log	Used to plan and record program testing, record the outcomes of testing and the changes made to solve problems.
User interface	The visual part of the database through which a user interacts with a computer or software. A good interface is intuitive and allows a user to easily enter the required data accurately. A user interface is implemented using screen forms with titles, labelled boxes for data entry, buttons to perform actions and other features to make interaction as easy as possible.

A few more guidelines

▸ Always make a plan for your answer before you start writing. Sketch this out so that you can refer to it throughout – remember to include an introduction and a conclusion and think about the key points you want to mention in your answer. In this plan, think about setting yourself some timeframes so that you can make sure that you have time to cover everything you want to – and, importantly, have time to write the conclusion!

▸ Try to keep your answer as focused on your key points as possible. If you find your answer drifting away from that main point, refer back to your plan.

▸ Make sure that you understand everything being asked of you in the activity instructions. It might help you to underline or highlight the key terms in the instructions so that you can be sure that your answer is clear and focused on exactly what you have been asked to do.

Sample answers

Look at the sample questions which follow and the tips on how to answer them well.

Worked example

Set task brief

You have been asked to produce a database to manage cinema bookings. You have identified that the cinema has shows (with a film title, rating and description) and it has customers who want to come to see the shows.

> In the real assessment, you will be given a more detailed brief.

Activity 1: Entity-relationship database

Produce an entity-relationship diagram (ERD) for the database by normalising the given data to third normal form.

Sample answer

You have drafted out an ERD which looks like this:

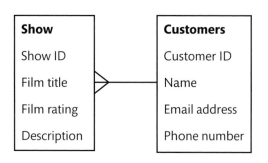

Show	Customers
Show ID	Customer ID
Film title	Name
Film rating	Email address
Description	Phone number

> This shows that the Customers table is a one-to-many relationship with the Show table, as one customer can go to see many different films. However, each show has more than one customer. Lots of people go and see each showing of the film, not just one. This is, therefore, a many-to-many relationship, which needs to be resolved with a link table. Adding a Sales table to link the Show table and the Customers table will resolve the many-to-many relationship.

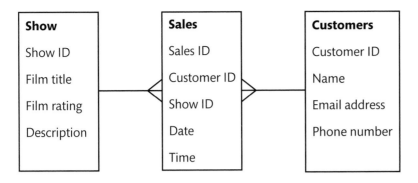

Activity 2: Data dictionary

Produce a data dictionary for your database using the given document.

In the real assessment you will be given a template table.

Sample answer

The first draft for the Sales table looks like this:

Data dictionary: Sales table			
Field name	**Key?**	**Datatype**	**Validation**
Sales ID	Primary	Integer	
Customer ID		Integer	
Show ID		Integer	
Date		Text, 6 characters	
Time		Text, 4 characters	

To improve this data dictionary, the Customer and Show IDs should be listed as foreign keys.

Date and time fields should have date datatypes, to ensure that they are automatically validated as the correct format for a date or time.

Activity 3: Design the user interface

For another task, you are asked to produce an interface design for the process of registering a new customer and making a sale.

Sample answer

Your first interface design is for the customer registration:

```
┌──────────────────────────────────────────────┐
│  Cinema system                                 │
│                                                │
│   Customer ID    ┌──────────────────────┐     │
│                  └──────────────────────┘     │
│                                                │
│   Name           ┌──────────────────────┐     │
│                  └──────────────────────┘     │
│                                                │
│   Email address  ┌──────────────────────┐     │
│                  └──────────────────────┘     │
│                                                │
│   Phone number   ┌──────────────────────┐     │
│                  └──────────────────────┘     │
│                                                │
│                      ┌──────┐                  │
│                      │  OK  │                  │
│                      └──────┘                  │
└──────────────────────────────────────────────┘
```

However, the Customer ID should not be entered by the user, as it needs to be unique. It should be created automatically (an Access AutoNumber field).

The next screen is the Sales screen where the film is selected:

```
┌──────────────────────────────────────────────┐
│  Cinema system                                 │
│                                                │
│   Customer ID    ┌──────────────────────┐     │
│                  └──────────────────────┘     │
│                                                │
│   Sales ID       nnnnnn                        │
│                                                │
│   Show ID        ┌──────────────────────┐     │
│                  └──────────────────────┘     │
│                                                │
│   Date           ┌──────────────────────┐     │
│                  └──────────────────────┘     │
│                                                │
│   Time           ┌──────────────────────┐     │
│                  └──────────────────────┘     │
│                                                │
│                  ┌──────────┐                  │
│                  │  BOOK    │                  │
│                  └──────────┘                  │
└──────────────────────────────────────────────┘
```

The Sales ID should be an AutoNumber field so that it is correctly shown as a field that the system displays rather than one that the user enters. However, the user would not know which Show ID to enter. This field would be better as a drop-down box which displays the film names.

It might also be a good idea to add a Cancel button to allow the user to back out of the transaction.

This design needs some improvement. The Customer ID would come from the previous screen so does not need to entered, just displayed.

In your assessment, you are also likely to be asked to complete other activities, such as the following.

- Activity 4: Testing plan
- Activity 5: Database development and testing (using data provided)

Activity 6: Evaluation of your database solution
Evaluate your solution.
You should consider:

- how well your solution meets the requirements of the scenario
- the quality, performance and usability of the database
- the changes made during the development and testing process.

Sample answer
This is your first draft:

I have worked very hard on this database and I am really happy with the result. Most of it works well and it does what it is supposed to do and could be used to book cinema tickets with a few additions. I think the user interface is ok but perhaps it needs a few more buttons to make it easier to use, like some 'Back' or 'Cancel' buttons on some forms. The report I produced could also be made better by tidying it up a bit. I didn't have a lot of problems creating the database. There were a few things I found difficult but I managed to sort them out.

The main problem with this evaluation is that is it too vague. For example, it says you are happy with the database but does not say why. You would need to say something like:

I'm happy with the database design as the tables are all related correctly and there is no duplication of data. I checked the design with the normalisation process. The data dictionary is also fully complete with appropriate data types and validation for all the fields where it can be used. This should help make sure that correct data is input, wherever possible. The queries I developed extract the correct data and have all the required fields and provide the forms and reports with the data that they require.

The forms are laid out reasonably well but would benefit from some of the labels and fields being adjusted in size and position, and including Cancel buttons would make them easier to use.

You would also need to provide more detail about how the development process went and the problems you had and how you overcame them. This is one reason why keeping a diary during the development process, in which you can note down these things, can really help when it comes to writing the evaluation.

Remember that when writing an evaluation you need to give specific details about:

- what you think is good (and why it is good) or went well with your database
- what you had difficulty with and how you overcame those difficulties
- what you would improve or correct given more time.

Using Social Media in Business 3

Getting to know your unit

Social media is a phenomenon of the internet age; nothing like it existed before. Its immense popularity has provided a new way for individuals, businesses and other groups to communicate with each other. For business users, social media provides a new way to interact with the public and customers. This unit is about the ways in which businesses can make use of social media, the methods and benefits of doing so and the issues and dangers that exist. Understanding how businesses can use social media successfully will be a useful skill to have when looking for work in the IT industry.

In this unit, you will explore different social media websites and consider the ways in which they can be used for business purposes, including the potential pitfalls. You will then develop and implement a social media plan for a business to achieve specific aims and objectives. You will also collect data on the business's use of social media and review the effectiveness of your social media plan.

How you will be assessed

This unit will be assessed by a series of internally assessed tasks set by your tutor. Throughout this unit, you will find assessment activities that will help you prepare for the live assessment.

For learning aim A, you will need to look into how social media can be used by businesses in general, while for learning aims B and C you will need to plan and implement the use of social media in a real or imaginary business. To pass this unit, you need to ensure that you have covered all the Pass criteria fully in the live assessment. To achieve the higher grades of Merit or Distinction, you need to ensure that you present evidence which meets the requirements of the individual assessment criteria. The Merit criteria require an assessment or a justification, so evidence which is merely a description will not be sufficient. For M2 for example, you will need to say why you made the decisions you did and why alternatives were rejected. Similarly, some of the Distinction criteria require an evaluation.

Assessment criteria

This table shows what you must do in order to achieve a **Pass**, **Merit** or **Distinction** grade, and where you can find activities to help you.

Pass	Merit	Distinction
Learning aim **A** Explore the impact of social media on the ways in which businesses promote their products and services		
A.P1 Explain the different ways in which a business can use social media. Assessment practice 3.1	**A.M1** Assess the different ways in which a business can use social media to attract a target audience. Assessment practice 3.1	**A.D1** Evaluate the business use of social media to interact with customers and promote products or services to a target audience. Assessment practice 3.1
A.P2 Explain the audience profiles of different social media websites. Assessment practice 3.1		
Learning aim **B** Develop a plan to use social media in a business to meet requirements		
B.P3 Produce a plan to use social media in a business to meet its business requirements. Assessment practice 3.2	**B.M2** Justify planning decisions made, showing how the plan will fulfil its purpose and business requirements. Assessment practice 3.2	**BC.D2** Evaluate the plan and use of social media in a business against business requirements. Assessment practice 3.2
B.P4 Review the plan with others in order to identify and inform improvements. Assessment practice 3.2		
Learning aim **C** Implement the use of social media in a business		
C.P5 Produce business-related content using appropriate features of social media which meet the requirements of the plan. Assessment practice 3.2	**C.M3** Optimise the content, format and features of social media which meet the requirements of the plan. Assessment practice 3.2	**BC.D3** Demonstrate individual responsibility, creativity, and effective self-management in the planning and use of social media in a business context. Assessment practice 3.2
C.P6 Review data obtained on social media usage and interaction. Assessment practice 3.2		

Getting started

Social media has had a huge impact on our lives. Consider how social media is used by businesses. Do you ever click on adverts you see on social media? Do you follow/like any businesses? Have you joined any Facebook groups? Which ones did you join and why?

 # Explore the impact of social media on the ways in which businesses promote their products and services

You probably already use social media sites, but this unit is not about the personal use of these sites. Instead, it is about the ways in which businesses can use social media to promote their products and services. However you have probably noticed that some things that you post on social media are more popular than others: they get more likes or shares, for example. Have you ever thought about why you like or share some posts but not others? For businesses, understanding what makes people interact with a post can really help them promote their business on social media effectively.

Social media websites

There are a wide variety of different social media websites, from the very well-known ones, such as Facebook™ and Twitter™, to the less well-known ones, many of which have a particular focus. Instagram™, for example, is a social media website where users can upload images taken with their phone, while LinkedIn® is used for making business contacts.

Business promotion using social media

Social media has become hugely popular and many millions of people have signed up to accounts on social media websites. Each site has its own particular features and the sites are constantly developing and adding new facilities to keep existing account holders engaged and to attract new members.

In general, each social media website has its own unique features and structure that make it different from the others.

▶ **Table 3.1:** Key social media websites, their features, structure and target audience

Social media website	Key features and structure	Target audience
Facebook™	• Connect to 'friends' – both real-world friends and acquaintances, and people you only know virtually through social media (often friends of friends). • Friends post status updates, photos/videos or links and interact with others by 'liking', commenting on posts or by sharing posts. • Dashboard view showing newsfeed, links to messages, events, friends, groups, pages, apps and adverts. • Groups – both public and private social groups for friends with a common interest, different communities. • Pages – clubs and societies as well as businesses may have a page which users can join to see their posts. • Newsfeed – a scrolling panel in the centre of the Facebook™ main display shows posts from you, your friends, groups and pages that you have liked. • Events – both public and private events can be organised with a dedicated page. • Targeted advertising and trending articles appear in a sidebar on the right of the page.	• Individuals who want to know what is happening in the lives of their friends and family. • People who want to follow particular interests using groups. • Businesses who want to promote their products and services.

▶ **Table 3.1:** – *continued*

Social media website	Key features and structure	Target audience
Google+™	<ul><li>Similar in concept to Facebook™.</li><li>Users can organise friends into 'circles' which are groups of friends with which certain content can be shared.</li><li>Updates from a user's circles are displayed in the central 'stream' (similar to Facebook™ newsfeed). It is a multi column displaying friends' updates, and different circles can be selected using a menu bar. Communities allow users to join in a conversation about a particular topic of interest (similarly to Facebook™ groups).</li><li>Collections allow you to group your posts by topic. Other users can then follow a collection rather than everything you post.</li><li>Hangouts allow users to take part in multi-user video conferences.</li></ul>	<ul><li>Individuals with a particular interest who want to follow a community of like-minded individuals.</li></ul>
Twitter™	<ul><li>Post short messages (max 140 characters) known as Tweets which are seen by your followers.</li><li>Follow other Twitter™ users to see their Tweets. Twitter™ is often used to follow celebrities and keep up to date with what they are doing.</li><li>Retweet posts that are considered interesting to your followers.</li><li>Suggestions for accounts to follow and current trends on the left of the page.</li></ul>	<ul><li>Individuals who want to know what is happening to celebrities and other people they are interested in.</li></ul>
Instagram™	<ul><li>Upload photos and short videos from your phone.</li><li>Use Geotagging to identify the location shown in the photo.</li><li>Filters can be applied to the photos to provide a variety of different looks.</li><li>Users can follow other people and see the photos they upload.</li><li>Users can connect their Instagram™ accounts to other social media accounts to share uploaded photos on those sites as well.</li><li>Simple newsfeed view, with a scrolling display of photos uploaded by the user or the accounts they follow.</li><li>Can only be accessed using mobile devices, not PCs.</li><li>Instagram™ has been owned by Facebook™ since 2012.</li></ul>	<ul><li>Individuals who want to share photos with friends and family.</li></ul>
YouTube™	<ul><li>Upload videos, and create your own video channel which others can subscribe to.</li><li>Carry out simple editing on videos.</li><li>Subscribe to YouTube™ channels created by individuals or companies with collections of videos on a particular subject.</li><li>There is a vast range of videos on YouTube™, including music videos, and instructional videos covering almost every imaginable subject.</li><li>For a business with a physical product, YouTube™ is an excellent place for product demonstrations.</li><li>YouTube™ has been owned by Google™ since 2006.</li></ul>	<ul><li>Individuals who want to upload videos.</li><li>Businesses that want to promote their product with a video.</li><li>People who want to watch music videos.</li></ul>
LinkedIn®	<ul><li>Upload a business-related profile showing your professional experience and qualifications.</li><li>Groups related to professional interests.</li><li>Company pages providing a detailed profile of a business.</li><li>Personal users can link to other contacts and network.</li><li>A good place to look for job opportunities.</li></ul>	<ul><li>Business people/ professionals and companies that want to network and make contacts.</li></ul>
Pinterest™	<ul><li>Pinterest™ is a relatively new social media site which saw a big increase in users during 2014–15.</li><li>Allows users to create a scrapbook (or pin board) type collection of website links, images and videos.</li><li>Users can follow each other so they see their newly added content (so-called 'pins').</li><li>Users can search and browse through any user's public pin boards.</li></ul>	<ul><li>People who are interested in, for example, crafts who want to get ideas from others.</li><li>People who want to collect ideas on a particular theme.</li></ul>

Many social media sites work with each other, for example you can link your Instagram account to Facebook™ so that whenever you post a photo on Instagram, it automatically posts on your Facebook™ too. You can also post your YouTube™ videos on Facebook™.

How businesses can use social media

There are a number of ways in which businesses can use social media websites to support their business aims and needs and these are discussed in the following sections.

Promoting products and/or services and creating an image or brand

Businesses, just like individuals, can set up free profiles on social media websites. They use them to promote their products or services, and to describe their businesses to customers. Social media allows them the opportunity to develop an online community of followers. The aim is that the business will post interesting content that their followers (potential customers) will interact with by commenting, liking or sharing the content.

Many businesses use social media to help create a **brand** or image for their products. This is about associating the product in people's minds with the kind of image the company wants to portray. For example, a company might want to promote a healthy or sports-orientated lifestyle brand, or they want to associate the product with quality, success or luxury, or they might want to give a product a quirky, out of the ordinary, alternative image. The goal is to attract customers from their target market to think positively about the product or service, and ultimately purchase it.

Key term

Brand – an aspect of a product or service that distinguishes it from other similar products. It can include, among other things, a logo, colour scheme and name. Companies often go to great lengths to develop a unique brand identity. Some of the best known brands in the world are McDonalds™' golden arches, Apple®'s symbolic apple logo and Nike®'s iconic 'swoosh'/tick.

Case study

Facebook™

Facebook™ was founded by Mark Zuckerberg in 2004 and originally limited to university students, but since September 2006 it has been open to anyone over the age of 13. After 2009 Facebook™ grew rapidly, and it had 500 million active users in 2010 and by September 2014 it had reached 1 billion active members. Facebook™ is the second most visited website in the world after Google™ and the third most visited site in the UK (after Google.com and Google.co.uk). After the US, the country with the largest number of Facebook™ users is India. However, Facebook™ is not as popular in every country as it is in the US and UK. In countries such as Japan, where local social media sites tend to be preferred, Facebook™ is still way ahead of other social media sites in terms of the number of users. In 2014, the percentage of US adult online users that used Facebook™ was 71 per

cent; its nearest rival was Linkedin™ with 28 per cent of internet users. Source: www.pewinternet.org

Facebook™ has had a huge impact on the way people communicate and relate to each other. It has changed the way that people stay in touch with individuals and about forthcoming events. Facebook™ has also had a political impact. For example, it is said that Facebook™ played a major role in the 2011 Egyptian revolution, allowing people to easily organise mass rallies.

In recent years, the growth of Facebook™ has slowed, perhaps because it is reaching saturation in many countries and other newer social media sites such as Instagram™ and Pinterest™ have grown more rapidly. However, these newer social media sites still have a long way to go to reach the number of active users that Facebook™ has.

Discussion

Think about some of the ways in which you could create a brand image for different products. For example, suppose you were asked to promote an expensive luxury car, a low-cost airline or personalised marshmallows. What type of image would you want to portray for these different products? How would you achieve that? Have a discussion about this with your class and decide on a brand image for a number of different products.

Communicating with customers

Using social media is an excellent way to communicate with customers, especially about unexpected or time dependant changes to the business' products or services. For example, many train and bus companies use Twitter™ to update passengers on delays, cancellations and route changes. Furthermore, the communication does not need to be one way as social media can be used to obtain customer feedback and to gather customers' opinions. This can be a much more cost-effective method of doing market research than traditional methods such as telephone or face-to-face interviews. It helps customers to feel that their opinions and ideas are valued by the company as they feel that they have direct access to the company.

Customer service

Businesses can use social media to provide good customer service, by resolving queries and managing issues through their social media profiles. This is a method of communication that many people are familiar with and can access quickly and easily. When customers have questions or problems with a product or service they can quickly message or post on the Facebook™ page of the company or send them a tweet on Twitter™. For businesses to use social media successfully for customer service, they need to ensure that their business profiles are monitored regularly (or constantly) and that customers are replied to quickly, otherwise it may look like the company does not care about their customers.

Features of social media websites tailored to business needs

There are a number of key features of social media websites that can be tailored to business needs. These are discussed in the following sections.

Social media profiles and advertising

Social media websites do not charge users (individuals or business) to create accounts. They make money by offering businesses paid advertising on their website. On Facebook™, paid-for (sponsored) adverts appear on the right sidebar of the main newsfeed when you are using a PC or a Mac. On Twitter™, paid-for tweets (promoted tweets) appear among the tweets from the people you follow in your Twitter feed. Social media websites offer advertisers special facilities such as adverts that only appear on the pages of users that meet certain **demographic** criteria, for example age or gender, or adverts that relate to the user's recent internet search history.

Key term

Demographics – measurements used to put people into different categories. One reason to do this is to understand their likes and dislikes more easily.

Social media websites therefore need to attract business users and provide a number of features aimed specifically at them. Many sites provide facilities for businesses to create pages and profiles for the business (both Facebook™ and LinkedIn® provide this). The profile tells the public about the business, what they do, their business aims and where they are located. Some sites also provide tools which show detailed demographic profiles of the people who visit a business's pages and how they interact with them. The best known example of this is Facebook™ Insights, which is a powerful tool for gathering data on the effectiveness of your posts and the profile of your social media audience. Twitter™ and Google™ also provide their own analytics tools. Facebook™ Insights is covered in more detail later in this unit.

If you want to place paid-for adverts on Facebook™, you can choose the audience you want the adverts to reach, in terms of demographics. For example, if you are a plumber, you really only want to advertise to local people so it would be useful to be able to target people based on their location.

You may have noticed that if you search for a product on a website like Amazon™, adverts for the product you have searched for start appearing on your Facebook™ page. Providing a link to a user's previous e-commerce site search history, and displaying related adverts on their page, is a business feature that Facebook™ offers to advertisers. The aim is to remind users of items they have looked at, but not yet purchased, in the hope that they will now purchase them. However, paid-for advertising is only a small part of what a business can use social media for.

Link

For more on Facebook™ Insights and analytic tools for social media see Data gathering and analysis.

Website and mobile device integration

Many people access social media via mobile devices rather than from laptops or PCs and this is a growing trend as people like to be able to communicate and stay 'plugged in' on the move. Most social media websites have mobile versions of their sites which are optimised for small screens. Mobile integration is important for businesses because it allows users to locate local services and may help businesses pick up passing trade. For example, restaurants and fast food outlets have the opportunity to attract trade from visitors to the area. Some specialist websites, such as Foursquare™, specialise in providing location-related information.

Link

For more on mobile device integration, see Mobile device integration in *Unit 7: Mobile Apps Development*.

Search engine optimisation

Social media has an important relationship with search engine optimisation (SEO). SEO is the name given to a range of techniques applied to a website to attempt to improve the ranking of the website (how close to the top it appears) in unpaid search results (in other words, the standard Google™ or Bing® search results rather than paid-for adverts). The theory is that when customers search for a type of product or service, they will be more likely to contact the one that appears first in the search results and are very unlikely to contact businesses that do not appear on the first page of results.

All businesses want to improve their search engine rankings. There are lots of things a business can do to their website to achieve an improvement in search engine ranking, but they should also have and maintain a Google+™ account. As Google+™ is owned

Using Social Media in Business

by Google™, the most widely used internet search engine, using a Google+™ account is likely to help improve a business's search engine ranking.

▶ **Figure 3.1:** The results of a search 'Search engine optimisation'

Some of the most important things a business can do to improve the search engine ranking of their website are listed below.

▶ Decide upon and use appropriate **keywords** within the content of the website.

▶ Update web pages regularly. Search engines assume websites which are not updated regularly are less likely to be relevant to people searching for something.

Link

Keywords are covered in the section on Keywords in Content planning and publishing.

Key term

Keywords – words that identify the key things that a business has to offer to customers and are likely to be used by potential customers when carrying out an internet search for a product or service.

▶ Use the most relevant keywords in the URLs and web page titles and to describe the site.

▶ Ensure that website text is properly spelt and uses correct grammar. Search engines assume that websites which have many spelling errors or bad grammar are not likely to be relevant.

▶ Encourage other people to add links from their website to yours (sometimes called 'inbound' links). If other businesses think your website is worth linking to then search engines assume that this is because there is a lot of useful information on your website and that it is worth others being directed to it.

▶ Make sure your site is mobile friendly. Google™ downgrades the rankings of non-mobile-friendly sites.

SEO is a huge topic, and large companies will spend a great deal of time and effort ensuring that their website is fully optimised. Search engines themselves provide guidance on how to achieve good results with their products. For example, search for 'Google webmaster guidelines' to see the advice that Google™ offers to websites on how to optimise their content.

Audience profile

An important concept in understanding how businesses can use social media is that of the 'audience profile'. The audience profile of a social media website describes the nature of the people who have registered profiles with the site, in terms of their age group, gender, geographical location and so on. Different social media websites have different audience profiles and, over time, the profile of a site's users can change.

> **Research**
>
> Run an internet search for 'social media audience profile'. This should produce some interesting results, but make sure that you are looking at recent information and also be aware that many results may only show data for the US. How do the profiles of sites differ? Pick a variety of different audience profiles (age, gender, location etc.) and find the site which matches the profile the closest.

For example, in 2015 research suggested that more men than women used Twitter™ but the reverse was true for Instagram™, which had more female users. Instagram™ also has a younger audience profile than most other social media websites. Pinterest™ has a much higher proportion of female users than any other mainstream social media website. Another example of the way in which social media usage has changed over time can be seen from research carried out in the US into the use of social media by teenagers. During 2015, the number of teenagers using Twitter™ fell, while the numbers using Instagram™ and Snapchat™ rose, although Twitter™ remained the second most important social media network for US teenagers (behind Instagram™).

LinkedIn®, on the other hand, with its focus on professional business relationships, was more popular with the over 50 age group than any of the other popular social media websites.

A key benefit to a business of using social media is the ability to identify the audience profile that they have attracted. Facebook™, Twitter™ and other social media websites provide tools which show the profile (in terms of demographics) of a page's audience. This is usage data which indicates the profile of followers. These analytic tools, such as Facebook™ Insights, also show businesses the effectiveness of individual posts in terms of the amount of interaction generated (that is, likes, comments or shares). This type of data is invaluable for marketing, but is either not available or difficult and expensive to collect using traditional types of media (TV, radio, newspaper and magazine adverts) and market research. Hence, social media has fast become a powerful tool for businesses in terms of promoting their products and services, because it allows them to easily understand who their target audience is.

Business uses of social media

There are so many people using social media on a daily basis (there are more than 1 billion active Facebook™ users) that businesses have potential access to a huge market for their products and services. Any business can create a profile on any number of different social media websites but a profile on its own is not enough – they need to encourage people to follow their pages and must interact with their potential customers. In other words, their profiles cannot be idle. They should be updated with regular new posts and they need to be engaging to invite customer interaction.

Content formats

Social media websites allow businesses to post a variety of different content. You can post text and images on most social media websites, and many sites such as

Facebook™ and YouTube™ also allow you to post videos. Facebook™ works well as a place for short promotional videos but, because of the dynamic nature of Facebook™ (that is, older posts move down your timeline), if a company wanted to post instructional videos of its products, YouTube™ would probably be a better choice because all your videos stay in place on your YouTube™ channel. The different social media websites can complement each other. For example, if a company provided customer service over Facebook™ and Twitter™ and a customer messaged asking how to do something, the reply could link them to an appropriate video on the company's YouTube™ channel.

Almost all social media websites allow you to include web page links in posts. This allows businesses to link their social media with their own website. For example, many businesses that use Twitter™ tweet a brief comment (remember tweets are limited to 140 characters) alongside a link to a web page or blog page article.

The Facebook™ Poll app allows posts to include a poll. This can be used in a number of ways, for example it can collect customer feedback on a new product or version of a product. There is also a Facebook™ Quiz app which can be used to create a simple knowledge quiz or a 'personality quiz'. For example, a 'personality quiz' could be used by a jeweller, who creates a 'What kind of jewellery suits your personality?' quiz that suggests different types of jewellery to potential customers based on the user's answers to several questions.

Content focus and developing an audience

As well as being able to post different formats of content, businesses can use social media to post content that focuses on a wide variety of different purposes.

▶ To be informative – that is, to describe a business's history, aims and objectives in order to help potential customers buy into an image/brand. Social media posts can also inform customers of important information quickly (eg changes to train arrival/departure times).

▶ To promote – that is, to advertise and promote the products, services and image/brand/lifestyle ethos of a business.

▶ To entertain – depending on the business, posting humorous or other entertaining and engaging content could appeal to potential customers.

▶ To make offers – businesses use social media to make special offers to customers. For example, they might offer 24 hour discounts to customers who have liked and shared the business's page or offer a prize to the ten thousandth person who likes their page.

▶ To provide customer service – this will normally be in response to customer posts on their page. Responding quickly and directly to customers on social media and solving their problems will make a business look efficient and effective.

Ultimately, the main reason for businesses to use social media is to attract more customers and to make more money by selling more products or services. However, a business that constantly uses a 'hard sell' **direct advertising** approach on social media may end up annoying its followers rather than encouraging them to purchase. A much better (and ultimately more profitable) approach to developing an audience for your business is by mixing posts that promote products and services directly (and special offer posts) with other content, related to the area of business that the company operates in, that is either informative or entertaining. This approach is a form of **indirect advertising**. For example, if a pet grooming business had a Facebook™ page, they could include posts related to issues to do with pets (such as pet health, grooming and food), photos of unusual pets, or links to amusing pet videos and other similarly pet-focused content that would be of interest to their target audience of pet lovers.

Key terms

Direct advertising – where a business uses adverts which tell you to buy their product or sign up to their service. They use a direct approach by simply telling you what the product/service is and suggesting that you purchase it.

Indirect advertising – is more subtle than direct advertising. It attempts to create a positive attitude towards the product/service in the mind of the customer through sponsorship (eg a company sponsors a particular TV programme), product placement and other methods (such as those that social media uses) to try to create a relationship with the customer.

This type of engaging content, focused on issues which will be of interest to their target audience, will help promote their social media streams and encourage people to like or share their posts (on Facebook™) or retweet them (on Twitter™). It will also help to create a positive image of the business in the minds of the people who follow them, giving the impression of a business that is not just interested in selling, but has a genuine interest in the subject area and is knowledgeable about it.

Keywords

The choice of keywords is an important concept that relates both to a company's website and the content they post on social media. In most cases, when someone is looking for something online, they use a search engine such as Google™ or Bing®. It is very important for a business's success on the web that, when someone searches for the product or service they provide, their website or social media pages are listed at or near the top of the search results. Keywords relate to the likely search strings (the text a person searching for the product or service types into the Google™ or Bing® search box) that potential customers would use. It is important to make sure that these keywords appear in the social media posts and profiles that a business creates and are used in the URLs and page titles of their website, as it will increase the likelihood that the business's website and social media profiles will show high up in search results. For example, the keywords for a freelance editor's website and social media are the services they offer, such as 'proofreading', 'copy editing' and 'project management', terms associated with their work such as 'publishing' and 'editor', and the name of the business.

Developing contacts

It is also important to develop contacts via social media. Businesses can use social media to keep up to date with their industry and with suppliers and competitors. By following their suppliers, competitors and industry experts on social media websites like Twitter™, a business can stay informed and also use this information to plan their marketing, product development and keep up to date with developments in technology. This can be a much better method of keeping up to date than having to trawl through a range of magazines and websites. A business can further develop their contacts (their online community) by sharing or retweeting relevant posts from other business or individuals. This will hopefully encourage other businesses to return the favour and occasionally share or retweet a post from them. Remember that one of the aims of a business's social media page is to provide material that will be of interest to their target audience, so other businesses' and industry experts' blogs can provide a useful source of the type of content that is needed.

> **Research**
>
> What kind of business would you like to run? Who would be the target audience? What kinds of content would they be interested in? Search on Facebook™ for groups related to that area of interest. Search Twitter™ to see if you can find any relevant accounts of related businesses, organisations or industry experts. Search the internet to see if there are any blogs related to these interests. All the content you find could form the basis of potential social media posts for your business.

Social media and company websites

Most businesses will have a company website as well as social media pages. Ideally, the two should link closely with each other. The colour scheme, text (including profile information) and graphics should be consistent across both the company website and all of their social media pages. Social media is dynamic, with content posted today and forgotten tomorrow, but a website is more stable. Although it should be updated regularly, this is the place where more static, detailed content should be presented. The company's website should include buttons to link to its various social media pages. Many social media websites provide HTML code to create these buttons and make them work, which businesses can use on their websites. Figure 3.2 shows Twitter™'s website resources page from which you can copy the HTML code required to put various types of Twitter™ button on your website.

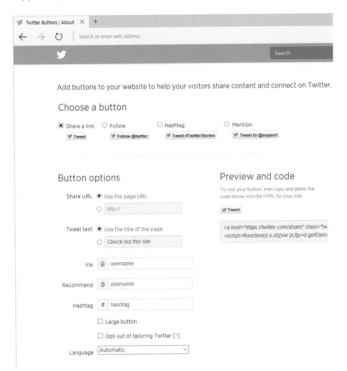

▶ **Figure 3.2:** Twitter™ enables businesses to add Twitter™ buttons to their website that link to their Twitter™ account

Where relevant, a business's social media posts should contain links to the company's website. For example, a business might post a 'teaser' photo of a new product on their social media pages, with a 'find out more' link to a page on the company's website, where more detailed product information is provided and the product can be purchased.

Another way to link a company's website to its social media pages is to embed social media feeds into the website itself. Facebook™ and Twitter™ provide HTML code that can be used to embed a newsfeed into a sidebar or another area of a website.

Risks and issues

While social media provides many excellent opportunities for businesses to promote their products or services, using social media is not without its pitfalls.

Time constraints and return on investment

Creating and running the social media presence of a business is time consuming, as it takes time to build up interest in a business on social media and results will not be achieved overnight. A business would probably need to have at least one person who dedicates a considerable amount of their time to social media marketing, and it may be that a small or even medium-sized business could not justify this expense when a positive effect on sales is not guaranteed. When any business invests time or money into a project, they need to consider the return on investment. In other words, they need to weigh the time and money spent on their social media marketing campaign/ customer service against the potential increase in sales that they might be able to achieve. It is quite hard to make this judgement prior to setting up a social media profile, so a business might need to run a trial in which they try out the use of social media over a reasonable period (say 6 to 12 months) and then review the results to see what the benefits to the company have been (for example, has there been an increase in sales or have their customer service ratings improved).

Negative comments

An issue faced by all businesses using social media is that people may make negative comments on their social media pages. Every business has customers that make complaints, but when customers complain via social media other customers can see the complaints and this can be potentially very damaging for the business's reputation. The only effective way to deal with negative comments is for the business to respond to them promptly and correctly. Often the correct way to deal with a negative comment is to offer an apology and some kind of solution to the problem. Dealing with negative comments promptly requires someone in the business being able to monitor all the business's social media pages regularly and deal with any comments, preferably within hours of them being made. This significantly adds to the cost of using social media for the business, and the question of return on investment is raised again. However, companies that deal with customer service issues promptly and effectively are likely to gain a good reputation.

Unforeseen consequences

There can be unforeseen consequences of posting content to social media. There is a very wide range of different opinions and beliefs among the general public, both within the UK and across the world. Sometimes, content which you find engaging and appropriate is felt to be inappropriate by others. It is very easy to post something on social media which you intended and thought was witty or sarcastic, but is viewed by others to be insensitive, crass or insulting. This unforeseen consequence of a post on social media can be very damaging to a business, particularly if the post and the offence people have taken to it goes **viral**.

There is also a danger that members of staff who post content on a company's social media pages might make comments or express opinions that are damaging to the company. This may be unintentional, and might be done with the intention of being friendly and helpful to a customer. For example, an employee dealing with complaints about a particular product, might, in an attempt to calm an angry customer, agree with the customer that the product is not ready for sale or contains serious flaws. As this will be seen publicly on social media, it could potentially be damaging to sales of the product and the company's reputation.

> **Key term**
>
> **Viral** – a social media post is said to have gone 'viral' if it is shared by numerous people who themselves share it (and so on). As more and more people share the post, the number of people who see it can increase into millions. Having a social media post go viral is often considered a good thing unless, of course, it is regarding a negative issue about a company.

Urban Outfitters

In October 2012, a serious storm called Hurricane Sandy hit the east coast of the US. It left 71 people dead and caused 71 billion dollars' worth of damage. US clothing retailer, Urban Outfitters, tweeted: 'This storm blows (but free shipping doesn't)! Today only...' with the hashtag #ALLSOGGY. Although at the time of the tweet the full extent of the devastation caused by the storm was not yet known, it was a tasteless and inappropriate tweet as no one wants to see a company trying to make money out of peoples' misfortune. This is widely quoted as an example of a social media public relations disaster.

Security issues

Using social media can create a number of security risks for a business. Cyber criminals are always looking for ways to attack and defraud companies and social media provides an opportunity for them. These risks can take a number of different forms.

▶ Malware – Cyber criminals may try to trick social media users into installing some kind of **malware**. For example, by posting something interesting and inviting, they encourage users to click on a link which then downloads malware. Alternatively, cyber criminals may trick users into giving away their login credentials. Businesses must therefore make sure that their employees are aware of these dangers and take extra care when using social media and engaging with customers. The business must, of course, also ensure that their anti-virus software is always up to date.

▶ Ransom/blackmail – A company, by raising its profile on social media, may attract the attention of cyber criminals who then target the company. This could potentially lead to a variety of attacks including those designed to extract a ransom from the company, for example a **denial-of-service (DoS) attack** on the company website (which is essentially blackmail).

▶ Company-sensitive and personal information – Members of staff may inadvertently give away company-sensitive information or personal information (about members of staff or customers). Alternatively, the information is stolen by cyber criminals who trick staff into giving away this information by messaging them through the company's social media pages with seemingly innocent requests. To protect themselves against these, and other, risks associated with social media, businesses need to ensure that their staff are fully trained in the use of social media and are aware of what they can and cannot do and say. This is usually spelt out in a social media policy document, which will be covered in detail later in this unit.

Link

To learn more about social media policies, see Developing a social media policy.

Key terms

Malware – an umbrella term for a range of different types of software that have a malicious intent. Malware includes viruses and Trojans and spyware, among others.

Denial-of-service (DoS) attack – an attack on a company's website which involves sending so many bogus requests to the server where the website is hosted that it is overwhelmed and cannot respond to legitimate requests. The likely purpose of the attack is either revenge or blackmail.

Make a list of the risks and issues that a business of your choice would face when using social media.

Look back through the topics covered in this section and think about how they relate to a business of your choice.

For each risk or issue that you identified, work out how your chosen business would mitigate the risk or deal with the issue.

Reflect

As you work on through this unit, it is important to demonstrate the kind of behaviour that has a positive impact on others and on your learning (that is, to be professional). Professionalism mean things like showing a clear division between your personal and professional use of social media, and completing work fully and on time. You may also have to work with others in your class, perhaps providing feedback for them on their social media posts and by playing the role of a customer commenting on posts they have made. You need to do this in a supportive and professional manner, demonstrate good etiquette and be polite and reasonable at all times.

Assessment practice 3.1   A.P1   A.P2   A.M1   A.D1

You have been asked to give a presentation to local small-business people about how they might be able to use social media to promote and benefit their businesses.

You need to prepare a presentation including speakers notes for the business people, in which you:

- explain the different social media websites and the audience profiles they attract
- provide an assessment of the different ways in which a business can use social media to attract a particular target audience
- evaluate the business use of social media to interact with customers and promote products or services to a target audience.

Plan
- What is the task? What am I being asked to do?
- How confident do I feel in my own abilities to complete this task? Are there any areas I think I may struggle with?

Do
- I know what it is I am doing and what I want to achieve.
- I can identify when I have gone wrong and adjust my thinking/approach to get myself back on course.

Review
- I can explain what the task was and how I approached the task.
- I can explain how I would approach the hard elements differently next time (ie what I would do differently).

B   Develop a plan to use social media in a business to meet requirements

Using social media offers businesses many benefits but, as outlined already, there are also risks and issues. Therefore it would be unwise for a business to start using social media without first forming a plan. A carefully managed social media campaign can avoid many of the pitfalls and can also help the business to clearly identify if the effort, time and money of running the campaign will be worth it.

Social media planning process

For a small business, such as a sole trader, the burden of planning and running a social media campaign will fall to the business owner. As part of the planning process, they should think carefully if they are going to have time to do all the things that will be required. In a medium or large company, there may well be one or more people dedicated to running the social media campaign, and in a really large organisation there could well be a whole team. Whether a whole team is involved in the planning or just one person, there are a number of things which need to be decided and planned.

- The specific business requirements – What are the business's requirements? What is the business intending to use social media for and what is it hoping to achieve by doing so? In a larger company, these questions will probably need to discussed with the sales and marketing team(s).

- Content planning and publishing – What kin d of content will the business post? How will the business obtain content to post, such as images and videos? What social media websites will the business have pages on? When and how frequently will the business post content?

- Developing online communities – How will the business go about developing an online community of followers? How will the business keep followers engaged once it has them?

- Enforcing social media policies – What will the business include in its social media policy? How will it ensure that employees comply with the policy?

Each of these areas of planning will now be looked at in more detail.

Business requirements

There are many ways in which a business can promote itself, for example newspaper, TV and radio, to name but a few. Before a business embarks on a social media campaign, it should consider what the benefits might be of using social media to promote its products and/or services compared with using other traditional methods.

Using social media may not suit all types of business. For example, a geographically-limited business selling a low-value product which cannot be easily differentiated from other similar companies except on price (such as a small grocery store) might not get much benefit from using social media. However, a business that sells a product which can be shipped worldwide and which can be differentiated from other similar products (perhaps by uniqueness or quality) is more likely to benefit from using social media (for example, a jewellery maker).

Requirements for the use of social media

Businesses need to consider the purpose of their use of social media, that is, what does the business want to get out of it? For example, do they want to use social media for the direct selling of a product and service, to create an image/brand, for customer service, to drive traffic to the company website or a combination of all of these? Without a clear idea of what the business requirements are, the social media campaign will not have a clear focus and is therefore not likely to be successful. Initially, it is better to have one or two simple and clearly defined requirements, rather than trying to do a wide range of things. Once the main requirements have been decided, the business also needs to consider who its target audience is, which social media websites are best suited to the business's products or services and what the aims of the business are.

Selection criteria – matching social media websites to businesses

Even if a business is suited to social media, not every social media website will suit every business. With so many different social media websites, businesses, especially small ones with limited resources, need to select the right social media websites for their business needs. They should focus their efforts (time and money) on those social media websites whose site profiles best match their aims.

▶ Facebook™'s dominant position in the social media market means that, for many businesses, a Facebook™ presence is a must.

▶ However, a business offering professional services to other businesses would probably want to include LinkedIn® in their social media pages. For individuals such as freelancers who offer professional services to other businesses, a LinkedIn™ profile will be of more use than a Facebook™ page.

▶ If a business's products or services target a largely female audience, then they might want to consider using Instagram™ and Pinterest™ as these social media websites have a higher proportion of female users than most of the others.

▶ A business that has a product or service which is highly visual in nature (eg a jeweller, fashion designer or wedding photographer) would be wise to look at social media websites such as Instagram™ for promotion because it focuses on images.

▶ YouTube™ would be a good choice for a business with a physical product which requires demonstration because it is a good place to showcase videos. For this reason, setting up a YouTube™ channel would also benefit video production and animation companies.

Any business should monitor the performance of its social media pages to ensure that its efforts are not wasted. If some pages constantly outperform others, then efforts should be focused on the most effective social media pages.

Success criteria and targets

It is important that the business considers how it will measure the success of using social media and the targets that it will set. Measuring success and setting targets is important because the business needs to be able to prove that the time and money spent by the business on using social media is having measurable benefits. Identifying criteria for measuring success means that a business needs to understand what the measurable benefits would be for that business of using social media. Largely, this comes down to fulfilling the requirements for using social media that the business decided upon. The extent to which they are successful in fulfilling those requirements is most easily measured by setting targets.

It is unlikely that any business will see significant results in a short timescale. It can take some time to build up followers and to develop an online community, particularly for new businesses or ones that have not used social media before. So the initial success criteria and targets that a business sets itself should probably be quite modest: for example, aiming to achieve a specified number of 'likes' or followers within 6 months of starting the campaign. If a business is using multiple social media websites it should set a target for each so that it can measure the performance of each social media stream individually. The target set should match the site's own terminology for interaction. For example, on Facebook™ 'likes' are normally considered to be a good basic measure of popularity, so a good example of a target for using this site might be 'achieve at least 500 page likes over the next 6 months'. Twitter™'s popularity, on the other hand, is often measured by the number of followers an account has. However 'likes' or the number of followers does not really measure interaction by users on individual posts, so setting targets for interaction such as (for Facebook™) 'achieve an average of 20 likes, comments or shares per post' can be used. Ideally, the business's social media targets should be 'SMART' (Specific, Measurable, Achievable, Realistic and Time-bound), so targets such as 'improve social media interaction' are not SMART, but the target 'increase the number of Twitter™ followers from 50 to 100 in three months' is SMART.

Timescales and responsibilities

When planning a social media campaign, it is important that the business decides who is going to do what within the team (if there is one) and creates an outline action plan for completing the tasks (that is, define who is responsible for each task and establish the timescales involved). There should be someone within the team who is responsible for setting the overall strategy for the campaign. They will probably work closely with the marketing and sales teams. There also needs to be people who will develop the content to implement the strategy (that is, set up the profiles/pages and produce content that will be posted) and there should also be people who monitor the social media pages and respond to comments.

	A	B	C	D
1	Day number	Day of week	Main task	Secondary task 1
2	1	Monday	Write and post blog post 1	Share blog post on social media
3	2	Tuesday	Brainstorm ideas for future blog posts	
4	3	Wednesday	Research possible guest authors	Get in touch with one or two possible guest authors
5	4	Thursday	Write and post blog post 2	Share blog post on social media
6	5	Friday	Start outreach campaign to connect with other bloggers	
7	6	Saturday		
8	7	Sunday		

▶ **Figure 3.3:** An action plan

If a business decides that they do not have the expertise in-house to develop a social media marketing campaign, they might bring in an external social media consultant to help them through the process, although this would obviously add to the cost.

The end result of the planning process is likely to be a proposal document outlining all the things listed above, along with the action plan. In a small company or sole trader this might just consist of some simple notes, but in a large organisation the proposal might need to be a much more formal document which is signed off (approved) by higher management who would need to agree the costs and resources involved.

Content planning and publishing

One of the biggest challenges in creating an effective social media campaign is to create content which not only reflects the company's image and products/services, but is also engaging for the audience. Users engage with content that they find interesting, useful or amusing and, by being engaged, they are more likely to interact with the content in some way: that is 'like' it, retweet it, comment on it or share it.

Target audience

When planning a social media campaign, one of the first things you need to do is to ensure that you have correctly identified your target audience. That is, you need to understand the types of people who are interested in your products or services in terms of demographics (for example, age, gender, interests or income). Once you have done this, you can think about how you will engage your target audience through your social media content.

> **Link**
>
> For more on target audience look back at Audience profile.

Simply posting special offers or details of products and prices is not really enough to attract an audience, and using social media for direct advertising is not likely to be very effective. A much better approach is to use indirect advertising and to consider what kinds of things are likely to engage your target audience. Indirect advertising via social media involves posting content that is informative and interesting to the target audience, rather than just sales-orientated. The business needs to consider what kinds of content the people who are likely to buy their products/services (that is, their target audience) might be interested in. For example, a company that sells audio equipment (for example, speakers and amplifiers) might post links to news articles about new advances in audio technology, the resurgent interest in vinyl records and people who have unusual or super-expensive audio set-ups. This content is likely to engage their target audience, who will then be more likely to interact with the content and ultimately to consider purchasing products from this audio equipment company.

Some of the content that a business will post will be in direct response to the comments made by others on their pages or related to current events. It is obviously difficult to plan this content beforehand. Nonetheless, other content will need to be planned, even if only in outline, so that the plan can be adjusted if things change. Some businesses, if they can afford it, will enlist the help of advertising or social media consultants to help them develop content.

A common concept in marketing is 'trans media story telling', where one campaign is stretched across multiple platforms, each with an element of the campaign that is not available on the other platforms, a bit like a digital treasure hunt.

> **Link**
>
> For more on focusing content to match a target audience, see Content focus and developing an audience.

Keywords

The need to include keywords in profiles and posted content has already been mentioned, but how does a company choose the most appropriate keywords? The question a company needs to consider is 'what will people type into the Google™ or Bing® search box when they are searching for the product or service we provide?'. This might sound like a simple question, but it is often more complex that it might at first appear and there might be a range of different search strings used. For example, imagine a company providing wedding photography and video services in the Cambridge area. What would people type in Google™ or Bing® when searching for that kind of service? Here are some possibilities:

- ▶ wedding photographer in Cambridge
- ▶ wedding photos in Cambridgeshire
- ▶ video and photos for weddings

- photographer for weddings
- wedding videographer
- wedding photography.

Therefore it would be important to ensure that the company used the following keywords (which all relate to their core services, industry and location) prominently on their website (that is, in their page titles and URLs) and in their social media profiles. The keywords would be: wedding(s), photographer, photography, video, videographer, Cambridgeshire.

Google Adwords™

One very useful tool for identifying the most likely search strings to be used is Google Adwords™. The service is aimed at people who want to use paid adverts on Google™, but you can research search strings for free. Researching keywords is useful because it helps you to understand the most popular search strings that people use to search for a particular business, product or service. Once you know the most popular search strings, you can ensure that you use the correct keywords in your social media profiles and on your website,

---

Step by step – Google Adwords™　　6 Steps

1 You need to register with Google Adwords™ (if you already have a Google™ account, you can just use those login credentials), then you can use the Keyword planner tool.

2 Go to the main page of Google Adwords™ at **www.google.co.uk/adwords/**

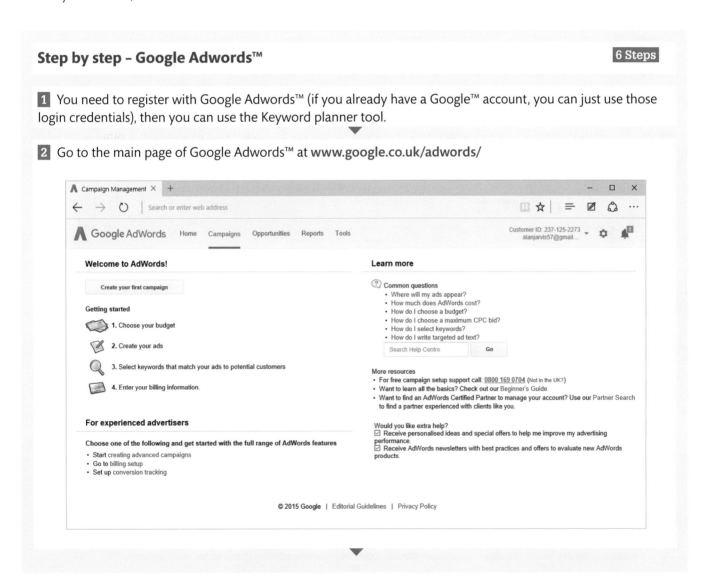

---

3 From the main page, choose Tools, then Keyword planner, which will then display the Keyword planner main page.

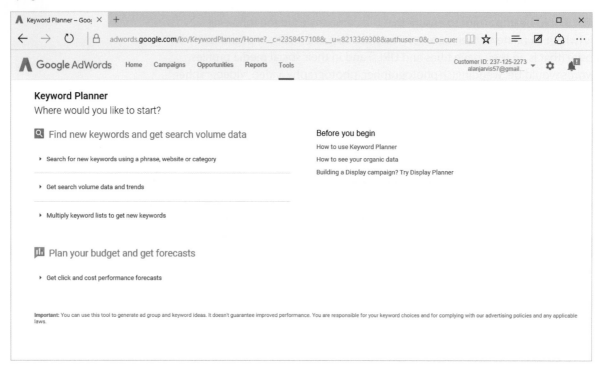

4 Choose Search Volume and Trends then enter a search string, for example 'Wedding photographers in Cambridge', then click Get search volume and you will see the results.

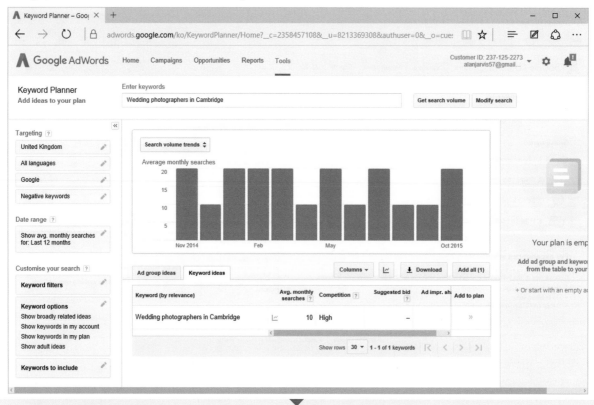

5 However, if you look at the volume and trends for 'photographers in Cambridge', you can see that the results are a little different, with an average of 40 searches per month compared with only 10 for 'Wedding photographers in Cambridge'.

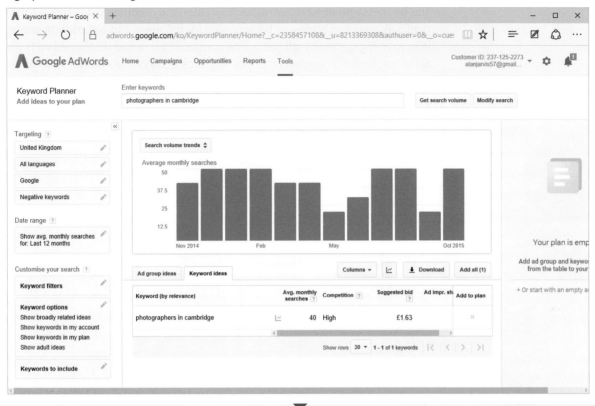

6 Being able to do this kind of research, and finding out exactly what people search for, is invaluable to a company in helping them decide what keywords they should use on their website and in their social media profiles.

Timing

Establishing the best time to post content that has been developed is another important consideration for anyone planning a business social media campaign. Social media is very dynamic, and if content is posted when your audience is not online they will most likely miss your post. A business, therefore, needs to identify those days and times when their target audience is most likely to be looking at social media. Once a business has sufficient people interacting with, for example, their Facebook™ page, then tools such as Facebook™ Insights will provide this information. If a business is starting from scratch, then research suggests that, for Facebook™, on Fridays or at the weekend in the early afternoon are when most people are on the site, whereas Twitter™ is more popular during the week. Late at night or early in the morning is when fewest people are using social media. However, if the business sells a product internationally, then different time zones will need to be considered.

The advertising of some products is suited for posting at a particular time of day. For example, for a pizza takeaway restaurant the best time to post on social media would be just before lunch or dinner time when people are likely to be hungry and thinking about what they should eat. Some businesses sell products which have a seasonal variety. For example, a garden centre might post articles about planting bulbs

Research

You have probably considered the idea of running your own business. How do you imagine people might search for your business on Google™? Use Google AdWords™ to research the search strings that people actually use. Based on your research, choose four or five keywords that you would use for your business.

in Autumn, lawn mower reviews in Spring and information on how to water your garden in Summer.

Publishing schedule

The business also needs to consider how often they should post material to social media. Posting too often can be annoying for followers, but not posting enough can lose your engagement with the online community you had developed with your target audience. Research suggests that posting once a day on Facebook™ is about the right amount while on Twitter™ approximately three tweets per day is best.

As part of the planning process for a social media campaign, a business should produce a publishing or posting schedule to show what content it intends to post and when (see Figure 3.4).

Social Media Content Schedule

Name: ....

Business: ....

Date: ....

	Date (Frequency of posting should be defined in your social media marketing plan.)	Channels (Enter all or name specific channels.)	Type of post (Sales, information, general interest, amusing.)	Content (Photo, video, web link, poll, questions, etc.)	Comments
1					
2					
3					
4					
5					
6					
7					
8					

▶ **Figure 3.4:** An example of a social media schedule

Ⅰ PAUSE POINT   Being able to develop plans with timescales and targets is an important skill in many areas, and social media is no exception. Due to the dynamic nature of social media, plans need to be flexible and relatively short term (months rather than years).

Set yourself five SMART targets for a social media plan for a business of your choice.

Hint   SMART objectives need to be Specific, Measurable, Achievable, Realistic and Time-bound.

Extend   Develop your social media plan further by outlining the target audience, what keywords you would use, and how you would time your posts.?

Developing an online community

There are a number of techniques that a business can use to help develop an online social media community. Posting content that will be of interest to the business's target audience and avoiding the 'hard sell' approach has already been mentioned, but there are many other promotional techniques that can be used.

People love to be asked their opinion, so asking questions, surveying opinion and requesting feedback is always a good way to engage with people. For example, a cake-making business could post 'our new flavour of cake is carrot and beetroot', but a more engaging post might be 'our new flavour of cake is carrot and beetroot, what do you think?' As well as engaging with the original post, people also like to respond to the comments left by other people. Perhaps an even better approach might be 'we are thinking of launching some new flavours, vote for your favourite', along with a Facebook™ poll. Another possibility is to link social media engagement with special offers, for example by offering a discount for customers who 'like' the company's Facebook™ page.

Of course, there is no point in asking your audience questions if you do not respond to them, so, to develop an online community, you need to monitor all your social media streams frequently and respond to any queries or requests promptly. If users post complaints or negative comments, then it is even more crucial that these comments are dealt with promptly and effectively.

Social media is not the appropriate place for detailed company and product information. This kind of information should be found on the company website. Social media posts should, where appropriate, provide links to the company's website. This allows people who are interested in finding out more to find it on your website, but avoids having to include a lot of information in a social media post that many people will not be interested in.

Developing a social media policy

As already mentioned, there are a number of risks and issues associated with the business use of social media. One way to help reduce some of the potential problems is to create a social media policy. This document lays down guidelines for the use of social media within a company and anyone in the company who is associated with the use of social media should be aware of the contents of the policy. Some of the things which should be included in a social media policy are detailed here.

Company image and philosophy

It is important that the way a company presents itself through social media reflects the image that the company would like the public to have of it, and this should be outlined in their social media policy. For example, a cut-price supermarket would be happy to post content about special offers and price comparisons with other supermarkets, whereas a high-end supermarket would not want to post comparisons with cut-price supermarkets or give their customers the impression that they were cheap, because their image would be that of offering a touch of luxury. Some companies also have particular philosophies that they want to put across to their target audience. For example, some companies might want to demonstrate that they are environmentally friendly or that they have high ethical standards: the Co-operative Bank is one such example .

Guidelines for content

The social media policy needs to state clearly what kind of content is acceptable to post and what is not. This will include things like ensuring that content is not offensive to anyone, and that it does not discriminate against anyone. It should use non-gender-specific terms (for example, police officer rather than policeman) and ensure that images show a mix of races. It may also cover guidance for staff such as never entering into arguments with customers, always showing respect for everyone's opinions, not making negative comments about competitors' products and ways of dealing with complaints or negative comments. The guidelines will also normally encourage people to be open, honest and respectful in their communications, and to never tell lies even if the truth is not what the customer wants to hear. For example, being honest about prices, delivery timescales or mistakes that have been made is encouraged.

Guidelines for confidentiality

There is likely to be information that every company wishes to remain confidential, at least for a specific period of time, and this information should not be included in social media posts or in replies to customer's comments. This may include a whole range of things such as details of new products that are currently in development, phone numbers of staff members, details of why products are priced a certain way and the profit margins that the company intends to make. The policy should make it clear to staff what information is confidential and should not to be made public.

Guidelines for security

As the security risks involved in using social media are quite high, the social media policy will need to contain information about how to keep account details secure, how to avoid malware infections and other security issues.

Link

To remind yourself of the security risks involved for businesses using social media, see Security issues.

Separating company and personal content

Most of the employees within a company will have their own personal social media profiles and it is very important that they do not confuse these with those they are managing for their employers. The social media policy will need to remind employees that they must never use the company's social media streams for personal messages or to get too personal in their interactions with customers. It may also restrict what the employees can say about their company on their own personal social media profiles. In addition, some of these rules and guidelines may be included in the contracts of employment that employees sign when they join the company.

Legal and ethical considerations

There are a number of legal and ethical considerations that a social media policy should cover. The use of tracking cookies to enable personalised or targeted adverts, and complying with copyright laws when posting images and other content that has been created by others are just two such issues. EU law requires the consent of the user before cookies can be stored on their device. You will probably have seen these message pop-ups when you first visit a website, asking you if you consent to cookies being stored. Images and videos help to make posts more engaging but, unless the assets are created in-house, the copyright on the assets needs to be checked: that is, the ownership needs to be checked and permission sought for use of those assets on a company's social media pages and this might require payment of a fee. The social media policy may well forbid certain practices which are considered unethical, such as using so-called **'Black Hat' SEO techniques**.

Key term

Black Hat SEO techniques – techniques that attempt to fool search engines into ranking a website higher than it would have otherwise been, by violating the search engines' terms of service and possibly by creating fake customer reviews.

Reviewing and refining plans

Planning the use of social media by a business is not a one-off event, but rather an ongoing process of review, feedback and refinement. By reviewing the quality, effectiveness and appropriateness of pages and posted content, a business can, over time, determine which approaches to social media posting are the most beneficial, enabling them to focus their efforts on these approaches in the future. Businesses will work with any clients and other relevant stakeholders, including the in-house team, to review and refine social media plans and they will need to consider the following.

Gathering feedback from a client and potential users

To review and refine social media plans, the main technique will be to gather feedback from clients and potential users (that is, the target audience). Some of the feedback from clients will come in the form of analysis from a social media analytic tool such as Facebook™ Insights. It will also be useful to look at whether the business has achieved the targets it set itself for interaction on its various social media streams and whether it has met the success criteria that it set.

Communicating with a client

Sometimes, a company will be managing its own social media plans, in which case there would not be a clients as such, only senior management that the social media team would need to report to. Larger companies may hire a social media consultant to manage their social media plans, in which case representatives from the hiring company are said to be clients of the consultant. In such cases, the consultant would need to discuss their plans with the client in order to gain their approval and to improve the plans further. The hiring company may need to sign off on certain expenses involved in the social media plans. Working with a client can be difficult as they might not share your opinions or might disagree with your ideas. The important thing is to listen carefully to what the client says, and to consider what their aims are for their social media campaign. Remember that the client will probably understand the particular business much better than you do, but their understanding of social media may be very limited, so you need to listen to their explanations of how the business works and match that up with your knowledge of social media. Ultimately, the client is in charge because it is their company being represented on social media, but they will have hired a consultant for their expertise so should listen to their advice and suggestions.

Scheduling and documenting meetings

To work effectively and successfully with a client, you should have regular meetings with them. In these meetings, you (as social media consultant) should present your ideas and plans as they develop, and listen to the client's feedback. It is important to document these meetings (that is, to take notes) so that you know what was discussed, what feedback you received and any decisions that were made, in order to act on these decisions.

Agreeing and adjusting timescales

When planning a social media campaign, either in-house or with a social media consultant, it is important to agree timescales for when certain tasks need to be completed (such as setting up social media streams) and when targets are expected to be met. As mentioned above, communication is the key to a good relationship between a client and a social media consultant. Assuming that the communication is good, it would be fairly straightforward to agree to any changes to timescales within a social media plan based on the latest updates from the social media consultant on progress, or in response to changes within the client's business.

Refining ideas and solutions

Through gathering feedback and looking at whether success criteria and targets have been met, a social media consultant and client can see how successful their social media plans have been. They can also determine whether there are any parts of the plans, the targets they have set or the timescales they are working to, that need to be refined or adjusted, in keeping with the business's aims for their use of social media. The review work they have done, and good communication throughout, should enable the client business and the social media consultant to refine their plans and come up with any new solutions together, as well as reach any compromises that are required, and to agree a modified version of the social media plan.

> **Reflect**
>
> Working with social media will require you to respond to feedback from a number of sources, including the client and target audience (social media users who have liked/followed your social media pages). Receiving feedback requires that you do not take feedback personally, but in a professional and objective manner. It will also require you to learn from your mistakes, or at least improve upon your initial work, and to be flexible about your ideas. Reflect on how you would receive feedback in a professional and objective manner and respond to negative feedback about your work.

C · Implement the use of social media in a business

Once you have created a social media plan, the next step is to implement it. You will need to select and use appropriate social media website tools and techniques to implement your social media plan.

> **Tip**
>
> You can practise using many of the tools and techniques required to implement a social media plan quite easily, because most social media websites will let you set up accounts and profiles for free, even if they are for an imaginary business.

Creating accounts and profiles

Once you have identified which social media websites are to be used by a business, you need to sign up for accounts, create and set up profiles, and then perform ongoing administration.

Step by step: Creating a page on Facebook™

`2 Steps`

1 Facebook™ allows anyone with a personal page to set up any number of separate business pages. To do this, click the Create page option in the drop down menu that can be accessed via the down arrow at the top of the main Facebook™ newsfeed page.

▼

2 You then need to select the type of page you want to create. You can choose from: Local Business or Place; Company, Organisation or Institution; Brand or Product; Artist, Band or Public Figure; Entertainment; Cause or Community. For example, if you wanted to create a page for a professional photographer, you could choose 'Artist, Band or Public Figure', then choose 'Photographer' from the drop down menu, enter the name of the photographer or their business name, and then click Get Started. Now you can work through the process of setting up the page.

Tip

The area provided for the cover image is long and thin, whereas most images taken with a digital camera are much closer to being square, so you may need to edit a photo to make it work well in the space. However, you can reposition which part of the photo appears on the cover once you have uploaded it. Given the shape of the space available, only images which fit across a thin, horizontal area will work well; for example a vertical full-length image of a person would not be suitable as a cover image.

Customisation and configuration of a company profile

The company profiles created for the various different social media websites being used should all tie together in terms of the company image they are portraying. This is achieved through the design scheme used, tailored to each social media website's specifications, and through the text used to describe the company. They should all also include the keywords that have been identified for that business during the planning stage.

Most social media websites require the use of a background image or banner on profile pages. On Facebook™, this is known as the cover image, while on Twitter™ it is called the header photo. The profile page should also have a company logo, known as the profile picture on Facebook™ and profile photo on Twitter™.

You may need to put some thought into the cover image and profile picture. An existing business may already have a logo which can be used for the profile picture. A sole trader who offers some kind of service where they will meet their customers in person (such as a decorating or house cleaning service) might, alternatively, want to use an image of the person who runs the business and delivers the service, to provide a personal touch. The cover image should represent the company and what it does in some way, or reflect the company philosophy.

Remember that in order to build brand identity and recognition (so that members of the public recognise your company), you should use the same photos, colour schemes and text on all of the social media streams that the business is using (that is, your pages should all follow the same business branding guidelines).

When setting up your Facebook™ page, you should enter as much information about the business as you can, using the About page. The profile About page helps people find your business. For example, if you enter a valid postal address for the business, then it will appear on Facebook™ Places and when people do a geographical search. Your company profile is important because the text that you include in the short description is visible to anyone viewing your page, along with the address of your website (which you should also fill in on the About page).

The Settings page is also important; you can find this by clicking the Settings link at the top right-hand side of the page. This controls many things about how your page works. The General settings, for example, allow you to develop a page, but keep it unpublished until you are ready for everyone to see it. You can also choose whether people can message you, if visitors are allowed to post to the page and a number of other things, including privacy settings.

Another very useful feature for business pages are Page Roles, which you can set up via the Settings page. These page roles allow other people to run the page and you can give them the ability to do various things such as edit the page, post content to the page and view the page's Facebook™ Insights account. This means that, within a business, different people can have different responsibilities with respect to social media. For example, you could have one person responsible for monitoring and responding to comments/messages and another person responsible for posting new content to the page. To set up another person who can edit the page you need to click the Page Roles link on the left of the Settings page.

An interesting feature of Facebook™ pages (introduced in February 2015) is the ability to set the Preferred Page Audience for your page. Anyone is still allowed to search for the page, but the page is more likely to be seen by people who match your target audience selections.

There are a number of other useful things you can control on the Settings page. For example, the Notifications option allows you to set up email or text message notifications when a variety of things happen on your page. For example, you could receive an email every time anyone comments on one of your posts or every time the page receives a message.

Content creation and publication

During the planning stage, an outline publishing schedule and social media plan should have been created. Now is the time to implement that plan but it is likely, due to the dynamic nature of social media, that the plan will need to be changed and adapted as a result of how the public responds to it and to current events. For example, if a business sells a product which is related to the weather (such as ice cream or umbrellas), then they might need to adjust their posting schedule depending on changes in the weather.

Posts which contain images are likely to be more engaging than those that just contain text so, as part of the content creation process, you will need to obtain suitable images. Photos of the products that the business sells should be used, or photos that reflect the service that the business offers. Also, photos that tie in with the business image and branding will also be useful. Photos need to be of high quality as poor quality photos will reflect badly on the products/services and should, therefore, be avoided. Remember that if you use photos that you have not taken yourself, you need to check the copyright situation and get permission to use them.

Carry out research to produce engaging content

You will also need to think about and research what kind of content will engage your target audience. There are two ways you can do this. You can carry out some market research by finding members of your target audiences, showing them some content ideas and asking them which ones appeal to them most and why. However, this can be quite time consuming. The other way is to use social media analysis tools such as Facebook™ Insights and look at how much interaction each post generates. You can then modify the kind of content you post, based on the analysis you receive.

Improving visibility of published content

There is little point in putting a lot of effort into creating content and posting it on social media if no one sees it. Therefore it is important that you post at the right times on the right days when the majority of your target audience is online. This is something that you can check with Facebook™ Insights, as explained later in the chapter. There are also certain specific things you should do when posting on Facebook™ and Twitter™ to make sure that your posts are seen by as many people as possible.

Facebook™ does not show an individual user every post from all of their friends and the pages that they have liked. Instead, it uses sophisticated algorithms to prioritise those posts it thinks will be the most interesting to them. This is based on research Facebook™ has done into what users like to see and do not like to see in their timeline. Understanding how Facebook™ does this will help improve the visibility of the posts you make.

▶ One important factor that Facebook™ uses to decide if your post should appear on an individual's newsfeed is the affinity between you (your business) and that person. This is the amount of interaction (likes, comments and shares) between you and that individual. Therefore, whenever an individual comments on one of your posts, you should respond to help build up the affinity between you and that person.

▶ Try to create posts which encourage people to comment on them. One way of doing this is to ask questions rather than make statements. This will also help to build up the affinity between you and your audience.

▶ Post about relevant and trending topics and add links to relevant content from other websites or industry experts. For example, if you are a photographer and Canon™ launch a new camera with some special features, comment on this and add a link to the relevant page on the Canon™ website. The Facebook™ algorithms see this kind of posting as interesting to your audience so there is a greater likelihood that your posts will be widely seen.

▶ Avoid hard selling. Posts which simply encourage people to buy your products/services are not considered to be interesting so these types of post are least likely to appear on your audience's newsfeeds.

> **Research**
>
> The way Facebook™ selects which post to show is, as you might imagine, quite a hot topic in the social media world. The algorithm Facebook™ uses is often called 'EdgeRank' and an internet search for 'Facebook Edge Rank' will produce a lot of articles on the subject. However, ensure that you read the most recent ones as Facebook™ develops and improves the algorithm all the time.

To improve the visibility of your tweets on Twitter™, you should consider doing the following.

▶ When replying to a Twitter™ follower who has made a comment, it is common to start your tweet with an @ sign and the username of the person you are replying to e g '@bertsmith Thanks for that Bert we will look into it and let you know'.

▶ These types of reply are not seen by all your Twitter™ followers, only by people who follow both you and the person you are following. If you want all your followers to see the tweet, then do not put the @username at the very start of the tweet.

Another way you can make sure that your posts are seen by your target audience is to use paid-for posts. A business would need to weigh up the cost of a paid advert campaign against the time and effort required to run a 'free' campaign. The two are not mutually exclusive, of course, and a business might well use a paid-for campaign to get their social media presence 'off the ground' and then maintain and develop the followers with a 'free' campaign.

> **Tip**
>
> It is very important to proofread posts before you actually post them. Posts with spelling mistakes or other errors will reflect very badly on the company. If possible, get someone else to check the posts (because it is much harder to spot mistakes in your own work), not just for spelling errors but also to ensure that the meaning of the post cannot be misunderstood and that it is not likely to cause offence to anyone.

Encouraging audience interaction

▶ The importance of encouraging audience participation has already been mentioned. Posts need to be phrased in a way that is entertaining and focused on your target audience without being pushy. Including images in posts is always a good idea as people respond better to images rather than text alone. The use of the **click bait** approach is not recommended as many social media users find it annoying and the Facebook™ EdgeRank algorithm does not favour it. Encouraging comments by asking questions is one way; you can also ask people to post photos of themselves using your product. Other possibilities include using surveys (which are useful for obtaining feedback on new product ideas) and quizzes.

> **Key term**
>
> **Click bait** – a term used for content that encourages users to 'click through' the post to see the linked content on an external website. Click bait content often uses sensationalist headlines such as 'You won't believe what happens next' to exploit the viewer's curiosity.

Integration of information across social media and the company website

For companies that sell their products through an website, one of the main goals of using social media will be to encourage people to visit their website and, ultimately, to purchase their products. Conversely, they will also want people who visit their website to like their Facebook™ page and follow them on Twitter™ and other social media websites. Therefore, a company's social media pages and the company's website should, as far as possible, be integrated in a number of ways.

▶ The company website should feature social media buttons to encourage visitors to like/follow their social media pages.

▶ The formatting of both the company website and the social media pages should reflect a consistent company branding style. For example, the background photos and profile images used on the social media page should match/reflect the images and colour scheme used on the company website.

▶ Social media posts should, where relevant, contain links to the company's website. For example, when a new product is launched, brief details can be given in a social media post, with a link to the product website page, where much more detailed information on the product can be found.

Overall, the idea is that a company's social media pages and their website should integrate with each other, and, of course, to develop brand identity they should have a consistent look to them.

Adapting and testing content on different device platforms

It is likely that you will develop and post content using a PC, but many of your target audience will view the content using mobile devices such as smartphones, tablets or notebooks. You can check which devices and web browsers your audience uses with analysis tools such as Facebook™ Insights. It is a good idea to check how your content looks on different devices, especially those with a much smaller screen, to ensure that your audience will see the posts in the way you intended them to. It is also worth bearing in mind that, as the account holder, the posts you make will often look different from how they appear in a user's newsfeed. For this reason, it is often useful to have a separate social media account available to help you to check how your posts appear to your audience.

> **Reflect**
>
> To work in the social media industry you will need good communication skills. Writing posts which are short but convey the intended meaning, and using the right tone and language, is a real skill. You also need to be able to respond to social media messages, which might include negative comments and complaints, in a positive and helpful way. Setting the right tone when replying to these types of messages is not easy, but you should try to be positive and helpful. Think about techniques that you could use to write short and clear posts and how you would respond positively and helpfully to negative comments.

Implementation of online community building

Ways to develop a business's online community have already been outlined. One approach to develop an online community further is to join other related online communities, rather than just staying within one business's own social media pages. This can be done in number of ways.

> **Link**
>
> Look at Developing an online community for more on how to develop an online community.

▶ Joining Facebook™ groups on relevant subjects, joining Google+™ communities or following appropriate accounts on Twitter™ can provide useful sources of information. For example, a photography business could join one of the many photography groups on Facebook™ or Google+™. While many groups frown on businesses posting advertising material, there is nothing to stop the business answering questions and making comments. Many bloggers tweet details of their latest blog posts and, by following relevant bloggers on Twitter™, businesses can keep up to date with interesting and relevant developments. This can also provide a good source of material for posting on your business's social media pages. Sharing (on Facebook™) or retweeting (on Twitter™) interesting relevant posts from other people and companies you have followed is a good way to develop your online community, and help develop the idea in people's minds that your business is knowledgeable and a useful source of relevant information.

▶ Tagging photos in Facebook™ is also a way of trying to encourage engagement. For example, suppose that a car dealer asks each person who buys a new car to have a photo taken with the car they purchase. They then ask the person if they would mind posting the picture on Facebook™ and tag the owner in the pictures (assuming they have a Facebook™ account). If they are happy, then the picture will not only go up on the company's Facebook™ page, but will also be seen by all the Facebook™ friends of the person who bought the car, thereby expanding the online community.

▶ Twitter™ hashtags provide a way to join in an online conversation about a specific topic. If a business sees a hashtag relevant to their company, then they can tweet a comment using the hashtag.

All of these suggested ways of developing an online community are designed to raise the profile of the business in the minds of people that follow their social media pages. Rather than annoying the business's target audience with pushy direct selling posts, the idea is to build up an impression of a business that knows what it is talking about and is up to date with all the latest information and developments, making this the sort of company that people feel they can trust and can do business with.

Monitoring and responding to comments and automating content posting

It can be difficult to keep track of all the different social media streams and to time postings at the optimum times. Fortunately, there are a number of different tools which can be used to help manage the task of running a social media campaign. One of the best known tools for this is called Hootsuite®, and as long as you only want to manage a maximum of three different social media streams it is free to use. Hootsuite® not only allows you to view your different social media streams on a single dashboard, but it also allows you to set up social media posts and set a time and date when you actually want them posted, on multiple streams if required. Being able to view all your different social media streams in one place is very useful because, as mentioned several times before, it is very important to respond promptly to comments that people make. Being able to monitor your social media streams in one dashboard means that you do not have to swap between separate browser pages all the time and you can integrate your approach to posting on the various streams more easily.

There are many other social media analysis and management tools available. Some of the best know free ones are:

▶ TweetReach™ – allows you to analyse how many times your tweets get retweeted

▶ Klout™ – uses a variety of measures to identify what people think of your brand and what kinds of post influence them the most

▶ Social Mention™ – allows you to monitor the use of different keywords across a wide range of social media websites

▶ TweetDeck™ – a Twitter™ management tool that allows you to schedule tweets, track hashtags and manage multiple accounts

▶ Google Alerts™ – allows you to monitor the internet for any mentions of your brand, your competitors or any keyword you choose.

Step by step – Hootsuite™

6 Steps

1 Here is a look at some of Hootsuite®'s features. If you log into Hootsuite® using your Facebook™ account you will see something like this.

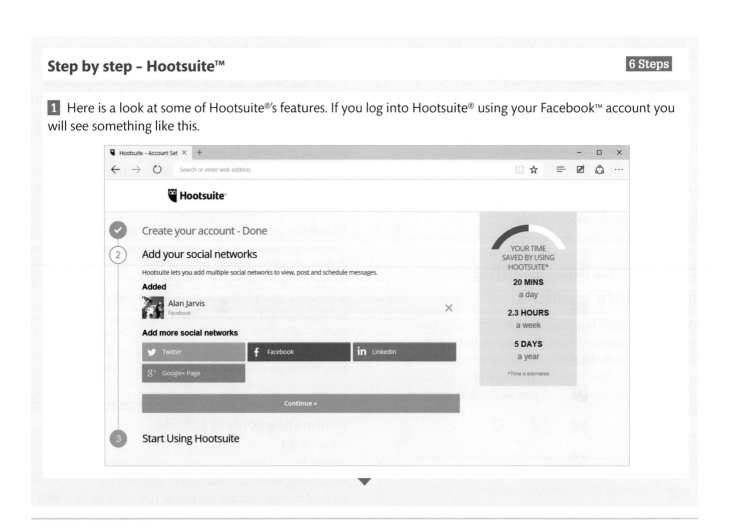

2 You then need to add your other social media pages using the buttons on the page. With the free version of Hootsuite®, you can only add three social media accounts. Hootsuite® has lots of features but one of the most useful is the ability to create a single message and have Hootsuite® post it for you on multiple accounts. When you open the main Hootsuite® dashboard the message creation area is at the top.

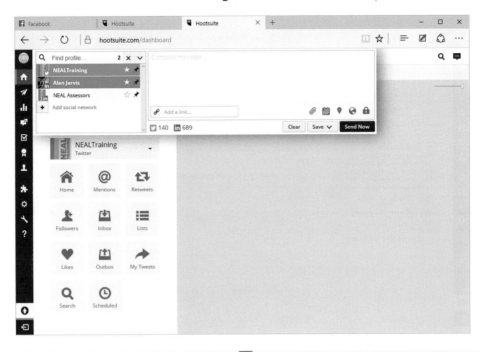

3 You can then type the text of the message you want to post and add links if required. The figure below shows both this and the scheduling option which allows you to choose a time when the post is made. You can, therefore, create posts at a time which is convenient to you but actually post them when your target audience are most likely to be online.

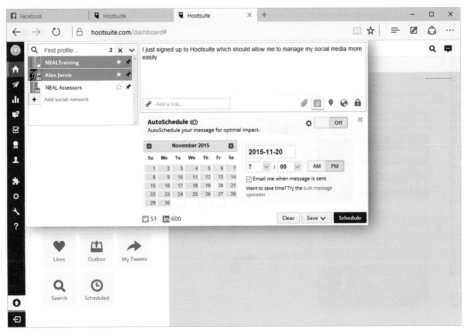

4 Another useful feature of Hootsuite® is the ability to create social media 'streams' and display them on your Hootsuite® dashboard. This means that, rather than having to visit each social media page to see what is going on, you can have all the updates from your social media accounts shown in one place. To set this up, click on the Home button on the panel that runs down the left-hand side of the dashboard and the 'Add a stream box' should pop up.

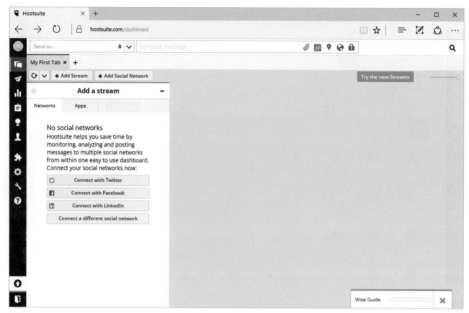

5 Choose the social media account you want to add the stream for (Twitter™ shown here), and then select what aspect of the stream you want displayed (home is a good starting choice). The figure below shows a Twitter™ stream added.

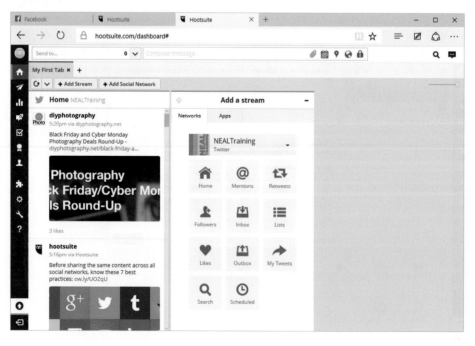

6 Further streams can be added to complete the dashboard and allow you to monitor multiple social media pages at once.

Data gathering and analysis

One of the major benefits of using social media over traditional methods of promotion is that tools are available to allow you to investigate how successful your posts have been and who your audience is. Facebook™, for example, provides a free tool called Facebook™ Insights which provides detailed data on the effectiveness of your social media efforts. Twitter™ provides Twitter Analytics™ (also called the Twitter™ Activity Dashboard), which provides data on how many tweets you have made and how many

people have seen them. There are also many other third-party tools available.

Google Analytics™ is a powerful tool for analysis of website traffic, but it does not provide any social media data. However, Google Analytics™ is a useful tool if the aim of using social media is to drive customers to your company website as it will show the source of these visitors, so that you can see how effective your efforts have been and how many people have 'clicked through' your social media pages to your website.

Step by step: Facebook™ Insights

`4 Steps`

1 Any business page can use Facebook™ Insights as long as they have more than 30 'likes'; you cannot use Insights on your personal Facebook™. The Facebook™ Insights link appears in the menu at the top of your Facebook™ page. Once you click on the link to Facebook™ Insights, the Overview page is shown.

2 The Likes box shows the total number of likes the page has received and the number received in the last week. The **Post Reach** shows the number of people who have seen your posts in the last week, and the **Engagement** box shows the number of people who have interacted with the page. In the lower part of the page, is a list of information on the last five posts on the page. This is particularly useful as you can see how effective individual posts have been in engaging with your audience, and the charts on the right give a visual impression of the effectiveness of each post. A link at the bottom of the recent posts table allows you to expand the table to see all posts. Down the left-hand side is a menu from which you can choose to see different data about your page. For example, the Page Views link will display a graph showing how many people viewed your page.

3 The default view shows you the page views over the last month, but you can change the period over which the views are shown on the graph at the top right-hand side of the page. This allows you to see the popularity of your business's page over time. Lower down on the page, it shows how many times people came to your Facebook™ page from other websites such as Google™ or your company's website. The Posts link will display charts which show when people who have liked your page are online. This information is very useful as it helps you to decide on the best time and day to post.

4 Another interesting page with lots of useful data is the People page. This provides data about the demographics of people who have liked your page (eg their age group, gender and location). In this figure, the page has a predominately male audience (69 per cent male compared with 30 per cent female) and 75 per cent of the people who liked the page are in the 18 to 34 age range (40 per cent are 18 to 24). There is a lot of other information that you can display with Facebook™ Insights. The Help menu, at the top right-hand side of the pages, contains information on how to use Facebook™ Insights.

The data that tools such as Facebook™ Insights or Twitter Analytics™ provide can help you to develop and focus a social media campaign in a number of ways.

- ▶ It can identify how much interaction each post you make generates. Posts that generate interaction are what you should be aiming for, and the data should help you see the types of post that are most successful in this respect. This means that you can concentrate your future efforts into developing the types of post that generate a lot of interaction and waste less effort on those that do not.

- ▶ You can also identify your audience profile in terms of age, gender and location. Once you know this, you can compare your actual audience with your target audience. If there is a significant mismatch (for example, your actual audience is much older than your target audience or your page attracts more males than you were aiming to), you can do one of two things. Either adjust the content you are posting to try to attract more of your target audience (that is, post more material that might be of interest to a younger audience and/or female audience), or adjust the profile of your target audience to match the one you have attracted. (This second option might also involve rethinking your product or service and would have many added complications, but sometimes might be necessary.)

- ▶ The data will reveal the location of your audience. If you run a geographically-limited business (such as a dog grooming service), then having lots of followers in the US or Japan is not particularly beneficial (although you might want to consider the possibility of setting up a blog). Therefore, it might be worth making your posts more locally focused. If your business can deliver its products by post and you attract a large non-UK audience, you might want to consider encouraging overseas buyers, for example by mentioning overseas shipping prices.

- ▶ You can monitor the number of likes and shares. This is useful if you have set yourself a target of achieving a certain number of likes or shares during a specified period of time. It is also a way of monitoring the success of the content you post and identifying which types of post achieve the most likes or shares.

Case study

Blogging

If your social media pages develop a lot of followers, you might want to consider setting up a blog on a particular subject. Bloggers post articles at regular intervals (often daily) which are more detailed and in more depth than social media postings. The blog articles are usually promoted to their social media followers by posting a link to the latest blog article. Bloggers who are really successful and have lots of followers can make money from adverts placed beside their blog articles. However, becoming a successful blogger requires a lot of commitment in terms of the time needed to develop the articles and build your audience.

Ⅱ PAUSE POINT

Tools such as Facebook™ Insights provide valuable objective data to help you to evaluate the success of your social media campaign and your progress towards the targets you have set. This can really help you understand what works well and what is not so successful, so that you can improve your own performance by focusing your efforts in areas you know have been successful in the past.

Prepare five posts, including a variety of content formats, for a business of your choice. Share these via a Facebook™ page that you have set up for a business of your choice. Get your classmates, friends and family to interact with the posts. Then use Facebook™ Insights to analyse how successful each post was in terms of interaction.

Hint

Look back through learning aim C for ideas about the kinds of content you could create for posts, and about how to use Facebook™ Insights.

Extend

Write a report on which post was most successful in terms of interaction and why you think this was. In your report, you should also discuss how your audience is composed in terms of demographics and location.

Assessment practice 3.2

`B.P3` `B.P4` `C.P5` `C.P6` `B.M2` `C.M3` `BC.D2` `BC.D3`

One of the small-business people you gave a presentation to for Assessment practice 3.1 has asked you to develop a social media campaign to promote their photography business. You need to:

- produce a plan for using social media to promote the business, justifying the choices you make and showing how they will meet the purpose and business requirements
- review the plan with others to refine and improve it
- produce appropriate social media content for the business in line with the requirements of your plan
- review data on social media usage and interaction and optimise the content and format/features of the social media website in use
- write an evaluation of the plan you created and its implementation that considers how well the business requirements were met
- demonstrate individual responsibility, creativity, and effective self-management in the planning and use of social media in the context of the photography business.

Plan
- What is the task? What am I being asked to do?
- How confident do I feel in my own ability to complete this task? Are there any areas I think I may struggle with?

Do
- I know what it is I am doing and what I want to achieve.
- I can identify when I have gone wrong and adjust my thinking/approach to get myself back on course.

Review
- I can explain what the task was and how I approached the task.
- I can explain how I would approach the hard elements differently next time (ie what I would do differently).

Further reading and resources

There have also been many books written on the subject. It is always wise to check the publication date of a book in such a dynamic area, as books more than a few years old are not likely to be relevant.

Kitchen, T. and Ivanescu, Y. (2015). *Profitable Social Media Marketing: How To Grow Your Business Using Facebook, Twitter, Instagram, LinkedIn And More.* CreateSpace Independent Publishing Platform.

Ryan, D. (2014). *Understanding Digital Marketing: Marketing Strategies for Engaging the Digital Generation.* London: Kogan Page.

Ryan, D. (2015). *Understanding Social Media: How to Create a Plan for Your Business thatWorks.* London: Kogan Page.

Steam, A. (2014). *Make Social Media Work for your Business.* CreateSpace Independent Publishing Platform.

Brown, M.J. (2015). *Social Media Marketing, 2nd Edition.* CreateSpace Independent Publishing Platform.

Websites

There are many blogs and websites related to social media. Some of the best known are:
- The Social Media examiner: **www.socialmediaexaminer.com**
- Buffer Social: **blog.bufferapp.com**
- Razor Social: **www.razorsocial.com/blog**
- Post planner: **www.postplanner.com/blog**

THINK ▶FUTURE

Simon Jones

First year journalism student

After school, I took a Media degree course as I found the subject interesting and I wanted to work in journalism. During my first year, we have completed modules in media photography, radio production and new media (which includes social media). The course has been hard work but I have enjoyed many parts of it and learnt a lot of new things. I know, however that this is a really competitive area and, to progress into a job in media, I am going to have to demonstrate excellent technical skills and creativity. I had a great opportunity to develop some of my skills with a holiday job in my uncle's builders' merchant business recently. It's a medium size business with five large builders' yards in the Wolverhampton area. He asked me to develop the company's social media presence as they only had a Facebook™ page and it hardly ever got updated. Work experience like this was a great opportunity for me as it allowed me to develop real-world skills to add to my academic studies.

Focusing your skills

Planning a social media presence

To be able to develop a social media strategy for the builders' merchant there are a number of things to consider.

- How well do you understand the business? Spend some time in the yards watching how the staff work and talking to customers to understand how social media might be able to work for the business.
- What does the company owner want to achieve by using social media? Is it realistic and achievable?
- What timescales are you working to?
- How will the staff be trained in the company's social media procedures?

Where to start? Once you have learnt as much as you can about the business, you need to formulate an outline social media plan covering the following.

- The purpose of using social media in the company. For example, you might decide that the main purpose is customer service, providing a method by which customers can enquire about stock levels. A secondary purpose might be to provide information to customers about new products and special offers.

- The social media websites you will initially use and why. For example, you might decide to use Facebook™ and Twitter™ as they provide the messaging facilities that you need to provide customer service.
- The requirement to create a company social media policy. Once it has been written, all of the staff who will use social media need to be made aware of it. It should include procedures for staff who will respond to received messages and information requests.
- An outline project plan showing timescales and tasks.
- Targets you will set and how you will monitor and evaluate the use of social media.
- Outline the type of content you will post. You could post about new stock coming in and, for example, articles about new innovations and techniques in the plumbing world.

You should discuss your plan with some of the staff who will implement it to see if they think it is feasible. Once you have a plan, you need to present it to the company owner for review. Your presentation will need to be professional and focus on the business benefits of what you propose. You are likely to need to make some refinements based on the feedback you get from the company owner.

Getting ready for assessment

Anita is working towards a BTEC National in Information Technology. For learning aim A, she was given an assignment which asked her to create a presentation aimed at local business people about how they can use social media in their businesses. Anita shares her experiences below.

How I got started

First, I created an overall structure for the presentation by listing the main things I needed to cover. These were:

▶ an outline of the different social media websites and their audiences
▶ the different ways in which businesses can use social media, along with some examples
▶ the risks and issues for businesses of using social media
▶ an evaluation of the business use of social media.

I collected all my class notes on this topic into a folder and divided them up into the sections listed above. I then chose a PowerPoint® slide template and created title slides for each section. I also did some research to find examples of businesses which use social media for different purposes, took screenshots of these and copied them into my presentation. I found this approach worked well as it gave me a structure around which to build the presentation.

How I brought it all together

I worked through my notes for each section and used a highlighter pen to pick out the main points. I used these as the bullet points on each slide of my presentation, making sure I didn't have more than about five or six small bullet points on each slide, otherwise the text would have become too small to read. I also checked that I just had the main points on the slides and I rewrote the rest of the text from my notes into the slide notes section, rewording them as if I was talking to an audience. I also added some further screenshots to illustrate the text.

In the section about target audiences and site profiles, I added some links to the external websites that I had used in my research. Once I had completed the presentation, I read it through as if I was actually giving it to an audience and I adjusted some of the slides to make them clearer. I added more information to the slide notes where I felt it was needed.

What I learned from the experience.

I found that the notes I made in class were fine on some topics but too brief on others. I wish I had been more consistent in my note-taking as I had to spend quite a lot of time doing research to find out about some topics which had been covered in class but where my notes were not adequate. I found the last section, the evaluation, hard to write. My first attempt was really just an explanation of the risks and issues of using social media. I had to take each point and think hard about how it might relate to a small business and their use of social media. In the end, I decided that this was hard to cover in the presentation slides themselves and that I needed to write most of the evaluation in the slide notes, where I weighed up the advantages and disadvantages of different aspects of social media use, relating these issues to a small business.

Think about it

▶ Are you taking class notes and collecting the handouts your teacher has given you? These will be really helpful when you come to write your assignments, so keep them safe and organised in a folder.

▶ There is a lot of information about social media on the internet. You can use this in your assignments but check that it is up to date as this is a rapidly changing sector. You can use direct quotes only if you clearly reference them; otherwise you will need to rewrite the information that you find in your own words.

▶ Making a plan for completing your assignments is important. You must hand your assignment in on time, so creating a plan with timings can help you make sure that you have everything ready by the deadline.

Programming 4

Getting to know your unit

Computer programs are at the very heart of modern organisations and businesses. They are vital to the delivery of products and services and they help organisations to respond to a business environment that is constantly changing. Studying this unit will transform you from a computer program user to a computer program developer who can design and program solutions to a variety of problems. You will learn to use computational thinking skills to analyse problems, identify patterns and break down complex tasks into more manageable chunks. Programming is all about problem-solving, and this unit will hone your analytical and problem-solving skills in preparation for employment or further study.

How you will be assessed

This unit will be assessed internally by a series of tasks that will be set by your tutor. Throughout this unit, you will find assessment practice activities that will help you to work towards your assessments. Completing these activities will not mean that you have achieved a particular grade, but you will have carried out useful research or preparation that will be relevant when you come to complete your final assignment.

In order for you to achieve the tasks in your assignments, it is important to check that you have met all of the Pass grading criteria. You can do this as you work your way through each assignment.

If you are hoping to gain a Merit or Distinction, you should also make sure that you present the information in your assignment in the style that is required by the relevant assessment criteria. For example, Merit criteria require you to review and justify and Distinction criteria require you to evaluate.

The assignments set by your tutor will consist of a number of tasks designed to meet the criteria in the table. The first assignment is likely to be a research-based written task that requires you to explain computational thinking skills and the principles of computer programming, while the second assignment will include practical activities such as:

▶ designing a software solution to meet client requirements
▶ developing a software solution to meet client requirements.

Assessment criteria

This table shows what you must do in order to achieve a **Pass**, **Merit** or **Distinction** grade, and where you can find activities to help you.

Pass	**Merit**	**Distinction**
Learning aim **A** Examine the computational thinking skills and principles of computer programming		
A.P1 Explain how computational thinking skills are applied in finding solutions that can be interpreted into software applications. Assessment practice 4.1	**A.M1** Analyse how computational thinking skills can impact on software design and the quality of the software applications produced. Assessment practice 4.1	**A.D1** Evaluate how computational thinking skills can impact on software design and the quality of the software applications produced. Assessment practice 4.1
A.P2 Explain how the principles of computer programming are applied in different languages to produce software applications. Assessment practice 4.1		
A.P3 Explain how the principles of software design are used to produce high-quality software applications that meet the needs of users. Assessment practice 4.1		
Learning aim **B** Design a software solution to meet client requirements		
B.P4 Produce a design for a computer program to meet client requirements. Assessment practice 4.2	**B.M2** Justify design decisions, showing how the design will result in an effective solution. Assessment practice 4.2	
B.P5 Review the design with others to identify and inform improvements to the proposed solution. Assessment practice 4.2		
Learning aim **C** Develop a software solution to meet client requirements		
C.P6 Produce a computer program that meets client requirements. Assessment practice 4.2	**C.M3** Optimise the computer program to meet client requirements. Assessment practice 4.2	**BC.D2** Evaluate the design and optimised computer program against client requirements. Assessment practice 4.2
C.P7 Review the extent to which the computer program meets client requirements. Assessment practice 4.2		**BC.D3** Demonstrate individual responsibility, creativity and effective self-management in the design, development and review of the computer program. Assessment practice 4.2

Getting Started

Many problems are solved by experienced programmers before they even touch their computer keyboard. Write down a list of the tasks and questions you think a programmer would consider when designing and building a computer program. At the end of this unit, look back at the list you have made and see whether you have missed anything, such as specific tasks or questions.

Examine the computational thinking skills and principles of computer programming

Programming is not just a question of learning how to use the programming language that is currently fashionable or in high demand. Programming is really about learning how to solve problems by thinking in a logical fashion and understanding what a programming language is, what it can do and how it is used.

Computational thinking skills

Successful computer programming relies on you exercising your computational thinking skills. These skills will help you to investigate a problem, analyse it methodically and identify potential solutions that you can further develop into working software applications. Computational thinking skills can be understood as four separate but interlocking steps, as shown in Figure 4.1.

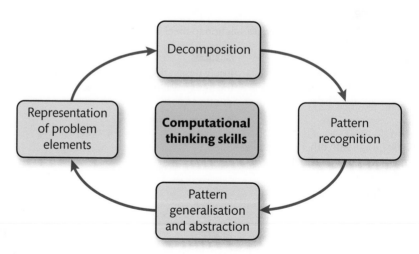

▶ **Figure 4.1:** Computational thinking skills

Decomposition

Decomposition is the process of breaking complex ideas down into smaller, more manageable parts. Sometimes this process may be called factoring. Generally, problems which are not decomposed prove to be more difficult to solve. The process of breaking a larger problem down into a number of smaller problems often improves the chances of success. This is chiefly because it allows you to focus on just one thing at a time, permitting its details to be examined more closely.

Everyone uses decomposition every day, often without realising. For example, the process of making a family meal involves:

1 choosing an appropriate recipe to follow
2 calculating the correct quantity of ingredients for the recipe and the family size
3 collecting appropriate ingredients
4 preparing the ingredients
5 cooking the ingredients in the right order
6 cooking the ingredients using the correct methods
7 cooking the ingredients for the correct duration
8 assembling the meal
9 putting the meal on plates, ready to be eaten.

In this way, a single problem (making a family meal) can be decomposed into at least nine sub-tasks, each of which could be further decomposed, if necessary, until the steps required to solve each task are relatively straightforward to understand. In programming, decomposition involves the following four stages.

Identifying and describing problems and processes

At this stage, you will list problems and processes concisely, using language that matches the problem's source. For example, if you are dealing with a financial problem, you should accurately use terms from the financial sector. This means that you need to be familiar with the technical language used in the business sector relevant to the problem.

Breaking down problems and processes into distinct steps

At this stage, you will decompose complex problems and processes into separate steps which, when taken together, can be reassembled correctly. There is no specific limit to the number of steps included or of levels to which you may decompose. You will simply continue to decompose each step until you reach an acceptable level of understanding. For example, the problem of calculating someone's net pay (salary after tax is deducted) is decomposed into several steps in Figure 4.2.

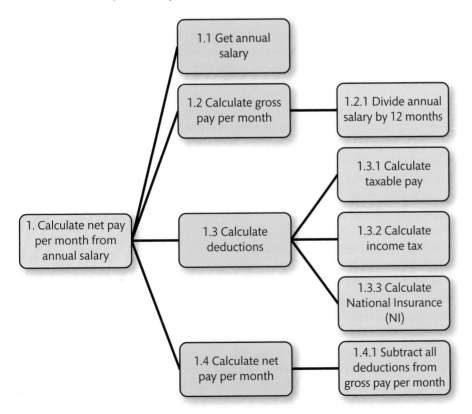

▶ **Figure 4.2:** Decomposing a single process into progressively smaller steps

Describing problems and processes as a set of structured steps

At this stage, you will document the problems and processes that you have decomposed as a set of structured steps. This should be straightforward enough to be followed by you or by others.

Communicating the key features of problems and processes to others

At this stage, you will discuss the problems and processes with others. This may include other programmers or the client. Once you have decomposed a complex problem, it is possible to start looking at the steps involved to see if there are any repeating patterns.

Reflect

As a programmer, your communication skills must be flexible. You will need to adjust your delivery to meet the needs of different audiences. For example, programmers will understand technical **jargon** while a client may not. On the other hand, the client may appreciate the use of business sector-specific language, but programmers may not.

You must be able to communicate a problem to others, because having a really clear understanding of the problem is essential to your eventual success in solving it. Albert Einstein is often quoted as having said, 'If you can't explain it to a six-year-old, you don't understand it yourself.'

Key term

Jargon – words or phrases used only by a particular group, which people outside that group find difficult to understand.

Pattern recognition

Pattern recognition is the ability to see recurring attributes within the same problem and between different problems. For example, a new problem may have features which are similar to problems that have been previously encountered and solved. Recognising these repeating patterns can make problem-solving much easier, as it can provide a good place to start.

Pattern recognition is a process based on five key steps.
▶ Identifying common elements or features in problems or systems. This involves:
  • examining problems or systems
  • listing elements or features that exist in each
  • highlighting those which exist in multiple places
  • recognising these as patterns.
▶ Identifying and interpreting common differences between processes or problems. This involves:
  • examining problems and processes
  • listing elements or features that exist in each
  • highlighting those which are unique to each
  • recognising these as differences.
▶ Identifying individual elements within problems. This involves:
  • examining problems to identify the inputs, processes (including selections and iterations) and outputs that are present.
▶ Describing patterns that have been identified.
▶ Making predictions based on identified patterns:
  • for each identified pattern, determine how they could be used in the future or how they may appear in similar situations.

Pattern generalisation and abstraction

In computing, abstraction is a concept whereby systems are split into different layers, with each layer hiding the complexity of the layer existing beneath it. This allows a programmer to use a feature without having to know exactly how it works: the irrelevant and intricate mechanics are simply 'abstracted' away or removed.

Pattern generalisation happens when relationships between patterns can be identified and simple conclusions can be drawn. For example, patterns can be identified even when, at first, it does not look like there are many similarities.

In forms of transport, for example, cars, buses and lorries, we can see similar elements repeating in the design patterns. Each vehicle includes four wheels, two axles, a chassis, a steering mechanism and so on. In order to problem-solve effectively, you must look beyond the obvious (in this case, the physical differences between the three forms of transport). Instead, try to identify the elements that are common and the relationships between these elements.

There are two parts to this phase of computational thinking.

First, identify the information required to solve an identified problem. You can achieve this by:

▸ knowing what information you need
▸ knowing your reasons for needing this information (the 'rationale')
▸ knowing the format in which this information needs to be provided
▸ knowing how soon this information is required to prevent the solution from being delayed.

Second, filter out the information not required to solve an identified problem. You can achieve this by:

▸ knowing what information is not needed, as this will be a distraction
▸ knowing (and justifying) why you have excluded this information.

Representing parts of a problem or system in general terms

To do this, you need to identify the:

▸ variables – these are the values in a problem or system that may change, typically input by the user or as the result of a required calculation
▸ constants – these are the values in a problem or system that do not change often or that remain fixed for a reasonable period of time (e.g. the base rate of income tax being 20%)
▸ key processes – these are the processes that are absolutely critical to understanding a problem or how a system works
▸ repeated processes – these are processes that occur multiple times within a problem
▸ inputs – these are the values entered into the system, including the units used and, potentially, any valid values or ranges (e.g. where gender is 'M' for male or 'F' for female, or where a house price has to be between £20,000 and £2,000,000)
▸ outputs – this is information presented to the user in a required format, generally specified by the client as part of their requirements.

Discussion

In small groups or pairs, think about an everyday process such as calculating the cost of decorating a room with fresh paint. Try to determine the variables, constants, key processes, inputs and outputs that are involved.

Uses of software applications

Software applications (often called 'applications' or 'apps') are programs that have been developed to carry out specific tasks, solve particular problems and fulfil identified user needs. There are many different ways to categorise applications: by type of software licence (free, commercial etc.), by computer platform (desktop, mobile etc.) or by use. Table 4.1 shows some software applications categorised by popular use, including the **implications** of their use.

Key term

Implications – the likely effects of something.

▶ **Table 4.1:** Uses and implications of software applications

Usage category	Needs which are fulfilled	Examples	Implications
Gaming	Videogames which can be used to entertain, educate or help recuperate after trauma.	Activision Call of Duty Bioware Mass Effect Ubisoft Assassin's Creed PopCap Peggle Microsoft Minecraft	Potential social isolation Health issues (has an impact on physical exercise) Mental wellbeing (as relaxation tool) Potential addiction
Entertainment	Applications that help users relax and enjoy various forms of media, e.g. music, video, books through downloading, streaming or both.	Apple iTunes Microsoft Media Player BBC iPlayer Amazon Kindle App	Potential social isolation *Ad hoc* viewing/listening (more flexible consumption)
Productivity	Applications such as spreadsheets, databases, word processors and presentation software which help workers complete tasks more efficiently, typically when working in administrative roles.	Microsoft Office Apache OpenOffice Adobe Creative Suite Google Drive/Apps for Work	Improved productivity New work skills New ideas and problem-solving techniques Greater efficiency Reduced costs
Information storage and management	Applications used to store and manage information safely (preventing loss) and enable rapid retrieval, typically via the internet.	Dropbox Google Drive Apple iCloud	Less risk of data loss Redundancy of data Flexible access to data
Repetitive or dangerous tasks	Applications used to automate equipment in environments which are hazardous to people or which replace monotonous manual tasks.	Energy industry Self-driving trucks (mining) Car manufacture Chemical processing	Reduced physical risk to individual More job satisfaction (fewer menial, repetitive jobs) Redundancy New work skills Improved productivity Reduced costs
Social media	Applications designed to connect you to other people, to aid communication and share ideas, events, pictures and videos.	Twitter™ Facebook™ Snapchat™ WhatsApp™ Pinterest™ Instagram™ WordPress™ Blogger™	Changes to communication skills Ability to discuss and share problems with others Ability to exchange ideas with others Security risks Risks to minors and vulnerable adults Potential addiction Improved contribution to important issues
Search engines	Applications that provide a facility for users to quickly and accurately search the world wide web for specific terms, returning meaningful results.	Google Microsoft Bing Yahoo! Search	Improved access to information Products and services found faster Less time wasting Risk of tracking and/or targeted advertising

Features and characteristics of programming languages

Hundreds of different programming languages have been developed since the mid-20th century. Original programs were written in machine code (**binary**) instructions that told the computer's processor exactly what to do, but this proved to be time consuming and very demanding on the programmers' skills. Although fast and efficient in execution, such programs took a relatively long time to create and complicated applications were considered a major undertaking.

Over time, newer **low-level** and **high-level languages** made programming a more understandable process. As a consequence, they reduced the production time of more intricate applications and systems software. Table 4.2 contrasts two different types of program code being used to output the same message screen, initially using low-level machine code and then using the high-level language, C++.

▸ **Table 4.2:** Outputting 'BTEC student' using low- and high-level program code

Low-level language	High-level language
'BTEC student' in Intel x86 machine code (shown in hexadecimal): B4 09 BA 09 01 CD 21 CD 20 42 54 45 43 20 73 74 75 64 65 6E 74 24	'BTEC student' in C++ source code: `cout << "BTEC student";`

While we can probably read the C++ code more comfortably, a computer can process the low-level equivalent much more easily as its machine code instructions talk directly to its **central processing unit (CPU)**. In comparison, the C++ code has to be successfully translated into machine code using a **compiler** before it can be executed by the CPU.

Uses and applications of high- and low-level languages

A computer's architecture is complex in construction. Low-level programming languages such as machine code (often written in binary, which is a base-2 system, or hexadecimal, which is a base-16 system) or assembly language hide little of this complexity from the programmer. In order to program the computer at this level, the developer must know the processor's architecture very well.

In comparison, high-level languages such as Microsoft Visual Basic .NET and C++ use abstraction to hide the complexities of the architecture from the programmer. In these languages, a single command may translate to hundreds of complex low-level instructions which the processor can understand.

Key terms

Binary – a number system that only uses the digits 0 and 1 to form numbers (also known as 'base 2'). For example, '5' in binary is 101 $(1 \times 4 + 0 \times 2 + 1 \times 1)$. Computer circuits have 'on' and 'off' states which can be used to represent binary 0s and 1s.

Low-level and high-level languages – in programming, the terms 'low' and 'high' refer to a language's position between being understood by a computer (e.g. binary is low-level) and understood by a person (e.g. natural languages such as English are high-level).

Central processing unit (CPU) – a computer's central 'brain'. Typically it controls the computer's resources, inputs and outputs and, most importantly, the processing instructions and data fetched from its random access memory (RAM).

Compiler – a special program which translates program code written in a high-level language into binary instructions which the CPU can process.

The majority of commercial programming languages used in the world today are high-level. This is because high-level languages:

1 improve programmers' productivity when writing program code
2 improve the readability of code
3 produce code that is easier to **debug**
4 allow for the use of more flexible program development tools
5 produce code that can be **ported**.

Research

The term 'bug' is popularly attributed to computer pioneer Grace Hopper who, in 1945, located a moth which had become trapped between the contact points in a computer's relay switch. Once she had removed the 'bug', the computer worked again.
In reality, though, the term is even older than this.
Do some research to see if you can identify its origin.

Low-level languages provide the ultimate control over computer hardware. However, they are time consuming and complex to use. In contrast, high-level languages abstract the difficulties of talking to the computer hardware directly and offer more rapid software development opportunities. However, the finished program is often less efficient, slower and bigger than it might be if produced in a low-level language.

Programming paradigms

Different types of problem have spawned different programming styles. Each style, known as a paradigm, aims to solve a problem in a different way, often to fulfil different user needs. Table 4.3 shows the most common types of programming paradigm.

Some programming languages can belong to multiple paradigms. For example, Ruby is commonly used as a scripting language, but it also has many features which are object-oriented. Microsoft's Visual Basic .NET, which many classify as an event-driven language, is also heavily reliant on the classes (e.g. buttons, forms and dialogs) that represent the core of the Microsoft Windows operating system. Consequently, it can also be considered OO.

▶ **Table 4.3:** Different programming language paradigms

Programming paradigm	Programming languages
Procedural	All programming languages are procedural

Features and characteristics

Procedural languages are often the first one learnt by a programmer. They are often considered to be a general-purpose tool and are used to create many different types of application. They are typically written as a set of well-defined steps which solve a set problem, e.g. performing a simple calculation in C, as shown in Figure 4.3.

If the steps become over-complicated, lengthy or repetitive, the programmer may choose to divide the steps into separate procedures, each with a single purpose that can be used multiple times.

The term 'imperative' can also be used to describe this type of language, but imperative languages tend to rely less on procedures.

```c
#include <stdio.h>
#include <string.h>

int main()
{
  int a;
  int b;
  int c;

  puts("Enter first number");
  scanf("%d", &a);
  puts("Enter second number");
  scanf("%d", &b);

  c = a + b;
  printf("%d + %d = %d",a,b,c);

  return 0;
}
```

▶ **Figure 4.3:** C program code displaying the sum of two inputted numbers

Programming paradigm	Programming languages
Object-oriented (OO)	• C++ • Microsoft C# • Oracle Java • PHP • Ada

Features and characteristics

Object-oriented programming is a popular modern approach to programming. OO languages rely on the concepts of 'classes' and 'objects' to solve real-world problems. Due to this approach, they are popularly used to design videogames, e-commerce websites, database systems and user interfaces.

In OO, objects are created from classes which are usually modelled on real-world 'things' such as customers, bank accounts, products, orders etc. Each class acts as a software blueprint, encapsulating (or containing) the thing's state (its data or properties) and behaviour (its functions or methods) in program code (see Figure 4.4). The programmer creates specific interactions between different objects in order to solve the problem. Because each class exists separately, they can easily be modified or adapted to reflect changes happening in the real world without having a negative effect on the whole solution. This makes OO languages very attractive to developers when they consider the demands of tackling ongoing maintenance.

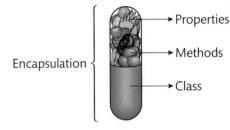

▶ **Figure 4.4:** Encapsulation

Programming paradigm	Programming languages
Event-driven (ED)	• Microsoft Visual Basic .NET, Pythion, Ruby, Java

Features and characteristics

This is a popular paradigm for the development of graphical applications which respond to events generated either by the system (e.g. system clock) or the user (e.g. a mouse click).

Event-driven programs typically work non-sequentially with users able to select the operations they want to perform rather than follow the preset inputs of a more rigid program structure.

Developers typically focus on programming event handlers, which is the code that specifies the actions to perform when a particular event is triggered via a listener. A listener is a process that waits for a certain event to happen. For example, if a File->Open menu option is clicked, a file open dialog will be displayed.

Programming paradigm	Programming languages
Machine	• Machine code • Assembly language (sometimes informally referred to as 'assembler')

Features and characteristics

These are the lowest level programming languages which offer control over the basic hardware of the machine. Machine code must be written for a specific CPU family, such as Intel x86 (32-bit) or x64 (64-bit). It cannot be run easily on different platforms without conversion to the new platform's CPU instructions or emulation of the original CPU's instructions.

Assembly language uses a series of people-friendly mnemonics to represent basic CPU instructions. Mnemonics are memory aids that help people to remember complex concepts, typically through visual representation or easily-remembered sayings or rhymes. In assembly language, mnemonics improve readability and increase productivity.

For example, when adding 4 + 2 in assembly language:

• mov means move, add means add and int means interrupt (int 20 terminates the program)
• ax and bx are registers (high speed memory areas) inside the CPU.

```
mov ax, 0004
mov bx, 0002
add ax, bx
int 20
```

These mnemonics come in the form of opcodes and operands.

Opcodes describe the operation being performed and operands are the values being processed by the operation.

In machine code, this same code expressed as hexadecimal looks like this:

In order to execute, assembly language needs to be translated to machine code using a special program called an assembler.

```
B8 04 00
BB 02 00
01 D8
CD 20
```

Machine languages are often used when speed is vital or when low-level access to computer hardware or communication with connected electronics is important. For example, it may be used in vending machines, head-up displays and videogames.

Programming paradigm	Programming languages
Markup	• HTML (Hypertext Markup Language) • XML (Extensible Markup Language)

Features and characteristics

Markup is a form of language used to specify the content formatting of a document in a structured manner using special tags. For example, in HTML <p> is used to denote the start and end of a paragraph, as shown in Figure 4.5.

```
<p>A new paragraph</p>
```

▶ **Figure 4.5**

▶ Other markup languages can be used to represent complex data structures in a platform-neutral manner, such as entries from a CD library stored in XML, as shown in Figure 4.6.

▶ XML is often used as the preferred format to transfer data between different computer systems and applications, such as when exporting and importing data between relational database systems that are normally incompatible.

```
<CD>
  <TITLE>Let's Dance</TITLE>
  <ARTIST>Bowie, David</ARTIST>
  <YEAR>1983</YEAR>
</CD>
<CD>
  <TITLE>Rubber Soul</TITLE>
  <ARTIST>The Beatles</ARTIST>
  <YEAR>1965</YEAR>
</CD>
```

▶ **Figure 4.6**

Programming paradigm	Programming languages
Scripting	• Perl • JavaScript • Ruby • PHP

Features and characteristics

Different types of scripting languages are used for different purposes.

JavaScript is used in web design to automate processes and add interactive features to web pages.

PHP is a popular server-side scripting language used to create complex online applications used in e-commerce.

Perl and Ruby are often used to automate system processes on a computer by linking and executing tasks that may have originally been run separately by a user. For example, Figure 4.7 shows a Ruby program to display the first 255 bytes of a specified file on screen.

```
#!/usr/bin/ruby

filename = ARGV[0]

aFile = File.new(filename,"r")

if aFile
  content = aFile.sysread(255)
  puts content
else
  puts "Unable to open file!"
end
```

▶ **Figure 4.7**

Comparing and contrasting programming languages

There are many factors to compare and contrast when considering different programming languages. These include the requirements (e.g. hardware, software and special devices), performance and ease of development.

Discussion

In small groups or pairs, discuss why you think you might need to compare programming languages and why it is important to have a variety of different languages. Write down the reasons you can think of. Now read on and see how many reasons you correctly identified.

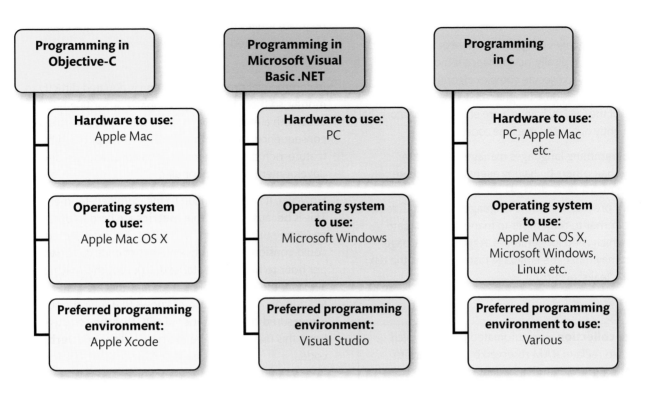

▶ **Figure 4.8:** Contrasting hardware and software requirements for selected programming languages

Hardware and software needed for running and developing a program

Some programming languages require specific hardware and software for running and developing a program. Preferred requirements for popular programming languages are shown in Figure 4.8.

Some programming languages, such as C, are considered to be 'cross-platform'. This means that it is supported on many different combinations of hardware and operating system. This is likely to explain why it is still so popular with commercial programmers, despite the fact that it was initially released back in 1972.

Special devices required

When programming solutions for external hardware, it is quite common to connect a desktop PC to a special device, typically a Serial Programming Interface (SPI) or Joint Test Action Group (JTAG). This special device is usually connected to the desktop PC via a universal serial bus (USB), serial or parallel cable, and it allows the developer to perform a process called in-system programming (ISP). ISP allows devices to be reprogrammed without being removed from their original circuit. For example, a common use of ISP is to re-program a mobile telephone in order to 'unbrick' (repair) it or unlock its features, as shown in Figure 4.9.

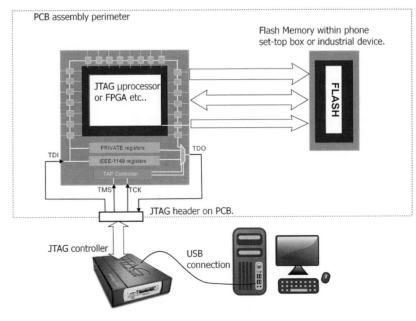

▶ **Figure 4.9:** JTAG interfacing a mobile telephone and a PC

Performance

Programming languages can perform more or less efficiently than one another. Typically, performance is measured by a language's ability to execute complex algorithms against a clock. For example, some programming languages make better use of the CPU by having more efficient translators that generate tightly optimised machine code.

Some programming languages manage RAM more efficiently than others by having aggressive **garbage collection** measures. Garbage collection is not a mandatory process and some languages, such as C, require the programmer to remember to manually deallocate memory which is no longer in use. Aggressive garbage collection may make the language faster but runs the risk of memory 'leaks' occurring.

> **Key term**
>
> **Garbage collection** – an automated process which attempts to reclaim RAM reserved by a program to store data, e.g. an identifier (variable or object) that is no longer needed.

Preferred application areas

Some programming languages are better suited for some areas of application.

- C is considered to be a general-purpose language, but it is particularly effective for controlling external hardware and electronics because of its low-level control of the computer system.

- Java is used to create applets for webpages and Android mobile apps. Its 'write once, run anywhere' (WORA) approach means it is incorporated into many different forms of home entertainment device, e.g. TV set-top boxes and Blu-ray players.

- PHP is used to create server-side applications for businesses in e-tail, e-commerce etc.

- C# is used to create videogames for Microsoft Windows and popular games consoles, particularly because of its ease of use with Microsoft's XNA, which is a popular set of tools used in videogame development and management.

- Objective-C is used to create mobile apps for Apple's iOS devices, i.e. iPad, iPhone etc.

Development time

Development time is an important consideration when choosing a programming paradigm. For example, as we have seen, programs written using machine code and assembly are efficient and execute very quickly, but development time when using these languages can be much longer than when working with high-level languages in modern integrated development environments.

In commercial programming, time is equated directly to money, so there is a strong emphasis on writing reliable code with a minimum of bugs as quickly as possible. As a consequence, programming languages supported by feature-rich development tools which claim to reduce development time are popular.

However, it can be difficult to measure development time. This is because acceptable **metrics** are hard to determine and agree upon within the industry. For example, you could consider the number of lines of code (LOC) written per hour to be an acceptable metric, but this may not consider the number of related bugs that are generated. In addition, if a programmer knows that their productivity is measured by the number of LOC that they create in an hour, this may encourage them to write overly **verbose** code.

> **Key terms**
>
> **Metric** – an agreed form of measurement that enables comparison and evaluation.
>
> **Verbose** – using more words or code than necessary.

Ease of development

As noted earlier, some programming languages are easier to use than others. This is because some languages present the software developer with advanced tools that can offer hints or auto-generated program code. For example, Microsoft Visual Basic .NET converts input forms created using drag-and-drop functionality into program code automatically.

The quality of other tools available within a programming language editor can also have an impact on the ease of development and a programmer's productivity. These tools include help systems, syntax highlighting and debugging tools.

- Syntax highlighting is a feature in many programming language editors which displays different programming constructs in specific colours. For example, a comment may appear in green, a string of text in red and so on. Most developers find the resulting code easier to read, understand and debug.

- Debugging tools offer the programmer a range of features that help them to identify bugs in their code and remove them. Popular debugging tools include traces, watches and breakpoints.

Programming constructs and techniques and their implementation in different languages

Programming language constructs are the building blocks used to create a program. You will use them in many different ways and apply various techniques to solve the problems you are given. One thing you will discover very early on is that many constructs and techniques are common across a number of languages, which means that your knowledge can be easily transferred between languages.

Code samples from a number of different popular programming languages have been used to help you compare and contrast their constructs and techniques. However, the larger code samples in this chapter have been written in Microsoft C#, which is a very popular language within the software development industry. As your skills progress, you should find it relatively simply to convert these code samples to another target language.

Command words

The concept of command (or reserved) words is at the core of most programming languages. These reserved words cannot be used by a programmer to name things (see Identifiers). Instead, they are used to command a specific action, such as 'open a file', 'clear the screen' or 'put text on the screen'. The quantity and purpose of reserved words can vary greatly between different programming languages but, as you become more experienced as a developer, you will start to identify recurring concepts.

Link

A list of reserved words for Java is shown in *Unit 7: Mobile Apps Development*.

Identifiers

An identifier is a programmer-friendly name which represents a quantity stored in the computer's RAM. Many types of identifier are used in programs, but some of the most common types are:

▸ a constant – this is an identifier representing a value that will not change while the program is running

▸ a variable – this is an identifier representing a value that may change while the program is running.

For example, when a person logs into a program, their name and password would typically be stored as variables, as these details would be different for each different user. However, a program calculating the price of a new television in a shop's electronic till would need to ensure that the current rate of value added tax (VAT) is added to the price. This value would not change for every sale, so it could be set as a constant.

In order to create (or declare) a constant or a variable, you must provide the programming language with two things:

▸ a name

▸ a data type.

You should always choose a sensible and meaningful name. For example, a good variable name for storing the user's name would be 'username'. Some names cannot be used because they are reserved by the language for a particular use, typically because they are a command word. These reserved words vary between different programming languages, so be careful.

There are many different naming conventions used in programming. CamelCase or snake_case are perhaps the two most popular in modern programming, for example if we want to store a user's age in years in C#:

| camelCase | int userAge; | The first word is in lower case. The initial letter of each successive word is capitalised. |
| snake_case | int user_age; | All words are in lower case. Words are linked with an underscore symbol. |

Most programming languages also contain the concept of local and global variables. The easiest way to think about this is to remember that global variables can be used *anywhere* in your program code. Local variables are *limited* to being used in the block of code (e.g. a function) in which they are declared.

> **Link**
>
> This also applies to mobile apps development, as shown in *Unit 7: Mobile Apps Development*.

Data types

Almost all programming languages support the concept of data types. A data type is used to define what kind of value a variable or constant can store, what operations can be performed upon it and its behaviour within the program. Most programming languages offer many different data types for the programmer to use.

The most common data types used are:

▶ character – this stores a single character (a character is a letter of the alphabet, a digit, a blank space or a punctuation mark)
▶ string – this stores a collection of characters
▶ integer – this stores a whole number (i.e. a number without decimal places)
▶ real (sometimes called floating point) – this stores a number with decimal places
▶ **Boolean** – this is a logical value which stores either true (1) or false (0).

> **Key term**
>
> **Boolean** – a form of logical data type named after the 19th century mathematician, George Boole.

Because these data types are quite common, it is possible to compare their implementation in different programming languages, as shown in Table 4.4.

Some languages are said to be strongly typed while others are weakly (or loosely) typed. This makes a fundamental difference to the formality of the programming language. Strongly typed programming languages require data and data types to be consistent when used.

For example, in Java, if a variable has been declared an integer, it should only be used to store integer variables, otherwise errors may occur. This is because Java is a strongly typed language. However, C is loosely typed: it will implicitly convert the data to the correct data type that the variable expects without the programmer needing to add any specific code to do so. This is a convenient feature, but it can lead to unexpected results.

> **Tip**
>
> Be careful when dealing with data types. Always think about the data you want to store and which data type is the most appropriate to use. Getting the data type wrong can lead to problems such as truncation of decimal places and incorrect rounding, both of which could be disastrous in an application dealing with money.

Statements

Statements are the core aspect of many programming languages. They define the basic actions that can be performed and often combine a number of language constructs.

Common examples of basic statement types with direct language equivalents are shown in Table 4.5. There are many similarities between them. For example, they are all are very **case-sensitive**, but only some of them require semi-colons to mark the end of a statement.

> **Key term**
>
> **Case-sensitive** – when a programming language recognises the difference between upper-case and lower-case characters, such as 'a' and 'A'. For example, if a command word is expected in lower case, an error will occur if it is unexpectedly written in upper case. Most modern programming languages prefer lower case.

▶ **Table 4.4:** Variable declarations using different data types in different programming languages

What to declare...	Programming language implementation in...		
	C	**C++**	**Microsoft Visual Basic .NET**
Initial (**character**)	`char initial;`	`char initial;`	`Dim initial As Char`
Username (**string**)	`char username[20];`	`string username;`	`Dim username As String`
Age (**integer**)	`int age;`	`int age;`	`Dim age as Integer`
Price (**real**)	`float price;`	`float price;`	`Dim price as Double`
Valid (**Boolean**)	`Not available`	`bool valid;`	`Dim valid as Boolean`

▶ **Table 4.5:** Statement types, their purposes and expressions in different languages

Statement type	Purpose		
Assignment	Store a value in an identifier (variable or constant).		
	Microsoft C#	**C++**	**Ruby**
	`userAge = 17;`	`userAge = 17;`	`userAge = 17`
Input	Allow input from the user, typically from the keyboard or a file.		
	Microsoft C#	**C++**	**Ruby**
	`userName = Console.ReadLine();`	`cin >> userName;`	`userName = gets`
Output	Generate output for the user, typically to the screen, a printer, a speaker, a file and so on.		
	Microsoft C#	**C++**	**Ruby**
	`Console.WriteLine("Hello");`	`cout << "Hello";`	`puts "Hello"`

Control structures

The algorithms that control programs are typically built using a combination of three basic programming building blocks known as control structures. These control structures are **sequence**, **selection** and **iteration**.

> **Key terms**
>
> **Sequence** – one action after another, none missed, none repeated.
> **Selection** – actions chosen based on a supplied condition which is evaluated to true or false.
> **Iteration** – actions repeated a number of times, typically until a condition is no longer true.

> **Link**
>
> The C# code for selections and iterations is very similar to the Java examples found in *Unit 7: Mobile Apps Development*.

Logical operations

Operators are special symbols used to perform special tasks in a program. Logical operations such as 'And', 'Or', 'Not' etc. operate on Boolean principles. They are used to combine conditions in 'if' statements and various loops. For example, a logical 'And' operator (&&) is shown in the C# 'if' statement condition in Figure 4.10. In this example, a customer will get free shipping if their order is worth more than £50 and if their address is less than 25 miles. Both parts of the condition must be true to qualify for free shipping.

Care should be taken when moving between languages. For example, in some languages (e.g. Visual Basic .NET) the single '=' sign is used to test for equality, while in other languages (Java, C, C++, C#, PHP) the '==' is used instead. Take the time to investigate the different types of operators available in your target programming language.

```
if (customerOrder > 50 && deliveryDistance < 25)
{
    Console.WriteLine("You have qualified for free shipping.");
}
```

▶ **Figure 4.10:** C# if statement using a logical And (&&) operator

Link

A detailed list of common Java operators (including logical types) is provided in *Unit 7: Mobile Apps Development*.

Subroutines, functions and procedures

Subroutines, functions and procedures are terms used in procedural programming, where code is split into a number of different modules. Each module may be called a subroutine, function or procedure depending on the programming language used. Each module is responsible for performing a single task and is typically somewhere between 5 and 50 lines of code in length.

The C# code shown in Figure 4.11 demonstrates the use of a programmer-defined function to calculate the area of a circle when given a specific radius.

```
class Program
{
    const float PI = 3.14f;

    static void Main(string[] args)
    {
        float radius;
        float area;

        radius = 10.0f;
        area = calcAreaCircle(radius);   // function call

        Console.WriteLine("Area of circle is {0}", area);
        Console.ReadKey();
    }

    //function declaration
    public static float calcAreaCircle(float radius)
    {
        return PI * radius * radius;
    }
}
```

▶ **Figure 4.11:** Code to calculate the area of a circle given the radius

The use of these modules means that code tends to be easier to write, read and debug. Code written in this way can usually be reused through multiple solutions and allows a single application to be divided and worked on by multiple programmers simultaneously, which means that development time can be reduced.

> **Tip**
>
> Almost all programming languages have library functions which programmers can use when solving complex problems. These allow the programmer to perform common but crucial tasks on data, such as formatting its appearance, finding the length of a string or the square of a number. You can also download and install third-party functions from reputable websites to expand programming languages.

Data structures

A data structure is a programming technique used to collect and organise data items in a formal structure, which helps the data to be processed efficiently. Although the availability of certain data structures vary between different programming languages, many are very common. These common data structures include string, array (one- and two-dimensional), stack, queue and record.

Sometimes, it is possible to program more efficiently through the selection and use of specific data structures, especially when this is combined with iteration control structures (loops). Software developers become familiar with different data structures as they learn about different programming languages. Here are some of the most common data structures.

String (or text)

This is a data structure which is used to store a collection of characters with one character minimally requiring one byte of RAM. Strings may be 'fixed length' (for example, only containing 10 characters), Alternatively, they can use a special 'terminator' character to mark their end. This may mean that a string requires an additional character to be included, but it allows them to have flexible lengths.

Each individual character in a string can be accessed by using its positional index. For example, in Table 4.6, Planet[2] is 'r'.

This example is demonstrated in C# strings in Figure 4.12.

▶ **Table 4.6:** Each character in a string has a positional index

Planet					
0	1	**2**	3	4	5
E	a	**r**	t	h	#

```
string Planet;
Planet = "Earth";

Console.WriteLine("Whole string is {0}", Planet);
Console.WriteLine("3rd character is {0}", Planet[2]);
```

▶ **Figure 4.12:** Working with C# strings

Some languages use a static one-dimensional array of characters to simulate a string, rather than using a specific string data type. However, their use is very similar.

Strings are commonly used to store simple text entered by the user, such as a username. Strings may also be used to enter more complex text for processing, such as the content of an email, instant message or tweet. The term 'substring' is used to describe a part of a larger string, for example 'Ear' is a substring of 'Earth'.

Array (one-dimensional)

Traditionally, this is a static data structure, which means that it has a fixed size. However, modern programming languages are generally more flexible and allow an array to be resized.

Typically an array can only store one type of data. Any type of data, such as integers, characters and Booleans, is acceptable.

If we wanted to store seven daily maximum temperatures in degrees Celsius for a local weather station, we would create an array of seven decimal numbers, as shown in Table 4.7.

▶ **Table 4.7:** One-dimensional array of seven decimal numbers

Temperatures						
0	1	2	3	4	5	6
12.50	10.45	12.30	14.60	17.70	11.20	12.50

This appears to be similar to a string. In fact, you can think of a string as an array of characters. As with a string, it is possible to access individual elements or items in the array by using the required index. For example, Temperatures[4] is 17.70. Figure 4.13 demonstrates the creation and access of this simple one-dimensional array in C#.

Array (two-dimensional)

A two-dimensional array is similar to a one-dimensional array, but it can store multiple rows of data. Imagine that we still wanted to store seven daily maximum temperatures in degrees Celsius for a local weather station, but that we needed to do this over three consecutive weeks. In this case, we would create a two-dimensional array of seven by three decimal numbers, as shown in Table 4.8.

▶ **Table 4.8:** Two-dimensional array

Temperatures							
	0	1	2	3	4	5	6
0	12.50	10.45	12.30	14.60	17.70	11.20	12.50
1	12.22	11.00	10.00	20.00	21.00	14.00	15.50
2	13.00	14.00	14.50	14.60	12.30	14.00	14.60

As before, it is possible to access individual elements or items in the array by using both indices, for example Temperatures[4][1] is the value found where column 4 and row 1 meet: 21.00.

> **Tip**
>
> The actual order of indices may vary between different programming languages. The general rule is that the element access order will reflect the declaration order of the array, i.e. you could not access an element in Temperature [1][4] as these indices do not reflect the declaration order of the array.

It is possible to use higher orders of dimensions. For example, a three-dimensional array could be used to store the twenty-one temperatures that we have stored for each of five different weather stations.

```
//create the array of decimal temperatures
float[] temperature = new float[7];

//initialise each element
temperature[0] = 12.50f;
temperature[1] = 10.45f;
temperature[2] = 12.30f;
temperature[3] = 14.60f;
temperature[4] = 17.70f;
temperature[5] = 11.20f;
temperature[6] = 12.50f;

//select Thursday's and output it
Console.WriteLine("Temperature on Thursday is {0} degrees C", temperature[4]);

//wait for keypress to continue
Console.ReadLine();
```

▶ **Figure 4.13:** C# one-dimensional array

Arrays can be split and joined. In some languages, this is called exploding arrays and imploding arrays. In languages where strings are stored as arrays of characters, the extraction of substrings and concatenation of different strings are practical uses of these types of operation. See String handling for more on substring extraction and string concatenation.

Stack (LIFO)

A stack is known as a **LIFO** data structure. It has two basic operations: Push and Pull (sometimes known as Push and Pop).

Stacks are a vital part of any computer platform's operating system, and they are a common tool for a programmer to use when developing solutions. Stacks are conceptually viewed vertically, as in Figure 4.14.

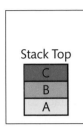 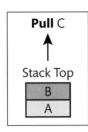 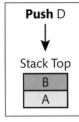 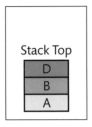

> **Figure 4.14:** Stack operations

You can see a stack operation in C# in Figure 4.15.

```csharp
using System;
using System.Collections;

namespace stack
{
    class Program
    {
        static void Main(string[] args)
        {
            char data;                      //single item of stack data
            Stack st = new Stack();         //our stack

            //push onto stack
            st.Push('A');
            st.Push('B');
            st.Push('C');

            //show the stack
            Console.WriteLine("Current stack: ");
            foreach (char ch in st)
            {
                Console.WriteLine(ch);
            }

            //remove from stack top - it should be "C"
            data = (char)st.Pop();
            Console.WriteLine("The popped value: {0}", data);
```

```
//push onto stack again
st.Push('D');

//show the changed stack
Console.WriteLine("Current stack: ");
foreach (char ch in st)
{
    Console.WriteLine(ch);
}

//wait for keypress to continue
Console.ReadKey();
        }
    }
}
```

▶ **Figure 4.15:** Stack operation in C#

Unlike an array, where elements may be accessed in any order, a stack can only be accessed in a last in, first out manner. This can be particularly useful when processing **recursive algorithms**. Stacks are often included in a programming language's library, complete with the necessary methods to process them.

Queue (FIFO)

In contrast to a stack, a simple queue is known as a **FIFO** data structure and has two basic operations:

▶ add (to tail of queue) or 'enqueue'
▶ remove (from head of queue) or 'dequeue'.

Only data at the head of the queue can be accessed and removed.

> **Key terms**
>
> **Recursive algorithms** – a piece of programming code that executes itself repeatedly until it reaches an end condition where the calculated result can be returned.
>
> **FIFO** – this stands for 'first in, first out'. It means that the first item of data added is also the first item of data that may be removed.

Like stacks, queues are a vital part of any computer platform's operating system. For example, you may be familiar with the concept of a printer queue. For a programmer, they are an excellent way of managing task processing.

Queues are conceptually viewed horizontally as shown in Figure 4.16.

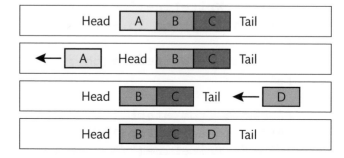

▶ **Figure 4.16:** Queue operations

Figure 4.17 demonstrates the creation and access of a simple queue in C#.

```csharp
using System;
using System.Collections;
using System.Linq;
using System.Text;


namespace queue
{
    class Program
    {
        static void Main(string[] args)
        {
            char data;                  //single item of queue data
            Queue q = new Queue();   //our queue

            //add to queue
            q.Enqueue('A');
            q.Enqueue('B');
            q.Enqueue('C');

            //show the queue
            Console.WriteLine("Current queue: ");
            foreach (char ch in q)
            {
                Console.Write(ch + " ");
            }

            //remove from head - it should be 'A'
            data = (char)q.Dequeue();
            Console.WriteLine("The removed value: {0}", data);

            //add to queue again
            q.Enqueue('D');

            //show the changed queue
            Console.WriteLine("Current queue: ");
            foreach (char ch in q)
            {
                Console.Write(ch + " ");
            }

            //wait for keypress to continue
            Console.ReadKey();
        }
    }
}
```

▶ **Figure 4.17:** C# simple queue

Record (or structure)

A record is a similar concept to an array. However, it differs because it can store a mix
of data types within its structure. For example, it can be used to store details, as shown
in Table 4.9.

Student				
StudentID	**Forename**	**Surname**	**Age**	**Enrolled**
2001	Preston	Myla	21	True

In this example, 'StudentID' and 'Age' are stored as integers, 'Forename' and 'Surname' are strings and 'Enrolled' is a Boolean. A C# implementation of a simple record structure is shown in Figure 4.18.

```csharp
using System;
using System.Linq;
using System.Text;

namespace ConsoleApplication1
{
    public class testStructure
    {
        //create the record structure
        struct Student
        {
            public int StudentID;
            public string Surname;
            public string Forename;
            public int Age;
            public bool Enrolled;
        };

        public static void Main(string[] args)
        {
            Student mystudent;     //declare mystudent of type Student structure

            //initialise the elements in the record structure
            mystudent.StudentID = 2001;
            mystudent.Surname = "Preston";
            mystudent.Forename = "Myla";
            mystudent.Age = 21;
            mystudent.Enrolled = true;

            //print the data in the record structure
            Console.WriteLine("ID        : {0}", mystudent.StudentID);
            Console.WriteLine("Surname   : {0}", mystudent.Surname);
            Console.WriteLine("Firstname : {0}", mystudent.Forename);
            Console.WriteLine("Age       : {0}", mystudent.Age);
            Console.WriteLine("Enrolled  : {0}", mystudent.Enrolled);

            //wait for a keypress to continue
            Console.ReadKey();
        }
    }
}
```

▶ **Figure 4.18:** C# simple record structure using 'struct'

You can also create an array of structures to store multiple instances of a record. For this reason, a record (or 'struct') can be seen as the basis for simple record storage in a database table or a binary data file.

String handling

Although strings are simply a collection of characters, they may still need to be processed. This task is commonly known by programmers as string handling. Programmers often need to perform certain operations on strings and most high-level languages have specialist library functions to help. Here are some common tasks, with C# practical code examples showing their implementation. Similar string functions exist in many other programming languages.

Finding the length of a string in characters

In Figure 4.19, the length property of the 'month' string object is used to access the string's number of characters. In this example, the string is the word 'January'.

```
string month = "January";
int length;

length = month.Length;
Console.WriteLine("{0} is {1} characters long", month, length);
```

▶ **Figure 4.19**

Examining single characters

In Figure 4.20, the output will be 'Character 3 of January is u'. This is because 'u' is the character in position 3. The string starts with a 'J' in position 0.

```
string month = "January";
char singleLetter;
int whichLetter = 3;

singleLetter = month[whichLetter];
Console.WriteLine("Character {0} of {1} is {2}", whichLetter, month, singleLetter);
```

▶ **Figure 4.20**

Extracting a substring

In Figure 4.21, the output will be 'Substring is ua'. This is output because we start extracting at position 3 ('u'), and we want to extract the next 2 characters, including the first one ('ua').

```
string month = "January";
string subString;
int startPos = 3;
int howMany = 2;

subString = month.Substring(startPos, howMany);
Console.WriteLine("Substring is {0}", subString);
```

▶ **Figure 4.21**

Concatenating two strings

Concatenation is the process of joining things together. In programming, it is used to describe the process of joining shorter strings together to form longer ones, for example 'Hello' and 'World!' to form 'Hello World!'.

In Figure 4.22, we are joining two strings: 'January' and 'has 31 days'. The output will be 'Joined string is January has 31 days'. This is output because we use the '+' operator to join the two strings together. Other techniques are available in C#, but this is perhaps the simplest to use.

```
string month = "January";
string saying = " has 31 days.";
string combined;

combined = month + saying;
Console.WriteLine("Joined string is {0}", combined);
```

▶ **Figure 4.22**

File handling

Data storage is a key aspect of modern programming. The ability to open data files for reading (i.e. getting data from a file) and writing (i.e. sending data to a file) in a programming language is essential. In order to use a file, it must be opened, and when you have finished it should be closed. Some programming languages require special commands to perform these operations. For example, C uses fopen() and fclose().

A simple form of file handling is the ability to read data from an ASCII or text file. This can be achieved in Microsoft C# using a few simple constructs, as shown in Figure 4.23.

```
using System;
using System.IO;
using System.Collections.Generic;
using System.Linq;
using System.Text;

namespace ConsoleApplication1
{
    class Program
    {
        static void Main(string[] args)
        {
            //exception handling
            try
            {
                // attempt to read the named file
                using (StreamReader file = new StreamReader("c:/customer.txt"))
                {
                    string line; //stores a single line of text read from the file

                    //loop which continues to read a line of text until
                    //end of file (EOF) is reached
                    while ((line = file.ReadLine()) != null)
                    {
                        //output the line of text read
                        Console.WriteLine(line);
                    }
                }
            }
            catch (Exception e)
```

```
        {
            //show user the correct error message.
            Console.WriteLine("Sorry, could not read the file.");
            Console.WriteLine(e.Message);
        }
        Console.ReadKey();
    }
}
}
```

▶ **Figure 4.23:** C# file handling demonstrating the reading of an ASCII/text file

In Figure 4.23, a simple C# 'while' loop is used to iterate through each line of the specified text file. As the line of text is read, it is output to the screen. Exception handling is used to ensure that the program does not fatally crash if the named text file cannot be found.

Most modern programming languages (such as Microsoft C#, PHP, Ruby and so on) also support connection to relational databases such as Microsoft SQL and MySQL. This supports more complex data handling.

Event handling

Event handling describes the complex process of using a specially written function or class method to perform set actions when a user event or system event is triggered. Examples of this include outputting the result of a calculation when a button is pressed on a screen form, or displaying a confirmation message when the screen resolution is changed.

Events are more commonly found in form-based applications, such as those which use **graphical user interface (GUI)** elements to allow the user to interact with the application. It is possible to create simple event-handling applications that work in the console or **command line interface (CLI)** environment, as shown in Figure 4.24.

Key terms

Graphical user interface (GUI) – a modern user interface comprised of windows and icons which is controlled by a mouse and a cursor/pointer. Examples include Microsoft Windows 10 or Apple OS X.

Command line interface (CLI) – an older style of text-based user interface that is still in use. Users interact with the computer via commands entered from the keyboard. Examples include Microsoft Command Prompt or a Linux terminal.

```
//Publisher - defines the event and the delegate
public class myClock
{
    //Defines the delegate, needed to define an event inside a class
    public delegate void SecondHandler(myClock clock, EventArgs evt);
    //Defines an event based on the delegate
    public event SecondHandler second;
    public EventArgs evt = null;

    public void Start()
    {
        //never stop!
        while (true)
        {
            //1000 milliseconds is 1 second
            System.Threading.Thread.Sleep(1000);
            if (second != null)
            {
                //raise the event (each second)
                second(this, evt);
            }
        }
    }
```

```
            }
        }
    }

    //Subscriber - accepts the event and provides the event handler (showClock)
    public class Listener
    {
        public void Subscribe(myClock clock)
        {
            clock.second += new myClock.SecondHandler(showClock);
        }

        //Event Handler - shows the clock in the top-left corner of the screen
        private void showClock(myClock clock, EventArgs evt)
        {
            Console.CursorLeft = 1;
            Console.CursorTop = 1;
            DateTime now = DateTime.Now;
            Console.WriteLine(now);
        }
    }

    //class used to test the event-driven clock
    class Test
    {
        static void Main()
        {
            //create a new clock object
            myClock clock = new myClock();
            //create a new listener object
            Listener myEventListener = new Listener();
            //link the event and the handler
            myEventListener.Subscribe(clock);
            //start the clock ticking...
            clock.Start();
        }
    }
```

▶ **Figure 4.26:** Using C# console events to create a real-time clock

In this example, a one-second event is used to provide a real-time clock on the console screen. This is an example of C#'s Publisher-Subscriber model. The Publisher defines the event and the delegate. Once the Publisher invokes or triggers the event, other objects in the program such as the Subscriber are notified. The Subscriber then accepts the event and provides an appropriate event handler. In this case, the appropriate event handler is a function which displays the clock in the top-left corner of the screen.

Link

Form-based event handling plays a significant role in developing mobile apps, as demonstrated in *Unit 7: Mobile Apps Development*.

Documentation of code

Program code should always be documented to good standards. Doing this will:

▶ make the code more readable
▶ help other programmers understand the code
▶ help when programmers are debugging the code
▶ aid with maintenance of the program code, especially if this will be performed by another developer.

Programmers can use various techniques to document their code. These techniques include:

▶ self-documenting identifiers – this means using meaningful names which explain the purpose (and sometimes the data type) of the value represented by the identifier

> **Tip**
>
> Rules on creating identifier names can vary greatly between programming languages. Some identifiers can only use certain characters (e.g. no spaces) or cannot start with certain characters (e.g. digits 0–9). In addition, stylistic advice is often given, e.g. do not abbreviate or use acronyms when naming identifiers.

▶ single-line comments – these are short comments that explain the purpose of a line of code
▶ multi-line comments – these are longer comments that explain the purpose of a more complex section of code or preface a separate section of code, such as a function, procedure or class
▶ use of constants – this means replacing multiple instances of fixed 'literal' values (numeric, text etc.) scattered throughout a program with named identifiers which may be modified at a single point in the program code.

Table 4.10 shows these most common techniques in C#.

▶ **Table 4.10:** Documentation of code in Microsoft C#

Documentation concept	Microsoft C#
Self-documenting identifiers	`int userAge;`
Single-line comments	`// stores user's age`

Multi-line comments	`/*`
	`This section of code validates the user's`
	`age when entered.`
	`*/`

Use of constants	`const double PI = 3.14159;`

> **Research**
>
> Many software publishers recommend standards for naming identifiers. For example, Microsoft provides online documentation containing advice and guidance on these technical issues in order to encourage good programming practices. Visit their Developer Network to find out about their recommended identifier naming conventions.

> **Link**
>
> Tools are also available which generate HTML documentation directly from comments placed in programming code. This is discussed further in *Unit 7: Mobile Apps Development*.

Principles of logic applied to program design

In computing, logic is the set of principles beneath the different elements of a program or system that allows the program or system to function. Successful program design benefits from the application of simple logic. This is more important than the ability to think in a particular programming language. Being able to think logically will help you to process data correctly, form complex conditions which enable you to test data appropriately and build powerful algorithms to solve even the most complex problems.

The principles of logic used in computing include mathematical logic, iterations, propositional logic and the use of sets. These concepts help programmers to understand problems more fully and build the logic that is incorporated into their programs.

Mathematical logic

Mathematical logic can be applied to help developers understand and accurately describe the basic facts in a problem and their relationships to one another. For example, inference is the process used to reach a logical conclusion from premises (situations) which are thought or known to be true. This can be seen in the following example.

▶ Premise: All meat comes from animals. This is true.
▶ Premise: Lamb comes from sheep. This is true.
▶ Inference: Therefore lamb comes from animals.

This inference is true because sheep are animals. False inferences are called fallacies.

The concept and use of inference is important when using programming languages such as Prolog ('Programming in Logic') to build simple knowledge bases which can be queried to reveal new facts.

Other logical concepts can also be considered. For example, consistency tries to see if a statement (and its opposite) are both true in order to determine whether there are contradictions in the statement.

Iteration

Iteration occurs when a computational procedure is applied to the result of a previous application.

Completeness

Completeness is a logical concept that states that you can 'prove' anything that is correct. Here is a simple assertion which uses the following symbols:

▶ Σ (the Greek letter sigma)
▶ Φ (the Greek letter phi)
▶ $\vdash$ (turnstile) means 'proves' or 'yields'.

Writing the assertion '$\Sigma \vdash \Phi$' means 'from Σ, I know that Φ'. More simply, it means that Σ 'proves' Φ.

There are many different forms of completeness, such as functional and semantic. In programming, completeness can be used to prove whether algorithms would successfully work given certain rules, goals and logic.

Truth tables

You can verify simple algorithmic logic through the use of truth tables. For example, a customer can only log in (L) to a system if they have a valid username (U) and password (P), and have not been locked out (O) within the last 30 minutes.

In a truth table for this example, 1 is used to represent 'true', while '0' means false. The '.' symbol means logical 'and'. The bar above the 'O' means logical 'not'. This means that we can express this logical expression as L = (U.P). $\overline{O}$ or 'successful login = username and password and not locked out'. After the expression is evaluated, we can prove the only combination which is valid, as shown in Table 4.11. The resulting expression could be converted to any target programming language, as its underlying logic is proven by the truth table.

▶ **Table 4.11:** A truth table showing possible combinations and the only valid permutation (row in bold)

U	P	O	L (U.P). $\overline{O}$
0	0	0	0
0	0	1	0
0	1	0	0
0	1	1	0
1	0	0	0
1	0	1	0
1	**1**	**0**	**1**
1	1	1	0

Propositional logic

Propositional logic is based on the simple concept that a sentence can be considered to be either true or false, but not both true and false. Consider these examples.

▶ The Sun is hot.
▶ Two plus three is six.

Both sentences are propositions and they have a truth value of either 'true' or 'false'. The first example is true because the Sun is indeed hot. The second example is a false proposition, because two plus three is five, not six. These types of simple sentences are known as basic propositions.

More complex propositions can be created using connectives. There are five basic connectives. Each one has a word and symbol form, as shown in the photos.

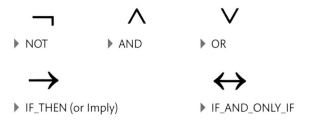

▶ NOT   ▶ AND   ▶ OR

▶ IF_THEN (or Imply)   ▶ IF_AND_ONLY_IF

These basic connective symbols allow us to represent complex expressions in a very mathematical fashion.

For example, the expression, 'If I have **m**oney **or** a **t**icket then I can watch a **f**ilm' could be expressed as: '(M ∨ T) ⟶ F'. In other words: F is true if M or T is true.

In another example, the expression, '**If** I have **no m**oney, then **if d**irect **d**ebit is due, a **b**ank **f**ine must occur' could be expressed as: '¬ M ⟶ (DD ⟶ BF)'. In other words: if M is false, then if DD is true, BF must be true.

Because such simple logic statements use a formal mathematical notation, it is possible to test their validity before any program code is produced. It is also possible to use propositional logic to derive new knowledge from existing facts.

A further revision called propositional dynamic logic (PDL) is used to demonstrate the function of algorithms. PDL is designed to present the states and the events of dynamic systems (such as working programs) in mathematically friendly notation. One of its most important features is its ability to check whether completed algorithms can complete with the desired state: that is, calculate the correct result.

Use of sets

Sets can be used to help organise data and define the interrelationships between different sets of data. This allows you to easily search and **filter** potentially complex data. Some programming languages have data types which support set-style functionality, and this logic can be used to form user permissions.

> **Key terms**
>
> **Set** – a collection of distinct objects. Sets can contain anything (e.g. names, numbers, colours or letters of the alphabet) and may consist of many different members.
>
> **Filter** – include or exclude certain values when running a search.

For example, you may have two groups of people with different access rights in a particular program. Set A is the Admin group, which contains John, Ahmed and Jo. This can be expressed as Set A = {John, Ahmed, Jo}. Set B is the Finance group, which contains Claire, Jo, Niamh and Phil. This can be expressed as Set B = {Claire, Jo, Niamh, Phil}. We can represent these sets as a Venn diagram, as shown in Figure 4.25.

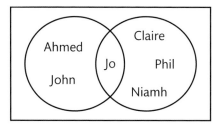

▶ **Figure 4.25:** Venn diagram showing two sets of people

There is a particular function in the program that can only be accessed by administrators (members of the Admin group) who work in the Finance department (members of the Finance Group). Looking at Figure 4.25, we can easily see that the only user who exists in both sets is Jo. This means that only Jo has access to this function.

Quality of software applications

When faced with the same problem, different programmers can arrive at very different solutions. This usually occurs because problem solving is a very personal process and most programming languages have enough flexibility to permit a variety of solutions to the same problem. However, the actual design and implementation of the software solution has a direct impact on its overall quality. The quality of a software solution is judged by assessing its efficiency or performance, maintainability, portability, reliability, robustness and usability.

> **Discussion**
>
> In small groups, share your experiences of having problems with unreliable software applications. Do you think that these problems could have been prevented? Why do you think these problems were not fixed before the application was released?

Efficiency or performance

The performance of an application is usually assessed by measuring the system resources consumed by the program. For example, CPU clock cycles, processor time, allocated RAM and the rate at which storage media is read from and written to. A complex process may be very

CPU intensive. It may be possible to revise the program code to be more economical, which, in turn, may improve performance (work faster) and use fewer resources (RAM and so on). This type of revision is common in programs which rely on speed, such as videogame programming (where screen frame rates can suffer due to inefficient coding) or talking to external devices in real-time systems where timing issues can be critical, for example traffic control systems or missile guidance systems.

Maintainability

Maintainability is the ease with which a program can be modified by present or future developers in order to carry out **corrective**, **perfective** or **adaptive maintenance**. For example, code that is written in a maintainable way will be easier to adapt or modify, and this will save both development time and money. There is always a trade-off to be made between writing code efficiently to reduce initial development costs and considering how long future maintenance will take.

> ### Key terms
>
> **Corrective maintenance** – fixing an error or bug that has been identified.
>
> **Perfective maintenance** – making an improvement to a program that enhances its performance
>
> **Adaptive maintenance** – making modifications to a program, by adding, changing or removing functionality to reflect changing needs.

Portability

Portability is a measure of the number of different computer platforms that the source code can target, such as hardware, operating systems and so on. Some programming languages, such as C, are particularly portable, as they have compilers that translate the existing code to the required target machine code on many different platforms. For example, a program written using Microsoft Visual Basic .NET may limit its execution to a Microsoft operating system, while programs written in C can be ported for use in Microsoft or Linux operating systems with few platform-specific code changes.

Reliability

The reliability of an application is determined by the overall accuracy and the consistency of its outputs across multiple runs. Consistency is particularly important in reliability testing. A program may calculate answers very accurately, but, if it cannot replicate this every single time it runs, it is not considered to be reliable. This is even more important in environments where people's safety depends on the reliability of a program, such as in safety systems in a power station or collision detection in aircraft traffic control systems.

> ### Discussion
>
> We have already seen a couple of examples where reliability is crucial. In pairs, discuss and write down three more examples of situations in which a program has to be completely reliable.

Robustness

Robustness is a measure of the program's code quality, particularly when the program is tested to ensure that extreme and erroneous data can be processed without causing the program to crash.

Usability

Usability is a measure of how user-friendly an application is to use. If the principles of user-centred design (UCD) have been followed, users will have been involved throughout the design process. Their ongoing evaluation will have helped to refine the design many times before being fully accepted. Popular techniques, such as rapid application development (RAD), permit the developer to quickly alter the layout, flow and interactivity schemes of an application to receive realistic interface feedback from the user. Although this form of rapid prototyping usually lacks the full functionality of the final product, it does provide the targeted user with a fairly-realistic 'look and feel' of the application quite early in the development process.

Usability includes a program's inputs, navigation and standards of output. The general appearance of the application can also have a bearing on this. For example, usability may suffer if the choice of colours or fonts is poor. Accessibility for users with disabilities or special needs should also be considered when thinking about usability, particularly for users with physical, visual or hearing impairments who may use **assistive technologies**. The broader study of human-computer interaction (HCI) can also inform the design of application interfaces, including how the user's psychology and, in particular, their behaviour, affects their use of the application.

> **Key term**
>
> **Assistive technologies** – hardware or software designed to assist users with a specific disability or special need, such as screen readers for users with visual impairments or learning disabilities.

❚❚ PAUSE POINT Can you explain what the learning aim was about? What elements did you find easiest?

> **Hint** Close the book and make a list of the features of computational thinking skills and the principles of computer programming.

> **Extend** How does the type of programming language affect the development of a software solution?

Assessment practice 4.1   `A.P1` `A.P2` `A.P3` `A.M1` `A.D1`

A local school is launching a campaign to promote programming. You have been asked to write a student-friendly blog post which explains and promotes the application of computational thinking skills when solving problems and developing software applications.

To make the blog post as helpful as possible for your target audience, you should explain the principles of computer programming, especially how different languages can be used to create solutions. You should also discuss the basic principles of software design and how they are applied to produce the high-quality software that your target audience needs and uses on a daily basis.

Conclude your blog post by analysing and evaluating the impact of computational thinking on software design and the quality of the software produced.

While you are writing your blog post, think carefully about your target audience and their level of knowledge about programming. Consider how you will explain technical concepts to an audience that may contain both experts and beginners.

Plan
- What is the task? What am I being asked to do?
- How confident do I feel in my own ability to complete this task?
- Are there any areas I think I may struggle with?
- Am I using appropriate language for the target audience?
- Do I understand the difference between analysis and evaluation?

Do
- I know what I am doing and what I want to achieve.
- I can identify where I have gone wrong and adjust my thinking or approach to get myself back on course.

Review
- I can explain what the task was and how I approached it.
- I can explain how I would approach the more difficult elements differently next time (i.e. what I would do differently).

Design a software solution to meet client requirements

The key point of any software solution is that it meets the client's requirements. If you do not or cannot achieve this, then it does not matter how attractive, user-friendly or efficient your solution is: you have not actually solved your client's problem.

Make sure that you really understand your client's requirements before you start. Once you have started to design and develop the solution, you should also return to the original client requirements at regular intervals. This will help you to keep your software development on course for success.

Software development life cycle

Designing a software solution is a cyclical process with clearly defined stages. Although many different versions of the software development life cycle exist and names may change, most stages are common and follow the same sensible order.

The software development life cycle (SDLC) is a **conceptual model**. It describes the stages used to manage the creation of a software solution from its inception through to its ongoing maintenance and eventual retirement or replacement. A typical SDLC is shown in Figure 4.26.

> **Key term**
>
> **Conceptual model** – a way of organising ideas and concepts in a logical fashion. Conceptual models often represent the ideas concerned in a visual manner that illustrates the relationships between them in a simple way that is easily understood.

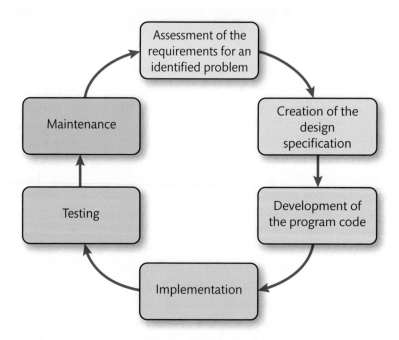

▶ **Figure 4.26:** SDLC conceptual model - there is a big overlap between development of the program code and implementation

The following step-by-step process shows how these six steps are applied in software development.

Step by step: Software Development Life Cycle (SDLC)

1 Assessment of the requirements for an identified problem

You must fully understand the client's requirements for an identified problem. If you do not have a clear understanding of what needs to be achieved, it will be difficult or even impossible to create a working solution. The requirements for a solution to the identified problem are usually drawn from the client's brief. Where details are lacking or clarification is needed, you must investigate in order to grasp what the client wants the program to achieve. This may involve a number of different investigation techniques including:

- direct questioning of users or employees about the tasks they perform, their work patterns and any difficulties that they encounter in their jobs
- observation of the manual process which is being computerised, such as completing a customer enquiry form or calculating the cost of an order
- examination of manual documents which need to be computerised. This might include data collection forms such as order forms, timesheets or stock lists, and outputs such as reports or charts.

Once the requirements are clearly set out, it is possible to decide what is within the scope of the project and what is not within the scope. From this, you can create the design specification.

2 Creation of the design specification

A full design specification needs to include the following items.

- The scope of the project: This is what is covered by your proposed solution and it may also be called the 'problem domain'. Defining a project's scope upfront helps a software developer to stay on track and avoid 'feature creep' – this means adding features which are not initially required, which will potentially delay completion of the solution.
- Inputs: These are the values being entered into the program and how these values will be entered (e.g. manually, automatically from a database).
- Outputs: This is the information generated by the program. You should include details about its format and layout.
- User interface: This is how the user will interact with the program (e.g. menu systems, use of keyboard and mouse, voice control, colour schemes and layout).
- Processes and algorithms: These include calculations being performed in order to generate the desired output from the data being entered, data being validated and so on.
- Timescale: This is how long the process will take, including targets to be completed during the duration of the project. It should also include agreed 'milestones', which are predetermined points in the process at which the developer can demonstrate how much progress has been made.

3 Development of the program code

Program code should be written in your chosen language, although sometimes a client will require a specific language. The choice will be based on the design specification and the specific requirements of the solution. As you have already seen, there are many different factors that will influence your choice of programming language. The documented inputs, outputs, processes, algorithms and user interface required should provide a software developer with a very clear vision of what the program is and how it should work. The developer has to take the design specification and use their chosen programming language as efficiently as possible to create working program code, using the most appropriate features of the selected language.

In a commercial environment, this is typically achieved using discrete steps, known as 'story points'. These break up the different parts of the program being worked on into hours of work, with one hour typically equating to one story point. This means that more complex features will equate to more story points.

Commercial software developers generally produce program code on a 60/40 basis. This means that they spend 60 per cent of their time coding and 40 per cent planning, debugging and testing.

4 Implementation

Implementation involves:

- selecting the most appropriate programming language (if this has not already been chosen by the client)
- selecting the development environment – the software tool(s) used to build the program, the operating system and sometimes the type of hardware
- coding the solution from the design specification
- debugging the code to ensure that simple bugs are identified and removed before formal testing starts.

5 Testing

Testing is an essential process that ensures that any program fully meets the client's requirements and operates in an accurate, reliable and robust manner.

There are two common types of testing: white box testing and black box testing.

- White box testing is usually performed by the developer who has produced the program. It involves tracing the **use cases** through the program code logic and completing **trace tables**.
- Black box testing is performed by a user following a use case. The user has no exposure to the program code and does not need to know how the program works. You, as the developer, are only interested in the outcome the user gets.

Testing enables the program to be refined (made more precise or exact) and optimised (made to work faster or more efficiently).

> **Key terms**
>
> **Use case** – a list of specific actions or events which occur between a user and the program. Possible use cases that occur when a customer tries to withdraw cash at an ATM include 'card rejected', 'PIN correct', 'PIN incorrect', 'card swallowed', 'cash dispensed' and 'no cash available'.
>
> **Trace table** – a table that tracks inputs, processes and outputs for each use case. It includes an expected result (what should happen) and an actual result (the result of the program), which can be compared and contrasted to identify unexpected outcomes.

6 Maintenance

Maintenance is an ongoing process. It results in correcting the program code based on testing and/or user feedback.

- Maintenance may adapt the original solution to meet changing client needs. For example, if a client originally required financial information in one currency and now requires it in multiple currencies instead, this would be an adaptation of existing code.

Alternatively, maintenance may expand the solution by including additional functionality. For example, if a client asks for completely new menu options to fulfil a totally new requirement, this would be an expansion to include additional functionality.

The whole process of the software development lifecycle may be repeated over and over again. The performance of any programmed solution will eventually decline over time as the client's needs or business circumstances change. Active maintenance can prolong a program's life, but, eventually, the cycle will restart and requirements for a new improved solution will need to be assessed.

Software solutions design

A software solutions design or specification is a formal document that is completed by the developers (with input from the clients and/or target users) before the actual programming starts. It should include a full breakdown of the problem-solving process that has been followed and all the suggested solutions. If written correctly, it should provide enough detail for a programmer who is unfamiliar with the problem to build the desired application using the preferred solution.

> **Tip**
>
> Remember that there may be more than one solution to consider for a single problem.

Problem definition statements

Problem definition statements are a key element of software solutions design. They are clear descriptions of the issues that exist, the people affected by the issues and the **constraints** which may have an impact on the solution. Typically, they are created during the initial investigation and discussion with clients by asking the five 'Ws': who, what, when, where and why? They help the developers to understand the problem, its scope and its constraints. In this way they help to focus the minds of the developers when they are solving the problem.

'What?', 'When?' and 'Where?' questions will help you to create a full summary of the problem to be solved and its complexity, as well as the benefits of and constraints on any proposed solutions.

- What is the **context** of this problem?
- What is the nature of the problem to be solved?
- What are the boundaries or scope of the problem?
- What requirements are defined by the client?
- What are the constraints that limit the solution that can be developed?
- What are the benefits of solving this problem?
- What is the impact of not solving this problem?
- What is the purpose of the required solution?
- What is the complexity of the problem we need to solve?
- What is the nature of the interactivity between the target users and the solution?
- What level of cooperation will the software designers receive from existing users and clients when solving the problem?
- What resources are available to solve this problem?
- When is the problem occurring? Can its timing be isolated? Is there a recognisable pattern?
- When does this solution need to be operational?
- Where is the problem occurring? Can its location be isolated? Is there a recognisable pattern?
- Where is the solution to be deployed?

'Who?' questions will help to identify the intended users of a software solution and the nature of the interaction that users will have with the software solution.

- Who is affected by this problem?
- Who wants this problem to be solved?

'Why?' questions will help to further identify the benefits of a software solution.

- Why does this problem occur? Can its cause be isolated? Is there a recognisable pattern?
- Why does this problem need to be solved?

> **Key terms**
>
> **Constraints** – restrictions on something. Constraints in a programming context include features of the programming languages, the technical skills of the developer, the platforms supported by the programming language and so on.
>
> **Context** – the setting or circumstances surrounding something. In software solutions design, the context will include details such as the background history of the problem.

Worked example: Writing a problem definition statement using a 'What?' question

A builders' merchant has a problem with the integration of their store and online systems. The developer asks the client, 'What is the nature of the problem to be solved?'

This is the problem definition statement that the developer creates based on the client's answers to this 'What?' question:

'A customer may have two different trade accounts which they can use within a branch store to buy goods on credit. However, when they visit our online store, they can only use the new type of account – older account types simply are not recognised and we have received complaints. We need to allow the customer to select which account they want to use to purchase our goods by choosing the correct account from an available list on screen.'

This problem definition statement is clear and concise. It describes the exact problem that needs to be solved using the correct terminology for the client's sector.

Theory into practice

Using the worked example, write problem definition statements that answer these questions.
- What are the benefits of solving this problem?
- What is the impact of not solving this problem?

Features of software

A description of the features of the proposed software solution is a core part of the solution design. This includes the main program tasks, any data storage that is required and the required inputs and outputs.

Main program tasks and input and output formats

When considering the required input and output values, you should also think about the formats that are required. For example, a developer has been briefed to create a simple program to convert an amount of pounds sterling (£) into US dollars ($) or euros (€) depending on the user's choice. The developer has created a visual representation of the required inputs, processes, outputs and data storage, as shown in Figure 4.27.

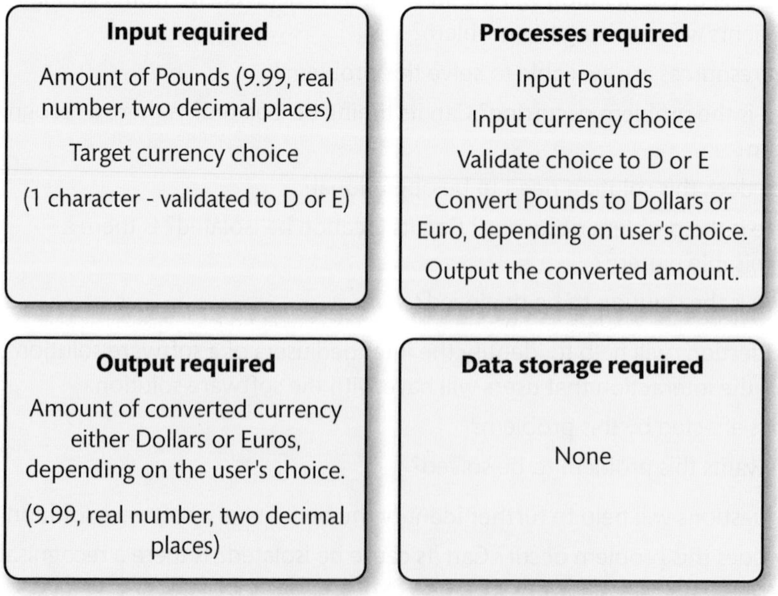

Input required	Processes required
Amount of Pounds (9.99, real number, two decimal places) Target currency choice (1 character - validated to D or E)	Input Pounds Input currency choice Validate choice to D or E Convert Pounds to Dollars or Euro, depending on user's choice. Output the converted amount.

Output required	Data storage required
Amount of converted currency either Dollars or Euros, depending on the user's choice. (9.99, real number, two decimal places)	None

▶ **Figure 4.27:** A quad diagram showing inputs, outputs and processes

The developer has listed all the inputs and outputs and noted their formats, particularly the quantity of decimal places to use. They have also included details of any validation that is required.

Diagrammatic illustrations

A solutions design will almost certainly contain a number of different diagrams, or diagrammatic illustrations. There are three common types that can be included, each of which focuses on aspects of the **user experience (UX)**. These are:

▶ screen layouts, showing how elements will be organised on the virtual 'page'
▶ user interfaces, showing how the user will interact with the application
▶ navigation elements, showing how the user will move between different virtual 'pages'.

These illustrations (see Figure 4.28) can be sketched out on paper or created electronically using specialised design tools, many of which are available online.

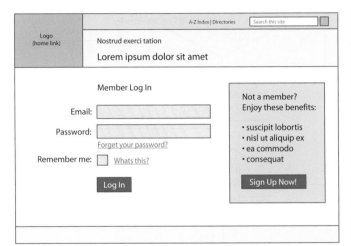
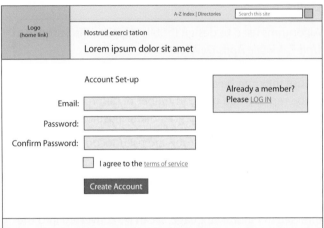

▶ **Figure 4.28:** Two potential screen layouts for the same application

Table 4.12 demonstrates the advantages and disadvantages of diagrammatic illustrations.

▶ **Table 4.12:** The advantages and disadvantages of diagrammatic illustrations

Advantages	Disadvantages
The creation process can be sped up when illustrations are created using electronic design tools.	Electronic design tools may require registration or purchase.
Can be easy to create and quick to change, especially if created electronically.	Can be time consuming if they have to be **iterated** through a number of design revisions.
Allow the designer to walk potential users through the flow of the application. This may help to identify any areas of confusion or difficulty while the design is being refined.	Can be difficult to replicate on-screen appearance exactly.
Allow the client to view prototypes of the intended user experience before the coding begins.	
Improve client involvement by helping to involve clients in the design process. This means that the final application has the best possible chance of fully meeting their requirements.	
Allow designers to try different ideas and get feedback on their ideas.	
Save development time, as developers do not have to repeatedly adjust the program code, especially as adjustments may introduce bugs.	

Screen layouts and navigation for mobile apps (a technique called wireframing) is discussed in *Unit 7: Mobile Apps Development*.

Algorithms

An algorithm is a set of instructions that is followed to solve a problem or perform a particular stage of processing in the overall solution, such as validating user inputs. Software applications may be made up of many different algorithms, implemented in the program code using a combination of many different programming constructs, functions and procedures.

Algorithms used to design mobile apps are discussed in *Unit 7: Mobile Apps Development*.

Because they can be difficult to communicate, algorithms may be represented using a number of different design tools, some which offer diagrammatic illustration.

The three most common tools are pseudocode, flowcharts and event diagrams or tables.

Pseudocode

Pseudocode is an informal outline of the algorithm, expressed in natural language. It can be converted into the target programming language. For example Figure 4.29 shows a simple validation of a user's age between 18 and 60. Pseudocode should not contain any programming language commands or syntax.

```
Do
    Ask user for their age

    Input user's age

    If age is less than 18 or
    greater than 60 then

        Output age error

    Else

        Output age accepted

    Endif

While age is not between 18 and 60.
```

▶ **Figure 4.29:** Simple validation of user's age

Flowcharts

A flowchart is a graphical representation of the algorithm, showing its actions and logic through a set of standardised symbols. Figure 4.30 shows the same algorithm as in Figure 4.29, but represented as an extract from a flowchart.

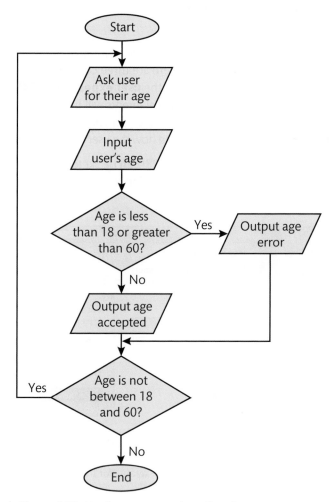

▶ **Figure 4.30:** User's age expressed as a flowchart

Event diagrams

Event diagrams or event tables are used to record events in a simple table. For each event, the following details are included in the table.

▶ The name of the container in which the responding object is located (e.g. Form1).
▶ The name of the object responding to the event (e.g. Button1).
▶ The event being responded to (e.g. Click).
▶ The event handler which is triggered by the listener (e.g. button1Action()).

Event tables can act as a useful checklist when building the GUI components of an application.

Although flowcharts can be created manually, many free online tools exist that support their creation in a user-friendly 'drag-and-drop' fashion.

Data structures

Any software solution should detail the different structures which may be used as part of any algorithm. These are different from data storage as data structures are stored in RAM while the application is executing.

Common data structures include arrays (one-, two- and three-dimensional), queues, stacks and records.

Data storage

Designing any software solution involves dealing with the persistence or continued existence of data. A computer's data storage in RAM is said to be 'volatile' or unstable because it is lost when power is removed, for example when the computer is switched off.

This means that, while it is fine to store data in RAM while the program is running, you need a more permanent (non-volatile) form of data storage to enable data to exist between program uses, especially when the power is removed. Non-volatile forms of data storage include magnetic storage, such as a hard disk, or a USB flash drive.

The most common form of non-volatile data storage is the data file. These are supported by most programming languages. Although the data file stores the data used by a program on non-volatile media, it does not store the instructions of the program itself. These are kept in separate files.

Data files may exist in many different formats. Common examples include:

▸ ASCII (American Standard Code for Information Interchange) or text

▸ Binary(where numbers are stored as a pure binary value not individual ASCII character codes)

▸ CSV (Comma Separated Value)

▸ XML (eXtensible Markup Language).

Table 4.13 demonstrates how the same customer data can be specified in in ASCII, CSV and XML for comparison.

The choice of the data file format is often influenced by its use. For example, if a data file is to be imported into a spreadsheet application (such as Microsoft Excel), CSV is a popular option. Data files can be used for many purposes, such as storing user records, a program's configuration information or its licence details.

Designing a software solution requires you to consider data storage in the following ways.

▸ What data storage is required to solve the problem (e.g. customer data and product data)?

▸ What should the files be called?

▸ How will the data be accessed (e.g. read, write or **append**)?

▸ If the data will be updated, deleted and so on, how will this happen?

▸ What file format will be used (e.g. ASCII, CSV or XML)?

▸ Where should the file be stored (e.g. media and folder name)?

> **Key term**
>
> **Append** – to add to the end of something. In a data file, it means adding new data to the end.

▸ **Table 4.13:** Comparison of different file formats used for simple data storage

Data file format	Data storage example	Notes

ASCII	```CustomerAcc Lastname Firstname Location```
	```000000001 Jones Alex London```
	```000000003 Willis Claire Swindon```
		The first row is used for headings. A tab is used to separate each value. A new line separates each customer's data.

CSV	```CustomerAcc,Lastname,Firstname,Location```
	```000000001,Jones,Alex,London```
	```000000003,Willis,Claire,Swindon```
		The first row is used for headings and each value is separated by a comma. A new line separates each customer's data.

XML	```<?xml version="1.0">```
	```<Customer>```
	``` <CustomerAcc>000000001</CustomerAcc>```
	``` <Lastname>Jones</Lastname>```
	``` <Firstname>Alex</Firstname>```
	``` <Location>London</Location>```
	```</Customer>```
	```<Customer>```
	``` <CustomerAcc>000000003</CustomerAcc>```
	``` <Lastname>Willis</Lastname>```
	``` <Firstname>Claire</Firstname>```
	``` <Location>Swindon</Location>```
	```</Customer>```
		The XML document starts with an XML tag stating its version. Each customer is 'blocked' or separated from others using a Customer start-tag and end-tag pair. Each piece of data is placed in a start- and end-tag pair describing the attribute, e.g. CustomerAcc.

More complex solutions may require many data files in order to function correctly. In some cases, particularly when searching functionality and when complex data relationships are needed, it may be more appropriate to make use of a relational database instead of data files.

Control structures

Control structures include sequences, selections and iterations. The validation algorithm shown in Figures 4.29 and 4.30 contains all three control structures. A software solution must clearly show the range of control structures selected and how they are used to solve complex problems as part of an algorithm. Flowcharts and pseudocode are good techniques to use for highlighting these details.

Data validation

You may have heard the expression 'garbage in, garbage out' (GIGO). This describes the general rule that the quality of the output is directly dependent on the quality of the input. If the input is rubbish, the output will also be rubbish. Validation is the process that checks to see if an inputted value makes sense and is reasonable before it is processed.

The use of checkboxes, buttons and list boxes usually limits input choices to sensible inputs. However, most programs still require validation to handle the probability of problematic inputs from the user, particularly when using traditional keyboard inputs.

> **Tip**
>
> Validation does not check to see if the data has been keyed in accurately. This is a separate process called verification.

It is very important to build validation rules into a solution. They will check whether different inputs are sensible and prevent inaccurate results, **run-time errors** or fatal application crashes.

> **Key term**
>
> **Run-time error** – a problem that occurs while an application is being used. These errors result in the application locking (refusing to accept user input) or crashing (terminating and returning the user to the device's menu or desktop).

There are several different types of validation.

Range check

A range check assesses whether data entered is within a valid minimum-to-maximum range. For example, if a customer is limited to buying up to ten of a particular item, then the valid range would be 0 to 10. Input outside this inclusive range would be considered invalid. Typical C# program code to perform this type of validation is shown in Figure 4.31.

```csharp
const int MIN = 0;      //minimum value of the range
const int MAX = 10;     //maximum value of the range

string strNumber;       //string to temporarily store our input
int qtyValue;           //our inputted quantity

//perform loop while quantity is outside range
do
{
    //input quantity
    Console.WriteLine("Enter quantity between {0} and {1}:", MIN, MAX);
    strNumber = Console.ReadLine();
    qtyValue = int.Parse(strNumber);

    //check is quantity outside range
    if (qtyValue < MIN || qtyValue > MAX)
    {
        Console.WriteLine("Sorry, the quantity entered is outside the allowed range");
    }

} while (qtyValue < MIN || qtyValue > MAX);

Console.WriteLine("Your quantity of {0} is valid, thank you.",qtyValue);

//@TODO other things with the quantity...

//wait for keypress to continue
Console.ReadKey();
```

▶ **Figure 4.31:** Validation routine for a defined range in C#

Of course, an input of 0 would indicate that the customer is not trying to purchase any number of the item. However, it is still a logically valid input and would pass validation.

Ranges do not have to be limited to numerical input. For example, the characters 'A' to 'F' could also represent a valid range.

Length check

A length check assesses how many characters have been entered. Some very well-known inputs have limited lengths. For example:
▶ short message service (SMS) texts are limited to 160 characters
▶ tweets were originally limited to 140 characters (derived from SMS length minus 20 characters for the user's unique address).

Figure 4.32 shows a C# extract which limits character input to a predetermined maximum length set by a constant.

```
const int MAX = 10;      //set maximum number of characters

string message;          //our message to input and process
int messageLength;       //our message's length in characters

//perform loop while string too long!
do
{
    //input string
    Console.WriteLine("Enter message (max {0} characters)", MAX);
    message = Console.ReadLine();

    messageLength = message.Length;

    //check its length
    if (messageLength > MAX)
    {
        Console.WriteLine("Sorry, your message of {0} characters is too long.",messageLength);
    }

} while (messageLength > MAX);
```

▶ **Figure 4.32:** Validation routine for a typical length check in C#

Presence check

A presence check assesses whether data is present – that is, whether it exists. For example, a user has to input whether they are 'male', 'female' or 'would prefer not to say' when completing a registration input form. The presence check validates that they have not left the entry blank or unselected.

Type check

A type check assesses whether the data entered is of the correct data type, as in Figure 4.33. For example, if the user has to enter their age, this would require the input to be an integer (a whole number). If input of incorrect data types is not prevented by the programmer, it can cause a fatal run-time error.

```
Age? A            (data type is character, this is INVALID)
Age?  16          (data type is integer, this is VALID)
Age? 01/09/16     (data type is date, this is INVALID)
```

▶ **Figure 4.33:** Example of a type check.

Format check

A format check assesses whether the data entered is in the correct format, for example, it checks that a string containing a UK postcode follows the format 'PO1 3AX'.

- PO is the area, such as GL (Gloucester) – this has to be capitals, alphabetic, 1 or 2 characters.
- 1 is the district, usually between 1 and 20 per area – this has to be up to 2 numeric digits.
- 3 is the sector, usually covering up to 3000 addresses – this has to be 1 numeric digit.
- AX is the unit, usually covering up to 15 addresses – this has to be capitals, alphabetic, 2 characters.

A format check on a postcode would apply these rules, as shown in Figure 4.34.

```
Postcode? GL2 4TH    (postcode is VALID)
Postcode? W1A 1AA   (postcode is VALID)
Postcode? GL2 24TH   (postcode is INVALID; sector can only be 1 numeric digit)
```

Figure 4.34: A format check on a postcode

Check digit

Typically, a check digit is a single character (usually a numeric digit) derived from an algorithm which is performed on a piece of data. The algorithm is designed to only generate this particular digit if the data (e.g. a string of characters) has exactly those characters and they are arranged in that specific order. Any incorrect character or swapping of character positions generates a different check digit value and fails the test. Check digits are mostly used to detect errors in inputted values such as barcodes, bank account numbers and software registration codes.

Key term

Modulus division – performing a division operation and returning the remainder rather than working out the decimal or fractional answer.

An ISBN-10 (10-digit International Standard Book Number) uses a check digit. For example, the previous version of this very book had an ISBN-10 of 1846909287. The last digit (7) is treated as the check digit. You can determine if this code is correct using the follow technique.

Step by step: Check digit validation

3 Steps

1 Multiply each digit by smaller and smaller positional weights, as shown in Table 4.14.

Table 4.14: Check digit for student book ISBN

Digits in ISBN	1	8	4	6	9	0	9	2	8	7
Factor of multiplication	×10	×9	×8	×7	×6	×5	×4	×3	×2	×1
Subtotals	**10**	**72**	**32**	**42**	**54**	**0**	**36**	**6**	**16**	**7**

2 Add up the subtotals in all columns:
10 + 72 + 32 + 42 + 54 + 0 + 36 + 6 + 16 + 7 = 275

3 Perform **modulus division** by 11:
275 MOD 11 = 25 remainder 0
Is there a remainder of 0? Yes, there is, which means that the ISBN is valid. Any other result means an incorrect ISBN has been entered

This technique identifies incorrect or transposed digits in the code. In the example given in the Step by step, the last digit (7) is considered to be the check digit.

Spelling

A spelling check assesses whether the words being entered can be found within an electronic dictionary – that is, that they are valid words.

Error handling and reporting

Many modern programming languages have syntax features which are designed to handle run-time errors when they occur. If they did not have these features, the application would crash or lock unresponsively.

A common error handling technique is the use of the 'try…throw…catch' expression that can be found in many languages, including C++, Microsoft C#, Oracle Java and PHP. This error handling technique works by trying an operation, catching any possible errors and (optionally) throwing an appropriate exception. This approach prevents the application from failing the operation in an uncontrolled way, as this would cause the application to crash completely.

An example of this error handling technique is shown in Figure 4.35 by illustrating the dangers of dividing by zero. In this example, the division operation is placed inside a try block, just in case the user has entered '0' (zero) as their second number. This has been done because dividing a number by zero can generate a serious error on a computer platform and may result in a run-time crash. By using the 'try…catch' block we are able to avoid this by displaying the exception that has been caught, which, in this case, is a 'DivideByZero' error.

```csharp
using System;
using System.Collections.Generic;
using System.Linq;
using System.Text;

namespace test
{
    class Program
    {
        static void Main(string[] args)
        {
            float num1;        // first number
            float num2;        // second number
            float quotient;    // result of dividing first number by second
            string strNumber;  // string to temporarily store our input

            quotient = 0;

            //get 1st number
            Console.WriteLine("Enter 1st number");
            strNumber = Console.ReadLine();
            num1 = float.Parse(strNumber);

            //get 2nd number
            Console.WriteLine("Enter 2nd number");
            strNumber = Console.ReadLine();
            num2 = float.Parse(strNumber);
```

```
    //try the division
    try
    {
        quotient = num1 / num2;
        Console.WriteLine("{0} / {1} = {2}", num1, num2, quotient);
    }
    catch (DivideByZeroException e)
    {
        //output the handled exception
        Console.WriteLine("Error exception caught was: {0}", e);
    }

    //wait for key press before finishing
    Console.ReadKey();
    }
  }
}
```

▶ **Figure 4.35:** A Microsoft C# example of error handling using try and catch blocks

Error reporting is an important aspect of software development. It may be directed towards the user, by telling them that they have made a mistake, or towards the developer, so that they can understand where a program has encountered an error and the nature of this error.

Common techniques for error reporting include:

▶ displaying an on-screen error message and/or error code

▶ appending the error details to an electronic log file which can be viewed separately

▶ sending an email to the developer which includes the error details.

Choice of language

There are a number of different factors that influence the choice of programming language for a software development project.

Client preference

Your client may express a preference for a particular programming language.

Suitability

Depending on the technical nature of the software development task, different programming languages may be more suitable in each case.

▶ If you were creating an e-Commerce solution, you would typically use PHP (PHP: Hypertext Preprocessor) or Microsoft's ASP .NET technologies. This is because these are server-side scripting languages. They offer the functions, features and libraries that enable the rapid development of this type of solution.

▶ If you were creating a video game, you might use Microsoft C# ('C sharp'). C# tends to be favoured because of its extensive .NET framework XNA, which enables video game development for Microsoft Windows, Xbox and Windows mobile phones.

▶ If you were creating program code to interface with electronic hardware, you could use C. These embedded systems make use of C's ability to access devices at a 'bare metal' level, as it can initiate, time and monitor electronic signals with ease in real-time. For this reason, C is a common programming choice for controlling the interfacing of the Raspberry Pi or Arduino with external devices.

Portability

Some programming languages are more portable than others. This means that the program code written can be compiled (translated to machine code or binary) for use on many different CPUs. C is a mature programming language and so countless compilers are available to translate it, including those which cross-compile from one hardware platform to another. For example, a C compiler on a Microsoft Windows platform (X86_64 processor) can create machine code to run on an Android (**ARM CPU**) device such as a mobile phone, tablet etc.

The popularity of Java has reduced some portability concerns. This is because Java code, when compiled into processor '**architecture-neutral**' byte code, can be run in Java Virtual Machines (JVM). These virtual machines exist within a wide range of devices, from mobile phones to set-top TV boxes.

Key terms

ARM CPU – a family of power-efficient CPUs created by ARM, formerly known as Advanced RISC Machines, that are used in a variety of electronic devices such as mobile telephones, tablets and portable game consoles.

Architecture-neutral – code which is not designed to run on a specific family of CPUs but, instead, is run in a virtual machine.

Maintainability

Even though maintenance is one of the later stages of the SDLC, it will influence the choice of programming language. It is unlikely that a programmed solution will never need maintenance. The most common causes of maintenance are bugs and changes to client or user needs. Maintenance can take time, so it is important that the target programming language encourages good developer practices such as readability and extensibility. These factors will result in program code which is easier to maintain, and this is especially useful if the person maintaining the software solution is not the original developer.

Extensibility

Extensibility describes a solution's ability to grow (or scale) as the needs of the client or the users change over time. Some programming approaches, such as object-oriented programming (OOP), are particularly extensible. This is because their class-based nature closely reflects real-world situations, processes and data, ensuring that the code is easy to adapt as needs change. For this reason, OOP languages such as C++ and C# are very popular.

Expertise

The technical ability of the developer is linked to their familiarity with a particular programming language. Unless external 'contract' developers are to be employed short-term for the duration of a project, the choice of language is constrained by available 'in-house' expertise.

Developers are often encouraged to expand their skill set and this means that they may be sent on study programmes by their managers as part of their continuing professional development (CPD). However, companies are often prepared to pay contract developers for expertise in new or in-demand technologies if their in-house developers do not have the required skill set to complete critical projects.

Time

The length of time spent on development is dependent on the complexity of the problem and the choice of programming language and tools used to solve the problem. Most modern development environments are designed to improve the speed at which a programmer can work. This is because improved productivity in the commercial sector is important in reducing costs.

Rapid application development (RAD) is a software development approach that enables programmers to produce code very quickly. This is achieved by using programming languages that allow the programmer to quickly create **prototypes** of the application. These prototypes can then be modified through an iterative process of client testing and review. This can reduce the length of time spent planning the project. RAD also relies on the use of reusable code snippets and drag-and-drop user interface creation. This means that programming languages that support RAD, such as Microsoft's Visual Basic .NET, can have a beneficial impact on development time.

Key term

Prototype – a working model of the desired solution or components of the solution. It may not have full functionality but allows clients and users to test and review the proposed solution. Their feedback then informs the next prototype and the process continues until the final product is ready.

Support

Many programming languages and development tools can be downloaded free from the internet. This allows developers to build commercial solutions with minimal costs. However, there may not be any technical support for these free languages and tools. They also may not be updated or maintained. For this reason, it is important when choosing a programming language to know that the technology will not be discontinued or become unsupported in the near future. This may mean that a developer may prefer to purchase a development tool that offers full manufacturer support, frequent updates and fixes and a vibrant community of users.

Cost

The development cost of a project can be linked to a number of factors. Many of these factors are directly or indirectly linked to the choice of programming language. Identifiable cost factors include:

- development tools
- programming skills required, either by training existing staff or hiring contract developers with the necessary language expertise
- licences required for languages, tools or distribution of the executable program code
- speed of development (the time taken to develop the software solution in the chosen language)
- ease of maintenance (the likelihood of bugs)
- ease of extensibility.

Calculating the cost of a project is a complicated task, and the choice of programming language plays a key part in cost estimations.

Reflect

Designing any application involves substantial amounts of planning, particularly in terms of investigating and understanding the client's requirements and the complexities of the chosen programming language.

Any proposed solution should not just list the software features you need to consider but should be an exhaustive examination of all the factors which have shaped your solution, including feedback from the client (if you have shared prototype designs) and your peers.

Recording your findings accurately and comprehensively throughout the solutions design (including the preparation of original assets) strengthens your problem solving by providing a solid foundation on which effective development may begin.

Predefined programs and code snippets

Sometimes it is possible to incorporate predefined programs or snippets of existing code within a solution. These must be documented as part of the software solutions design so that future developers know what they are dealing with. Many software development environments offer prewritten snippets of code which can be referenced or simply 'dropped' into a solution while it is being developed. In addition, third-party code may also be downloaded and incorporated with little technical difficulty.

The use of predefined programs and code snippets has its advantages and disadvantages, as shown in Table 4.15.

Developers should always check that their use of a predefined program or code snippet does not breach the terms of use defined by the original developer. For example, a developer may provide their code 'free for use' as long as it is *not* used in a commercially developed solution. If another developer uses this code in a commercial product that they are producing, they would be acting illegally.

▶ **Table 4.15:** Advantages and disadvantages of using third-party code in a solution

Advantages	Disadvantages
Saves development time.	Code may introduce potential errors if not tested appropriately.
Saves money (if program/code snippets are free and do not require additional licensing).	Code may not be modifiable (in some cases, the original developer may explicitly prevent modification).
Code is likely to be pretested so should be bug-free.	May result in unforeseen compatibility issues.
Code is likely to be written in an efficient and maintainable way.	They may no longer work with the developer's solution if the predefined program/code snippet is updated.
Code may offer additional functionality which may be useful in the future.	Predefined programs may contain malware, especially if downloaded from a disreputable source.
	There may be no support from the original developer.
	They may be discontinued or abandoned.

Ready-made and original assets

Modern programs usually have a media-rich presentation and incorporate a wide range of high-quality assets to enhance their appearance, user interface and functionality. Typical digital assets may include:

▶ graphics – such as PNG (Portable Network Graphics), BMP (Bitmap) or JPG (Joint Photographic Experts Group)
▶ animations – such as HTML5 (Hypertext Markup Language 5th major version), Adobe Flash SWF (Small Web Format) and animated GIFs (Graphics Interchange Format)
▶ audio – such as WAV (wave), MP3 (Moving Picture Experts Group Audio Layer 3)
▶ video – such as AVI (Audio Video Interleaved), MP4 (Moving Picture Experts Group 4 Part 14)
▶ **typefaces** and **fonts** – such as Arial, Times New Roman, Verdana.

Key terms

Typeface – the design of an alphabet, i.e. the actual shapes of the letters and symbols. 'Arial' and 'Times New Roman' are examples of typeface.

Font – a word used to describe the digital file that contains the typeface. For example, arial.ttf is a TrueType font file. Many people use the terms 'typeface' and 'font' interchangeably.

Assets used by a program should be included in the software solutions design as a key resource. They are grouped by category and the following details are listed for each asset:

▶ filenames (and paths)
▶ file formats
▶ file sizes
▶ dimensions/resolution in pixels (for digital graphics)
▶ duration (for digital audio and video)

▶ frames (for animation)
▶ FPS (frames per second – for animation and video)
▶ notes on their purpose/usage in the program
▶ any licence information that is required, e.g. original copyright.

Tip

When using any digital asset, you must acknowledge its copyright. Sometimes, you may need to request formal permission to include the asset from the copyright owner. This may involve paying a licensing fee for the copyright owner. In the UK, copyright is defined by the Copyright, Designs and Patents Act 1988.

Feedback from others

A key aspect of the software design process is taking feedback from peers and your client. Designing an application is an iterative process – that is, one that repeats a particular process a number of times until it gets closer to completion. Feedback can be used to refine the next iteration of the process.

Gathering feedback on screen layouts, user interface, navigation, algorithms and so on will help you to refine your ideas. It allows you to identify and remove aspects of the design which do not work well and to identify and keep the ideas that users like. It will also help you to gain confidence in your problem-solving abilities, encourage you to consider alternative design ideas and strengthen your ability to make decisions and justify changes to others.

Link

Feedback is also a key ingredient for the robust testing of mobile apps, as shown in *Unit 7: Mobile App Development.*

Test plan

Testing should form part of the software solutions design. A test plan should detail how you are planning to test your program, step by step, and it will include several use cases. Each use case tells the story of a user's successful or unsuccessful interaction with the program. Use cases include details of:

▶ the test data entered
▶ the operations performed
▶ the order of the operations performed
▶ the user's response to the program's prompts.

Test data is usually found in one of three possible states:

▶ typical/normal – data within the acceptable range that the user would usually enter
▶ extreme – unlikely data at the edges of the acceptable range
▶ erroneous – data which should not be entered (e.g. text rather than numbers).

Link

For more about test data, see *Unit 5: Data Modelling*.

Test data should be realistically selected, where appropriate. For example, it can be taken from values provided by the client, especially if you are automating a manual process, such as order processing, for your client.

Technical and design constraints

Your problem-solving skills may be limited by a variety of technical and design constraints. These constraints should be reflected in the software solutions design and may include the following.

▶ Connectivity – which devices or network connections are required for your application? This is particularly important where special hardware is needed (e.g. for input, storage or output) or if the application has to have an active network connection.
▶ Memory storage – are there RAM requirements that your program's digital footprint must not exceed?
▶ Programming languages – has the programming language been preselected by the client? This may happen if they have experience with applications written in particular programming languages.

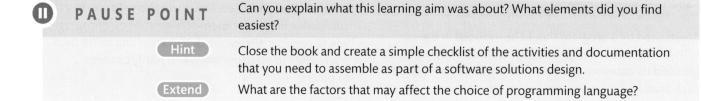

PAUSE POINT Can you explain what this learning aim was about? What elements did you find easiest?

Hint Close the book and create a simple checklist of the activities and documentation that you need to assemble as part of a software solutions design.

Extend What are the factors that may affect the choice of programming language?

C Develop a software solution to meet client requirements

Once the software solution has been designed, documented, reviewed and agreed, it is time to implement the design to produce a working application. If your design is detailed, you should find it relatively straightforward to convert it to appropriate code in your target programming language.

Software solutions development

Software solutions development can be a time-consuming process. However, modern development tools have removed many difficulties for both novice and experienced programmers. You will have many options available to you when developing your application. Choosing your development environment is your first step.

Development environment

The software development process uses integrated development environments (IDEs). IDEs help to improve productivity by allowing developers to manage projects and edit, compile, debug and execute code, all from within the same software suite.

> **Link**
>
> For more on IDEs, see *Unit 7: Mobile Apps Development*.

Sometimes, the IDE is specific to the chosen programming language. For example, Microsoft Visual Basic .NET uses the commercial Visual Studio or free Visual Studio Express editions, as shown in Figure 4.36.

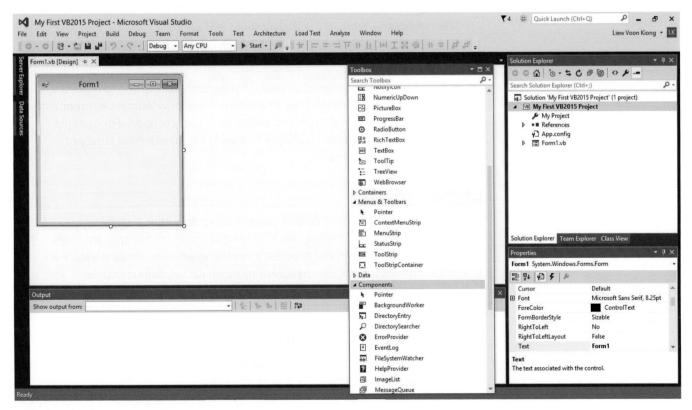

▶ **Figure 4.36:** Microsoft Visual Basic .NET IDE

Other programming languages do not have a specific IDE, and this may influence the choice of programming language. Popular languages such as C, C++ and PHP can be developed using a variety of development environments. These environments may even be made up of a number of disparate elements. For example, PHP could be developed using either of the following set-ups:

▸ a Linux operating system, Nano text editor, Apache HTTPD Web Server with PHP5 modules installed

▸ a Microsoft Windows operating system, Notepad++, Microsoft IIS Web Server with Windows PHP binaries installed.

Either of these solutions would provide a suitable environment for a developer working with PHP.

> **Link**
>
> Common development environments for mobile apps are discussed in *Unit 7: Mobile Apps Development*.

Library routines, standard code and user generated subroutines

The chosen development environment should offer access to library routines, standard code and programmer-defined subroutines. These can be used to make the program more efficient.

Many development environments will contain features to help programmers generate code more quickly. These include the following.

1 Boilerplate code – outline 'skeletons' of standard code which act as a starting point for programmers from which to code their application.

2 Automatic code completion – pop-ups which suggest code that may be used by the programmer to finish their current line of code, often offering a number of different options, complete with definitions and uses.

3 Code snippets – short sections of code which can be dropped into a program from a library of prewritten routines, often including commonly used tasks.

All of these features are designed to save the programmer time and to make the development process more intuitive. In addition, many development environments provide access to online resources containing third-party support. For example, Microsoft's MSDN (Microsoft Developer Network) has an extensive library of resources and active forums.

> **Link**
>
> IDEs are used in all kinds of development. For example, *Unit 7: Mobile App Development* examines the popular IDEs used to create mobile apps for Apple iOS and Android devices and provides a worked example of creating a software application for a specific user need. For more on IDEs in different contexts, see *Unit 6: Website Development* and *Unit 8: Computer Games Development*.

Testing software solutions

As soon as obvious bugs, such as syntax errors, have been successfully removed from a program using the debugging tools available in your programming environment, software solutions can be tested. This involves following a simple step-by-step process, using a test plan and test data.

Worked example: Testing software

Step 1: Ana creates a test plan and selects suitable test data, which includes typical, extreme and erroneous data.

Step 2: Ana feeds her sample test data and user choices into a trace table. She then records the outcomes that she expects to see.

Step 3: Ana feeds her sample test data into the live program and records the actual outcomes.

Step 4: Ana compares the expected and actual outputs to see whether they are different.

Step 5: Ana identifies any discrepancies and revisits the program code to fix the semantic errors that the test has identified.

Step 6: Ana retests the program to see if the changes she has made to the code have fixed the errors. If they have not, she should then repeat the process until the errors are solved.

Other types of testing would include the following.

▶ Compatibility testing – testing the application within different environments, such as on different operating systems and/or different hardware platforms (desktop PC, Apple Mac, mobile phone, tablet and games console).

▶ Stability testing – also known as load or endurance testing; this checks that the software solution performs continuously well, time after time, without issues.

▶ Functional testing – a black box style of testing which ensures that the software solution meets the functional requirements that the client originally presented.

Link

To test software, you need a test plan and test data, which are discussed earlier in this unit. Testing software is also discussed in *Unit 5: Data Modelling* and *Unit 7: Mobile Apps Development*.

Syntax errors are the mistakes in the source code that the programming language's translator cannot pass or resolve, which the translator reports for the developer's attention. These occur when the program code breaks the language's rules or structure, for example when invalid symbols are used or reserved words are incorrectly spelled.

Semantic errors in statements are often more difficult to identify and fix than syntax errors. This is because their syntax is fine, so they are not reported by the translator. However, they are an 'error in logic or meaning', which means that they do not perform the task that you intended.

Tip

Fixing errors in a version of a program (often called a 'build') can unintentionally break aspects of the program that previously worked. Always make sure that you test a program fully every time it is fixed, rather than just testing the aspects that the most recent changes were intended to fix.

Improving, refining and optimising software applications

As a developer, you can use a number of methods to refine and optimise your software solution. These include:

▶ annotating code, as this will allow developers to repair or debug the program and will improve its maintainability

▶ program compilation for a designated platform or environment

▶ reviewing the quality of the program in terms of its reliability, usability, efficiency, maintainability and portability

▶ undertaking user testing and getting feedback from users on their experience

▶ making use of the outcomes of testing and feedback in any planned perfective or adaptive maintenance, e.g. using errors found during formal testing to target code which needs fixing or following user feedback to identify aspects which need improvement

▶ documenting any changes to the design and solution, e.g. changes to program code, required inputs, formatted outputs, data storage etc.

Link

See *Unit 7 Mobile Apps Development*, for a specific example of these methods in developing mobile apps.

Reviewing software solutions

You should always review and evaluate your software solutions once they have been developed. You may find that the following questions are useful when reviewing your solution.

▶ How suitable is it for the intended audience and purpose?
▶ Does it meet the client's original needs?
▶ How user friendly is it?
▶ Is the software solution of a high quality? Is it:
  • reliable
  • efficient in performance
  • easily maintained
  • portable to other platforms?
▶ Did the selected programming language contain constraints that compromised the solution?
▶ Were there any other constraints that affected the solution? These may include:
  • available time for development or testing
  • your personal skills and knowledge
  • issues when using languages on particular platforms.
▶ What are the strengths and weaknesses of the software solution?
▶ How could you improve the solution? Think about this in terms of the improvements that you would make in the short term, the medium term and the long term.
▶ Could the software solution be optimised by:
  • improving robustness, i.e. making the program more resilient against user errors, bad inputs etc. and preventing it from operating erratically or fatally crashing
  • improving efficiency of the code, i.e. making the program execute faster, use fewer resources or simply feel more responsive to the user
  • expanding functionality, i.e. improving the user's experience by incorporating new options, user customisation or adding new tasks for the application to process?

Link

Reviewing is also discussed in more detail in *Unit 7: Mobile Apps Development*.

Reflect

Evaluation is a key skill that you will develop in your work as a programmer. Take what you have learnt from evaluating others' programs and codes and practise evaluating your own. You may find this difficult at first because you will have to look at your own work as though it were someone else's and identify its weaknesses as well as its strengths. However, doing this will improve your programming skills and performance and will develop your ability to make and justify well-informed recommendations. It will also give you more confidence in making decisions as you will be able to analyse your own reasons for making or recommending a particular decision.

Assessment practice 4.2

B.P4 B.P5 B.M2 C.P6 C.P7 C.M3 BC.D2 BC.D3

You are a programmer in a development team, and you have just been introduced to a client who wants your team to develop a bespoke program to meet their company's changing needs.

The client has no fixed ideas about how the problem can be solved or which programming language should be used. However, they have provided a list of the required inputs, a description of the outputs that must be created and the actions that the application must perform.

Investigate this problem and analyse its features. When you think that you understand it to the best of your ability, produce a comprehensive design for a computer program to meet these client requirements.

Ensure that you review the design with others (including the client) and use their feedback to drive improvements to your proposed solution. You should justify all of your design judgements, demonstrating that the solution you have created will be effective and fully meets the client's needs.

Once the design has been signed off by the client, your line manager asks you to implement the design and develop the software solution.

Use a suitable programming language and appropriate features of the chosen development environment to produce the code required. In addition, you need to select library routines and design subroutines to improve the efficiency of your program.

Create and implement a sensible test plan to thoroughly test your program. You must check the code's functionality, stability and compatibility. Once testing is complete, refine your solution by annotating it correctly to enable effective repair and debugging.

Review your code in terms of its reliability, usability, efficiency, maintainability and portability. Use review feedback from users to make changes to the solution and document the rationale behind each improvement.

Finally, you should evaluate the design and the finished optimised program, comparing them with the client requirements to see whether you have fully met their original needs.

You should demonstrate individual responsibility, creativity and effective self-management throughout all the stages of the software development project.

Plan

- What is the task? What am I being asked to do? Do I understand the client's needs?
- What is my starting point for this task? What is the most important thing to know?
- How confident do I feel in my own abilities to complete this task?
- Are there any areas I think I may struggle with, especially technical areas? If so, do I know how to research these?
- Are there any resources or worked examples which would help me to complete this task?
- Before I start to write the code, how well do I think my proposed solution is described in the software design?

Do

- I know what it is I am doing and what I want to achieve.
- I will use this as an opportunity to try new techniques and improve my problem-solving skills.
- I can use feedback and review comments to identify when I have gone wrong and adjust my thinking or approach to get myself back on course.
- I know who to ask for feedback on the ideas I have generated.
- I am prepared to optimise my solution based on identified requirements and user feedback.

Review

- I can explain what the task was and how I approached it, justifying my decisions at all stages.
- I can justify the changes I have made based on feedback I have received.
- I can explain how I would approach the hard elements differently next time (i.e. what I would do differently).

Further reading and resources

Books

Pilone, D. and Miles, R. (2008) *Head First Software Development* (O'Reilly Media) ISBN 9780596527358.

Greene, J. and Stellman, A. (2013) *Head First C#, Third Edition* (O'Reilly Media) ISBN 9781449343507.

Hogan, B.P. (2015) *Exercises for Programmers: 57 Challenges to Develop your Coding Skills* (Pragmatic Bookshelf) ISBN 9781680501223.

Websites

Tutorials point: **www.tutorialspoint.com/index.htm**

Codeacademy: **www.codecademy.com/**

THINK ▶FUTURE

Dan Hardy

Junior
Programmer
in a software
development
team

I've worked in the team for just over a year. In that time, I've worked on various programs and I've already learnt so much. Some of the programming tasks we tackle are very complex – I've found that I can't just sit at my keyboard and start writing program code without thinking about the solution properly. When I first started, my manager encouraged me to draw flowcharts to break down difficult business logic into simple steps. I find this approach really works, and I end up returning to my flowcharts a lot while I'm working on the next part of the problem.

When I started, I only knew Microsoft C#. I was worried when I was asked to develop in other languages like Java and PHP. After playing around with these languages, though, I discovered they had similar syntax to C#, and many of the C# concepts I knew were easy to translate. I guess you could say I started to identify the repeating patterns!

When I have to describe to my friends what programming is like, I tell them that it's mainly about problem-solving. I spend a lot of my time refining complex problems into simpler ones and trying to spot any patterns in the problems I deal with.

Focusing your skills

Being adaptable

There are many different programming languages used in computing and the industry is constantly evolving. It is really important that you keep your skills and knowledge as up to date as possible. To get a position as a junior developer in a software development team, you have to be able to adapt yourself and your skills to meet market needs and to keep up with current programming trends.

Here are some questions to ask yourself to help you do this.

▶ Which programming languages are in demand right now?

▶ What kinds of skills are sought after? Is there a particular interest in specific operating systems or specific types of applications?

▶ Are there any other skills related to programming that are in demand, such as knowledge of web technologies or relational databases?

▶ What experience of and exposure to different programming languages is expected of a junior developer? What skills are mentioned in software development job descriptions and vacancies?

▶ Can I transfer my programming skills to new languages and different development environments?

Getting Ready for Assessment

Nisar is working towards a BTEC National Extended Certificate in Information Technology. For learning aims B and C, he was given an assignment which asked him to design and develop a software solution to meet client requirements. This is Nisar's experience of developing his software solution for assessment.

How I got started

I started out by revisiting the design for my software solution. I had written it specifically to meet the client requirements that I had been given. I'd already reviewed the design with some of the other students in my class, and this helped me to make important improvements to my proposed solution. Now I just had to implement it.

I realised that the quality of my design would determine how quickly I could get started on building the software solution. Luckily, I'd documented the necessary inputs, outputs and processes really well in the design, so I'd definitely recommend taking the time to do this properly. This helped me to set up the identifiers and data files really easily. The algorithms I'd drawn could be converted to selections and iterations in my target language with very few changes needed, and I could convert the pseudocode I'd written into comments to document my software solution.

I also found that looking back on some of the smaller programs that we had developed in class was helpful. They demonstrated how I should tackle some of the trickier challenges like data file handling. By the end of the assignment, I was really glad that I'd kept my notes!

How I brought it all together

Once I'd debugged and documented the program code, I started to review its functions and features against the original client requirements. I identified areas where I had deviated from the original design, although I found that this was mainly because of technical constraints with the programming language I'd chosen. I thought about my reasons for deviating from the design and then justified them.

I included a section on optimisation, noting down all the improvements that I had made to the code in order to improve the user experience and make it as close as possible to the solution that the client had originally requested. I also improved my report by evaluating the final design and program code against the client requirements, making balanced judgements about how well the final program had met their expectations.

What I learnt from the experience

I realised that building a detailed design was really helpful when I started to produce the program code. I also learnt that looking back at my design frequently was important. This allowed me to refresh my understanding of the client requirements throughout the development process, and this made it pretty easy to make sure that the program I developed met their requirements and was optimised to meet them in the best way possible.

Think about it

▶ Do you know the difference between reviewing, justifying and evaluating?
▶ How will you demonstrate your creativity and individual responsibility when designing, developing and reviewing your computer program?

Data Modelling 5

Getting to know your unit

Every organisation is constantly faced with situations that require decisions, so producing alternative solutions to decision making is very important. Each decision has an impact, which can be positive if an effective decision is made, or negative if a poor decision is made. This unit explores how complex spreadsheets can support decision making in organisations by showing the consequences of alternative choices before they are actually made. You will find out how to design, develop and test a spreadsheet before responding to user feedback to make it better.

How you will be assessed

This unit will be assessed internally by means of a series of assignments set by your tutor. Throughout this unit, you will find assessment practice activities that will help you work towards your assignments. Completing these activities will not mean that you have achieved a particular grade, but you will have carried out useful research or preparation that will be relevant when it comes to your final assignment.

In order to complete the tasks in your assignment successfully, it is important to check that you have met all of the Pass grading criteria. You can do this as you work your way through the assignment.

If you are hoping to gain a Merit or Distinction, you should make sure that you present the information in your assignment in the style that is required by the relevant assessment criteria. For example, Merit criteria require you to analyse and discuss, and Distinction criteria require you to assess and evaluate.

The assignment set by your tutor will consist of a number of tasks designed to meet the criteria in the table below. The assignment is likely to consist of a written report but may also include:

▸ practical activities, to design and develop a data model to fulfil a client's requirements
▸ design documentation to plan your spreadsheet
▸ logs to record your spreadsheet development and testing.

Assessment criteria

This table shows what you must do in order to achieve a **Pass**, **Merit** or **Distinction** grade, and where you can find activities to help you.

Pass	Merit	Distinction
Learning aim **A** Investigate data modelling and how it can be used in the decision-making process		
A.P1 Explain the stages involved in the decision-making process for data modelling. **Assessment practice 4.1**	**A.M1** Analyse how the features of spreadsheet software contribute to the decision-making process. **Assessment practice 4.1**	**A.D1** Evaluate how the features of spreadsheet software contribute to the decision-making process. **Assessment practice 4.1**
A.P2 Explain how the features of spreadsheet software are used to support the decision-making process. **Assessment practice 4.1**		
Learning aim **B** Design a data model to meet client requirements		
B.P3 Produce designs for a data model which meets client requirements. **Assessment practice 4.2**	**B.M2** Justify decisions made, showing how the design will fulfil its purpose and client requirements. **Assessment practice 4.2**	**BC.D2** Evaluate the design and optimised data model against client requirements. **Assessment practice 4.2**
B.P4 Review the designs with others, to identify and inform improvements. **Assessment practice 4.2**		
Learning aim **C** Develop a data model to meet client requirements		
C.P5 Develop a data model to meet client requirements. **Assessment practice 4.2**	**C.M3** Optimise the data model to meet client requirements. **Assessment practice 4.2**	**BC.D3** Demonstrate individual responsibility, creativity, and effective self-management in the design, development and review of a data model. **Assessment practice 4.2**
C.P6 Test the data model for correctness, functionality and acceptance. **Assessment practice 4.2**		
C.P7 Review the extent to which the data model meets client requirements. **Assessment practice 4.2**		

Getting started

Data modelling involves using a spreadsheet or another app to mimic a real-life situation in which business decisions need to be made. It allows all options to be considered by predicting likely outcomes. Can you list some examples of real-life situations where a data model would be useful?

A Investigate data modelling and how it can be used in the decision-making process

Before you can design or create a spreadsheet to meet client requirements, you need to understand what data modelling is and how it is used. This section takes you through the stages in the decision-making process before moving on to the spreadsheet features that you will use to create your data models. Data modelling is used to help consider alternative choices. You will find out how to evaluate models and how to document your choices, justifying your decisions.

Stages in the decision-making process

There are many stages that you will explore in the decision-making process which include:

▸ understanding the scenario
▸ identifying information and sources
▸ recognising the factors affecting the quality of information
▸ analysing information
▸ identifying alternatives and the consequences of implementing them
▸ making and justifying decisions
▸ communicating decisions to others.

Understanding the scenario

The **scenario** is the situation in which the data model is needed. If you do not understand this there will inevitably be problems with the usefulness of your spreadsheet. In summary, the scenario lets you understand what your spreadsheet needs to be able to do.

Key term

Scenario – the situation or context within which you will need to create your data model.

The first stage in this process is to know who wants the spreadsheet, why they need it and what they want it to show. To understand the choices they need to make, your spreadsheet must be able to help their decision making by showing what is likely to happen from each possible alternative and therefore which of the choices is the best option. For example, if the decision-making process is being used to decide upon the price of a new product, the spreadsheet would need to be able to explore all the choices. These would include how many are made, how many are sold, quantities and costs of components, other costs (such as business premises or staff wages), the profit wanted for the product and the retail prices to the trade and the public.

Identifying information and sources

Every data model needs information, so, for this stage in the decision-making process, you will need to know where your information will come from and how reliable it will be.

Information required

This is the information required for the spreadsheet. You need to identify all the information needed for the spreadsheet data model including, for example, the profit to be made by producing a new product, or your model cannot work. When you know what information is needed, you can identify where it will come from.

Tip

You could list the information you have identified as being needed for your data model in one column of a spreadsheet and each of their sources in the next column. This can be used as a checklist to ensure that nothing is missed.

Information that is already available

Some of the information you need for your data model will already be available from the scenario. You should read the scenario carefully to identify this information.

For example, you may be able to identify the number of potential customers or the costs involved in producing the new product.

Additional information needed

There may also be additional information that your data model needs that is not given in the scenario. You will need to find out where this information can be found, that is, the source of this information. For example, if you are planning a data model that needs historical weather information for regions in the UK, then an internet search for 'download UK regional weather' would bring up the UK Met Office website, which provides a wide choice of downloadable data. In a product development scenario, the additional information needed could be how much are customers willing to pay for the product or the form of advertising that will be most effective.

Sources of additional information

You must identify the sources of any additional information that you will need for your spreadsheet data model. If these sources are from the internet, be careful to record exactly where they are located. There are likely to be lots of paper-based sources too. Try looking in the learning resource centre at your place of study or visit your local library. It might be possible to get the additional information that you need from primary sources such as interviews or questionnaires that you carry out yourself, but if you do, be very careful to make sure that you are querying the right people and that you have a good number of responses. For a new product, market research is often used to source additional information.

> **Discussion**
>
> The internet and paper-based sources are both good sources of information. What other sources can you identify? How reliable are these sources?

Requirements for verifying the information sources

All of the information you use for your spreadsheet needs to be trustworthy and reliable so that you can be confident that your data model will be useful and accurate. Verifying your information sources involves making sure that they are good and usable. To do this, find out who has provided the information and how old it is. If you have never heard of the information provider before, research them to find out who they are and why they have made the information accessible. Be especially cautious of organisations who are selling goods associated with the information. Also, most information gets less useful as it gets older, so always try to discover how old the data is. If it is two or more years

old, think carefully about whether it is still relevant and good enough for your model. For a new product, verifying sources of information would involve identifying the core market for the product and gathering market research data from this group.

Factors affecting the quality of information

The currency and accuracy of the **data** are the most important factors affecting the quality of the **information**. It could also be influenced by other external factors.

> **Key terms**
>
> **Data** – the raw facts and figures, in an unorganised state. Often there is a massive amount of raw information and it is usually difficult to understand.
>
> **Information** – produced when data is processed and presented so that it has meaning.

Currency of data

The currency of data is how recent it is. As stated above, older data tends to be less useful than up-to-date, recently produced data. Try to avoid old data that has lost its currency as it may make the information that you use for your data model a lot less useful.

Accuracy of data

The accuracy of data is how error free it is and also how detailed it is. Accurate data can be processed into a good and useful model. Try to avoid inaccurate data as the errors will produce poor results from your data model.

External factors

An external factor is something that is outside your data model but which may still influence it. External factors can be anything that may have an effect on how good your information is. For example, a car manufacturer could have a data model to predict the sales of their vehicles throughout the year based upon sales from the last decade. An external factor, such as a rival manufacturer bringing out a new model with very similar specifications at a much better price in the last two years, would make this data model very inaccurate.

Analysing the information

Analysing information is an important skill that is used by many IT professionals in a wide variety of jobs. These range from a helpdesk manager who needs to understand the support needs of the users of a network to a systems analyst planning a new software development project. So how is information analysed? The most important part of analysis is to understand what data needs to be collected and how it will be processed in order to find out the required information.

Worked example: Temperature and sunshine level changes

You are asked to produce a chart to identify trends in changes in temperature and sunshine through the years, on a monthly basis. The purpose of this data model is to produce information needed by an ice cream manufacturer to help them to decide how much ice cream to produce. What data is required to make this model work?

Step 1: Decide what each axis on the chart will be used for. For this model, use the y-axis for temperatures and sunshine hours and the x-axis for the months and years.

Step 2: Identify the data that is needed to make this work. You will need figures for both temperatures and sunshine hours for each month of each year. Ideally, this data should go back at least 50 years so will probably need to be be found in several separate data sets. The data sets need to be practical to import into the spreadsheet that you intend to use (eg Microsoft® Excel®).

Step 3: Identify where the data can be found. An internet search shows that the UK Met Office has some useful sets of weather data.

Step 4: Open the most suitable-looking data sets to check that they contains the required data.

Step 5: Download a data set to confirm that it can be used in Excel®.

Identifying alternatives

Always remember that any analysis of information that you produce is likely to be one of several possible solutions. Good practice is to carefully consider all the known alternatives before recommending or implementing a solution. To do this, you could try to approach the analysis from a different direction. Are there any other ways in which the information could be presented or calculated? Are there alternative data sources that you could use?

Identifying consequences of implementing the alternatives

Once you have identified alternative methods of information analysis and sources of data, you must be able to make a sensible decision about which to use.

A good starting point for making this choice is to identify the quality of the information produced from implementing each of the alternatives. What would be the consequences of using each of the alternatives? Would the information be any better? Is it more, or less, reliable or current? Would it take longer to produce the data model, or less? Is the data more, or less, expensive?

Making a decision

After identifying the consequences of implementing each of your alternatives, you should be able to understand which are the best and worst alternatives and therefore choose the one which has the best balance of quality and practicality.

Justifying the decision

You must be able to justify your choice of information. Understanding the consequences of implementing the alternatives should have provided good, solid reasons for why you made your choice. These reasons will need to be explained and justified as part of your assessment for this unit.

Communicating decisions

Communicating decisions to others is always important. It is essential for everyone involved in the data modelling project to be informed of your decisions, using the most appropriate methods of communication for each group of people.

Client

The client is the person from the scenario who wants to use your data model when it is ready. They know what is required and need to be kept up to date with your decisions. You may not communicate with the client every day but, instead, you may have regular meetings and give weekly or fortnightly reports. Good ways to communicate with the client are in person at meetings, in a report attached to an email or over the telephone. You may also consider sending letters if the client likes this form of communication.

Supervisor

Your supervisor needs regular updates on progress and an early heads-up or warning of any problems that develop. This is so that they can support you and are easily able to update anyone else who needs to know how the project is progressing. Most of the communication with your supervisor will probably be in the form of face-to-face conversations in the workplace. You may also communicate with them via email or telephone or at regular meetings.

Project sponsor

The project sponsor is the budget holder and is likely to be a manager in the organisation. Most communication with the project sponsor will be through your supervisor. Your supervisor, or you in certain circumstances, will communicate with the project sponsor in person at regular meetings, or through updates via email or telephone.

Spreadsheet features used to support data modelling

This section goes through the spreadsheet features that you will use to support your data modelling. The examples and techniques for this unit use the Microsoft® Excel® spreadsheet software app.

Entering and editing data

Data in a spreadsheet is kept in cells. Each cell looks like a rectangle in the spreadsheet. Every cell has a reference, so that it can be used in calculations. The cell reference is the column letter (from above the cell) and a number (from the left of the cell), for example B2.

Entering data is easy: simply select the cell then type. To complete the data entry you can tap the <Enter> key or use the <Arrow> keys to complete the data entry and move on to another cell in the direction of the arrow.

You edit data when you change something inside a cell. To do this, you need to select the cell then start the editing mode.

PAUSE POINT	Can you explain the stages involved in the decision-making process for data modelling?
Hint	Draw a diagram to show the sequence of the stages.
Extend	What communications would be made at each stage? How would each be communicated and to whom would you send them?

You can also choose to replace what is in the cell by selecting the cell, then typing just as if the cell was empty. This is followed by pressing the <Enter> key or one of the <Arrow> keys.

Formatting data

There are many ways in which you can format the data in a spreadsheet, for example to change colour or appearance. First you need to select the cells containing the data. Then you can apply the formatting to the cells.

> **Link**
>
> See the Layout and presentation section for details on how to use formatting techniques.

Using formulae and functions

Formulae are calculations which start with = to let the spreadsheet know that the cell contains something that needs to be worked out. For example, typing = A2 * B4 would multiply the numbers in cells A2 and B4 together and the answer would be shown in the cell containing this formula.

Functions are more complex calculations which are already inside the spreadsheet, waiting to be used, for example =COUNTIF(B1:D1000,'Pass') which would show how many cells contain the text 'Pass' in the three thousand cells from B1 to D1000.

Step by step: Entering a function   4 Steps

1 This step by step shows how to enter a function into cell E4 to find the average of the numbers in cells A1 to C4. Select the cell in which you want the function. Type = to start the function. Type the first few letters of the function. You will see a list of functions beginning with the letters you have typed. Use the <Down arrow> key to highlight AVERAGE.

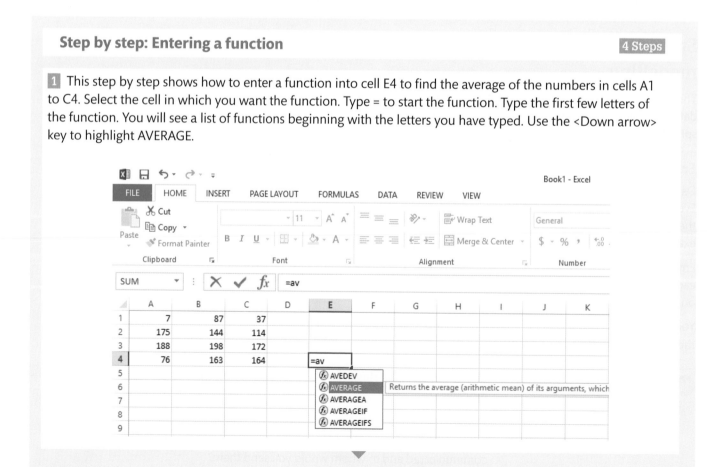

2 Use the <Tab> key to select AVERAGE. Notice how this also types the open bracket for you. Alternatively, you could double left click on AVERAGE at step 1.

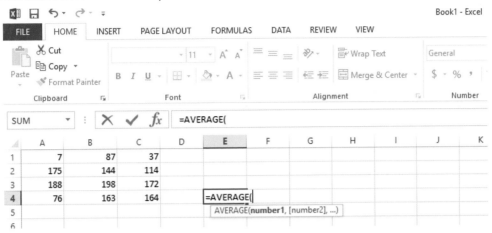

3 Select the cells which are to be averaged. You can drag the mouse over these or use the <Arrow> keys to select one corner (C4) then hold a <Shift> key to highlight the required cells using the <Arrow> keys to move to the opposite corner (A1). Notice how there is a prompt under the function 'AVERAGE(number1,' (with what you are currently entering in bold), to let you know which cells the function will work on. In the example here this is A1:C4.

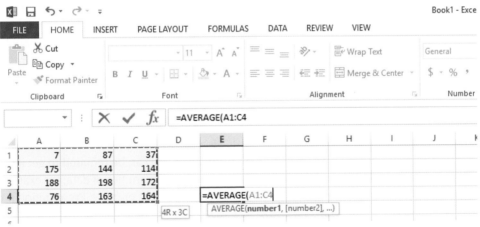

4 Use the <Enter> key to complete the task. Excel will put in the last) to finish the function for you.

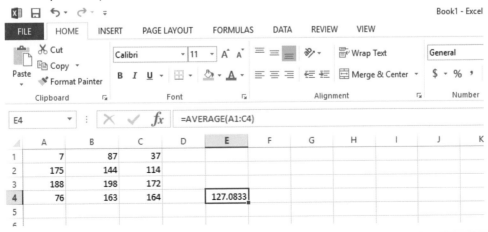

Validation and verification of data

Many mistakes can be made when data is typed into a spreadsheet. Two ways of reducing data entry errors are validation and verification of data. The computer can help with validation and provides some support for verification.

Validation

Validation occurs when data entry is checked to make sure that it is OK (valid). Excel® allows you to set up validation for a cell to check for any of the following:

▶ whole numbers

▶ decimal numbers

▶ dates

▶ times

▶ text length

▶ data entries that are too big or too small (outside a range).

You can also use a list box to choose from pre-set choices for the data entry.

Excel® allows you to set up checks for data entry problems such as:

▶ duplicate entries

▶ spaces before, after or in the data entry.

There are many other ways in which you can set up calculations and check for data entry problems.

Verification

Verification is when data entry is checked to make sure that it is correct (verified). A computer does not have the intelligence to make sure that something typed in is actually correct. The best way to verify data entry using Excel® is to type the same data in twice. The second entry can then be checked against the first by an Excel® function or conditional formatting to warn the user if the two entries are different.

Analysing and interpreting data

You will need to carefully explore the data you find in order to get useful information from it. This is similar to analysing the information (as outlined in the section entitled Stages in the decision-making process), but here the analysis is from the bottom up. Previously, we started with the required information, analysed it to discover what data was needed and then processed it to produce the required information. Now you need to analyse the data to find out how to process or interpret it to get the required information.

Data can be very large and often takes the form of an enormous table of numbers in a spreadsheet. An effective data model will analyse these numbers to interpret them into something more understandable. Sorting and filtering can bring some order and sense to large data sets. Functions can be used to count, find the average and carry out other processing actions, while conditional formatting can show interesting items and charts and can be a very effective way of helping people understand the meaning of the data. All of this requires some analysis or understanding of the data before the power of the spreadsheet can be used to bring it to life.

Presenting data

How data is presented is always important and a lot of time and skill can be required to get it right. There are often large quantities of data, for example, a hundred thousand items or more. Presentation is one of the tools used to bring meaning to this data.

As a general rule, less is more when presenting data. Simple summaries are often much more useful than lots of detail. A data modeller makes the calculations and processes the data to produce these summaries. It is a good idea to group related information, use font sizes and colour consistently, use charts where they add value and ensure that it is possible to print the summaries sensibly on a page.

Charts can be an excellent way to present data. Again, the skill here is to produce information which actually means something. Figure 5.1 shows how much easier it is to understand the larger combination chart in which the two sets of rain data are shown as stacked columns and the three sets of sunshine and temperature data are shown as lines. The smaller chart shows all five sets of data as lines and is not as easy to interpret.

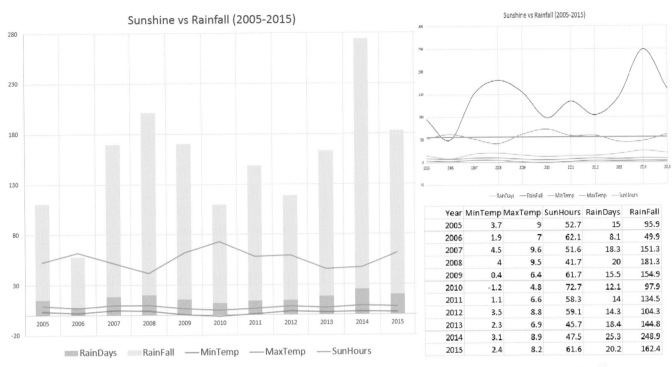

Figure 5.1: Same data, different charts (left: larger combination chart; right: smaller chart where all five data sets are lines)

Year	MinTemp	MaxTemp	SunHours	RainDays	RainFall
2005	3.7	9	52.7	15	95.9
2006	1.9	7	62.1	8.1	49.9
2007	4.5	9.6	51.6	18.3	151.3
2008	4	9.5	41.7	20	181.3
2009	0.4	6.4	61.7	15.5	154.9
2010	-1.2	4.8	72.7	12.1	97.9
2011	1.1	6.6	58.3	14	134.5
2012	3.5	8.8	59.1	14.3	104.3
2013	2.3	6.9	45.7	18.4	144.8
2014	3.1	8.9	47.5	25.3	248.9
2015	2.4	8.2	61.6	20.2	162.4

PAUSE POINT   List the features of spreadsheet software and explain what they do.

Hint   Create a two-column table with features listed in one column and an explanation of what they do in the other.

Extend   Explain which spreadsheet functions can be used to help the decision-making process. How and why are they helpful?

Using data modelling to consider alternatives

When a data model has been set up, it can be used by the data modeller to identify possible alternatives and to choose the best of them. This is usually done by testing different input values.

Identifying the inputs required for the model

The inputs required for a model are used for the 'what if' analysis of possible alternatives, such as: What if we increase our prices by 20 per cent? The key here is to try out a range of possible inputs to find the balance needed to produce acceptable outcomes.

The range of outputs that can be produced

Outputs produced by the model could be viewed on-screen, printed or exported. On-screen is best for exploring possible input combinations, printed is best to share the best alternatives with others and exported is best for further reporting using other apps. A good data model

will produce easily understandable outputs which clearly show the meaning of the data to meet the requirements of the client.

Alternative solutions

A good data model will be able to generate several possible solutions. Each of these will need careful consideration so as to justify your choice.

Benefits and limitations

What are the benefits and limitations of each alternative solution? These need to be carefully considered so as to identify and justify your preferred choice. You can produce a table showing the benefits and limitations of each alternative solution to help identify the most appropriate.

Impacts and consequences

What are the impacts or consequences of each alternative solution? Factors to consider are:

▶ risk (does a solution produce more or less)
▶ differences in timescales
▶ differences in costs.

Identifying the best decision or compromise

Your data model may not be able to find a perfect solution. You need to weigh up the benefits and limitations of the alternative solutions very carefully in order to find the one that fits the users' needs best or involves the least amount of compromise.

Evaluating models

You need to consider many factors (see Figure 5.2) when evaluating your model including:

▶ how well it reflects the scenario
▶ the decisions it supports
▶ whether it can be improved
▶ if the model could be extended.

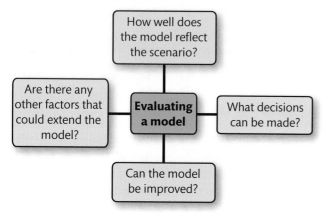

▶ **Figure 5.2:** Evaluating models

How well the model reflects the scenario

When evaluating your data models, a good starting point is how well each of them mimics the given scenario. Carefully check each aspect of the scenario to confirm that it is included in the model. How well do the calculations match the scenario? Is it possible to check these calculations against values from the scenario?

Decisions that can be made using the model

The data model is there to support decision making, so what decisions does the model actually help you make? Are these decisions useful to the decision maker? Are there any decisions that the decision maker might need to make that are not supported by the model?

Whether the model can be improved

Evaluate how the model could be improved. Most models have potential for improvement, often at a cost in terms of time, expense or practicality. You need to be able to identify whether the model can be made better and weigh up the benefit or the extra value of these improvements against any extra time or costs these improvements would involve.

Other factors

Consider whether there are other factors that could be used to extend the model. There might be another data set that could be added to the model to improve the information it provides. Are there any other apps that could receive an export of data from your model to further extend its usefulness? An example of this would be a database using a query to join the export with other data to compile a report.

> **Tip**
>
> Try to think 'outside the box' to identify anything else that adds to the potential of the data model.

Documenting and justifying decisions

This documentation will summarise the situation (scenario) and will include your information sources, the factors you considered and the methods used to reach your decisions. It must include appropriate justification of those decisions.

Summarising the situation

You should start your documentation with a section that sets out the context for the report by outlining the scenario, the need for the data model and your role in this process.

Your documentation should have structure, that is, start with an introduction, then give the detail and end with a summary.

Identifying information sources

Include a section which identifies the sources of the data that you used for your model. Make sure that you state clearly where your data sets came from, the data they provide and how useful they are for the model.

> **Tip**
>
> A diagram could be used to communicate your sources of information.

Indicating factors considered

Your documentation needs to indicate the factors that you considered when planning your data model. This could include your current skills, the time within which you need to complete the model and any other constraints. You could include a sub-heading for each factor with a paragraph or two to explain why you thought the factor was relevant and any impact it had on your planning.

Methods used to reach decisions

You should include a section which outlines the different methods that you used to reach your decisions in your chosen model. For example, what calculations did you use to process the data into information? How did you show the information output from the model?

Justifying choices

Make sure that you justify:

▶ your choice of information sources

▶ the factors considered

▶ the methods used.

The justification could be included in each section and also summarised at the end of your report.

Reflect

Reflect on what you have covered in learning aim A and consider what you will need to record during the design, development and testing of your data model. This should include gathering feedback from others.

It is important to plan ahead and set yourself relevant targets and timescales. Reflecting on how well you achieved these after completing a project will help you plan for the next one.

Assessment practice 5.1

A.P1 A.P2 A.M1 A.D1

You have a job as a junior programmer in the head office of a retailer called W-Ready that specialises in selling weather-related goods at open-air events from a number of mobile shops, based in different parts of the country. W-Ready prides itself on selling goods that respond to the weather (for example umbrellas, waterproofs, wellies and hot soup at events where rain is expected or sunglasses, sunhats, ice creams and cold drinks during hot weather).

The purchasing manager, Ellie, wants to improve her decision making related to pre-ordering, so as to save the company money by enabling them to negotiate better prices from suppliers and reduce wastage and the need to store stock.

Ellie has requested that the programming team in which you work should produce a data model to help her to make purchasing decisions. She is not sure that a spreadsheet would be the right platform for this, so she has asked you for a report that evaluates the role of spreadsheet data modelling in the decision-making process.

Your report needs to include:

- the stages involved in the data modelling decision-making process
- explanations of how each stage would help focus on Ellie's requirements and maximise the usefulness of the model
- the features of spreadsheet software that can be used to support the decision-making process, including how they can be used in data modelling
- an analysis and evaluation of how spreadsheet software features would help support Ellie's decision-making.

Your report should be a comprehensive, detailed explanation of the stages involved in the decision-making process. It should consider how a systematic approach using valid information leads to informed decisions that can be justified. It should evaluate the use of advanced spreadsheet features and functions in data modelling to clearly show how this contributes to the decision-making process.

Plan
- What is the task? What am I being asked to do?
- What are the success criteria for this task?
- What am I learning? Why is this important?
- How will I approach the task? Are there any areas I think I may struggle with?
- How confident do I feel in my own ability to complete this task?
- Do I need clarification around anything?

Do
- Have I spent some time planning out my approach to the task at hand?
- Am I confident that I know what I am doing and what it is I should be achieving?
- What strategies am I employing? Are these right for the task? Are they working? If not, what do I need to change?
- I understand my thought process and why I have decided to approach the task in a particular way. I can explain this reasoning when asked.
- I can set milestones and evaluate my progress and success at these intervals.
- I understand when to consider and when to be decisive (reflection versus action).

Review
- I can explain what the task was.
- I can explain how I approached the task.
- I can say whether I met the task's criteria (ie whether I succeeded).

B Design a data model to meet client requirements

In this section, you will learn and practise the techniques needed to design your data model. You will start with the functional specification where you will define exactly what is required, and then progress to planning the spreadsheet that you will create to meet these client requirements. Finally, you will need to review your plans and adjust your designs to resolve any issues that you may find.

Functional specification

Your functional specification will be a document which needs to define everything that the data model needs to include so as to meet the client requirements. It should include

▶ the nature of the problem
▶ the functions that the model must perform
▶ the user interface
▶ any constraints (that is, limiting factors)
▶ the success criteria.

Nature of the problem

The nature of the problem makes a good introduction to your specification document as it puts the data model into context. The scenario should be summarised along with the users' needs and the client's broad expectations for the model (that is, what information they intend to get out of it).

Functions the model must perform

All spreadsheet functions that the model needs to perform must be listed in the specification along with enough detail to clearly define each of them. For example, whether the model needs to calculate averages or to count how many items are present in a data set.

User interface

You will need to include everything that is required from the **user interface** in the functional specification. This information should be taken from the scenario and user requirements.

Diagrams are not appropriate in the functional specification, because the specification should define and explain what is required. However, the design documentation (which will be described later) shows how you will implement your data model and, for this, diagrams are useful. In summary, the functional specification will specify what is needed from the user interface, but does not include the actual design for the user interface.

Constraints

Constraints need to be listed and explained in the functional specification. An obvious constraint to data modelling is the amount of time you have been allocated to produce your data model. Another will probably be the software available to you to implement your model. Make sure that you include all the constraints that you can identify in your functional specification.

Success criteria

This section defines what is needed to confirm that the data model is acceptable and complete. If you are employed as a data modeller who completes data models for clients, meeting the success criteria usually triggers the payment for a job because it indicates that it is finished.

An often overlooked but important part of the specification is the definition of the success criteria at the outset. This is very good practice as all interested parties are then clear on exactly what the data model must deliver before the model is produced. Identifying success criteria means understanding what benefits a business needs to get out of the data model (that is, the information that they require) and agreeing on client requirements.

 PAUSE POINT List all the constraints that you might expect for a data modelling project.

 Hint Think about anything that might hinder achieving a perfect data model.

Extend How would an IT professional, working for an organisation, deal with these constraints?

Spreadsheet model design

Your designs for your data model will show how you are intending the spreadsheet model to look and work. These designs will help you to communicate to everyone involved in the project how the model will look and function. They will also be useful for you, to make sure that you are clear about what you are required to produce.

Worksheet structure diagrams

You will need to produce worksheet structure diagrams to show:

▶ the layout and presentation

▶ data processing

▶ data entry and validation

▶ navigation

▶ the output of your planned data model.

Layout and presentation

Your layout diagrams should show how you will structure the spreadsheet. They will show where the inputs and outputs are to be located as well as where the spreadsheet will keep any data needed by your model. All the worksheet pages should be shown here along with details of what each of them will contain.

Presentation diagrams should show how you plan to communicate the information that the data model produces. It should include your choice of chart type(s) and where they will be held in the spreadsheet.

Processing

The processing section diagrams need to outline the calculations (formulae and functions) and other actions, such as copying data, which the spreadsheet will carry out. These could be simple **block diagrams** to show where your calculations will be, along with what they do.

Any macro coding will require **program flowcharts** or **Jackson Structured Programming (JSP) structure diagrams** to show how your code will work. Macros are the code you write to program a spreadsheet to carry out certain actions on command. Macro code for Excel® is called Visual Basic® for Applications (VBA) and is very similar to the Visual Basic .NET (VB.NET) programming language.

Data entry and validation

You will need diagram(s) to show the data entry and validation for your data model. These will clearly identify the cells or forms where data is typed. You could annotate the diagram(s) to explain any validation you plan so as to minimise mistyping and other data entry errors.

Key terms

Block diagram – a simple diagram that uses rectangles to represent the parts of a system (such as a section of program code) to show how it is structured. These diagrams communicate how the parts fit together without the need for unnecessary detail.

Program flowchart – a diagram using shapes and lines to show where decisions (branches) are taken, when inputs and outputs are made and where the code can end. These diagrams show the routes that can be taken through program code.

JSP structure diagrams – Jackson Structured Programming (JSP) structure diagrams are a type of a block diagram used to show how programs are structured. They have lines joining the blocks to show the sequence, decisions and iterations.

Navigation

Your navigation diagram(s) will probably be quite simple and use block diagrams to represent the worksheets in your planned spreadsheet and arrows to show how the user can move from one part of the data model to another. The actions needed for these navigations should be included in these diagrams (for example, clicking on a button, pressing a key on the keyboard or clicking on other parts of the spreadsheet).

Output

The outputs from your data model are important because they convey the meaning derived from your data model, so they need to be carefully planned. These diagrams should clearly show what information is being output along with where they can be found in the data model.

You can produce mock-ups of any charts that you are planning, including annotations, to clarify any features you will include in them. Carefully choose the chart types that you think best convey the meaning(s) of your information. Block diagrams with annotations can be used to communicate how you have planned the printed or on-screen outputs from your data model.

Test plans

You will need to produce a test plan for the data model that shows your choice of test data, the purpose of each test and the results you expect to get from each test.

You can use your functional specification to structure the test plan, ensuring that the tests cover all aspects of your data model. Table 5.1 on the following page shows an example of the headings that you could use in your test log to record outcomes of testing.

▶ **Table 5.1:** Test log

Test number	Test description	Test data	Expected result	Actual result	Test passed	Action taken	Re-test number

Test data

The most effective testing uses carefully chosen test data to confirm each calculation, produces the correct answers, finds conditions that respond as expected and finds that bad data does not break the model.

Purpose of the test

Every test must have a purpose that should be recorded in the 'Test description' column of your test log. Knowing the purpose of the test is especially important to help you focus your efforts when testing the model. If a test has no purpose, there is no point in doing it.

Expected result

The expected result of every test needs to be calculated or predicted before the test is run. Test data results can be calculated separately before using your model so that, when they are put through your spreadsheet, you can recognise whether each test has been passed or not.

If a test has not been passed, you should first check your pre-test calculation to confirm the expected result. The data model will then need some adjustment and the test should be re-run to confirm that the correction has solved the problem. All of this needs to be recorded in the test log.

> **Link**
>
> For more on testing see section Testing the data model solution.

Reviewing and refining data model designs

You should now have a design for your data model which is the result of a lot of research, thought and planning. In a business, you would usually carry out this work in a team. Collaborative working like this usually brings positive contributions from each person in the team so as to produce the best design for your data model.

Once you have a design for your data model, you would share this with the client, other stakeholders and any other potential users. You would then work as a team to improve the quality, effectiveness and appropriateness of your designs based on their feedback.

Gathering feedback from clients and potential users

You will find it particularly useful to gather feedback from both the client and potential users on the extent to which your design meets their requirements. Client feedback is a good starting point for reviewing and refining your design, simply because they know what they want (because they defined the requirements) and are well placed to communicate with you on how well your planning is meeting those requirements. Potential users should be able to give feedback on how easy or difficult they think your model would be to actually use in the workplace.

Communicating with clients

The methods of communication that you use with clients will need to be appropriate for each situation. Emails are quick and easy and allow you to attach the design documents for the client to look at when it suits them. Similarly, emails are an easy way for the client to respond. However, it is best to avoid communicating complex issues or problems via email as this can lead to misunderstandings. It is better to use email to arrange a meeting to deal with such issues. Verbal communication, especially in a meeting, can be very effective as issues which are raised can be discussed and agreed effectively, with any confusions being ironed out on the spot. You could send an email to confirm agreed actions after a meeting.

Meetings

Meetings can be the most powerful type of communication, although more time consuming due to the need to set up the meeting, hold it and to document it afterwards. Scheduling a meeting needs to be carefully arranged to fit in with the diaries of all the attendees, but also needs to be held before any issues it will raise might become critical.

Risks, Actions, Issues and Decisions (RAID) logs can be used to document the meeting. A copy should be sent to each attendee after the meeting to confirm what was discussed and to ensure that agreed actions and outcomes are accurately understood.

Timescales

The timescales for implementing your data model should be agreed by all concerned in the data modelling project (that is the client and the data modellers) and will depend on what is possible and practical. There might be a need to adjust these timescales if you encounter problems during the planning or implementation stages. In this case, all the project stakeholders should be informed and new timescales should be agreed.

Refining ideas and solutions

The feedback you receive from clients and potential users, when they review the design of the data model, will almost certainly result in the need to refine your ideas and solutions to produce a better, more useful and realistic plan for the data model.

Review and feedback

Changes will need to be made to your planning documentation by updating the design specification, based on the reviews and feedback.

Link

For more on review and feedback see Reviewing and refining the data model solution.

Reflect

You will have reviewed your data model using feedback from professionals on the quality of the data model and its suitability to meet the original design requirements. The views of other people are very valuable as they can bring a fresh and honest opinion on the real worth and usefulness of your work.

Think about how you would respond positively to negative feedback about your data model from a client or potential users.

 PAUSE POINT   How will you review your designs with others, to identify improvements?

Hint   Create a list of all the people who you could ask to review your data model designs, along with what each person would be best at identifying.

Extend   How would you get your reviewers to communicate their findings to you?

C   Develop a data model to meet client requirements

Having designed and planned your data model, you can now begin to build up your spreadsheet skills by finding out how to use Excel®. Once you have developed your model, it will need to be thoroughly tested and any problems will need to be fixed before being reviewed and undergoing further refinement. This project work will provide great opportunities to improve the quality of your written documentation and other communication skills.

Developing a data model solution

You will need to develop and practise your skills at using the Excel® data processing features. You will need to be able to create formulae and functions and forms for data entry which have the required layout to aid presentation and which meet the output requirements.

Processing features and requirements

Excel® offers many useful processing features to enable you to fulfil your processing requirements. These features are discussed in this section.

Formulae

Excel® makes it very easy to enter simple arithmetic formulae to add, subtract, divide and multiply.

All you need to do is to type =, select one of the cells for the formula, type the arithmetic sign, select the other cell in the formula then use the <Enter> key, for example = A3 * B3.

Link

For more on formulae see the Using formulae and functions section.

A formula can have more than two **arguments** (terms), for example = A3 * B3 / C3, and can mix cell references with numbers, for example = 2 * B3 / C3.

When you have more than two arguments, you might find the result of a formula is different from what you expect. This will be due to **BIDMAS (or BODMAS)**, otherwise known as the precedence of operators.

> **Discussion**
>
> What is the answer to 3 + 4 * 5? What answer does Excel® give to this simple formula? Why?

> **Key terms**
>
> **Argument** – part of a calculation (formula or function) that represents a number or value. An argument can be a cell reference such as A2 or a value such as a number, say, 12, or it can be text, say, Richard.
>
> **BIDMAS (or BODMAS)** – stands for Brackets, Indices/Orders, Divide, Multiply, Add, Subtract and is used to remind us of the order in which a formula is worked out (otherwise known as the precedence of operators).

Worked example: BIDMAS

> From BIDMAS, we can see multiplication is worked out before addition and that brackets are worked out first before multiplication.
>
> 4 + 5 * 6 works out to be 34 because 5 is multiplied by 6 before 4 is added.
>
> If you want the answer to be 54, the formula needs brackets, (4 + 5) * 6 so that 4 and 5 are added together first (because they are in brackets) before being multiplying by 6.

Relative and absolute cell referencing

The formulae used so far in this unit have all been relative, for example A3, which are easy to enter and good when you want to copy and paste a formula, because the cell references adjust in the pasted formulae. In Figure 5.3, the formula was entered into cell D3 as =C3 * B3 and, when it was copied and pasted into cells D4, D5 and D6, the formula adjusted so that each time it multiplied the two cells to the left.

These are known as relative cell references because a copied formula changes to keep the relative positions. In the example, the second cell to the left gets multiplied by the first cell to the left.

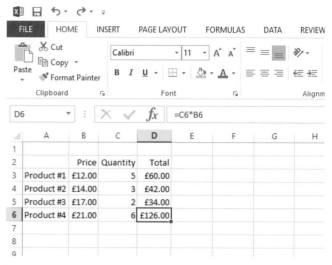

▶ **Figure 5.3:** Relative formula copy

For many formulae, relative addressing is perfect and good for copy and paste. However, other formulae need to also use absolute cell referencing to prevent some parts of the formula from changing when using copy and paste. In Figure 5.4, the formula was entered into cell E3 as =D3 * $E$1 and, when it was copied and pasted into cells D4, D5 and D6, the absolute part of the formula, $E$1, stayed the same so that, each time, this was multiplied by the cell to the left.

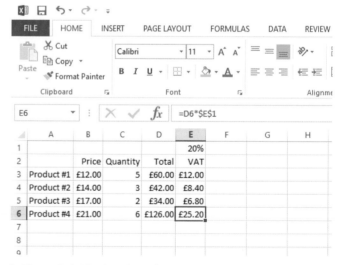

▶ **Figure 5.4:** Absolute formula copy

These are known as absolute cell references because they do not change in a copied formula.

Closer examination of an absolute cell reference shows two $ signs, one before the column letter, the other before the row number. These can be used for more control over copying. For example, if $E1 is copied and pasted, the column letter (E) will stay the same, while the row number (1) will change as a relative cell reference.

Tip

In Excel you can use the <F4> key to put the $ signs into a relative cell reference to make it absolute.

Functions

A function is a complex calculation that is built into Excel®. Every function has a name and usually needs arguments inside brackets following the name.

To use a function you need to type = followed by the first part of the function name. You can then select the function you want, making sure that the terms (arguments) needed by the function are there, and then press the <Enter> key: for example, = AVERAGE(A1:C4).

Link

For more on functions, see the Using formulae and functions section.

Many IT professionals use the prompt that Excel® shows under a function as it is being entered to help remind them what each argument does. The arguments in a function are separated by commas. When a comma is typed, the prompt changes to describe the current argument.

There are around 400 functions in Excel ®, so it is easy to carry out calculations for almost any type of data model. Excel® also allows programmers to use macro Visual Basic® for Applications (VBA) code to add their own functions to this collection. Figure 5.5 shows some of the general functions available in Excel® being applied and Table 5.2 lists some general functions in Excel® and examples of how they can be used.

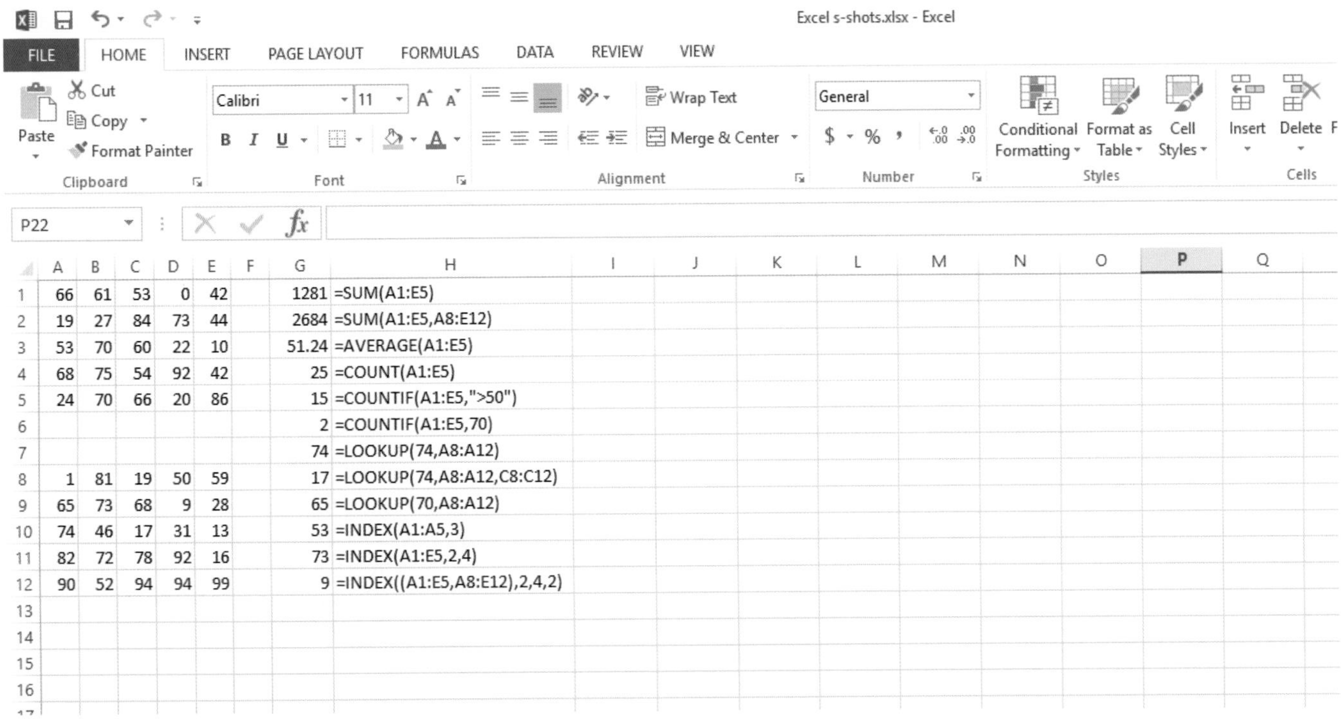

▶ **Figure 5.5:** Examples of general functions in Excel®

▶ **Table 5.2:** General functions in Excel®

Function	Arguments	Why it is used	Example of how it can be used
=SUM(Number1 [,Number2],...)	Number1 is a cell or number or range of cells Number2 is an optional further cell, number or range of cells	To add the arguments together.	• =SUM(A1:E5) • To add all the numbers in the cells from A1 to E5. • =SUM(A1:E5,A8:E12) • To add all numbers in the cells from A1 to E5 and A8 to E12.
=AVERAGE(Number1 [,Number2], ...)	Number1 is a cell or number or range of cells Number2 is an optional further cell, number or range of cells	To show the average of the arguments.	• =AVERAGE(A1:E5) • To average all the numbers in the cells from A1 to E5.
=COUNT(Range1 [,Range2], ...)	Range1 is a cell or number or range of cells Range2 is an optional further cell, number or range of cells	To count how many numbers are in the range(s).	• =COUNT(A1:E5) • To count how many numbers are in the cells from A1 to E5.
=COUNTIF(Range, Criteria)	Range is the cells that are searched to count how many of the criteria are found Criteria is what is counted	To count how many cells in the range meet set criteria.	• =COUNTIF(A1:E5,'>50') • To count how many numbers in cells A1 to E5 are bigger than 50. • =COUNTIF(A1:E5,70) • To count how many 70s are in the cells A1 to E5.
=LOOKUP(Value, Lookup [,Result])	Value is what is looked for Lookup is where to search and must be in order, from low to high Result is an optional range for what gets shown by this function and must be the same size as the Lookup range	To find a value and show either the best match or, optionally, whatever is in the Result cell corresponding to where the value is found in the Lookup range. See Figure 5.6 for examples of VLOOKUP() and HLOOKUP() functions.	• =LOOKUP(74,A8:A12) • To find 74 in the range A8 to A12, as there is an exact match, 74 shown. • =LOOKUP(74,A8:A12,C8:C12) • To find 74 in the range A8 to A12 and show the match from C8 to C12. As there is an exact match, 17 is shown. • =LOOKUP(70,A8:A12) • To find 70 in the range A8 to A12, as there is no exact match, 65 is shown.
=INDEX(Ref, Row [,Col] [,Area])	Ref is the cell range and needs brackets if more than 1 range is used Row is the number of the cell in the range which is to be shown Col is optional for when the cell range is a rectangle Area is optional for when there is more than 1 range to select which area is to be used	To show what is in a cell in a range.	• =INDEX(A1:A5,3) • Shows 53 as that is inside cell A3 as row 3 is the third row of the range A1 to A5). • =INDEX(A1:E5,2,4) • Shows 73 as that is inside cell D2 as row 2 is the second row of the range A1 to E5) and col 4 is D (fourth column of A1 to E5). • =INDEX((A1:E5,A8:E12),2,4,2) • Will show 9 as that is inside cell D9, row 9 is the second row of the second range A8 to E12) and the fourth column is D.

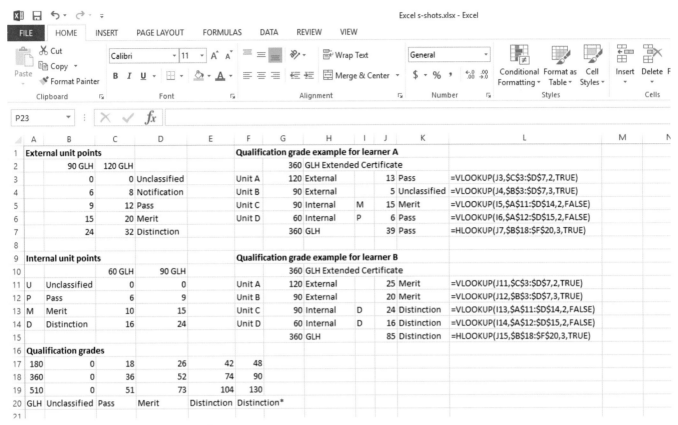

▶ **Figure 5.6:** VLOOKUP() and HLOOKUP() functions

▶ **Table 5.3:** Other lookup functions (see Figure 5.6: VLOOKUP() and HLOOKUP() functions, for examples)

Function	Arguments	Why it is used	Example of how it can be used
= VLOOKUP(Value, Table, Col [,Lookup])	Value is what you are looking for in the table Table is where you are looking for the value Col is the column in the table for the result Lookup is optional, choose between True (approximate match for numbers) and False (for an exact match)	To find something in a range of cells to bring back a result matching the find. V (vertical) lookup is used when the left column of the table holds what you are looking for. This is a good alternative to nesting lots of IF() functions as it is much easier to use.	• =VLOOKUP(J3,$C$3:$D$7,2,TRUE) • Shows 'Pass' as that is inside cell D5 as row 5 is the row where 13 (from J3) is found in the first column of range C3 to D7 and column 2 in the table is D. • The TRUE in the function is for approximate match which allows 13 (from J3) to be found. • The range C3 to D7 is entered as $C$3:$D$7 so the function can be copied and still point to the same table. • =VLOOKUP(I5,$A$11:$D$14,2,FALSE) • Shows 'Merit' as that is inside cell B13 as row 13 is the row where 'M' (from I5) is found in first column of range A11 to D14 and column 2 in the table is B. • The FALSE in the function is for exact match as only 'M' (from I5) is to be found. • The range A11 to D14 is entered as $A$11:$D$14 so the function can be copied and still point to the same table.
=HLOOKUP(Value, Table, Row [,Lookup])	Value is what you are looking for in the table Table is where you are looking for the value Row is the row in the table for the result Lookup is optional, choose between True (approximate match for numbers) and False (for an exact match)	To find something in a range of cells to bring back a result matching the find. H (horizontal) lookup is used when the top row of the table holds what you are looking for. This is a good alternative to nesting lots of IF() functions as it is much easier to use.	• =HLOOKUP(J7,$B$18:$F$20,3,TRUE) • Shows 'Pass' as that is inside cell C20 as column C is where 39 (from J7) is found in the first row of range B18 to F20 and row 3 in the table is 20. • The TRUE in the function is for approximate match which allows 39 (from J7) to be found. • The range B18 to F20 is entered as $B$18:$F$20 so the function can be copied and still point to the same table.

Discussion

Figure 5.6 (VLOOKUP() and HLOOKUP() functions) shows some examples of how these functions are used. Consider the following discussion points which all relate to this spreadsheet.

- Why are the functions in L3, L4, L7 looking for approximate matches?
- Why are the functions in L5, L6 looking for exact matches?
- What function could be used in cell J5 to look up the points for this 90 GLH (Guided Learning Hours) unit?
- What function could be used in cell J6 to look up the points for this 60 GLH unit?
- Can you write a function for cell J5 which can then be copied to cells J6, J13, J14 to give accurate results?
- Can you write a function for cell L3 which can then be copied to cells L4-L6, L11-L14 to give accurate results which cater for External/Internal and the number of GLH? (You could insert column(s) to provide interim calculations to simplify your function.)
- What function would you use in cell J7? Can this be copied to cell J15?
- What function would you use in cell G7? Can this be copied to cell G15?
- How could you apply conditional formatting to cell G15 to validate the unit GLH numbers?

Logical functions

These functions use logic to decide upon a choice of outcomes. The logic is anything that results in a true or false result, for example comparing two values to find which is greater (larger) than the other. See Figure 5.7 for examples of logical functions.

◢	A	B	C	D	E	F	G
1	**Bargain Hunt**						
2	**Red team**	Runners up	=IF(B14<B7,"Winners","Runners up")				
3	Profit item #1	£20	Golden gavel	FALSE	=IF(AND(B3>0,B4>0,B5>0),TRUE,FALSE)		
4	Profit item #1	-£10		No	=IF(OR(B3<=0,B4<=0,B5<=0),"No","Yes")		
5	Profit item #1	£25					
6	Profit bonus item	£5		Some loss	=IF(NOT(D3),"Some loss","All profit")		
7		£40	Total				
8							
9	**Blue team**	Winners	=IF(B14>B7,"Winners",IF(B14=B7,"Draw","Runners up"))				
10	Profit item #1	£12	Golden gavel	TRUE			
11	Profit item #1	£5		Yes			
12	Profit item #1	£34					
13	Profit bonus item	£19		All profit			
14		£70	Total				
15							
16							
17							
18							
19							
20							

▶ **Figure 5.7:** Logical functions

▶ **Table 5.4:** Logical functions (see Figure 5.7 Logical functions, for examples)

Function	Arguments	Why it is used	Example of how it can be used
=IF(Condition, IfTrue [,IfFalse])	Condition is anything that can be worked out as true or false IfTrue shows if condition is true IfFalse it is optional what to show if the condition is false	When a cell needs to show one of two possible results.	• =IF(B14<B7,"Winners","Runners up") • To test if the contents of cell B14 is less than what is in cell B7 to show "Winners" if true or "Runners up" if false.
=NOT(Condition)	Condition is anything that can be worked out as true or false	To flip (invert) a true condition to false or a false condition to true.	• =NOT(D3) • To invert the contents of cell D3. • D3 is showing false, so the example here returns a true. • This is used as the condition of the IF() function in cell E6.
=AND(Condition1 [, Condition2], ...)	Condition1 is anything that can be worked out as true or false Condition2 is anything that can be worked out as true or false	To show true if each of one or more conditions are true.	• =AND(B3>0,B4>0,B5>0) • To test if the contents of cells B3, B4, B5 are each more than zero (0), returns true if all of these are above zero. • This is used as the condition of the IF() function in cell E3. The = is not needed here as the AND() is inside the IF() function.
=OR(Condition1 [, Condition2], ...)	Condition1 is anything that can be worked out as true or false Condition2 is anything that can be worked out as true or false	To show true if any of one or more conditions are true.	• =OR(B3<=0,B4<=0,B5<=0) • To test if the contents of cells B3, B4, B5 are each less than or equal to zero (0), returns true if any of these are zero or below. • This is used as the condition of the IF() function in cell E4. The = is not needed here as the AND() is inside the IF() function.

Nested IF functions

Nesting means that you have a function inside another function. The inside function is worked out first so this result can then be used in the main function. Nested IF() functions can be used for a cell showing one of three possible outcomes. See Figure 5.7 and Table 5.4 for an example of this where cell C9 contains an IF() function to answer which team won by comparing the total of the Blue team (B14) to find if it is greater than the total of the Red team (B7). If true, "Winners" is shown, If not true, the nested IF() function responds to a draw (B14=B7), showing "Draw" if true or "Runners up" if false.

Figure 5.7 and Table 5.4 show examples of how NOT(), AND() and OR() functions can be nested inside IF() functions. Most functions can be nested inside another function. The result given by the nested function is used by the main function.

> **Tip**
>
> Nested IF functions can be used for more than three possible outcomes, but this is not recommended as it is easy to make mistakes and hard to solve any errors in the result. It is much better to use VLOOKUP() or HLOOKUP() for a cell that needs four or more possible outcomes.

Goal seek

Goal seek is a feature of Excel® that allows you to select a cell holding a calculation then choose the answer you want from this cell by selecting another cell that can be changed to provide the answer. Excel® will then work out what needs to be in the changeable cell to provide the answer.

Step by step: Using Goal Seek

4 Steps

1 This step by step shows how to use Goal Seek to adjust the number in a cell to produce a required result in a calculated cell. The example here is a very simple data model used to explore the costs of a manufactured product. Firstly, set up the data model using calculations and functions as shown here.

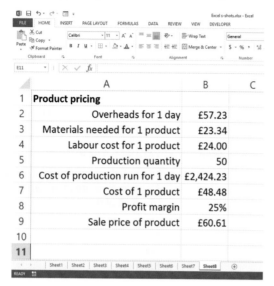

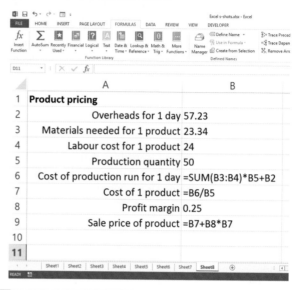

2 Market research has shown that the maximum sale price could be £60, so this data model is to be used to find out how many products need to be produced each day to meet that price. Cell B9 is selected then the Goal Seek option is taken under the What if Analysis drop-down menu in the Data toolbar.

3 The Goal Seek dialog box is completed to set B9 to 60 by changing B5.

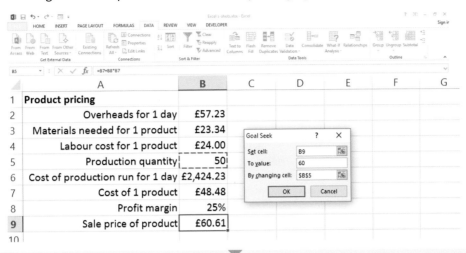

4 The OK button is used to run the Goal Seek resulting in the data model showing the production run size to meet the price of £60. The target production quantity is shown with a decimal part, so would need to be rounded up to a whole number for a practical run size of 87 products per day.

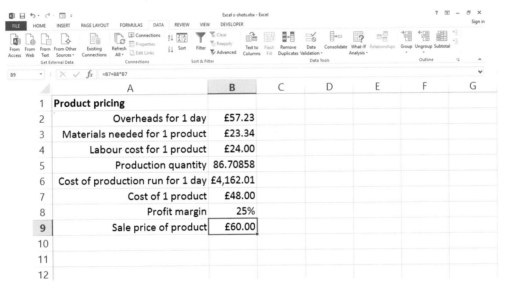

What if

What if is a feature of data models that allows you to explore different possibilities by changing numbers in cells that are used by the formulae and functions of the spreadsheet data model. As the calculations are almost instantaneous, it is very easy to explore options such as: 'What if we increase the cost of a product?' or 'What if our sales decrease by 10 per cent?'

Good data modelling design will group together the cells used for key numbers used in the model and also have the key outputs close so it is easy to see the outcomes from different inputs without having to scroll to other parts of the spreadsheet. These What if explorations can be made by simply typing over existing values in a data model's cells. Excel® also offers some tools under the What if Analysis drop-down menu in the Data toolbar which include Scenario Manager, Goal Seek and Data Table.

Step by step: Using What if scenarios

6 Steps

1 This step by step shows how to set up a What if scenario using the same data model shown in the Using Goal Seek step by step. Cell B8 is selected and then the Scenario Manager option is taken under the What if Analysis drop-down menu in the Data toolbar.

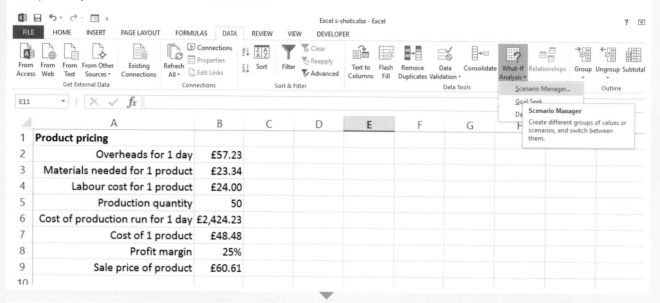

2 Once you have the Scenario Manager dialog box, use the Add ... button to add a scenario.

3 The scenario can be given a name so that it can be easily selected when completed. The cells that can change are selected. They will all have values, not formulae. The Comment defaults to who is using the spreadsheet and date, but can be changed to summarise the values used in his scenario.

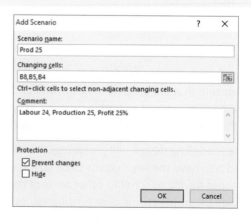

4 Using the OK button moves from the Add Scenario dialog on to the Scenario Values dialog so that the values to be used in the selected cells for this scenario can be set. Press the OK button once this is complete. More scenarios can be added with different values which are of interest to the model.

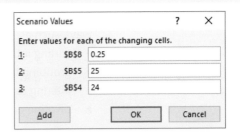

5 Any of your scenarios can then be selected from the Scenario Manager. Press the Show button to set the spreadsheet cells to that scenario's values.

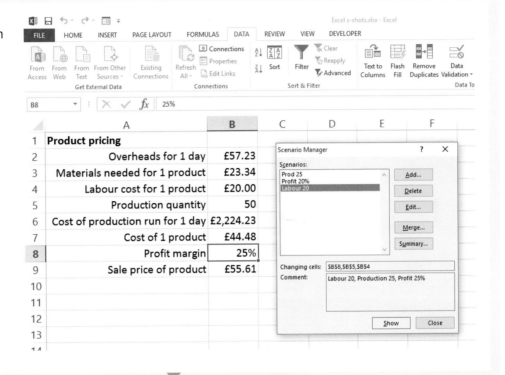

6 The Scenario Manager has a Summary button which can create a new worksheet with a scenario summary. The summary has controls around it to control how much of the summary is shown.

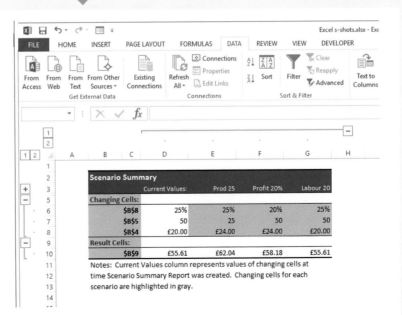

Data manipulation

Data manipulation is a feature of spreadsheets which lets you see the data in different ways, such as:

- sorting into a different order
- grouping to bring similar or related items together
- filtering to only see the items you are interested in
- pivoting data to rearrange the rows and columns.

Sorting

Sorting a range of cells is useful in many ways. You might want to order items showing the cheapest at the top and the most expensive at the bottom, or list names ordered by surname or by first name. Sorting will also show duplicates as they would be next to each other.

A two-level sort will group the items together on the first-level sort. For example, this could be by the first level, department, then by the second level, surnames in alphabetical order.

Multilevel sorting can have more than two levels. For example, a three-level sort could group staff members by (1) location then by (2) department then by (3) surname. To do this, select the data and then use the Sort button in the Data toolbar to bring up the Sort dialog box, as shown in Figure 5.8.

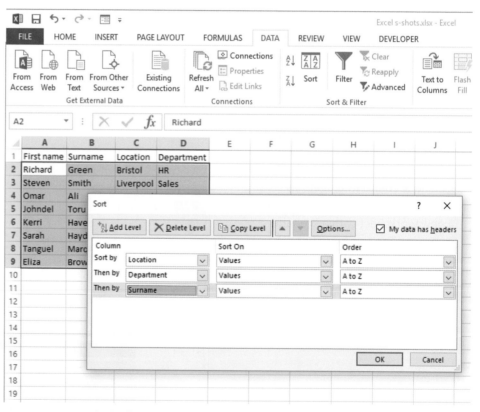

▶ **Figure 5.8:** A three-level sort

Grouping

Grouping is an Excel® feature, similar to outlining in a word processor, making it easy to show or hide groups (sections) of your data. At the bottom of each group, there will be a section where functions show useful information such as the subtotal, average or count.

Step by step: Grouping

1 This step by step shows how to enter and explore the set of data shown in the figure below, which can be downloaded from the UK Met Office website.

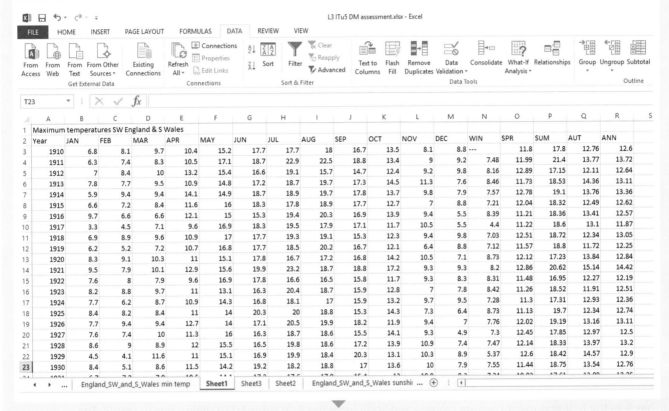

2 You need to insert a new column that holds data that can be used for grouping. We will use this column for another set of years so we can group by decade. Insert the new column to the left by placing the cursor anywhere in the current column A, then either right click, select insert, select entire column or use the keyboard by pressing <Alt> <I> then <C>. Type '1910' (the first decade), into A3, then copy down to A12 (all the years to be in this group). Repeat this for the other decades, so that each group has the start year for that decade in the A column.

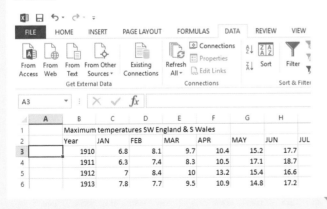

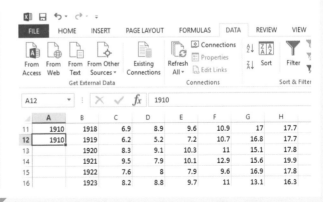

3 Place the cursor anywhere in the data, eg B3, then click on the Subtotal button in the Data toolbar. Excel® will highlight the data it finds around B3 and show the Subtotal dialog box. You can choose the function used for each group, (Sum, the default is shown in this screenshot). If you want more statistics, you could insert rows between the subtotals and groups later. Use Add subtotal to check boxes in this dialog box to select all columns where you want the function. Click the OK button to complete.

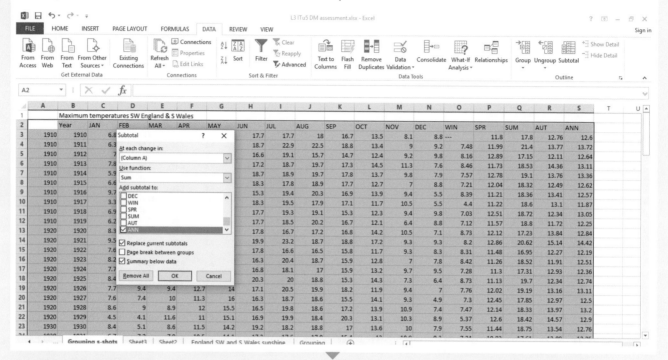

4 You now have subtotals and Excel® has also grouped your data. In this example, the =SUBTOTAL() function has 9 as the first argument because we selected SUM from the Add subtotal to dialog box in step 3. The grouping is shown to the left of the row numbers with the numbers (1, 2, 3) used to select how much of the grouping you can see on the spreadsheet.

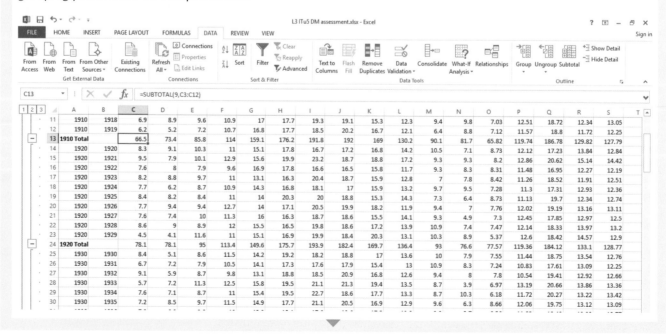

5 Click on the 1 in grouping to see just the summary row for all the whole group.

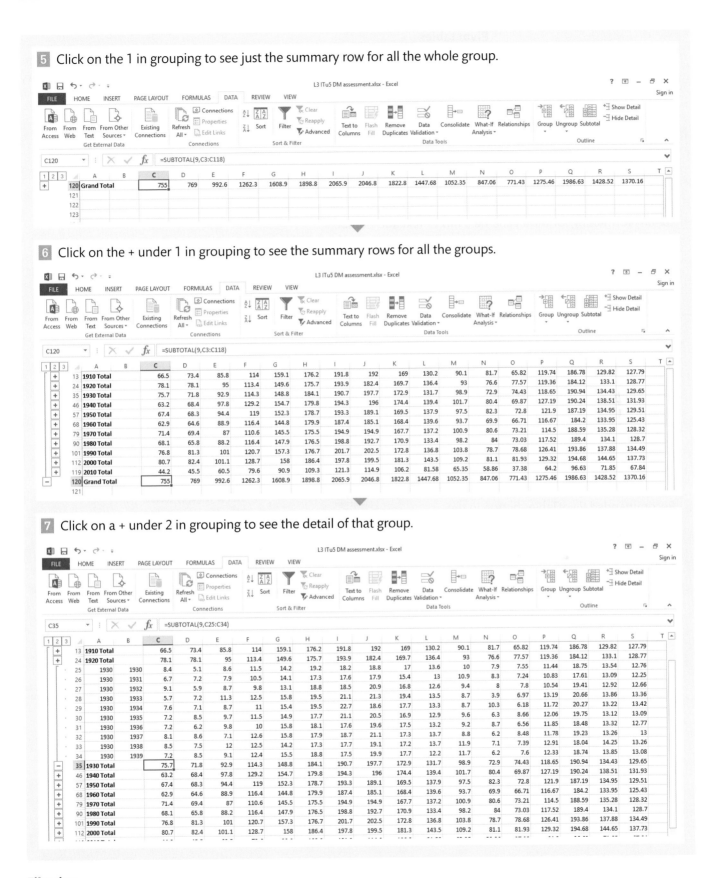

6 Click on the + under 1 in grouping to see the summary rows for all the groups.

7 Click on a + under 2 in grouping to see the detail of that group.

Filtering

Filtering allows column headings on a set of data to reduce (filter) the rows shown in the spreadsheet.

Pivot tables

Excel® pivot tables help you to explore large spreadsheet data sets by copying the parts you want to a sheet where you can choose row and column headings for this summary and apply further filtering if needed.

Step by step: Pivoting data

4 Steps

1 This step by step shows how to insert a pivot table into a spreadsheet and how to create a pivot chart. You need some data in your spreadsheet for the pivot chart to use. The data should have column headings (no need for any formatting for these) and be a mix of text and numbers.

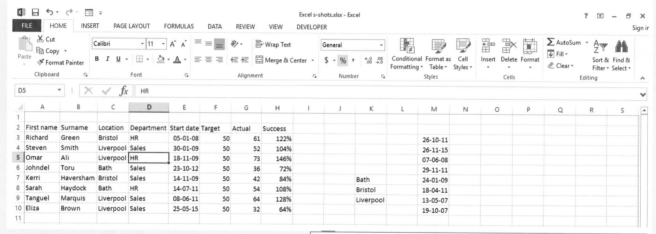

2 Select any cell in your data then use the Recommended PivotTables button in the Insert toolbar. This has two major advantages over using the PivotTable button: it checks that your data is suitable for use as a pivot table and it gives you some previews of potential layouts for your pivot table. Select the layout closest to what you want, then use the OK button.

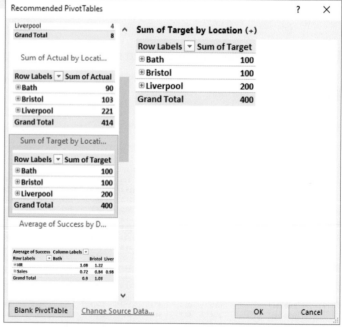

3 A new worksheet is created for the pivot chart you chose.

You can rearrange the pivot table by dragging fields in the PivotTable Fields control to the right of the pivot table display. The example here needs formatting in the Sum of Success column to show the numbers as percentages. To do this, right click on the column, select Value Field Settings, then select Number Format, where you can set the format of this column to percentage. The Grand Total and sub-totals of this column would be more meaningful as averages.

To do this, right click on the column, select Summarize Values By, and then select Average.

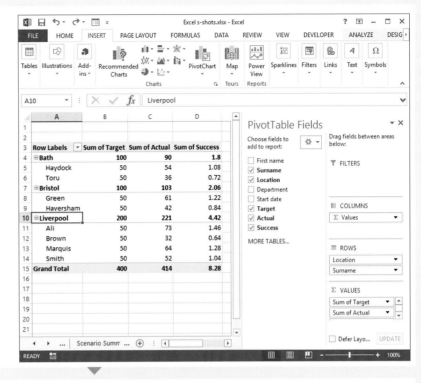

4 You can create a chart from your pivot table by simply clicking on the Pivot Chart button in the Insert toolbar. This chart is dynamic, with buttons that you can use to change the view of the data charted. The example shown here allows you choose which Locations are shown.

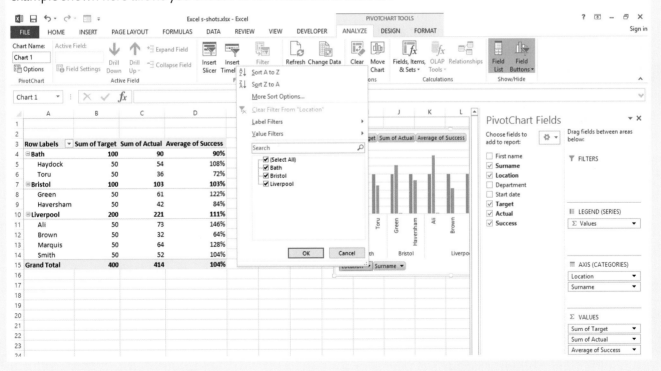

Importing data

When data is brought in from another source, it is said to be imported into a spreadsheet, usually as a file that the source app saved in a format that Excel® can recognise. Imports are usually **text files** as these do not include any extra formatting information that would not be recognised by the spreadsheet. Each line of the text file will be a row in the spreadsheet, so there needs to be a method used by the spreadsheet to break the line into cells. There are two methods used to define cells in a row: fixed width and delimiter characters.

▶ Fixed width is very simple, for example first 8 characters into the first cell (column), 3 characters into the next, and so on.

▶ Delimiter characters are used in the text file between items of data to indicate how to allocate them to cells. Tab delimited files use <Tab> to separate the data in each line and are usually given a **TSV** extension when saved. **CSV** is the other commonly used import data file type, with commas used to delimit items of data.

Step by step: Importing data

7 Steps

1 This step by step shows how to import a text file that has been downloaded from the Met Office website into an Excel® spreadsheet. Select the cell (A3) where you want the top left corner of the data import. Click on the From Text button in the Data toolbar to bring up a dialog box where you can select your data file.

2 After you have double clicked on the text data file, the wizard starts. You see a preview of the text file. The text data file shown here starts with some lines of text describing the data, and these do not need to be imported into Excel®.

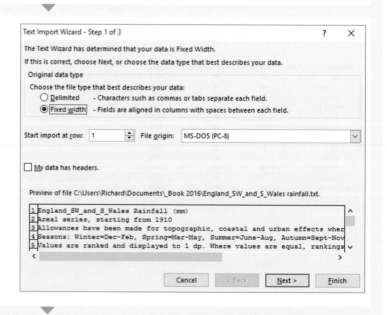

3 Scrolling down the text data preview shows that the data actually starts on line 8, so the Start import at row 1 needs to be changed to row 8. Select Delimited (as there are spaces between data items in the text file), then use the Next button.

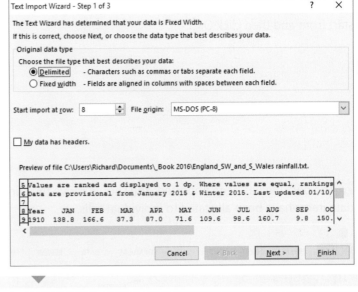

4 The Delimiters need to be set to Space and the Treat consecutive delimiters as one need to be selected as there are variable numbers of spaces between the data items. The preview shows where the data will be divided into cells when imported into the spreadsheet.

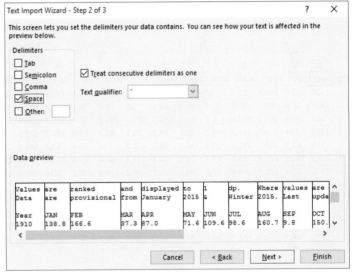

5 You could fine tune the formatting that Excel® will apply to the cells when the data file is imported at step 3 of the wizard. You can leave the default settings and then click Finish.

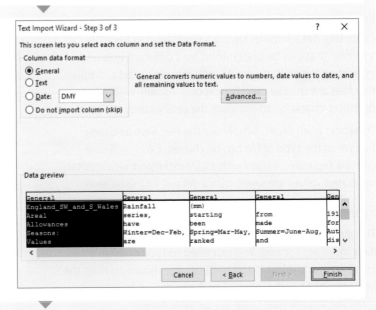

6 Confirm cell (A3) is where you want the data import to start from and then click OK.

7 The data file has been imported. You should move the cursor around some of the cells to check that the text data items have been allocated to individual cells.

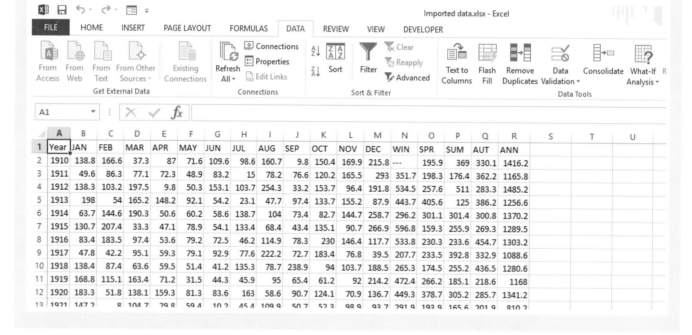

Exporting data

Exporting data involves saving a worksheet in Excel® in a format that can be understood by a different app and importing it into that app. As with importing data, simple text files are usually used for exports, usually with a delimiter character to separate the cells as they get saved.

To export from Excel®, simply use the File, Save as dialog box when the type of file can be chosen. Excel® will save comma separated values with a CSV extension, whereas tab separated values are saved with a default TXT extension.

Autofill

The autofill feature of Excel® is there to automatically enter data into cells for you. You just need to type enough into Excel® to start, select it and then use the mouse to drag the bottom right handle (corner) of the selection to where you want the autofill (see Table 5.5 Excel® autofill).

▶ **Table 5.5:** Excel® autofill

Initial selection	Extended series
1, 2, 3	4, 5, 6,..
9:00	10:00, 11:00, 12:00,..
Mon	Tue, Wed, Thu,..
Monday	Tuesday, Wednesday, Thursday,..
Jan	Feb, Mar, Apr,..
Jan, Apr	Jul, Oct, Jan,..
Jan-07, Apr-07	Jul-07, Oct-07, Jan-08,..
15-Jan, 15-Apr	15-Jul, 15-Oct,..
2007, 2008	2009, 2010, 2011,..
1-Jan, 1-Mar	1-May, 1-Jul, 1-Sep,..
Qtr3 (or Q3 or Quarter3)	Qtr4, Qtr1, Qtr2,..

Replication

Formulae and functions often need to be replicated into new rows or columns of data. In most situations, this will be using copy and paste or dragging the bottom right handle of the highlighted cell(s) containing the calculation(s). Replication is often needed after data is imported to recreate any calculations that were lost in the text file.

Using macros and buttons to initiate procedures

Macros are the program code that can work with your spreadsheet to automate actions. Excel® provides a rich programming environment called Visual Basic® for Applications (VBA) which can match many dedicated programming languages for capability. You can use buttons or other objects such as images to initiate macro code procedures as well as allocating key press combinations to start your programs.

> **Research**
>
> Using macros is a massive topic that deserves further research, reading and practice.

Many VBA programmers use Excel® to record a macro where they carry out a spreadsheet operation they want to automate. The code produced by this recording can then be edited into exactly what the programmer wants and can be copied to another part of the VBA program code where it is needed.

To use macros, you need the Developer toolbar which Excel® does not show by default. This toolbar can be shown by using the File, Options menu to bring up the Excel® Options dialog where you select the Customize Ribbon option. The Developer checkbox under Customize the Ribbon options has to be ticked and then you use the OK button to exit Excel® Options to return to the workbook where the Developer toolbar will now be shown.

The Developer toolbar has a button with which you can start recording your actions as a macro. This changes into a button to stop recording when you have completed your macro. It is a good idea to practise your actions before

recording a macro to reduce mistakes. The actions that you record can be just about anything that can be done to the spreadsheet with the mouse or keyboard.

The Developer toolbar has a button named Visual Basic which can take you to the VBA macro code environment. This environment will run as a separate app to your spreadsheet and will end when the spreadsheet is closed. Many programmers use the VBA macro code environment to edit their macros to delete mistakes in a recording or to add more functionality to their macro programs.

Data entry and validation

Data entry and validation requirements and methods include:

▸ using data entry forms

▸ restricting data input to acceptable values

▸ protecting cells by hiding, locking and password protecting

▸ ease of use techniques

▸ automated data transfer between sheets or applications

▸ adding user prompts and messages.

Data entry forms

Many users prefer to enter or edit a large spreadsheet with a data entry form to show all the entries in one form, rather than needing to scroll around the rows and columns. A data entry form is quickly and easily produced by Excel®. All you need to do is select a cell anywhere inside some data with column headings, then click on the Form button. Recent versions of Excel® do not include the Form button in the toolbars by default, so you will need to customise a toolbar yourself (see the Step by step).

A data entry form can be used to find a particular record for editing or deleting by using the Criteria button on the form. Searching can use the * and ? wildcards to help find the required records. A search for Pet* would bring up everything starting with Pet, for example Pete or Petra, because the * wildcard represents any number of characters. A search for Pet? brings up everything starting with Pet which is four characters long, for example Pete but not Petra, because the ? wildcard represents one character.

Step by step: Creating a data entry form

1 This step by step shows how to add a Form button to the Excel® toolbars and use this to bring up a data entry form for some worksheet data. The data entry form is then used to find a record in the data. Click on Customize Quick Access Toolbar.

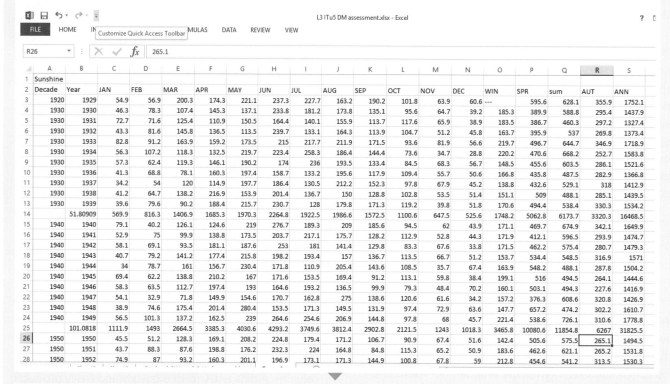

2 Click on More commands from the Customize Quick Access Toolbar menu to bring up the Excel® options dialog box showing the Quick Access Toolbar options.

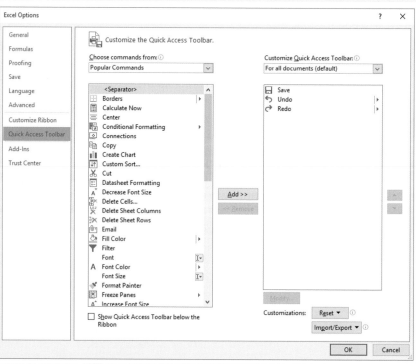

3 Select Commands Not in the Ribbon from the Choose commands from drop-down list box. This shows the buttons that you can add to the toolbar. Scroll down these so that the Form button is visible.

4 Click on the Form button then use the Add button to include this in the Quick Access Toolbar.

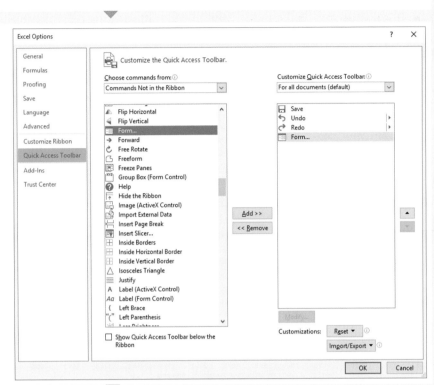

5 Click on the OK button. You now have the Form button in the Quick Access Toolbar.

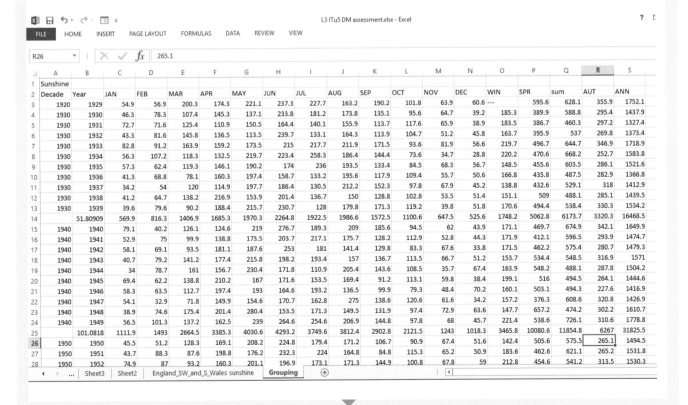

6 Now that you have the Form button available, you can show the data entry form. To do this, select any cell inside the data in the worksheet then click on the Form button.

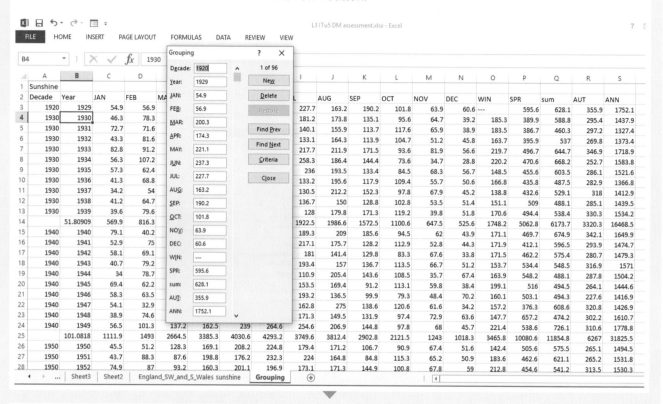

7 You can use the Criteria button to find a record row in the data. To do this, click on the Criteria button; the form clears. Type '1950' into the Decade text box.

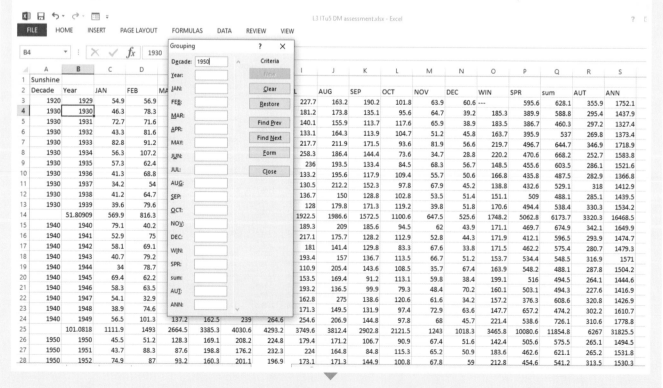

8 Click on the Find Next button. The data entry form shows the first record which has 1950 in decade. Notice that the cursor does not move in the worksheet behind the form. You could edit any of the cells shown in the data entry form. The Find Next button can be used to show the next record in the data entry form, or the Find Prev to show the previous record. Use the Close button when you are finished with the data entry form.

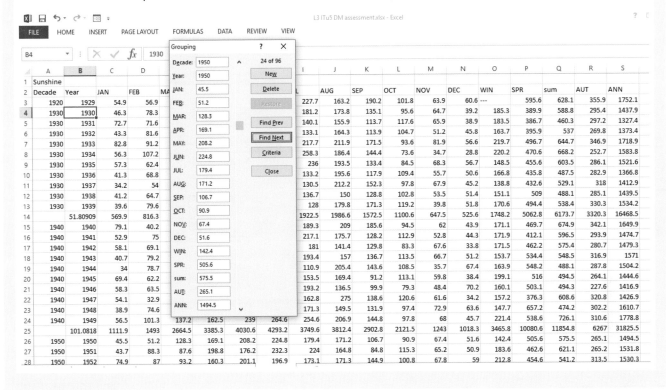

Restricting data input

Most errors in a data set are from mistyping. Excel® can help reduce these typos by restricting data input into selected cells to acceptable values.

Step by Step: Restricting data input to acceptable values   2 Steps

1 To do this, first select the cells where you want to set validation on data entries then use the use the Data Validation drop-down menu on the Data toolbar to select Data Validation. In the dialog box you can choose what to allow to be entered into the selected cells.

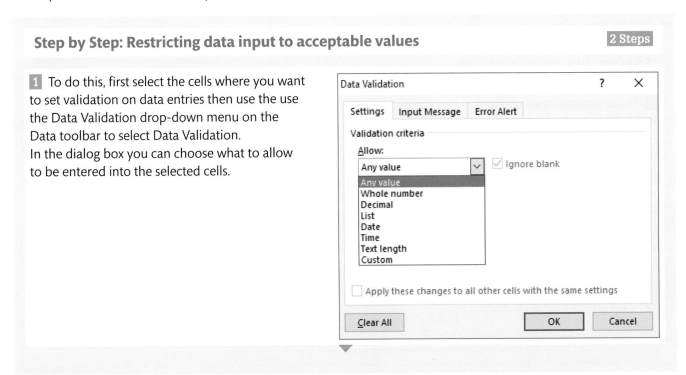

2 The Data Validation dialog box gives good control over messages to the user on what data can be entered and to alert them to any mistyping with a message on what to do about it. You can restrict data entry into the cells to a list. The result of this example is to let the user choose from a drop-down list of values from cells K6 to K8 when clicking into cells C2 to C9.

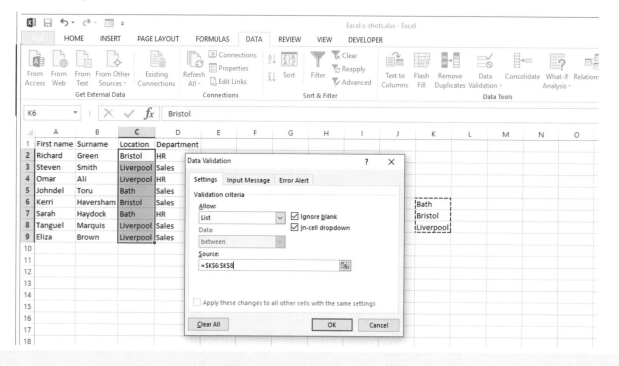

Protecting cells

Many spreadsheets holding data and calculations use cell protection to prevent users accidentally typing over calculations and to help data entry. Protecting cells can assist data entry by only allowing the user to select cells which are unprotected. This can make the spreadsheet much quicker to use as the <Arrow> keys jump to the next cell where data is to be input.

Step by step: Protecting cells

2 Steps

1 To use protection, you need to format all the cells which can be edited then use the Review toolbar to protect the worksheet. Cells available for editing are selected; a right click brings up the Format Cells dialog box then you need to select the Protection tab. You can then choose to select Locked to lock the cells or, as shown here, deselect the Locked checkbox to unlock cells.

2 When all the cells needed for editing have been formatted as not locked, you can use the Review toolbar to click on Protect Sheet to bring up the Protect Sheet dialog box. Here you can untick the Select locked cells checkbox so that the user is restricted to the cells that have been formatted as unlocked. You can also set a password using this dialog box. (To remove the protection, use the same button on the Review toolbar, which will now show Unprotect sheet.) Cells can also be protected by hiding the row or column so that they cannot be seen or easily selected.

Ease of use techniques

Excel® offers you a good choice of techniques to make a spreadsheet easier to use. These include drop-down menus and list boxes. A drop-down menu lets you choose from a list of choices when entering data into a cell. This makes data entry faster and errors less likely as you would not be able to mistype.

Before you can set up a drop-down menu, you need to have the menu choices entered into a range of cells with no gaps. Select the cells to have the drop-down menu, then use the Data Validation in the Data toolbar to bring up the dialog box (see step 1 of Step by Step: Restricting data input to acceptable values). Click on List in the Allow drop-down list of this dialog box to show Figure 5.9 where you can select the source cells holding the menu choices (=$B$3:$B$6 in this example). Click on the OK button to complete.

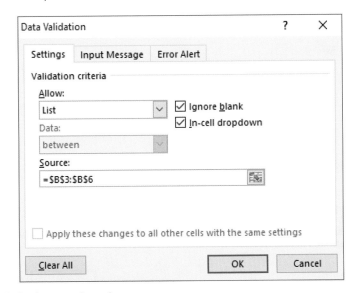

▶ **Figure 5.9:** Setting up a drop-down menu

Automated data transfers

There are many methods used to automate data transfer between sheets and applications.

Simple formula

If all you need is to show and use data from one worksheet with another worksheet in the same spreadsheet (workbook), you can use a simple formula. To do this, select the cell where you want the other worksheet data, type = then select the cell in the other worksheet with the data. Use <Enter> to complete. You can easily copy and paste this into other cells if needed. This simple formula will also work between spreadsheets. If you do this, be careful not to move or rename the spreadsheets involved. When you open the workbook spreadsheet containing these formulae, you will be prompted to update the links to the original (source) workbook (see Figure 5.10).

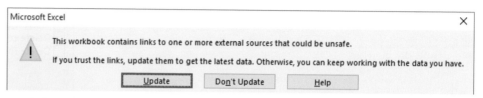

> **Figure 5.10:** Update links prompt

Linking

A common method for automating between apps is to use linking. A section of an Excel® spreadsheet can be copied and then **Paste Special** can be used to paste this into Word® as a link (see Figure 5.11) There are several choices of how you want the linked spreadsheet to appear in the Word document. Each time the document is opened, you will be prompted on whether to update the link to show current information in the document.

A macro can be used to automate data transfers. As the macro is program code, you have several options for tweaking the data transfer, for example by adding calculations, formatting cells, or by deleting rows or columns.

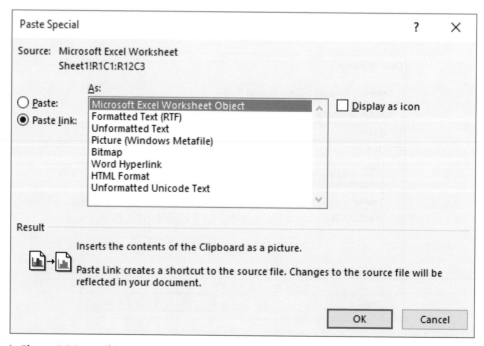

> **Figure 5.11:** Excel® link pasted in Word®

User prompts and messages

Adding user prompts and messages helps to make your spreadsheets more user-friendly and also to reduce errors, as the prompts help inform users what they should be doing to the various parts of your data model. As already seen in the Ease of use techniques section, prompts can be added to data validation.

Macro code can include message boxes which pop up when that part of the code is run if you think it useful to bring something to the user's attention at that point, for example to make sure that a data file is where it is expected to be and ready to import into the data model.

Layout and presentation

Excel® offers many options to help you choose the layout and presentation of your data model. You can:

▸ change the font size and style
▸ merge cells
▸ select colours
▸ include borders
▸ use shading
▸ use conditional formatting.

All these options require you to highlight or select cells before formatting them. There are other layout and presentation options such as graphics, headers and footers which require other approaches (see Figure 5.12).

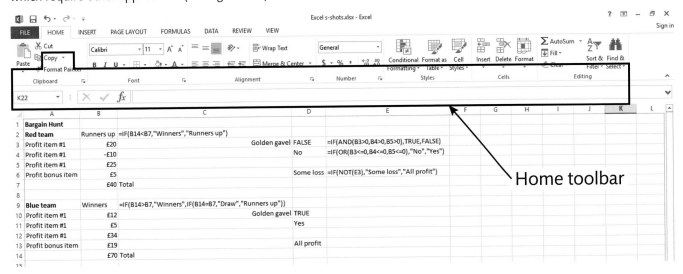

▸ **Figure 5.12:** Home toolbar formatting

Font size and style

Having the correct font size and style is essential for emphasising the more important text in a spreadsheet and for making the data model more easily understandable. Using a larger font size makes the text more prominent. Using different styles can be used to differentiate between fonts of the same size: **bold** is more prominent than ***bold italic***, which is more prominent than 'normal', which is more prominent than *italic*. **Bold** and ***bold italic*** are often essential when light coloured text is shown over a dark background because, otherwise, this can be very difficult to read.

Excel® gives some choices for copying a font size and style to other cells with the format painter or with paste special. To use the format painter, start by copying the cell with the formatting that you want to use, click on the Format Painter button and then click on the cell that needs the new format. You can do this to many cells by double clicking on the Format Painter button; this will remain active until you tap the <Esc> key.

To use paste special, you also start by copying the cell with the formatting that you want to use. You can now highlight the cell(s) you want to format, then bring up the dialog box by either clicking on the Paste Special button (in the right click menu) or typing <Alt> <E> then <S> (see Figure 5.13). Select Formats then OK. The paste special can be repeated to format other cells without needing to re-copy the original cell. When completed, you tap the <Esc> key to clear the copy.

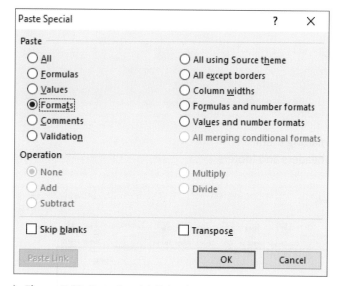

▶ **Figure 5.13:** Paste Special dialog box

Cell layouts

Colour

Colours are easily set by selecting the cells to be formatted and then clicking on the Font Colour or Background Colour drop-down menus to choose the colour.

Merging cells

Merging cells can be useful for centring a heading over several cells. Select the cells to be merged and then click on the Merge and Centre drop-down menu in the Home toolbar. You will now have three merge choices plus the option to unmerge.

- ▶ Merge and Centre will merge the highlighted cells, and any text in the leftmost cell will be centred in the merge.
- ▶ Merge Across will merge the highlighted cells and any text in the leftmost cell will keep its alignment in the merge: for example, if it was right aligned before, then it will end up right aligned in the merged cells.
- ▶ Merge cells is similar to Merge Across in that the alignment is kept. It differs if more than one row of cells are selected for the merge in that they are merged into one cell, whereas Merge Across merges each row.

For all of these merge options, text in the (top) leftmost cell is kept and text in the other selected cells is lost.

Borders and shading

Borders and shading can be set after selecting cells by bringing up the dialog box (see Figure 5.14). Either right click on them to select Format or click on the Borders and Shading drop-down menu in the Home toolbar to see the Borders menu, where you can click on More borders. To use the Border tab of the Format Cells dialog box, select the style and colour you want and then click on one of the Presets, click in the Border diagram or use a Border button.

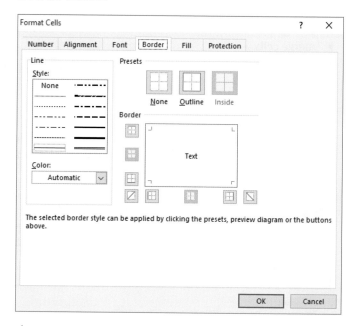

Figure 5.14: Border dialog box

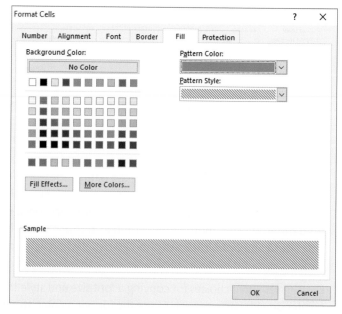

▶ **Figure 5.15:** Fill dialog box

See Figure 5.15 for the background and shading options. This is shown by clicking on the fill tab of the Format Cells dialog box. Here you can click on a background colour or choose a pattern fill colour and style. The OK button completes any choices using this dialog box.

Conditional formatting

When you have a large data set and need to be able to identify certain items of data, for example especially large or small values, conditional formatting is very effective. Select the cells and then use the Conditional Formatting button in the Home toolbar to bring up the options.

There are many conditions you can apply to format cells that match your criteria (see step 1 in Step by step: Setting up conditional formatting). You can have several conditional formatting rules on the same range of cells, so that you can look for different things such as below a chosen value or above average. This can result in almost any formats for matching cells including font, bold, italic, colour and background. Many spreadsheets use red for bad data and green for good, but anything is possible as long as it matches the user's requirements.

Step by step: Setting up conditional formatting   2 Steps

1 This shows how to enter conditional formatting to colour cells red if they are below a given value. Select the cells where you want the conditional formatting and then use the Conditional Formatting drop-down menu in the Home toolbar to show the available options.

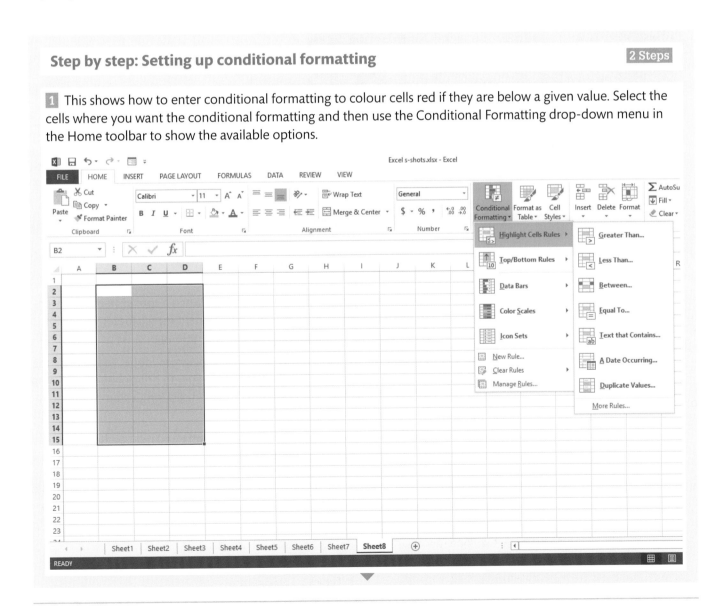

2 Select the Highlight Cells Rules then Less Than. Excel® shows the Less Than dialog box where you type '0', the number that triggers the conditional format. The default for less than is red. Other colours for cells that meet the trigger can be chosen from the drop-down menu. The OK button completes setting up this conditional formatting.

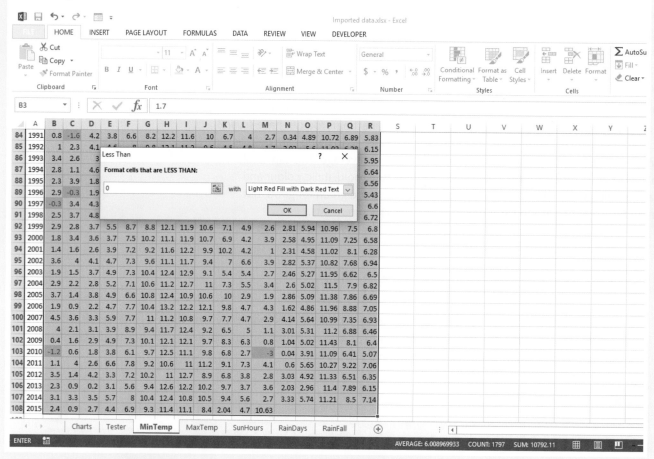

Headers and footers

It is often useful to add headers and footers, especially when a spreadsheet will cover several pages if printed. Even a single page print will benefit from a footer with fields giving information such as filename or date and time of printing.

Figure 5.16 shows the dialog boxes involved in setting a custom footer. To start, use the Sheet Options drop-down menu in the Page Layout toolbar to bring up the Page Setup dialog box. From here, select the Header/Footer tab then click on Custom Footer to bring up the Footer dialog box.

The Footer dialog box has three sections for the left, centre and right of the footer. You can click inside any of these sections then mix typing and fields from the buttons (Figure 5.16). For example, the left section has a field for Page (number) then 'of' was typed then the field Pages (number of pages). A header can be set using these dialog boxes in just the same way. The OK buttons complete these dialog boxes to save your changes.

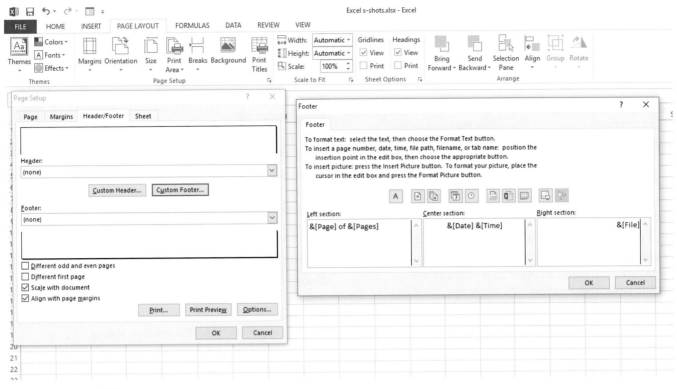

▶ **Figure 5.16:** Excel® footer

Graphics

You can use graphics other than charts to add diagrams, photos, logos and so on to your spreadsheet. The simplest method for this is to copy the graphic and then paste into the spreadsheet. Once pasted, you can use the mouse to move and resize the graphic. Right-clicking on a graphic object allows you to format any shadows, edges or other aspects of the graphic, for example a line around it.

You can also find a large collection of graphical objects under Shapes in the Insert toolbar, which allows you to enter rectangles, lines or call-outs to your spreadsheet.

Output requirements

Your data model needs to meet the client's requirements in terms of worksheet layout and output from charts and graphs. Your design documentation defines what was agreed with the client for each of these features.

Worksheet layouts

The worksheet layout design should include some detail about what it will be used for and a plan for how the data and calculations will be grouped and kept. Graphics can add meaning to the data model and logos will personalise it. Colours, borders and shading help to make the information more accessible and can also match any corporate style that the client has. You should refer to your designs for all of these aspects of the worksheet layout while implementing your data model to ensure that it meets the client's needs.

Charts and graphs

The types of charts and graphs that you will use for your data model should have been outlined in the planning documentation. You might need to tweak these designs when your actual data is used to produce the charts, to help you communicate your findings more clearly.

Testing the data model solution

You will use both formative and summative testing to test your data models. You should include tests for functionality and user acceptance.

Formative testing is carried out as the model is developed. Each calculation and function should be checked after it is entered to confirm that it gives the expected result.

Summative testing is carried out when the model is completed to confirm that it works as expected.

Testing

Your data model needs thorough testing to establish whether:

▸ the solution meets all the requirements of the functional specification
▸ the **underlying logic** is correct
▸ all the functions and formulae work correctly.

All this testing should be recorded in the test log with outcomes and corrective actions should be taken.

> **Key term**
>
> **Underlying logic** – how the spreadsheet will process the data into information. This is more of an overview of what the processing is to achieve, rather than the detailed calculations which actually implement the underlying logic.

Meeting the requirements

You will need to check that your data model solution meets all the requirements of the functional specification. To do this, return to the original user requirements and carefully plan tests to ensure that everything that was wanted is present and works well.

A common problem with large projects is that they can sometimes lose sight of what was actually required at the start of the work. For example, a data model might be required to predict monthly sales, but implemented to predict weekly sales.

Underlying logic

Testing is needed to check that the underlying logic of the model is correct. You will need test data with the expected outcomes pre-calculated so that, when you test the model, you can compare the actual results with what was expected.

The underlying logic should be tested with data that would be expected to produce a wide range of outcomes so that you can confirm that the model works as expected.

Functions and formulae

All the functions and formulae in the spreadsheet must work correctly, so (as far as practical) each must be tested. If there are a large number of calculations which have been copied from a row or column, then you can carefully check the originals and the first few copies and the last few for correct working.

Another way to check a large number of calculations is to use the Show Formulas button in the Formulas toolbar, which enables you can see the calculations rather than their results. This test is useful because you can see if anything looks wrong, for example a number in amongst the formulae (where someone has typed over a calculation).

Other factors

During testing, there are other factors to consider. These include:

▸ the selection and use of appropriate test data
▸ finding suitable users for solution testing
▸ gathering feedback from users
▸ completing the test documentation.

Test data

As already explained, the selection and use of appropriate test data makes a big differenc e to how well your data model is tested and therefore to how useful it is.

Valid data is needed to prove that calculations produce correct and reliable results. Valid data consists of any test data which is expected to produce a good output.

Invalid data is used to find out what this does to the data model. Invalid data is test data that is obviously wrong, for example a date entered as 35/5/2016. Ideally, it would be rejected from the checks you have set on the data entries.

Erroneous is similar to invalid, except that it should pass as valid, even though it is wrong, for example a misspelt word or a number that was wrongly entered. This should be handled by the model without crashing or producing system error messages.

Extreme data should be used to check the limits of the model. Ideally, this would be at both the low and high limits of what is acceptable, just inside and just outside. As in all the other tests, the model should respond to these extremes as expected. If it does not, then any differences need to be corrected.

Users

Users are an important part of your testing, so you need to select suitable users to test your solution who are able to communicate their findings to you. Gathering feedback from users will enable you to respond to their findings.

PAUSE POINT   How will you test the data model for correctness, functionality and acceptance?

Hint   Create notes under the subheadings correctness, functionality and acceptance on what you would test.

Extend   In addition, state what your test data will need to achieve for each type of test.

You should be particularly interested in how users find the effectiveness, presentation, performance and users of your data model.

Test documentation

Your test logs will document what you did and what happened: that is, which tests were passed and the remedial actions you took to rectify any failed tests.

Try to design this test documentation so that it looks professional and is able to communicate the thoroughness of your testing and the reliability of the model. To do this, the documentation must be completed during every test and the outcome must be carefully recorded.

> **Link**
>
> For more on test documentation see Test plans.

Reviewing and refining the data model solution

As the project nears completion, there will still be some improvements or refinements that you can make to the data model, in order to fully meet the client requirements.

Refining the model

Refining the model may need to take into account any issues raised during testing. Each of these issues must be carefully considered and evaluated. How much impact would they have on improving your spreadsheet? You will have a limit on how much time is available, so you will need to weigh up the expected benefits against the practicalities of implementing them. For example, calculations in the model might be optimised to simplify the inputs, processing or outputs.

There could also be an opportunity to refine the model to take account of the feedback and client requirements. Other people can be a valuable source of ideas and can also identify problems in the model that you did not notice or anticipate. You will again need to evaluate whether it is practical to make refinements based on the feedback at this time.

Document any of the issues raised that were not practical for you to implement at this time as ideas for extending your model.

> **Reflect**
>
> Evaluating the outcomes of your work is necessary to help you to produce high quality, justified recommendations and decisions. Your evaluations are essential to achieve the highest grades for this unit and to maximise the quality of your data modelling spreadsheet solution.
>
> Evaluate what you could have done better and what improvements you could make if you had time.

Extending the model

Always include in your documentation any ideas you have which could be used to extend the data model. This section will be useful to communicate an evaluation of your understanding of the user requirements, the current value of your spreadsheet solution and the future potential of your data model.

The future potential of your data model could be realised by extending the model. What could be added to the model to make it more useful? Would more (or less) user inputs offer more possible outcomes or make it easier to use? Could the meanings of the data model outputs be enhanced using charts or different formatting?

 PAUSE POINT   How can a data model be optimised?

Hint   Create notes under the subheadings testing, user feedback, inputs, calculations and outputs.

Extend   Identify an appropriate use for each of the different Excel® chart types.

Assessment practice 5.2

`B.P3` `B.P4` `C.P5` `C.P6` `C.P7` `B.M2` `C.M3` `BC.D2` `BC.D3`

Your job as junior programmer at W-Ready is going well and the purchasing manager, Ellie, has accepted your report evaluating the role of spreadsheet data modelling in decision making.

Ellie would like the data model to include collections of real data on weather, such as minimum/maximum temperatures, hours of sunshine, average rainfall and number of rain-free days, along with predictions for the future, so as to produce useful information on which she can base her purchasing decisions.

She particularly wants to be able to compare the temperature, sunshine and rainfall for any month she selects and to control how many years of back data are used to make predictions for the next two years.

Plan

- Do I need to be working with anyone else? If so, what is my role? What am I contributing?
- Do I have any existing knowledge around the task at hand?
- What resources do I need to complete the task? How can I get access to them?
- How much time do I have to complete the task? How am I going to successfully plan my time and keep track of my progress?
- What aspects of the task do I think will take the most/least time? How will I balance these?

The programming team are to produce a spreadsheet for Ellie, and your team leader, Salim, has given you the task of producing the following documentation for the project.

- A functional specification to clarify and define the data model.
- Design documentation including:
  - designs for the data model meeting client requirements
  - review of your designs including feedback from Ellie and others in the programming team
  - improvements to your designs
  - justification of the decisions you made
  - how your chosen design will fulfil its purpose and client requirements.
- Testing logs to record your spreadsheet tests and any actions you took to resolve problems.

You will need to use appropriate methods to inform Ellie and Salim of the design improvements to confirm that they both agree with these changes to the specification. These will be documented as screenshots, recordings or witness statements.

You are then asked by Salim to create and develop a data model to fulfil your design using a range of appropriate and advanced spreadsheet features and functions.

Carry out comprehensive testing and seek user feedback to refine and improve your data model. Make sure that the model is thoroughly tested to prove that it meets Ellie's requirements and keep your testing log up to date.

Produce a report on your spreadsheet to:
- evaluate the effectiveness of the alternatives you considered along with ways they could be improved if you repeated the task
- review the extent to which the data model meets client requirements
- explain how you optimised the data model to meet client requirements.

This report will evaluate the decisions and processes that you applied throughout the design, development and testing stages along with their impact on the effectiveness of the final solution. You should evaluate your alternatives along with their impacts and consequences and justify the selection that produced the best decision or compromise.

Your evaluation should be a systematic and accurate review of your own skills and performance and how this improved the effectiveness of the solutions. Identify where you took responsibility for your own work (for example, identifying potential issues and how you resolved them, the improvements you made and how you kept the work safe and secure) and explain how you made responsible use of any copyrighted content.

Document any creative or innovative approaches you took to this problem solving. Evaluate your final design and produce well-considered, justifiable suggestions for future improvements to your data model.

Do

- I can seek others' opinions.
- I am open to change.
- I can make connections between what I am reading/researching and the task, and identify the important information.
- I am recording my own observations and thoughts.
- I am recording any problems that I am experiencing and looking for ways/solutions to clarify queries.
- Am I utilising all the support available to me?
- What am I struggling with? Do I know how to overcome this?
- I can question my own learning approach.
- I can identify when I have gone wrong and adjust my thinking/approach to get myself back on course.

Review

- I can explain which elements I found easiest and hardest.
- I can explain how I would approach the hard elements differently next time.
- I can describe my thought processes.
- I can explain the skills that I employed and the new ones I have developed.
- I can make informed choices based on reflection.
- I can explain what I have learned and why it is important.
- I can explain what success looks like.
- I can use this experience in future tasks/learning experiences to improve my planning/approach and to monitor my own progress.
- I can identify how this learning experience relates to future experiences (ie in the workplace).
- I realise where I still have learning/knowledge gaps and I know how to resolve them.

Further reading and resources

Alexander, M. (2015). *Excel Macros For Dummies*. New Jersey: John Wiley & Sons.

Harvey, G. (2013). *Excel 2016 For Dummies (Excel for Dummies)*. New Jersey: John Wiley & Sons.

Laing, R., Hawkins, R. and Mayne, M. (2015). *Microsoft Excel Basics*. London: Flame Tree Publishing.

Websites

Microsoft® Office® help and training: **www.support.office.com**
This is a comprehensive website supporting Excel® and other MS apps.

Stack Overflow: **www.stackoverflow.com**
This website provides Excel VBA macro programming support.

Excel Easy: **www.excel-easy.com**
This website offers general Excel support.

Excel Functions: **www.excelfunctions.net**
This has a good choice of Excel step-by-step support.

THINK ▶FUTURE

Billy Stephens

Systems analyst in a large bank.

I've been working for a large bank for ten years now, progressing from junior programmer to systems analyst, responsible for a team of six programmers. My role is varied, interesting and busy. I have to communicate with users, their managers and my programming team to understand the users' needs so as to design suitable programs that my team will then produce.

Data modelling is part of my role. We produce spreadsheets that meet the users' needs. This is usually a much smaller task than a full programming project, which would require a language such as C#, and it can be delivered a lot more quickly. There is a steady demand for small spreadsheet-based data models so that users can explore 'what if' scenarios with a lot more flexibility than our program projects usually deliver.

Our spreadsheet models often use data that is downloaded from our main systems so that users have up-to-date information to examine. Obviously, we try to avoid our users needing to type in large amounts of data as this is time consuming, error-prone and unnecessary. We usually set up some cells so they can explore percentage changes in the data and include charts to help them easily understand the information that our models produce.

Focusing your skills

Data analysis

Data and information are everything in the modern workplace. Computer systems are used by every organisation to input, store and process data and output information. It is important to be able to recognise the data required to produce useful information along with the processing required to do this. There are very good opportunities for people who are able to identify such data to pursue careers as systems analysts.

Here are some simple tips to consider.

- What data is available?
- Can the data be used as it is? That is, does it need to be typed in, or can it be imported into your data modelling app?
- Does the data need more content? That is, by typing or by combining with other data.
- Make sure that you understand how the processing is going work.
- Make sure that you know what information is required: that is, the content and how it will be presented.

Spreadsheet creation

The spreadsheet is a great app for creating data models. There is flexibility on how the model can be structured because of the enormous collection of functions available and there is a wide range of possible ways of showing the information using charts and cell formatting.

Spreadsheet creation can be a good route towards many career opportunities involving systems analysis and programming.

Here are some useful tips.

- Practise using the spreadsheet to become familiar with the calculations, functions, charts and formatting options before planning your data model so that you know the options open to you.
- Plan your spreadsheet before you start work on the data model.
- Produce a test plan to clarify your understanding of what is required from your data model.
- Check every calculation as you enter it.
- Use paste special to control how you copy and paste, especially values, formulae or formats.
- Save your work regularly and use save as to make a copy of your model before making major changes.
- Check that printing works well, is easily readable and does not spill over onto unwanted pages.

Getting Ready for Assessment

Kerri is working towards a BTEC Level 3 National Extended Certificate in Information Technology. She was given an assignment with the following title: 'Investigate data modelling and decision making' for learning aim A. She had to write a report with these sections:

▶ stages involved in the decision-making process for data modelling with explanations
▶ features of spreadsheet software that can be used to support the decision-making process and how they can be used
▶ an analysis of how spreadsheet software features help decision making
▶ an evaluation of how spreadsheet software features contribute to the decision-making process.

Kerri shares her experience below.

How I got started

I set about using several search engines to research spreadsheet data modelling on the internet. The websites I thought most useful were bookmarked into the two browser folders I made for data modelling and for spreadsheets.

Next, I visited the central library to check out the books available for some background reading. This was quite difficult as most of the titles were about databases, but I did find one which I took home for a fortnight. I quite like books because I find flipping through the pages a quick and effective way of skipping past what I don't want and finding what I need.

I met up with one of the IT team at my centre for half an hour to talk through what they do with spreadsheets to support their managers. This introduced me to something called the Cube which is a pivot table they use to hook into their network data sources.

How I brought it all together

I created a Word® document for my report with headings for each of my sections. I also added an introduction, a summary and a bibliography section. I typed my name into the header and page numbers into the footer.

The stages involved in the decision-making process for data modelling section just involved reading my research and typing it up. My section on the spreadsheet features needed quite a lot of hands-on time with Excel® to get familiar with what could actually be done with this app. I focused on four features, which I illustrated with my own screenshots.

▶ The analysis of spreadsheet software features helping decision making section was a mixture of my hands-on experience with Excel® and the discussions around using the Cube.
▶ My evaluation of how spreadsheet software features contribute to the decision-making process simply recycled my previous research with extra depth and my thoughts on how these work together.

What I learned from the experience

The biggest surprise was meeting the IT team member and seeing what can actually be done in a modern system, especially the way charts were used to present information. My report writing is a little stronger now and I'm a lot better at using Excel®.

Think about it

▶ Do you have a plan with timings so that you can complete your assignment by the submission date?
▶ Is there a workplace or organisation that you can visit as part of your research?
▶ Which features of a spreadsheet are most suitable for supporting a data model?

Website Development 6

Getting to know your unit

The internet has grown and developed so much within the last decade, enabling new ways of communicating and sharing information. It has transformed the way in which people use information technology. Millions of web pages are created daily so it is important that they are engaging and capture the interest of the public. Website developers need to understand how to resolve complex problems and develop innovative solutions.

The evolution of the worldwide web has brought about more exciting opportunities for businesses and individuals. Businesses can now sell goods and services online, which extends their customer base, potentially worldwide. Individuals can communicate with people anywhere in the world cheaply and affordably. The worldwide web also caters for individuals who have physical disabilities. For example, a person with a visual impairment can browse the web using new accessibility tools.

As the worldwide web evolves, information technology professionals must evolve with it. In this unit you will learn the fundamental principles and key concepts of website design and development. The skills you acquire will benefit you if you wish to further your studies in higher education or prepare for employment in the website development sector.

How you will be assessed

This unit will be assessed by a series of internally assessed tasks set by your tutor. Throughout this unit, you will find activities that will help you work towards your assessment. Completing these activities will not mean that you have achieved a particular grade, but you will have carried out useful research and preparation that will be relevant when it comes to your final assignment.

In order to complete the tasks in your assignment successfully, it is important to check that you have met all the Pass grading criteria. You can do this as you work your way through the assignment.

If you are hoping to gain a Merit or Distinction, you should make sure that you present the information in your assignment in the required style. For example, Merit criteria require you to analyse and discuss, and Distinction criteria require you to assess and evaluate.

The assignment set by your tutor will consist of a number of tasks designed to meet the criteria in the table. This is likely to consist of a written assignment but may also include activities such as the following.
▸ Explaining how websites are used and the principles that underpin them.
▸ Using different design techniques to provide innovative solutions to complex problems.
▸ Creating a website based upon your design documentation.

Assessment criteria

This table shows what you must do in order to achieve a **Pass**, **Merit** or **Distinction** grade, and where you can find activities to help you.

Pass	Merit	Distinction
Learning aim **A** Understand the principles of website development		
A.P1 Compare the principles of website design used in two websites, including their suitability for the intended audience and intended purpose. Assessment practice 6.1	**A.M1** Analyse how the principles of website design are used to produce creative, high performance websites which meet client requirements. Assessment practice 6.1	**A.D1** Evaluate how the principles of website design are used to produce creative, high performance websites which meet client requirements. Assessment practice 6.1
Learning aim **B** Design a website to meet client requirements		
B.P2 Produce designs for a website that meets client requirements. Assessment practice 6.2	**B.M2** Justify the design decisions, explaining how they will meet the users' needs and be fit for purpose. Assessment practice 6.2	
B.P3 Review the website design proposals with others to identify and inform improvements. Assessment practice 6.2		
Learning aim **C** Develop a website to meet a client requirement		
C.P4 Produce a website for an intended audience and purpose. Assessment practice 6.2	**C.M3** Optimise a website to meet client requirements. Assessment practice 6.2	**BC.D2** Evaluate the design and optimised website against client requirements. Assessment practice 6.2
C.P5 Test the website for functionality, compatibility and usability. Assessment practice 6.2		**BC.D3** Demonstrate individual responsibility, creativity and effective self-management in the design, development and review of a website. Assessment practice 6.2
C.P6 Review the extent to which the website meets client requirements. Assessment practice 6.2		

Getting started

Think about some of your favourite websites. What is it about them that makes them your favourite? Is it the colour, the positioning of elements, or the font type used? Working in small groups, list some of your favourite websites and note down what you think it is that makes them stand out from the rest.

A Understand the principles of website development

Websites have changed tremendously throughout the years. When the web was first developed, it was used by scientists in research institutes to share ideas. Early websites included **hypertext** and hyperlinks as a way of moving through all the text. In today's world, websites are still used to share ideas, but the web has evolved into something essential to our way of life.

> **Key term**
>
> **Hypertext** – text that contains links to other bits of text.

Purpose and principles of website products

Websites are now so much more than simple links that provide information. Consider a very basic news website. It is full of up-to-date content such as videos for streaming, polls where visitors can publish their thoughts, and even basic games. Websites and the businesses that run them are now in competition against one another to get you to view their products. Therefore, website developers need to understand the purpose and principles of website design so that they can make websites which are fit for purpose but also stand out in people's minds for the right reasons.

Purpose of websites

Websites have different purposes and perform different functions. Traditionally, websites were used to provide information. However, content based technology called Web 2.0 has been developed to enable users to interact and add their own content, knowledge and opinions. Web 2.0 technology has enabled the development of the following.

▶ Wikis – places where all users can contribute to information, the biggest example of which is Wikipedia, an encyclopaedia website where anyone can contribute to any article and even create new ones.

> **Theory into practice**
>
> In this unit you will come across many technical terms. Go online and develop your own wiki that will serve as a glossary for all the terms you come across within this unit. This can be shared with your class and you could all contribute to it.

▶ Blogs – online journals that include tools for readers to comment and contribute. Anyone can become a blogger and create a blog, most of which are public (although there are some private ones).

▶ Social networking – websites such as Facebook™, LinkedIn® and Twitter™ that allow people to communicate by creating a profile. These social media websites provide tools that enable users to correspond by posting status updates or tweets. They can also have private conversations and play games. Users are encouraged to make 'friends' with other users, although most people using Facebook™ are friends with people they know in real life and friends of friends online. On Twitter™, you follow celebrities and well-known figures as well as friends, but the celebrities are unlikely to follow you. There are other social media websites that offer more specific services, such as Flickr™, which allow users to share and rate photographs.

▶ Online applications – online applications allow users to use programs via the internet, rather than purchasing a program and installing it on a local computer. This means that the applications are accessible anywhere and are often free or have a small subscription fee. Google Docs™ is a good example of an online application.

▶ Podcasting – a way of making audio or video files available on the internet that can either be listened to or viewed. A podcast is saved to either a PC or a mobile device where a user can listen to or view the content while they are on the move. A podcast will be treated as a sound file (audio podcasts) or a film (video podcasts are also known as vodcasts).

Product and/or service-based websites

▶ **Table 6.1:** Examples of product and/or service-based websites

Service	Example types	Target audience	Key benefits
Commerce	• eBay™ • Amazon™ • online banking	• consumers	Allows users to carry out transactions easily and conveniently on PCs and mobile devices.
Real-time information	• 24/7 news updates • travel information • weather reports	• information seekers	Provides immediate up-to-date information. For example, mobile phone apps can send notifications to inform you of recent news reports or train arrival times.
Communication	• blogs • Skype™ • email • online gaming	• social networkers • information seekers • online gamers • adult and teenage consumers	You can receive immediate replies from anyone at no additional cost to your broadband or mobile fee.
Download services	• music downloads • film downloads • software downloads • gaming downloads • streaming services	• information seekers • entertainment seekers • online gamers • adult and teenage consumers	Flexibility and convenience of downloading different mediums to your PC or mobile device. Moreover, you can also now stream online content to your television, computer or mobile device.
Virtual learning environments (VLEs)	• Moodle • Pearson's ActiveLearn Digital Service • Blackboard®	• information seekers • consumers (teachers and learners)	Many benefits as learners have the flexibility of downloading information from the comfort of their own home. Moreover, learners can submit homework/ assignments online or be set independent study tasks.

Requirements of websites

The following are key requirements of all websites.

▶ User-friendly – It is easy to use and understand. Understanding how to produce a user-friendly website will significantly improve the way in which visitors are able to understand and use your website in terms of layout, design and the content.

▶ Consistent – Consistency, that is, keeping things the same, is a key principle of website design. Consistency can apply to many different things within website design. For example, consistency in the colours and font typography you use, the positioning of links on pages and the style and images you use. An inconsistent approach to website design makes for a website that will ultimately frustrate users. Consistency makes for an intuitive and user-friendly website.

▶ Navigational – It is important that any website you develop is easy for users to navigate and find the information that they require. Think of a website's navigation like a road map to all the different areas and information contained within the website. A consistent navigation system will help your users to find the information they require more quickly. It is also important not to add in unnecessary levels of navigation.

▶ Customisable – New technologies have made it possible to customise website interfaces for website users. The benefit of this is that you can attract new users and keep existing users more engaged with your website. For example, consider the way in which some websites allow you to set your location on them. One advantage of doing this is that you can get regular news headlines about your specific area or receive local weather reports.

▶ Responsive – Responsive websites are those that are optimised to automatically adapt to the layout of the web browser you are using, whether on a PC or mobile device, without the need to resize or scroll excessively.

▶ Bandwidth utilisation – With many on sensitive data mobile contracts, designers must recognise how their content will be used and how many will view the viability of the service that they offer.

Principles of website design

Millions of websites are built on a daily basis, so more emphasis is now given to the principles of good website design. Following these standard principles is important as it allows every website the opportunity to be successful in a market which is very competitive. When you combine these principles of good design with elements of innovation and creativity, your website has every chance of being successful. In terms of business, if you get the website right, the business is more likely to succeed.

▶ Usability – This is the ease of use of a website, that is, how user-friendly it is. For example, an important element of website usability is ensuring that website content is flexible and works on all browsers and devices.

▶ White space/spacing – This is the space on web pages that is left untouched and white. Website developers utilise white space to separate design elements such as text, graphics and other elements. Unless you utilise spacing, your web pages will look cluttered and messy, and it would be hard for visitors to interpret which words relate to which images and understand what they are looking at. Therefore, when designing a web page, it is crucial to use spacing between elements so as not to overwhelm and confuse website users.

▶ Site layout – This means giving consideration to where elements go on a web page and how content will be spread across a website. For example, where the header, navigation links, text and graphics will appear on the page. The layout used for one web page should be consistently used across all the pages on a website, where similar content is being included. For example, headers should be positioned in the same way on all pages. A good site layout is one that is uncomplicated, has clear navigation and is intuitive and user-friendly.

▶ Accessibility – Website developers must ensure that websites are correctly designed and developed to enable all users to have equal access to information. This is important as it removes barriers that would otherwise prevent a person with disabilities from using a website. The BBC is an example of a website that provides excellent website accessibility. It includes features that advise users on how to customise their computer set-up and remove barriers to using the website. People with poor vision can change the font size and colour. In addition, it provides accessible games for children with motor and cognitive disabilities. **Alexa Traffic Rank** consistently rates the BBC website in the top 100 websites worldwide. One reason for this is the excellent way that it caters for all users.

Key terms

Alexa Traffic Rank – ranks websites based on a combined measure of page views and the number of visitors. From this, it creates a list of 'top websites' averaged over three-month periods.

Serif – a type of font that has embellishments at the ends of letters. An example of a serif font is Times New Roman.

Sans serif – The word 'sans' is French meaning, 'without'. Therefore a sans serif font is one without embellishments at the ends of the letters. An example of a sans serif font is Arial.

Link

The World Wide Web Consortium is committed to ensuring that the web is accessible for all, regardless of their disability. Find out more about their Web Accessibility Initiative at **www.w3.org/WAI/**

▶ Navigation – It is important that users can navigate their way easily around a website. The navigation must be intuitive and simple to use. Good navigation on websites involves making it obvious where website links are and being consistent across the whole website. There should be an intuitive structure of pages.

▶ Typography – The type of font used on websites is important. Websites need to have clear and legible text in order to be user-friendly and accessible. There are two main types of font families: **serif** and **sans serif**. Most websites utilise a sans serif font such as Arial because they have no embellishments to the letters, making them clearer and easier to read.

Research

Research how typography is connected to disabilities such as dyslexia. When building a website, what font would you use and why? Consider what else you could do as a website developer to ensure that all users can access your website regardless of disability.

▶ Alignment – Alignment is how elements are positioned on a web page and how they interact with each other. For example, if you place an image on a web page which is aligned to the left and the supporting text was aligned to the right of the page, this would suggest to users that there is no relationship between the two elements, whereas, if they were both aligned left, there would appear to be a connection between the two elements.

- Clarity – Clarity, being clear, is key to good website design. It is pointless choosing a visually appealing design if users cannot understand it because it is not clear. Therefore, any website you develop must communicate what you want it to say clearly, but also have clarity of design and layout. For example, if you want a user to contact you, you should provide a visible email address or phone number. Asking users to fill in forms takes additional time and does not put the user first. Good design matters, but good communication matters more.

- Consistency – Consistency means keeping elements within your website the same throughout. This is considered one of the most important principles in website design. Website consistency involves using the same page layout, the same font and the same design and colour scheme, throughout. An inconsistent website is unintuitive and difficult to navigate.

- Accuracy – Everything included in the website needs to be accurate: that is, it should be correct and meaningful. To keep information accurate and current, websites should be updated regularly. Moreover, it is important that the information provided on websites is checked for factual errors as well as spelling and grammatical mistakes.

- Content – The content of the website includes the text, graphics (diagrams, artworks and photos) as well as media and objects. Content needs to be accurate, consistent in style (where appropriate), and you need to ensure that you have permission to use any content that you did not create from scratch.

- Media and objects – Some websites include interactive content, such as videos, background sounds, Flash images and **applets**. Media elements are used to captivate and grab the attention of website users. The use of media must be appropriate as its overuse can slow down a website, clutter the appearance of web pages and put off some users.

> **Key term**
>
> **Applet** – a mini software application that can be built into a web page, for example a calculator that can be used by website users upon clicking a button on a web page.

- Simplicity – Websites which are simplistic in their design are often the most visited. They manage to combine the content they need to get across with a clear and simple, easy-to-use design that attracts users back because they know they will get what they need from it without fuss. It is important when developing a website that you do not overcomplicate the design by introducing too many elements on the pages.

▶ **Figure 6.1:** Google.com home page

PAUSE POINT

Alexa Traffic Rank ranks websites based on a combined measure of page views and the number of visitors. In August 2015, Google.com (see Figure 6.1) was measured to be the most heavily visited website during that year. Consider what makes this website so appealing and popular. Print out screenshot(s) of Google.com and annotate them in terms of how the principles of good website design apply to this website. Alternatively, if you do not wish to use Google.com, consider another website that you think is good and identify where the principles are applied.

Hint

Use the snipping tool within Windows (go to the Windows menu, All apps, Windows accessories, Snipping tool) to 'snip' parts of the website that adopt a principle of good website design. This is easier than printing screenshots and then cropping images.

Extend

Consider additional principles of good website design that you believe are important. Explain what these principles are together with an annotated image to explain your reasoning.

Media and objects

Media and objects are used within websites to draw in and engage website users. As mentioned above, media includes videos, audio and interactive content. Moreover, objects such as applets, PDFs and Flash can be embedded into web pages. There are a number of factors you should consider when using media and objects.

▸ Position – Where should you put media or objects on a web page? As media and objects are used to grab the attention of users, they need to be placed somewhere where they can easily be seen, but you need to consider how prominently you want to position them.

▸ Colour – Colour is an integral part of website design, especially when you are embedding object elements such as Flash. Flash is a form of animation used to attract the attention of users. However, too many vibrant colours can be off-putting to users. You should also consider users who suffer from photosensitivity. Therefore, when using colours you should use them appropriately so that they are not overwhelming.

▸ Contrast – Contrast is used to differentiate between two or more elements on a web page. For example, if you were using a Flash image embedded in your web page, and the background used a key colour of the Flash image, it would be difficult for the user to see the Flash image clearly. Therefore you should use contrasting colours to differentiate the elements of a web page.

▸ Size – Screen size is a big concern when developing a web page. Media and objects are used to capture the attention of users. However, if you embed a video on the web page that takes up most of the screen, this will have implications on where the rest of your content will go, and users will have to scroll to see it. Therefore, sizing of media and object elements is important, and

this should be thought through during the design phase. You will need to consider how the object will appear on a mobile. Will it work on a mobile?

▸ Appropriateness – When using media and objects, you must consider whether they really add anything to the effectiveness of your webpage. Although media and objects are useful to draw users' attention, the downside is that the inclusion of media and objects means that your web pages will take longer to load, especially on a mobile and they might not be compatible with every browser. Therefore, you have to consider the appropriateness of using media and objects, and whether their inclusion will actually be beneficial to website users.

Tip

Professionalism is a key attribute not only for website developers but in any walk of life or job. One important aspect of professionalism is having good etiquette. Etiquette is a code of behaviour that dictates how we should behave within society and at work. It all comes down to manners, that is, how we behave and present ourselves. It is crucial to be professional and have good etiquette when seeking employment.

Creativity and innovation

With so many websites being developed on a daily basis, and businesses now heavily reliant on websites, it has become very important that websites are creative and innovative if they want to draw in customers. However, websites should not be different just for the sake of being different. Website developers must have a creative side and deliver interesting designs that capture the imagination of users, while still adhering to the principles of good website design. However, there are techniques and certain layouts which can be used to make a website, 'stand out' while still conveying information in an appropriate way.

Unconventional layouts

In the past most websites tended to fit to a standard layout template, which, to an extent, is fine because then they all follow the principles of good website design. However, there still needs to be room for creativity and innovation. A vast number of websites are being created so new websites need to stand out. The art of website design is still evolving and good, new ideas can still be found. Recently, there has been an increase in unconventional website layouts through 'out-of-the-box' thinking on the part of the website developers who came up with them.

Here are some examples of creative and innovative websites.

Ice & Sky

Go to education.iceandsky.com. The Ice & Sky website follows in the footsteps of Luc Jacquet and the Wild-Touch project. What makes this website creative and innovative is that it uses unique animations to help tell the story, combined with an out-of-the-box-thinking layout. Notice how the links appear at the bottom and the main link 'Discover' is prominently displayed in the middle of the web page.

> **Link**
>
> To find out about Luc Jacquet and the Wild-Touch and Ice & Sky projects put these terms into a search engine.

p2 Media

> **Discussion**
>
> The internet and paper-based documents are both good sources of information. What other sources can you identify? How reliable are these sources?

Now go to the p2 Media website at www.p2media.de/. This website makes good use of space by having scrolling pages for the different links within the website. In essence, it uses several home pages and scrolls through each one on a timer. This is an interesting way to present a website and is quite unconventional compared with most websites that you may come across.

Golden ratio

It is not known who discovered the golden ratio, but it is a mathematical concept that has been used for over 2000 years. This ratio has, either intentionally or unintentionally,

been used to make designs **aesthetically pleasing**. The golden ratio has been used in:

- nature
- science, including astronomy
- art, including painting
- architecture.

The golden ratio can also be applied to website design. This ratio is based on a simple mathematical equation which produces a **ratio**. It produces a special number which is equal to 1.618 (or 1.62 rounded up to two significant figures). This special number is found by dividing a line into two sections so that the longer section divided by the smaller section is also equal to the whole length divided by the longer part: a/b = (a+b)/a or for example 31/24 = (31+24)/31. This number of 1.62 (2sf) can be applied to web design to set the width of the main content and side bar columns.

> **Key terms**
>
> **Aesthetically pleasing** – something which is visually engaging or appealing to the senses of sight and hearing. Usually such things are considered beautiful or attractive.
>
> **Ratio** – a way of concisely showing the relationship between two quantities. A ratio is represented by separating the two quantities with a colon (:). For example, a ratio of 1:2 is one quantity compared with something which is twice the first amount (twice as much).

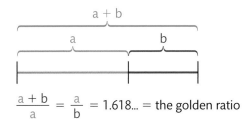

$$\frac{a + b}{a} = \frac{a}{b} = 1.618... = \text{the golden ratio}$$

▶ **Figure 6.2:** The golden ratio.

Two quantities are in the golden ratio (see Figure 6.2) if the *ratio* of the values is the same as the ratio of their *sum* to the larger of the two quantities. It is often symbolised using phi (Φ), after the 21st letter of the Greek alphabet.

> **Research**
>
> Find examples of where the golden ratio of 1.62 appears within science (including astronomy), art (including painting), architecture and nature.

Search engine optimisation

Search engine optimisation (SEO) is a set of techniques used to maximise the number of visitors to a website. By applying the techniques of SEO, a website developer can ensure that their website appears high on the list of results returned by a search engine for related search terms. SEO is very important to businesses as users of search engines tend to click on the first relevant link they come to. By appearing at the top of a search engine, they are likely to maximise the potential of advertising their products and services. There are books and courses available that can help you optimise your website so that it appears first on search engine results lists, although achieving this is not always as easy as it may at first appear. Outlined here are a number of the techniques that website developers use to optimise their websites for search engines. Remember that Google down-grades non-mobile-friendly sites.

Indexing (meta tags)

Search engines use the entered search term/phrase to find websites in its database which include that term/phrase, rather than searching the whole internet each time. Search engines utilise 'spiders' to trawl the internet for new websites to include in their databases, with the intention that all websites will be included in the databases. The spiders examine each web page that they encounter and send information about that page back to the search engine to be stored in its database. This process is called 'web crawling'. There can be disadvantages to web crawling, because sometimes a web crawler will attempt to spider your website aggressively. which will result in a server overload. Therefore only limited crawling should be carried out.

To ensure that the spiders list a website correctly, website developers include meta tags in the coding of a web page. Meta tags are embedded into the **<head>** section of a web page. These meta tags are used to provide search engines with information about a website. The text in these tags is not displayed within the web page. Instead, it tells search engines (and other web services) specific information about the page. Although the meta tags are not displayed on your website, it is sensible for them to be the same as your web page headings (assuming that these are sensibly titled) to tell people what the purpose of your website is and what products or services you offer.

Keywords

A keyword is a word or phrase that can be put into a search engine so that it will return matching and relevant results. Businesses often use market research companies to see what keywords or phrases best reflect their business, products and services. You should bear the following goals in mind when selecting keywords:

▶ use keywords that accurately describe the business, products or services

▶ use words/phrases that people actually type into search engines when looking for something online

▶ use the most relevant keywords in the URLs and web page titles and to describe the site; for example, you should use the keywords in the meta tags, the titles and body of the text on the pages and even in the image filenames.

> **Key term**
>
> **<head>** – an HTML tag which is used to provide data about an HTML document (web page).

All this, when used correctly, can help to improve your ranking on the search results page.

> **Link**
>
> For more on keywords and SEO generally, see *Unit 3: Using Social Media in Business*.

Importance of updates

In order to ensure that your website is relevant, it must be updated regularly. Search engines can determine how often your website is updated. If a website is updated regularly, then the search engine considers it a consistent source of new information. As a result, the website is more likely to be placed higher in the search results.

Factors affecting website performance

There are a number of different factors that affect the performance of a website. If performance is adversely affected, websites can load slowly or fail to load completely. If your website does not respond quickly, you are likely to lose users to more responsive websites. Performance is key to the success of a website.

Where scripting runs

Scripting can either run on the web server (server-side scripts) or on the local client machine (client-side scripts). Server-side scripting is used for advanced interactive features such as connecting to a database. It works by the user requesting a web page from the server. The script in the page is interpreted by the server to suit the needs of the user, and then is sent to the device. The downside of server-side scripting is that, when a user makes requests over the network to the server, it can slow down the experience for the user and place more load (strain) on the server.

Client-side scripting is when the script is executed on the user's computer, and does not connect to a server. Client-side scripting is useful as it can provide extra interactivity within web pages without the need to connect to a web server.

Browser compliance

All web browsers were not created equally. Each web browser will render code differently. This means that when the code of your website is loaded within a web browser it can be interpreted in a different way by that web browser to the way it would be interpreted by another web browser. For example, how your website looks in Firefox® may not be how it looks in Internet Explorer®. Some pages will load faster than others depending on which web browser you use. In addition, some elements of web pages may not be supported, depending on which web browser you use. As a website developer you may be asked to develop a website which is compliant for two or three web browsers. Your job would therefore be to develop a website that appears consistently in all of these web browsers. Different web browsers all have their own advantages and disadvantages. For example, Chrome™ is good for HTML5 support, whereas Firefox® is good for its website developer add-on options. It is important to realise that, when using a web browser, there is not necessarily an even playing field. Each one is different and unique in its own way.

Server-side factors

Some of the factors affecting the performance of websites are server-side: that is, they relate to the capabilities and capacity of the web server being used and whether it has been bought or is rented.

- Bandwidth availability – This determines how much traffic can be handled by the web server; specifically, how much content can be downloaded at any one time. Bandwidth can be thought of as a pipe from the web server to the users. The bigger the pipe, the more that can be sent down it. Conversely, the larger the content to go down the pipe, the fewer bits of content that can go down it at any one time. The larger the web page and its associated files, the less users can download from it at any one time.

- File types – By using smaller file types which use **compression** methods, the website will have a faster download time. When deciding on which file types to use, a website developer must make a judgement in order to balance quality and file size, because the higher the quality, the larger the file size.

- Number of hits – The number of web page hits can have an effect on web page performance. For example, if too many people are on the same web page at the same time, then it can overload the web server and slow down the website's performance.

> **Key term**
>
> **Compression** – where a mathematical calculation is performed on a file in order to 'squash' it and make it smaller.

Client-side factors

Some of the factors affecting the performance of websites are client-side: that is, they relate to the capabilities of the user's computer system. If the capabilities of the user's system are poor, those people using that system might not be able to access certain websites, particularly those that suffer from poor server-side performance.

- Upload and download speeds – The speed of the user's internet connection will determine how quickly they are able to download or upload web pages.

- Processor speed – As the connection speed will determine the rate of download, so the computer's components will affect the speed with which the content is displayed and with which users can interact with it. You must take into consideration that a user's device may not have a fast processor or large memory capacity and so website developers must decide between high user specification requirements and a high number of visitors. Sites that rely heavily on client-side scripting such as JavaScript can put a significant load on a user's CPU.

Categories	Connection Method	Description	Typical Speed
Fixed line narrowband	Dial-up	This was the traditional method of connection. It uses the existing analogue telephone lines and it remained popular for many years. However, in 2013 BT turned off dial-up internet access service, in favour of broadband.	56 Kbps
	ISDN (integrated services digital network)	ISDN was used to generate faster speeds than dial-up. It still used a phone line to which digital lines needed to be connected. However, ISDN is slowly being phased out for much faster connection methods.	128 Kbps
Fixed line broadband	DSL (digital subscriber line)	Using digital lines, DSL was introduced. It is the most common method to provide a broadband service. The most common in the UK is ADSL (asynchronous digital subscriber line).	1 Mbps to 8 Mbps
	Broadband	This technology is constantly being developed and faster speeds are conceivable in the near future.	Cases of up to 100Mbps in England
	Fibre optic	This connection method utilises visible light as a transmission method. This is significantly more efficient and reliable than typical broadband which uses copper wires to send electrical signals.	Up to 1000Mbps
Wireless broadband	Mobile broadband	Mobile broadband is a wireless communication technology that uses mobile phone networks and can generate internet access to almost anywhere. This service is usually accessed through a mobile phone (smartphone).	Internet speeds vary. 384kbps to 30Mbps for 3G (3rd Generation). 4G speeds can go to 1000Mbps (1Gbps)
	Wireless hotspots	Wireless hotspots are places such as shops and cafés, which offer you free access to their broadband connection. You may need to be a member to get the password for the wireless connection.	Depends on the internet service provider and how many people are logged on

---

Research

Working in small groups or in pairs, research the differences between fibre to the home (FTTH) and fibre to the building (FTTB). How do these technologies work? What are the advantages and disadvantages of each?

▶ Cache memory – Cache memory may be the memory that your computer has. The bigger the memory the faster the computer will run. The cache memory is used to reduce the average time needed to access the memory. This means that the more memory you have, the quicker your computer is at dealing with the website you are accessing. The cache used by websites may be on the physical (eg hard drive in the form of temporary files) storage as well as within the computer's RAM.

▶ Browsers – As discussed in the section on Browser compliance, web browsers were not created equally. Some web browsers can affect the speed at which a web page can load.

▶ Interactivity – When you incorporate interactive elements into a web page, such as Flash images or games which are embedded, this can affect the speed at which the website can be loaded. The more interactivity a website has, the more time is needed for your computer system to download all the information. With new technologies such as 4G, 5G and fibre optics, this is less of a problem. Previously, it took time for the information to download and, consequently, was used sparingly. Now interactivity is standard and users tend to expect it within websites.

You have applied for an apprenticeship with a website development company, where you hope to prove to the recruitment manager that you are a competent website developer. Competition for the job is high, so you have been set a preliminary report-writing task to gauge your understanding of website development principles. Applicants who perform well in this task will progress to the next stage of the recruitment process.

You are to identify two websites with a similar theme, and compare the principles of website design that each website employs. It has been recommended that you take screenshots of any part of the website if you wish to back up your reasoning. You must conclude your report by analysing each website's suitability for their intended audience and purpose.

You should take this further and fully evaluate the way in which the principles of website design are used to produce creative, high performance websites which meet client requirements. You are free to choose which websites to use within your evaluation.

Plan

- What is the task? What am I being asked to do?
- How confident do I feel in my own abilities to complete this task? Are there any areas I think I may struggle with?

Do

- Have I spent some time planning my approach to the task at hand?
- Am I confident that I know what I am doing and that I know what it is I should be achieving?

Review

- I can explain what the task was and how I approached it.
- I can explain how I would approach the hard elements differently next time (i.e. what I would do differently).

B Design a website to meet client requirements

Once you understand the principles behind good website design, you will need to put this knowledge into practice by designing a website.

Website design

The website design process involves a number of steps which, if they were to be skipped, would cause major problems when the website **goes live**. There is a saying: 'If you fail to plan, you are planning to fail.' This saying very much applies to website development, but also to any design and development project.

> **Key term**
>
> **Goes live** – describes the first time a website has been uploaded to a web server and is made available to the public.

Problem definition statement requirements

Before a website can be built, a website developer must elicit as much information about the requirements of the website as they can from the client. The more information a website developer has about the client's requirements,

the more likely they will be to fulfil the requirements effectively. All the information about the requirements for the website will be collated within a problem definition statement.

Intended audience

Web designers must always have two sets of needs in mind: those of the client and those of the users. The client is the person who has commissioned the website and, usually, they are also the person who holds the purse strings. If the client is not happy with the website, you (the website developer) may not get paid for your work.

The users are the visitors to the website. They need to be attracted to the website initially, and then encouraged to revisit to make more purchases, to look at new content or take part in discussions on forums. One aim of websites is to persuade their users to bookmark the website, which increases the probability of them returning on a regular basis.

Full summary of the problem to be solved

A website developer will need to understand the full problem to be solved. This will require communication between the developer and the client. There are a number of ways in which this can be done. A commonly used method of requirements gathering is called SQIRO. SQIRO stands for sampling, questionnaires, interviews, research and observations. A website developer will use these techniques with the client so as to gather as much information as possible to fully understand the problem that the creation of the website is intended to solve.

Constraints

A client will need to understand the constraints of the website. The constraints are the limitations the website could have. Typical constraints of websites often include:

▸ money
▸ timescales
▸ staff training
▸ levels of security
▸ support and maintenance contracts.

Benefits

The reason why a client will approach a website developer is for the potential benefits that a website will bring to their business. The benefits for a business of having a website include:

▸ advertising for your products/service and of the business worldwide
▸ less expensive than printed media, radio and television advertising
▸ more accessible (24/7, 365 days a year) (you do not need to turn away customers because it is closing time since a website is accessible to customers at all times)
▸ other websites may link to you, spreading the word about your business's products or services
▸ it gives you the opportunity to gain long-term clients. (There is a difference between a client and customer. A customer is someone who walks in and buys something. A client is a regular customer who will often return to your website, which can help your business grow.)

Nature of interactivity

Most modern websites involve interactivity: that is, they are **interactive websites**. You risk losing users if you have only a **static website**. It is important to decide how much interactivity will feature on a website. Too little interactivity and users may lose interest, too much interactivity and they may feel overwhelmed. It is important to get the balance right.

For e-commerce websites, the web designer also needs to decide how online transactions will be performed. There are two parts to this issue.

1 How will the user browse the catalogue? For example, how will the items be listed in the catalogue? Consider e-commerce websites such as Amazon™. Amazon™ has items which are catalogued in a hierarchical fashion, where you can filter your preferences, such as the relevancy, date added, price (in ascending or descending order) and customer reviews.

2 How will users make purchases? Before a user will purchase an item, the website will need to register their details and credit/debit card information. This information is encrypted using a method called **transport layer security (TLS)**. PayPal™ uses such a method because it stores all your financial information, such as credit card details, so you do not need to give these to the website you are purchasing from.

Key terms

Interactive website – involves some level of activity from a simple feedback form to a database that personalises the website for each individual visitor. Changes can be made to the website 'on-the-fly'.

Static website – one with no interactivity, which is usually just a presentation of information. Changes to the website have to be hard-coded into the website.

Transport layer security (TLS) – is a protocol that makes certain that there is privacy between communicating applications and their users on the internet. TLS is the successor to the secure sockets layer (SSL) method.

Purpose requirements

Once all the available information has been gathered, the requirements are then generated. It is important that all the requirements that are gathered are SMART. When we refer to SMART requirements, we are saying that the requirements are as follows.

▶ **S**pecific – Targets a specific area of improvement.
▶ **M**easurable – It is possible to measure whether a requirement has been completed, that is, you can verify its completion. It is best to avoid any requirements that cannot be verified as complete.
▶ **A**chievable – The requirement must be achievable.
▶ **R**ealistic – The requirement can be realistically achieved with the available resources.
▶ **T**ime-constrained – The requirement can be achieved within the timeframe allocated.

Design ideas and prototyping

By this stage, you should understand the client's requirements for the website and what it needs to do. Therefore you can use design tools to design a website which can be presented to the client for approval. Once the design has been approved, it can be used to create a website that goes live. It is important to consider the principles of good website design when you create a website and ensure that these are incorporated within it.

> **Link**
>
> Look back at the Principles of website design to remind yourself of the fundamental principles which should be applied to any website design.

When developing any IT product, including websites, it is not uncommon for developers to build a prototype. This is usually done so that the user can have an idea of what the website will look like as well as what it will do. The idea for prototyping comes from engineering, where a prototype is often built before the construction on an assembly line to produce many copies.

Several tools can be used to ensure that all areas are considered when designing websites. By producing a thorough design, using the tools presented in this section, and using this design to communicate with your client, you can ensure that your client is happy with your plans before you build the website. This should reduce the problems that you would encounter if there was a mismatch between client expectations and the actual outcomes.

Diagrammatic illustrations

To convey the concept of a website, you might use one or more of the following tools.

Mood boards

The aim of a mood board is to produce something with the same feel as the website (see Figure 6.3). It is a useful way of focusing the design and demonstrating initial ideas to the client. Think of a mood board as a sketchbook where you can collate images, different typographies, fonts, artwork, sample layouts and so on. The mood board can be presented to the client who can decide what they like and do not like on it. Their feedback and amendments to the mood board can then help to focus the website developer on what the website should look and feel like.

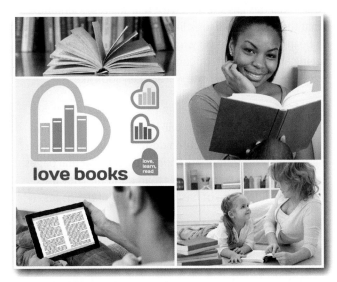

▶ **Figure 6.3:** Mood board picture example

 **PAUSE POINT**   Think of a website that you would like to develop. It could be for your favourite TV programme, your favourite computer game or an idea that you have for a business. For this website develop a list of:
- 10 SMART requirements for the website
- 10 website requirements which are not SMART.

Hint   Working with a peer, compare your requirements and work together to see if they are correct or not.

Extend   What do you feel would be the implications for the design and development of a website if you did not have SMART requirements governing it?

Storyboarding

Storyboarding is key to structuring a website clearly and is a way of expressing a navigational design (see Figure 6.4). Storyboarding is not just used in website design; it is often used in the design of moving images such as animations or films.

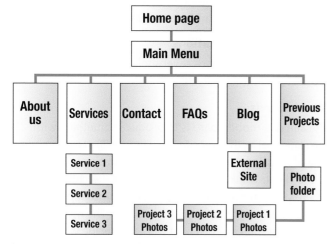

▶ **Figure 6.4:** Storyboard image artwork

Realistic representation

Your initial designs should give a realistic representation of what the website will look like. This is where it is important to be in communication with your client so that, upon seeing all your design documentation, the client can envisage what the website will actually look like.

Wireframe

To visualise what the pages will look like before building them, designers create screen designs or wireframes (see Figure 6.5). Wireframes are mock-ups of the actual pages, concentrating on layout rather than content. They also usually include some of basic **attributes** of the pages.

> **Key term**
>
> **Attributes** – additional information about your wireframe. For example, which font you will use, which font size you will use, where the sidebar will appear, alignment and so on.

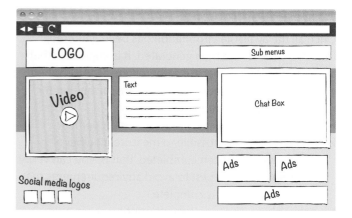

▶ **Figure 6.5:** Wireframe artwork

Site map

A site map is a list of pages of a website that is accessible to crawlers or users. It can be a document, in any form, which is also used as a planning tool for the website design, or a web page that lists the pages on a website. It also shows the relationship between the pages, representing how they are linked together.

Search engine optimisation

When designing a website the developer will need to consider the best way to maximise the number of users who visit the website. Therefore, it is important that the design conveys an effective solution which users will want to keep returning to. Websites which receive more traffic are more likely to be ranked highly in search engine results pages, which will be beneficial to the business because users are likely to click on the first relevant link they see. A good design is not in itself enough to get more users visiting a website, although it might mean that those who find the website will return. To get more users visiting your website in the first place, you need to employ SEO techniques to ensure that your website appears at the top of search engine results pages.

> **Link**
>
> For more on SEO see Search engine optimisation.

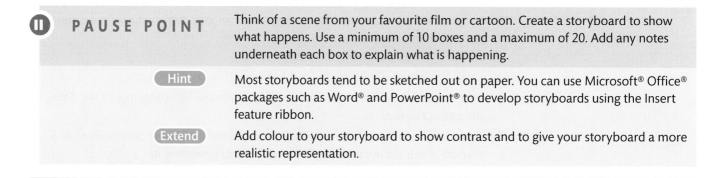

PAUSE POINT — Think of a scene from your favourite film or cartoon. Create a storyboard to show what happens. Use a minimum of 10 boxes and a maximum of 20. Add any notes underneath each box to explain what is happening.

Hint — Most storyboards tend to be sketched out on paper. You can use Microsoft® Office® packages such as Word® and PowerPoint® to develop storyboards using the Insert feature ribbon.

Extend — Add colour to your storyboard to show contrast and to give your storyboard a more realistic representation.

Alternative design ideas

Alternative design ideas should be considered and thought through in case problems are identified with your preferred design and also to give clients more choice in terms of the design they decide to go with. Alternative design ideas can be presented within your mood board and in storyboards. Once the client is happy with a particular design, you can focus on this design in a wireframe. Consideration must be given to design compatibility with mobile devices; this is something that will need to be discussed in the requirements stage. It is common these days for businesses to develop mobile-friendly versions of their websites. However, for smaller businesses, it might not be possible to develop a separate mobile website so the one website needs to be suitable for viewing on desktop computers and on mobile devices. With HTML5 it is now more common to develop a responsive website that dynamically adjusts elements to work in any size browser/screen without having multiple versions to maintain.

Discussion

Using your PC, go to uk.pearson.com to be consistent with screenshots and notice the design (see Figure 6.6). Now using your smartphone or tablet device, go to **uk.pearson.com** (see Figure 6.7). Can you see the difference? Notice how the two websites look different despite being the same website. This is done for user convenience and compatibility. Discuss, in your class, how you think a website developer would go about making this possible?.

Client-side scripting design

Client-side scripting refers to websites where the script is executed client side (by the user's web browser) instead of server side (on the web server). JavaScript is a programming language that enables client-side scripting and can be used to create interactivity within web pages.

Prior to coding or scripting, appropriate designing must take place. This must be done to inform a website developer of the function that the website must perform. When they have all available design documentation, the website developer can then create the website.

Flowcharts

Flowcharts are diagrams that are used by software developers to represent a solution to a given problem. Flowcharts involve boxes of different kinds, used to represent different things, and arrows that show how the boxes relate to one another (see Table 6.3 and Figure 6.8).

▶ **Table 6.3:** British Computer Society (BCS) flowchart symbols with descriptions

Flowchart symbol	Description
⬭	An oval shape represents a start or end point
⟶	An arrow is a connector that shows the relationship between representative shapes
▭	A rectangle shape represents a process
▱	A parallelogram represents where an input or output will take place
◇	A diamond shape represents where a decision will be made

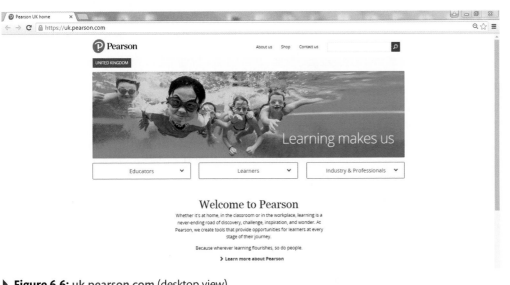

▶ **Figure 6.6:** uk.pearson.com (desktop view)

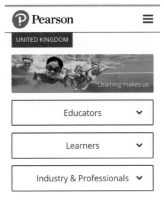

▶ **Figure 6.7:** uk.pearson.com (mobile view)

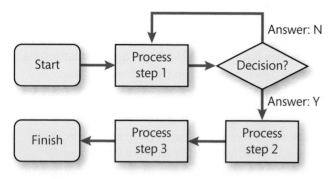

▶ **Figure 6.8:** A flowchart example

Pseudocode

Pseudocode helps programmers develop **algorithms** by forming an intermediary step between an explanation in English (or another natural language) and the coding language. By using pseudocode, a designer can plan what the code will do, without having to worry about ensuring that the correct words and syntax are used.

Ready-made and/or original assets

Assets include animations, graphics, audio and videos. All of these assets can be embedded within a web page to provide additional interactivity, information or context.

Ready-made assets

It is important, if you are using pre-existing, ready-made assets, that you seek the owner's permission to use their assets on your website, as there could be copyright issues. If you do not seek the owner's permission to use an asset, you will be in breach of the UK's Copyright, Designs and Patents Act 1988. The maximum penalty for breaking this law is a possible prison sentence and/or a large fine. Therefore it is essential that you get permission from the owner of any asset that is not copyright free before using it in your website. Getting permission will sometimes, but not always, involve paying a fee.

Original assets

It is simpler to use original assets: that is, ones that you have created yourself from scratch. Any animations, graphics, audio or video that you create yourself can be embedded within your website without any possibility of infringement of copyright, as long as they are not based in any way on someone else's work. (You are the copyright owner of these assets.) You do, however need to be careful of certain issues when creating your own original assets, for example photographs. If you take photographs of people, you need them to sign a model release form that gives you permission to use the photograph that they appear in as you wish.

Obtaining and using feedback from others

When you have completed your website designs it is important to gather feedback from others (including the client and potential users) to see if the designs meet the requirements and could be refined in any way to make them better. This is a crucial part of the design and development process because if issues were found with the design after the developer starts building the website this is likely to lead to delays. Also the website may not be as good as it might have been, because time and cost constraints might mean that compromises have to be made. Therefore, it is important to obtain feedback on designs before they are implemented, to determine if any refinements need to be made.

The feedback stage is also an opportunity to identify any technical and design constraints. By identifying them at this stage, you will be able to come up with alternative

▶ **Table 6.4:** Pseudocode example and JavaScript equivalent

Pseudocode	JavaScript
Age = input from user	Age=prompt("Enter age", "");
If age>= 18 then	If (age>=18)
Print onscreen "Hello World"	{document.write("Hello World");}
Else	Else
Print onscreen "I am x years old"	{document.write("I am " + age + " years old");}

design solutions to overcome any constraints, before it is too late to do anything about them. In addition, the website development process is recursive, meaning that you can go back and adapt the designs to factor in the feedback of others before going ahead with development, not just once but repeatedly until the design is right (keeping in mind time and cost constraints, of course).

One method of obtaining feedback is to use a questionnaire. Questionnaires can be used to gather feedback and determine areas of strength and areas in need of improvement. Questionnaires use two main types of questioning, **quantitative** and **qualitative**.

Examples of quantitative questioning

▶ On a scale of 1–10 how would you rate the overall aesthetics of the website?
▶ Could you navigate through the website effectively? With answer options such as 'Yes, easily', 'Yes', 'Yes with difficulty', 'No', 'No, it was very difficult'.
▶ Did you find the pop-up boxes a distraction or were they beneficial? With answers options such as 'Distraction' or 'Beneficial'.

Examples of qualitative questioning

▶ What did you enjoy most about the website?
▶ How could we improve your website experience?
▶ Do you have any feedback about the website you think we should be aware of?

> **Key terms**
>
> **Quantitative questioning** – questions have a definitive answer, either a numerical value or specific answers in ranges. It focuses on statistical analysis.
>
> **Qualitative questioning** – questions do not have definitive answers. It provides answers as to how or why and is used to gauge opinions and get more detailed feedback.

> **Link**
>
> For more on quantitative and qualitative questioning see Test users and user feedback in *Unit 7: Mobile Apps Development*.

Using the test information

It is recommended that you get several people to test your website. This is because someone may identify an issue not noticed by yourself or your other testers. However, you cannot test forever as you will be bound by time and budget constraints. Therefore, once you have the information, you must use it to refine the website, where necessary. Any errors that are spotted must be changed. For example, if a link within the website does not work as expected, this must be resolved. It is also an opportunity for the website to be tested on different web browsers

---

⏸ PAUSE POINT

Part 1:
Create a wireframe for a website based on a theme of your choosing. This wireframe will be for the homepage. Be sure to include all necessary attributes in your design and to apply the principles of website design.

Part 2:
Develop a questionnaire for potential users about your homepage which poses five quantitative questions and five qualitative questions.

Part 3:
Ask a peer in your group to complete your questionnaire about your homepage. They should answer your quantitative and qualitative questions and critique your wireframe design, citing any areas in need of improvement. (If you are able, ask more than one person to complete your questionnaire; this could include family and friends.)

Part 4:
Based on the questionnaire feedback, make any necessary or beneficial refinements to your wireframe design for the homepage.

Hint
If you are developing your wireframe using a package such as Microsoft® Word® or Excel®, remember to change the page orientation to landscape to give you more room. Also, annotate your designs effectively using the Comments feature within the Review section of the ribbon.

Extend
Explain how your website fulfils the fundamental principles of website design. Annotate your wireframe design indicating where you have adopted these principles.

and on different mobile devices. Different web browsers render code in different ways, which is why some websites look different depending on which web browser you are using.

This test data is invaluable, as you can then refine the website and streamline it to make sure that it is fit for purpose and meets the needs of the client.

Discussion

In small groups or in pairs, discuss why it is important to get other people to test your website. What do you feel are the implications of not doing so? Furthermore, what are the potential problems of testing a website yourself only?

Testing plan

A testing plan is used to test functionality. In other words, a testing plan is used to check that all parts of the website work as they should. Sometimes, this is referred to as 'black box' testing as it focuses on functionality as opposed to the internal mechanics or workings of a program. This is where, prior to the website being built, a series of tests or test data is developed so that, when the website *is* built, the test data can be used to see if all parts of the website work as they should.

Research

Compare black box testing to white box testing. What are the differences between the two?

Link

For more on black box testing see Testing a mobile app in *Unit 7: Mobile Apps Developments*.

The elements that occur within a test plan are:
▶ test number
▶ purpose of test
▶ additional data on test eg which web page
▶ test data
▶ expected results.

Link

For explanations of these elements of a test plan see Test plans in *Unit 5: Data modelling*.

Tip

When developing your test plan, change your page orientation to landscape. This will give you more space and enable you to type more.

Example testing plan

Remember to test all parts of the website and not just those elements that appear on the home page. It is important to test a range of features and attributes of the web pages, not just the links. For example, you should test whether images appear but also test for browser compliance: that is, ensure that it looks correct in different browsers. See Table 6.5 for part of an example test plan.

▶ **Table 6.5:** Example test plan

Test number	Purpose of test	On page	Test data	Expected result
1	Test the home button	about.html	Left click	Load home.html
2	Logo.gif	home.html	Load page	Appears in the centre of the page
3	Test the alt/title tag of Logo.gif	home.html	Hover over Logo	Tool text tip appears

Link

Refer to *Unit 4: Software Design and Development Project* for more details on testing.

Technical and design constraints

Constraints are limitations or restrictions that may make it more difficult to design and develop a website. They may limit the scope or complexity of the website you design. Constraints tend to fit into two categories: technical and design constraints. Some of the possible constraints are outlined here.

PAUSE POINT Develop a series of 10 tests which could be used to test the functionality of a website of your own choosing.

Hint If you are not comfortable using tables in Word® to do this, consider using Excel®, which is just as effective.

Extend Work with a peer within your group to see what additional tests they have thought of, and apply these to your test plan. This will help both of you to have a wider range of tests in your test plans.

Technical constraints

▶ IT staff – The skills needed for the creation of the website might not be available, meaning that staff would need to be trained or recruited to complete the required design and development work.

▶ IT equipment – The website might require specialised hardware or software that may need to be bought in or installed before the website design and development can proceed.

Design constraints

▶ Financial – The client's requirements for their website might not be feasible within their budget. A budget will have been agreed with the client and you have to work within that budget. However, if the client wants features that would cost more than the budget, you can present this information to the client. They may choose to increase the budget so that they can have the additional features or they may compromise on the features to keep the budget the same.

Theory into practice

When undertaking a project which requires you to be time constrained (it needs to be built by a specified date), it is important that timescales are built in to ensure that the final website is completed on time.

When working in the IT industry, it is extremely likely that you will be given tasks that need to completed within a specified time frame. Therefore, you have to set relevant targets with deadlines for when each target needs to be achieved. This must include contingency planning, such as taking into consideration the feedback from others (and so having to make improvements), as well as the possibility that you might be ill for a few days.

1 Write a list of sensible targets which could be given specified deadlines for the process of designing and developing a website: that is, milestones within the design and development.

2 Once you have this list of milestones, allocate amounts of time for the completion of each of these stages.

3 Put each stage into a schedule, using the amount of time allocated for each stage, to determine the dates by which they would need to be completed (using an end date of your choice).

4 Write a list of factors that might affect your ability to complete your milestones on time, such as being ill.

▶ Flexibility – You need to design a website to work on different platforms (both on desktop computers and mobile devices), then you will need to consider this constraint when designing the website.

Legal and ethical considerations

We need to consider the legal and ethical considerations involved when designing and developing websites. For example, there are laws that protect an individual's intellectual property and those that ensure that an individual's personal data is not released.

Copyright, Designs and Patents Act 1988

The Copyright, Designs and Patents Act 1988 protects all original works such as music, art, writing and programming code once it is tangible, which means once it is in a fixed form (for example, a music album is released or a book is published). These original works are the intellectual property of the individuals who created them. As the internet has become such an important part of everyday life, the question of whether websites are subject to protection under copyright laws has often been discussed. It is now accepted that a website becomes tangible once it is coded and saved onto storage media, so websites are now protected by copyright.

Data Protection Act 1998

The Data Protection Act 1998 was designed to protect sensitive data held in databases. It was originally passed in 1984, with an update in 1998, which was brought into effect in 2000. It is upheld by the Information Commissioner's Office. Every business that stores data (that is, information about customers), must register and state the data they plan to hold.

There are eight principles of the Data Protection Act 1998 (see Figure 6.9). The data subject is the person to whom the data refers. Under the act, the data subject has several specific rights, including:

▶ the right to compensation for unauthorised disclosure of data

▶ the right to get inaccurate data corrected or removed

▶ the right to access data and apply for verification or erasure where it is inaccurate.

Prior to development, a website designer must consider how the Data Protection Act could affect their website. For example, a website that collects users' data, such as an enquiry form asking for personal information (eg your surname, forename and phone number) should include a Privacy Policy that informs website visitors how you retain, process, disclose and purge their data in line with the act.

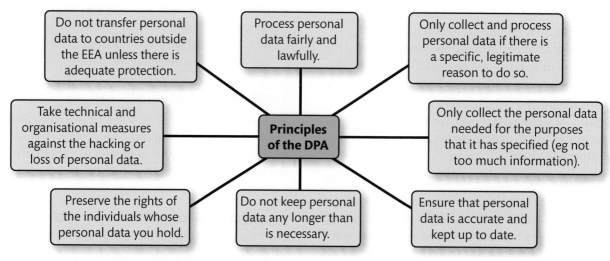

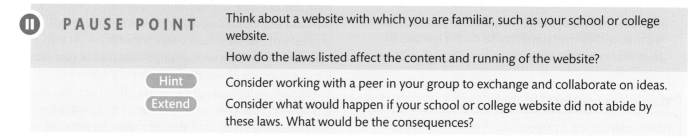

▶ **Figure 6.9:** The eight principles of the Data Protection Act 1998

⏸ **PAUSE POINT**   Think about a website with which you are familiar, such as your school or college website.

How do the laws listed affect the content and running of the website?

Hint   Consider working with a peer in your group to exchange and collaborate on ideas.

Extend   Consider what would happen if your school or college website did not abide by these laws. What would be the consequences?

Common tools and techniques used to produce websites

It is important that, once appropriate designs have been approved and completed, different tools and techniques for development are explored in order to meet the client requirements.

HTML

HTML (hypertext markup language) is the most commonly used markup language, so much so that all others are just about extinct. It forms the basis of all worldwide web pages, even if other languages are used for parts of them.

HTML uses a system of tags (indicated by angle brackets < and >) which contain the instructions. Almost all instructions come in a pair of open and closed tags enclosing the content to be affected, for example `<font color="red">Some text</font>` would produce 'Some text'. Note that American spelling is used in HTML. HTML pages should start with `<html>` and end with `</html>` tags to declare the language being used.

HTML5

HTML5 is the current hypertext markup language standard used for structuring and presenting content on the worldwide web. Website developers should always work to the current standard so, when developing your web pages, you should code using this standard. Tags for changing the font are no longer required in HTML5; instead, cascading style sheets (CSS) should be used. It is likely that there will be subsequent updates, leading to HTML6, which will then become the new standard that website developers should use.

HTML5 was finalised by the **World Wide Web Consortium (W3C)**. HTML5 has a larger set of technologies that allows for more diverse interactivity and more powerful websites and applications.

Link

For an introduction to HTML5 elements and tags, see HTML5 Introduction at www.w3schools.com

Key term

World Wide Web Consortium (W3C) – an international community that develops open standards for the use of HTML5 to ensure the long-term growth of the worldwide web.

Tables

Tables used in HTML begin with the `<table>` tag. Tables should not be used to structure websites (which has been done in the past), because it causes accessibility and browser rendering issues. Instead, the `<table>` tag should be used only to present a table on a web page. For example, if you are presenting the opening times of a shop.

Forms

Forms are used in website development to collect user input. There are different ways of collecting user input using forms.

▶ Text field – This defines a one-line input field for text input.

```
<form>
  Please enter your first name:<br>
  <input type="text" name="firstname">
  <br>
  Please enter your age:<br>
  <input type="text" name="age">
</form>
```

▶ Text area – Allows you to have more user input.

```
<form>
  <textarea name="textarea"> Please enter your text here</textarea>
</form>
```

▶ Submit button – Defines a button for submitting a form to a form handler.

```
<form action="test_page.php">
  Where were you born?:<br>
  <input type="text" name="birthplace">
  <br>
  Where do you currently live?:<br>
  <input type="text" name="livingplace">
  <input type="submit" value="submit">
</form>
```

▶ Radio buttons – Radio buttons let a user select one of a limited number of choices.

```
<form>

  Are you sure?
  <input type="radio" name="validation" value="yes" checked>YES
  <br>
  <input type="radio" name="validation" value="no">NO
</form>
```

▶ Check boxes – As opposed to radio buttons, which only let you select one of a limited number of choices, check boxes allow you to select more than one choice.

```
<form>

  I own the following:<br>
  <input type="checkbox" name="games">Playstation<br>
  <input type="checkbox" name="games">XBox<br>
</form>
```

Navigation

Navigation is a way of moving around a web page to find what you need. At first, the worldwide web was restricted to simply using hyperlinks. However, as time has progressed and technology has advanced, new ways of navigating a website have been developed.

▸ Menus – Menus can appear anywhere within a web page, but most website developers tend to place them towards the top of a web page. Instead of traditional hyperlinks, these menus are more attractive and aesthetically pleasing. Visitors to a website can click on a menu and it will redirect them to the page they are looking for. Alternatively, sometimes when you hover over a menu a sub-menu will appear (see Figure 6.10).

▸ **Figure 6.10:** Menu and sub-menu

▸ Hyperlinks – Hyperlinks are links that, when clicked on, take you to a particular part of the website (an internal link) or they will take you to another website (an external link). Hyperlinks can be text, images or buttons.

▸ Anchors – Anchors are used to redirect a visitor to a certain part of a web page. For example, if you are reading a long document online, at the beginning of the web page there will be links to the beginning of each section within the document. By clicking on one of these section links you will be redirected to the precise point in the web page that you require.

Interactive components

Interactive components are used as a means of enhancing the look and feel of a website. However, a web page should not be littered with too many interactive components because they increase the download time and can make a website look amateurish. Interactivity involves two-way communication between the user and the computer. In other words, it requires input from the user which provokes a response from the computer. This could include giving feedback, searching a catalogue of products or purchasing a product from a website. To have a full catalogue of products would require a database and server-side scripting.

Research

What are the components involved in server-side scripting? Research, compare and contrast 'PHP' with 'ASP'. Which do you believe is best suited for server-side processing?

▸ Hot spots – A hot spot is an area of an image that acts as a hyperlink. When a person clicks on a hot spot, a hyperlink takes the user to another web page.

▸ Pop-ups – These are small internet windows that pop up on your screen to get a user's attention (see Figure 6.11). Sometimes they can be considered annoying or dangerous. They are often used by advertisers. The first

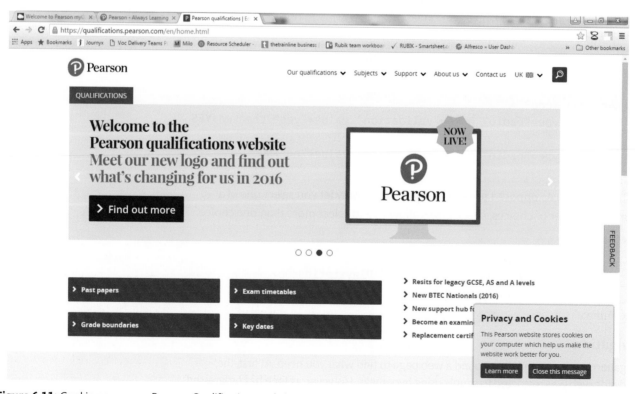

▸ **Figure 6.11:** Cookie pop-up on Pearson Qualifications website

time you visit a website, a pop-up will appear to tell you that cookies for that website will be downloaded to your PC (this is now a legal requirement) and you have to accept them to continue using the website. The cookie that is downloaded remembers that you have visited the website, so the next time you visit it the pop-up will not appear. However, the cookie might have tailored the website based on any customisable choices you made last time you visited.

- Buttons – These look like command buttons in that, when you press them, they will depress like a conventional button. Buttons have different purposes, one of which can be to take you to another web page.

- Rollover images – A rollover image is a secondary image loaded into your web page to display when a user on your website rolls their mouse over (rolls over) a certain image within your website. It is used to make your website more interactive. For example, some clothing websites display one image of a piece of clothing but when you roll over the image another view of the piece of clothing is shown.

Colour schemes, styles and templates

- Modern web design, within HTML5, uses templates with built-in colour schemes and styles. There are templates which are free to download and some that you have to pay for. These templates are built using a technique called cascading style sheets (CSS), which is discussed further in the next section.

- What makes an appropriate or pleasing template is subjective, that is, a matter of opinion. Quite often the colour scheme and styles used by your website will determine its theme. Therefore for you must choose appropriate colours and styles for the type and content of your website. For example, if you are producing a website for a nursery, it would make sense to use a playful font and a variety of bright colours, whereas, if you are producing a professional corporate website, then a more minimalistic look using a small colour palette and contrasting backgrounds is considered best.

Discussion

Investigate different colour combinations that you could use for a website which is education based. Think about accessibility issues such as colour blindness. Discuss, in a small groups, which colour combinations would be best suited and explain your reasoning. Use the BBC website for more information.

Cascading style sheets

It is good practice to use the same layout and styling throughout a website. Cascading style sheets (CSS) are used to ensure standardised formatting across a website. CSS allows you to create a standard layout and style which can easily be applied across all the web pages within a website. They are cascading in that when you make a change in one place within a website this change will be cascaded to all the web pages within the website that use that style. This makes altering and maintaining the design of the website much easier. For example, in HTML to change the font colour of all the titles in a website to red would have involved changing each one individually. But now, using HTML5 and CSS, only one value would need to be changed, and the change would be immediately applied throughout the website for every title.

Link

For more on how to apply CSS to web pages see Using cascading style sheets.

The World Wide Web Consortium

The World Wide Web Consortium (W3C) is a body which promotes the standardisation of web design, especially of HTML. It aims to ensure universal accessibility of the web. For example, they promote the need for all websites to be displayed on a variety of browsers and resolutions so that they are usable by people with special needs. The W3C produces guidelines and tools for standardising websites which contribute towards increased accessibility. HTML compliance plays an important factor in this because if we use outdated HTML coding techniques or conventions this prevents a website from becoming fully accessible.

Link

For more on the W3C and their Web Accessibility Initiative visit their website: **http://www.w3.org/WAI/**

Accessibility features

- Alternative tags (alt tag) – An alt tag is a text alternative for an image or object on your web page (see Figure 6.12). If the image cannot be displayed the **alt** tag will be read in its place. The alt tag will be read by screen readers and other website readers as an alternative to the image itself. This is a necessity for blind users who use the internet, as the screen reader will tell the blind user what the image is, by reading the alt tag aloud. Therefore alt tags need to meaningful: that is, say what is shown in the image in the context of the text on the page.

▶ **Figure 6.12:** As you can see by hovering over the magnifying glass, the title tag is clearly stated as 'Search'. This means that a screen reader will be able to read this and a blind person will know what this icon is.

▶ Zoom features – Web browsers have a feature which allows the user to zoom in or out, making the content on the screen larger or smaller depending on their preference. This is particularly useful for users who have poor vision.

▶ Text-to-speech – For visually impaired users, text-to-speech (TTS) is very useful. It is a type of speech synthesis application that is used to create a spoken sound version of the text in a web page.

Platform compatibility

When developing websites, it is important that they are tested across a range of different platforms, particularly if it is part of the client's brief that the website should be usable on these platforms. These platforms can be broken into three categories:

▶ web browsers

▶ operating systems

▶ mobile devices.

When testing a website, you must ensure that it has a consistent appearance across these different platforms. The consequence of not doing this is that your website may display incorrectly on one or more web browsers, using a particular operating system or on certain mobile devices. Consider that every user visiting your website may use a different combination of browser and operating system, or be using a mobile device. Therefore, you must cater for all platforms and test your website to ensure that it appears the same across them all.

Obviously, developing a website to be compatible across multiple platforms is expensive, so this is an important constraint and consideration for clients and website developers. It might be that, initially, a client decides to focus on ensuring compatibility with only the most popular web browsers and the most popular mobile device operating systems, with the intention of ensuring compatibility with the others once the website has been established successfully on the most popular ones.

Embedding and compression of assets into suitable file types

Compression is a way of making a file smaller so that it uses less disk space. By using smaller file types that use compression methods, the website will have a faster download time making it more user-friendly. When deciding on which file types to use, a website developer must make a judgement in order to balance quality and file size because the higher the quality, the larger the file size. Once you have put your assets into the appropriate file types, they can be embedded within your web page. However, consideration also needs to be given as to what type of asset you are going to select.

Image files

There are two image file types available: bitmap and vector.

Bitmap file types include .gif and .jpeg. A .gif file has a maximum palette of 256 colours, and should, therefore, be used when the quality of the colour images is not that high and for images that do not contain many shades of colour. A .jpeg has a larger colour palette and is, therefore, better for high-quality colour images that include a lot of shading.

For a comparison of bitmap and vector images, see Table 6.6.

Digital sound files

Sound travels in waves. Natural sound waves are continuous and analogue. Digital sound waves are sampled at regular intervals with gaps, which are so small that the human ear cannot detect them. Once these signals are combined, the whole piece is a series of waves that denote the characteristics of the sound. As a computer can only understand 0s and 1s, the value of each part of the wave is converted into a binary value, for example 0000, 0001, 0010, 0011. These values are then translated by the computer into sound output.

There are several types of sound file type available, each with its own method of sampling and compression. A .wav file has a high sample rate, which means that the sound quality is closest to that produced by actual instruments, but it has a relatively large file size. A .mp3 file tends to have a lower sample rate and therefore produces a smaller file size. (This is how MP3 players manage to store such a high volume of music.) However, there is a loss of quality with .mp3 files compared with .wav files, depending on the compression rate chosen. The higher the compression rate, the smaller the file size, but this is at the cost of some fidelity. Consideration must also be given to the types of music **plug-ins** that a user is likely to have, as this may restrict the choice of compression rate available.

> **Key term**
>
> **Plug-in** – Software that will play specific types of files. For example, modern versions of web browsers like Internet® Explorer® come with Flash® Player which is a plug-in to allow the user to play Flash® animations.

Digital video and animation files

Videos and animations can seriously affect the speed at which a website is able to load and, in general, should be used sparingly. Both video and animation file types can produce very large file sizes.

Traditionally for users to be able to view videos or animations embedded within a web page, they used to have to click on them and download them. Due to the size of the files, this would often take a relatively long time and control a large proportion of bandwidth during the download, even with a high-quality internet connection. Files like this also take up a large proportion of web server space. However, with the advent of HTML5, more videos are being embedded into web pages which can now show animations and video without the need of a plug-in. Therefore, there is no longer the requirement for constant plug-in updates and this means that videos and animations will run much more quickly and seamlessly.

Exporting digital assets

Once your digital assets have been created and developed using an appropriate file type, these files can then be exported for website use. When exporting your files, you should develop a folder directory which will store all your assets including images, sounds, videos and animations, as well as CSS files. This will mean that all your files will be stored appropriately and you will be able to refer to them when you code your website solution.

▶ **Table 6.6:** Comparison of bitmap and vector images

Feature	Bitmap	Vector
Nature of file type	Each pixel is saved individually with its location, colours and other details.	Coordinates of points and curves are saved as a mathematical equation.
File size	Generally has a large file size.	Generally has a small file size.
Resizing	The image will become pixelated.	The image will retain clarity.
File formats	.bmp, .gif, .jpg, .png	.pdf and .eps.
Created by	Programs such as Microsoft® Paint and Adobe® Photoshop®.	Programs such as Adobe® Illustrator® and CorelDRAW®.
Used for	Usually used in web pages as they are rendered by all graphical browsers.	Often used for graphics such as logos which need to be resized.
Shapes	N/A	Drawn in Adobe® Flash®.

Develop a website to meet client requirements

Once your website design is complete, when it has been tested, when all the assets have been prepared and when the client has approved it, the website can be built.

Website development

The first element that needs to be created to build an interactive website is the structure. This will provide a solid basis for the content, which can then be easily inserted. Extra features, such as interactivity and audio-visual elements can then be added. Once the website has been built, all elements must then be tested to ensure that they are functioning correctly. Once the website developer is happy that there are no bugs in the website, it can be uploaded to a web server and go live on the internet. This section will cover the creation of interactive websites.

Using cascading style sheets and accessing CSS from HTML

Cascading style sheets (CSS) allow you to create a standard layout and style which can be easily used on each web page in the site. Due to this standardisation, it is also easier to alter and maintain the site. For example, in HTML to change the font colour of all the titles to green would involve changing each one individually. When using CSS, only one value would need to be changed, and the change would immediately be applied (cascaded) throughout the whole site for every title.

CSS can be written into the HTML in three different ways: inline, header and external.

Inline

The CSS is defined in the same area of the code as that to which it is to be applied.

```
inline.html
1    <!DOCTYPE html>
2    <html>
3    <body>
4
5    <h1 style="color:red; Font-family: Courier New; font-size: 40pt;">
6    This demonstrates an example of inline CSS Heading</h1>
7
8    </body>
9    </html>
```

Header

The CSS is defined in the head section of each web page and applied throughout the website.

```
header.html
1     <!DOCTYPE html>
2     <html>
3     <head>
4     <style>
5     H1 {
6     Background: red;
7     Color: white;
8     Font-family: Times New Roman;
9     }
10    </style>
11    </head>
12    <body>
13    <h1>An example of header CSS</h1>
14    </body>
15    </html>
16
```

External

The CSS is defined in a separate file, which all web pages can reference. This is a .css file, rather than a .html file. The line, which can be put in the head of the HTML to link to the external CSS pages, is shown in Figure 6.13.

```
  external.html    styles.css
1      <!DOCTYPE html>
2     <html>
3     <head>
4        <link rel="stylesheet" href="styles.css">
5     </head>
6     <body>
7
8     <h1>This demonstrating what happens to the header tag</h1>
9     <p>This is demonstrating what happens to the paragraph tag</p>
10
11    </body>
12    </html>
```

```
  external.html    styles.css
1     body {
2         background-color: grey;
3     }
4
5     h1 {
6         color: green;
7         font-size: 25pt;
8         font-style: italic;
9         font-weight: bold;
10        font-family: Arial;
11        text-align: center;
12
13
14    }
15
16    p {
17        color:white;
18    }
```

See the examples in Figure 6.13 and Figure 6.14.

▸ **Figure 6.13:** Example 1 of external CSS being applied

Example of h1

Example of h2

▶ **Figure 6.14:** Example 2 of external CSS being applied

Other features of CSS

CSS can be used to alter the layout and formatting of any web page. Here are some examples of the hundreds of properties that can be changed.

These properties use the external method of applying CSS.

▶ Changing the background colour:

```
     Body
     {
          Background-color:yellow;
     }
```

▶ Changing the background image:

```
     Body
     {
     Background-image: url('picture.jpg'); }
```

▶ Formatting text:

```
1    <!DOCTYPE html>
2    <html>
3    <head>
4      <link rel="stylesheet" href="styles.css">
5    </head>
6    <body>
7
8    <h1>How to format text using CSS</h1>
9
10
11   </body>
12   </html>
```

These properties use the header method of applying CSS.

```
1    H1
2    {
3    Font-family:serif;
4    Font-style: italic;
5    Font-weight: bold;
6    Font-size: 50px;
7    color:red;
8    }
9
```

▶ Applying borders:

```
1    <!DOCTYPE html>
2    <html>
3    <head>
4    <style>
5    p.border1 {
6        border-style: groove;
7        border-width: 5px;
8    }
9
10   p.border2 {
11       border-style: double solid;
12       border-width: medium;
13   }
14
15   </style>
16   </head>
17   <body>
18
19   <h1>How to apply borders</h1>
20
21   <p class="border1">Example of Border1</p>
22   <p class="border2">Example of Border2</p>
23
24   </body>
25   </html>
```

▶ Applying padding:

```
  Padding.html
   1      <!DOCTYPE html>
   2      <html>
   3      <head>
   4      <style>
   5      td {
   6          padding: 15px;
   7      }
   8      </style>
   9      </head>
  10      <body>
  11      <h1>Table Padding</h1>
  12      <table>
  13        <tr>
  14          <th>Firstname</th>
  15          <th>Lastname</th>
  16          <th>Sex</th>
  17        </tr>
  18        <tr>
  19          <td>Michelle</td>
  20          <td>Rowden</td>
  21          <td>Female</td>
  22        </tr>
  23        <tr>
  24          <td>Michael</td>
  25          <td>Bean</td>
  26          <td>Male</td>
  27        </tr>
  28        <tr>
  29          <td>Kelvin</td>
  30          <td>Andrew</td>
  31          <td>Male</td>
  32        </tr>
  33      </table>
  34      </body>
  35      </html>
```

Step by step: Creating a simple CSS Page   4 Steps

1 Open Notepad++ or similar text editor. Save the file as myCSSwebpage.html.

▼

2 Enter this code and then save the file.

```
   1      <!DOCTYPE html>
   2      <html>
   3      <head>
   4      <title>My First CSS</title>
   5      <link rel="stylesheet" href="myCSS.css">
   6      </head>
   7      <body>
   8      Here is some normal text.
   9      <br>
  10      <h1>Here is the text with CSS tags.</h1>
  11      </body>
  12      </html>
```

▼

3 Create another new file and save it as myCSS.css. Enter the following code and then save the file.

```
1  h1 {
2    font-family: Arial;
3    color: red;
4    font-size: 20pt;
5  }
6
```

▼

4 Navigate to where the.html file is saved using My Computer. Then double click your html file to open in your browser.

PAUSE POINT

Following on from the Step by step, complete the following.

1 In myCSS.css, change the font to Wingdings. Save the .css file and refresh the .html file in the browser.

2 In myCSS.css, change the colour to blue and the size to 100pt. Save the .css file and refresh the .html file in the browser.

3 Now that you have done this, save an image from the internet and embed this into your css.

4 Develop the website to have different alignment of content.

Hint   Use the external method of CSS as it is easier to separate the HTML from the CSS. Sometimes, this makes development of your website easier.

Extend   Consider how to position your elements on your web page so that it is not restricted to alignments.

CSS box model

Key term

Pixel perfect – is a term used in the design sector to describe graphics that are accurate to the very last pixel.

CSS is used to create layouts on web pages. Using this method, the pages can be viewed in any web browser or at any resolution and the integrity of the design should remain. This is because the layout is recalculated on each opening. The resulting web page can therefore be designed very accurately, and can be **pixel perfect**.

The CSS box model structures the web page in a similar way to a table. Margins, borders, padding and content are each defined (see Figure 6.15 for an example).

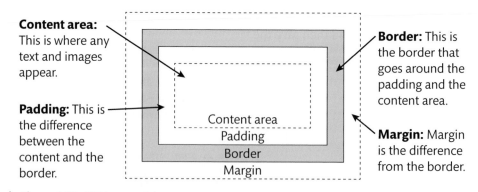

Content area: This is where any text and images appear.

Padding: This is the difference between the content and the border.

Border: This is the border that goes around the padding and the content area.

Margin: Margin is the difference from the border.

▶ **Figure 6.15:** CSS box model

▶ Content area – Where the text and images which will be displayed on the web page should be placed. There can be more than one content area on a web page.

▶ Padding – The blank space around the content area, which ensures that the content is not displayed right up to the edges of the border.

- Border – The design surrounding the padding and content area, which defines the edge of the box.
- Margin – The blank space around everything so that the box does not display right up to the edges of the screen.

The padding, border and margin are optional and, if not defined, are set at a default value of zero. At this value they would be invisible.

HTML

It is important to realise that HTML evolves throughout time, and the most current up-to-date version of HTML is HTML5. In HTML5 there are new tags that have been introduced, and some tags that were present in previous versions have been removed.

Research

Research the differences between HTML 4.01 and HTML5. What are the new tags which have been brought in, which have been removed and what are the other differences? What do you feel the challenges are of using HTML5?

Table 6.7 describes some common HTML tags, their purpose and examples.

▶ **Table 6.7:** Common HTML tags

Open tag	Close tag	Purpose	Example
`<font>`	`</font>`	Changes text. Open tag can have parameters such as colour, size, face.	`<font face="Arial" size="16">Text</font>`
`<strong>`	`</strong>`	Makes text bold.	`<strong>Text</strong>`
`<em>`	`</em>`	Makes text italic.	`<em>Text</em>`
`<li>`	`</li>`	Creates a list with bullet points.	`<li>first item</li>` `<li>second item</li>`

`<table>`	`</table>`	Creates a table (`<tr>` creates rows and `<td>` creates columns).	`<table border=1>`
			`<tr>`
			`<td>top left</td>`
			`<td>top right</td>`
			`</tr>`
			`<td>bottom left</td>`
			`<td>bottom right</td>`
			`</tr>`
			`</table>`

`<img>`	No close tag	Inserts an image. One of the rare tags that is not in a pair.	`<img src="Images\logo.gif">`
`<a href>`	`</a>`	Creates a hyperlink. Can be used around text or an image.	`<a href="index.html">Go to home page</a>` `<a href="index.html"><img src="Images\logo.gif"></a>`

Doc types

The `<!DOCTYPE>` declaration must be the very first thing in your HTML document, before the `<html>` tag. This is not an HTML tag. Instead it is an instruction to the web browser about what version of HTML the page is written in. When creating a web page you should always add the `<!DOCTYPE>` declaration to your HTML documents, so that the browser knows what type of document to expect. When using a rapid application package (RAD) such as Adobe® Dreamweaver®, this automatically puts it in for you. When coding a web page using a text editor, you will have to put this in manually.

The most up-to-date doc type is in HTML5 and looks as follows.

```
1    <!DOCTYPE html>
2    <html>
3    <head>
4      <title>Title of the document</title>
5    </head>
6
7    <body>
8      The content of the document......
9    </body>
10
11   </html>
```

Client-side scripting

Even though HTML is the basis of all web pages, as a language it is quite limited and so other languages need to be brought in to create more advanced features on web pages. A client-side scripting language is used to write code that is embedded into the HTML. When the web page is downloaded onto the user's browser, the script is run on the user's computer.

> **Link**
>
> To remind yourself of what client-side scripting is, see Where scripting runs.

VBScript® and JavaScript® are client-side web languages. This means that the code is executed using the user's computer and not the web server. This frees up the processing power which would otherwise have been used on the server. Both languages can create interaction on a website, for example forms, searching and even games. Although VBScript® and JavaScript® are used to create extra functionality within web pages, they are different and have different uses. VBScript® is a simplified version of Visual Basic® that Microsoft® developed to deal with the static nature of websites. The disadvantage of using VBScript® is that it is only supported in Internet Explorer®, whereas JavaScript® offers cross-platform support for most web browsers. Table 6.8 below denotes some of the differences between the two languages.

▶ **Table 6.8**

JavaScript®	VBScript®
Tends to be the default scripting language for most web browsers	Not the default language of choice by website developers
Offers cross-platform support for nearly all web browsers	Supports Internet Explorer® only
(+) is used for addition as well as concatenation	& is used for concatenation
Case sensitive	Not case sensitive
{ } are used to denote functions	Uses Function and End Function

Embedding client-side script into a web page

Follow the process that follows to embed original client-side scripts into web pages to provide more interactivity and improve the usability of a website.

Step by step: Creating a simple catalogue search using JavaScript®

4 Steps

1 Using Notepad++ or a RAD tool such as Dreamweaver®, create a catalogue web page with three products.

▼

2 Below the <body> tag, enter the following code.

```
1    <!DOCTYPE html>
2    <html>
3    <body>
4    <script>
5    necklace = 1
6    chocolates = 2
7    toy = 3
8    product=prompt("Please enter search product", "")
9    if (product=="necklace")
10   {document.write("Item found. Catalogue number " + necklace)}
11   else
12   if (product=="chocolates")
13   {document.write("Item found. Catalogue number " + chocolates)}
14   else
15   {document.write("Item found. Catalogue number " + toy)}
16   </script>
17
18   </body>
19   </html>
```

▼

3 Amend your code to match your three products.

▼

4 Run the web page in a browser to test if it works for all three products. (It needs to be viewed in Windows® 10 and the latest version of a popular web browser.)

⏸ PAUSE POINT

Client-side scripting can be used to provide different kinds of interactivity for web pages. Using resources such as the internet or books, see if you can create the following functionality within a web page.

1 Place today's date in the header of a web page.
2 Place the current time in the footer of a web page and make it work in real time.
3 Using a form text field, enable it so that when you type in text and press the <Tab> key it will convert the text to uppercase.
4 Display an alert when someone visits your website.
5 Create a hit counter.

Hint   Consider working in pairs to see if you can come up with the correct solution. Website developers often work together to develop solutions to problems.

Extend   Try to embed the JavaScript® coding into an external file (this is similar to the way in which you would create a CSS external file). Research how this would be done, and what advantages it would have.

Use of scripting languages

A scripting language such as JavaScript® has many uses. Some of the uses of JavaScript® are outlined below.

Alerts

Pop-ups to alert the user to something.

```
1    <!DOCTYPE html>
2    <html>
3    <body>
4
5    <script>
6    alert('This is what an alert message looks like.');
7    </script>
8
9    </body>
10   </html>
```

Confirming choices

Confirming choices is a form of **validation**. This gives a user the opportunity to check if they are sure that they clicked the correct option.

```
1    <!DOCTYPE html>
2    <html>
3    <body>
4
5    <button onclick="confirmChoice()">Click and see what happens</button>
6    <script>
7    function confirmChoice() {
8        confirm("Press a button");
9    }
10   </script>
11
12   </body>
13   </html>
```

> **Key term**
>
> **Validation** – an automatic computer check which ensures that data entered is sensible and reasonable.

Browser detection

Used to determine what browser you are using.

```
1    <html>
2    <body>
3
4    <script>
5    document.getElementById("demo").innerHTML =
6    "Name is " + navigator.appName + ". Code name is " + navigator.appCodeName;
7    </script>
8
9    </body>
10   </html>
```

Creating rollovers

Rollovers add more visual interactivity. A web page can use rollover images or, in this case, buttons.

```
1    <html>
2    <body>
3
4      <img onmouseover="makeBigger(this)" onmouseout="normalImage(this)" border="1" src="lobster.gif" alt="lobster" width="50" height="50">
5    <script>
6    function makeBigger(x) {
7        x.style.height = "80px";
8        x.style.width = "80px";
9    }
10       function normalImage(x) {
11        x.style.height = "32px";
12        x.style.width = "32px";
13    }
14      </script>
15
16   </body>
17   </html>
```

Handling forms

Handling forms allow users to fill in forms and submit them, either for the website to process or by email to an inbox. This example enables a user to disable and enable a drop-down list using JavaScript®.

```
1    <html>
2    <head>
3
4    <script>
5    function disablecombobox() {
6        document.getElementById("selectFish").disabled=true;
7    }
8    function enablecombobox() {
9        document.getElementById("selectFish").disabled=false;
10   }
11   </script>
12   </head>
13   <body>
14
15   <form>
16   <select id="selectFish">
17      <option>Shellfish</option>
18      <option>Monkfish</option>
19      <option>Skate</option>
20      <option>Prawns</option>
21   </select>
22
23   <input type="button" onclick="disablecombobox()" value="Disable list">
24   <input type="button" onclick="enablecombobox()" value="Enable list">
25   </form>
26
27   </body>
28   </html>
```

Validating input

Validating input is a technique used to see if a user has entered text within a textbox. Here is an example.

```html
1  <html>
2  <head>
3
4  <script>
5  function validateEntry() {
6      var x = document.forms["validation"]["forename"].value;
7      if (x == null || x == "") {
8          alert("You cannot have a blank field.  Please type in your forename");
9          return false;
10     }
11 }
12 </script>
13 </head>
14 <body>
15
16 <form name="validation" action="validation_blank_field.asp"
17 onsubmit="return validateEntry()" method="post">
18 Forename: <input type="text" name="forename">
19 <input type="submit" value="Submit">
20 </form>
21
22 </body>
23 </html>
```

Constructs

Constructs are syntactically permissible parts of a program, and must be used in accordance with the rules of the programming language you are using. As with any code, scripting languages need to use the correct construction in order to work. This includes the **syntax**. It is important for any programming language that the syntax is correct. In the example below, the **dot operator** is used to allow an object to use a method.

```html
1  <html>
2  <body>
3
4  <script>
5  str="First Message"
6  document.write(str.replace(/First/,"Second"))
7  </script>
8
9  </body>
10 </html>
```

Key terms

Syntax – a set of rules that is unique to each programming language, which defines the combination of symbols considered to be correctly structured within that language.

Dot operator – is a full stop (.) used to define what method an object will use.

Array – a collection of indexed variables, each of which has a single value.

Here is a list of various constructs.

- Loops – Loops are useful if you want to run the same code repeatedly, each time with a different value. Loops can often be used with **arrays**.
- Decision making – This is the process of using a statement whereby the user is forced to make a choice on a web page. For example, are you sure you want to exit this page? The options being either 'Yes' or 'No'.
- Functions – A function is a block of code designed to perform a particular task . This can be executed when something calls it into action.

```
1    <!DOCTYPE html>
2   ⊟<html>
3   ⊟<body>
4   ⊟<script>
5    function hello()          <!--This is where the function is named-->
6   ⊟{
7    alert("Hello World!")
8   ├}
9   └</script>
10
11   <input type="button"
12   onclick="hello()"        <!--This is where the function is called-->
13   value="Click here!">
14
15  ├</body>
16  └</html>
```

▶ Parameter passing – Parameter passing occurs when a value is passed to a function and then the function uses it while it is running.

▶ Handling events – Events are 'things' that happen based upon user interaction or something that the browser does. For example:
  • an HTML web page has finished loading
  • an HTML input field was changed
  • an HTML button was clicked.

▶ Methods – A method is an action that can be performed by an **object.** The image below shows how the method to UpperCase is used to force the whole word to be in upper case.

```
1    <!DOCTYPE html>
2   ⊟<html>
3   ⊟<body>
4   ⊟<script>
5    hw="Hello World"
6    document.write(hw.toUpperCase())
7   └</script>
8
9   ├</body>
10  └</html>
```

> **Key term**
>
> **Object** – an object is a type of data that knows things about itself (its properties) and knows how to do things (methods).

Other issues involved in website development

Once you have developed your website using client-side scripting languages, there are a few other things you need to consider before your website development will be complete.

Compatibility with mobile and tablet devices

It is important when you develop a website that you consider how to make your website compatible with mobile and tablet devices. This is called **responsive web design (RWD)**. RWD involves using CSS and HTML5 to resize, hide, shrink, enlarge or move the content to make it look good on any screen. There are a number of methods of RWD for making a website compatible with mobile and tablet devices.

> **Key term**
>
> **Responsive web design (RWD)** – makes your web pages appear correctly (look good) on all types of device, including desktop PCs, mobile and tablet devices.

Effective use of tools and techniques

There are many scripting languages such as HTML, JavaScript®, CSS and it can be quite overwhelming to use the techniques associated with using them to produce websites. There are additional tools available that can help you to produce websites more easily, for example the rapid application development (RAD) package Adobe® Dreamweaver®. These RAD packages allow you to create websites very quickly. For example, if you wanted to centre some text you would simply highlight the text and click on the central alignment button. The code for this change would automatically be generated for you. This may seem great and more effective to use. However, you do have more control over your website when you code it manually using a text editor.

Uploading of files to a web server

To allow a website to be seen by the public across the internet, it must be uploaded on to a web server (going live). The process of uploading involves a protocol called File Transfer Protocol (FTP). Uploading files via FTP (commonly known as FTPing) can be done directly through a web browser or by using a program such as FileZilla®.

It is not only the web pages that must be uploaded onto the web server, but all the associated files including media assets and CSS files. This is because these files are not embedded into the web pages. Instead, they are linked to them but remain as separate entities.

> **Reflect**
>
> Working to time and schedule is important when developing a website. Timeframes are often defined at the outset of a project. Someone will need to take responsibility for ensuring that all parts of the project are delivered on time. For example, set amounts of time will be given to the requirements stage, the design, the coding, testing and so on. Strong leadership is important to oversee all of these stages. If one of the stages takes too long, or is incorrect, then this has a knock-on effect on the following stages. Therefore it is important, when managing a website project, that there is strong leadership and good communication.

Website review

After your website is built, it is essential to review it to ensure that it is suitable for its intended purpose and audience, and meets all the client's requirements. This can also identify any areas for further improvement.

Quality in comparison with other similar websites

Once your website has been completed it is useful to compare your website against similarly themed websites. Remember that millions of websites are created daily, so you have to do more than your competitors to make your website stand out. Comparing your website against similar websites will enable you to identify areas where your website stands out positively (compares favourably). There may also be elements of other websites that are better than yours or that work particularly well which could be incorporated into your own. You can take ideas from these websites to use for future improvement of your website. You might also identify areas in need of improvement in the other websites. Therefore, when further developing your website, you can use strong features from similar websites and leave out those features which you have identified as in need of improvement. This research will help you to produce a website which will stand up to competition from similar websites.

Suitability for intended purpose and audience

Your website will need to be reviewed to establish whether or not it is suitable for the purpose and audience for which it was intended. Quite often this will involve carrying out some form of market research to get feedback from potential users and discussions with the client to see if they are satisfied with the overall website. Remember that, while you may have been hired to develop a website for your client, ultimately it is other people that will be using it and these are the people that you (as well as the client) need to cater for. It is possible that the client might not fully understand the design preferences of the intended audience of the website, in which case your user feedback may help to inform both you and the client about how the website could be improved.

Suitability against the client requirements

During the beginning of the website development lifecycle, one of the first elements to be generated was a list of requirements. These SMART requirements state what the website must be able to do and how it should work. In order to know if the website development has been successful, it is important to compare the original requirements against the final developed website. There will need to be an appraisal to establish whether or not you have been successful in fulfilling the original requirements. If you find that there are some requirements that have not been fulfilled, then these areas can be optimised and developed further to meet the client requirements fully.

> **Reflect**
>
> Taking individual responsibility is a crucial behaviour attribute, whether in the IT industry or any other walk of life. There are always times when we fail to meet expectations. This is human nature and there is nothing wrong with it as long as we take responsibility for our own actions (we are accountable for them). The most important thing is that, when this does happen, a person understands what went wrong and puts measures in place to ensure that it does not happen again.

Legal and ethical constraints

Your website will need to be reviewed to ensure that it complies with any legal and ethical considerations. For example, it has already been mentioned that websites must be fully accessible. This means that your website must have elements such as:

- having alternative tags embedded within images
- having clear navigation
- ensuring documents/web pages are understandable
- not using colour alone to provide meaning

Moreover, your website will need to be reviewed to ensure that it does not break current legislative laws, in particular the Data Protection Act 1998 and the Copyright, Designs and Patents Act 1988.

Strengths and improvements

You may notice that websites evolve and change with the times. Good websites recognise that they have to stay up to date with the latest trends in good design and cater for the needs of all users. Therefore, once your website has been developed, it is important to identify areas of strength and any areas in need of improvement within your website.

Consider a social networking website such as Facebook™ which has millions of registered users. The Facebook™ website has continuously evolved, considering feedback from others and making improvements. As a website developer, you will seldom be satisfied with the end product and should always try to find ways of improving and adapting your website.

However, it should be noted that there are limits on the improvements you can make to websites. Web developers cannot always take on board all comments and feedback because they may be constrained by time and budget. Therefore you need to carefully select which improvements can be made. These decisions need to be considered within the website development team and with the client. You should consider which improvements will be of the greatest benefit to the website and which will be most beneficial to the client's business. Other improvements should be set aside for now but be planned as part of future development at a later date.

Website optimisation

As well as reviewing the website, it is essential that the website is fully tested to ensure that it is fit for purpose and works correctly. There may be elements within the website which do not work as intended and therefore need to be optimised in order to fulfil the client's requirements.

Your website can be optimised so that it runs more quickly and efficiently. The following are ways in which your website can be optimised to run much more effectively.

▶ Reduce HTTP requests:
  • this can be done by using CSS instead of images, wherever possible
  • combine multiple style sheets into one
  • reduce scripts that run on the page.
▶ Compress large web files:
  • compression reduces the bandwidth used by your web page, thereby reducing the HTTP response time; there are online tools which enable you to do this.
▶ Avoid WYSIWYG resources:
  • WYSIWYG (**W**hat **Y**ou **S**ee **I**s **W**hat **Y**ou **G**et) are website resources that enable you to create a website quickly by inserting website objects; although they

make it easy to build a web page, they do create messy code which can slow down your website considerably.

▶ Optimise Images:
  • oversized images can take longer to load, so it is best to optimise your images to the required size.
▶ CSS Delivery:
  • an external style sheet is the best method to optimise a website to its full potential; as only one external stylesheet is required, it reduces the size of your code and creates less code duplication.

These are additional areas of website optimisation that a user can test for and which would increase the performance of your website.

Performance and user testing

Performance and user testing is perhaps one of the most crucial forms of testing. This is used to test the functionality of a website and to ensure that everything works as expected. It is at this stage that you can use the test plan that was developed during the design stage and extend it to show the actual results and comments.

> **Link**
>
> Look back at Testing plan and, in particular, Table 6.5 Example test plan. You should use your test plan for user testing to show the actual results.

> **Tip**
>
> Remember to develop your test plan in a landscape orientation. This will give you more room to complete your testing and keep all related information together on one row.

▶ **Table 6.9:** Example test plan with results

Test number	Purpose of test	On page	Test data	Expected result	Actual result	Comment/screenshot
1	Test the home button	About.html	Left click	Load Index.html	SUCCESS	It worked as expected. No further action required.
2	Logo.gif	Index.html	Load page	Appears in the centre of the page	SUCCESS	The logo appeared in the centre of the page as expected. No further action is required.
3	Test the alt/title tag of Logo.gif	Index.html	Hover over logo	Tool text tip appears	FAILURE	It failed to work. When I hovered over the logo, nothing appeared. Screenshot 1
3B	Test the alt/title tag of Logo.gif	Index.html	Hover over logo	Tool text tip appears	SUCCESS	On this attempt it worked. I failed to put in the speech marks of the alt tag. Now works as expected. Screen shot 2

Remember that your test plan can also be used to check interactivity and compatibility with other web browsers. For example, if you have included any client-side scripting, such as including the time and date, then this should be tested. Remember that your website will be viewed in different web browsers. Consequently, the way in which your website may appear in one web browser may not be the same in another. Therefore, you will need to ensure that you complete your test plan in two or three different web browsers. When something does not work as expected, then this should be commented upon in the 'Comments/screenshot' column.

> **Tip**
>
> The Snipping Tool in Windows® is really useful for snipping images of your screen to show your screenshots of the website, whenever you have a test success or failure. To access it, go to the Windows Start screen, click on All apps, scroll down and click on Windows Accessories, then scroll down and click on the Snipping Tool.

Obtaining and evaluating feedback from others

Testing can take many different forms. As in the design stage, you could develop questionnaires to elicit feedback from others to help you refine your initial designs. You should obtain feedback from potential users of the website, in particular.

It can be hard to be critical about something which you, yourself, have developed. Therefore it is important that, when your website has been developed, you obtain feedback from your client, potential users and peers to see if the website works correctly, whether it meets the client's requirements and whether it is suitable for its intended purpose and audience.

Your initial design questionnaires can be adapted to elicit user feedback about the developed website using quantitative and qualitative questions. The feedback that you get will help you to identify where improvements can be made to your website. Be aware that you need to evaluate the feedback you receive about your website. Hopefully, most of it will be relevant and useful but it is possible that some of it is inappropriate or not helpful. For example, a client might feed back that the website does not have a particular element that was not in the brief.

It is unreasonable and outside the scope of the website requirements for them to request this feature at this late stage. However, you may need to consider developing this feature if the client is willing to wait for the website and to pay for additional features.

> **Theory into practice**
>
> When asking your client and potential users for feedback on your website, it is likely that not all of the feedback will be positive. As an IT professional, it is necessary to have a 'thick skin' while also remaining objective and being professional. Remember that within the computing industry reputation is very important. Therefore, understanding how to respond to outcomes and how to communicate effectively are key attributes of a website developer.
>
> Once your website has been completed, you will need to present and launch the website that you have developed. You will need to provide clear and comprehensive feedback on the product, and show how it fulfils the original requirements that were defined in the design stage.
>
> 1   Consider how you will be positive in the face of negative criticisms of your website. List three things that you would do to deal with negative feedback in a constructive way.
>
> 2   Consider how you will effectively present your completed website to the client. Summarise what tools you will use to present your website and what you will include in the presentation.

> **Reflect**
>
> Once the website development has been completed, you will need to provide a justification and rationale of the decisions made. It is important that when doing this you refer back to the original requirements and the design documentation. By carrying out an evaluation of the outcome of your work, you can convey to the client that a high-quality product has been developed because you are able to justify your decisions based on all the processes that have been undertaken.
>
> Carry out an evaluation of your website development outcomes.

Assessment practice 6.2   `B.P2` `B.P3` `C.P4` `C.P5` `C.P6` `B.M2` `BC.D2` `C.M3` `BC.D2` `BC.D3`

You were successful in the first part of your interview. The recruitment manager was very impressed by your report on the principles of website design. As a result, you have been placed on probation and given a twelve week trial, where you have been asked to work on a website project.

You will be responsible for the design, development and testing of the website. It is hoped that, if you do a satisfactory job, the recruitment manager will authorise you to pass your probation and provide you with a full-time job.

Design stage

Your client is a local county council who want a website to advertise a town. The website that you produce will be used to promote the area and improve tourism. Therefore you will need to highlight the positive aspects of the town so as to attract visitors to the website.

A set of client requirements will be provided. You will need to produce design documentation including mood boards, storyboards, wireframes and flowcharts (to show any client-side scripting). You will work with a peer to review your designs and identify any areas in need of improvement. You will need to document the review that your peer completes for you so you will need to develop a questionnaire which you can give to them to elicit their feedback. It is important that the questionnaires ask a variety of questions so as to highlight areas of strength in the designs and identify those areas in need of improvement.

Be sure to include a completed test plan which you can use to test your developed website. This will need to be populated with a minimum of 20 tests.

After your designs have been reviewed and any improvements made, you will need to fully evaluate the design and justify the decisions that you made, explaining how it would meet the needs of the client.

Development stage

Using your design documentation, you are to produce a website which will fulfil the client requirements. As you develop your website, make sure that you test it as you go along. Be sure to use the test plan that you completed.

Once you have completed your website, review it by getting your peers to critique it. Therefore, you need to use questionnaires to gauge their thoughts and opinions. Be sure to optimise your website based on their feedback, by making the changes that they suggest (assuming they are good ideas). It is recommended that you keep before and after versions, annotating where the changes have taken place.

Finally, you should evaluate both the design and the final website that has been developed. This will mean looking at the overall process undertaken and identifying what went well and what did not go so well.

Throughout the whole process, you will also need to demonstrate individual responsibility, creativity and effective self-management. This is important, as the recruitment manager is eager to know that you have the necessary traits of being able to work responsibly, professionally and under pressure to fulfil the role of a web developer.

Plan

- What is the task? What am I being asked to do?
- How confident do I feel in my own abilities to complete this task?
- Are there any areas I think I may struggle with?

Do

- Have I spent some time planning my approach to the task?
- Am I confident that I know what I am doing and that I know what it is I should be achieving?

Review

- I can explain what the task was and how I approached it.
- I can explain how I would approach the hard elements differently next time (ie what I would do differently).

Further reading and resources

Flanagan, D. (2011). JavaScript: *The Definitive Guide (Definitive Guides), Sixth Edition.* Cambridge: O'Reilly Media.

McFarland, D. (2015). *CSS: The Missing Manual, Fourth Edition.* Cambridge: O'Reilly Media.

McGrath, M. (2011). *HTML5 in Easy Steps, Seventh Edition.* Southam: In Easy Steps Limited.

Websites

www.csszengarden.com/
This website allows anyone to explore different CSS templates which can be applied to a website design.

www.webpagesthatsuck.com/
This website analyses well and poorly designed websites.

https://validator.w3.org/
The Markup Validation Service (W3C) allows you to validate website content for free. This website enables you to check for errors and ensure that your website is W3C compliant.

www.codecademy.com/
Includes free videos and training tutorials on how to develop websites.

www.w3schools.com/
A useful starting point for anyone who wishes to learn how to use HTML, CSS and JavaScript to produce websites.

THINK ▶FUTURE

Michael Bean

Junior Website Developer

I've been working as a website developer for over three years now. I was fortunate to take an apprenticeship position with a company that hired me to learn on the job while I undertook my BTEC National in IT. The experience I gained while working at college and in the workplace has been invaluable. I was so pleased to become a full-time employee with the company I am at, as it gives me opportunities to develop my creative and artistic skills when creating websites. As well as this, there is a challenging, problem-solving side to the job where I have to develop solutions to problems that occur. Sometimes, these problems can be quite simple to solve. Other times they need more thought but, as I am working within a team, there are people I can talk to, and together the problems quickly develop into solutions.

If there is one thing I would like to pass on to aspiring web developers it would be to always remember to place the needs of the client first. If the final website does not suit their requirements or does not fit the audience, then the client is within their rights to reject it. The client's needs must be balanced with the users' needs too. The client needs a website that people will want to visit, which draws them in and grabs their attention. Balancing these needs can be challenging, at the best of times. However, when you develop a website from the very beginning to its completion, it is a very satisfying achievement, and one which gives me pride in what I have done.

Focusing your skills

Designing a website

It is important to be able to design a website before you go ahead and actually develop it.

- What are the main methods in gathering feedback from your client?
- What are the implications if you fail to gather the requirements for the website?
- As a website developer, you are put under constraints. What might these constraints be? And what effect could they have on the development of the website?
- Finally, once you have gathered all the requirements, what design methods should you employ? To whom should these designs be presented?

Creating a website

Once you have received all necessary feedback and the design stage is complete, you can go ahead with developing your website.

- What would you consider to be the best method of developing a website? Would you use a rapid application development package such as Dreamweaver® or would you use a text editor?
- If your testing revealed that your home page does not look right or render properly in another web browser, what steps would you take to resolve this issue?
- What steps should you take if your client does not like the initial look of the website?
- How would you upload the final website to the worldwide web?

Getting ready for assessment

Kelvin is working towards a BTEC National in IT. He was given an assignment with the following title: 'How website principles are utilised to creative effective websites' for learning aim A. As part of this assignment, he was provided with a real-life scenario which he may encounter when he attends interviews for the role of a website developer. The assignment is based on a Word® report explaining how two websites utilise website development principles. Kelvin will also need to:

▶ give an explanation of how the principles embedded within his chosen websites meet the client requirements

▶ give a comprehensive evaluation of how website principles incorporated within his chosen websites have been utilised to create a creative, high performance website.

Kelvin shares his experience below.

How I got started

First I collected all my notes on this topic and collated them into a folder, for easy reference. My first task was to select two websites which I could compare. This proved more challenging than I expected because I wanted to select a website which included the majority of the elements that I had learnt about in my lessons.

Once I had selected the websites, I printed out screenshots of the web pages onto paper. I began to highlight areas where website principles had been incorporated. This helped me enormously when I began to bring it all together to produce my assignment. I also highlighted areas where website principles were not incorporated appropriately. I made brief notes, in the margin, of the implications this could have on website visitors.

How I brought it all together

I decided to use Microsoft® Word® and to use a sans serif font such as Arial. I had learnt that sans serif fonts are easier to read, especially for people with learning difficulties such as dyslexia. I wrote a short introduction, identifying the two websites I was going to discuss in my report.

▶ I produced a screenshot of the home page of each website.

▶ I produced screen grabs of the elements of the web page where I wanted to give further explanation and analysis. I found that the Snipping Tool in the All apps, Windows Accessories section of the Start menu really helped me extract elements of the websites easily.

▶ I explained how each of the websites was suitable for their intended audience and purpose.

▶ I gave an evaluation of how website principles contributed to creating two websites which were highly effective and creative.

I ended with a brief conclusion giving my overall thoughts on the websites. This helped to summarise my findings.

What I learnt from the experience

I found the task more challenging than I initially thought it would be. I began to research websites which gave me full coverage of all the principles I had learnt about in lessons. I did spend too much time on this, and this meant that I had less time to complete the report. This meant that my evaluation was not as detailed as I would have liked. I feel that the report would have benefited from having more detail about the way in which website principles are used to create high performing websites.

I also chose two differently themed websites. With hindsight, I think it would have been better to choose two similarly themed websites. If I had chosen two similarly themed websites I believe comparing them would have been easier and would have felt more natural than comparing two completely different websites. I would also consider that both of the websites did not need to be great, as then there would have been more to compare about them.

Think about it

▶ Have you written a plan with timings so you can complete your assignment by the agreed submission date?

▶ Do you have notes on all the elements of website principles that you have been taught?

▶ Have you included screenshots to give extra clarification to any justifications you have given?

▶ Is your information written in your own words with quotations from books, journals and websites and is it referenced clearly?

Mobile Apps Development 7

Getting to know your unit

Mobile devices are everywhere and their impressive sales are primarily driven by the innovative apps that keep their users educated, informed and entertained. The mobile applications sector enjoys a thriving commercial ecosystem and it can be profitably targeted by small start-ups and larger corporations alike.

Developing a mobile application is typically the result of having a good initial idea or solving an essential problem; making that mobile application really successful comes from an appreciation of the intricacies of mobile devices, the various forms of functionality available and how apps are designed to be intuitively usable. The ability to create such applications is a highly sought skill and will help you, as a software developer, gain a competitive edge.

How you will be assessed

This unit will be assessed internally by two tasks set by your tutor. Throughout this unit, you will find assessment practice activities that will help you work towards your assessments. Completing these activities will not mean that you have achieved a particular grade, but you will have carried out useful research or preparation that will be relevant when it comes to your final assignment.

In order for you to complete the tasks in your assignments successfully, it is important to check that you have met all of the Pass grading criteria. You can do this as you work your way through the assignments.

If you are hoping to gain a Merit or Distinction, you should also make sure that you present the information in your assignments in the style that is required by the relevant assessment criteria. For example, Merit criteria require you to review and justify and Distinction criteria require you to evaluate.

The assignments set by your tutor will consist of a number of tasks designed to meet the criteria in the table. The first assignment is likely to consist primarily of a research-based written task that requires you to investigate mobile apps and mobile devices, while the second will include practical activities such as:

▶ designing a mobile app that utilises device functions
▶ developing a mobile app that utilises device functions.

Assessment criteria

This table shows what you must do in order to achieve a **Pass**, **Merit** or **Distinction** grade, and where you can find activities to help you.

Pass	Merit	Distinction

Learning aim **A** Investigate mobile apps and mobile devices

Pass	Merit	Distinction
A.P1 Explain how the purpose of a mobile app and the needs, preferences and characteristics of the user affect its design and the provided features. **Assessment practice 7.1**	**A.M1** Analyse how the implementation and design of mobile apps is affected by the intended user, current technologies and the purpose of the app. **Assessment practice 7.1**	**A.D1** Evaluate how the effectiveness of mobile app implementation and design are affected by the intended user, current technologies and the purpose of the app. **Assessment practice 7.1**
A.P2 Explain the impact of current technologies on the design and implementation of mobile apps. **Assessment practice 7.1**		

Learning aim **B** Design a mobile app that utilises device functions

Pass	Merit	Distinction
B.P3 Produce designs for a mobile app to meet identified requirements. **Assessment practice 7.2**	**B.M2** Justify how decisions made during the design process ensure the design for the app will meet identified requirements. **Assessment practice 7.2**	**BC.D2** Evaluate the design and optimised mobile app against client requirements. **Assessment practice 7.2**
B.P4 Review the mobile app designs with others to identify and inform refinements. **Assessment practice 7.2**		

Learning aim **C** Develop a mobile app that utilises device functions

Pass	Merit	Distinction
C.P5 Produce a mobile app that meets the design criteria. **Assessment practice 7.2**	**C.M3** Optimise a mobile app that meets the design criteria. **Assessment practice 7.2**	**BC.D3** Demonstrate individual responsibility, creativity and effective self-management in the design, development and review of a mobile app. **Assessment practice 7.2**
C.P6 Test a mobile app for functionality, usability, stability and performance. **Assessment practice 7.2**		
C.P7 Review the extent to which the mobile app meets the identified requirements. **Assessment practice 7.2**		

Getting Started

Developing mobile applications requires the knowledge and application of many different skills. Write down a list of the tools and techniques you think you will need in order to create innovative mobile applications. When you have completed this unit, see if you have missed any obvious skills, tools or technologies from this list.

A Investigate mobile apps and mobile devices

Before starting to develop mobile applications, it is important to gain an appreciation of the range of devices and functionality available. Many design decisions are shaped by the freedoms and constraints of the target devices. In this section, we will investigate different types of mobile app, the devices on which they work and the features, characteristics and options that will shape your development path.

Types of mobile apps

Mobile applications (more commonly known as mobile apps) are programs designed to work on smartphones, tablet PCs and emerging wearable technology such as watches and glasses. An app is typically developed as one of three general types outlined in Table 7.1.

Native and hybrid applications require specialist software (and sometimes hardware) in order to be developed successfully. For example, Apple® iPad® and iPhone® apps are normally created using Apple®-specific software and hardware which guarantees development standards and practices.

In direct contrast, web applications can be developed using simple text-editor tools such as Microsoft® Notepad and may work equally well from within web browser client software running on a desktop PC, games console or

mobile device. By being so versatile, they reward greater investment (time, money etc.) by developers because the potential user base is much larger.

Generally speaking, when choosing which type of mobile app to develop, there is a trade-off between development time and cost, the required functionality and the level of user experience required.

Discussion

If you have a mobile device, you are likely to have encountered a wide variety of different mobile applications. Think about these apps, especially their appearance and functionally, and determine whether they are likely to be native, web or hybrid apps. Discuss your conclusions with your class.

Context of mobile apps

Mobile apps are created to fulfil many different user needs, and this defines their context and purpose. Each app is designed to provide the user with a specific tool, experience or enhancement that their basic mobile device does not already provide (or do well). The overall interface design, development challenges and actual use once installed on the mobile device is dependent on the type of app.

▶ **Table 7.1:** The three types of mobile app

Native apps	Web apps	Hybrid apps
• Programmed for, and installed on, a specific mobile platform. • Can take advantage of all (permitted) functionality available in the device, eg location, camera, contacts. • Typically mimic manufacturer's 'official' apps, drawing on the user's prior experience for ease of use.	• Remote applications, typically running on a server. • User typically interacts with the application through a mobile device's web browser. • No application or data is typically installed on the device. • Assess to device functionality is limited. • May visually mimic the devices's usual interface.	• Usually cross-platform compatible. • Typically uses website components that are 'wrapped' inside a native application. • Assess to device functionality may be limited. • May be seen as a more cost-effective development approach, especially when multiple types of mobile device are being targeted.

▶ **Table 7.2:** Common categories of app context and purpose

Context	Purpose and features	Examples
Locale	Apps designed to provide you with geographical information based on their current location (eg maps, GPS route finders, augmented reality (AR) experiences).	Google Maps™, Wikitude™, Yelp Monocle™, Google™ Sky, Aurasma™
Utility	Apps provided to help configure or maintain your device (eg file manager (adds or removes files), backup tools (backup to the cloud), system monitors).	Glary Utilities™, CCleaner™, WinZip™, AVG® AntiVirus for Android™
Productivity suites	Apps giving office-style functionality for word-processing, spreadsheets, slideshows, databases. They provide the user with facilities to write letters or reports, create presentations, calculate project costings etc.	Adobe® Acrobat®; Microsoft® Office®, Office 365® and OneNote®; Dropbox™
Immersive full screen	Apps using the screen display exclusively to fully draw you into their experience (eg games).	Temple Run 2™, Candy Crush Saga™, Angry Birds™, Fruit Ninja™, Minecraft: Pocket Edition™
Lifestyle	Apps designed to enrich your life (eg healthy recipes, DIY, interior design, gardening, travel). They may provide step-by-step visual instructions and narrative, 3D mock-ups and links to commercial websites.	Craftsy™, Gumtree™, TripAdvisor®, Etsy™, Evernote™, Google Translate™, eBay™
Social	Apps designed to connect you to other people, to aid communication and share ideas, events, pictures and videos.	Twitter™, Facebook™, Snapchat™, WhatsApp™, Pinterest™, Instagram™, WordPress™, Blogger™
Entertainment	Apps that provide media content (eg music players, video streaming, podcasts, e-book readers).	YouTube™, BBC iPlayer™, Spotify®, Shazam™, SoundCloud™, Kindle™, Audible™
Widgets	Apps that take up very little of the mobile device's screen display which provide quick access to live data or settings (eg news tickers, quick device settings, search facilities, calendar and appointments).	Feedly™, Flashlight apps, Todoist™, BBC News

Building apps for each of these categories poses different challenges to the mobile app developer.

In simple terms, the mobile app you design and its features will be determined by the task(s) that it must perform and the personal preferences and needs of its targeted user.

Identifying specific user needs can be difficult, but there are some key points and questions to remember.

▶ User needs – what functionality does the user need from the app? Which features are required?

▶ User preferences – how does the user want to use the app? How does the user want to interact with the app? How does the user want to navigate the app's functions and features? What visual style should the app offer?

▶ User characteristics – how should the app cater for different types of user, eg age of the user, technical expertise of the user, disabilities such as visual impairment or hearing difficulties, the physical environment in which the app is used, the breadth of user configuration that the app offers, the level of help and assistance the app provides?

Answering these types of question builds a profile of the app's intended users and helps to shape both its design and included features.

You have probably experienced occasions where you have downloaded two similar mobile apps that claim to do the same job; their design, effectiveness and usability will help you evaluate which to keep and which to remove.

Theory into practice

Podcasting has become a popular form of entertainment in the last few years and there are many different podcast apps available for the popular mobile platforms.

Select three different podcast apps for a selected mobile platform and investigate their design, functions, features, performance and usability.

Which one would you recommend to a friend? Explain and justify your reasoning.

Mobile device integration

Mobile devices come in many different shapes and sizes (smartphones, tablets, wearable technology). In addition, their features and functions also vary greatly. This is partly due to the fact that mobile manufacturers wish to distinguish their products in the marketplace and the integration of specific sensors (fingerprint security, for example) can be an attractive selling point. When designing a mobile app, it is necessary to be aware of these different characteristics and the implications they may have for both design and development.

Mobile device functions

As a developer, you cannot guarantee that a mobile device has a particular function when designing and developing an application so it is recommended that you check the operating system to see if the function is available. However, key functions such as vibration, headphone and speaker output, touch screens, microphone and still and video cameras can generally be guaranteed across any modern mobile device, irrespective of the manufacturer.

▶ **Figure 7.1:** Spirit Level mobile app using an orientation sensor

User interface

A user interface (often abbreviated to UI), is the combination of software and hardware that a user interacts with to perform set tasks. The software part of the UI includes the underlying operating system and the selected mobile app itself. The hardware of the UI is represented by input devices (such as touch screens, physical buttons, camera and microphone) and output devices (such as screen, speaker and vibration).

Mobile apps development is challenging because there are many limitations that the designer and programmer need to navigate successfully in order to create a rewarding UI interactive experience. These challenging characteristics include:

▶ limited (or potentially variable) screen size
▶ limited keyboard/keypad input mechanism
▶ limited processing power (although in modern smartphone devices this has rapidly improved).

The use of alternative input mechanisms such as voice, touch control, complex gestures (pinch, stretch and swipe) and physical effects (shake and tilt) require extensive thought before they are used in an app, in order to produce a user-friendly experience. When used well, for example in a sketching app that allows the user to shake the device to wipe the picture clean, the results are pleasing and the experience is highly intuitive. When designed poorly, for example controlling a nimble playable character using poorly judged touch screen controls, the results can be imprecise and frustrating for users.

▶ **Table 7.3:** Common mobile device functions, what they are and how they are typically used

Mobile device function	What it is	How it is used
Accelerometer	A motion sensor measuring the force applied to the device on all three axes (x, y and z), excluding gravity.	Used to track motion such as shaking the device and tracking the difference between a user walking or jogging.
Magnetometer	A positional sensor measuring the ambient magnetic field.	Used to create a compass.
Thermometer	An environment sensor measuring ambient or internal temperature, typically in degrees Celsius (°C).	Used to measure room temperature or the temperature of the mobile device itself.
Barometer	An environment sensor measuring air pressure usually in either hectoPascal (hPa) or millibars (mbar).	Used to measure air pressure in a room. Also used to measure altitude, to make GPS more accurate when height is important.
Photometer	An environment sensor measuring the ambient light levels in lux (lx).	Used to auto-adjust screen brightness depending on external light conditions to improve readability and conserve power.
Orientation	A motion sensor calculating tilt and orientation (see Figure 7.1). This uses the accelerometer.	Used to change the orientation of an app's display when a device is changed from being held in a portrait to landscape manner, or to create a spirit level.
Global positioning system (GPS)	A positional sensor using triangulating satellites or cellular base stations to calculate a real-world location.	Used to track the physical location of the mobile device for providing location-sensitive information (eg nearest restaurant or petrol station) or services (finding friends), live maps and route finding.

Even devices in the same family (for example Apple® iPhone® or iPad®) may have slightly different UI options, so you should never really take any feature for granted without researching it properly.

Variable features may include the type of touch screen (**resistive** or **capacitive**-based, single or multi-touch), dedicated physical buttons or just a very small screen. Mobile app developers need to think about how their application will function within the constraints of different user interfaces (and on different hardware) in order to support their targeted users effectively.

> **Key terms**
>
> **Resistive touch screens** – use two layers (usually glass and plastic) covered in an electrical conductive material (usually Indium Tin Oxide (ITO)). The two layers are kept apart until a finger or stylus presses them together, which causes a localised change in electrical resistance. This type of touch screen is cheaper to manufacture than capacitive touch screens but is not very sensitive and cannot support multi-touch gestures.
>
> **Capacitive touch screens** – use two spaced layers of glass that are both coated with minute ITO capacitors. When the user's finger touches the screen, it changes the screen's local electrostatic field. This type of touch screen is brighter and more sensitive than resistive touch screens, and supports multi-touch gestures. However, the structural complexity of the screen raises its production costs.

Operating system

Mobile devices are controlled by their operating systems (OS) in a similar fashion to notebooks and PCs. Similarly, just as notebooks and PCs offer different operating systems (Microsoft® Windows®, Linux™, Apple® OS X®), the majority of the mobile device marketplace is divided between those devices running the Google™ Android™ OS (see Figure 7.3) and those using Apple® iOS (see Figure 7.2).

Both mobile operating systems support similar functionality but the way in which a developer makes use of each function as their app runs is often quite different, and this can also vary between versions of a mobile device OS. For example, it is quite common for a new OS version to 'break' a mobile app that was previously working because it has changed some small detail or setting.

In addition, the programming language used to build the app for each OS is typically different and provides its own challenges, rewards, advantages and disadvantages.

Traditionally Android™ apps are written using Oracle®'s Java™ (although C or C++ may also be used), while Apple® iOS apps are created using Objective-C.

▶ **Figure 7.2:** Apple® iOS

▶ **Figure 7.3:** Google™ Android™

Device permissions

Mobile app developers will often want to access particular data or functionality contained in a mobile device in order to make their apps more appealing to customers. Mobile device manufacturers take security and the integrity of their devices very seriously; therefore, apps often need to be granted permission to use data and functionality within a device through manual user intervention.

You may well have experienced this yourself. A pop-up prompt will appear asking if the mobile app you are using may access your location, read your contacts or phone status, and even access your network (see Figure 7.4). Some mobile apps, such as podcast players, may even need permission to download data if not connected to a wireless network, simply because mobile network data charges can be expensive.

As a mobile app developer, you should not plan for your app to rely on data or functionality that might not be granted by the user.

▶ **Figure 7.4:** An operating system asking permission from the user for the app to access their Contacts information

Mobile app programming

As a mobile app developer your choices, including the programming language you must learn and the integrated development environment in which you build your application, are typically predetermined by the OS of the mobile device for which you intend to build your app, as shown in Figure 7.5.

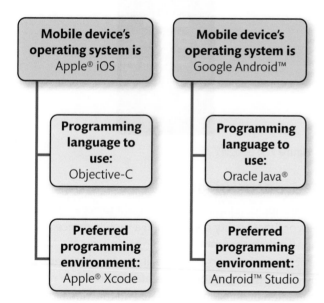

▶ **Figure 7.5:** Determining the development tools and programming language

Programming languages

Java® is an established and popular programming language, which is over 20 years old and is used in billions of devices worldwide. The Android™ **software development kit (SDK)** uses Java® as the basis for building its mobile apps. Objective-C, a superset of an older language called C, has been around since 1983 and is the main language used by Apple® for its desktop OS X® and mobile iOS operating systems.

Despite being different programming languages, Objective-C and Java® are both **object-oriented programming languages** and are similar, in terms of their structure and syntax. As a result, you may find that becoming confident in one will be beneficial for learning the other.

Developing for Android™ is essentially free, although a one-off $25 registration fee is required for publishing free or commercial apps that are to going be distributed through Google Play™. Apple® iOS development appears to be more expensive as it requires a $99 registration fee annually.

Programming environments

The role of the modern programming environment is represented by an integrated development environment (IDE). The IDE provides developers with a comprehensive suite of tools, typically including:

▶ project management tools – to create, organise and manage your apps

▶ design tools – to create user interfaces, typically using 'drag and drop' techniques

▶ fully featured text editor – to key-in, edit and save your app's source code

▶ code completion – helpful auto-complete to speed-up development

- compiler – to translate your app's source code so it works on its target mobile device
- syntax highlighting – colouring different elements of program code to improve readability
- documentation tools – for adding comments explaining how your app works
- debug tools – to assist with identification and removal of program errors
- emulation tools – demonstrating your app running on a virtual mobile device
- testing tools – to show your app's performance, usage of resources etc.
- deployment tools – to transfer an app to its electronic store or physical mobile device.

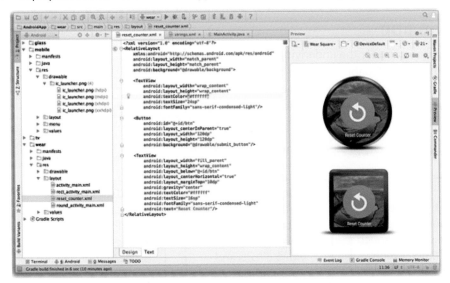

▶ **Figure 7.6:** Android™ Studio is the official IDE for Android™ application development

 **PAUSE POINT**   Can you explain what the learning aim was about? What elements did you find easiest?

> Hint   Close the book and make a list of the different types and categories of mobile app available.

> Extend   Which factors affect the design and features of a mobile app?

Assessment practice 7.1   A.P1   A.P2   A.M1   A.D1

Following in your footsteps, another junior developer is joining your development team next week. Although they have some programming experience, they have very little experience of developing mobile applications but are expected to learn very quickly.

You have been asked by your line manager to prepare and deliver an induction presentation that explains how the design of a mobile application is affected by its intended purpose and the needs, preferences and characteristics of the target users. In addition, you have been asked to provide an overview of current mobile technologies, explaining how these affect the design and implementation of such apps.

You should conclude your presentation with a worked example that analyses the design and implementation of some sample mobile apps, given these influencing factors, and which evaluates how they might have an impact on the effectiveness of the design and implementation.

Plan
- What is the task? What am I being asked to do?
- How confident do I feel in my own abilities to complete this task?
- Are there any areas I think I may struggle with?

Do
- I know what I am doing and what I want to achieve.
- I can identify when I have gone wrong and adjust my thinking/approach to get myself back on course.

Review
- I can explain what the task was and how I approached the task.
- I can explain how I would approach the hard elements differently next time. (ie what I would do differently).

Design a mobile app that utilises device functions

It is best practice to design your mobile application thoroughly before practical development takes place. In this section, we examine the design considerations and actions that you should make when designing your mobile application.

Analyse requirements for an app

Your first step when designing a mobile app is to consider the underlying computing requirements. Some of these are concerned with the capabilities of the device, while others focus on what the app needs to do (its core functionality) and the specific needs of the user. We can break this down using a quad diagram, which is a simple visual tool that focuses on four simple areas (see Figure 7.7).

It should be possible to complete a quad diagram for any prospective mobile app.

Device capabilities	**Input required**	**Output required**	**User's needs**
Functions such as accelerometer, GPS, tilt sensor, etc.	How user interacts with the app, e.g. voice, touch screen, timed events.	How the app provides feedback to the user, e.g. vibration, audio, video effects and transitions, etc.	Particular considerations, e.g. location-based services, accessibility issues, responsiveness, accuracy, etc.

▶ **Figure 7.7:** Quad diagram for app requirements

Worked example: Traffic lights

A simple mobile app is needed which will teach the correct colour sequence of a UK traffic light (a mandatory aspect of the UK driving test). Users should be able to see a timed animation of the UK traffic light sequence and be able to play a simple game where they predict which light will be next in the sequence by touching the correct light. Correct responses should be greeted with a congratulatory round of applause; incorrect responses should make the device vibrate. Accessibility options should be included for users with colour vision deficiency. The traffic lights are reset to the main menu via a simple shake gesture.

Step 1: Analyse and identify elements for each requirement category.

Step 2: Complete a quad diagram to organise your thinking.

Device capabilities	**Input required**	**Output required**	**User's needs**
Accelerometer to detect user shake action.	Touch screen for traffic light selection, menu options and navigation.	Feedback through animated visuals, sound effects (applause) and vibration.	Accessibility options for users with colour vision deficiency, eg different shapes (square, circle, triangle) for each light?

Step 3: Check that all elements have been correctly identified and categorised.

Designing a mobile app

Creating appropriate documentation is an important and necessary part of the mobile app design process. If you are developing individually, it helps organise your thoughts and planning. If working as part of a team, it helps to communicate ideas, share problem solving and identify potential problems as they emerge.

Design documentation should minimally contain:
▶ actual user requirements
▶ a proposed solution.

User requirements

User requirements define the problem you are trying to solve. In fact, no attempt at problem solving should be made before you fully understand what it is that the user actually wants. Sometimes, it is necessary to narrow down user requirements based on available resources or simply confirm your understanding of them more comprehensively, usually by asking additional questions of the client or through market research of potential users.

Proposed solution

The proposed solution represents a blueprint of how the mobile app is going to be built. The design documentation should include all the details of the blueprint. In order to create a comprehensive software blueprint, there are many elements that you must include. These elements are outlined in the sections below.

Description of program tasks

The description of program tasks is a list of the core functionality of the mobile app, generated from the actual user requirements.

The tasks performed need not be listed in a chronological order; this is often impossible to achieve as functionality on a mobile application may be accessed in different ways. However, it should be comprehensive, meet the user's requirements as fully as possible and be usable as a 'to do' checklist once formal development begins.

Target platform(s)

The platform should identify the:
▶ required mobile device(s)
▶ operating system(s) including the targeted version
▶ type of app (native, web or hybrid).

Mobile devices include various smartphones, tablets or wearable technology but you may also need to specify particular versions. For example, if your app needs a front and rear-facing camera to work properly, this may limit it to certain models. Some apps may be designed for particular screen sizes; if this is true, make sure that the design documentation makes this clear.

In addition, although your mobile app development will certainly target a specific operating system (e.g. Android™ rather than Apple® iOS), you must ensure that any key software feature that you have used is not operating system version specific (eg Android™ 6.1) unless it is unavoidable. Doing so will limit potential users or force them to upgrade their operating system, if this is possible; some devices will simply become too outdated.

Screen layouts and navigation

Visual design is the cornerstone of good mobile app development. Visual design includes the principles of good screen layout and intuitive user navigation.

▶ **Figure 7.8:** Android™ wireframe examples

Many designers use graphical mock-ups of devices, along with their screens and widgets to prototype an app and receive feedback before any lines of program code are actually written. There exist online design suites that permit developers to prototype their screen layouts and navigation using simple 'drag and drop' functionality. The industry term for this process is **wire-framing** (see Figure 7.8).

> **Key term**
>
> **Wire-framing** – an important step in the screen design process, helping the developer to plan layout and user navigation using paper-based or electronic models of the devices and their visual components.

Algorithms

An algorithm is simply a set of instructions that can be followed to solve a problem or perform a calculation. Apps may be made from many different algorithms, implemented in the program code using a combination of many different programming constructs, functions and procedures. Algorithms used in mobile apps may be represented using a number of different design tools such as:

▶ pseudocode – an informal English-like outline of a program which can be converted to the target programming language

▶ activity charts – also known as unified modelling language (UML) activity diagrams, these demonstrate user activity flow through a coordinated set of actions, for example using a standard notation to login, purchase an item or book an appointment

▶ flowcharts – a graphical representation of the program, showing its actions and logic through a set of standardised symbols.

These design tools are not specific to mobile app development. The skills that you build up using them can easily be transferred to other programming environments.

Link

For more on different programming environments, see *Unit 6: Website Development* and *Unit 8: Computer Games Development*.

Control structures

The algorithms that control mobile apps are typically built using a combination of three basic programming building blocks or control structures.

These control structures are sequence, selection and iteration.

1 Sequence – one action after another, none missed, none repeated (see Figure 7.9).

▶ **Figure 7.9:** A sequence

2 Selection – actions that are chosen based on a supplied condition which is evaluated as true or false (see Figure 7.10).

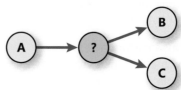

▶ **Figure 7.10:** A selection

3 Iteration – actions repeated a number of times, typically, until a condition is no longer true (see Figures 7.11 and 7.12).

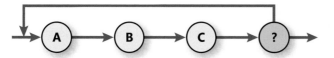

▶ **Figure 7.11:** Post-conditioned iteration (or loop)

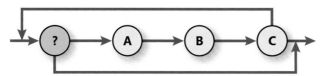

▶ **Figure 7.12:** Pre-conditioned iteration (or loop)

Data validation

Mobile apps typically use widgets such as on/off switches, pickers and list boxes for input, removing (as much as possible) the need for traditional keyboard input.

When text-based input does occur, it usually needs to be validated. Validation is simply checking to see if something makes sense before it is processed: for example, 'Age' must be entered using numeric digits only.

An inputted 'Age' of 21 is acceptable, but a value of F4 or typing 'twenty one' is not. Building validation rules, which check whether different inputs are sensible, into a program is very important as failing to do so can cause inaccurate results or, more severely, a **run-time error** or a fatal application crash.

Integration of device capabilities

If specific device capabilities are required (functions, interface aspects, operating system features or certain permissions) they should be documented as part of the design. It is important to know how, when and where they will be used in your app.

Alternative solutions

Few solutions exist without alternative approaches that also have some merit. A critical part of the design document should be coverage of different design solutions and delivery plans for the app. These may approach the solution from the opposite direction, target different devices or potentially require more or less resources (time, money, expertise) to complete.

Having alternative solutions should see you exhausting possibilities and, crucially, having a contingency plan in place should events not go according to plan during development of your chosen solution.

Resources and assets

Your design should detail any existing resources and assets that need to be incorporated into your app such as predefined code (yours and/or from a third-party library) and media assets. Your media assets may include:

▶ images (eg .jpg or .png image files)
▶ video (eg .avi, .mpg, .mov video clips)
▶ audio (eg .wav, .mp3, .au, .aiff audo files).

Care should be taken to ensure that media assets are suitably processed before inclusion. For example, they should be cropped to appropriate size and **optimised** for efficiency. Listing them as part of the design documentation also acts as your checklist for content preparation.

> **Key term**
>
> **Run-time error** – a problem that occurs while an app is being used, typically resulting in it locking (refusing to accept user input) or crashing (terminating and returning user to the device's menu or home screen).

> **Key term**
>
> **Optimised** – optimised assets are created using file formats which are more efficient as they require less storage space. This can result in improvements in performance and a smaller digital footprint on the device's resources. Examples include using .jpg images rather than .bmp files as these use data compression to reduce file size.

Test and review schedule

Scheduling robust testing and reviews is a critical part of the design process. As we will see, the planning of thorough test plans and the selection of suitable test data is essential for ensuring that the app you have built performs reliably and as expected on the targeted device(s).

Review is best achieved through the analysis of selected user feedback. The aim of reviewing your mobile app design is to help improve and refine it before it is developed and then formally released. By reviewing the design, you should be able to iron out any defects or niggles before development.

Constraints

Constraints are limiting factors that are encountered on a personal or team level or imposed by your targeted platform.

For example, you may be constrained by time, development costs, the available technology, or simply by your own technical expertise or that of your team.

You may also discover that your design is constrained by the selected platform. The permissions, capabilities and limitations of the operating system or hardware may force you to make particular design decisions.

Legal and ethical considerations

Legal and ethical considerations must be taken into account as part of your design documentation, particularly those relevant in the United Kingdom. The Data Protection Act 1998 (DPA) in particular should determine the way in which your application handles personal data. Privacy is important to users, so you must think about how your application collects, deals with, controls and secures personal data, and if it is absolutely necessary to collect specific types of data in the first place.

Ethically, there are concerns over data that can be shared by companies who develop apps. The personal data that is collected could be used to influence insurance, credit, education or employment decisions. As noted previously, modern mobile devices generally rely on permissions to prevent the users' personal data from being used by the companies who own the apps without their consent but, ultimately, the developer's guiding ethics are the final protection.

In addition, pay attention to potential issues such as copyright infringement, especially with regard to the use of media assets such as images, video and audio files. Although media assets can be easily incorporated into your mobile app, they retain their original creator's copyright and remain their intellectual property (IP), not yours.

> **Research**
>
> Visit the Information Commissioner's Office (ICO) for further reading on recommended codes of practice for mobile app developers, including ensuring users' privacy.
>
> To access this website go to: **ico.org.uk**.

> **Research**
>
> Visit the UK's legislative website and learn about the Copyright, Designs and Patents Act 1988. To access this website go to: **www.legislation.gov.uk**.

❚❚ PAUSE POINT   Can you explain what the learning aim was about? What elements did you find easiest?

 How do you define the design requirements for an app?

 Which elements should be included in the documentation of a proposed solution?

C Develop a mobile app that utilises device functions

Once the design of a mobile app has been reviewed against the user requirements and accepted by the client, it is possible to start the physical development process. There are a number of different phases to work through that will challenge you to develop a rewarding range of practical and technical skills in mobile app development.

Content preparation for mobile apps

Mobile apps are assembled using assorted forms of digital content, typically including program code, visual layouts, sound files, images (icons, pictures, animation) and video.

Before you build your mobile app, it is a good idea to prepare this content, that is, your resources, so that you have them ready to put straight into your app.

Step by step: Content preparation for mobile apps   `5 Steps`

1 Select appropriate applications and techniques to prepare your resources (see Figure 7.13).

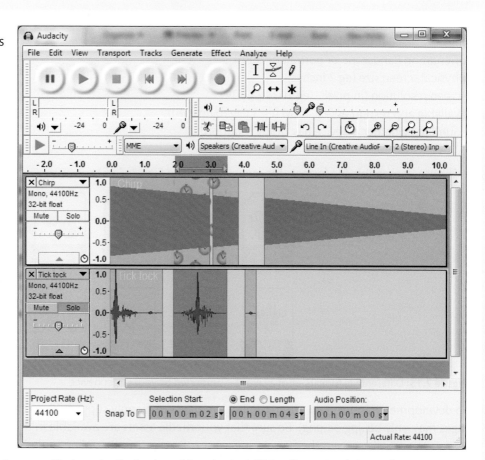

▶ **Figure 7.13:** Audacity® is a popular, open source, audio recorder and editing suite

Your code development options are likely to be limited to either Android™ Studio or Apple® Xcode. However, there are many different options for editing images and audio files, including online utilities, freeware and commercial software. Most editing processes have suggested workflows that encourage best practice in order to achieve the best results for the specific devices you are targeting with your app.

2 Consider how different device attributes will affect your content when it is used (see Figure 7.14).

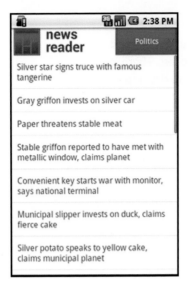 

▶ **Figure 7.14:** Same app, different device sizes and orientation

Things to consider include:

- orientation (landscape or portrait or both)
- physical screen size (eg 7 inches)
- screen resolution (in pixels) (eg 1024 x 600)
- available app resources (e.g. RAM (eg 1 Gigabyte (GB))
- sound (eg whether a device has Dolby® support).

3 Choose compatible file formats for media assets (see Figure 7.15).

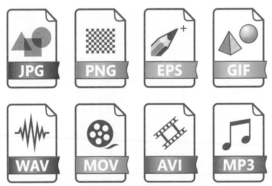

▶ **Figure 7.15:** Different file formats – not all may be supported by your target device

App development (and certain programming languages) may only support files in a particular file format (eg images may only be .jpg or .png). Be sure that your media assets are available in the correct format. If they are not, you can usually convert them using specialist software or using online tools. You should also consider the effects of user interaction on assets. For example, a user zooming-in on a raster image will experience the image appearing 'blocky' or overly pixelated, whereas vector images (if supported) do not suffer from this issue.

4 Optimise content as appropriate (see Figure 7.16).

▶ **Figure 7.16:** Optimising an image by cropping

Apply sensible optimisation to:

- program code (eg removing unnecessary sections of pre-written ('boilerplate') code that IDEs often provide as a helpful starting point

- reducing file sizes of media assets by using compression techniques such as saving images as .png or .jpg files, selecting the most efficient format for a particular type of content or cropping parts of files that are not needed.

You should always remember that there is a trade-off between optimisation levels and quality (be too aggressive and the quality of your content will suffer).

▼

5 Think about security.

Some data or assets may contain sensitive information. Consider using encryption tools to protect them and the target users of your app from cyber attack. Encryption is typically an arithmetic algorithm that scrambles sensitive data using a user-defined key. If the data is encrypted, it is considered to be safe from third-party prying because it cannot be correctly unencrypted without the user's key.

Reflect

Designing any mobile app involves substantial planning, particularly in terms of investigating and understanding the target users' requirements and the complexities of the target platforms. Any proposed solution should not just list the actions you need it to perform but should include an estimate of the amount of time each step requires for development.

Recording your findings accurately and comprehensively throughout the design and content preparation stages strengthens your problem solving by providing a solid foundation on which effective development may begin.

Tip

Always keep your user keys (passwords) safe and change them regularly. Even encrypted data could be at risk if passwords are not secure.

Link

For more on graphics (raster and vector images) see section Developing Computer Games (Worked Example) in *Unit 8: Computer Games Development*.

Developing a mobile app

This section will take you through the process of developing a mobile app to meet identified user requirements and, as part of that journey, introduce you to the key concepts that form a mobile programming language and the development environment used to build it. This example uses Android™ Studio and the Java® programming language.

Reflect

Good communication skills are necessary for investigating and recording the target user's requirements. This may involve written and verbal communication, evidenced through activities such as conducting personal interviews, sending and responding to emails and the creation of formal design documentation for the mobile app.

Target users often know what they want in terms of a product but have very little technical awareness of the mobile app development process. You will have to reflect and learn how to adjust your verbal delivery to avoid the use of unnecessary jargon and find the language and technical level most suitable for the intended audience.

The following example will show you how to design a simple temperature conversion application that will allow the user to convert between readings in degrees Celsius and degrees Fahrenheit. The basic design can be seen in Figure 7.17.

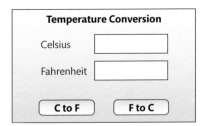

▶ **Figure 7.17:** A simple design for a temperature conversion app

In order to create this app you will need to download and install the Java® SDK and a copy of Android™ Studio, both of which are freely available. The Java® SDK should be installed first, followed by Android™ Studio.

Link

Download Java® SDK from **www.oracle.com**

Download Android™ Studio from **developer.android.com**

Once you start Android™ Studio and create a new project, you are usually presented by a new project window (on the left). If not, select the Project vertical tab and then expand 'res' and then 'layout'.

Clicking on the content_main.xml entry should display your empty app with the default 'Hello World!' TextView in the central pane, as shown in Figure 7.18.

▶ **Figure 7.18:** Android™ Studio design view, showing the default 'Hello World!' TextView

Android™ Studio's design view works on a simple 'drag and drop' principle, so you should be able to move the selected TextView freely around on the app's main form.

Android™ Studio has a number of different classes that may be used to place objects on the app's main form. These are shown in the Palette to the left of the central design pane. Classes are grouped into the following types.

▶ Layouts – control how the contents of a form are organised (eg in a table, in a grid, in rows).

▶ Widgets – different types of form element that are used to build the app's interface, allowing the user to input data, make selections and see output (eg TextViews, Buttons, CheckBox).

▶ Text Fields – specific types of TextView for defined jobs (eg Password, E-mail address, Telephone number).

▶ Containers – ways of grouping form elements together.

▶ Date & Time – different types of form elements related to the device's calendar and clock (eg DataPicker, TimePicker, CalendarView, TextClock, AnalogClock).

▶ Expert – complex types of form element for the more advanced app developer.

▶ Custom – a specialised class created by the developer or a third-party widget.

When you drag and drop a class from the Palette onto the form, Java® creates a solid object (a concrete instance of that class) which has a name, properties (things that describe it) and methods (things that it can do). Android™ Studio is also generating an XML (eXtensible Markup Language) file which describes the app's appearance as you make each change and addition; this is viewable on the Text tab at the bottom of the screen.

You will now delete the 'Hello World!' TextView and replace it with content based on your temperature conversion app design. This is shown in Figure 7.19.

▶ Edit the form's properties so that it resembles the design shown in Figure 7.19.

▶ **Figure 7.19:** The main form with additional Java® objects dragged from Android™ Studio's Palette

Each object can be edited by changing its properties (notice the Properties window in the bottom-right hand corner of the Android™ Studio IDE). Properties controls each object's visual appearance and allows you to alter their size, typeface and colour. It is also possible to double-click on a form object to edit its text and ID.

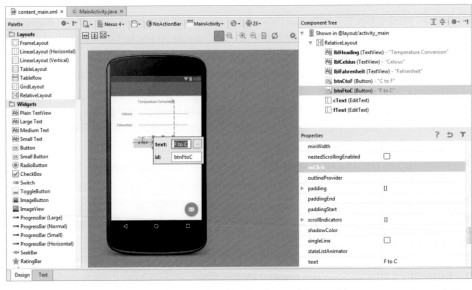

▶ **Figure 7.20:** Android™ Studio design view, showing form objects with new properties and IDs

You may have noticed that each object on your app's main form has a default name (or ID), for example textView, textView2, editText, editText2. Although this is helpful, it does not generate readable program code so it is a good idea to rename them sensibly. Do this by double-clicking on each object; a small dialog will pop up allowing you to change their IDs, as shown in Figure 7.20.

Make sure the new IDs match the list of objects, as shown in the Component Tree window in Figure 7.20.

Programming constructs

Now pause and focus on the Java® programming language in which Android™ apps are written.

Reserved words, local and global variables, constants and assignment

Java®, like most programming languages, has a number of reserved words. Reserved words are fundamental parts of the language which *cannot* be used by you for naming things. A list of common Java® reserved words is found in Table 7.4.

▶ **Table 7.4:** Alphabetical list of Java®'s reserved words (some are version specific)

abstract	continue	for	new	switch
assert	default	goto	package	synchronized
boolean	do	if	private	this
break	double	implements	protected	throw
byte	else	import	public	throws
case	enum	instanceof	return	transient
catch	extends	int	short	try
char	final	interface	static	void
class	finally	long	strictfp	volatile
const	float	native	super	while

When you name things, you are creating identifiers. There are two types of basic identifier – variables and constants. As the names suggest, variables store values which your app can manipulate. Constants store values that cannot change while the app is running.

Discussion

Mobile apps often use many variables and constants. Imagine creating a friendly app to calculate your wages for a part-time job. In a small group, discuss which values would be stored in variables and which would be constants, making sure that you justify your decisions.

In order to declare a variable we need to specify its name and its **data type**. Developers must select the most appropriate type for the data they wish to store. Table 7.5 shows Java®'s primitive data types and examples of different declarations.

Key term

Data type – the kind of data that we want to store in the mobile device's RAM. Storing each type of data requires different quantities of RAM. For example, the data type needed to store a number is different from the one used to store a character and will require different amounts of RAM. Exact names of data types can vary between different programming languages, so be careful to select the right one.

In each declaration we are saying:

data type   variable name   =   value

The = sign (or assignment operator; see Table 7.5) is used to store the value in the named variable. The first time you do this is called an 'initialisation'; afterwards it is simply called 'assignment'. Variables may change their value many times as your app runs.

Link

For more on RAM see Memory and storage in *Unit 8: Computer Games Development*.

Table 7.5: Java®'s primitive data types, their features and example declarations

Data type	What it is	Min – max range (where appropriate)	Default value	Example declaration
byte	8-bit signed two's complement integer	-128 to 127	0	`byte age = 17;`
short	16-bit signed two's complement integer	-32,768 to 32,767	0	`short qty = 10000;`
int	32-bit signed two's complment integer	- 2,147,483,648 to 2,147,483,647	0	`int largeqty = 100000;`
long	64-bit signed two's complement integer	-9,223,372,036,854,775,808 to 9,223,372,036,854,775,807	0L	`long vlargeqty = 100000L;`
float	single-precision 32-bit IEEE 754 floating point		0.0f	`float wages = 2814.20f`
double	double-precision 64-bit IEEE 754 floating point		0.0d	`float salary = 28140.20d`
boolean	Boolean 1-bit state; true or false	true or false	false	`boolean alive = true;`
char	single 16-bit Unicode character	'\u0000' to '\uffff'		`char initial ='A';`

Most programming languages have the concept of local and global variables. The easiest way to think about this is to remember that global variables can be used anywhere in your app's code. Local variables are limited to being used in the block of code in which they are declared. However, Java® does things a little differently as you will see.

Operators

Operators are special symbols used to perform special tasks in most apps. If you are already familiar with symbols such as using * for multiply, then you are familiar with an arithmetic operator. Java® has a number of these and it is a good idea to familiarise yourself with them. The most commonly used operators in Java® are shown in Table 7.6.

Table 7.6 : Common Java® operators, showing their grouping and purpose

Java® operators	Name	Operator group	Purpose
+	Add	Arithmetic	Adds two values giving their sum
-	Subtract	Arithmetic	Subtracts one value from another giving their difference
*	Multiply	Arithmetic	Multiplies two values giving their product
/	Divide	Arithmetic	Divides one value by another giving their quotient
++	Increment	Arithmetic	Increases a value by 1
--	Decrement	Arithmetic	Decreases a value by 1
==	Equal to	Relational	Tests where two values are equal
!=	Not equal to	Relational	Tests whether two values are unequal
>	Greater than	Relational	Tests whether one value is greater than another
<	Less than	Relational	Tests whether one value is less than another
>=	Greater than or equal to	Relational	Tests whether one value is greater than or equal to another

Key term

Operator – a special symbol (or multiple symbols) which tells the program to perform specific arithmetic, relational or logical operations on its data. Operators must be used in a specific order of precedence (this describes which is executed first). You may be familiar with this concept from using BIDMAS (or BODMAS) (Brackets, Indices/Orders, Divide, Multiply, Add and Subtract) in mathematics.

Table 7.6: – *continued*

<=	Less than or equal to	Relational	Tests whether one value is less than or equal to another
=	Simple assignment	Assignment	Assigns a value to a variable, not to be confused with the double equal sign which tests equality
&&	And	Logical	Performs a logical And operation
||	Or	Logical	Performs a logical Or operation
!	Not	Logical	Performs a logical Not operation

Research

It is not possible to list all of Java®'s operators here. Visit the following online resource to find out about the other operators that exist and gather examples of their usage:

www.tutorialspoint.com/java/java_basic_operators.htm

Control sequences

Recall the three control structures introduced earlier: sequence, selection and iteration.

When you are building a mobile app, sequences are represented by any block of Java® program code that executes line-after-line, with none missed or repeating.

Research

You can quickly experiment with the code samples shown by visiting a free, online Java® compiler. When you have keyed in the program code you want to try, simply click on the "Compile" and "Execute" options. You may even save your code for future use.

Visit **www.tutorialspoint.com** to try this out and discover new coding techniques, for example nested if statements and conditional operators.

Link

For more on sequence, selection and iteration see Control structures.

Selections are built using either an if...else or a switch statement. Which one you use depends on what you are trying to achieve.

A simple if...else statement has a condition that evaluates to either true or false. As shown in Figure 7.21, the actions in the first block are executed if the condition is true, otherwise the actions in the (optional) else block are used. The output from two test runs of this Java® code is shown in Figure 7.22.

```java
1   import java.util.Scanner;
2
3   public class NumberTest {
4
5       public static void main(String []args) {
6
7           int number1;
8           int number2;
9
10          Scanner keyboard = new Scanner(System.in);
11          System.out.print("Enter 1st number: ");
12          number1 = keyboard.nextInt();
13          System.out.print("Enter 2nd number: ");
14          number2 = keyboard.nextInt();
15
16          if (number1 == number2) {
17              System.out.println("Numbers are the same!");
18          }
19          else {
20              System.out.println("Numbers are NOT the same!");
21          }
22      }
23  }
```

▶ **Figure 7.21:** Java®'s if...else statement

```
Enter 1st number: 4
Enter 2nd number: 5
Numbers are NOT the same!

Enter 1st number: 78
Enter 2nd number: 78
Numbers are the same!
```

▶ **Figure 7.22:** Output from two different tests of Java®'s if...else statement

Java®'s switch statement is a useful way to check for multiple values at the same time, as shown in Figure 7.23. It is also possible to add a default check in case no listed options are matched. Output from four test runs of the switch statement is shown in Figure 7.24.

```java
1   import java.util.Scanner;
2
3   public class BankAccount {
4
5       public static void main(String []args) {
6           int option;
7
8           Scanner keyboard = new Scanner(System.in);
9           System.out.println("1 - Bank Balance, 2 - Account Query, 3 - Payments");
10          System.out.print("Enter option 1, 2 or 3: ");
11          option = keyboard.nextInt();
12          switch (option) {
13              case 1: System.out.println("You have chosen to see your balance");
14                      break;
15              case 2: System.out.println("You have chosen to make a query");
16                      break;
17              case 3: System.out.println("You have chosen to make a payment");
18                      break;
19              default:System.out.println("You have not chosen a correct option!");
20
21          }
22      }
23  }
```

▶ **Figure 7.23:** Java®'s switch statement

```
1 - Bank Balance, 2 - Account Query, 3 - Payments
Enter option 1, 2 or 3: 1
You have chosen to see your balance

1 - Bank Balance, 2 - Account Query, 3 - Payments
Enter option 1, 2 or 3: 2
You have chosen to make a query

1 - Bank Balance, 2 - Account Query, 3 - Payments
Enter option 1, 2 or 3: 3
You have chosen to make a payment

1 - Bank Balance, 2 - Account Query, 3 - Payments
Enter option 1, 2 or 3: 8
You have not chosen a correct option!
```

▶ **Figure 7.24:** Output from four different tests of Java®'s switch statement

Iterations (sometimes called loops) are represented by one of three common statements (for, while and do...while). Figures 7.25 to 7.27 show Java®'s for, while and do...while loops for a particular example. Figure 7.28 shows that the output from all three loops is identical.

```
 1▾ public class ForLoop {
 2
 3▾     public static void main(String []args) {
 4          int counter = 0;
 5
 6▾         for (counter = 1; counter <= 5; counter++) {
 7              System.out.println("BTEC National");
 8          }
 9      }
10  }
```

▶ **Figure 7.25:** Java®'s for loop

```
 1▾ public class WhileLoop {
 2
 3▾     public static void main(String []args) {
 4          int counter = 1;
 5
 6▾         while (counter <= 5) {
 7              System.out.println("BTEC National");
 8              counter++;
 9          }
10      }
11  }
```

Figure 7.26: Java®'s while loop

```
 1▾ public class DoWhileLoop {
 2
 3▾     public static void main(String []args) {
 4          int counter = 1;
 5
 6▾         do {
 7              System.out.println("BTEC National");
 8              counter++;
 9          } while (counter <= 5);
10      }
11  }
```

▶ **Figure 7.27:** Java®'s do...while loop

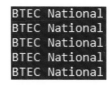

Figure 7.28: Output from all three loops is identical

Although all three loops generate the same output, they have all worked differently. Ideally, you would use for loops when you know that code needs to repeat a fixed number of times. While loops may not even run once (they are pre-conditioned) and do...while loops always repeat at least once (they are post-conditioned).

Loops repeat based on their controlling condition being true. In the example shown in Figures 7.25 to 7.28, the controlling condition is the counter variable having a value less than (or equal to) 5. When the counter reaches 6, the condition is no longer true and the loop ends.

Functions and procedures

Another key component of a mobile app is the concept of a function or procedure. **Functions** and **procedures** are common features in procedural programming while, in **object-oriented** programming, they are essentially represented by the methods which occur with the class.

> **Tip**
>
> The temperature conversion app is relatively straightforward and should just make use of a basic sequence control structure. When you start designing more complex apps, the other constructs (sequence and iteration) will become important, so remember the if, switch, for and while statements shown here.

> **Key terms**
>
> **Function or procedure** – a function is a block of code, ideally between 5 and 50 lines in length, which has a single defined purpose. Although written just once, it can be executed many times during a program by using a function 'call', reducing the need for repeated code. In some programming languages, the terms 'function' and 'procedure' are used interchangeably, but, in others they are very different concepts: a function typically returns a calculated value while a procedure performs a single identifiable task.
>
> **Object-oriented** - Java®, which we use to create Android™ apps, is categorised as a class-based, object-oriented programming (OOP) language. In OOP, objects are created from classes that are usually modelled on real-world 'things'. Each class acts as a software blueprint, encapsulating (or containing) the thing's state (its data or properties) and behaviour (its functions or methods) in program code.

Objects and classes

Classes are a fundamental aspect of every Android™ mobile app solution created using Java®. Classes are used to represent the physical components that you use to build an app. For example, each item in the Android™ Studio Palette (screen components such as forms, Layouts, Widgets, and Text Fields) represents a different class that you can use.

Once the class is dragged to the form, a concrete instance of that class is created, which we call an object. Try to think of a class as a design pattern, something like a jelly mould, stencil or cookie cutter; one jelly mould (the class) can be used to make many jellies (the objects).

Each object has associated methods and properties and can interact with other objects to perform a task. Commercial apps will use a wide range of classes, many of which may be freshly created by their developers.

Event handling

Once you have created the visual design for your app's interface and named objects sensibly, the next step is to code the algorithms that calculate the outputs or actions needed. In the case of our temperature conversion app, this means converting between a temperature input in degrees Fahrenheit to an output in degrees Celsius and vice versa.

These calculations are executed when a user presses one of the two buttons we have added to the app's main form. When the user presses a button (or performs any action the operating system recognises) it triggers a specific event – in this case, what is commonly called an 'on click' event.

In order to link the event trigger to the calculations, you need to build an event handler. There are many ways to achieve this in Android™ Studio. The most traditional method involves registering a listener method for each button that will run a specifically coded **event handler** method.

Revisit the Project explorer pane, expanding 'Java' and then 'MainActivity'. Clicking on this should display the Java® program code, which will have been automatically created for you. You will need to insert the highlighted code shown in Figure 7.29 to add appropriate event handlers that will respond to user inputs and calculate the desired outputs, in order to get the right screen components.

> **Key term**
>
> **Event handling** – describes the process of using a specially written function or class method to perform set actions when a user or system event is triggered. For example, outputting the result of a calculation when a button is pressed or displaying a device's 'low battery' warning indicator when it falls below a certain charge level.

```
import android.support.design.widget.Snackbar;
import android.support.v7.app.AppCompatActivity;
import android.support.v7.widget.Toolbar;
import android.view.View;
import android.view.View.OnClickListener;
import android.view.Menu;
import android.view.MenuItem;
import android.widget.Button;
import android.widget.EditText;

public class MainActivity extends AppCompatActivity {

    @Override
    protected void onCreate(Bundle savedInstanceState) {
        super.onCreate(savedInstanceState);
        setContentView(R.layout.activity_main);
        Toolbar toolbar = (Toolbar) findViewById(R.id.toolbar);
        setSupportActionBar(toolbar);

        FloatingActionButton fab = (FloatingActionButton) findViewById(R.id.fab);
        fab.setOnClickListener((view) -> {
            Snackbar.make(view, "Replace with your own action", Snackbar.LENGTH_LONG)
                    .setAction("Action", null).show();
        });

        addButtonCtoFListener();      //call method to add listener to CtoF button
        addButtonFtoCListener();      //call method to add listener to FtoC button
    }
```

▶ **Figure 7.29:** Adding new code to your app

The new (highlighted) lines shown in Figure 7.29 perform two actions.

1 They import various Java® code packages that we need for our app to compile into our program.

2 They call two listener methods, one for each button on the app's form.

Your next task is to create the Java® code for the two event listener methods, Each will include an event handler that:

▶ gets the value entered into a TextField on the app's form

▶ performs the correct calculation

▶ puts the results back into the other TextField on the app's form.

Figures 7.30 and 7.31 show the new code for each listener and handler. You should note that the Java® code for the addButtonCtoFlistener method is annotated to demonstrate best practice.

```
/*
 * Class method adding a Listener to
 * the CtoF button to enable responding to
 * events
 */
public void addButtonCtoFListener() {

    //Create button object representing CtoF button on form
    Button btnCtoF = (Button)findViewById(R.id.btnCtoF);

    /*
     * OnClick listener for CtoF button will
     * call its associated event handler to perform
     * the CtoF calculation
     */
    btnCtoF.setOnClickListener(new OnClickListener() {
        public void onClick(View v) {
            float celsius;        // Inputted Celsius value
            float fahrenheit;     // Calculated Fahrenheit value

            //alias Celsius input box
            EditText cValue = (EditText) findViewById(R.id.cText);

            //grab celsius value from input box, converting from text to floating point
            celsius = Float.valueOf(cValue.getText().toString());

            //perform conversion of Celsius to Fahrenheit
            fahrenheit = (celsius * 9.0f / 5.0f) + 32.0f;

            //alias Fahrenheit input box
            EditText fValue = (EditText) findViewById(R.id.fText);

            //convert calculated Fahrenheit floating point value to text
            String fahrenheitText = Float.toString(fahrenheit);

            //put the converted Fahrenheit text value into the Fahreneit input box
            fValue.setText(fahrenheitText);
        }
    });
}
```

▶ **Figure 7.30:** Java® code for the addButtonCtoFListener method (annotated)

```
public void addButtonFtoCListener() {

    Button btnFtoC = (Button)findViewById(R.id.btnFtoC);

    btnFtoC.setOnClickListener(new OnClickListener() {
        public void onClick(View v) {
            float celsius;
            float fahrenheit;
            EditText fValue = (EditText) findViewById(R.id.fText);
            fahrenheit = Float.valueOf(fValue.getText().toString());
            celsius = (fahrenheit - 32.0f) * 5.0f / 9.0f;
            EditText cValue = (EditText) findViewById(R.id.cText);
            String celsiusText = Float.toString(celsius);
            cValue.setText(celsiusText);
        }
    });
}
```

▶ **Figure 7.31:** Java® code for the addButtonFtoCListener method (not annotated)

Code annotation

As you have seen, it is important to ensure that your code is suitably documented. Annotating code essentially means inserting developer-readable comments throughout your code. Although these comments are removed during the compilation process and therefore inaccessible to the user, their inclusion is good practice.

The purpose of annotating your program code with meaningful comments is to improve its readability and aid understanding. This can be especially important when programmers are asked to redevelop apps that were originally written by others.

Your comments should make clear how your code relates to its real-world application, not explain the syntax of the actual reserved words used. The actual techniques used to comment on program code vary between program languages.

Java® uses a combination of multiline and single line comments, and this is shown in Figure 7.32. Another popular use of annotation is to 'comment out' program code that the developer wants to keep but not compile, possibly as they test new ideas or identify code which is not working correctly.

```java
1    public class HelloWorld{
2
3        /*
4            Main function
5
6            Program to test program output
7
8            Written by A. Jones
9            Version 1.0
10
11       */
12       public static void main(String []args){
13
14           // Output welcome message
15           System.out.println("Hello World");
16
17       }
18   }
```

▶ **Figure 7.32:** Multiline and single line comments

The use of meaningful identifiers is also a key aspect of code annotation as the representation names you have chosen are said to self-document.

Some SDKs and third-party tools can generate web page documentation automatically from your program code if it is formatted in the correct fashion. For example, Oracle®'s Javadoc tool performs this function for Java®.

Utilise device capabilities

Android™ and Apple® support mobile app developers by providing **application programming interfaces (APIs)** and **frameworks** that permit apps to receive motion data from integrated device hardware such as gyroscopes and accelerometers. Android™ calls this the Sensors framework while Apple® refers to their implementation as the Core Motion framework.

Key terms

Application programming interface (API) – this acts as a library of pre-written routines that provide the developer with access to other systems (such as databases), the operating system of a device or its actual hardware. The aim of an API is to make the development process easier by abstracting (hiding) the complexity of the software and hardware systems beneath.

Framework – a particular set of development tools that can be accessed via its API.

Interrogate device status

A key part of mobile app programming is the ability to interrogate the device's status. Different types of status may be checked by the developer, including important statistics such as its physical location, battery level or orientation (that is, whether it is portrait or landscape). For example, Android™ uses a useful BatteryManager class, which provides a method for querying battery and charging properties.

Research

Many examples can be found that provide the Java® code necessary to interrogate an Android™ device's status. Visit the **www.tutorialforandroid.com** website that demonstrates how the battery level of such a device may be checked.

Investigate this code, adapt it and incorporate into your own projects.

Although you do not need to perform this type of interrogation in your introductory temperature conversion app, being able to do so is an important skill.

Orientation of device

Your app needs to auto-detect the orientation of the physical device on which it is running (and when it changes). It does this by querying the screen's rotation. The device's normal rotation is derived from its screen format: for example, if the screen is naturally tall (portrait) and the device is turned sideways (landscape) its rotation value will either be 90 or 270 degrees depending on the direction it was turned (clockwise or anticlockwise). Helpfully, Android™ supplies an appropriate class called 'Display' within its API to assist developers determine the screen rotation, size and refresh rate.

Apps can also force the orientation mode by automatically changing the device's rotation to fit a portrait or landscape view, although this is not generally considered to be good practice.

Research

Investigate Android™'s 'Display' class and its methods by visiting **developer. android.com**

Creating an executable for a target device

You can deploy your app to either an emulated device or the actual physical device you have targeted.

Emulated device

Key term

Android™ virtual device (AVD) – a software emulated version of a particular physical device, running within a host operating system such as Microsoft® Windows® or Apple® OS X®.

Using an emulated device is useful because it lets you test the compatibility and performance of your app on types of device to which you may not have physical access, for example different smartphones, tablets, TVs and pieces of wearable technology. In Android™ Studio, you can achieve this by creating an **Android™ virtual device (AVD)**. To create an AVD it is necessary to specify the hardware, and the version of the Android™ operating system being used (4.X KitKat, 5.X Lollipop or 6.0 Marshmallow).

Android™ Studio allows you to create multiple AVDs and then choose which one you want to use when developing your app. This allows you to test your app easily on many different physical devices. The device can be chosen through the available hardware definitions, as shown in Figure 7.33.

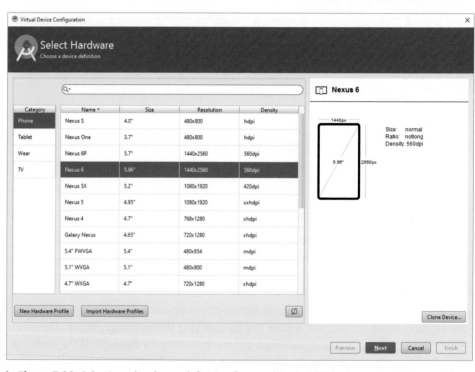

▶ **Figure 7.33:** Selecting a hardware definition for a real Android™ device

It is then possible to select an Android™ system image to use. Android™ Studio will have some images already installed but you may download others as you need them (as shown in Figure 7.34). In order to run your app successfully using an AVD, you must use a system image that is compatible with the programming or hardware features you have used.

Each system image is typically available in different virtualisation options: x86 (32-bit), x64 (64-bit) or ARM (Advanced Reduced Instruction Set Computing Machine). ARM is generally the slowest but is more likely to be independent of virtualisation options set in your host PC's BIOS (Basic Input Output System) (these should always be modified with caution).

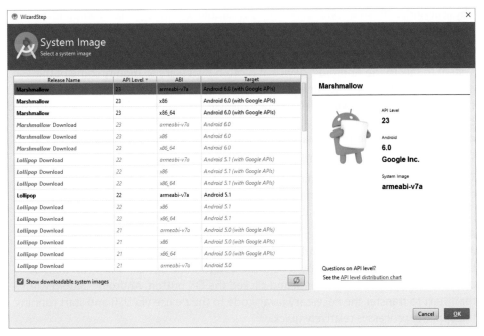

▶ **Figure 7.34:** Selecting an Android™ system image for the AVD

It is then possible to tailor various options to your personal preferences, as shown in Figure 7.35.

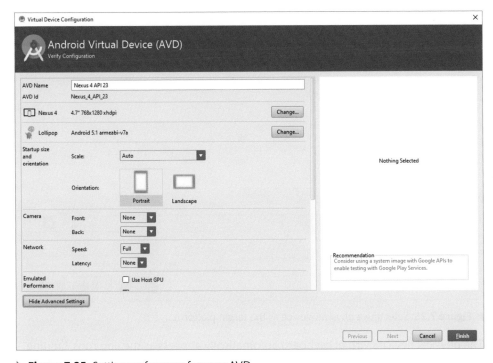

▶ **Figure 7.35:** Setting preferences for your AVD

Figure 7.36 shows the AVD running in Microsoft® Windows® 10.

Physical device

The other technique for testing your Android™ app is to connect the system upon which you are developing it (for example Apple® Mac® or Microsoft® Windows® PC) to a

▶ **Figure 7.36:** An AVD running in Microsoft® Windows® 10

▶ **Figure 7.37:** Android™ device connected via USB cable

physical Android™ smartphone, tablet, or wearable technology via a compatible USB (Universal Serial Bus) cable, as shown in Figure 7.37.

In addition to installing the correct Android Debug Bridge (ADB) driver for your host system to talk to the Android™ device, it is often necessary to modify some of the device's settings in order to run your app. This often involves enabling options for USB or running apps not downloaded through Google Play™, and only has to be performed once. These developer settings can vary from device to device, and may even be deliberately hidden to prevent accidental damage, so you are advised to check the correct procedure with the device's manufacturer before attempting this.

The primary advantage of running your app on the target physical device is that you will get the truest impression of its performance and behaviour. Many devices also have developer debug tools that can assist your live testing.

As a developer, you just need to select the connected Android™ device (not an AVD) once you have clicked Android™ Studio's green 'run' app button. If the device is successfully connected, it should be listed as a running device, which can then be chosen. Once you have selected it and clicked the OK button, Android™ Studio will then start to transfer the necessary Java® code to the device via USB and start running the app; the process is relatively quick.

Figure 7.38 shows that a physical device has been selected as the target platform and Figure 7.39 shows the temperature conversion app transferred and running on a physical device.

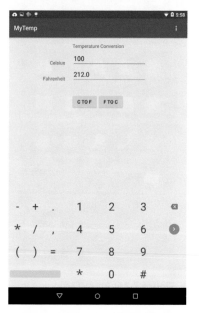

▶ **Figure 7.39:** Your app transferred and running on a physical device

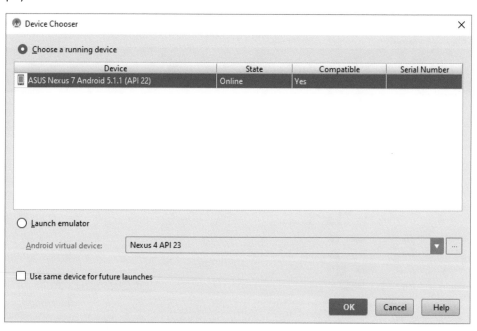

▶ **Figure 7.38:** Selecting a physical device as the target platform

The physical device's virtual keyboard automatically appears as the app runs, limiting the user to entering only numbers. This happens because of the design decision to choose 'Number (Signed)' text fields.

Although a quick test seems to indicate that the app is working correctly (100 degrees Celsius is indeed equivalent to 212 degrees Fahrenheit), your next step should be to review your efforts through a process called quality control.

Quality control

Quality control is a process that reviews the standards of manufacturing applied during production. Its aim is to deliver the best product or service for a customer. For a mobile app, this essentially means measuring how well the design was implemented during development for the target device(s).

Quality control is an intrinsic part of the mobile app development process, helping you to assess the resulting standard that your development process has achieved and, crucially, to identify areas of potential improvement. Quality control should be performed before formal testing starts. An overview of quality control is shown in Table 7.7.

▶ **Table 7.7:** Quality control areas of concern, key questions and considerations

Area	Question	Consider...
Efficiency and performance (This is called application 'profiling')	How does your app impact on the resources of the mobile device? Can we identify any issues affecting performance?	• use of RAM allocation • use of device storage media • use of central processing unit (CPU), particularly in terms of its percentage share • use of system and application processes that may highlight performance bottlenecks • use of graphical processing unit (GPU), especially when rendering user interface (UI) elements • use of battery, comparing drain of similar applications • temperature constraints – mobile devices can shutdown to protect components during periods of heavy use (especially when recharging) if they become too hot.
Maintainability	How easy is it to modify or improve your app? Have you programmed the app appropriately?	• recommended standards of coding • levels and usefulness of code annotation • structure and organisation of your program code • extensibility of your solution • use of programming constructs, functions, procedures, data types, classes and the device's code framework.
Portability	Which devices are compatible with your app? How could you improve the potential compatibility?	• devices which will correctly run your app • devices which do not run your app (and identify the reason(s) why) • devices which run your app but have minor issues (and what can be adjusted to improve portability) • any unexpected compatibility issues which you had not anticipated • whether your app's actual portability meets the platforms targeted in the design phase (including specific versions of the operating system).
Usability	How easy is it for a user to interact with your application? How can you improve the user experience?	• adherence to manufacturer guidelines, ie Apple® iOS and Android™ recommended design principles and standards • capturing user feedback, both good and bad • identifying common likes and dislikes • requesting user feedback for improvement • identifying whether the app meets the user requirements targeted in the design phase.

Links

- For more on RAM, CPU and GPU see the section on Hardware in *Unit 8: Computer Games Development*.
- For a reminder of what is meant by 'user interface (UI)', see User interface.

Quality control is best achieved through manual (rather than automated) review and can be a self-reflective process. Formal testing will examine feedback from a wider range of users.

Testing a mobile app

Testing is widely recognised as an essential process that ensures that any mobile app you develop meets the requirements that were identified during its design, and that it operates in an accurate, reliable and robust manner. Testing should be performed every time the app is updated, so the process should be seen as cyclical; this is shown in Figure 7.40.

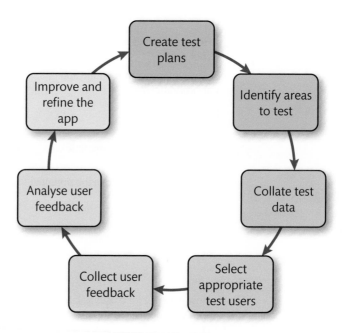

▶ **Figure 7.40:** The cyclical stages involved in robust testing of a mobile app

Test plans should detail in a step-by-step fashion how you are planning to test your mobile app. This will include the identification of several 'use cases'. Each use case attempts to tell the story of a user's interaction with your app (successful and unsuccessful) and typically includes a combination of:

▶ test data being entered
▶ operations being performed
▶ the order of the operations being performed
▶ the user's responses to your app's prompts.

Test data typically can be found in one of three possible states.

▶ Normal – data within the acceptable range that the user would normally enter.
▶ Extreme – unlikely data at the edges of the acceptable range.
▶ Erroneous – data which should not be entered (eg text rather than numbers).

Another concept that you may encounter as part of the test plan is the idea of white and black box testing. White box testing is usually performed by the developer by tracing the use cases through the program code logic and completing **trace tables**. A black box test is performed by a user by following a use case. The user has no exposure to the program code and does not need to know how the app works, whereas you, as the developer, are only interested in the outcome that the user gets.

Areas which need to be tested include the following.

▶ Functionality – all functions in the app should work as expected.

▶ Acceptance – the app should be fit for purpose: that is, it should meet the identified user requirements.

▶ Installation – covers the app's initial installation (typically from an app store download), its updating and its eventual removal.

▶ Performance – how the well the app behaves and impacts upon the target device(s).

▶ Usability – the app should be intuitive to use and its interface quickly mastered by its users; getting a positive response from testers is often a key part of an app's success.

▶ Compatibility – the app should work consistently well across different models and brands of device.

Test users and user feedback

It is advisable that you select test users who have had very little to do with the development process. This will ensure that their observations are honestly expressed and without the bias that project involvement typically brings. Users should be drawn from a random population sample, ideally with mixed levels of technical experience.

User feedback must be collected from the user. This may be achieved using a variety of fact-finding techniques including:

▶ direct observation

▶ one-to-one interviews

▶ focus groups

▶ questionnaires or surveys

▶ automated error reports generated by the app itself.

Collecting user feedback can be both time-consuming and expensive, so techniques have to be used wisely. A common (and cost-effective) technique is the logging of feedback from confirmed users using online app stores because it is free and unsolicited (for example from Apple®'s App Store or Google Play™). The release of free Alpha or Beta (very early) releases of an app to selected users is also a useful tactic to consider.

Feedback should, ideally, be a mixture of quantitative and qualitative data which can be collated and analysed to produce useful information and identify patterns and trends in the user experience, which can highlight faults and areas for improvement.

Quantitative data – data that specifies quantities: that is, it can be measured and written as numbers, percentages or proportions. For example, '50 per cent of users experienced no issues while using the app'.

Qualitative data – are represented by reasons, opinions and motivations and can be used to explore (and make sense of) quantitative data. For example, 'users found the application difficult to navigate and text hard to read on smaller devices'.

Key term

Trace table – a table created by the developer, through white box testing, which charts the changes in program variables as a use case is performed. The trace table would have entries for each use case with expected (what should happen) and actual (what does happen) outcomes. Comparing these outcomes helps the developer assess whether the app is working correctly.

Discussion

Look at the two examples of quantitative and qualitative results. Can a link be found? Is the reason why 50 per cent of users experienced issues when using the app (quantitative result) explained by the problems encountered with the navigation and text size (qualitative result)? Discuss in small groups.

Table 7.8 Shows quantitative and qualitative questions in a questionnaire.

▶ **Table 7.8:** Quantitative and qualitative questions

Question 10a	How was MyApp's user interface?	☐ poor ☐ acceptable ☐ good ☐ outstanding
Question 10b	Please explain your reasons ...	

For example if users' feedback suggested that while some found the user interface 'attractive and with a bright colour scheme' (qualitative data), you also find that '60 per cent of users judged the user interface 'poor' (quantitative data), then there is clearly a usability issue in your app's design.

If the supporting data is not available, it might be necessary to return to those users and investigate their unsatisfactory responses to find the underlying cause. Superior fact-finding should always ask for reasons and not just record a score.

Improving and refining your app

The process of improving and refining your app is guided by analysing the combined results of your testing (that is, done by the developer) and the received user feedback.

Issues to tackle should include:
▶ ensuring that the app has all the agreed functionality described in the design
▶ fixing run-time errors, bugs or application crashes to improve reliability
▶ fixing inaccurate calculations and outputs
▶ improving responsiveness
▶ improving user interface (eg colour scheme, typeface, font sizes, images)
▶ improving user navigation and app flow
▶ increasing speed/performance
▶ reducing the app's use of device resources by further optimising assets or simply programming more efficiently
▶ improving the compatibility of the app with different models/brands of mobile device.

Reflect

You will have reviewed your app using feedback from fellow professionals and test users. The views expressed by others are often very useful as they are typically unbiased, providing a neutral judgement about the design and implementation of your app. Learn to respond to outcomes and take this feedback in your stride. This will enable you to react in a mature fashion that leads to improvements in both the end product and your problem solving abilities.

Any changes made to the app should be recorded in a change log, which is a document written by the developer that details the fixes and improvements made for each version of the app. A version number is used to clearly identify each successive release. This uses a 'major.minor' system, for example:
▶ MyApp ver 1.0 – first major release
▶ MyApp ver 1.1 – minor update, fixing menu (from user feedback), improving compatibility
▶ MyApp ver 2.0 – major update, includes additional functionality.

As you can see, minor versions increment when small updates and fixes are committed (for example MyApp ver 1.1). Many minor releases may occur between major updates. In contrast, major updates represent large changes to the app functionality, features or code (for example, MyApp ver 2.0). You may also have personal experience of later app releases introducing brand new errors and bugs. This is quite common and a hazard that every developer faces when trying to remedy an identified problem; in fixing a bug, they sometimes introduce others.

Lessons learned from developing a mobile app

It is important that you reflect and evaluate the effectiveness of the app that you have developed. This review encourages you to ask yourself the following questions.

▶ How well has the solution met the user requirements identified in the design document?
  Think about: how has your app met the targeted user requirements, which elements has it achieved and which elements are missing or incomplete?

▶ Which issues arose during testing and your refinement of the app?
  Think about: the issues you should have anticipated, how you could have prevented these problems from occurring, which coding techniques or device features could have been used better?

▶ How could the app be improved to meet the user requirements more closely?
  Think about: the testing and user feedback, the aspects that could be added or refined.

▶ With hindsight gained through your testing and user feedback, if you were to repeat the task, were there alternative solutions that should have been implemented instead?
  Think about: the testing, user feedback and the alternative designs in your design document.

Whatever the outcome, there is always room for improvement when developing a mobile app. One of the key parts of the learning process (and of developing better apps) is learning from your mistakes.

Reflect

Mobile app developers need to develop and demonstrate behaviours that fit the professional nature and expectations of the industry. Some key attributes you must adopt are:
- giving respect to others, especially their opinions when they are giving you essential feedback
- communicating appropriately with a target audience, providing and accepting open and honest ideas and opinions
- having an open mind to new ideas and alternative solutions and not being afraid to try new techniques to improve a solution or the target user's experience
- a commitment to personal improvement, by developing both new knowledge and practical skills
- the desire to achieve excellence through the standards of problem solving applied and the mobile apps created.

Ⅱ PAUSE POINT   Can you explain what the learning aim was about? What elements did you find easiest?

> **Hint**   Describe the general steps of developing an app from a design.

> **Extend**   What is the difference between quality control and formal testing?

Assessment practice 7.2

`B.P3` `B.P4` `C.P5` `C.P6` `C.P7` `B.M2` `BC.D2` `C.M3` `BC.D3`

You have been asked by your line manager to lead a development project for the design and implementation of a new mobile app that generates quotations for a landscape gardener. This involves selecting the prices of services that are involved (eg gardening, paving, planting, mowing) and the costs of goods (eg seeds, plants, bushes) that are to be included. Prices for the various services should be selected from local businesses although they should be easy to configure in the app itself. A standard rate of VAT is also expected.

Intending to demonstrate best practice to a newly recruited junior developer, you start by producing designs for a mobile app that meet the requirements you have identified. As part of your design process, you should review the design with your peers to identify opportunities for improvements or refinements. Before commencing development, you should justify and evaluate your design decisions to your junior colleague by explaining how they meet the identified requirements.

Once the design has been agreed, you must produce the mobile app from your design, testing it for functionality, usability, stability and performance. The working app should then be reviewed to ensure that it meets identified requirements and is optimised as necessary.

A final evaluation should be made of the optimised mobile app, comparing and contrasting it to the client requirements.

Plan
- What is the problem I am being asked to solve? Do I understand the client's needs?
- How confident do I feel in my own abilities to complete this task, in terms of design and coding?
- Are there any technical areas I think I may struggle with? If so, do I know how to research these?

Do
- I know what it is I am doing and what I want to achieve.
- I can identify through feedback and review when I have gone wrong and adjust my thinking/approach to get myself back on course.
- I am prepared to optimise my solution based on identified requirements and feedback.

Review
- I can explain what the task was and how I approached the task, justifying my decisions at all stages.
- I can explain how I would approach the hard elements differently next time (ie what I would do differently).
- I will use this as an opportunity to try new techniques and improve my problem solving.

Further reading and resources

Banga, C. and Weinhold, J. (2014). *Essential Mobile Interaction Design*. New Jersey: Addison Wesley.

Lee, W-M. (2012). *Beginning Android 4 Application Development*. New Jersey: John Wiley & Sons.

Burd, B, (2015). *Android Application Development All-in-One For Dummies*. New Jersey: John Wiley & Sons.

Lowe, D. (2014). *Java All-in-One For Dummies*. New Jersey: John Wiley & Sons.

Ray, J. (2015). *iOS 8 Application Development in 24 Hours, Sams Teach Yourself*. Indianapolis: Sams Publishing.

Websites

Develop apps for Android™: **http://developer.android.com/**
This enables you to get started with Android Studio.
Develop apps for Apple®: **https://developer.apple.com/programs/**
The Apple Developer Program.
Mobile Development Tutorials: **www.tutorialspoint.com/**
Mobile Development Made Easy (for Android™, Apple® iOS etc.).

THINK ▶FUTURE

Elizabeth Shaw

Junior Developer in a mobile app development team

I've been working on mobile apps for about two years and during this time I have been involved in developing many different apps, some for Android™ and others for Apple® devices. Although the technologies and languages are quite different, the design principles are generally very similar. Although sometimes my preferred design is pitch-perfect, this often isn't the case and I have to review the design with considerable input from my colleagues. I have to be mature about this and take suggestions and feedback in a positive way although often it will mean going back to the drawing board and trying other ideas.

Of course, sometimes I don't agree with my colleagues and I have to justify the decisions I have made during the design process. As long as I can prove that my ideas meet the identified requirements this is usually ok. Essentially, I am demonstrating my creativity and taking an individual responsibility for my efforts, something which my colleagues openly encourage.

Focusing your skills

Reviewing mobile app designs

It is important to be able to review the designs of a mobile app, both individually and with others, in order to ensure that they meet the identified requirements. Here are some questions to ask yourself to help you do this.

- What are the implications of implementing a poorly thought-out design?
- Which requirements need to be identified and addressed by your design?
- How can you justify the decisions that you made during the design process?
- How you would record the feedback you receive from others and how might you use it to improve the design?
- Finally, for each requirement you have identified, work out how you can ensure that it is dealt with in your design and review.

Designing a mobile app – questions on design requirements

The design for your mobile app has been reviewed by others. What happens next?

- If the mobile app design is poorly received and serious shortcomings have been identified in your understanding of the problem and/or your design, you will need to revisit the original client requirements.
- If the mobile app design is generally well received but issues have been identified with elements of your designs that rely on specific devices, platforms or the presence of integrated hardware, you may wish to refine your ideas.
- If the mobile app design is very well received, consider that there may still be room for improvement and seek advice and guidance from others who may have more practical experience than you.

Getting ready for assessment

Florence is working towards a BTEC National in Information Technology. She was given an assignment which asked her to give a presentation on 'mobile apps and mobile devices' for Learning Aim A. She had to cover all the different areas of mobile apps and mobile devices, with a particular emphasis on which aspects affect the design and implementation of mobile apps. Florence shares her experience of completing this assignment below.

How I got started

Having researched the different types of mobile app (including the different categories of app and whether they are native, hybrid or web apps), my next step was to think about how the users' needs determined the app's design. To do this, I asked a relative for an app that they would like on their mobile phone. I made notes of their needs (what they wanted it to actually do), their preferences (how they wanted it to look and work) and their characteristics (how they wanted to use it) and tried to link this to a potential design, explaining my decisions in terms of their requirements.

Another aspect I had to explore was how current technologies impacted on the design and implementation of mobile apps. I looked back at apps operating on various devices (for size comparison) and from differently aged models (older and newer phones).

I tried to analyse this further by selecting a number of different apps and comparing their design and implementation across various types and models of device. I managed to create a list of different aspects that enabled me to compare and contrast these really well.

In order to achieve the highest grade, I realised I had to make some judgements about the effectiveness of these apps. I conducted and documented a consumer test with my family and friends, asking them to compare a popular app across a number of different devices. They gave me a lot of feedback about the usability of each app and I collated this into a set of results which I used to rate each app. It was then possible to draw some conclusions about the users' needs, the purpose of the app and the technologies available in each device in order to evaluate how the app's overall design and effectiveness had been directly affected.

How I brought it all together

I typed my findings into a document and used this to create slides and notes which formed my presentation. I created some tables and charts to help me to explain my findings. This reduced the amount of text I needed to add and made the presentation look more interesting and professional.

I ensured that I had proofread each page carefully and practised the presentation with a family friend who pretended to be the target audience. This helped with my nerves and timings on each slide. When they became confused over some of the technical terms I had used, I simply changed them or added a quick explanation. At the end of the report, I added a set of URLs for the audience so that they could find out more information.

What I learned from the experience

I realised that, although my class notes provided a good starting point, it was essential to understand what I was being asked to do before I started work on the assignment. This proved to be good practice for developing mobile apps: always understand the problem fully before you start work on it.

I also learned that collecting other people's opinions was a very useful way of getting honest feedback and this helped me to rethink my own views on certain apps and mobile devices. Even when I didn't particularly agree with them, I still found their feedback interesting, something which will be useful when I receive feedback on my own app.

Think about it

▶ Do you know the difference between explaining, analysing and evaluating?

▶ Can you respect other people's feedback even when you do not necessarily agree with it?

Computer Games
Development 8

Getting to know your unit

Assessment
You will be assessed by a series of assignments set by your tutor.

The UK games industry is one of the fastest growing job markets today. The UK is a world leader in producing amazing, interactive experiences for desktop PCs, consoles, and handheld and mobile devices. The computer games industry is a team-based and fast-moving area that involves many different job roles. The production of computer games requires an understanding of the whole process from concept art through to formal testing. You may want to become a games programmer, concept artist or 3D animator but, for whichever role you want to focus on in the future, you will have to a good understanding of the entire games development process first. In this unit, you will investigate how and why people play games, what is changing in games hardware and development, and how to design and create games.

How you will be assessed

This unit will be assessed by a combination of theory, design and practical tasks set by your tutor. Throughout this unit, you will find assessment practice activities that help you work towards your assessment. Completing these activities will not mean that you have achieved a particular grade, but you will have carried out useful research or preparation that will be relevant when it comes to your final assignment.

In order for you to complete the tasks in your assignment successfully, it is important to check that you have met all of the Pass grading criteria. You can do this as you work your way through the assignment.

If you are hoping to gain a Merit or Distinction, you should make sure that you present the information in your assignment in the style that is required by the relevant assessment criteria. For example, Merit criteria require you to analyse and discuss, and Distinction criteria require you to assess and evaluate.

The assignment set by your tutor will consist of a number of tasks designed to meet the criteria in the table. This is likely to consist of a written assignment but may also include activities such as:
- writing an article about the current trends in gaming
- designing a game from a set client brief
- creating and testing a 2D or 3D game level.

Assessment criteria

This table shows what you must do in order to achieve a **Pass**, **Merit** or **Distinction** grade, and where you can find activities to help you.

Pass	Merit	Distinction
Learning aim **A** Investigate technologies used in computer gaming		
A.P1 Explain social and technological trends of computer games. Assessment practice 8.1	**A.M1** Discuss how current and emerging technologies impact on how games are designed and developed to meet the requirements of the users and the larger computer games industry. Assessment practice 8.1	**A.D1** Evaluate the impact of current and emerging technologies on the design and development of computer games to meet the requirements of the users and the computer games industry. Assessment practice 8.1
A.P2 Explain how current and emerging technologies impact on computer games design and development. Assessment practice 8.1		
Learning aim **B** Design a computer game to meet client requirements		
B.P3 Produce designs for a computer game that meet client requirements. Assessment practice 8.2	**B.M2** Justify decisions made, showing how the design will fulfil its purpose and client requirements. Assessment practice 8.2	**BC.D2** Evaluate the design and optimised computer game against client requirements. Assessment practice 8.2
B.P4 Review the designs with others to identify and inform refinements. Assessment activity 8.2		
Learning aim **C** Develop a computer game to meet client requirements		
C.P5 Produce a computer game to meet client requirements. Assessment practice 8.2	**C.M3** Optimise a computer game to meet client requirements. Assessment practice 8.2	**BC.D3** Demonstrate individual responsibility, creativity and effective self-management in the design, development and review of a computer game. Assessment practice 8.2
C.P6 Test a computer game for functionality, usability, stability and performance. Assessment practice 8.2		
C.P7 Review the extent to which the computer game meets client requirements. Assessment practice 8.2		

Getting Started

It is important to understand all of the different roles involved in the computer games development workflow. Write down a list of all the different jobs that you think are involved in the making of a computer game, splitting your list into different categories, such as artistic or technical.

A Investigate technologies used in computer gaming

Computer and video games are big business and a continuing source of exciting and creative jobs that require strong IT skills and original ideas. The next big successful title could be just around the corner and one of the most exciting elements of the computer games industry is how small teams with great ideas can become international success stories. Different **genres** can grow out of new titles and create entire new fan bases of dedicated gamers, sometimes forming strong communities of players. Many of the recent game genres have grown out of innovative technologies such as virtual reality, augmented reality, new operating systems and advances in streaming.

Gaming trends and society

The original gaming device was a cathode ray tube amusement device in 1947. There have been nearly seven decades of gaming developments since then and people access and enjoy computer games in many different ways. These different trends have led to an ever-evolving industry that seeks to bring interactive entertainment to all areas of society, whether they are casual gamers wanting a few minutes of distraction with Angry Birds™ or hard-core gamers who eagerly anticipate the newest release of the Halo® series.

▶ **Figure 8.1:** A scene from a video game

Popular genres

Innovation and originality are keys to the success of a game publisher and players are always willing to explore different genres of games. One of the most popular genres in gaming is the First-Person Shooter (FPS) genre where the player sees through the eyes of a character and must fight through different levels to achieve a particular goal, for example Call of Duty®. Genres can grow and change, they can spawn sub-genres that take the original definition of a genre and spin it off in a different direction, or they may become hybrid genres that take elements of other genres and merge them together. An example of this is an online FPS, such as Star Wars™ Battlefront™, which features many players fighting at the same time. This game has all the features of an FPS game but it also fits into the **massively multiplayer online (MMO) game** genre. So it could be called an MMOFPS. To muddy the waters further, this game also allows you to switch to third-person mode so that you can see the character you are playing.

> **Key terms**
>
> **Genre** - a genre is a category of computer game that describes the style of play, types of challenges and the perspective of the player.
>
> **Massively multiplayer online (MMO) game** – a game played by multiple players, across the internet, all online at the same time.

Role-playing games (RPGs) have been popular since before games were created digitally. Classic pen and paper games such as Dungeons and Dragons™ saw players work against a dungeon master, having chosen a particular character and, as the game progressed, their character would grow and improve as they made choices. This role-playing concept works very well in computer game format and some RPGs, such as The Elder Scrolls V: SKYRIM®, have had massive success. Other games developers have noticed the appeal of RPG game players improving their characters and have been adding this feature to titles from other genres, such as Call of Duty®, enabling them to 'level up' and receive perks and rewards.

The nature of constant change within computer games, of borrowing of ideas from other genres and adapting to player feedback, means that it is impossible to write a definitive list of genres.

▶ **Figure 8.2:** Games bring people together as a common interest and popular pastime

Types of player

As computer game titles can be categorised into different genres, it is also important to consider different types of player. When a game studio pitches an idea for a new title to a publisher, one of the most important factors they have to consider is the audience of the game they want to make. It is impossible to make a game that will please everyone as players have different tastes and interests, and psychologists such as Richard Bartle and David Keirsey have even made academic studies into how and why people play games. The table below (Table 8.1) looks at the main factors that determine the types of player.

The table above represents basic demographics, that is, measurements used to put people into different categories so that their likes and dislikes can be understood more easily. However, there are other considerations to look at when designing games.

In recent years, as home broadband speeds have increased, online games have soared in popularity and the previous generation of home consoles (PlayStation 3™, Xbox 360®) were designed to appeal to people who wanted to play together in engaging, online worlds. Our most recent generation of consoles (Wii U™, PlayStation 4™ and Xbox One™) have all included the ability to play online and stream content so that other people can watch the play and comment on the skills of the players.

Research

How do people play games together? Try to list as many different ways in which traditional games (pen and paper, board games etc) and computer games provide multiplayer activities.

Key terms

Casual gamers – people who only play games for short periods of time and prefer simpler games.

Immersive – a term which refers to how focused you are on the experience that you are having. An immersive game will keep your attention for long periods of time and block out distractions. It should make you enjoy the game more, but only if you have the time to spend on it.

Franchise – a series of game titles that feature the same world, the same characters or the same setting.

▶ **Table 8.1:** Main factors that determine the different types of computer game players

Age range	In the UK, games are rated by PEGI. PEGI decide what is appropriate for different age groups. Game designers will tend to create bright, cartoon adventures for younger players and darker, more realistic worlds for adult players.
Gender	Despite being commonly considered to be a 'boy thing', gamers are split between male and female, with roughly 60 per cent of players being male and 40 per cent female. Game designers often design children's games for a specific gender, but the older the target audience gets, the less targeted to a particular gender the content becomes.
Time commitment	Possibly one of the most important factors is how much time a person is willing to spend playing a game. This can affect the design of a game greatly. **Casual gamers** will happily load a game for a few minutes at a time. They may play on mobile devices while travelling or download digital games that cost a lot less than boxed games. Casual gamers will not be particularly loyal to one genre, worried about saved games or necessarily interested in sequels.
	Players who want a much more **immersive** experience will spend hours exploring their favourite worlds. They will be loyal to particular brands and spend a lot of their spare time playing games. Immersive gamers may also be referred to as 'hard-core gamers'. Some people may criticise the time they spend on games, but is it any different from spending hours watching TV?
Theme choice	The content or style of a game and any ideas that tie all of its features together are called its theme. People may choose a game based on its story, setting or design. There are many different game themes: a fantasy adventure, a realistic war game, a puzzle game with fun characters or a game that follows the stories and characters from a well-known film or book **franchise**.

Game production

The production of a game is a complicated event. It usually begins with an idea being pitched by a **game development studio** to a **game publisher**. This pitch will contain an overall concept of the game with details about the characters, **game mechanics** and who the game is being designed for, that is, the audience. Without an identified audience, there would be no financial incentive for making the game. Sometimes the publisher will approach the studio with an identified audience or game genre and/or theme and ask them to create a game for that market. After the studio has been given the funding to start development, they will begin by creating **concept art** that illustrates the graphical style and theme of the game (see Figure 8.3).

> **Key terms**
>
> **Game development studio** – a team of people who create computer games.
>
> **Game publisher** – a company that releases games to shops or online platforms, and pays for development.
>
> **Game mechanics** – the way a game world works, its features and its rules such as double jumps or collecting items.
>
> **Concept art** – drawings and paintings created before a game is developed to show how the game world should look and feel.

▶ **Figure 8.3:** Concept art by Ewon Harding

The concept art will be referenced throughout the game's development so that everyone on the development team knows what the game should look like, and the kind of feelings that the game should be evoking in the player.

Mainstream publishers

Some publishers are large international companies, known as mainstream publishers, such as Electronic Arts (EA™ Games) or Nintendo®. These mainstream publishers are responsible for funding the production of many different game titles at the same time. Smaller publishers, such as Telltale Games®, will usually specialise in one particular genre and will often release only one game at a time.

Indie games

When development of a game is started before it has a publisher, it is known as an indie game. Studios who make indie games fund the development themselves. This means that they do not have the same restraints placed on them by publishers during development so they can make their own decisions about the content and style of the game. This often leads to innovative and original game designs but it also means that the studios can struggle to pay the bills, as they do not make any money until the game has a publisher. When a studio has proved that there is a market for their game, through research or testing, a publisher will fund their project. Good examples of successful indie games are Minecraft™, Super Meat Boy™ and No Man's Sky™.

Indie games are able to start making a profit when they find a publisher. Often the profit is fed back into the development of their next game, before it gets a publisher. Indie games usually get published as digital downloads because getting a game disc printed, boxed and shipped to game shops all around the world costs a lot of money. It is partly because there are so many good indie games now that digital download providers (such as Steam™, PlayStation™ Store) have become so popular. Mainstream publishers will now decide before development if a game is going to be printed on disk or released through a digital platform. If they expect to sell to a wide audience then they will make the investment in a boxed game sold in a shop, but if the game is more niche then it may only be released digitally, as there is a greater financial risk in printing on disc because it costs more.

Crowdfunding

Indie developers are able to raise funds directly from players through crowdfunding websites such as Kickstarter™ or Indiegogo™.

Crowdfunding is a recent phenomenon and it has really exploded over the last ten years to a point where it has gone from being a gimmick, which could be used to top up the finances of a struggling studio, to a viable means of funding large-scale projects. Virtual reality hardware such as the Oculus Rift™ would not exist without crowdfunding. Equally, some very successful games have been funded through this model, for example Broken Age™, which was one of the first games to raise far more funding than it asked for. Star Citizen™ is the most successful crowdfunded game to date, having made over £25 million.

The crowdfunding model differs from traditional game development not only in how the money is raised but also in the inclusion of 'stretch goals'. This means that developers will commit to a certain scope for the game, but given additional funding they would make additional promises. These 'stretch goals' may be different platforms for release, extra levels or a virtual reality mode. One of the disadvantages of crowdfunded games is the delays to titles, over which customers have no control, as extra features can push back delivery dates and people can often wait a long time for their games.

Free-to-play

Another model of game production is the free-to-play model, which has become a mainstay of mobile apps games development. Using this approach, smaller studios and publishers release games for free and then include a number of paid-for upgrades or features. The idea is that players will get hooked on the game when they can play it for free and will then be willing to spend money unlocking extras. These free-to-play games are also known as freemium titles. Some players find it frustrating to begin a game that they think is free only to find later that they have to pay to keep playing. Publishers of free-to-play games can avoid making players pay for the games after a certain period by placing adverts in the games, which pay for the cost of development.

> **Link**
>
> The development of mobile games apps is covered in *Unit 7: Mobile Apps Development*.

Artificial intelligence

Artificial intelligence (AI) is the name given to the programming that makes machines (or non-playable characters (NPCs), in the context of games) seem like they are thinking for themselves.

Programmers have to think about how an NPC in a game should react to where they are or what they are supposed to be doing. A soldier guarding a gate should be looking in certain directions but should have moments where their attention lapses so that the player can sneak past. All of this character behaviour has to be coded into the game.

Modern game AI has developed to the point where enemies are able to have realistic reactions to players: such as an enemy blocking an attack in a fighting game, or more strategic behaviour such as enemies responding to patterns in the player's choices by avoiding a 'duck and cover' attack or trying to flank enemies, in multiplayer games. The more sophisticated the AI, the more complicated the programming required to create it.

Search algorithms

Different **algorithms** are used when designing AI and programmers often use search algorithms, such as the A* Algorithm, which is a path-finding algorithm. A search algorithm allows the AI attached to a NPC to solve problems, such as the problem of where to go next. The problem of deciding the best route to take from one point to another is quite easy for humans: we look at the area around us and decide the best way to get somewhere using the smallest amount of effort. It is not as easy for an NPC (often an enemy) in a game; the NPC has no real concept of where it is or where it should be. Therefore, when a player is seen by the enemy at the end of a hallway that contains several crates, barrels and piles of rubble, it needs an algorithm to figure out how to get down the hallway to the player. The A* Algorithm would break the hallway and obstacles down into a series of steps and work out the best set of steps to get the NPC from its starting point to its goal. There would be a choice of different routes to take and the algorithm uses mathematical optimisation to work out the best route to take.

> **Key term**
>
> **Algorithm** – a set of instructions that are executed in order to solve different computer problems.

Mathematical optimisation

Mathematical optimisation is the selection of the best solution to a problem when given a selection to choose from. It forms a part of all AI and is often tied to a game's difficulty setting. Most game NPCs would have the ability to get rid of a player quickly, if programmed correctly, but that would render the game impossible. Therefore, a game's difficulty setting will change the possible solutions available to NPCs, from a simple approach such as lowering the enemy's health value or making a less powerful adversary, to more sophisticated AI such as the enemy being able to change tactics.

Logic

An important factor in creating realistic AI is considering the logic and patterns of behaviour that a human would normally follow. Does the enemy behave in a way that is logical and reasonable? If it emerges in the testing phase of a game's development that the answer is no, then the AI programmers must go back to their code and improve it until a player is not puzzled by the behaviour of an enemy. This is a difficult task as games are very complex, interactive software applications and it is hard to predict what players might do in a game. In fact, players often cheat by finding an 'exploit' or vulnerability in a game's AI. This often leads to developers having to find a fix that they then patch onto the game as a download after the game has been released.

Emerging technology

One of the things that makes the computer games industry so exciting is the rapid pace of development and new ideas that change our game playing experiences. New ideas are driven by improvements and innovations in the hardware and software that we use to play games.

> **Research**
>
> What improvements to games hardware have been made in the past few years? Have a look at the technical specifications and features listed by different hardware manufacturers and see if you can come up with a list of the technological features that define the current generation of games platforms.

Virtual reality

One of the fastest growing areas is virtual reality (VR). Back in the 1990s, VR was set to be the next big thing but the headsets were very expensive and the processing power was too slow, so the technology never took off. However, more recently crowdfunding has brought about the first version of the Oculus Rift™ headset, which has proved to be an incredible success and spawned imitators from Valve™ and Sony®.

▶ **Figure 8.4:** Virtual reality is creating a whole new way of engaging with games

VR in its current form consists of two screens, one over each eye, with special lenses that magnify the screens so that they fill your field of vision (see Figure 8.4) . Added to the headsets are accelerometers, which measure which direction you are looking in, and gyroscopes, that measure how much you have turned your head. Often a positional tracker is paired with the headset, which follows your head's position in space so that you can move forwards and backwards. This positional tracker can be combined with motion controllers, and even a treadmill, to create total movement in a virtual world.

Augmented reality and wearable technology

Microsoft® have taken a different approach to the new headset phenomenon and have focused on augmented reality (AR) instead of VR. AR uses cameras to capture the real world and layers virtual game assets over the top, so that they appear to exist in the real world (see Figure 8.5).

AR already existed on various mobile apps and in game form on the Nintendo® 3DS™ and PlayStation Vita™ but Microsoft®'s HoloLens™ seeks to outdo them all by creating engaging experiences with virtual characters in the real world.

Once you have exhausted all the games on your PC, console, mobile and handheld games devices, you can look to smart watches to top up your gaming urges (see Figure 8.6). The Apple® and Android™ smart watch app stores both have a growing range of simple games, which you can play on your wrist. These games are restricted by the size of the screen that they are played on, but sometimes a physical restriction can be the catalyst for an amazing game idea. Lifeline™ is an example of an Apple® Watch® game, where the player receives messages from an astronaut stranded on an alien moon. The game's interface is simple text but it is an engaging and exciting story with delays built in so that players are not staring at their watches for hours on end.

▶ **Figure 8.5:** Whilst virtual reality places you in a different world, augmented reality brings virtual objects into our world

▶ **Figure 8.6:** The Apple® Watch gives you access to apps on your wrist

Digital distribution

It is not just headsets that are changing the way we play games. Digital distribution platforms such as Steam™, GOG™ and PlayStation™ Store have changed how we buy games. One of the most dominant games providers, Steam™ by Valve™ is also one of the best places to get indie games, which can often cost a lot less than console disc-based titles. Disc-based games are often priced the same as their digital equivalents on the console's own digital stores, as there are not any incentives for console publishers to discourage their audience from buying games in a traditional shop, because if the shops cease to exist then there are fewer places to buy the console.

Steam™ has created its own operating system (OS). Steam OS is a free, **Linux**®-based OS that prioritises gameplay and is available on 'living room' PCs. 'Living room' PCs are compact PCs that are connected to a TV and are designed to be used in a similar way to a traditional games console, by using the digital platform as the main source of content.

Streaming

Streaming has become a huge part of games culture with websites such as Twitch™ and YouTube™ making gameplay videos highly popular because they enable people with limited budgets the opportunity to preview a game that they might be interested in buying. Many people are used to streaming music and films to different devices, and games can be streamed too, using services such as PlayStation Now™. Subscribers can rent games for set periods and download them to their device, be it a console, PC or a smart TV.

Discussion

Which of these emerging technologies would engage you as a gamer? Discuss, in a group, who you think these emerging technologies would engage and whether or not new audiences for games may grow out of these emerging technologies.

Security of integrated services and multiplayer environments

As game systems become more reliant on digital services and streaming content, there is an increased requirement for users to share their personal data with the services that they are using. Most of the digital platforms require stored credit card details and they will often ask customers to connect their social media sites so that customers can share details of what games achievements they have gained or levels they have completed. This presents a big security risk, as the information could be used by criminals to steal a customer's identity. For example, Sony® was the victim of a series of cyber attacks in 2014. All the companies offering games platforms have to be very careful that new updates and upgrades to their software do not inadvertently create a breach that criminals can exploit.

MMO game providers can also be the targets of hackers and they often have less security in place than an online bank or shop. It is important that they protect their user's data because, despite being a game rather than a bank, they are still holding the same level of sensitive personal data about customers.

Players do not just have to worry about the security systems in place on MMO games, but they also have to be careful about the information that they give out if they are having conversations with strangers in the game through text or voice chat. Criminals are able to get a lot of information out of players without them realising it, by pretending to be friendly. Before they know it, the player's password has been guessed and they are locked out of their own account. (This could be their login for an MMO such as World of Warcraft® or a digital distribution account such as Steam™ or Google Play™.)

Gaming technology

Keeping up to date with games technology, and how it is changing, is one of the main challenges for anyone involved in the computer games industry.

Benefits and limitations of different platforms

Players face the added challenge of choosing which platform to invest in. While developers may often want to create games for the most popular platforms, each one comes with its own benefits and limitations.

Hardware

Most gaming hardware is made of the same core components to allow digital information to be displayed on screen and interacted with by the player.

Central processing unit

The central processing unit (CPU) is the brains of the computer. It carries out all of the instructions sent to it by a computer program using thousands of tiny switches to perform arithmetic, logic and input/output. In the case of a game program, the CPU is responsible for working out all of the game's system requirements. Most modern PCs use an Intel® or AMD CPU and the performance of PC games (such as that of Steam™ titles) is dependent on the power of the processor. For example, The Witcher® 3 is a a huge open world RPG with very good graphics and its minimum system requirements include an Intel® Core™ i5 processor that runs at a speed of 3.3GHz (a fast processor which is not sold cheaply), but its recommended requirement is an even more expensive Intel® i7 processor running at 3.4Ghz. Given this, many PC gamers will overclock their

▶ **Table 8.2:** Benefits and limitations of different platforms (then update subsequent table numbers)

Platform	Type	Benefits	Limitations
Windows® PC	Personal computer or laptop (desktop)	Easy games development; broad user base; access to Steam™	No standardised technical specifications; some games will not run on lower spec PCs
Mac®	Personal computer or laptop (desktop)	Works with most digital platforms; powerful systems with fast CPUs	Fewer games are released for Mac®
PlayStation 4™ and Xbox One™	Console	Hugely popular consoles; strong hardware; OSs dedicated to playing games	Can be expensive to develop for; getting disc distribution requires working with large publishers
Nintendo® Wii U™	Console	Large fan base; not too many titles on the shelves	Very specific tablet-based controls mean that games cannot be ported onto other systems
Apple® iOS devices (phones and tablets)	Mobile devices	Hugely popular with owners willing to invest in higher priced games than non-iOS® mobile apps	All products have to be approved by Apple® who can have quite strict standards; development usually restricted to Mac® unless using a games engine
Android™ devices (phones, tablets and notebooks)	Mobile devices	Much cheaper development costs than Apple®; open source system	So many different types of devices means quality testing can be difficult
Adobe® Flash®	Web-based platforms	Easy to animate and create great visuals on	Flash® does not have simulated physics; due to security concerns, many browsers are discontinuing their Flash® support
HTML5	Web-based platforms	Supported on all web browsers, desktops and mobile devices; no plugins necessary	No built-in support for 3D, gamepad or to save games

CPUs. 'Overclocking' means to force the CPU to run faster than its recommended manufacturer speed and, while it can be done with stability by changing the voltage, this will invalidate the warranty and put your PC at risk.

Games consoles are able to use slower CPUs because they optimise their games to run with fewer details. For instance, they may use less real-time shadows or lower-resolution textures. They also do not have to worry about running large operating systems in the background, like Windows® or OS X®.

Mobile devices, such as smart phones, run with much slower CPUs, which is why they are unable to run large-scale games with complex graphics.

Link

For more information about CPUs, see *Unit 4: Programming*.

Graphics processing unit

A graphics processing unit (GPU) works alongside the CPU and its sole responsibility is to manage the production of images on the display. The more complex the graphics, the more work for the GPU. When playing PC games, the GPU can be part of the main **motherboard** but is more commonly a separate card connected to the motherboard through an expansion slot. Most GPUs have their own separate random access memory (RAM) (see below) and PC games will often specify the minimum power of the GPU needed by a game to run. Consoles also have their own GPUs, as do mobile devices.

Key term

Motherboard – a circuit board within a PC that connects all the main components.

Memory and storage

Memory is split into two different types: read-only memory (ROM) and random access memory (RAM). ROM is used in games as storage for the game's software. This is usually a DVD or Blu-Ray disc, (downloaded games from Steam or mobile app stores are stored on a hard drive or flash memory) but cartridges were used in the past in consoles and handheld devices. RAM storage is used to temporarily store data when the processor is working on it, and the more RAM available, the faster things usually run. Consoles and mobile devices use the amount of RAM they have as a selling point of their systems whereas on a PC it is a lot cheaper and easier to upgrade the amount of available RAM.

Long-term writable storage, unlike ROM that is read only, usually comes in the form of a hard drive or flash memory that will store not only the game data itself but also user-based data such as game saves and leaderboards. As games get more popular and people want to change devices when new models come out, cloud storage for game data has become a staple feature of consoles. Letting players store game data and game saves in the cloud means that they are able to continue playing from the same point if they upgrade or change their machine.

Output

Sound and display graphics are major elements of games and, as such, form the biggest share of the output. Gaming PCs and consoles use TVs or monitors to display the graphics but some, like the Wii U™, will have secondary screens for displaying additional information or providing a screen to use when someone else wants to watch TV. Smartphones and tablets are currently in a hardware war to outdo each other's display capabilities, with 1080 pixel screens becoming the standard and 4K screens providing unbelievable detail on a device that you can carry around in your pocket.

Sound is important, as it is one of the main ways in which the game communicates with the player without distracting them with text. A positive sound effect will inform the player that something good has happened and part of a game's learning curve is to remember which sound effects mean which benefits or punishments.

Another output of a game could be haptic feedback, which is a physical sensation such as a tremble or vibration, which is usually provided by controllers (see Figure 8.7).

▶ **Figure 8.7:** Game controllers can provide a rumble feature which provides extra feedback about events in game

Input

The way in which a player inputs information into a game is more crucial than any other aspect of software for computer games. The slightest delay in the interpretation of input by a game could mean the difference between life and death for your character.

Many PC players will argue that keyboard and mouse controls are better than those of a gamepad controller, but it really comes down to personal preference. Keyboard and mouse controls offer more customisability but players can use gamepad controllers when sitting on a sofa rather than at a desk.

Recent developments in voice and kinetic controls have created new and innovative ways to control games that not only challenge designers to come up with new ways to input instructions into games, but also open gaming up to people with physical disabilities who may struggle to hold traditional gamepads.

Touch input has become a big consideration as games for mobile devices have become more commonplace, because users will need to use the touchpad of their smartphone or tablet to play games. Some gamepads now include touchpads so that casual gamers are tempted to move across to console titles.

Connectivity

As we move into a time where society is always online, gaming devices are required to stay connected to the internet as much as possible. This allows operating systems to perform fixes and updates and for games to download patches to deal with bugs and exploits. PCs and consoles maintain their connections through local area networks (LAN) or wireless connections, while mobile devices can also enjoy wireless through mobile data network connections.

> **Link**
>
> For more on new hardware technologies, see the Emerging technologies section.

Software

Games are software applications, written using a programming language, and run on an operating system. They are a lot more complicated than most software applications but they are written using many of the same programming processes and techniques.

> **Link**
>
> For more information about programming processes and techniques, see *Unit 4: Programming*.

Operating systems

PC games are run on either a Windows®, Mac® OS X® or Linux® operating system. These operating systems differ in popularity and this is the main deciding factor in how many games are made for these systems. While most family homes will have run a Windows® PC, Linux® is a more specialist operating system and Apple® Mac®s are traditionally used by designers. If the priority use of the operating system is not gaming, then fewer games will be made using that operating system. However, digital platforms have started to change this.

PC operating systems are made to work on a number of different hardware configurations (on various different PCs, laptops and notebooks), unlike console operating systems which are designed with far fewer features and for one specific piece of hardware (one version of a console, eg Xbox One™). Console operating systems are known as proprietary systems, which means that the hardware manufacturers create them, and the source code is kept private and is not intended for use anywhere else. Most mobile devices run on either Android™ or Apple® iOS, but some run on Windows®. A newer operating system is Steam OS by Valve™ which has been designed for PCs that are primarily being used for gaming.

Programming languages and graphics options

The programming language in which the game is written can also vary quite a lot depending on the platform that it is intended for. The dominant language for developing games is C++, which is an **object-oriented language** that has been popular for nearly thirty years. Other languages that use a similar structure are C# and Java. C# is used within games engines and Java is used to create Android™ games. Different programming languages tend to be tied to different platforms. Some languages are described as 'light weight' and will only run within a games engine, such as JavaScript. These 'light weight' scripting languages rely on existing assets and features to keep the amount of code low and to produce games quickly, but they may run slower as a result.

Graphics software also needs to be considered. Systems use application programming interfaces (APIs) for managing the tasks related to the software and the GPU. The APIs are largely sets of routines and protocols for making the development of games easier. DirectX® is a Microsoft® graphics API and OpenGL® is the open source alternative.

Device drivers

Device drivers are another important type of software used for running games. The drivers are responsible for identifying the hardware devices that have been connected to the operating systems. Drivers tell the PC, console or mobile devices which hardware is trying to communicate with it and how it should work. This is how peripheral devices connect to games, such as newer controllers, microphones or even dance mats. Console manufacturers such as Nintendo® or Sony® will often release extra hardware devices in order to prolong the lifespan of the system and keep players interested.

Audio options

Audio is another important area of software. The music and sound effects are a massive part of the feeling and ambience that designers want to create for a game and one of the best ways to evoke feeling in a player is through music. A game will have different music in the different levels and these will be similarly themed to generate a common link across the game. Sound effects are used to teach players when they have done something positive or negative. Music files can be quite large and developers have created a number of different file formats in order to make the games run more smoothly, especially for online games. These file types are WAV, MP3, FLAC and AAC.

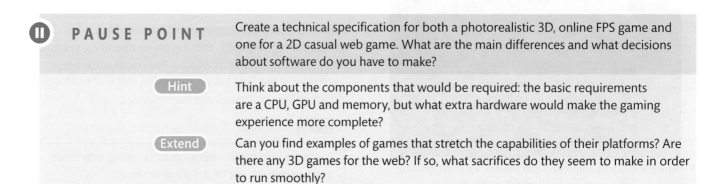

PAUSE POINT   Create a technical specification for both a photorealistic 3D, online FPS game and one for a 2D casual web game. What are the main differences and what decisions about software do you have to make?

Hint   Think about the components that would be required: the basic requirements are a CPU, GPU and memory, but what extra hardware would make the gaming experience more complete?

Extend   Can you find examples of games that stretch the capabilities of their platforms? Are there any 3D games for the web? If so, what sacrifices do they seem to make in order to run smoothly?

Games engines

Writing a computer game from scratch is a large undertaking and can involve writing thousands of lines of code. One way to make this easier is to use a games engine. A games engine is a piece of software, which is designed to make games. Most games engines are a combination of designer and programming environments in which the user is able to place all of the graphical assets for a level and then write the code that makes it interactive. There are a number of popular games engines in use today. Some of these are proprietary, meaning that they are only available to particular publishers or the large games studios that own them. However, some others are available to anyone, either for free or for a subscription fee. Popular games engines for multiple platforms are Unreal® Engine 4 or Unity® (see Figure 8.8), which are able to build games for PC, consoles, the web or mobile devices. Other engines are designed for one particular platform, for example XCode® is designed for Apple®'s iOS.

> **Figure 8.8:** The Unity® Game Engine is a powerful application used to build games quickly and efficiently

Rendering engines

One of the main jobs of a game's engine is **rendering.** This is usually done through one or more virtual cameras that point at the actions within the game that the players need to be focused on. The speed at which the game is rendered is measured in frames per second (FPS). The faster the FPS, the smoother the game appears to the player. When a gaming system is not powerful enough to run the game that the player has loaded, the FPS is usually the first casualty and a game may appear to run slowly or lag.

Physics engines

As all computer game worlds are virtual, all of the events and rules that occur within them have to be programmed. Some of the hardest elements to create involve the laws of **physics** that need to be applied to the world. Most games engines include built-in physics that takes the responsibility away from the programmers and allows

Key terms

Rendering – the process of converting game assets and environments into 2D images that can be displayed on a screen.

Physics – in the real world, gravity, mass and other laws of physics apply naturally but in a world created by a computer programmer the laws of physics have to be made to apply through coding the game correctly.

Collision detection – the process of checking to see which game objects have collided with each other.

for faster game production. Other engines that do not include built-in physics can use APIs to add physics. An example of this is the Box2D physics engine that was used to create Angry Birds™, one of the most popular physics-based puzzle games ever made. Another physics engine is the Havoc® physics engine, which has been used in many popular 3D games such as Assassin's Creed®.

Collision detection

Once the objects in a game world have physics, they have the ability to collide with one another. Working out the correct way for objects to collide which each other, and what occurs afterwards, is known as **collision detection** and is another important role of a games engine. Objects in a game world may have solid colliders surrounding them so that game characters are not able walk through them. These colliders may be the sides of a building, the floor or even invisible walls to stop a player falling off the edge of the game world. The player's character will also be surrounded by a collider that detects where their boundary is and stops them from moving through walls. A game character, whether it is 2D or 3D, has a very complex shape and it would be too taxing on a system to make every part of their body a collider. Instead, a capsule-shaped collider is often placed around them (see Figure 8.9) which is why, if you are careful, you can sometimes see a character's arm or leg moving through a solid wall in a game. The more you learn about how games are made the easier it is to spot things like this when you are playing them.

Scripting

A games engine will always provide the ability to add code in order to make things happen in the virtual world that has been created. Code is added using a **scripting language** such as JavaScript, or a full programming language like C++. The Unreal® Engine contains a visual scripting language called Blueprints. This is an easy way to create interaction without having to write lines of code.

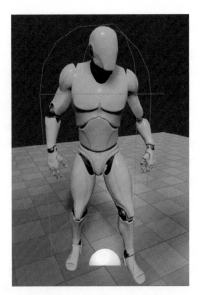

▶ **Figure 8.9:** Character surrounded by capsule-shaped collider in Unreal® Engine to enable collision detection

Graphical nodes are used to create movement, interaction and game mechanics like health or ammunition. Blueprints is similar to Scratch, a visual scripting language used to teach programming, but Blueprints provides a lot more functionality. The downside of using a visual scripting language is that the more

Key terms

Scripting language – a programming language that requires a separate application to run, such as a games engine or web browser.

Graphical nodes – colourful blocks used to represent the different functions of a programming language used to add easy interaction.

complex the game's mechanics, the larger the amount of nodes on screen, and it can soon look like a scramble of lines and nodes. If this happens, it would be better to switch to C++ and write the game in traditional code.

Animation

The final responsibility of the games engine is animation. Animation involves making different elements in the game move. There are two types of animation: vertex-based animation (which moves parts of a 3D mesh or 2D sprite) and skeletal animation (which uses a rigged character and sets of different animation cycles). An example of vertex-based animation would be a door opening when the player approaches it or a floating coin spinning around.

The image below (Figure 8.10) illustrates skeletal animation in the Persona system within Unreal® Engine. A character created in 3D can be rigged with a set of virtual bones that are, in turn, attached to different parts of the mesh. When a virtual bone is moved or rotated, the mesh connected to it will also move. The player will never see the bones but the engine knows that they are there and understands how they are supposed to act. The 3D character modeller will rig the character in a design software application such as Autodesk® 3D Studio Max, weight the bones so that the mesh is connected properly and then create different animation cycles such as a walk cycle, run cycle, jump cycle etc. These cycles are a single animation that ends at the same position as it starts so that it can be repeated for as long as the game requires the character to do that action. For example, when a player is pushing forward on the gamepad, the game will repeat the run cycle for as long as the player pushes forward. When a character is imported into the games engine, the animation cycles will be imported too.

▶ **Figure 8.10:** Skeletal animation in the Persona system within Unreal® Engine

PAUSE POINT

Games development can be an expensive process but much of the software mentioned so far is free for learners to use or does not cost anything until a game is published and has made a certain amount of money. Can you find out what the costs are for the software discussed so far?

> Hint   The websites for each of the different software are the best places to start.

> Extend   We have discussed game engines, 3D modelling software and operating systems, but graphic design software plays a large part in games development too. What additional software might you need?

Assessment practice 8.1   A.P1   A.P2   A.M1   A.D1

A mainstream games publisher is interested in creating a new game franchise that will have different titles that embrace the latest developments in current games technology. They want to show that they understand the needs of gamers and the different devices on which they can play. They also want to be seen as being part of the next phase in gaming. They have asked you to make a presentation to one of their development studios to help them understand the opportunities that are available.

They want a presentation which:

- explains the current social trends of computer games, including:
  - Different types of players.
  - Who buys what games?
  - How have habits have changed over time.
- explains the technological trends of computer games.
  - What emerging technologies are being developed in the computer games industry?
  - How are existing technologies being used alongside new ones?
- discusses how current and emerging technologies impact on how games are designed and developed to meet the requirements of the users and the larger computer games industry.
  - How is this changing the games that people buy?
  - How have game designs changed to meet them?
  - Who is investing in this technology and what will they gain?
- evaluates the impact of current and emerging technologies on the design and development of computer games to meet the requirements of the users and the computer games industry.
  - What technologies have failed in the past?
  - Are people playing games differently?

Plan

- What am I being asked to do?
- What information do the designers need?

Do

- Am I getting the most up to date information?
- Can I look at how past technology has impacted on game design?

Review

- I can explain what parts of researching the presentation were the hardest.
- I realise where there are still areas of the industry where I have knowledge gaps.

B   Design a computer game to meet client requirements

Designing a computer game is a complex process involving team members with many different specialist skills. The design phase is vitally important and rushing this stage can lead to many problems for the development team, or even the players further down the line. However, game development studios are not always in charge of their own deadlines, for example if they are working on a commission for a large publisher. Often they will be given the contract on the understanding that they meet very specific deadlines, so an efficient but also effective design process is crucial.

Computer games design processes and techniques

Understanding the formal methods used to design a game is very important. Each member of the team is trained in their own specialism (art, asset creation or programming) but they all have to understand all the steps in the game design workflow. The first stage of the game design process is the creation of a high-concept design document that will outline all of the game's unique features, storyline, characters and mechanics. This document is then expanded into a game design document (GDD), which covers all of the detailed design specifications for the entire game including how it will be made, how many levels there will be, how the game world works etc. The GDD is then shared between every member of the team and extra documents are written, for example a style guide and a technical specification. These two documents contain even more detailed designs for the specialist teams who will be working on the art or the programming sides of the game.

Mathematical techniques and processes

Maths and logic are a core element of programming and as such they form a crucial part of games design. The technical specification outlines all of the code that is required for the game, the platforms and languages that are being used, as well as details of the developers who will be responsible for creating them. The processes required for creating the functionality of the game and the maths that will make it happen must be considered thoroughly.

Calculations

Calculations are present in all software. Every time we click a mouse button or a gamepad trigger there are lighting fast calculations being performed in order to figure out what should happen as a result. Games use maths in a variety of different ways. The mathematics of graphics is one of the most common uses of this as geometry (the area of mathematics that deals with shape, size and space) is used to position 2D and 3D assets in a virtual world and then manage how they move, rotate and interact with one another. Geometry deals with points, lines, planes and solids and this transfers directly to the 3D modelling of objects where we create vertices, edges, faces and meshes. Games will use geometric calculations as part of their game mechanics. So, if we are playing an FPS where a player must fire a bullet at a target, geometry is used to calculate what happens if the player shoots at a particular angle and from a particular distance. Where would the bullet hit the target if fired in that direction, at that angle and from that distance? Geometry is used to establish

which shots would achieve the desired result and which shots would miss. In geometry, the point where a line cuts through a plane is called the intersection, and it would be this value that decides whether the player has been successful or not.

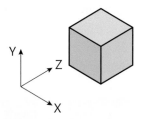

▶ **Figure 8.11:** All 3D game objects have a position in 3D space which is measured on an XYZ co-ordinate

2D and 3D space

The various different points in game space that need to be monitored, such as the location of a power-up or the exit to the level, will be stored as a vector. A vector is a mathematical way of representing the point in terms of its location on the x, y and z coordinate axes. Based on its distance from the game world's centre point (0,0,0), you can consider the vector value to be the object's address in the game world. Vectors are written as (x,y,z), always in that order, so that all developers and functions within the game understand the vector's location.

Vectors have two main abilities: they can move (or transform) from one place to another or they can be rotated into a new position. The way in which a vector rotates is decided by its pivot point. A spinning coin may have a central pivot whereas a door would pivot from one side. Vector values are also used to describe a direction that something is going to move in, so, if a platform was going to move to (0,0,10), it would move 10 units in the z direction but stay in the same position on the x- and y- axes.

You already know that maths is used in games, for example path-finding algorithms such as the A* algorithm, but it is also used as part of a game's physics. While all objects will have a vector to store their position, some will be marked as physics objects and they will have another vector for velocity, acceleration and mass. These vectors decide the direction in which an object is moving, how quickly it is moving, whether it is speeding up or slowing down and its mass.

Visual styles, graphics processing and editing techniques

The GDD will set out all of a game's design details in terms of how the game should look, and a large part of the design process is dedicated to this.

Worked example: Gravity

Now have a look at how a game would use maths to add gravity to a falling object. Most games will have a game loop function that runs continuously. Every time the game changes frame, the game loop function will run. Some engines call this an 'Update function' or an 'EventTick'.

Now set a numerical value for the gravitational field strength. Both Unreal® and Unity® game engines use a value of about 9.8 m/s^2 (metres per second per second), so the velocity of the object increases by 9.8 m/s every second in free fall. This is the same as the gravitational field strength on Earth.

Setting the gravitational field strength value to 9.8 and giving an object physics means that in every game loop we would say:

If the object is still falling, keep on increasing the velocity by the gravitational field strength.

Which would mean, while the object has not hit the ground, make it fall faster until it does.

Can you see a fault in this approach so far?

The game loop function loops every time the game changes frame and gravity causes an acceleration of 9.8 m/s each second. This means that the game's gravity is going to be stronger than standard Earth gravity because it is going to increase the falling velocity more often than 9.8 m/s each second. The game's programmers would have to calculate the game's likely frames per second and work out a smaller amount of gravity to add with each game update, or only add 9.8 m/s to the falling velocity after one second has passed.

Visual styles

While there are still a few text-based adventure fans out there, the majority of games are incredibly visual products and their individual art styles and design can often be one of the main selling points for the game. For example Limbo™, by Playdead™, studios is a monochromatic game (black and white) with soft lighting and all the characters are silhouettes (see Figure 8.12). This creates an amazing atmosphere of isolation and tension when playing the game and the art style is so important that every person working on the game had to consider it at all times. This means that the style guide for the game would have been of vital importance, especially to the asset designers.

▶ **Figure 8.12:** A screenshot from the Playdead game, Limbo™, showing its unusual visual style

Graphics processing

Objects in a game will have a texture or sprite applied to them via a shader. Also known as a material, the shader is a piece of code that defines how the object should be rendered graphically. It will set out properties such as the object's colour, texture, reflections, metallic value or outlines. Shaders are very important for maintaining a consistent graphical style across an entire game. They come into effect during the graphics processing stage of designing a game, before all the objects are rendered into 2D images that are then animated onto the screen, because the shaders decide how the objects should look.

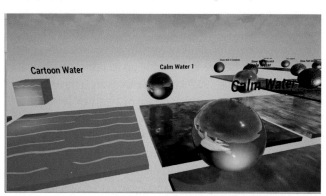

▶ **Figure 8.13:** Different effects can be created using shaders to allow the game developers to achieve the world designed by the concept artists. Screenshot provided by Ross Everson

Editing techniques

There are many different visual or art styles used in games and this is a major part of what makes games so popular to different audiences. Players may like **cel shaded** games such as Borderlands™, an abstract art style such as The Unfinished Swan™ or a paper craft style such as Tearaway™.

The art style of the game could be reliant on particular editing techniques. Editing techniques are the tools and features of graphic design software used to manipulate images to get certain effects. This would be the responsibility of texture artists, who may employ a particular technique, such as using a cartoon art style, to create the textures for objects in the game. These textures are created in a professional image-editing software application such as Adobe® Photoshop®.

Platform

Given that platforms vary in terms of capabilities and features, the target platform for a game is a big consideration for the designers. If a game title is intended for one particular platform, then it must be designed to take full advantage of that platform. For example, PC games should take advantage of keyboard and mouse controls as they are the most configurable controllers available and players can decide exactly where they want to map action buttons. Equally, games for the Wii U™ should take advantage of its tablet controller, which has its own touch-screen display that can be used to display extra information and provide additional interaction with the game.

Other titles are designed to be played on multiple platforms. If a game is designed for smartphones, will it work on Apple® iOS, Android™ and Windows® phones? If it does, will it connect to all of a player's game centre social networks and allow players to compare scores or challenge each other? Will it scale up to tablets such as the iPad® or the Nexus® 9? All of these questions have to be answered during the design phase of a game's production. Crowdfunded games may have stretch goals to expand their titles to different platforms after initial design, while games that are funded by mainstream publishers will have set agreements with different platforms before the game is made and they will only expand a game to new platforms if it has done well in sales.

Delivery

Games are designed for either physical or digital delivery, that is, their distribution to customers will either be by means of a physical product (a disc) or digitally (via a download or online streaming). If it is physical delivery, then there will be set deadlines for when the game code needs to be supplied to the factory responsible for printing the discs and game boxes. There will also be an additional amount of time allocated to distributing the game to shops around the world in time for release.

Games that are delivered digitally through platforms such as Steam™ or PlayStation™ Store will be given a deadline for digital distribution but it will not require as many steps to make it ready for the player. The choice of delivery method will often depend on the size of the game and the platform for which it is intended. Mobile games must have digital delivery, as smartphones and tablets do not have disc drives. There is the option for both on PC and consoles. Digital games are usually smaller. However, increasingly gamers like to have the choice of delivery method: a hard copy on disc that they can keep or the convenience of downloading their next game.

Game assets

A game asset is an element of the game that is created outside of the games engine and which has been imported into the engine. The asset may be a visible object that makes up part of the game environment, or it may be a sound effect that plays at certain times during the game. Game assets can be 2D or 3D and they can be graphical, audio or **triggers**. The assets are the building blocks of the game, that is, the game objects.

Gameplay features

A game's design has to cover all elements of the gameplay features. The GDD should cover all of these elements and ensure that the developers understand exactly how everything should work in a game. The following sections outline the different features of gameplay that are designed for a game.

Interaction model

How is the player interacting with the game? Is it through an avatar, that is, a virtual character who represents the player, or is it through some omnipresence, an invisible hand of god, which controls events in the game and of which the game world's inhabitants have no awareness? The type of interaction sets a variety of design decisions, such as the position and viewpoint of the game's camera, the way information is delivered to the player and how NPCs are interacted with.

Case study

Forest Jump

Consider a 2D platformer game called Forest Jump where a character must jump forever upwards through a forest canopy. The image below shows a scene from the game with labels indicating the types of asset involved.

The character is an asset made up of animated **sprites** that make her appear to jump and run.

The background is a static asset showing the forest background which never changes.

The trees are sprite assets and there are branch assets that have colliders so that the player can land on them.

Each time the player presses the jump button, a springy sounding audio asset is played and when the player reaches the top of the canopy of trees they pass through an invisible trigger asset that tells the game's code that the level has been successfully completed.

The character is an asset made up of animated sprites that make her appear to jump and run.

The trees are sprite assets and there are branch assets that have colliders so that the player can land on them

When the player reaches the top of the canopy of trees they pass through an invisible trigger asset that tells the game's code that the level has been successfully completed.

Each time the player presses the jump button, a springy sounding audio asset is played.

The background is a static asset showing the forest background which never changes.

▶ **Figure 8.14:** A 2D game uses sprites for all its assets

The assets are created using various different tools. 3D assets are created in a 3D modelling software package, such as 3D Studio Max by Autodesk®, and the GDD needs to generate enough concept art for the 3D modellers to be able to create the assets. There is usually a full asset list in the appendix of a GDD, but additional small environmental assets are often added during development as long as they conform to the overall visual style of the game.

▶ **Figure 8.15:** Examples of 3D assets

Participation

What exactly is the player taking part in? Is it a single player campaign where they follow a story alone? Is it a multiplayer game and, if so, is it a local multiplayer or online multiplayer game? If it is an online multiplayer game, is it a player vs environment (PvE) game where groups of people work together against AI enemies or is it a player vs player (PvP) game where they battle each other in different modes? These decisions will radically change the design of the game. A network programming team is needed for multiplayer games in order to write the code and set up game servers that players will connect to.

Narrative

Does the game have a story? If so, then is it a linear story which will have the same events and outcomes every time, or is it a story with branching narrative where the player's choices affect the outcome of the story? Branching narrative requires multiple scenes and levels to be designed, some of which may never be seen by the player depending on what decisions they make. A story treatment is written as part of the GDD and then, if the game has dialogue, a script will be written for each part of the game. The designers need to decide if the game dialogue is spoken, in which case voice actors must be hired, or onscreen text needs to be produced. While players prefer audio dialogue to having to read text onscreen, it makes it difficult to release the game in multiple countries around the world because, for every different language region that you want to release your game in, all the dialogue has to be translated and re-recorded. This is part of a process called localisation and can be very expensive.

Game setting

Lots of decisions have to be made about the setting of a game and some of these may affect what genre the game is marketed as. The physical setting refers to how the game world is made up. Is it 2D or 3D? How are objects scaled in the world? What are the boundaries and are there invisible walls to stop the player wandering off the path?

Next the temporal setting needs to be decided. When does this game exist in time? Is it in our past, our present or our future? Once that has been established, we need to know how quickly time is going to pass in the game. Is it real time where every game minute is a real-world minute or will time speed up and slow down depending on the events unfolding?

The environmental setting decides where the game is set. Is it in our world or a fantasy world? Is it on a distant planet or inside a microscopic universe? The environmental setting can also dictate what the world is like in theme or culture. It could be a post-apocalyptic world ravaged by zombies or it could be a world under the sea at risk from an environmental threat. Lots of settings in games are repeated from title to title but elements of originality can still be found even in the most clichéd of settings.

We are used to novels and films telling us stories of emotional highs and lows such as love, loss and betrayal. Games are able to take on an even greater emotional journey by letting us make our own decisions about what happens in the story: this is the emotional setting. What can be more heart breaking than watching your character lose the one they love when it was your decision-making that led them to this loss? Games that manage to immerse us in their worlds and combine this with great emotional plots are always well received, and are responsible for moving games forward as an art form rather than just pure entertainment.

Ethical decisions are also a cause of great emotion in games. The designers may choose to give a game an ethical setting by putting the player in a situation where they have to make an ethical choice. For example, it could be between saving one life or a million, or it could be whether or not to perform criminal activities to further

a cause but, whatever it is, ethical decision-making can make games incredibly immersive and rewarding. A good example of this is Papers, Please™, a 2D job simulator where you take on the role of an immigration office official checking who is allowed into the country. Once the sob stories start flowing, the bribes are not far behind and the game becomes a series of ethical dilemmas where the player must either risk losing their job for a deserving stranger, or feed their own family.

Goals

The designers decide the main purpose or objective of a game and players will not engage with a game unless it has a point. The designers will decide how the goals are broken down into different levels within the game. Often there is an item that the player has to retrieve or a fellow character who needs rescuing, and this is the goal of the game.

Challenges

The challenges that the player must overcome in order to achieve their goals are the next focus of the designers. What are the actual threats or hazards that the player must face? This stage of the design will see the creation and allocation of NPC enemies to different areas in the game as well as the design of environmental hazards, such as falling floors or jets of fire, which need to be circumnavigated to get to the goal.

Rewards

The designers will come up with a list of potential rewards for the player. One of the most commonly found game rewards are experience points or XP. Players will receive XP for defeating enemies or using a particular skill effectively. Once they have enough XP they may be able to spend it on levelling up or new skills, depending on how the game is designed. Other rewards could be unlockable areas within the game, or, perhaps, additional time or a temporary power-up that can be saved and spent in a future level.

Player actions

What can the player do? Can their character perform basic movements like walk, run and jump? Do they have a more sophisticated set of skills such as magic spells, wielding powerful weapons or teleporting across worlds? All these decisions, while easily made, have far-reaching consequences. For instance, if you give the character the ability to fly, what is to stop them from just flying right to the end of the level over the heads of all the enemies that have been put in their path? Player actions have to be designed to give the player the tools they need to complete the game, but not too easily. Some game designers will not introduce all of the player's abilities at the start of the game, but allow them to be gained, one by one, as the rewards of different levels. There is a style of game design called Metroidvania where the entirety of the game world is available from the very beginning but some parts are only accessible after certain tools or abilities are won by the player. The name comes from the classic games, Metroid and Castlevania, which had this design.

Rules

Once a character's abilities are decided, the rules of the game must follow. If the player is able to make their character jump, then how high? Can they double jump? Wall jump? The movements of a player significantly affect their progression through the game world, and the movement rules need to be carefully considered. A player's valid moves are the ones that they are allowed to make and the game should ensure that no invalid moves are made accidentally. The rules of a game world do not just apply to the player character, they also apply to enemies, and they decide the physics of the game world as well. If a character has magic, for instance, is it limitless or will they have to top it up with something like mana potions? If that is the case, then how many mana potions should there be per level, and how many can a character hold? All this has to be designed and decided before building the game.

Feedback

The way in which a player is aware of their progress is crucial in a game. The way in which software communicates with humans is a field of study called **human computer interaction (HCI)** and it is never more crucial than in games design. The last thing you want as a player is for your attention to be taken off your object of focus in a game. If you are fighting a boss, you do not want an indicator to start flashing in the middle of the screen and block your view. Games use a head-up display (HUD) to show information in a discrete and unobtrusive way. The more subtly information is fed back to players, the better the feedback, although it does need to be clear.

> **Key term**
>
> **Human computer interaction (HCI)** – the study of how people interact with machines, and the best possible ways to design interfaces between people and machines.

Difficulty

The difficulty of a game, or degree of challenge, sets out how hard it is going to be for a player to complete the game. Many games use a difficulty curve where the game starts easily and gets progressively more difficult the further through it the player gets. This may be actioned through enemy strength or a number of hazards in a

level. Many games allow the player to set the overall level of difficulty at the start of the game depending on their confidence, and some games will release a new difficulty level once the game has been completed on its hardest setting.

Game mechanics

The mechanics of the game include all of the functional game elements that need to be designed and are taught to the player, through either a tutorial level, dialogue or trial and error. Game mechanics may include an inventory system that lets players collect items, a crafting system that combines items to create new ones, or a scoring system whereby different accomplishments generate higher scores and win conditions. A win condition is the rule that sets the circumstances in which the player wins either an individual level or an entire game. In the classic arcade game Donkey Kong™, the win condition is reaching the princess at the top of the scaffold tower. Other titles, such as strategy games, may have more complex win conditions, whereby you must beat the enemy within a certain time frame using only particular resources.

Game structure

The actual structure of the game includes the number of levels, **cut scenes**, enemies and the progression that the player must make to complete the game. This is shown in a number of design documents, such as storyboards which show simple drawings of the sequence of events in a game, flowcharts, diagrams that explain how different rules or algorithms will work, and activity diagrams that show the way in which a player navigates the game from the opening menu to the final credits.

> **Key term**
>
> **Cut scene** – a cinematic sequence in a game that tells part of the story. Cut scenes can be a separate movie clip or can be shown during a level.

Quality

Games should be designed in such a way as to ensure that they are as high quality as possible, otherwise they will receive poor scores when reviewed and sales will be low. A game's compatibility with its platform needs to be considered during the design phase. For instance, if a game is being made for a touch-screen device, how many different buttons will the player be able to cope with at once? If a game is being developed for multiple platforms, then it must not rely on specific platform features that are not common to all of the platforms it is being designed for.

The performance of a game is also a consideration, as the designers making a game for a device with a lower specification GPU and CPU would not be able to design photorealistic graphics and hours of cut scenes with audio dialogue, because the system would not be able to handle it.

In addition, the designers have to consider the gaming experience at all times during the design stage. Why would people play this game? What is unique about it? How does the level being designed compare to the previous level? Does it have anything new or interesting for the player to engage with? Bad games are games where these kinds of question have not been asked or answered, and where the player is not considered enough.

Design documentation

The game design documentation (GDD) is passed from team to team throughout the games development process. It is of crucial importance and will be referred to constantly by artists, asset creators, programmers and testers.

Audience, purpose and client requirements

The GDD must begin with an overview of the requirements that the client has set out. The client will be the publisher for most games, but for crowdfunded games it will be the backers. Their requirements may include a series of milestones, at certain dates, that the client wants you to meet, or a particular emotion or atmosphere that they want the game to evoke.

The design will then go on to specify the audience requirements, that is, who exactly is the game for and why would they want to play it? Pinning down the target audience is crucial; it is nearly impossible to design a single game that will cater for everyone. There are so many

different types of player buying games today and the game designers have to be acutely aware of this. Almost every decision they make when preparing the design document should consider the audience and, because of this factor, it must open with a very clear specification of whom the game is for.

The audience for a game is worked out by looking at various demographics, that is, categories of people based on their age, gender, spending power, education, location and family status. The amount of time that they spend playing games and their gaming experience is also important. You could design a simple platform game in the style of Super Mario Brothers™ for a child based on simple game mechanics, but you could also design a similar game for a 30–40 year old who had enjoyed the original games and wanted to enjoy a nostalgic experience. A game studio might identify its audience based on similar titles that a particular audience has previously enjoyed, sometimes in a bid to steal market share from a competing publisher or platform.

There may also be a specific purpose to a game as well. While most games are designed purely for entertainment purposes, sometimes a developer will create a game that is designed to introduce a new peripheral device, such as a motion controller, educate the player in how to train their brain or learn to play an instrument, or help to advertise a new film or TV series. Creating games for marketing purposes, nearly always creates weak games because their design and development is rushed so that they can be released in time to advertise the new film or TV series that they are tied into. If you wait too long to release a game for marketing purposes, then all interest in that film/TV series diminishes, so games are rushed out to market without being properly designed or tested. It is only when the game is begun at the early stages of a film or TV series' development that it stands a chance of being a quality title.

Case study

A sample client brief

Frodo Games, an international publisher, has asked your development studio to make a game that serves as a prequel to the popular children's TV series *Seb's Teds* which follows the adventures of a young boy and his teddy bears. The TV production company that owns the rights to *Seb's Teds* are letting you use the names and images from the show on the understanding that

the game will contain no violent scenes, does not portray Seb or any of the Teds acting aggressively, and maintains the ethics and morals that the show is known for.

- What game mechanics would you consider appropriate for this title?
- Write a description of the audience for this game.

Legal and ethical considerations

There are several laws covering the design and production of computer games and these need to be considered when looking at a game's design.

Copyright

The most important law to consider is the copyright law that protects creative works made by an individual or a company and stops other people from copying them and making money from the copies. The copyright laws cover game content such as characters, places and specific game designs, but the creation of clones in gaming is as old as the games industry itself. Consider the mobile hit Flappy Bird™. As soon as that became popular, it was very quickly followed by Flappy Shark™, Flappy Duck ™ etc, which are clones of the original game with just enough difference that the developers could not be sued for breach of copyright. The trouble is that the law does not protect the look and feel of a game; only the intellectual creation itself is protected so many popular games are cloned and rebranded. However, the developers doing the copying will not have access to the original game code so it will always be an approximation of the original instead of a complete copy. Part of the problem is that it is argued that the functionality of one game is very much like another or similar to hundreds of other titles that have a small element of the game in question. If so many characters run, jump and shoot, would the creator of the first game that contained a character running claim that all other games have stolen their copyright? Games contain lots of elements that fall under copyright protection, for example the images, titles, names and the design of the levels themselves. All this comes under the term intellectual property (IP), which is used to describe the content within a game as well as the game itself. You might hear a publisher bragging about a 'brand new IP' which means a new title that has not had any previous games out and is all-original. A game tied to a film cannot claim to be a new IP, because the film has the IP; neither can a sequel.

Consumer rights

As computer games become a common part of our daily lives, existing laws have been adapted to consider games. One of these laws is the Consumer Rights Act 2015, which gives customers stronger rights as the consumers of (ie the people who buy) video games. UK residents can now claim a refund or repair if the digital content that they have bought, that is the game, is not working or is of unsatisfactory quality. Poor quality is often a consequence of a publisher rushing the development to meet deadlines and not testing the game properly. Interestingly, this does not just cover digital games that need to be paid for, but it also covers disc-based games and games that are free to download. Therefore freemium titles also have to be of a decent quality or the developers are obliged to fix the defective product. This is a good example of the law changing to include new products and patterns in society. Game designers have to stay up to speed with the constant changes in law and the differences between the laws of different countries.

Licence fees

Games designers have to consider other laws when releasing their games and a lot of these are to do with the financial side of games development. If a game is going to be released on a platform such as a console, they will have to pay a licence fee to the console manufacturer to get their game released for that system. Therefore, if a game is made for PlayStation 4™, then the developer would have to pay Sony® a licence fee. This would be paid on the understanding that the game was of sufficient quality to appear on Sony®'s system as the company's reputation would be damaged if inferior products were released. This agreement would be made using a legal contract that sets out the responsibilities and actions of both parties.

Royalties

Another financial consideration is the payment of royalties. If a game is made using a commercial engine such as

---

Ⅱ PAUSE POINT

Have a look at the blog www.gamerlaw.co.uk

Now imagine that you have created an amazing new game that is unique in its story, features and visual style.

Find out how you would be protected by copyright law.

Hint   Copyright law protects 'the expression of an idea' but not 'the idea itself'. How will this protect you?

Extend   What will happen if you release your game in different countries?

Unreal® Engine, there may be an understanding that games can be published for free, but, if they earn over a certain amount in profit, then they must start giving a percentage of the game's profits to the commercial engine. Music within a game will also be subject to royalty payments in the same way that it is for a film or TV show. In terms of royalties for the actual developers, they tend to be paid an agreed fee at certain stages of the game's development and, after it has been released, they do not have any claim to the profits. A few games publishers do offer royalties to developers, but it is not commonplace.

Digital rights management

Digital rights management (DRM) is another legal consideration for games developers. This is the area of law that concerns itself with how digital products are used and shared. Once a game has been purchased as a download, is it acceptable to copy this to other devices in the same household or to give copies to friends, or even sell copies? If you bought a DVD of a game you could lend it to friends and later sell it on, but you would only ever have the one copy. Different companies take different approaches to DRM. Apple® will let you set up family networks that share apps, while Google™ lets you log into as many different devices with your Android™ account as you want. Steam™ forces you to authenticate whichever machine you log into with Steam™ and, if another user is on there, you can request access to their game library. Microsoft® originally announced that the Xbox® One™ would have a constant internet connection to check the DRM of any game played. This was introduced so that they could monitor which games people were playing and for how long. They tried to spin it to customers as a way to get constant updates, but this received such a backlash from players that they quickly changed their mind. Their competitor Sony® introduced a 'virtual couch' that lets friends play each other's games whenever they are both online.

Ethical considerations

No specific law covers the ethical considerations of games design, but it is something that games designers have to think long and hard about. If they are representing a particular country or culture, are they doing it in a way that is ethically acceptable? (For example, they should not suggest that all the people from a particular religion are violent. They cannot discriminate or portray stereotypes

in games.) If they are putting the player in a questionable situation, are they clear that they appreciate that this is an ethical question and not something that the player should just accept? Questions about violence and sex in video games are always present in the media and many games have been accused of provoking all sorts of real-world crimes. Therefore games designers have to think very carefully about what they are depicting in their games and who could be influenced by them.

Game design

The following features should be included in the design documentation for a game.

▶ Type of gameplay – a definition of what the game involves, eg FPS, MMO, RPG.

▶ Data dictionary – a table showing all the data used in the game, its type (eg number or text) and its purpose.

▶ Algorithm design – designs for the game's functions and features using **pseudocode**.

> **Key term**
>
> **Pseudocode** – a way of writing code without it being in a specific programming language.

▶ Storyboards, flowcharts and an activity diagram – all show the structure of a game, how the game should look and flow.

▶ Visual style:
  - world – the type of terrain, style of architecture and style of objects
  - characters – player, enemies and other NPCs
  - feedback interface – how information is communicated to the player
  - perspective – 2D, 3D, first-person, third-person, scrolling, aerial, context-sensitive.

▶ Full motion video – used for cut scenes and menus.

▶ Asset lists – graphical, audio, video.

▶ Gameplay features – what features make this game original and unique.

> **Link**
>
> For more on gameplay features, see the section on Gameplay features.

Worked example: Hazman

Here is a sample of the game design for a strategy game called Hazman. (The full design documentation would be a lot longer and more detailed.)

Type of gameplay – a point and click strategy game for PC that sees a young hero clearing chemical spills in industrial areas around the world. As the game goes on, Hazman starts to suspect that these incidents are not accidents after all and a conspiracy theory soon leads to a dramatic rescue.

The player will quickly assess an area and race against the clock to find the right solutions to clearing up the different spillages. The gameplay is a combination of solving coded puzzles by mixing the right chemicals together and 'escape-the-room' style puzzles to get the hero and any good NPCs to safety.

Data dictionary – each level will have the following data requirements.

Name	Data type	Data length	Scope	Purpose
LevelNumber	Integer	1–99	Public	Stores the current level number that the player has reached.
MovementSpeedMax	Float	0–25	Public	Stores the current movement speed based on input from player.
PlayerScore	Integer	0–4	Public	Stores the current score of the player.
ChemicalTypes	Integer	0–9	Public	Stores the amount of different chemicals that can be spilled in current level.
ExitPosition	Vector3	(0–999,0–999,0–50)	Public	Stores the position of the level exit.

Algorithm design – the game level will be split into tiles, with 4 rows by 4 columns. Each spilled chemical will start on one tile and, as the game progresses, will spread onto more tiles until the player becomes stranded.

Pseudocode:

```
LevelGridArray{0000,0000,0000,0000};
On Game Start
  While ChemicalTypes>0 - Set random grid element to 1, ChemicalTypes--
On Game Loop
  For Each Chemical - Spread to next available empty grid space till array full
```

Storyboards – the opening cut scene for the game will be a series of still cartoon panes that tell the story of the first chemical spills. Additional cut scenes will be made after release, available as downloadable content.

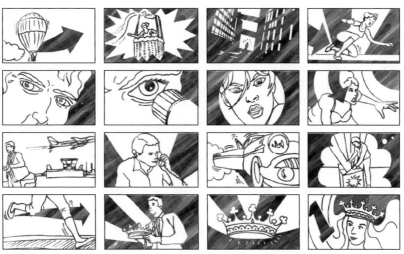

▶ **Figure 8.16:** A storyboard is a visual plan of how aspects of the game should look, usually showing cut scenes

Visual style – the game's style will be highly stylised cartoon visuals with thick black outlines around all assets. All floor tiles will have simplified textures and the chemicals will have a unique colour that is bright and has a shiny surface. The characters will only be seen from above and they will have exaggerated proportions (large heads and eyes, a small torso, short limbs and large feet). The HUD will display the time prominently on the top right and messages will be presented to the player in the centre of the screen (gameplay will pause until the message is discarded by the player).

The game will have a top down perspective throughout gameplay where the player clicks on different tiles to activate the puzzles and solutions. Where a solution is a success, a **context-sensitive perspective** will zoom in on the player's character whose animation will change to celebration mode.

Full motion video – there will be a cut scene at the start and end of the game. This will be an MP4 containing static images and the game's theme tune.

Asset Lists

Graphical	Audio	Video
Player sprites	Level specific theme tune	Opening cut scene
Floor tile sprites	Spillage Sound Effect (SFX)	Closing cut scene
Wall sprites	Creeping chemical SFX	
Hazard sprites	Death SFX	
Crates sprite	Win SFX	
NPC sprites	Time running low SFX	
Chemical sprites	Countdown SFX	
Menu textures		
HUD textures		

Gameplay features – the game is puzzle based. The first four levels will contain chemical puzzles where each chemical has an antidote, made up of ingredients that Hazman must collect, which will be spread around the level. Once these ingredients are mixed together, the level will be complete. The next four levels will involve escape-the-room puzzles where there are no antidote ingredients, but Hazman must assemble items to escape from the room. For instance, he will need to get a key from a monkey in a cage, and, once he opens the cage with a crowbar, the monkey will jump to a higher shelf out of reach, Hazman must then find a banana to tempt the monkey down and retrieve the key.

> **Key term**
>
> **Context-sensitive perspective** – this is when the in-game camera changes to focus on something that the player has selected or a change that they have caused.

Development choices

There are many different decisions that the development team need to make as they embark upon the creation of a computer game.

Platforms and programming languages

A number of different factors decide how a game is made and one of the most crucial of these is which platform it is being developed for. If the developer knows in advance that the game is only going to be released on one specific platform, then they will be able to find out the language that the platform is designed to be used with along with all the different games engines that can be used to create games for that platform. If they know that they are going to release the game onto multiple platforms, then they must use a games engine that supports all of these different platforms, or risk increasing the development time, because they would have to start from the beginning for each intended platform.

If you are writing games purely in code, then an integrated development environment (IDE) is used. This is a system, such as Visual Studio®, which supports one or more programming languages and is able to find errors in the program and, once finished, package the code into an executable application. A games engine will use an IDE to write the code portions of the game or it will have the IDE built in. For example, a console game that is going to be exclusively for the PlayStation 4™ could be written in C++ and all of the input and output will be designed specifically for the PS4™. It could be written in the Visual Studio® IDE. It is not possible to build levels and arrange assets visually in an IDE alone, which is why games engines are used.

If a game were going to be released on PC, Mac® and Linux®, then it would be best to create it on a games engine that supported all three platforms as it would be difficult to write the game code to work on three different operating systems directly in code.

Some programmers are able to use a simple text editor to write code and make games. In the 1980s, it was possible to buy magazines which contained code samples for players to copy to create their own games on systems such as the ZX Spectrum or Commodore 64.

C++ is the most widely used programming language for games. C# is a derivative of C++ but it is missing some features and does not run as fast. However, it is very useful for writing game mechanics for engines such as Unity® because it is easier to understand, but still powerful. Java is another object-oriented language, which can run slowly due to the way it is translated for any platform. It has not been embraced by games console developers for this reason, but it is the best way to write programs for Android™ without using a games engine, because the Android™ system is based on Java. Scripting languages like JavaScript and HTML5 are widely used for making web games because they are quick to run and small in file size. Older languages such as Python™ or Delphi® are not really used in professional games development but are very useful for learning how to program.

Application programming interfaces

The design of the game should also include reference to any application programming interfaces (APIs) that are going to be used. An API is a code library that has been written for use in other programs in order to quickly add extra functionality. It may be that the game needs to communicate with an external service, such as Apple®'s iOS Game Center for Developers to take advantage of online leaderboards, or it could be that the developers want to add a virtual reality option so the Oculus Rift™ API might be used. When a programmer wants to use an API, they reference it at the top of the code where it is needed in an 'Include or Using statement'. After the API has been included, the programmer can reference it whenever they want during development.

Computer game development kits

If a game is being designed for PC or web, then it is quite straightforward to test the code during development and the designers will ensure that the correct hardware is present before the build begins. If the game is being built for a console however, the development team will need to buy a console development kit for whichever platform they are designing it for. A console development kit is a version of the console that can connect to a PC and have test builds of the game deployed directly onto the console, to test how it works on the system for which it is being designed. This is the best way to test a game for a console and it ensures that all of the controls work, that the game loads and saves correctly and that any communication with the console's online capabilities work correctly. Some console manufacturers sell development kits while others are willing to lend them out to developers, especially ones they have worked with before.

Intended platform/media for delivery

An important question for developers to ask themselves considers which features of the intended platform the game will take advantage of. You may want to keep all the game's features common to all platforms or have specific functionality designed for individual platforms. These features should be included throughout the game, and should also be promoted in the marketing for the game as unique selling points.

In addition, the intended rating of the game needs to be considered during the design process (see Table 8.3). If a game is going to have a PEGI rating of 7 then it may have violence but the violence must be unrealistic (ie something that could not happen in real life, like a magic spell or a piano falling on someone and them recovering instantly). The rating makes a huge difference to a game's design and everyone involved in the design needs to know what the intended rating is so that they can make their designs age appropriate.

Another consideration is whether a game will be delivered as a digital download or a boxed game. If it will be released as a digital download, then there needs to be a series of graphical assets created for the game's entry on the download page. Digital platforms will also ask for a number of differently sized icons: these are graphics that can be resized, and graphics that can be used as part of a marketing promotion or sale (boxed games also need graphics for online advertising). All of these images have to be provided by the game's development team. If it is going to be a boxed game, then it also needs to have box art drawn up, an image to go on the printed disk and any instructions or promotional codes that are going to be included inside the game box.

▶ **Table 8.3:** PEGI games ratings, for more information visit **www. pegi.info**

3	Suitable for ages 3 and older. May contain very mild violence in an appropriate context for younger children, but neither bad language nor frightening content is allowed.
7	Suitable for ages 7 and older. May contain mild or unrealistic violence (eg violence in a cartoon context), or elements that can be frightening to younger children.
12	Suitable for ages 12 and older. May contain violence in either a fantasy context or a sporting action, profanity, mild sexual references or innuendo, or gambling.
16	Suitable for ages 16 and older. May contain explicit or realistic-looking violence, strong language, sexual references or content, gambling, or encouragement of drug use.
18	Unsuitable for persons under 18. May contain extreme or graphic violence, including 'violence towards defenceless people' and 'multiple, motiveless killing', strong language, strong sexual content, gambling, drug glamorisation, or discrimination.

Animation timeline

Different parts of a game will involve various different animated sequences. Animated characters will have a series of animation cycles that they will play on repeat when the character performs different actions. For example, walk cycles, run cycles, idle cycles and so on. The artists will draw single frame images of each position needed in the animation.

Cut scenes within a game involve assets used within the game, so the artists will create storyboards that follow the cut scene and may create a timeline showing the order in which assets are needed for that scene.

Production schedule

The schedule for a game is recorded in a number of different ways. The project milestones are set up first. The milestones are a list of stages that the project will go through, and the dates by which they need to happen. The art stage is followed by asset creation, mechanics implementation, level building and testing. Completion of these milestones may trigger the publisher to pay the development studio a portion of their fee, while any delays could result in a reduction in payment.

The GDD will contain a more detailed breakdown of the schedule. This may be a Gantt chart, which is a kind of bar chart that displays all the different tasks that need to be carried out to complete the project, who is doing them and when they need to be completed. The team may use project

management software to create and share the schedule. It is usually a live document that is regularly updated and adapted based on changes during development.

Resources

Games cannot be designed without various pieces of hardware and software and this can be one of the biggest expenses for a games studio, especially if they are making a game for the first time. Every developer in the team will need access to a PC and the appropriate software. 3D modelling software is very expensive, as is graphic design software, but they can be purchased on a monthly basis which means that the studio only has to pay for what they need. However, this is not a good long-term approach. The PCs required for games development need to have a good enough hardware specification to be able to model and animate in 3D.

Graphic designers and concept artists will need additional resources such as graphics tablets in order to complete their tasks (see Figure 8.17). They will also require traditional drawing equipment (pencils, pens and paper) and scanners to make these images digital so that they can be shared.

▶ **Figure 8.17:** A graphics tablet is an invaluable tool which provides a lot more accuracy than a mouse

In addition to these resources, a games studio will need a building to work in, and they will need to pay for utilities such as electricity, gas and broadband internet to function as a business.

Test plans

After a game has been created, it must be tested thoroughly. Players will not be happy if they have paid for something that does not work properly. Testing is taken very seriously and, while a lot of people imagine it to be tremendous fun to play games for a living, professional games testers need to be able to understand both the design documentation and the programming code because this is what they will use as a reference when they are creating and executing their tests. The test plans they write need to check the playability, performance and quality characteristics of the game.

There are a number of different strategies that can be used when planning the testing of a game, and the producer or project manager will be responsible for employing a test manager who will then choose the most appropriate tests. There are various types of testing documentation that can be used to plan the tests and then record the results.

The test plan covers the development of the entire game and makes sure that there are no flaws in the product that is eventually released. This is a very large-scale task and if any problems are found during testing the test plan will ensure that they are recorded and fixed. Games that are released with flaws or errors in them do not sell very well and receive poor reviews from games journalists.

Each test will have a test case, which is a particular

scenario that the tester will undertake to try out a feature of the game, or a command, under certain conditions. These conditions might be the direction of movement or the number of items in an inventory. It is important that the test cases cover as many different scenarios as possible so that there is nothing that the player could do when the game is sold that has not already been tried during a test.

The test plan is used as a test log, where all of the outcomes are recorded and an indication of what needs to be done to correct any errors is added. If a problem is found, the tester may take a screenshot to use as test evidence. This screenshot is then passed on to the developer who will use it to get a clear idea of the problem and then fix it. Once all of the testing is complete, a test report is written to show where problems were found, what has been fixed, and to summarise any vulnerabilities in the software or issues that might resurface. Once a game has been tested to a satisfactory level, it will then be released for sale.

Case study

Working out mesh constraints

The official documentation for Unreal® Engine 4 states that the maximum vertex count for a level in a mobile game is 65,000 vertices per mesh. So what does this mean? A 3D object in a game is created in software such as Autodesk® 3D Studio Max and is referred to as a mesh. Meshes are made up of single points called vertices and every vertex in a virtual world has to be calculated and positioned. If a simple cube mesh has 8 corners, then it has 8 vertices. If you divide the maximum possible amount of vertices, 65,000, by 8, you get 8125. This means that you could only have 8125 cubes in a mobile game.

It does not seem like that big a deal until you consider that a typical console character can be over 80,000 vertices: this is too many for a mobile game. Any character in a game will instantly increase the vertex count, especially if they are animated, as this requires more vertices in order to stop the mesh looking strange when it moves.

The next consideration is the number of bones used in animated characters. A standard human skeleton rig in an animated 3D character has 60 bones. The upper limit for bones in a mobile game according to the Unreal® Engine 4 documentation is 75 per mesh. This means that if you use the typical skeleton rig for animated characters, then you may not have enough bones left to have any other animated characters in the game.

Therefore designers working on mobile games will do a number of things to make sure that they can have multiple animated characters in their games. First, they will design the game with a very basic art style so that the meshes use as few vertices as possible. The more curves an object has, the more vertices it will require. So designers will create objects and characters with as many straight edges as possible. If you look at 3D games on old consoles, you will notice how the designers have avoided creating curves because they were limited in the number of vertices they could have.

Developers will also use level of detail (LOD) groups. This is a process where a simpler version of a 3D model is put into a game level when it is far away from the player, but, when you get closer to it, a more detailed version of the mesh is swapped in. For example, the less detailed version of a house may be a flat cube with images of windows and doors, but, when the more detailed version is swapped in, the house has doorframes, handles, window ledges and window frames.

Finally, developers can design their characters so that they are either not animated at all (they could still rotate or move), or they have simple skeletal rigs (no finger bones or feet bones, for example). Characters in mobile games tend to have cube-shaped feet and hands, which developers tend to get away with because these characters are viewed on small mobile device screens.

Constraints

The constraints of a platform are the limitations that designers have to consider when producing the design documentation. These limitations can have far-reaching effects on how the game is going to play.

Platform limitations – hardware

Perhaps the biggest concern for designers is what the hardware can cope with. A high specification gaming PC with an Intel® i7 processor, 16GB of RAM and a powerful graphics card will not have any difficulty running any game that is thrown at it but if a game is being designed for a less powerful platform then the abilities of the hardware will directly affect the game design.

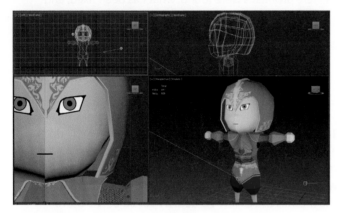

▶ **Figure 8.18:** A 3D Character designed for animation. Screenshot provided by Dan Bennett

Platform limitations – software

The software on a system does not produce as many constraints to games designing as the hardware does, but the version of an operating system that is being used may cause some problems. Mobile operating systems are updated all the time and if a game is not compatible with a few older versions then the designers will lose a portion of their target audience. Apple® fans often complain that new system updates make their hardware redundant and force them to upgrade, and that this also reduces the number of games available to them because a newer game, marked on the app store for a higher iOS version, will not even appear to them.

Reviewing and refining designs

Producing the design documentation for a game is not something that you do once per game and then make no changes. A game's design should be reviewed as often as possible, and the more time set aside in the schedule for looking at the designs and for seeing if they can be improved, the better.

Primary feedback

After the initial design documentation is completed, a game's designs will be shown to clients and other interested parties, potential players or any licence partners, to see what they think of them. They will be asked about the quality, effectiveness and appropriateness of the designs for the intended audience. Sometimes, a number of **prototypes** are made as part of the design process and these will be demonstrated to potential users via the internet or at gaming conventions. Designers have to be careful about showing too much too soon because a lot can change during the design stage. However, much can be gained from knowing what your potential audience thinks about your ideas. It provides you with feedback with which to review and refine your designs.

> **Key term**
>
> **Prototypes** – small test game levels used to make sure that the key features of the game are working and to illustrate to clients and potential customers what a game will be like.

Client communication

Prompt and professional communication with the client is crucial for the design team to show that they are on top of the project and that they are not hiding any slipped deadlines or major problems. Whether by email for brief exchanges, or face to face with the client for important discussions, the design team has to be in regular communication with their client. Many games studios subcontract some areas of the design and development to different studios and this can cause a breakdown in communication which may result in a weak final product. In 2013, a highly anticipated game received very low review scores and disappointed the gaming public because it did not contain scenes that had been in the promotional material. A group of gamers took the developers and publishers to court. The publisher blamed the developer but the developer claimed that it was the responsibility of the publisher. It is possible that these problems could have been avoided if there had been better communication between the developers and the publisher.

Meetings and timescales

Whenever different teams within a developer are working together, and when they are working with a publisher or subcontracting elements of the development, it is important to have regular meetings and to keep records of these meetings in the form of minutes, decision logs and action lists. In the games industry, one form of **project management** used is called Agile Scrum. This approach requires the teams working together on a creative project to meet every day for 'daily scrums' where they discuss the current progress and identify any changes that need making.

Key term

Project management – different methods and procedures used to keep a project on track and under budget by minimising and mitigating risks and issues.

When changes to the designs are made, either due to feedback or because of review work within the design team, the timescales for the overall development must be updated to include how long the new changes will take to implement.

Updating the design documentation based on feedback and reviews means that a new copy must be distributed to the entire development team as soon as the changes are approved. Alternatively, a live document can be edited which everyone has access to.

Refining ideas and solutions

When the design for a game is started everything is possible, but then, necessarily, it is slowly refined down into a more specific and sophisticated design that players will want to play. Through making prototypes, it is possible to see which ideas work or are popular, and then to refine them down to the best possible version. The game's designers will choose their refinements by selecting the most successful (popular or effective) features, and by removing elements that proved too difficult to get working properly in the prototypes. The game's publishers and potential customers will be shown the prototypes and asked for feedback, which will then inform their ideas. Problems in the game's design that are revealed by prototypes require solutions which, once found, are then included in the design refinements. It is hard to find out which features were cut out of popular games as the games studios tend to keep these details to themselves, but the internet is full of rumours of features that might have been.

Theory into practice

Media and communication skills

The games industry is at the forefront of creative media and technology. Given this, its working practices tend to be driven forward by dynamic individuals and cutting edge software. You have to be able to use excellent communication skills to ensure that your role in the game's design and development is as efficient and effective as possible. Below are lists of the written and verbal skills required to work successfully in the games industry.

Written skills:
- be able to use email to share or request information
- create design documents that colleagues can easily interpret
- write reports detailing a project's progress for clients
- create presentations with visual aids to assist understanding.

Verbal skills:
- be able to communicate effectively one to one with colleagues and subordinates
- be able to communicate and work effectively as part of a team
- be able to communicate effectively in both informal and formal situations.

How effective your verbal skills are will depend on how well you use tone and body language, as well as what you actually say, to remain professional and convey information. This is especially important when you are giving presentations or talking to clients. You have to use positive language and be able to reassure your audience that you are in control and you understand the scale and scope of your presentation topic. You must use the appropriate technical language when talking to people, especially when presenting information across different teams. If you use too much technical jargon with non-technical colleagues, the discussion may be lost on them.

1 You must always consider how you are responding to people. Are you being supportive? Are you making sure that everyone is getting the chance to talk, not just the loudest person at the table? If you are good at resolving arguments or conflict in teams, or managing the expectations of clients, then a leadership role in games development could be in your future. Make a list of ways in which you can develop your written communication skills.

2 Write a list of tips for yourself on how to communicate effectively in the following situations:
   - when discussing the design of a game with teammates
   - when delegating design tasks to subordinates (people that you manage)
   - when presenting the design of a game to clients.

Write down ideas for how you would be supportive to teammates and subordinates in a design team and how you would make sure that everyone's opinions and ideas were heard.

C Develop a computer game to meet client requirements

Programming a computer game can be very different to creating an office software application or a web application but there are still similarities.

Just as a software application uses code to create menu structures and events, so does a game: it can dictate the flow of the game from the loading screen, and it accesses files in similar ways for game saves. When games programmers are deciding how to proceed from the design documents that they have been given, they usually have the first decision made for them: which programming language they should use. This decision tends to be taken out of their hands because the choice of platform will decide how the game is going to be built. There are still some choices available to the programmer but they are narrowed down a lot. Some computer games development companies will have a particular house language that they insist that everyone uses. The implementation of the programming will depend on the language that is being used but also on the complexity of the game.

Principles of computer games development

Before development begins, there is a basic understanding shared amongst the development team about the principles of games development. When working on a game all team members, regardless of their individual role, have to understand every step of the process in order to ensure that they are working at the optimum level.

The design documentation should have been distributed to the entire team before the development phase. Certain technical diagrams, also known as **schematics**, are delivered to the people who are responsible for the production of those elements. If a 3D game has a third-person character, then they will require a 3D mesh that has been rigged, a series of animations, a state machine to control the transitions between animations, space and a player control program that reads input from the player and changes the animations, movement and rotation of the player character accordingly.

Computational processes

Various computational processes are used as part of games development. These processes happen discretely in the background of the development process and during runtime when the game is playing. One example of this is the **rendering engine**, a system that is responsible for changing the massive data set that represents the objects, textures and players in a game and converts them into a series of 2D images that are rapidly changed. We believe we are viewing a world in 2D or 3D and seeing it move but, as with TV, film and traditional animations, we are watching a series of flat images being quickly animated before our eyes. That is why, when a system slows down or **lags**, the images can freeze (we are stuck on one image waiting for the next one to render).

The screenshot below (Figure 8.19) shows how a rendering engine can also add effects on top of the world that we are

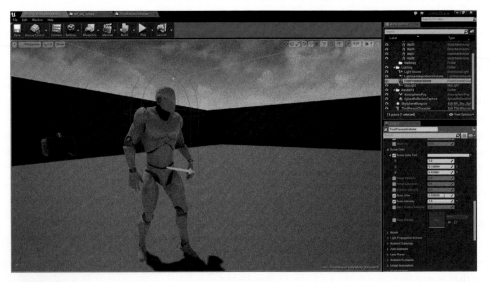

▶ **Figure 8.19:** Camera effects can be added to a game

Step by step: Production of a third-person 3D game using a games engine　4 Steps

1 The **3D modeller** is given concept art and detailed designs for the player character. As the character seen most in a third-person perspective game, it will have lots of vertices allocated to it. The modeller will understand, based on the animation schematics, how the character will need to move so they will create the mesh with movement in mind. This means that when the animator takes over, they will receive a model that has the rigged bones ready for animation and is modelled in such a way that allows for all the required animation. Imagine that a human character had been modelled and nobody had told the modeller that one of the animations sees the character reveal a tail that they had been hiding. If the tail was not modelled and rigged, it would not be able to feature in the game.

▼

2 The **animator** will use the animation schematics to create all of the different **animation cycles** that have been requested. In **photorealistic games** with big budgets, the animators will use **motion capture** studios, where actors perform the animation movements while wearing motion capture suits. This speeds up development but costs a lot of money.

▼

3 The animator will then hand the animated rigs over to a **technical artist** who will put the animated character into the games engine and create a state machine, which is a system that decides when one animation should change into another, for example when a character should go from standing to walking and from walking to running. The technical artist does not need the animator to explain all of the animations created to them because they can see them in the design documentation and perform their part of the job easily.

▼

4 Once the animations have been completed by the technical artist, they are handed over to the programmer who has been writing code to make the animations change on the push of a button or pressure on an analogue stick. This example is for the production of a third-person 3D game using a games engine. The process would differ depending on the type of game and size of team.

Key terms

Schematics – a technical diagram showing the content and function of game elements.

Rendering engine – the software in a games engine that converts virtual worlds into 2D images which are then animated.

Lag – a delay or reduction in the game's frame rate.

3D Modeller – a job role that involves the creation and texturing of 3D objects.

Animator – a job role that involves the creation of movement in game objects.

Technical artist – someone who works between the technical and design teams and understands both.

Animation cycles – different motions that characters will use on repeat such as running and jumping.

Photorealistic games – games that try to look as lifelike as possible.

Motion capture – a process where real-life motion is converted into data that can allow game characters to move in the same way.

being shown. It might be a temporary effect tied into the game's story or an artistic decision that is made later, but post-processing effects can be added to change the overall look and feel of a game. The example in the screenshot shows a film-grain effect being added to make a game seem more 'old world'.

Physics engines are an important computational process that can affect the speed at which a game runs. If a game uses too many physics objects, then the game can slow quite significantly.

Lighting is another crucial computational process and the real-time creation of shadows is a process that can slow a game down significantly or require that it is only played on a very powerful machine. Some PC games allow you to change the quality settings in order to run a game on a slower specification. One of the first things to get turned off will be real-time shadows. As with game physics, something that happens easily in the natural world takes a massive amount of calculations and processes to simulate in a game world. Shadow quality can, usually, be changed. A hard-edged shadow looks unrealistic in most situations, but more realistic than an object that does not cast any shadows. Soft-edged shadows that fade into the light are a lot more realistic, but require the shadow to be rendered a number of times and therefore take a lot more computational power.

Applying mathematics

When a game is being developed, all the objects which require physics will have it applied. This is usually done in a games engine but, when the game is written just using code and assets, the physics will be an API which is then applied to objects that require physics in the code.

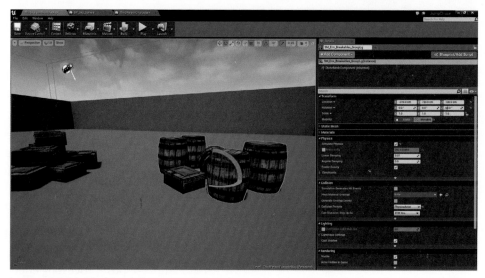

▶ **Figure 8.20:** The barrels have got physics activated in the game engine

The screenshot above (Figure 8.20) shows how a games engine applies physics, with a simple tick box and then the application of various different settings, such as how much mass the object has. The image also shows the three different vector values that are applied to the position, rotation and scale of the object. These vectors all contain three values which correspond to the *x*, *y* and *z* coordinates of 3D space. The object is selected using the rotate tool and each of the three axes are presented as a direction in which it can be rotated.

The application of maths while the game is running is dependent on the features of the game. One common maths function that is applied to game objects is called lerp, which stands for linear interpolation. This is movement from one position to another and is used on moving platforms, simple enemies and health bars, for example.

Prototypes and engines

If the development is taking place in a games engine, the correct choice of engine must be made. There are many to choose from and, as most of them include a purchase price or payment of royalties, it is important to get the choice correct from the start. Two of the most popular engines, Unity® and Unreal® Engine, have achieved their success by being able to port games onto multiple platforms, whereas other engines such as Cocos2D-x™ are aimed at one particular platform.

▸ **Figure 8.21:** Game mechanics should be tested in small prototype levels

Once the games engine has been decided upon, a number of rapid prototypes will be created to test and show off some of the game's unique features. These prototypes will be used to check the feasibility of a feature, explore the timescales needed for development or to solve problems and to identify issues early on. The prototypes will sometimes be used to create trailers or promotional materials for the game, but developers need to be careful because players have long memories and if the final product seems too different from early footage then complaints will be likely.

Tools and techniques for development

There are many different tools and techniques used in games development, and the more mature the industry becomes the more creative developers are getting.

The image below (Figure 8.22) shows landscape sculpting, which is a technique available in many games engines whereby a large flat mesh is created and the developers are given various sculpting tools in order to create a realistic landscape.

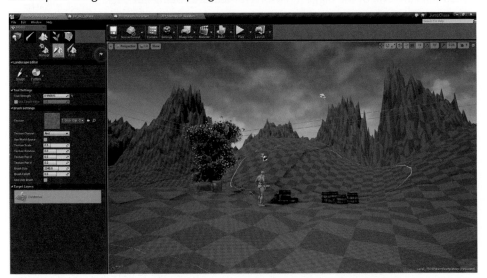

▸ **Figure 8.22:** Landscape sculpting can save huge amounts of development time

A multi-layered landscape material will then be applied which allows the environment designers to colour in the landscape with different textures that will represent, for example, rock, sand and grass (see Figure 8.22).

Another technique is high-to-low poly modelling whereby a 3D modeller will create a highly detailed version of a mesh and then create a texture from the model that is then applied to a low-poly mesh. Doing this creates the impression of detail without having to render complex shapes.

Choosing the right tools and techniques depends on the type of game in development but also the experience of the development team.

Quality assurance

The quality assurance (QA) process begins during the game design with the designing of the test plans, and as development begins the testing team will start to grow. The testing process is not just about finding problems – it is also about suggesting potential fixes and refinements. Testers are more commonly known as QA technicians and it is a very responsible role that requires people with meticulous attention to detail. Testers should not just be people who enjoy playing games, but people who are able to think of all of the different ways that a game can be broken, and are able to follow formal processes to document every problem that they find in a way that can be understood by the programmers.

The testing is split into different phases and begins with unit testing all of the individual technical elements of the game. This is followed by alpha testing the first complete build, beta testing the next release after bugs have been fixed and then a final quality test to ensure that everything is working. Sometimes the developers will offer a beta build to the public for testing, as this gives them the chance to get much more feedback.

Technical constraints

While we have already looked at the design constraints that can affect how the game will look and feel, a number of technical constraints may affect the development stage. The game will have a set budget and this will dictate how much time can be spent on development, as most of the team will be on fixed-term, temporary contracts. Players often ask why games do not have all the features it is possible to have and budget constraints are one of the biggest reasons for features being cut back.

The size of the servers will affect the development of an online multiplayer game. The number of players who can access the game online at one time is known as the maximum concurrent players. If the server is unable to cope with all of the potential players across the world, then the workload may be split between multiple servers for set areas such as, for example, Europe and North America.

Developing computer games

In this section, we will follow the step-by-step development of a third-person game called Jump Chase where the player has to race through different levels to get to the end goal within a set time limit. Known as a platformer or platform game, this style of game has always been a popular design.

Worked example: Creating Jump Chase

Visual style

As a platform game relies on precise jumps and timing, the perspective works best with a third-person avatar so that the player can judge all their jumps carefully. The game is being made in Unreal® Engine 4 and, as the screenshot below shows, the sample third-person character template contains an animated character mesh which is followed by a camera. That camera has its own settings and this includes field of view, or area of vision, which is the extent of the area that the camera captures. A wide field of view will let the viewer see more of the scene but this may scale down automatically if the display being used does not have enough resolution to support it.

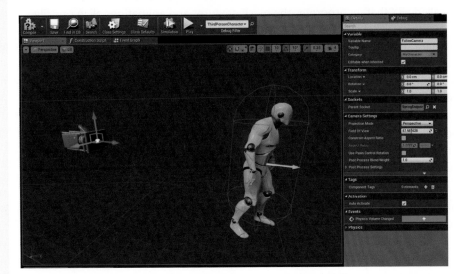

> **Link**
>
> For more about avatars and omnipresence see the Interaction model section.

▶ **Figure 8.23:** The field of view is set by the camera that follows the player's character in this third-person game

Input methods

In Jump Chase, the player needs to be able to control the main character as easily as possible and there are a number of input methods available for this, depending on which controller the game will use. This game is played on PC, which means that it could be controlled by a keyboard/mouse or by a gamepad.

▶ **Figure 8.24:** Player input can be mapped to keyboard, controllers or even both

The default settings for the third-person template in Unreal® Engine supports mouse and keyboard but it would be relatively easy to add gamepad support as well. While many different gamepads can be purchased for PC, the majority of them tend to have the same configuration so that they will work with the bulk of PC games. The code for the character will not specify a particular key or button but instead it will be named, for example MoveForward, Jump, LookUp. These labels are then mapped to one or more keys, so the walking movement may be mapped to the W, A, S and D keys. Some games allow menu options to provide customisable keys so that the player can choose exactly which keys they want to use. Some players may prefer the keys to be spread out, but some prefer them closer together. It can also work better for left-handed players to move the controls to the I, J, L and M keys. This feature is not usually available on console games, even though you can plug in a keyboard, but players are given control configuration choices in some games. Games consoles are sold with their own bespoke controllers and the designers will normally have used all of the button options available.

Asset integration

Once assets have been created for Jump Chase, they will need to be imported into the games engine. 3D modelling software exports meshes in a format called FBX that incorporates the mesh, textures and animations all in one file.

- Graphics:

  Graphics can be created in two different ways, using raster images or vector images. Raster images (known as **bitmaps**) are made up of a series of pixels and it is important when making games to keep the number of pixels in an image (its resolution) as low as possible without losing quality. This will make the game run more smoothly. A raster image with very few pixels will be a small file size but will have a very blocky style known as pixel-art style. The more pixels there are, the smoother the image. In Jump Chase the designers will need to make raster images for the textures applied to the 3D models and for the game's interface.

Vector graphics use points and lines to define an image. Vector graphics take more computational power to work with so are not used as frequently in games, and very few games engines support them. Even though vector graphics scale better, it takes less memory and processing to use a series of differently sized bitmaps.

- Texture mapping: All of the meshes that are imported into Jump Chase will have textures applied to them as set in the software in which they were created. One way to make a game run at a faster frame rate is to have different assets share the same texture file. This can be done when one asset, say, a floating platform, uses the top half of an image file for its metal texture and another asset uses the bottom half of the image. This means that two assets only need one image file. Textures are mapped to 3D meshes, which means that each flat surface on the mesh is tied to a particular part of an image file. If you think about a textured die, each face of the die would have a square in the image file and these squares would be mapped to each polygon in the mesh.
- Animation and video: The main character in Jump Chase is going to have different animation **cycles**. The default character has an **idle cycle**, a jump cycle, a walk cycle and a run cycle. The state machine uses the idle cycle as its **default setting** and, when the jump button is pressed, it will transition into the jump cycle.

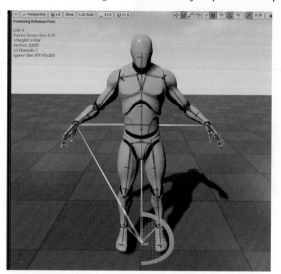

▶ **Figure 8.25:** Game characters can be rigged with bones to allow them to contain multiple animations

The walk and run cycles are blended together so that, when a speed value stored on the Jump Chase character changes (when the player pushes or releases one of the movement buttons), it will transition from idle to walk and then run, depending on how long the movement button has been pressed. All of these animations are used with the skeletal rig that is inside the mesh. Figure 8.25 shows what that rig looks like and how the games engine can be used to manually create new animations, if needed.

Other animations may be used in Jump Chase such as cut scenes or scripted events that move the story forward. Cut scenes will usually be recorded animations that are imported into the engine as a video file or, similar to scripted events, a series of animations controlled by the games engine. Unreal® Engine uses an animation system called Matinee that allows the developer to use existing assets and levels to create animated sequences, which are observed by cameras in the level. Therefore the player will lose control of the character while the cut scene or scripted event takes place.

- Audio: Audio is crucial to the experience of playing a game. The virtual world is made much richer by music and sound effects that create memories and by educating the player in how the world works. As for graphic assets, sounds can be imported into the games engine after they have been created in other software such as Logic®, Audacity® or GarageBand®. The level in Jump Chase will have fast-paced, frantic music that indicates that there is a time limit, but there will also be a constant ticking sound until the time runs out.

▶ **Figure 8.26:** Audio can have 3D properties so that it can become louder the closer you get to an area

Sound assets can be 2D or 3D. 2D sound assets are heard by the player at its volume setting and cued to play as programmed by the developer. Sounds can use triggers, so when the player steps into a certain area, such as a creepy forest, they walk through an invisible trigger and a sound effect will play (the cry of an owl, for example).

3D sounds work in the same way but they are location specific, so as the player approaches the sound will get louder and as they move past it the sound volume will diminish. In Jump Chase, there will be a creepy building and the sound of someone laughing coming from inside a room that cannot be opened, just to add a sense of horror to the level and to keep the player motivated to move forward. The sound clips have to be synchronised to the visual displays so that they happen at the right time. This is especially important when sound is being used for spoken dialogue as the character mesh has to move its mouth at the same time.

Artificial intelligence

Now that Jump Chase has some assets in place, this is a good point to start prototyping some of the more advanced features to ensure that they work correctly. The game features some roaming robots that will move around the ground and make sure that if the player falls down then there is still a challenge as they try to get back onto the platforms above.

The roaming robots will use a path-finding algorithm, a search algorithm, that needs to be tested in a prototype. The robots will consider the landscape to be a **grid** that is divided into separate **nodes**.

The code needs to be written such that the robots move between two different points. We need a way of working out the best way to move from one space to another and the breadth first search (BFS) algorithm can be used. BFS is an algorithm that shows the shortest route between objects on a grid. It does this by taking one step at a time and finding links between the different grid nodes. This is similar to a theory called six degrees of separation that says everything is six or fewer steps away, so that any two people can be connected, through a common experience such as being in the same film or going to the same school, by a maximum of six steps. BFS creates a queue of all of the nodes that are connected to the current node and then loops through them, one at a time, to see if they are connected or have been explored.

In C++, the programming language that the Unreal® Engine uses, the BFS algorithm would look like this.

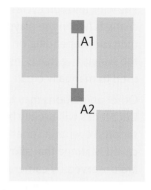

▶ **Figure 8.27:** Grids are used in games to map levels for AI characters to traverse

```
//Loop until node queue is empty
while (!nodeQueue.isEmpty()) {
        //remove node ID from queue
        int visitedNode = nodeQueue.removeFromQueue();
        //check all connected nodes in a loop
        for (int newNode = 1; newNode <= n; ++newNode)
        {
          //check to see if the newNode is connected and if it has been
          visited
          if (isConnected(visitedNode , newNode) ) {
                if(!hasBeenVisited[newNode ]){
                        //add to queue
                        nodeQueue.addToQueueEnd(newNode);
                        markAsVisited(newNode);
                }
          }
        }
}
```

Key terms

Grid – a network of lines that is projected onto a game level in order to split it into logical sections.

Node – a point where lines intersect.

Link

For more about path-finding search algorithms, see the section Search algorithms.

This code snippet shows a section of the BFS algorithm where it is checking through all of the nodes connected to the current node and seeing if they have been visited yet. The robots in Jump Chase will do this before they move. Once the code loop has finished and created a list of nodes to move through, the robot will then make its moves.

More advanced features

- 3D rendering: Jump Chase has a 3D environment with sculpted landscape and audio. This is created in Unreal® Engine and the platforms will be 3D meshes created in Autodesk® 3D Studio Max.

- Save game states and player progression: Another advanced feature is creating save files or auto-save points. Many modern games auto-save all the time, especially online titles. Third-person platform games like Jump Chase tend to use checkpoints, parts of the level that once reached are automatically returned to if the player's character loses a life. A checkpoint location will be stored in a save file locally on the player's system or on a server if it is an online game.

  Local file saves are also used to save progression information in Jump Chase. Details about how far the players have reached and how quickly they completed the challenges are added to leaderboards. The game will also use an achievement system so that when a player achieves certain goals in the game, such as completing it on the hardest level of difficulty, they will be able to see a trophy on the achievement screen.

- Multiple players: Games developers have to think very carefully about any multiplayer or networked features they are going to put into a game. Multiplayer games contain many advanced features such as player matching, which is a system that finds different people around the world who are of a similar level to you and will provide an appropriate challenge for you. Players do not like to be pitted against opponents who are too strong or too weak for them as this makes the experience unsatisfying.

  Ensuring that network connections are maintained is important, but this is not something that is in the developer's control. Game publishers will be responsible for creating servers that online games connect to, and the reliability and availability of these servers is dependent on how much money is spent on them. The servers have an important function in allowing the player's systems to communicate with each other and in maintaining any online leaderboards and achievements.

This example is designed to give an overview of a developed game but is too complicated to be created by a single learner or a small team. The scope of this unit is to provide an understanding of the whole process and to create a simple working game that will provide an understanding of how to create something that could be developed into a wider, working title.

Testing computer games

Once the development is completed to a point where testing can begin, it is important to get started as the more time that can be given to testing, the better the final product will be. The focus of the testing is split into four areas that look to answer the following questions.

▸ Playability – do all the features in the game work? Can the player do everything that they should be able to do? Is it possible for the player to get stuck anywhere?

▸ Compatibility – does the game work on its intended platform? Does it load and save appropriately? Do all the system's controllers work with the game?

▸ Stability – can the game be played from start to finish without breaking? Is the frame rate consistent throughout?

▸ Acceptance – do the players enjoy the game? Is the challenge at the right level?

Testing tools

Games engines and IDEs contain tools that help with the testing phase of games development. Figure 8.28 shows a statistics window that can show details of all of the assets in the scene and how they are being rendered.

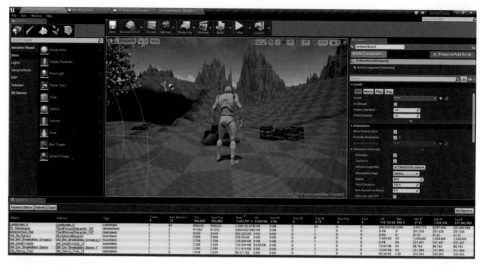

▶ **Figure 8.28:** A statistics window

Other tools include debugging tools like breakpoints and watch values that allow the programmers to automatically stop the game at certain lines of code within a function to check to see which values are being stored. This will be useful if a particular game feature is not working correctly because it will help the programmer or tester to solve the problem (or **bug**) by processes of elimination. When the programmer knows where the game is going wrong, they can figure out how to fix it.

Feedback

Feedback from testers, clients and players is very important and this is why end user testing or user acceptance testing is crucial. Testing by players may be done by small focus groups at the development studio, in larger sessions at games conventions or a game may be opened up to the public as part of an open beta. It is common for small testing groups to have to sign non-disclosure agreements (NDAs), which are contracts that prevent them from revealing details about the game. This way, if anything is taken out of the final version of a game, the public will never know about it.

End user testers will be asked to consider the following.

▶ Effectiveness – how well does the game play? How good are the controls?

▶ Presentation – does the game look good? Does the art style work well?

▶ Performance – does the game run smoothly? Has it lagged at any points?

▶ Accessibility – how easy is the game to control? Is the difficulty level manageable?

▶ Portability – does the game work well on different platforms? Does it work well on different screen sizes?

▶ Robustness – can you break the game? Can you get stuck anywhere?

▶ Purpose – do you understand what you are meant to be doing in the game? Do you understand why you are doing it?

Refinements

The feedback gained from users will go into making refinements to the game, but the scale of refinement depends on how much time is left before the final deadline and may also be dependent on the budget. Small changes to layout and challenge level can be considered but anything that requires new meshes or characters will be impossible after the beta stage of development. Some console games developers, when criticised on the performance of their games, have blamed the differences between console development kits and the retail versions of the consoles that players have at home. The disparity can be because the retail versions are updated more frequently than the console development kits in order to solve security issues. But if the console development kits do not have these updates, then developers are essentially having to test their games on slightly different systems which can lead to problems.

Theory into practice

Skills, knowledge and behaviours

If you want to work in the computer games industry, you need to develop the following skills.

Planning and recording
- You need to be prepared for the massive workload that is involved in the games development process. You must have skills that include the ability to set your own targets, consider timescales and decide how you are going to get feedback from colleagues.

Reviewing your own work
- You must be adept at reviewing your own work and be willing to admit when something is not as good as it should be. Teamwork is not the place for ego and if you cannot put your hands up and ask for help when something is not going to plan, then working in creative teams such as games development studios is not the right place for you.

Responding to feedback from others
- You must be able to collect useful feedback from other creative professionals and end users, which means putting your product in the hands of critics and being able to listen to both positive and negative feedback.
- You must be able to look at the feedback that you receive and compare it against the original requirements of the brief. If an end user is demanding unrealistic functionality, then their feedback is not that useful, but if someone is in your target audience and they are not enjoying the game, you must find out why and try to see if you can do something to improve their experience.

Reviewing computer games

After a game has been tested, it will then be reviewed. The review of a game is usually completed by the development team and the games publisher. It could be tempting to skip the review stage if deadlines are pressing but it is a really important step as it is an opportunity to evaluate the entire design and development process.

Quality

The reviewer will first comment on the quality of the game. How well is it made? They will consider the textures, the animations, the game mechanics, everything. Players tend to pay around £40 for a console or PC game or half that for a digital download game for PC. They expect to get a quality product for their money. This means that all the controls need to work well with the game, the graphics need to look good and the challenge levels need to be appropriate for the intended audience. All of these aspects will be checked by the reviewer.

Suitability for audience and purpose

The reviewer will consider who the audience is for the new game. They will make comments about whether or not the game has been designed with the audience in mind and to what extent the audience will be satisfied by the title. It is not just a question of age here – it could be a focus on the ability of the players, their intelligence or their history with that franchise of games. If a sequel comes out that does not refer back to the original story or move the story forward, then it is not considering its audience, it is just trying to make more money without giving the audience what it wants and expects from a sequel. The game must also be reviewed against the original purpose intended for the game.

Original requirements

The reviewer will also look at the original requirements of the game. They will look back to the original high-concept design document and comment on whether or not the game has met the outcomes that it originally set out to achieve. It may be that changes and refinements during development have changed some things, but a game should generally end up in a similar state to how it was originally conceived and designed.

Legal and ethical constraints

The games publishers should get a legal team to review the game and its content if there is any chance that it breaches any legal constraints such as copyright law or ethical considerations. Smaller development studios will not have the luxury of their own legal team and may have to check potential legal issues themselves or pay for legal advice from an external firm.

Technology constraints

Once the game has been made, its technical requirements will be confirmed and the reviewers will be able to check to see if these cause any problems. In the previous generation of consoles, the Xbox 360® used DVD discs and if a game was too big it would spill onto a second disc, which meant more expensive boxes were needed and players would be frustrated at having to change game disc halfway through the game. PC gamers pay very close attention to the recommended technical specifications so that they can play their games without having to sacrifice graphics or quality. When the quality team reviews the game, they will set out the minimum technical requirements for the game and the recommended requirements, as they will be advertised.

Strengths and improvements

A game is always sold on its strengths, and the reviewers will make sure that they are fully aware of everything that the game does well and anything that is not perfect. If a game is found to have an issue and it is too late to make fixes or refinements, then the developers must produce a **patch**. Games which have been shipped by the time problems are found will have what is called a 'Day 1' patch. A 'Day 1' will automatically download and install the fix when the player goes to play the game for the first time, but only if the player's system has internet access and the game knows to check for patches whenever it loads. Patches can continue to be delivered to the player's system long after the game has been released, but the longer the delay between fixes, the more dissatisfied the player will be.

Platforms and compatibility

The review team will look at all the different platforms that a game has been developed for and ensure that it works correctly and runs effectively on those platforms. There may be a certification testing phase where game code is sent to console manufacturers or digital distribution platforms to ensure that the game's install process works properly and that it makes proper use of any system features that it needs, such as network access or game saves.

External reviews and quality characteristics

Video games are big business, with millions of pounds a year being spent on games development and even more being spent on research into new hardware systems and advances in technology. Games journalism is crucial to both players and developers because the review scores that games are given before they are released can make or break it. While the games magazine industry is starting to fade, games websites are more popular than ever and players will often look to IGN.com, Kotaku.co.uk and Gamespot.com to decide what their next purchase is going to be.

Some games reviewers have got into trouble in the past for giving positive reviews to highly flawed games and have been accused of being influenced by games publishers through being given trips and lavish gifts. This has led to an increase in popularity of Metacritic.com, a site that gives a single score for a game based on the average of the scores from many different review websites. It also allows users to give a score to games, so that the opinion of the audience, as well as that of the critics, can be seen.

Further reading and resources

Game software to download for free

Unreal® Engine 4 – **www.epicgames.com** (free for personal and educational use).

Unity® 5 – **www.unity3d.com** (free for personal use, educational fees vary).

Autodesk® 3D Studio Max – **www.autodesk.com/education** (3 year licences for free for students and educators).

Tutorials

Brackeys.com – brackeys.com excellent free tutorials.

Pluralsight Creative – **www.pluralsight.com** subscription based video tutorials.

Articles

Richard Bartle – 'Hearts, Clubs, Diamonds, Spades: Players Who Suit MUDs'. **http://mud.co.uk/richard/hcds.htm**.

David Keirsey – 'Please Understand Me II' (1998); **www.keirsey.com/**.

Now that you have shown your knowledge to the games publisher about different games platforms, you have been asked to design a game. The publisher wants you to create a game for the web using the recent WebGL plugins that are available on the main games engines.

Remember that WebGL allows developers to create whole 2D and 3D games that will run in a web browser

In your design, you must show that you understand the constraints of designing for a web platform and that nothing is asking too much of the system.

The game's design is your choice. The publishers are open to seeing your ideas but they have specified the following requirements:

- a PEGI rating of 7 or lower
- either a 2D or a 3D design
- a third-person player character.

You should produce a GDD document and a set of design documents that justify your design decisions, showing how they fulfil the purpose of your game and meet the client's requirements. You will need to review the designs with others to make refinements.

You might create the following:

- storyboards
- level designs
- a summary of game mechanics
- game screen mock ups.

Having completed the design for your WebGL game, it is now time to create it. You have been asked to produce two working levels for the game that you have designed with a welcome menu and a game over screen.

Remember that you have learnt how long and complicated the game development process can be. Do not be too ambitious in your design. You can achieve high grades with a simple game design that works well.

You must ensure that the game is optimised for web delivery, which means that textures should be minimal resolution, any 3D meshes should be low poly and any audio should be kept to a minimum. Keep a production diary of your development and testing which records your organisation and self-management.

After you have created the game levels, you must test it fully and produce a review for the clients that evaluates the design.

Plan

- What am I being asked to do?
- What sort of game would the audience want?
- What resources do I need to complete the task?

Do

- Have a got a full set of design documents?
- Have I thought about everything that needs to be designed?
- I can identify when I have gone wrong in my game production and get myself back on course.
- I am recording my own observations and thoughts in a production diary.

Review

- I can consider all constraints involved in a web game.
- I realise where I might not fully appreciate how many assets I need to create to make the game look professional.
- I can explain the skills that I employed and the new ones which I have developed.
- I can explain what success looks like.

THINK ▶FUTURE

Gemma Kellner

Games programming university student

I'm an undergraduate student on a Games Programming degree course at university. I'm currently in my second year and, so far, I have learnt how to write games code in different scripting languages, use 3D modelling software and improve my maths so that I can code more efficiently. My course is a lot of hard work and I know that when I finish I am going to have to make myself really stand out in order to get a job in a very competitive industry. I spend my free time working on my art skills, so that when I am sent art assets I have a better understanding of how they will be used in the game and affected by the code that I write. I'm studying hard to ensure that I understand the entire workflow of games development. I will also be entering Game Jam events to network and improve my technical skills, such as writing code that will create the game's rules, the player controls and the win conditions.

Focusing your skills

Planning a game's development

It is important to consider the platform and audience for any game that you plan to make.

- Consider the timescales, how long have you got to complete your project?
- Have you done any market research? Is your idea that unique?
- Why is it fun? Would people be constantly stimulated playing your game?
- What is visually appealing about your game?
- Who is the game aimed at?
- How long would people need to play for? Is that amount of time realistic?

Working in a professional games studio

Professionalism

- To be professional is to understand that nothing is personal and that everyone is working together for the combined good of the game. You must put player satisfaction first and be willing to put the extra time in to ensure that this happens. You need to demonstrate your professionalism by being truly expert in your specialist area and delivering what you promised. You have an individual responsibility to do your job in a thorough and timely manner.

- Communication skills are key to being a good professional. You must use face-to-face meetings, phone calls and emails in appropriate situations, and make sure that your team and clients feel comfortable at all times. You must demonstrate good etiquette to colleagues, always be polite and never be overly personal.
- You may need to demonstrate leadership skills. Taking on a leadership role makes you even more responsible for your product. If you are a leader, then you are accountable for the team that you are leading and it is up to you to organise and motivate them to get the job done.

Evaluating outcomes

- You must be able to evaluate how well the product has met the original requirements of the client brief. You may be asked to make any recommendations about taking the project forward or decisions about last minute patches or refinements. Your recommendations must be based on considered review and reflection.

Evaluating targets

- You must be able to evaluate the targets that you set yourself or that your team leader set. Did you meet your targets? Was there enough time? Would you have approached a problem differently given more time? You must be able to ask yourself these kinds of question to obtain insights into your own performance.

Getting ready for assessment

Rupert is working towards a BTEC National in Information Technology. He was given an assignment that asked him to write a blog about 'Social Trends in Gaming' for learning aim A. He had to cover all the different areas of gaming trends in order to explore the changes in recent years and make some comments about where gaming could go, based on emerging technologies.

Rupert shares his experience below.

How I got started

I made a list of all of the different areas I needed to cover, from my class notes, and created individual blog pages for each of the headings. My headings were: Genres, Players, Production, Multiplayer, AI, Emerging Tech and Security.

It made me feel more organised to have all of the pages ready before I started, even though lots of blank pages were a bit daunting. I made sure that I had tagged the pages with the titles too, so that people searching through my blog would be able to find the information they needed quickly. I then went through all the notes I had made in class and wrote the appropriate tags on the top of the pages. For example, when I had made notes about the Oculus Rift™ being good for first-person shooters, I wrote 'emerging tech' and 'genres' on top of the pages. This meant that I could order my notes ready for writing them up in the blog. Some of the note pages had multiple tags written on them and I photocopied these so that I could keep separate stacks of notes for each blog section.

How I brought it all together

I then typed up my notes into the different sections of the blog but I made sure that I wrote it in a more structured way than the notes. My notes were originally just for me, so I had to make sure that they made sense to anyone reading them. A blog does not have to be written formally, like an essay, but it should be grammatically correct and make sense.

Then I found lots of images that supported what I was writing about and put them into each section, taking care to arrange them so that the pages flowed nicely. I kept notes of where I got my images from and referenced them in my blog.

I finished each page with URLs linking the reader to websites where they could find more information.

What I learnt from the experience

I learnt that I can write a lot from keeping good notes in class, from lectures and discussions. My handwriting is bad, so some of my notes were stored on my phone because our tutor trusts us to make notes that way. I was able to cut and paste these notes because they were already text. I think that in future I will keep all my notes this way and I might save up for a tablet, as it would be easier and quicker to type on.

I also learnt that there is a lot of information on the internet about games trends and not all of it is true. There are a lot of opinions online, and if you find out some information you should make sure that it is posted on a few different sites to check that it is likely to be true.

Think about it

▸ Have you been keeping notes in classes so that you can refer back to them when writing assignments?

▸ Do you have a list of reputable games-related websites that you can trust to give you reliable information?

▸ Have you been keeping a note of all the places you got information from so that you can reference it?

Glossary

<head> – an HTML tag which is used to provide data about an HTML document (web page).

3D Modeller – a job role that involves the creation and texturing of 3D objects.

4G – stands for 4th generation and is intended to replace 3G for accessing the internet at much higher speeds via mobile.

Adaptive maintenance – making modifications to a program, by adding, changing or removing functionality to reflect changing needs.

Aesthetically pleasing – something which is visually engaging or appealing to the senses of sight and hearing. Usually such things are considered beautiful or attractive.

AIO – an all-in-one (AIO) device is one which is multifunctional. They are also known as MFDs.

Alexa Traffic Rank – ranks websites based on a combined measure of page views and the number of visitors. From this, it creates a list of 'top websites' averaged over three-month periods.

Algorithm – a set of instructions that are executed in order to solve different computer problems.

Alt text – alternative text for an image or other media, for example on a web page or in an e-book. The alternative text is read by screen readers to tell the user what the image or other media depicts. Alternative text therefore needs to be descriptive and concise.

Amortise – gradually write off the initial cost of an asset over a period of time, because regular payments are made.

Android™ virtual device (AVD) – a software emulated **v**ersion of a particular physical device, running within a host operating system such as Microsoft® Windows® or Apple® OS X®.

Animation cycles – different motions that characters will use on repeat such as running and jumping.

Animator – a job role that involves the creation of movement in game objects.

Append – to add to the end of something. In a data file, it means adding new data to the end.

Applet – a mini software application that can be built into a web page, for example a calculator that can be used by website users upon clicking a button on a web page.

Application programming interface (API) – this acts as a library of prewritten routines that provide the developer with access to other systems (such as databases), the operating system of a device or its actual hardware. The aim of an API is to make the development process easier by abstracting (hiding) the complexity of the software and hardware systems beneath.

Architecture-neutral – code which is not designed to run on a specific family of CPUs but, instead, is run in a virtual machine.

Argument – part of a calculation (formula or function) that represents a number or value. An argument can be a cell reference such as A2 or a value such as a number, say, 12, or it can be text, say, Richard.

ARM CPU – a family of power-efficient CPUs created by ARM, formerly known as Advanced RISC Machines, that are used in a variety of electronic devices such as mobile telephones, tablets and portable game consoles.

Array – a collection of indexed variables, each of which has a single value.

Assistive technologies – hardware or software designed to assist users with a specific disability or special need, such as screen readers for users with visual impairments or learning disabilities.

Atomic – in this context, atomic means broken down into individual parts. For example, in terms of its suitability for a database field a person's name is not atomic because it can be broken down into title, first name, middle names and surname.

Attributes – additional information about your wireframe. For example, which font you will use, which font size you will use, where the sidebar will appear, alignment and so on.

Bandwidth – the available amount of data transmission capability.

BIDMAS (or BODMAS) – stands for Brackets, Indices/Orders, Divide, Multiply, Add, Subtract and is used to remind us of the order in which a formula is worked out (otherwise known as the precedence of operators).

Binary – a number system that only uses the digits 0 and 1 to form numbers (also known as 'base 2'). For example, '5' in binary is 101 $(1 \times 4 + 0 \times 2 + 1 \times 1)$. Computer circuits have 'on' and 'off' states which can be used to represent binary 0s and 1s.

Bit – short for binary digit. Bit is the smallest component of data represented as a zero (0) or a one (1).

Bitmaps – images that are made up of individual pixels that together display a picture.

Black Hat SEO techniques – techniques that attempt to fool search engines into ranking a website higher than it would have otherwise been, by violating the search engines' terms of service and possibly by creating fake customer reviews.

Block diagram – a simple diagram that uses rectangles to represent the parts of a system (such as a section of program code) to show how it is structured. These diagrams communicate how the parts fit together without the need for unnecessary detail.

Bluetooth – wireless connection which has a limited range.

Boolean – a form of logical data type named after the 19th century mathematician, George Boole.

Brand – an aspect of a product or service that distinguishes it from other similar products. It can include, among other things, a logo, colour scheme and name. Companies often go to great lengths to develop a unique brand identity. Some of the best known brands in the world are McDonalds™ golden arches, Apple®'s symbolic apple logo and Nike®'s iconic 'swoosh'/tick.

Broadband – a high-speed transmission technique, whereby a wide band of frequencies are used to transmit messages. It commonly refers to internet access via a range of networks including DSL, WiFi, 3G and 4G. Today, broadband is a very familiar term in the UK and all of our digital devices, such as smartphones, games consoles and internet-enabled TVs use broadband to connect to the internet and share data all the time.

Bug – a problem in code that causes errors or glitches in a game.

CAD – computer-aided design software which is used for detailed technical drawings. It is used to help design cars and buildings.

CAM – computer-aided manufacturing is done by machines that use software to operate tools and machinery for manufacturing, so providing greater precision and accuracy.

Candidate key – a field or combination of fields which could provide a unique identifier for a table. Typically in a table there may be several candidate keys which could be chosen as the primary key for the table.

Capacitive touch screens – use two spaced layers of glass that are both coated with minute ITO capacitors. When the user's finger touches the screen, it changes the screen's local electrostatic field. This type of touch screen is brighter and more sensitive than

467

resistive touch screens, and supports multi-touch gestures. However, the structural complexity of the screen raises its production costs.

Case-sensitive – when a programming language recognises the difference between upper-case and lower-case characters, such as 'a' and 'A'. For example, if a command word is expected in lower case, an error will occur if it is unexpectedly written in upper case. Most modern programming languages prefer lower case.

Casual gamers – people who only play games for short periods of time and prefer simpler games.

Cel shaded – is a type of non-photorealistic rendering. It is designed to make 3D graphics appear to be flat. It is often used to mimic the style of comic books.

Central processing unit (CPU) – a computer's central 'brain'. Typically it controls the computer's resources, inputs and outputs and, most importantly, the processing instructions and data fetched from its random access memory (RAM).

Click bait – a term used for content that encourages users to 'click through' the post to see the linked content on an external website. Click bait content often uses sensationalist headlines such as 'You won't believe what happens next' to exploit the viewer's curiosity.

CNC – computer numerically controlled (CNC) machines are automated using software programs to carry out precision production of parts used in manufacturing and construction.

Collision detection – the process of checking to see which game objects have collided with each other.

Command line interface (CLI) – an older style of text-based user interface that is still in use. Users interact with the computer via commands entered from the keyboard. Examples include Microsoft Command Prompt or a Linux terminal.

Compiler – a special program which translates program code written in a high-level language into binary instructions which the CPU can process.

Composite key – the combination of fields which can uniquely identify each record in a table (also known as a super key).

Compression – where a mathematical calculation is performed on a file in order to 'squash' it and make it smaller.

Concept art – drawings and paintings created before a game is developed to show how the game world should look and feel.

Conceptual model – a way of organising ideas and concepts in a logical fashion.

Conceptual models often represent the ideas concerned in a visual manner that illustrates the relationships between them in a simple way that is easily understood.

Constraints – restrictions on something. Constraints in a programming context include features of the programming languages, the technical skills of the developer, the platforms supported by the programming language and so on.

Context – the setting or circumstances surrounding something. In software solutions design, the context will include details such as the background history of the problem.

Context-sensitive perspective – this is when the in-game camera changes to focus on something that the player has selected or a change that they have caused.

Corrective maintenance – fixing an error or bug that has been identified.

CPU – central processing unit which acts as the computer's brain to process instructions.

CRM – customer relationship management system.

CSV – comma-separated values is a file type which stores records in a line and presents data in plain text as individual fields, where each field is separated by a comma.

CSV file – a simple text file that can be used to transfer data between apps. A comma is used between each item on a line to separate them, so if they were imported into a spreadsheet they would go into different cells. Hence CSV stands for 'comma separated values'.

Cut scene – a cinematic sequence in a game that tells part of the story. Cut scenes can be a separate movie clip or can be shown during a level.

Cycle – instructions or operations which are repeated.

DAB – digital audio broadcasting, which converts audio broadcasts to digital signal to reduce atmospheric and other interference.

Data – the raw facts and figures, in an unorganised state. Often there is a massive amount of raw information and it is usually difficult to understand.

Data cleansing – ongoing checking of data for accuracy, currency and completeness.

Data engineer – someone who designs and produces database programs known as information systems.

Data type – the kind of data that we want to store in the mobile device's RAM. Storing each type of data requires different quantities of RAM. For example, the data type needed to store a number is different from the one used to store a character and will require different amounts of RAM. Exact names of data types

can vary between different programming languages, so be careful to select the right one.

Database – a collection of data which can be in digital or paper form, such as a telephone directory.

Database transaction – a complete set of actions required to complete some task in a database. Transactions related to database systems, such as withdrawing money from an ATM machine or booking an airline ticket, are made up of several steps such as authentication of the user, selecting the required item and paying for a purchase.

Datatype – Datatypes are used in both programming and in database development as the definition of the type of data that is to be stored (in the case of database) in a field. The most commonly used datatypes are text and number, but there are variations on these and other datatypes too.

Debug – the process of identifying an error (or bug) in a program code and removing it.

Default setting – the setting selected by the games engine when nothing else has been input by the developer or, if the game is running, by the player.

Demographics – measurements used to put people into different categories. One reason to do this is to understand their likes and dislikes more easily.

Denial-of-service (DoS) attack – an attack on a company's website which involves sending so many bogus requests to the server where the website is hosted that it is overwhelmed and cannot respond to legitimate requests. The likely purpose of the attack is either revenge or blackmail.

Dependent on – one field depends on another if you can only find out the unique value of the second field if you know the value of the first one. For example, if you know the Product ID, then you can find the description and the price.

Direct advertising – where a business uses adverts which tell you to buy their product or sign up to their service. They use a direct approach by simply telling you what the product/service is and suggesting that you purchase it.

Dot operator – is a full stop (.) used to define what method an object will use.

Driver – a routine program used to operate peripheral devices such as monitors and keyboards.

Early adopter – an individual who feels compelled to obtain the latest products and technology as soon as they become available. For example, robotic vacuum cleaners, smart TVs and watches.

Efficiency – a measure given to undertaking a task or activity with least wastage of time, materials or labour.

Email host – an internet provider that offers an email service to its users.

Encrypting – converting data into a code to avoid it easily being accessed by unauthorised users. Specialist software is used to encrypt data.

Engagement – the number of people who interact with a post in some way (like, comment or share it). Post reach is good, but engagement is much better because it means that, not only did people see your post, but they found it interesting enough to interact with it in some way.

Ethical – relating to the knowledge of moral principles: that is, how we behave.

Event handling – describes the process of using a specially written function or class method to perform set actions when a user or system event is triggered. For example, outputting the result of a calculation when a button is pressed or displaying a device's 'low battery' warning indicator when it falls below a certain charge level.

Extranet – an intranet system which can be accessed by authorised external users to retain data security.

Fibre optics – a collection of very fine strands of silica glass which use light to transmit data at high speeds.

FIFO – this stands for 'first in, first out'. It means that the first item of data added is also the first item of data that may be removed.

Filter – include or exclude certain values when running a search.

Flash – authoring software used to create and play animated images.

Font – a word used to describe the digital file that contains the typeface. For example, arial.ttf is a TrueType font file. Many people use the terms 'typeface' and 'font' interchangeably.

Foreign key – the primary key from a record in a table at the 'one' end of a one-to-many entity relationship, which is used as a field in records in the table at the 'many' end, to provide the link between the records.

Framework – a particular set of development tools that can be accessed via its API.

Franchise – a series of game titles that feature the same world, the same characters or the same setting.

Function or procedure – a function is a block of code, ideally between 5 and 50 lines in length, which has a single defined purpose. Although written just once, it can be executed many times during a program by using a function 'call', reducing the need for repeated code. In some programming languages, the

terms 'function' and 'procedure' are used interchangeably, but, in others they are very different concepts: a function typically returns a calculated value while a procedure performs a single identifiable task.

Game development studio – a team of people who create computer games.

Game mechanics – the way a game world works, its features and its rules such as double jumps or collecting items.

Game publisher – a company that releases games to shops or online platforms, and pays for development.

Garbage collection – an automated process which attempts to reclaim RAM reserved by a program to store data, e.g. an identifier (variable or object) that is no longer needed.

Genre – a genre is a category of computer game that describes the style of play, types of challenges and the perspective of the player.

Goes live – describes the first time a website has been uploaded to a web server and is made available to the public.

GPS – the global positioning system (GPS) is an accurate worldwide navigational and surveying facility. It uses the signals from orbiting satellites to work out the position of the device.

Graphical nodes – colourful blocks used to represent the different functions of a programming language used to add easy interaction.

Graphical user interface (GUI) – a modern user interface comprised of windows and icons which is controlled by a mouse and a cursor/pointer. Examples include Microsoft Windows 10 or Apple OS X.

Grid – a network of lines that is projected onto a game level in order to split it into logical sections.

GUIs – graphical user interfaces are those which allow users to interact with a digital device using graphical icons.

Hardware – computer equipment that you can physically touch. It includes computers and other digital devices themselves and also peripheral devices such as the keyboard, monitor and mouse.

Hardwired – a permanent connection between components of an IT system with dedicated wired cabling. Modern buildings are often purpose built with the cables integrated into the fabric of the building and internet connections are provided for direct connection of non-mobile digital devices such as PCs, servers and machinery.

HTML – stands for hypertext markup language and is used to create web pages.

Human computer interaction (HCI) – the study of how people interact with machines,

and the best possible ways to design interfaces between people and machines.

Hypertext – text that contains links to other bits of text.

Idle cycle – the animation that a character displays when the player is not moving them. A character in an idle cycle may stand still and breathe or tap their foot after a few seconds.

Immersive – a term which refers to how focused you are on the experience that you are having. An immersive game will keep your attention for long periods of time and block out distractions. It should make you enjoy the game more, but only if you have the time to spend on it.

Implications – the likely effects of something.

Indirect advertising – is more subtle than direct advertising. It attempts to create a positive attitude towards the product/service in the mind of the customer through sponsorship (e.g. a company sponsors a particular TV programme), product placement and other methods (such as those that social media uses) to try to create a relationship with the customer.

Information – produced when data is processed and presented so that it has meaning.

Input mask – a database instruction which restricts or controls the type, format or amount of data entered.

Interactive website – involves some level of activity from a simple feedback form to a database that personalises the website for each individual visitor. Changes can be made to the website 'on-the-fly'.

Interface – a point where two (or more) systems meet and interact. In computing, an interface is a device or program enabling a user to communicate with a computer.

Internet – the networking infrastructure which enables communication and access to information between internet-enabled digital devices with potentially infinite range.

Intranet – a local network website where access is restricted to internal users, such as within an organisation.

ISDN – stands for integrated services digital network.

Iteration – a repetitive process, usually something done repeatedly until it is correct.

Jargon – words or phrases used only by a particular group, which people outside that group find difficult to understand.

JSP structure diagrams – Jackson Structured Programming (JSP) structure diagrams are a type of block diagram used to show how programs are structured. They have lines joining the blocks to show the sequence, decisions and iterations.

Keywords – words that identify the key things that a business has to offer to customers and are likely to be used by potential customers when carrying out an internet search for a product or service.

Lag – a delay or reduction in the game's frame rate.

Latency – the 'delay' experienced, for example, when playing online games. High latency results in you seeing the movements you made to a character a longer period of time after you made them.

LIFO – this stands for 'last in, first out' and it describes how data is treated in some data structures. It means that the last item of data pushed on is also the first item of data that may be pulled back off.

Linux® – an operating system (OS) which is released 'Open Source', meaning that the source code that creates it can be downloaded and adapted by anyone. Due to its adaptability, it is very popular and comes in lots of different versions such as Steam™ OS.

Logical model – takes the concepts and applies rules (logic) to the concepts (including verifying them with normalisation) and adding details such as the nature of the relationship which exists between customer and order (via the primary and foreign keys).

Low-level and high-level languages – in programming, the terms 'low' and 'high' refer to a language's position between being understood by a computer (e.g. binary is low-level) and understood by a person (e.g. natural languages such as English are high-level).

Malware – an umbrella term for a range of different types of software that have a malicious intent. Malware includes viruses and Trojans and spyware, among others.

Massively multiplayer online (MMO) game – a game played by multiple players, across the internet, all online at the same time.

Metric – an agreed form of measurement that enables comparison and evaluation.

MFD – a multifunctional device, such as a smartphone, a camera which connects to the internet or a printer which also scans and photocopies. They are also known as AIOs.

MIS – management information system.

Modulus division – performing a division operation and returning the remainder rather than working out the decimal or fractional answer.

Moral – principles about what is right and wrong behaviour.

Motherboard – a circuit board within a PC that connects all the main components.

Motion capture – a process where real-life motion is converted into data that can allow game characters to move in the same way.

Netiquette – a word derived by combining internet (net) with correct behaviour (etiquette); it is especially related to online discussions and forums but also emails.

Node – a point where lines intersect.

Object – an object is a type of data that knows things about itself (its properties) and knows how to do things (methods).

Object-oriented – Java®, which we use to create Android™ apps, is categorised as a class-based, object-oriented programming (OOP) language. In OOP, objects are created from classes that are usually modelled on real-world 'things'. Each class acts as a software blueprint, encapsulating (or containing) the thing's state (its data or properties) and behaviour (its functions or methods) in program code.

Object-oriented language – uses code that is organised into objects, which can be used to make it run in a fast and robust manner.

Object-oriented programming languages – a modern programming approach (paradigm) to software development that works by modelling real-world problems and simplifies complex processes into the basic interactions that exist between different objects: for example, a customer and their bank account.

Open source – Open source software has its source code available for the general public to use and modify as they desire, free of charge. This is rather than the source code being kept as a commercial secret by the company that created it. Open source software is meant to be a collaborative effort by programmers who give their time to develop the application.

Operator – a special symbol (or multiple symbols) which tells the program to perform specific arithmetic, relational or logical operations on its data. Operators must be used in a specific order of precedence (this describes which is executed first). You may be familiar with this concept from using BIDMAS (or BODMAS) (Brackets, Indices/Orders, Divide, Multiply, Add and Subtract) in mathematics.

Optimised – optimised assets are created using file formats which are more efficient as they require less storage space. This can result in improvements in performance and a smaller digital footprint on the device's resources. Examples include using .jpg images rather than .bmp files as these use data compression to reduce file size.

Patch – a series of code fixes that are downloaded and applied to the game code in order to fix problems.

Perfective maintenance – making an improvement to a program that enhances its performance.

Photorealistic games – games that try to look as lifelike as possible.

Physics – in the real world, gravity, mass and other laws of physics apply naturally but in a world created by a computer programmer the laws of physics have to be made to apply through coding the game correctly.

Ping – a test of end-to-end connectivity, which times the return of an ICMP packet between two hosts.

Pixel perfect – is a term used in the design sector to describe graphics that are accurate to the very last pixel.

Platform – the operating system which enables applications or programs to operate on a digital device.

Plug-in – software that will play specific types of files. For example, modern versions of web browsers like Internet® Explorer® come with Flash® Player which is a plug-in to allow the user to play Flash® animations.

Ported – written using one computer architecture, but compiled for use on another. This is also commonly known as cross-compiling.

Post reach – the number of people who see a particular post.

Primary key – a field which can uniquely identify one and only one record in a table.

Program flowchart – a diagram using shapes and lines to show where decisions (branches) are taken, when inputs and outputs are made and where the code can end. These diagrams show the routes that can be taken through program code.

Project management – different methods and procedures used to keep a project on track and under budget by minimising and mitigating risks and issues.

Proprietary – In the context of software, proprietary means the software is owned by a commercial organisation which develops it and sells a licence to use the software. Microsoft® Office® is an example of proprietary software, whereas Open Office is a free-to-use open source office software suite.

Prototype – a working model of the desired solution or components of the solution. It may not have full functionality but allows clients and users to test and review the proposed solution. Their feedback then informs the next prototype and the process continues until the final product is ready.

Pseudocode – a way of writing code without it being in a specific programming language.

QR codes – quick response codes which provide direct links to, for example, websites or make a payment, using a QR code reader app such as Red Laser.

Qualitative questioning – questions do not have definitive answers. It provides answers as to how or why and is used to gauge opinions and get more detailed feedback.

Quantitative questioning – questions have a definitive answer, either a numerical value or specific answers in ranges. It focuses on statistical analysis.

Query – a way of interrogating data by applying a set of criteria.

RAID logs – Risks, Actions, Issues and Decisions (RAID) logs are often used in project work to record things that could go wrong (Risks), what needs doing (Actions), problems (Issues) and the agreements made (Decisions).

RAM – stands for random access memory and is a form of computer memory.

Ratio – a way of concisely showing the relationship between two quantities. A ratio is represented by separating the two quantities with a colon (:). For example, a ratio of 1:2 is one quantity compared with something which is twice the first amount (twice as much).

Recursive algorithms – a piece of programming code that executes itself repeatedly until it reaches an end condition where the calculated result can be returned.

Rendering – the process of converting game assets and environments into 2D images that can be displayed on a screen.

Rendering engine – the software in a games engine that converts virtual worlds into 2D images which are then animated.

Resistive touch screens – use two layers (usually glass and plastic) covered in an electrical conductive material (usually Indium Tin Oxide (ITO)). The two layers are kept apart until a finger or stylus presses them together, which causes a localised change in electrical resistance. This type of touch screen is cheaper to manufacture than capacitive touch screens but is not very sensitive and cannot support multitouch gestures.

Responsive web design (RWD) – makes your web pages appear correctly (look good) on all types of device, including desktop PCs, mobile and tablet devices.

Router – an electronic device that enables data to be transmitted between networks.

RSI – repetitive strain injury.

Run-time error – a problem that occurs while an application is being used. These errors result in the application locking (refusing to accept user input) or crashing (terminating and returning the user to the device's menu or desktop).

Sans serif – The word 'sans' is French meaning, 'without'. Therefore a sans serif font is one without embellishments at the ends of the letters. An example of a sans serif font is Arial.

SAP – systems, applications and products is a data processing system.

Scenario – the situation or context within which you will need to create your data model.

Schematics – a technical diagram showing the content and function of game elements.

Scripting language – a programming language that requires a separate application to run, such as a games engine or web browser.

Serif – a type of font that has embellishments at the ends of letters. An example of a serif font is Times New Roman.

Set – a collection of distinct objects. Sets can contain anything (e.g. names, numbers, colours or letters of the alphabet) and may consist of many different members.

SLR camera – a single lens reflex (SLR) camera uses a lens which captures the scope of the image you actually see. They are a type of camera used by keen amateur and professional photographers. Digital SLR cameras are known as DSLR cameras. They have a much larger, better-quality sensor, capturing a better image than traditional cameras.

Software – applications or programs which are installed onto a digital device. They enable us to carry out certain functions such as word processing or creating spreadsheets, using media, accessing websites or playing computer games.

Software developer – someone who contributes to producing computer programs (software applications) or computer games.

Software development kit (SDK) – a suite of software tools provided for developers to create an application for a specific platform, for example Java® SDK for Android™. The SDK usually contains application programming interfaces (APIs), tools such as compilers and debuggers, reference documentation and code samples.

Specification – this describes, in depth, the make up of an IT system.

Sprites – images used to represent characters and objects in a 2D game.

SQL – stands for structured query language and is a special purpose programming language used for managing data in relational databases. SQL is a standard language (developed by ISO, the International Organisation for Standardisation) used by all the main database programs.

Standalone computer – a computer not reliant on any other computers or digital devices to function; therefore it can be used independently.

Static website – one with no interactivity, which is usually just a presentation of information. Changes to the website have to be hard-coded into the website.

Sync – is short for 'synchronise' or 'synchronisation' which means to match up and pull together, for example, to make sure that multiple devices have the same copy of the relevant files in many places.

Syntax – a set of rules that is unique to each programming language, which defines the combination of symbols considered to be correctly structured within that language.

Technical artist – someone who works between the technical and design teams and understands both.

Text file – a text file is a simple document with no formatting. They are just text, unlike apps such as Excel® or Word® which create documents that have lots of extra information (formatting) such as page size, fonts, images and tables which makes the document more complex and can be opened by an app that understands that format.

Trace table – a table created by the developer, through white box testing, which charts the changes in program variables as a use case is performed. The trace table would have entries for each use case with expected (what should happen) and actual (what does happen) outcomes. Comparing these outcomes helps the developer assess whether the app is working correctly.

Transport layer security (TLS) – is a protocol that makes certain that there is privacy between communicating applications and their users on the internet. TLS is the successor to the secure sockets layer (SSL) method.

Trigger – invisible collisions in a level that will prompt (trigger) a function or event.

TSV file – a simple text file that can be used to transfer data between apps. A <Tab> character is used between each item on a line to separate them, so if they were imported into a spreadsheet they would go into different cells. Hence TSV stands for 'tab separated values'.

Typeface – the design of an alphabet, i.e. the actual shapes of the letters and symbols. 'Arial' and 'Times New Roman' are examples of typeface.

Underlying logic – how the spreadsheet will process the data into information. This is more of an overview of what the processing is to achieve, rather than the detailed calculations which actually implement the underlying logic.

URL – stands for uniform resource locator and is the term given to the address of a website.

Use case – a list of specific actions or events which occur between a user and the program. Possible use cases that occur when a customer tries to withdraw cash at an ATM include 'card rejected', 'PIN correct', 'PIN incorrect', 'card swallowed', 'cash dispensed' and 'no cash available'.

User experience (UX) – a measure of how the user interacts with the program and their satisfaction when using it.

User interface – the part of the data model that the user interacts with. This includes click-on buttons, other controls and any screen outputs that they can view, print or export.

Validation – an automatic computer check which ensures that data entered is sensible and reasonable.

Verbose – using more words or code than necessary.

Verification – verification is the process of checking that something is correct. Normalisation is the process used to verify the database design.

Viral – a social media post is said to have gone 'viral' if it is shared by numerous people who themselves share it (and so on). As more and more people share the post, the number of people who see it can increase into millions. Having a social media post go viral is often considered a good thing unless, of course, it is regarding a negative issue about a company.

Viral (advertising/marketing) – unsolicited and infectious marketing tactics using social media to attract interest.

WiFi – a system that enables connection over the internet between wireless internet-enabled devices.

Wire-framing – an important step in the screen design process, helping the developer to plan layout and user navigation using paper-based or electronic models of the devices and their visual components.

World Wide Web Consortium (W3C) – an international community that develops open standards for the use of HTML5 to ensure the long-term growth of the worldwide web.

Worldwide web – also referred to as the Web, is a method of accessing information over the internet.

Index

3D modelling 451, 453-4
4G 7, 27, 28

A

abstraction 222, 225
Access® 87
    forms 123, 147-56, 159-63
    importing data 134-6, 144
    password control 163-5
    queries 125-39, 145-56, 149
    relationships 108-10
    reports 157-9
    tables 89-91, 108-10, 116-17, 138-9, 143-4
    validation 116-19, 122
accessibility 76-7
assistive technology 12-13, 23, 73, 251
    user interfaces (UIs) 16, 142
    websites 338, 357-8, 372
action queries 122, 133-9
activity charts 390, 442
advertising 62-3, 188, 194
algorithms 258, 350, 390
    games 425, 442-3, 458
analytics tools 186, 200
Android™ Studio IDE 386-7, 396-8, 404, 408-9
animations
    games 432, 446, 447, 451, 456-7
    websites 359
anomalies (databases) 103, 107-8
antivirus software 53
Apple® Xcode IDE 387
application programming interfaces (APIs) 407, 445
applications software 17-18, 226
arguments 294-7, 306
arrays 237-9
artificial intelligence 425, 458
assembly language 229
assets (digital) 267, 391
    games 436-7, 439, 444, 446, 456-7
    website design 350, 358-9
assistive technology 12-13, 23, 73, 76, 251
attributes 104-6, 108
Access® fields 88-9, 90-2, 111, 115
audience
    databases 114
    games 423, 440, 462
    social media 185-6, 187, 188, 193, 205-7, 214
    websites 345, 372

audio files 359, 430, 436, 457
augmented reality 426
automated tasks 12, 122, 208-11, 320
automation 226
    business processes 61-4
availability 23, 30

B

backup and recovery procedures 52, 102, 226
bandwidth 27-8, 35, 337, 343
BIDMAS/BODMAS 294
big data 21, 61-2
blogs 44, 207-8, 214, 336
bluetooth 7, 11, 26
booking systems 59
Boolean operators 234, 235-6
brand image 184, 188, 199, 203, 205
broadband 7, 27-8, 43, 344
browsers 343, 344, 349, 358, 366
BSI codes of practice 76
business applications 9-10, 58-64, 182-91, 280-1, 337

C

C 228, 232, 235, 264, 270
C# 229, 232, 235, 264, 445
C++ 227, 229, 235, 270, 430, 445
cabling 26, 28
cascading style sheets (CSS) 354, 357, 360-5, 371
cascading updates/deletes 108, 110, 114
cells (Excel®) 283, 294, 318, 322-3
charts and graphs 286-7, 325
clients
    communications 200-1, 283, 292, 448
        feedback 267, 292, 327, 350-1, 374, 460
        requirements 290, 327, 372, 433
client-server database systems 87
client-side scripting 343, 349-50, 366-71
cloud computing 39-41, 59, 60
cloud storage 38-9, 40-1, 429
code (programming) 18-19, 227-46, 252-3, 430 see also programming
code annotation 406
code snippets 266-7, 270
    documentation 247
codecs 36
codes of practice 56, 74, 76
collaborative working 8, 40-1, 59, 60, 292, 346

collision detection 431
command line UIs 16, 19, 245
command words 233
communication skills 224, 396, 449
clients 200-1, 283, 292, 448
communications technology 7, 8, 10-11, 33, 337 see also data transmission
Companies Act (2006) 55
compatibility
    equipment 24, 31
    platforms 349, 358, 371, 459
    software 21, 70
compilers 227
completeness 248
compression 35-6, 343, 395
computer architecture 227-8
Computer Misuse Act (1990) 54-5, 75
concatenation 239, 243-4
conceptual models 111, 119
connectivity 24, 26-36, 31, 43, 344, 429
console development kits 445
constants 225, 233-4
constraints 96
    data modelling 290
    games 447-8, 454, 462
    mobile apps 392
    social media projects/ design 190
    software development 255, 268
    website design 346, 352-4
constructs
    mobile apps 399-403
    programming 233-46
    website development 370-1
Consumer Rights Act (2015) 441
content 192, 194-8, 205-6, 393-5
control structures 235, 260, 391, 401-3
copyright 77, 200, 267, 350, 392, 441, 462
Copyright (Computer Programs) Regulations (1992) 75
Copyright, Designs and Patents Act (1988) 75, 267, 350, 353, 372
correctness 114, 140-2
costs 24, 31, 42-3, 45, 47, 63, 353
CPU (central processing unit) 227, 343, 427-8
Creative Commons licence 77
creative industries 10, 62
crowdfunding 424-5, 426, 436, 440
CSS (cascading style sheets) 354, 357, 360-5, 371
customers 185, 200

D

dashboards 68, 69

data
  collection and analysis 61–2, 65–8, 281, 286
  compression 35–6, 343, 395
  conversion 113
  entry 122–4, 283–4, 291, 313–19
  manipulation (Excel®) 304–9
  security 50-6, 77
  storage 259

data dictionaries 115–16, 120–1, 140–1, 143, 168, 442–3

data modelling 68–9, 280–3 *see also* Excel®
  analysis and design 287–93

decision-making process 280–3, 288–9
  evaluation and testing 288–9, 326–8
  information inputs and outputs 280–1, 287–8, 291
  specifications 290–1
  spreadsheet features and solutions 283–6, 293–325

data processing 12

Data Protection Act (1998) 55, 75, 114, 353–4, 372, 392

data structures 87–9, 115–16, 237–44, 259

data transmission 26–36, 54 *see also* communications technology

data types 89, 115–16, 234–5, 399–400

database design and development 111–21 *see also* Access®

data structures 89–96, 103–10, 143–6
  evaluation and testing 140–2, 163, 166–9
  extracting data 125–35, 137–40, 146–58
  importing and manipulating data 96–102, 135–9
  security 163–5
  user interfaces (UIs) 122–4, 159–63

databases 67–9, 87

debug 228, 232, 253, 264, 460

decision-making data models 12, 280–3, 288–9

decomposition 222–4

demographics 185, 187, 214, 440

design

data modelling 287–93

databases 102, 111–21, 122–4
  games 433–40, 442–9
  mobile apps 388–92
  website design 347–50

design specifications 252–3

development environments 269–70

device permissions 385–6

devices (digital) 4–8

drivers 15, 430
  mobile apps functions 383–5
  peripherals 10–14

diagrammatic illustrations 257–8, 291, 347

digital cameras 6

digital certificates 52

digital distribution 424, 426, 436

digital rights management (DRM) 442

Disability Discrimination Acts (1995, 2005) 76

documentation

data modelling 288–9

database design 114, 169
  games 434, 437, 440–4, 448
  mobile apps 389–92
  programming 247, 266–7, 271, 406

domains (databases) 88–9

E

ease of use 23, 30, 69, 251, 319
  mobile apps 411
  online systems 43, 45, 46
  testing 142, 169
  websites 337, 338

e-commerce 34, 264, 337, 346

education applications 7–8, 58, 337

efficiency
  IT systems 24, 31
  mobile apps 411
  software 249–50

electronic data capture (EDC) 6–7

elements
  mobile apps 397
  programming 222, 224–5, 238, 240, 257
  web pages 339–40, 348–9, 360

email protocols 33

embedding script 366–7

emerging technologies 21–2, 426–7

encryption 32, 34–5, 52–3, 54, 395

entertainment systems 5–6, 59, 226

entity relationships 94–6, 111–12, 121

ERD (diagrams) 94–5, 168

Equality Act (2010) 76

errors 232, 263–4, 270–1

ethics 72–5, 200, 353, 392, 442, 462

European Union Directive on Data Protection 114

evaluation 113–14, 167–9, 272, 288

event diagrams 258

event handling 245–6, 404–5

event-driven (ED) languages 229

Excel®

arguments 294–5

automated data transfers 320–1

cells 294, 318, 322–3

charts and graphs 325

conditional formatting 323

data entry and editing 283–4, 312–19

data import and export 310–12

data manipulation 304–9

filtering 307

formatting and layout 321–5

forms 313–17

formulae 284, 293–4, 313, 326

functions 284–5, 286, 295–9, 313

macros 291, 313, 320–1

pivot tables 308–9

scenarios 299–303

toolbars 313, 314–15

usability techniques 319, 321

extensibility 265, 327

F

Facebook™ 182, 184, 193, 198, 199
  Insights 187, 197, 207, 211–14
  posting 188, 206–8
  settings 202–5

feedback
  clients 292, 326–7, 372
  questionnaires 351, 374, 413–14
  reviewing designs 267, 292, 350–1, 392
  user testing 271, 326–7, 351–2, 373–4, 412–13, 439, 460

fibre-optics 7, 28, 344

fields 88–9, 90–2, 111, 115

files 244–5

formats 19–20, 259, 358–9, 394, 430
  permissions 52, 102, 153

financial services 58

firewalls 53

First-Person shooter (FPS) games 422

five Ws 255

flowcharts 258, 291, 349–50, 390, 442

format and layout
  Excel® 321–5
  website design 338–41, 360–5

formative testing 326

forms
  Access® 123, 147–56, 159–63
  Excel® 313–17
  HTML 355
  JavaScript® 369

formulae (Excel®) 284, 293–4, 326

4G 7, 27, 28

Freedom of Information Act (2000) 55

freemium titles 425, 441

front-end *see* user interfaces (UIs)
functions 236-7, 403
    Excel® 284-5, 286, 295-9, 326

G

games 226, 264
    artificial intelligence 425
    audience 423, 440, 462
    constraints 447-8, 462
    design process 433-40, 442-9
    development 450-9
    documentation 434, 437, 440-4, 448
gameplay features 424, 434, 436-40, 442-4
genres 422-3
    technology and platforms 426-31
    testing 446-7, 459-63
games consoles 423, 427, 428, 430
games engines 431-2, 441-2, 445, 452-3, 459-60
games industry 424-7, 436, 445, 463
Google™
    Adwords™ 195-7
    Analytics™ 211
    Android™ 385-6
Google+™ 183, 207-8
GPU (graphics processing unit) 428
graphics
    Excel® 286-7, 325
games 432, 434-6, 442, 444, 455-7
    software 430
GUIs (Graphical User Interfaces) 14, 15-16, 19, 245

H

hackers 50
hardware 4-6, 102
    communications 26-32
    games 424, 426-9, 430, 448
    mobile apps 382, 384-5, 407-8
    peripherals 10-14
    programming implications 228-9, 231-2, 264
health and safety 77
Health and Safety (Display Screen Equipment) Regulations (1992) 75
high-level languages 227-8
Hootsuite™ 208-11
HTML (hypertext markup language) 230, 354-6, 365-7, 371
HTML5 354, 357, 445
http (hypertext transfer protocol) 33-4
hybrid apps 382
hyperlinks 336, 356

I

identifiers 233-4
identity theft 8, 427

image files 358-9
imperative languages 228
implementation 24-6, 31-2, 47, 63-4, 252, 254
importing data
    Access® 122, 134-6, 144
    Excel® 310-12
indie games 424
Information Commissioner's Office (ICO) 56, 74
input devices 10-11, 12-13, 384-5
input masks 67, 69, 122
inputs 225, 256, 388-9, 429, 455-6
    data modelling 280-1, 287
Instagram™ 183, 187, 193
in-system programming (ISP) 231
integrated development environments (IDEs) 269-70, 386-7, 444-5, 459-60
integration 47, 64
integrity 96, 102, 103, 114, 386
interactivity 344, 346, 356-7, 436-7, 439
internet 22, 27, 38-43, 336, 343
IT systems
    costs 24, 63
    digital devices 4-14
    ethical issues 72-5
impact on organisations 60-1
implementation and testing 24-6, 63
    performance and efficiency 23-6, 29, 32, 35, 64
    security 26
    selection criteria 23-5
iterations 235, 237, 248, 260, 391, 402-3

J

Java® 229, 232, 265, 385-6
    annotation 406
    control structures 401-3
    event handling 404-5
    programming constructs 399-403
    statements 401-3
JavaScript® 230, 366-71, 445
Joint Test Action Group (JTAG) 231

K

keys 95-6, 108
keywords, search engine optimisation (SEO) 186-7, 188-9, 195-7, 342

L

LANs (Local Area Networks) 29
latency 35
layouts
    data models 321-5
    mobile device screens 390
    website design 338-41, 348-9, 360-5

legislation 54-5, 74-6, 114, 353-4, 372, 392, 441-2, 462
library functions (programming) 237, 270
LinkedIn™ 183, 187, 193
logic 248-9, 425
logical models 95, 111, 120, 326
logical operations 92-3, 111-13, 235-6
loops 235, 237, 260, 391, 402-3
low-level languages 227-8

M

machine code 227, 229
macros (Excel ®) 295, 313, 320-1
mainframe computers 5
maintenance 250, 252, 253, 265, 411
malware 50, 191, 267
manufacturing applications 9-10
marketing through social media 62-3, 182-91, 194, 199, 201-14
markup languages 230
    HTML (hypertext markup language) 354-6, 357, 365-7, 371, 445
    XML (extensible markup language) 397
massively multiplayer online (MMO) games 422, 427, 437
mathematical logic 92-3, 111-12, 235-6, 248, 425
mathematical optimisation 425
mathematics of graphics 434, 452
menu based UIs 16
meshes 447, 450-1, 453-4, 456
Microsoft Visual Basic .NET 227, 229, 232, 235, 269
migration (IT systems) 25-6
mobile apps 382-3, 426
    constructs 399-403
    design 388-92
    development 393-411
    documentation 389-92
    games 425, 448
    programming environments 386-7
    testing 408-10, 412-15
mobile broadband 27, 344
mobile devices 5, 371, 382
    attributes 394
    executable programmes 408-10
    games 428
    hardware and operating systems 383-6, 390
    sensors 384, 407
modular programming 236-7
multi-user systems 14, 102

N

naming conventions 121, 234
narrative 437-8

native apps 382
navigation (user interface)
    Access® 159–60
    data modelling 291
    mobile apps 390
    websites 337, 338, 355–6
navigation systems 6
netiquette 73
networking operating system (NOS)
    14–15
networks 29–32
news services 58–9
non-playable characters (NPCs) 425, 436
normalisation 103–7, 111, 114, 121, 168
numerical modelling 68

O

object oriented programming (OOP) 229,
    265, 386, 403, 430
Objective-C 232, 385–6
Oculus Rift™ 424, 426, 445
online communities 43–8, 199
    development 184, 189, 192, 207–8,
    445
online systems 38–43, 58–60, 336
    implementation 45, 47
    netiquette 73
    security 45–6, 48, 50–6, 59
    usability 46
Open Accessibility Framework (OAF) 76
open source code 18
open source database systems 87
operating systems 14–15, 16–17
    games 429–30
    mobile apps and devices 385–6, 390
    programming requirements 231
operators 111–12, 234–6, 294, 400–1
optimisation 373–4, 395, 425
    search engine (SEO) 186–7, 188–9,
    195–7, 200, 342, 348
output devices 10–11
outputs 225, 256, 388–9, 429
    data modelling 287–8, 291, 325

P

PANs (Personal Area Networks) 7, 29
password control 52, 163–5
pattern recognition and generalisation
    222, 224–5
PEGI ratings 445–6
performance
    games 427, 439–40, 447, 460
    IT systems 17, 21, 23–4, 29–30, 32, 35
    mobile apps 408, 410–13
    social media 193
    software 232, 249–50, 254
    websites 343–4, 373–4

peripheral devices 10–14
Perl 230
personal IT applications 8–9, 382–3,
    422–3
phishing 50, 51, 62
PHP (Hypertext Preprocessor) 229, 230,
    232, 264, 270
physics (games) 431, 451, 452
Pinterest™ 183, 193
pivot tables (Excel®) 308–9
plagiarism 65, 77
platform games 454–9
platforms
    game design platforms 444–5, 450
    games 426--31, 436, 448, 463
    hardware 207, 229, 231, 265, 270
    mobile apps 382, 390
    operating systems 14–15
    websites 358
playability 447, 459
player actions (games) 438–9, 459
plug-ins 359
podcasts 44, 336
Police and Justice Act (2006) (Computer
    Misuse) 75
portability 228, 250, 265, 410
primary data 65
privacy 45–6, 72, 77, 354, 392, 427
problem and process analysis 223–5, 255
problem definition statements 255,
    345–7
procedural languages 228, 236–7
procedures 236–7, 403
productivity
    business 26, 47, 59, 64, 226, 383
    IT systems 32
    software developers 228, 232, 269
professional codes of practice 56, 74
programming
    code snippets 266–7, 270
    constructs 233–46
    data structures 234–5, 237–44
    documentation 247, 406
    logic principles 248–9
    paradigms 228–30
    software and hardware requirements
    231
    testing 268
    thinking skills 222–5
programming environments, mobile apps
    386–7
programming languages 227–33, 370,
    430
    games 444–5
    mobile apps 385–6
    selection 264--6, 272

project management 290–3, 353, 446,
    448–9
Prolog (Programming in Logic) 248
propositional logic 248–9
proprietary database systems 87
proprietary source code 18–19
protocols 33–6, 52–3
prototyping
    databases 124
    games 448–9, 452–3, 458
    information systems 113
    rapid 251, 265
    website design 347–50
pseudocode 258, 350, 390, 442–3
public key cryptography 52–3, 54
publishing schedules (social media) 198,
    206

Q

qualitative data 65, 351, 413–14
quality
    games 439–40, 447, 454, 461–2
    mobile apps 410–12
quantitative data 65, 351, 413–14
queries (database) 67, 92–3, 97–9
    Access® 125–33, 145–56
    SQL (structured query language)
    96–102
questionnaires 66, 351, 374, 414
queues 237, 240–1

R

RAD (rapid application development)
    265
RAID (redundant array of independent
    disks) 14, 102
RAID (Risks, Actions, Issues and Decisions)
    logs 292–3
RAM (random access memory) 232, 259,
    428–9
real-time operating system (RTOS) 14
records 88–9, 237, 241–3
referential integrity 96, 103, 108, 110,
    114, 166
relational algebra 92–3, 111–12
relational database design and
    development 111–21 see also
    Access®
    data structures 89–96, 103–10, 143–6
    evaluation and testing 140–2, 163,
    166–9
    extracting data 125–35, 137–40,
    146–58
    importing and manipulating data
    96–102, 135–9
    security 163–5
    user interfaces (UIs) 122–4, 159–63

relational database management systems (RDBMS) 87–9, 112–13
relations 88–9, 138–9, 143–4
relationships (database design) 114
reliability 65, 250
remote working 41–2, 59
rendering 431, 435, 450–1, 458, 459–60
replacement 47, 64
requirements 252–3
    data modelling 290, 326–7
    database design 113, 114, 169
    games 433, 440, 462
    mobile apps 388–9
    websites 345–7, 372
responsive websites 337, 349, 371
retail industry 9, 58
reviewing and refining designs
    data modelling 292, 327
    games 448–9, 460–3
    mobile apps 414–15
    software solutions 272
    website development 372–3
risks 8, 50–1, 190–1, 292–3
role playing games (RPG) 422
royalties 441–2
RSI (repetitive strain injury) 75, 77
Ruby 229, 230, 235

S
scenarios 280, 290, 299–303, 447
schematics 450–1
screen layouts 348–9, 390
scripting 343–4, 366–71
    languages 230, 430, 431–2
SDK (software development kit) 386, 396
search engine optimisation (SEO) 186–7, 188–9, 195–7, 200, 342, 348
search engines 226
secondary data 65
security 26, 32, 50–6, 64, 191
    databases 102, 114–15
    mobile apps 395
    online 34–5, 40–2, 46, 48, 199–200, 427
    operating systems 15
    password control 52, 163–5
security applications 63
select operation 92, 97–9, 235, 391, 401–2
semantic errors 271
sequences 235, 391, 401
Serial Programming Interface (SPI) 231
servers 5, 454, 459
server-side scripting 264, 343
set theory 249
settings (games) 438

shopping 9, 58
single user operating systems 14
site maps 348
smartphones 8, 382, 383, 428, 429
Snapchat™ 187
social media 8–9, 43–4, 182–4, 226, 336, 372, 427
    audience 185–6, 187, 188, 193, 205–7, 214
    company profiles 201–5
    content 187–8, 192, 194–8, 199, 205–6
    marketing applications 182–91, 199, 201–14
    policies and planning 190–1, 192–201
    testing 207
software 17–18, 249–50
software development life cycle (SDLC) 252–4
software solutions
    design specifications 254–60
    development 269–72
    evaluation and testing 270–2
sound files 359, 429, 430, 436, 457
specifications 23–4, 252–5, 434
    data models 290–1, 326
    games 434
    networks 31–2
spreadsheets for data modelling 283–6, 293–325 see also Excel®
SQL (structured query language) 87, 92–3, 96–102, 112–13
stability 459
stacks 237, 239–40
statements 234–5, 401–3
Steam™ 426–7
storage devices 10–12, 13–14
storyboarding 348–9, 442–3
streaming services 337, 427
strings 237, 239, 243–4
subroutines 236–7
summative testing 326
surveys 65–6
syntax 232, 270–1, 370

T
tables 88–9, 94–5, 102, 104–7, 111
    Access® 138–9, 143–4
    HTML 355
tablets 382, 383, 429
task automation 12, 122, 208–11
test plans 270–1, 291–2, 392
    databases 140–2
    games 446–7, 454
    mobile apps 412–13
    websites 352, 373

testing 32, 268, 291–2, 351–2
    data modelling 326–8
    database design 113, 166–9
    games 445, 447, 454, 459–63
    mobile apps 408–10, 412–15
    social media 207
    software 252, 253, 270–1
    websites 373–4
thinking skills (programming) 222–5
third-party code 266–7, 270
3D modelling 451, 453–4
touch input 384–5, 429
trace tables 253, 413
transactional data 59–60
truth tables 248
tuples 89
Twitter™ 183, 187, 198, 206–8, 211, 214

U
Unity® 431, 445, 452–3
Unreal® Engine 431–2, 442, 447, 452–3, 455–8
usability 23, 30, 43, 45, 46, 69, 251
    data models 319
    databases 142, 169
    mobile apps 411
    websites 337, 338
USB (Universal Serial Bus) 11, 26
use cases 253, 413
user acceptance testing 459, 460
user experience 23, 30–1, 63, 257
    games 437–40
    online systems 45–6
user interfaces (UIs) 15–16, 19, 69–70, 290, 321
    data entry 113, 114, 122–4, 159–63
    games 436–9
    mobile devices 384–5
    navigation 159–60
    testing 141–2, 166
users 64, 396
    feedback from questionnaires 351, 413–14
    feedback from testing 271, 326–7, 351–2, 373–4, 413–14, 439, 460
    feedback on designs 267, 292, 350–1, 392
    needs 23, 30–1, 45–7, 63, 383
    requirements 65–6, 113, 114, 326, 389
utility software 17

V
validation
    Access® 115–19, 122
    data modelling 286, 291, 317–19
    information systems 66–7, 140–1
    mobile apps 391

programming 260–3
  website development 368, 370
variables 225, 233–4
VBScript® 366
vectors 434, 452
verification 67, 103, 122, 281, 286
virtual reality 426
viruses 50, 51, 53
Visual Basic® for Applications (VBA) 291, 295, 313
visual scripting 432
Visual Studio® 269, 445
visual styles 435–6, 442, 444, 455
VOIP (voice-over-the internet) 33
VPNs (Virtual Private Networks) 30, 41, 42

W
WANs (Wide Area Networks) 29–30
wearable technology 382, 383, 426

web 21–2, 336
  browsers 343, 344, 349, 358, 366
  page protocols 33–4
web apps 382
Web Content Accessibility Guidelines (WCAG) 76
websites 189, 207, 336–8
  CSS (cascading styles sheets) 354, 357, 360–5
  design 338–42, 345–50, 353–4
  development 354–9, 365–71
  HTML (Hypertext Markup Language) 354, 357, 365–6
  performance 343–4
  prototyping 347–52
  testing and review 372–4
  uploading 371
WiFi 7, 28
wikis 44, 65, 336

wireframes 348–9, 390
wireless connectivity 11, 26–7, 28, 344
workflow, game design 434, 446
working practices 38–40, 41–2, 47–8, 60, 64
worksheet structure 291, 325
World Wide Web Consortium (W3C) 76, 354, 357
worldwide web see web

X
XCode® 431
XML (extensible markup language) 230, 397

Y
YouTube™ 183, 188, 193